356186

Small Business Management: A Casebook

Small Business Management

A Casebook

By

W. Arnold Hosmer
Professor of Business Administration, Emeritus
Graduate School of Business Administration
Harvard University

Frank L. Tucker
Professor of Business Administration
Graduate School of Business Administration
Harvard University

And

Arnold C. Cooper
Associate Professor
Krannert Graduate School of Industrial Administration
Purdue University

1966

Richard D. Irwin, Inc.

Homewood, Illinois

First Printing, January, 1966

*Case material of the Harvard Graduate School of Business Adminis-
tration is made possible by the cooperation of business firms who
may wish to remain anonymous by having names, quantities and
other identifying details disguised while maintaining basic relationships. Cases are prepared as the basis for class discussion rather than
to illustrate either effective or ineffective handling of administrative
situations.*

Library of Congress Catalog Card No. 66–11808
PRINTED IN THE UNITED STATES OF AMERICA

To Elizabeth Hosmer

To Dorothy Tucker

To Jean Cooper

PREFACE

The inspiration for this book has come from the achievements of executives of small business enterprises. No one can ever know all the significant types of small enterprises or all the range of problems which may arise in any one. Years are not long enough. But it is possible through acquaintance with these men and through careful inquiry into the opportunities before them and the problems they meet to gain a familiarity, a "feel," for small enterprises as a segment of our business structure.

A careful analysis of the available statistics on small business is essential. But the statistics alone cannot give a fully balanced insight into small enterprises as a segment of industry.

The better managed small firms include many of the most profitable industrial and commercial enterprises in our whole business structure. It is unfortunate that statistics do not fully reveal this fact. The early history of large corporations shows that most of them have developed from one or more enterprises which were in operation while still small. Growth into a large corporation, however, is not the sole form of success; every year a substantial number of firms grows beyond the boundary of small enterprises, with continued success, and others are highly successful even though remaining small.

Tragedy is also a part of small business—tragedy in varying degrees in spite of all efforts by those concerned. The statement that the difficulty is in management is true in many instances but it is not true in all.

The direct management possible in small firms and effective use of the strategy of size can be strong factors in competition. Possibly the most hopeful solution to the problems facing small enterprises as a whole is to record the administrative methods used by the most successful small firms, as a means of wider dissemination of these methods among small enterprises as a whole.

In the cases included here, we have sought through balance in the types of companies presented an opportunity for young men to study problems of administration as they have existed in these firms and to acquire a "feel" for administration in small enterprises.

For two of the authors our interest has grown over a period of more than thirty years, as we have become progressively more familiar with the opportunities, the problems, and the achievements of small firms.

Both of us have been, and are, directors or other officers of small firms. The activity of the third author has been of somewhat shorter duration, but he also knows small firms and the executives who carry responsibility in their operation.

A course for which most of these cases were developed was first given at the Harvard Business School in 1958. From the beginning, the course has been fortunate in the ability of the students who elected it, in their increasing numbers, and in their contributions to the development of the subject. Professor Cooper has a comparable course at Purdue University which has shown similar results in the ability, the numbers, and the contributions of the students.

Most of the cases present issues which have arisen in manufacturing enterprises, since these firms have issues involving all of the functional areas, whether marketing, product development, finance, production, or otherwise. Typically these issues extend into all fields and require integration in seeking a solution.

All of us have taught this course at the Harvard Business School, and Professor Cooper has used most of this material in his course at Purdue University.

We wish to thank Dean Stanley F. Teele for his support at the initiation of the course and during its early years, and Dean George P. Baker for his continued interest and support. Professor Cooper also wishes to express appreciation to Dean Emanuel T. Weiler.

Some of the cases are disguised at the request of the cooperating executives, but the facts are real and the decisions had to be made. Since some are disguised, we cannot express our thanks to each personally, but we do appreciate the assistance of all those in each firm who helped us, and also the privilege of making public in this form the facts they gave us.

The members of the Smaller Business Association of New England have contributed greatly to our work. At the "February Conferences" and at morning sessions of annual meetings, it has been a privilege— and a challenge—to take up cases with groups of men, all of whom were executives of small companies. It is also interesting to meet friends in the halls and in more or less formal conferences where most of the talk is about small business.

Mr. Melvin Zurn, Mr. Everett Zurn, Mr. Frank Zurn, and their associates at Zurn Industries, Inc. have encouraged us throughout this task. Even though their company has expanded somewhat beyond the pale, by special dispensation they are members of the lodge of executives of small firms. One part of their assistance has been through establishing the Zurn Fellowship. Three men have held this Fellowship during the final, or thesis, year of their work for the degree of Doctor of Business Administration at the Harvard Business School—Professor John E. Walsh, Jr., Washington University, St. Louis; Professor Arnold C. Cooper, Purdue University, one of the authors of this volume; and Dr. Seymour Tilles, Vice President, Boston Safe Deposit and Trust Company. One condition of the Zurn Fellowship is that the thesis be planned and written to be of use to executives of small enterprises. A fourth thesis on "The Strategy of Size" is currently under way. All of these theses are based on inquiries among practicing executives, including those in the cases, as well as on familiarity with the literature.

Some of the cases and notes in this volume were originally developed for use elsewhere than in this course. We thank Professors Robert W. Austin, Paul Donham, Pearson Hunt, Thomas C. Raymond, Herbert F. Stewart, Lawrence E. Thompson, and Charles R. Williams, as well as Messrs. Robert Russell and Wrede Petersmeyer for permission to include cases or notes written by them or under their supervision.

The approach to the problems and opportunities of small enterprises, recorded in this book, has profited through the hard work of a notably able group of Research Assistants. The first four worked under the supervision of Professor Hosmer and the fifth under that of Professor Tucker. B. Robert Wood is now an investment counselor with Franklin Cole and Company, Incorporated, New York; Professor Cooper was first engaged in this effort as a Research Assistant; Karl H. Vesper is now Director of Case Development, Design Division, Mechanical Engineering Department, Stanford University. Mr. Alexander Jenkins, III, developed, while here, the conception of serving two small companies as Treasurer, and at the beginning as Chief Accounting Officer. He is now Treasurer and a Director of Orion Research, Incorporated, of Cambridge, and Treasurer and a Director of Ocean Research Equipment, Inc., Falmouth, Massachusetts.

Mr. Charles M. Leighton, who worked with Professor Tucker, is in charge of coordinating several companies as Group Manager for Bangor, Punta Alegre Sugar Corporation.

We appreciate the assistance of all these persons in what has been a most interesting task.

November, 1965

W. ARNOLD HOSMER
FRANK L. TUCKER
ARNOLD C. COOPER

TABLE OF CONTENTS

Notes and Readings

AN INTRODUCTION

Many books have been written about the administration or management of business. We have prepared here a work devoted to the management of small businesses.

Why should this segment of our economy be worthy of special consideration?

The statistics of small business attest to its importance. Approximately 95 percent of all concerns in the country have less than 100 employees. Firms with fewer than 500 employees make up more than 99 percent of the total business community. Small manufacturing firms in these two categories account respectively for 20 percent and 40 percent of all manufacturing employment. Many small firms perform services or manufacture products which are not economically feasible for larger companies. In so doing they supply not only the general public but also every large company. Few segments of the economy could function, few major contracts could be completed, few production lines could roll without products, parts, and services supplied by small business.

But why a book devoted to the management of small business? Is the art of managing these enterprises different from that used by the managers of large firms?

Yes! The art of management in small firms is different in significant ways. In this book we are dealing with companies typically with total personnel of 10 to 100. The management teams are small, typically 3 to 10. They can be cohesive, and they can maintain close contact with facts and decisions in all parts of the business to a degree impossible in large companies. The analytical tools of management are used, but in an environment which creates different demands and provides different opportunities for the administrator.

Management problems probably show a wider variation in these small companies than in large companies, a reflection, in part, of "the individual flavor" of small firms, many of which show to a marked degree the influence of the founders.

Many small firms, but by no means all, operate with limited financial resources. Most of them have more limited numbers of management personnel in relation to business done than large companies, a fact which further emphasizes the breadth of experience in small firms.

1

In applying the strategy of size the management teams of small companies often need to apply an added bit of imagination, technical competence, speed, and flexibility to attain success in their specialized field. To a degree not generally recognized the managers of small firms are required to demonstrate personal abilities greater than are required of their competitors in large firms.

To repeat, there is a definite art, significantly different in a number of ways, which is required in the successful management of a small enterprise.

And why should I, as a prospective professional manager, study this specialized field of small business?

Many business students will actually enter the field. Working in a small firm is rewarding both in terms of personal satisfaction and of financial gain. The more successful of small businesses are among the most profitable firms in existence. Both salaries and capital gain opportunities for the management teams are often substantial. The personal satisfactions of working and meeting the challenge in the small business situation are equally rewarding to most men who enter the field. The experiences of the men involved in the firms described in this book will themselves speak further to these points.

However, knowledge of the small business field is also important to the executives of large companies. In sales, in purchasing, and in other activities, large companies compete with small enterprises in some areas and cooperate with them in others. All enterprises are parts of the same business structure.

In many industries, for example, furniture, clothing, and electronic instrumentation, firms of all sizes compete directly, and not always to the disadvantage of the small firms. In the automotive and steel industries, there is substantially no small company competition in production. But gasoline and automobiles reach customers principally through the cooperation of small dealer firms. In steel, any company which sells directly not only to large users such as the automobile companies, but also to the vast group of machine shops, forging, and tool and die shops, must meet the competition of independent local distributors selling products of other steel companies. It may be highly useful for executives of large companies to know something about the strategy of size and other factors which enable small competitors or distributors to be especially effective.

In purchasing, the situation is similar, at least in part. Bethlehem Steel has over 30,000 suppliers, General Motors has spoken of its "26,000 Partners," Caterpillar Tractor has 7,500 suppliers worldwide large companies have comparable numbers. Most of the suppliers are small. The plant manager and purchasing agent of the large firm must be as concerned with the operating problems of their small suppliers as they are with their own production line. They must worry about these suppliers' manufacturing problems and be prepared to render aid and assistance if necessary to help them meet the shipping dates on which the large company's production schedules are dependent. They must also know how to render this help without infringing on the independence of the small firm.

It well behooves the manager of the larger organization to be as knowledgeable about small company types of problems as he is about those in his own organization. The success of many executives of major corporations is based on their ability to get a level of performance from small suppliers, sales firms, and service organizations equal to or better than that exacted from the men on their own payroll.

In addition to working contact with smaller firms, the man who chooses to join a major corporation, or a bank, investment firm, or large service company, will wish to invest a portion of his income to build his estate. There is no need to dwell on the profit which could have been obtained from an investment in a firm such as Texas Instruments, Xerox, or Polaroid when it was still small. However, many small firms have attained less outstanding success, and some have failed. The evaluation of investment opportunities in this area requires a knowledge of the workings of a small business, a "feel" for its potential, a sympathy with its problems, and an appreciation for its strategies which can only come from a study of the small business field.

This book provides the basis for such a study.

The companies described here have been chosen because they have problems which are multi-functional in nature. The management team of a small firm is rarely allowed the luxury of solving one problem at a time. It must usually deal with a series of interrelated issues which cut across several functional areas. The preponderance of manufacturing companies in the book is due to the fact that such organizations are unique, in that their management is involved in every business function: research and development, production, control, finance, marketing, and human relations. Research firms, marketing firms, and service firms each are involved in several of these functions, but, in order to provide a learning experience which will be as inclusive as possible, we have selected cases which present in most instances a relatively broad spectrum of problem areas. We believe experience with these broad cases can be valuable to readers with a variety of career objectives and their usefulness is not confined to those who are primarily interested in manufacturing firms.

The multi-functional character of these cases is the reason why we have not chosen to list them under various sub-headings in the Table of Contents. Although various categories could be developed, we believe that most of the cases are so broad that such categories would be arbitrary and probably not very useful. The cases are, however, listed in an order which we believe to be useful for teaching purposes.

The art of management in small companies is explored, not by the use of extensive text, but by a sequence of case studies of actual companies. Although some of the companies have been disguised, the events described actually occurred. The financial statements are those of the company at the time of the case, and the facts given are those then available to the executives, as fully as they could be recorded. The decisions involved in each case were actually faced by the management of the company concerned.

How does the use of cases differ from the reading of text in studying the art of managing small enterprises?

In the process of establishing a course of action in a business situation, the men involved must perform several basic operations. Information must be gathered, enough to allow for reasonable analysis of the situation, but not at the expense of unnecessary time, delay, or other costs. The data which have been gathered must be sorted and evaluated by the varying degree to which they bear on the situation. Finally, a decision must be made.

In the cases included here the process of gathering information has been completed, to the extent practical for case purposes. However, the reader will find that additional data about the industry, competition, or the economy will sometimes be valuable in the determination of the best course of action for the company concerned. General knowledge and experience are always, of course, applicable.

The challenge and the value of studying actual cases reaches full force with the process of sorting and evaluating the data available. Each case includes a number of facts which bear on the decision with varying force, and some which may be entirely irrelevant. It is the responsibility of the student, as it is the duty of a member of management in an actual business situation, to separate, sort, and evaluate the various pieces of information available to him.

Each case requires that a decision, and possibly more than one decision, be made. By this time the student, like the businessman, has determined the degree to which each of the several available facts bears on the decision or decisions. The ultimate requirement in each case, again as in each business situation, is for the formulation of a specific course of action for the people, or company, involved. The decision at certain times may be to seek additional information. If so, what information? How will it be gathered? What will be the cost, both in terms of actual expense and in the value of time lost? If a specific question is answered, what bearing will it have on the ultimate decision as to a course of action? One must guard against seeking additional information which is of a marginal nature and which, though comforting to the decision maker, requires an expenditure of time, effort and funds beyond the value of the new data.

Thus the student arrives, as does his business counterpart, at the point where he must select a specific course of action. He must be prepared, in the classroom, to defend his recommendations over the objections of often skeptical classmates who differ in their views. No student, and no professor, can claim to have the best solution to any case problem, just as it is impossible in the actual business situation to be certain of having chosen the "best" course of action. However, careful analysis of the situation, knowledgeable evaluation of the facts, and hardheaded but imaginative reasoning, can produce a course of action which can be recognized as "better" than less realistic alternatives. If a business manager can continue to make a "better" choice in each of a series of consecutive decision-making situations he will soon be rewarded by finding his company ahead of the competition, more profitable than the average, and recognized as a leader in its field.

Successful management of a business is the process of recognizing a need or opportunity, and taking appropriate action. The management team must analyze the opportunity and the relevant information, gather more data if necessary, arrive with all due speed at a reasonable course of action, and carry out that course of action creatively and forcefully, altering it if necessary as additional information becomes available. The process of carrying out the course of action is difficult, if not impossible, to duplicate in the classroom, even with the case method. However, the student will, under this method, duplicate much of the experience of his business counterpart in analyzing the data and choosing a course of action in each case situation. He will become action-oriented in that a decision or decisions must be made, and, to the extent that he is challenged by his classmates or professor, he will be forced to defend his reasoning, and thereby, to live with his decisions.

Small Business Management
CASES

1. DILLON FABRICATING COMPANY, INCORPORATED*
Identifying Administrative Problems and Taking Action

Alan Green had held the position of vice-president of the Dillon Fabricating Company for almost a year in November, 1958. He had been hired in early 1958 by the president, Richard Newman, to direct the company's manufacturing operations. The Dillon Fabricating Company was located in Crampton, Ohio, and was a relatively small company engaged in the custom fabrication and assembly of steel products ranging from large building sections and steel pressure vessels to small, mass-produced, contract items such as metal brackets and stampings. Employment in late 1958 approximated 115 persons.

Richard Newman had purchased a controlling stock interest from the Dillon family in October, 1957. Shortly thereafter, there had been a number of changes in management structure and a general realignment of job responsibilities. Previously, Alan Green's job had been filled partially by William Burke, son-in-law of the former president, the elder Mr. Dillon. Despite an apparent demotion, Mr. Burke had chosen to remain with the company as vice-president in charge of plant maintenance, although he had made it well known throughout the company that he was extremely dissatisfied with the new management.

Alan Green initially had spent much of his time becoming acquainted with the actual mechanics of the business and the personnel involved. As he became more familiar with the situation, he had been able to assume greater responsibilities. In November, 1958, in addition to his responsibility in manufacturing, he had been asked to take charge of the company's purchasing and to handle negotiations with the labor union. Despite the many duties he was performing, Alan had found time to give thought to the company's competitive strengths and weaknesses. He was aware that the situation presented a wide range of possible courses of action and was considering what suggestions, if any, he might make to Mr. Newman about strengthening the company's competitive position. He had also been advised that a block of 200 shares of the company's stock had been offered for sale at a price of $20 per share, and he was considering the possibility of acquiring these shares as an investment.

Company History

The enterprise was established by Arthur and Bruce Dillon, who had started it in 1938 as a small metalworking shop. The company was incorporated in 1941, at which time the Dillon brothers were joined by their father, John Dillon, who became president. Mr. Dillon had been associated with Central Iron and Steel, a medium-sized local company, for over 20 years but had left the company because of personal differences with some of the management. A third son, James, joined the company shortly afterward, as did William Burke, a son-in-law. Substantially all the management positions had been filled by the Dillon family since the early 1940's, with the exception of Philip Hobson, who had been employed as secretary and office manager.

All the Dillons were intensely interested in engineering and devoted most of their time to the technical aspects of the company, rather than concentrating on business or administrative matters. It was generally conceded that many jobs were accepted because they presented especially challenging engineering problems rather than being particularly attractive from a profit standpoint. This policy was exemplified by a company brochure which proudly proclaimed: "If It's Made from Metal, Dillon Can Make It." Little concentrated sales effort had been devoted to the company's products; the great bulk of sales was handled over the telephone by James Dillon and by one salaried salesman. Most sales arose as a result of customer inquiry rather than from active solicitation on the part of company personnel.

The actual manufacturing activities of the company were run by one plant superintendent and three foremen who were given responsibility for directing the company's work force of approximately 85. Scheduling of production was done on an informal basis between the superintendent and the foremen. Delivery promises, which were frequently subject to wide errors, were made as the result of informal guesses about the shop capacity and job complexity by one of the engineers, the superintendent, and the foreman concerned. No systematic production control system was used. Instead, each job was entered by number in the superintendent's notebook, which contained notations as to the promised delivery dates and reasons for delay, if any.

The company's costs were collected on an individual job basis and were broken down into totals for direct labor, direct material, and engineering. Prorated figures for shop overhead, general administrative expense, and selling expense were then added and the total cost compared with the estimated amount to determine if the job had been profitable. One shop overhead rate was used throughout the company. The rate was based on direct labor dollars and was revised at the start of each fiscal year on the basis of the actual experience of the previous year. No labor breakdowns had ever been made by operations, however; and it was extremely difficult to pinpoint the reasons for differences between actual figures and estimates. Despite the apparent lack of modern management techniques, sales had grown substantially during World War II and had leveled off between $1.5 million and $2.2 million per year during the postwar period. With the exception of one year, 1955, the company had shown a profit. Over its almost 20 years of existence, the company had acquired the reputation of being able to do a good technical job on practically any type of order, but it had been criticized frequently for inadequate service and late delivery. Information on the company's operations is contained in Exhibits 1–1 to 1–6.

The company was primarily a job shop and contract manufacturer and had been divided into three main departments. Exhibit 1–7 shows the arrangement of the company's plant and property.

The fabrication department, or "big shop," as it was referred to by members of the organization, served as a steel plate [1] and structural steel [2] shop, with facilities to handle heavy structural and special plate jobs. Miscellaneous light custom-built items employing structural sections were also manufactured in this area. During the war, the shop produced a wide range of defense orders for the government which fell entirely into the plate fabrication category. Postwar plate sales were concentrated heavily in various jobs, such as boilers and tanks, and were made largely to public utilities. The increase in construction activity following the war caused the company to accept a number of

---

[1] The fabrication of metal plate products consisted primarily of cutting, bending, rolling, and welding or bolting together individual sections of metal plate up to one-half inch thick to form items such as metal boilers, tanks, and test chambers.

[2] Structural fabrication consisted primarily of cutting structural steel shapes (beams, columns, angles, etc.) to specified lengths, and assembling them by bolting, welding, or other means into sections which were used as the framework of buildings and other structures.

Exhibit 1-1

DILLON FABRICATING COMPANY, INCORPORATED

ANNUAL INCOME STATEMENTS *

	1942	1943	1944	1945	1946	1947	1948	1949
Net sales	$306,239	$884,945	$1,493,935	$1,648,380	$1,125,948	$1,499,422	$1,678,223	$1,525,473
Manufacturing costs	227,005	699,858	1,152,395	1,328,499	917,474	1,253,922	1,382,632	1,314,719
Gross profit	79,234	185,087	341,540	319,881	208,474	245,500	295,591	210,754
General and administrative expense ..	37,719	65,694	92,899	111,193	82,727	96,934	111,306	99,887
Direct sales expense	4,701	30,644	19,452	29,219	18,753	30,839	43,067	57,643
	$ 42,420	$ 96,338	$ 112,351	$ 140,412	$ 101,480	$ 127,773	$ 154,373	$ 157,530
Operating profit	36,814	88,749	229,189	179,469	106,994	117,727	141,198	53,224
Plus: Other income	1,686	2,132	3,407	7,407	13,263	8,315	21,690	4,257
	$ 38,500	$ 90,881	$ 232,596	$ 186,876	$ 120,257	$ 126,042	$ 162,888	$ 57,481
Less: Other expenses	4,628	6,983	4,060	5,532	8,958	19,385	11,860	15,368
	$ 33,872	$ 83,898	$ 228,536	$ 181,344	$ 111,299	$ 106,657	$ 151,028	$ 42,113
Less: Contribution to profit-sharing fund	—	—	—	—	—	21,295	25,291	6,831
Profit before taxes	$ 33,872	$ 83,898	$ 228,536	$ 181,344	$ 111,299	$ 85,362	$ 125,737	$ 35,282
Less: Taxes†	16,952	60,295	169,211	134,357	50,533	38,474	53,052	12,181
Profit after taxes	$ 16,920	$ 23,603	$ 59,325	$ 46,987	$ 60,766	$ 46,888	$ 72,685	$ 23,101
Less: Dividends	—	—	—	—	—	—	—	—
Earnings Retained for Year	$ 16,920	$ 23,603	$ 59,325	$ 46,987	$ 60,766	$ 46,888	$ 72,685	$ 23,101

Exhibit 1–1—Continued

ANNUAL INCOME STATEMENTS

	1950	1951‡	1952	1953	1954	1955	1956	1957	1958
Net sales	$1,899,202	$1,801,605	$2,100,105	$2,228,705	$1,879,776	$1,815,424	$1,852,918	$2,249,949	$1,736,532
Manufacturing costs	1,644,813	1,512,565	1,730,795	1,845,525	1,652,196	1,590,684	1,620,494	1,887,022	1,429,451
Gross profit	254,389	289,040	369,310	383,180	227,580	224,740	232,424	362,927	307,081
General and administrative expense .	98,682	114,235	170,317	172,326	157,358	200,000	152,936	229,511	213,857
Direct sales expense.	61,026	46,399	47,509	72,608	57,953	45,658	49,829	61,403	68,926
	$ 159,708	$ 160,634	$ 217,826	$ 244,934	$ 215,211	$ 245,658	$ 202,765	$ 290,914	$ 282,783
Operating profit	94,681	128,406	151,484	138,246	12,269	(20,918)	29,659	72,013	24,298
Plus: Other income	5,783	9,626	10,074	8,927	7,676	10,315	10,722	12,104	11,518
	$ 100,464	$ 138,032	$ 161,558	$ 147,173	$ 19,945	$ (10,603)	$ 40,381	$ 84,117	$ 35,816
Less: Other expenses	21,321	14,387	22,453	16,247	17,165	36,286§	23,195	23,153	17,754
	$ 79,143	$ 123,645	$ 139,105	$ 130,926	$ 2,780	$ (46,889)	$ 17,186	$ 60,964	$ 18,062
Less: Contribution to profit-sharing fund	11,157	—	—				—	—	—
Profit before taxes ...	$ 67,986	$ 123,645	$ 139,105	$ 130,926	$ 2,780	$ (46,889)	$ 17,186	$ 60,964	$ 18,062
Less: Taxes†	26,915	67,429	80,580	71,679	1,192	(22,283)	5,304	20,437	7,404
Profit after taxes	$ 41,071	$ 56,214	$ 58,525	$ 59,247	$ 1,588	$ (24,606)	$ 11,882	$ 40,527	$ 10,658
Less: Dividends ...	—	—	—	—	—	—	—	9,340	2,335
Earnings Retained for Year	$ 41,071	$ 56,214	$ 58,525	$ 59,247	$ 1,588	$ (24,606)	$ 11,882	$ 31,187	$ 8,323

* Fiscal year ending November 30 for years 1942–51. Changed to September 30 for years 1952–58.
† Excess profits tax in effect: 1942–46, 1951–53.
‡ Figures for 10 months only.
§ Includes $20,692 of bad debts charged against income.

Exhibit 1–2

DILLON FABRICATING COMPANY, INCORPORATED

INCOME STATEMENTS
(Years Ending September 30)

	1956		1957		1958	
Net sales		$1,852,918		$2,249,949		$1,736,532
Material	$1,122,714		$1,371,996		$937,720	
Productive labor	175,421		220,405		209,811	
Plant overhead*	322,359		294,621		281,920	
Cost of goods sold		$1,620,494		$1,887,022		$1,429,451
Gross profit		$ 232,424		$ 362,927		$ 307,081
Direct sales expense		$ 49,829		$ 61,403		$ 68,926
Salaries, officers	$ 71,471		$ 74,946		$ 76,018	
Salaries, other	36,437		38,183		39,851	
Other†	45,028		116,382		97,988	
General and administrative expense		$152,936		$229,511		$213,857
Operating profit		$ 202,765		$ 290,914		$ 282,783
Plus: Other income		$ 29,659		$ 72,013		$ 24,298
		10,722		12,104		11,518
Less: Other expenses		$ 40,381		$ 84,117		$ 35,816
		23,195		23,153		17,754
Profit before taxes		$ 17,186		$ 60,964		$ 18,062
Less: Taxes		5,304		20,437		7,404
Profit after taxes		$ 11,882		$ 40,527		$ 10,658
Less Dividends		—		9,340		2,335
Earnings Retained		$ 11,882		$ 31,187		$ 8,323

* Includes: Engineering, supervision, nonproductive labor, supplies, depreciation, taxes, utilities, insurance, repairs, maintenance (etc.).
† Includes: Telephone, telegraph, travel expenses, professional services, office supplies (etc.).

EXHIBIT 1-5

DILLON FABRICATING COMPANY, INCORPORATED

COMPARATIVE BALANCE SHEETS

(September 30)

	September 30, 1956		September 30, 1957		September 30, 1958	
Cash		$ 13,414		$ 62,365		$ 73,920
Marketable securities, at cost*				29,133		20,195
Accounts receivable (net)		211,712		131,786		156,785
Notes receivable		1,401				
Inventories		518,597		581,269		460,376
Prepaid items		4,552		1,613		4,264
Total Current Assets		$749,676		$806,166		$715,540
Other Assets		$ 872		$ 734		$ 617
Land	$ 5,606		$ 5,606		$ 5,606	
Small tools	2,788				12,445†	
Building and equipment	386,291		393,145		402,925	
	(274,793)		(300,064)		(319,658)	
Total Fixed Assets		$119,892		$ 98,687		$101,318
Total Assets		$870,440		$905,587		$817,475
Accounts payable, trade		$ 67,189		$ 49,080		$ 34,040
Notes payable, bank		50,000		50,000		
Mortgage (current portion)		10,422		10,955		5,673
Accruals		25,935		33,293		34,470
Income taxes payable		5,304		30,437		7,404
Total Current Liabilities		$158,850		$173,765		$ 81,587
Mortgage payable‡		$ 78,665		$ 67,710		$ 63,452
Common stock§ (par $5.00)		93,400		93,400		93,400
Retained earnings		539,525		570,712		579,036
Total Equity		$632,925		$664,112		$672,436
Total Liabilities		$870,440		$905,587		$817,475

* 1957—debentures of listed industrial corporation, sold at a long-term capital gain of approximately 10 percent. 1958—common stock of listed industrial corporation, cost $20,195; approximate market, November, 1958, $24,000.

† Leasehold improvements (net).

‡ Secured by fixed assets—monthly payments: 1957, $1,220 plus 5 percent interest; 1958, $750 plus 5 percent interest.

§ Authorized: 20,000 shares; issued and outstanding, 18,680.

Exhibit 1-4

COMPARATIVE INDUSTRY RATIOS, 1957

	Current Ratio	Net Profits on Net Sales	Net Profits on Tangible NW	Net Profits on NWC	Net Sales to Tangible NW	Net Sales to NWC	Average Collection Period	Net Sales to Inventory	Total Debt to Tangible NW	Inventory to NWC
	Times	%	%	%	Times	Times	Days	%	%	%
Structural steel fabricating companies (101 companies)*............	3.93	6.42	21.64	43.98	5.21	8.75	34	8.5	64.9	50.1
	2.60	3.84	14.93	25.90	3.24	4.73	47	6.2	82.1	81.3
	1.95	1.76	6.62	11.60	2.31	3.75	60	4.2	147.2	99.4
Metal stamping companies (85 companies)*............	4.83	5.98	15.83	29.41	4.11	9.18	25	10.3	26.8	46.0
	3.04	4.14	10.09	17.33	2.49	5.01	35	6.2	54.5	71.8
	2.07	1.80	4.20	9.07	1.77	3.37	42	4.6	82.2	101.7
Iron and steel sheets, strips, bars, and plates (60 companies)†....	5.88	4.46	19.19	26.71	5.25	7.89	24	11.1	41.8	58.4
	3.55	2.68	7.75	12.78	3.27	4.38	32	5.7	71.3	82.1
	2.41	.80	3.93	5.53	2.36	2.75	40	3.2	114.0	110.1

* Manufacturing companies.
† Wholesaling companies.

The center figure for each of the lines of business is the median. The other two figures in each line are quartiles. When any figures are listed in order according to their size, the median is the middle figure (same number of items from the top and the bottom), and the quartiles are the figures located one-quarter and three-quarters down the list.

SOURCE: Dun & Bradstreet, Inc., *14 Important Ratios in 72 Lines of Business, Year 1957.*

Exhibit 1–5

DILLON FABRICATING COMPANY, INCORPORATED

Annual Sales by Categories
(Years Ending September 30)

	1954	1955	1956	1957	1958
Structural and plate	$1,079,940	$ 911,879	$ 962,955	$1,344,471	$1,127,233
Production shop . . .	389,750	304,203	312,213	256,589	177,594
Warehouse steel . . .	138,109	114,905	97,437	70,529	55,584
Commodities	363,723	309,329	235,971	141,250	102,367
Direct shipments . .	—	183,428	248,543	439,333	274,917
Total Sales . .	$1,971,522	$1,823,744	$1,857,119	$2,252,172	$1,737,695

orders for structural fabrication in addition to the existing plate business. Starting in 1948, the volume of structural work performed had climbed rapidly, with the result that in the early and mid-1950's the dollar volume of production in this department had been divided rather evenly between the two types of work.

Essential differences between these two types of jobs had somewhat reduced the flexibility of the department's labor force. Workers trained to perform plate fabrication were typically more skilled than structural fabrication men. It was possible for plateworkers to work on structural orders whenever a change in the composition of the company's work so demanded, but it was not always possible for structural workers to perform plate jobs, due to the higher level of skill required. This condition had resulted in attempts to maintain a workload evenly balanced between the two types of work, and it was thought that the work in the big shop had seldom been divided so that either type of business represented more than 70 percent or less than 30 percent of the department's total output. These figures were merely estimates, however, as no differentiation had been made between structural and platework for accounting purposes. While it had been possible to maintain a fairly steady employment level by this practice, it was thought that the efficiency of the department had suffered somewhat due to the existence of these two different types of work.

The majority of all jobs received by the big shop were built to customer's specifications, but occasionally the company had been called on to perform complete design and engineering services on an order. Jobs on which Dillon Fabricating might be required to provide design and engineering services were thought to be found more frequently among platework than among structural orders.

The production department handled light-gauge materials and was

Exhibit 1–6

DILLON FABRICATING COMPANY, INCORPORATED

ANNUAL DISTRIBUTION OF SALES, LABOR, AND MATERIALS*
(Fiscal Years Ending September 30)

	1954	1955	1956	1957	1958
Total sales	$1,895,475	$1,829,675	$1,856,125	$2,252,173	$1,737,696
Material	1,134,269	1,122,768	1,125,863	1,371,996	937,740
Labor	155,899	147,942	153,826	194,013	189,839
Total: Material and labor	$1,290,168	$1,270,710	$1,279,689	$1,566,009	$1,127,579
Total contribution	605,307	558,965	576,496	686,164	610,117
Structural and plate sales .	$1,079,940	$ 911,879	$ 962,955	$1,344,471	$1,127,233
Material	559,478	469,049	520,253	688,280	483,928
Labor	112,708	95,576	103,512	148,256	163,847
S&P: Material and labor	$ 672,186	$ 564,625	$ 623,765	$ 836,536	$ 647,775
S&P contribution	407,754	347,254	339,190	507,935	479,478
Production shop sales	$ 389,750	$ 304,203	$ 312,213	$ 256,589	$ 177,594
Material	208,523	141,795	148,186	130,113	90,472
Labor	46,217	42,536	45,627	39,288	19,389
Production shop: Material and labor	$ 254,740	$ 184,331	$ 193,813	$ 169,401	$ 109,861
Production shop contribution	135,010	117,872	118,400	87,188	67,733
Warehouse steel sales	$ 138,109	$ 114,905	$ 97,437	$ 70,529	$ 55,584
Material	96,720	77,919	68,268	46,475	36,544
Labor	3,822	3,280	3,021	2,582	2,497
Warehouse steel: Material and labor	$ 100,542	$ 81,199	$ 71,289	$ 49,057	$ 39,541
Warehouse steel contribution	37,567	33,706	26,148	21,472	16,043
Commodities item sales† .	$ 363,723	$ 309,329	$ 235,971	$ 141,250	$ 102,367
Material	289,960	204,268	197,287	119,954	79,559
Labor	3,622	4,773	5,468	3,887	3,606
Commodities: Material and labor	$ 293,582	$ 209,041	$ 202,755	$ 123,841	$ 83,165
Commodities contribution	70,141	100,288	33,216	17,409	19,202
Direct shipment sales† ...	—	$ 183,428	$ 248,543	$ 439,333	$ 274,917
Material	—	164,668	221,267	387,174	247,238
Direct shipment contribution	—	$ 18,760	$ 27,276	$ 52,159	$ 27,679

* Prepared by the company accountant.
† Direct shipments not separated from commodities until April, 1955.

equipped to produce a wide variety of products in the sheet metal line. The department contained a continuous production line consisting of a moving overhead conveyor, degreasing and painting booths, and two infrared drying ovens. Several other pieces of equipment, such as shears, stamping presses, brakes, and a cold forming mill for light-

Exhibit 1–7

DILLON FABRICATING COMPANY

PROPERTY AND FACILITIES, CRAMPTON, OHIO

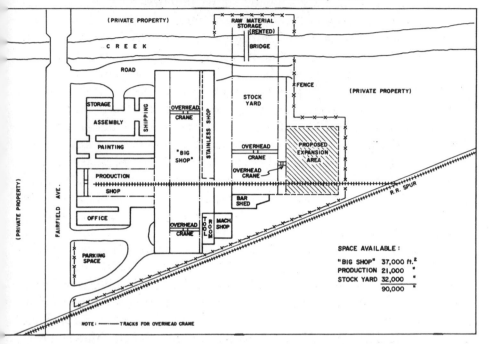

gauge strip steel were also located in the department. The shop was particularly suited to high-volume production of similar items. Special efforts had been made to keep all machinery reasonably portable to provide the flexibility necessary for efficient production of a variety of different types of metal products. Production line operations since World War II included such items as product display racks and stampings for the retail trade, collapsible metal ironing boards, bed rails, and roll-formed mirror supports for the furniture industry. It was estimated that under favorable conditions products with a sales volume of $500,000–$600,000 could be manufactured in this shop with its existing equipment.

The stainless department was located in a section of the big shop and consisted of a small group of highly skilled personnel with the few items of equipment necessary to supplement the facilities of other departments to properly fabricate and assemble special custom-built items of stainless steel, aluminum, and special alloys. The department had been formed after the war and had produced a wide variety of specialties for the dairy, textile, and chemical industries. Included among these products were specially designed aluminum tanks and custom-made stainless steel vats for chemicals.

In addition to the three departments mentioned above, the company also performed a quasi-wholesaling function for structural steel items and construction "commodities" such as metal sash and window frames. This function had been an outgrowth of the increase in structural fabrication jobs done by the company since the war. In the immediate postwar period when steel had been in short supply, the company had adopted a policy of stocking an inventory of the fastest-moving structural angles, sheets, beams, and bars. These were resold from stock to smaller local shops which were unable to obtain raw materials from the mills because of the small size of their orders. In the years immediately following the war, the company had done a sizable volume of this business with what was termed the walk-in trade; but as steel became more plentiful and local service warehouses came into being, this part of the company's business had dropped sharply. Nevertheless, an inventory of representative items valued at from $50,000–$75,000 had been maintained to provide service to the walk-in trade.

The company also carried an inventory of "commodity" items such as steel and aluminum sash and window frames. The local industry practice in soliciting bids on structural fabrication jobs was to request that a quotation include not only the structural members for a given construction job but also the sash and doors required. Management reasoned that a price advantage on structural jobs could be obtained by stocking some of the faster-moving items rather than by buying the specific items needed from a specialized commodity jobber. Consequently, the company had built up a commodity inventory which was used for the company's structural bids and also permitted occasional sales of commodities to walk-in customers. Storage of the commodity inventory in the rear of the big shop had somewhat reduced the amount of space available for fabrication of structural and plate orders. It was estimated that the commodity inventory usually ran somewhere from $60,000–$80,000 in value. The turnover, however, was not rapid, and it was suspected that the inventory contained a number of slow-moving or even obsolete items. A set of perpetual inventory cards had been set up for control purposes but had not been effective. It was not uncommon for physical checks on the inventory to disclose variances of as much as +20 percent from the card figures.

The company had negotiated agreements with three steel mills to ship structural shapes not requiring cutting or fabrication directly from the mill to the construction site in sufficient time to be used with the fabricated structural sections shipped by Dillon Fabricating. These direct shipments were billed to Dillon rather than to the contractor but were included as a part of the package provided by the company on structural jobs. The Dillon Fabricating Company received a discount of about 10 percent on direct shipment orders.

The personality of the elder Mr. Dillon had tended to dominate the affairs of the company from the time of its incorporation. A devoted engineer, he found little time for administration, preferring to leave these matters to others. No clear delineations of responsibility and authority had ever been made, however, with the result that few in the organization were willing to make administrative decisions without discussing the situation personally with Mr. Dillon, senior. Mr. Dillon tended to be quite lenient in his dealings with the men, a practice which had transmitted itself through the plant superintendent and the various foremen into a policy of consistently yielding to practically all demands of the work force. The enforcement of discipline became extremely lax, and several overt instances of favoritism had reduced the morale of the shop to a low level in the early postwar period.

Relations between management and the labor force had deteriorated gradually, and finally in 1950 the company was organized by representatives of a strong international union. Mr. Dillon was both surprised and hurt that the men had voted to join a union, and he chose to leave all labor relations to his sons. The union presented a number of demands, all of which were accepted by the company.

Major clauses in the contract included: provisions for collection of union dues by the company, restrictions on the type of work which could be done by union members,[3] comprehensive provisions covering overtime payments for hours worked in excess of 40 hours per week, paid holidays, vacations and company-paid accident and death benefits. All work was to be on a straight hourly basis, and any form of incentive payment was forbidden.[4] Management would be permitted to assign men to different types of jobs over a period of time, but workers were always to be paid the highest rate of any job held. With regard to layoffs and promotions, it was agreed that seniority would govern, subject to equal worker ability. In the case of a layoff, a senior worker would be given the right to replace a junior worker, regardless of the job, if he could perform satisfactorily in that job for three work-

---

[3] For instance, no union member could perform fabrication, installation, or erection work at a construction site within the jurisdiction of another union without express written consent.

[4] An incentive plan had been introduced in 1947, but lack of clarity in the accounting records had led to demands for abolition of the system.

ing days. A detailed grievance procedure, leading to arbitration in extreme cases, was also included.

Both lockouts and strikes were expressly forbidden unless either management or the union acted so as to defy an arbitration decision. The contract further permitted the union to reopen negotiations, on the subject of wages only, on an annual basis. Negotiations with the union were handled by Bruce Dillon until his death in 1953, at which time the responsibilities were assumed by William Burke. While relations had been far from ideal, few stoppages of work had occurred as a result of labor difficulties.[5]

Management Changes 1957–58

Stock ownership of the company was concentrated largely in the hands of the family, with Mr. Dillon, senior, owning well over half of the outstanding shares. During the summer of 1957, Mr. Dillon had decided to retire from the active conduct of the business and therefore had let it be known in local circles that a controlling interest in the company was for sale. Some time later, Richard Newman expressed interest in the company. Mr. Newman subsequently acquired an option on 51 percent of the stock, and after investigating the matter more fully he had exercised the option in October, 1957, and became the new president and controlling stockholder of the Dillon Fabricating Company.

Mr. Newman was forty-five years old and had spent several years with a cousin in the management of an ice cream and dairy specialty company in Wisconsin. He had been active in all major areas of the company, but particularly enjoyed the financial aspects of the business. He had spent much of his spare time becoming familiar with the stock market, and over a period of years had become a relatively successful investor.

Control of the dairy firm was held by Mr. Newman's cousin, however; and although the business had been successful, Mr. Newman decided to leave his cousin and search for a company of his own. Mr. Newman's wife had been born in Crampton, and while the couple were visiting the area in the fall of 1957, Mr. Newman had heard of the Dillon Fabricating Company from a local stockbroker and thought the situation might warrant further investigation. Examination of the company's financial records convinced Mr. Newman that he should

---

[5] Two stoppages of work, both of about one week's duration, had occurred in mid-1953 and early 1954.

take out an option on Mr. Dillon's shares. Mr. Newman contacted a wide range of sources in attempting to acquire useful information on the company. Discussions were held with the company's bankers, important customers, key suppliers, several competitors, and a local industrialist who owned approximately 20 percent of the company's stock but was not related to the Dillons.

"It seemed to me that the business had great potential," Mr. Newman explained. "Despite the fact that sales were only what had come in the front door, the company's volume had grown. Given a certain amount of push, it would seem that sales could be raised substantially; and what's more, the capacity was available to handle an increased volume. Everyone I talked with was optimistic about the company's prospects except for some competitors, and I think they were just trying to scare me off. When you consider that profits have been shown almost consistently over the years and then see the salaries the Dillons were paying themselves,[6] the situation looked pretty good," he added.

As a result of his investigations, Mr. Newman exercised his option on 51 percent of the company's stock for the sum of $290,000, or approximately $30 per share. "I think it was a good buy for me," he stated. "I was able to buy control of the company for a price a bit below book value and significantly below replacement cost of the facilities. Considering the company's potential, I think I got a very good deal."

One of Mr. Newman's first moves was to ask each key employee for a list of duties and responsibilities. After the information thus gathered had been analyzed, Mr. Newman decided that a number of management changes were necessary. These moves had resulted in the hiring of some new employees and had entailed a number of changes in the responsibilities of the family members in the organization.

Sales and estimating duties, which had been handled almost entirely by James Dillon, were divided into two main areas—plate sales and structural sales. Charles Cooper, who had formerly handled structural sales but had left the company, was rehired to handle the sales and estimating for structural fabrication jobs, commodities, warehouse steel orders, and direct shipments. Plate sales and plate estimating remained under James Dillon. Purchasing had been handled by Arthur Dillon, and William Burke had been responsible for manufacturing and labor relations. "Arthur just had to go," explained Mr. Newman. "He never really recovered from his brother's death and had

---

[6] The company had been paying annual salaries totaling about $60,000 to the four members of the family active in the business.

taken to drinking heavily, even on the job—you just can't run a business like that." The scope of Mr. Burke's job had been sharply curtailed by Mr. Newman because his job description appeared to be extremely nebulous.[7] "It didn't seem to me that he was doing much of anything around here," he said. Mr. Burke's job was accordingly changed from general manager of manufacturing operations to supervisor of the company's plant maintenance activities.

During this period of management readjustment, Mr. Newman asked Alan Green if he would consider joining the company as its manufacturing vice-president. Alan had known Mr. Newman for a number of years and was interested in further investigating the situation. Alan was thirty-five in 1958, and his experience at that time included three years as a production worker for a large chemical company, four years at college, where he received a degree in civil engineering, two years at the Harvard Business School, and two years with a large eastern manufacturing company. After his graduation from the business school in 1955, he was employed as assistant to the president of one of the three largest appliance manufacturers with offices in New York. After one year he was transferred to operations, where he acted as a department manager of a metalworking shop performing a number of stamping and deep-drawing operations. He had been in this job for a year when Mr. Newman offered him a position as vice-president of the Dillon Fabricating Company.

The prospect of joining the Dillon Fabricating Company appealed to Alan on several counts. He saw the job as a means of joining a company in a position where he would be able to contribute more directly to the company's performance than he could in a large organization. He was not entirely satisfied with his position at the large company and thought the new job would provide an excellent means for him to prove his real worth. Salary was no deterrent, for Mr. Newman offered to match or even exceed his salary from the larger company. Finally, Alan had grown up in the Ohio Valley and had always wanted to return to this area. "I guess it was a combination of both positive and negative factors," he explained. "I saw this as a chance to help build something worthwhile on a first-hand basis, and I just wasn't satisfied with big company life in New York."

Alan joined Dillon Fabricating in January, 1958, and soon found himself fully occupied with his new job. He enjoyed his work a great

---

[7] Mr. Burke's job description contained the statement, "the details of production are of no personal concern to me until trouble actually arises." He further added that, in his opinion, it was imperative that a solution to the then-existing production management void be found.

deal and made special efforts to become acquainted with the company's operations and shop personnel. Mr. Newman soon placed him in complete charge of the company's entire manufacturing operations, the job performed up to that time by William Burke. He also assumed responsibility for the purchasing function on the resignation of Arthur Dillon.

In addition to personnel changes in the company's operating organization, Mr. Newman also effected several changes in the company's board of directors. All members of the Dillon family who had been members of the board, including Mr. Burke, a son-in-law of the elder Mr. Dillon, were asked to resign in early 1958. Mr. Newman appointed his father-in-law, George Martin, to one of the vacant positions. Mr. Martin was a well-known business and political figure of the region and had served as a director of a local bank for a number of years. The broker who had handled Mr. Newman's acquisition of the company was also elected to the board. The company lawyer and a local insurance salesman remained on the board, and Mr. Newman assumed the chairmanship. One seat had been left vacant. While Mr. Newman had not decided on a replacement, he thought he would seek to fill the position with any one of several well-respected members of the local community. Explaining his moves, Mr. Newman stated, "I felt that the changes in the board would enhance the company's prestige in the community and would help us establish some important contacts. I also couldn't afford to have people on the board who were bound to disagree with me, as the Dillons were. To put it another way, I wanted people who would give my ideas an official rubber stamp."

The Dillon family felt that many of Mr. Newman's actions had been open to question. Despite the fact that Mr. Newman owned 51 percent of the company, they expressed the opinion that some of the organizational changes had been highly arbitrary, and often had voiced feelings of resentment over the way the situation had been handled. Mr. Newman was aware of this resentment but felt it was necessary in the company's best interests. "I've tried to work with them, but we just don't see eye to eye," he stated. "They were used to a loose organization that was plainly haphazard and inefficient, and I just can't operate that way. I've taken some steps in the realignment of responsibilities which I hope will strengthen the organization, and I have a few more in mind for the future." He explained that both James Dillon and William Burke had negotiated firm employment contracts with the company which expired in October of 1959. However, he thought it was likely that both of these men would resign on or before that date. Realizing that the departure of James Dillon would leave the company without a plate estimator, Mr. Newman had taken steps to locate a suitable replacement. Both he and Alan had talked with several promising prospects and thought that little trouble would be experienced in obtaining a competent plate engineer. No action had been taken to obtain a replacement for William Burke.

Despite the growing friction between Mr. Newman and the Dillon family, Alan Green had found Mr. Newman quite easy to work with. "We get along pretty well together," he explained. "Richard's first love is finance, and he seems to be pretty sharp at it too. He recently invested some of the company's excess funds in securities which have done very well since we bought them. Richard has said that he's relying heavily on me to run the production end of the business, and he has pretty much let me handle it by myself. Of course, I naturally discuss important matters with him first—in fact, I usually spend about an hour a day filling him in on the operating picture. He's just not a production man, and I don't think he has any real desire to learn the detailed operating side of the business," Alan added.

Mr. Newman believed he could be most helpful to the company as an overall manager and outside contact man. He usually arrived at the office at about 8:30 A.M., an hour after work began in the shops. On arriving at work, he spent about an hour opening and reading all company mail, after which it was distributed to others in the organization. Reading national publications such as *Business Week* and the *Wall Street Journal* typically consumed another hour of Mr. Newman's day. He had never made it a practice to call periodic management meetings, but usually spent several hours a day talking with members of the organization doing what he described as "checking to see if my orders are being carried out." He generally spent another hour a day discussing the company's current operations and problems with Alan Green.

Several days out of the week he attended local civic functions such as Rotary meetings, Chamber of Commerce gatherings, and various luncheons and dinners of civic importance. He believed that this amounted to missionary selling and that it might be possible to increase company sales by "pulling a few strings here and there." Mr. Newman received no periodic formal reports, with the exception of the company's quarterly financial statements, but preferred to keep current on important developments through personal contact with the officers of the company. He relied heavily on Alan Green for current information on the status of the company's manufacturing operations.

The Situation in November, 1958

The recession of 1957–58 had severely affected the Dillon Fabricating Company. Sales had dropped from $2.3 million in the fiscal year ending September 30, 1957, to $1.7 million for the similar 1958 period. The backlog of orders had also declined substantially, and it was estimated that the company's facilities were operating at about 50 percent of capacity in November, 1958. Despite the severe drop in sales, a small profit had been realized for the year, something which Mr. Newman felt represented a significant accomplishment in the circumstances.

The type of work in the company's shops had also changed during the 1958 fiscal year. The majority of orders during most of 1958 had been for platework, but during the latter part of the year the company had failed to receive a number of plate orders on which bids had been submitted, and structural steel jobs became predominant in the company's operations. Competition had intensified considerably in the structural market, however, and the company found that it had become necessary to substantially reduce its profit margins in order to obtain business.

"Structural fabrication can be a dog-eat-dog business," explained Charles Cooper, the company's head structural estimator and salesman. "It's not at all uncommon for the contractor to divulge quotations to bidders in order to beat the price down. You just can't bid blind in this game. You have to know your customers. We would never think of bidding as low a price to a contractor we know will try to chisel our price as we would to one we know we can trust. Competition is pretty rough now, and many times the man who finally gets the bid finds his margin so low that he wishes that he'd never seen the order at all. All in all, this business has been reduced to a production race. The company that can turn out the tonnage can generally do pretty well."

Mr. Cooper further stated that in periods of intense competition it was not always possible to submit structural bids on a complete job without separating the fabrication and commodity figures.[8] "Most contractors these days want us to break down our bids so they can

---

[8] Mr. Cooper estimated that typical structural orders were broken down on a dollar value basis into about 80 percent fabrication and 20 percent commodities. By commodities he meant sash, doors, and other metal trim.

chisel not only on the structural portion but also on the commodities," he said. "By doing this, they can get the local jobbers specializing on commodities to quote prices. Most of these outfits are pretty small and have much lower burden rates than we do, so they can be pretty rough on prices. Quite frequently, we have received the award on a structural job only to lose the commodity portion to local dealers."

He went on to explain that William Burke had recently drawn up a proposal for expansion and modernization of the company's structural facilities. Essentially, the proposal called for moving most of the structural work out of the big shop to the nearby stock yard and expanding operations to the far corner of the company's property.[9] Additional material handling facilities were suggested, and a revised layout for the rearrangement of structural facilities was included. The resultant arrangement was intended to convert the outdoor area into a modified type of production line and reduce material handling costs over existing methods. The project would involve an estimated capital expenditure of about $30,000 and an estimated annual savings in the neighborhood of $16,000, 55 percent of which would be direct [10] and 45 percent indirect [11] in nature. It was estimated that the proposed layout would increase the structural fabricating capacity of the company by 25 percent over the existing layout.

The company was in active competition with a number of local and regional firms for orders in structural fabricating work. Chief among these was Central Iron and Steel, a medium-sized fabricator with sales running around $10 million a year. Central was a well-established, efficient company, which had built up a good reputation for service among the area's contractors. The majority of the company's competitors in this type of business, including Central, were considerably larger than Dillon and had tended to concentrate more heavily on structural fabrication than on platework. Mr. Cooper had reviewed William Burke's proposal for increasing the company's structural output and thought that its adoption would greatly strengthen the company's competitive position. "If we can revamp our layout and lower our costs a bit, I think we can really give Central a run for their

---

[9] See Exhibit 1–7. Proposed expansion area is shaded in the diagram of the company's property and facilities.

[10] Direct savings were defined as direct reductions in labor costs and were expected to arise from increased mechanization.

[11] Indirect savings were defined as savings arising from the increased availability of space in the big shop which would ultimately lead to increased efficiency and lower costs on platework.

money. They have always pretty much had things their way, and I'd just love to see them hurting a bit," he stated.

In late 1956, Mr. Cooper had resigned his position with the company but had been rehired in 1958 by Mr. Newman. "I just couldn't stand seeing our customers continually getting kicked in the teeth with poor service any more," Cooper explained. "Things are better now, though—not perfect but better. We operate on a more business-like basis, and it's finally possible to get somebody to make a decision or help you with a problem. Getting new management has definitely helped the company."

While the structural fabrication portion of the company's business had been subject to frequent periods of intense price competition, the same pattern was not usually typical of plate fabricating. "Plate-work has traditionally been more stable," said James Dillon, who was in charge of the company's plate sales and estimating. "Efficient material handling is the important thing in structural work. It's a high-tonnage, constant flow, line type of operation," he explained. "It's an easy business for people to get into and doesn't require the skill or investment to get started that plate does. Of course, this is one of the problems. Because people can enter the field relatively easily, there are a great many producers, and in slow times competition for the available business can get pretty cutthroat. Now plate is much steadier from a profit standpoint. You still have to be competitive and adjust your prices to market conditions, but know-how and quality are much more important than in structural. It's less of a tonnage proposition and involves more skilled workmanship. There is quite a bit more labor cost per pound of material in a plate job than in a structural order. There is less competition, too. Central will do platework sometimes, but they're mainly a structural shop.

"Know-how and personal relationships with customers are very important," he continued. "The company has demonstrated a proven ability to apply its experience and handle particularly hard jobs, and our quality is consistently better than most of our competitors. Maybe that's one of our problems. We do such a good job that our costs tend to be on the high side, and we have doubtless lost some orders for this reason."

James Dillon thought the company needed some additional equipment to supplement its existing plate facilities. "The shop can do only light platework [12] with the equipment we have now," he explained. "In order to make this company a really versatile plate fabricator, it

---

[12] "Light" plate referred to steel plate less than one-half inch in thickness.

would be necessary to install automatic welding equipment, heavier bending rolls, and a larger brake. All this would cost in the neighborhood of $75,000 to $100,000, I'd say."

Sales of production shop items in November, 1958, consisted almost entirely of mirror supports produced on contract for a local furniture factory. The supports were made from strip steel, which was automatically cut to length and bent into shape by the shop's cold forming mill, after which they were placed on an overhead conveyor, automatically degreased, painted, and shipped. Although the company had been manufacturing supports for this particular customer since 1957, relationships had never been entirely satisfactory. The customer had given the company only short-run contracts and had exerted pressures for successively lower prices. When Mr. Newman suggested the possibility of negotiating monthly contracts in 1958, the customer became extremely aggravated, and it was later learned that inquiries concerning the prices and delivery of the necessary manufacturing equipment had been made. No action was taken on the matter, however, and the company continued to produce mirror supports throughout the year. Mr. Newman thought it possible that the customer might commence its own manufacturing operations on mirror supports at some time in the future but was not alarmed over the immediate prospects of cancellation due to the relatively large investment required for facilities to produce these items.

Walter Hale, foreman of the production department, thought the situation existing in the shop required the solution of problems in a number of troublesome areas. Walter had been with the company for five years and had been foreman of the production shop since 1954. "The production shop and the big shop are as different as night and day," he explained, " and trying to run them in the same plant has caused a lot of problems. This shop is a high-volume, production line operation where an order contains thousands of similar pieces, while the big shop's work is all on large, complex individual orders that require a lot of fitting and adjusting.

"My men look out in the big shop and see what they think is a lot of loafing going on out there with people standing around and talking. On the other hand, the fabrication workers look in here and see a simple, repetitive operation in a nice clean shop, while they're out in the big shop, handling rusty steel all day. This work requires less highly skilled workers than the big shop, and the wage differential would normally be fairly significant. With that union in here, though, the gap has narrowed to the point where it is a sore spot with some of the men. It's also likely that the high wages in this shop have worked to our disadvantage, since none of the area's other production shops are unionized."

He further believed that the use of a single overhead rate throughout the company had contributed to the low level of business in the production shop. "The company overhead rate of 160 percent may be realistic for the big shop, but it adversely affects our volume. We are competing for jobs with shops which have rates below 100 percent, and that extra loading has probably lost us a number of orders. Sure, we're operating at way below capacity now, so our actual rate is probably pretty high, but when business picks up again that rate will start to hurt us. It seems to me that the actual burden rate for capacity operations in this shop wouldn't be more than 80 or 90 percent at the most."

The possibility of manufacturing a proprietary item in the production shop interested Walter Hale. "We used to have a good item in that ironing board, but we never kept up with the times and eventually lost the business," he explained. "What this shop really needs is one or two salesmen devoting their time to selling for us. The company never has been too strong on selling anyway, but least of all for this department." In Walter Hale's opinion, the new management had taken a number of beneficial steps during 1958. "Mr. Newman is a pretty sharp financial man," he said, "and he and Alan Green have put this company back on a businesslike basis and cut out a lot of needless expenses. Unfortunately, though, I don't know if everybody appreciates the improvements that have been made since they came in. I'm afraid the men in the shop have lost confidence in them. They don't see the improvements that have been made. All they know is that we're hungry for work and might be facing a layoff. Then they talk to some of their friends at Central Iron and find out they're on a 44-hour week. Some of them are pretty discouraged. Alan thinks the men are loafing, and they probably are, but you can't expect a man to break his back turning out an order just so he can work himself out of a job! You need a good backlog of work to get the most out of the men."

Referring again to the new management, he said that while he believed a number of significant improvements had been made during the past year, it frequently had been difficult for many people in the organization to interpret the actions of Mr. Newman and Alan Green. "It seems to many of us that this is a pretty big company for two men to try to do everything all by themselves, especially if they don't have much familiarity with this sort of work," he explained. "Many of us have been here a long time and could contribute our experience if only we were consulted from time to time. We'd like to be able to help. It's getting so the right hand doesn't know what the left hand is doing around here. This has made the job of foreman particularly tough here," he continued. "The union considers us members of management, but we certainly aren't members of the management team. The few supervisory meetings we do have just act as vehicles for them to tell us how we should be doing things. They call them conferences, but the word has a pretty hollow ring to me. Usually, they do all the talking, and we do all the listening. I don't say much at these meetings any more."

As time passed during 1958, Alan Green found himself more and more involved in his job. Much of his time was devoted to the purchasing function, but he had made it a practice to keep current on the general status of jobs in the shop by daily talks with Frank Madison, the plant superintendent. Much of the remaining time was spread over a number of areas which included some work on checking and preparing bids, handling labor relations, and general public relations work in the community. He also spent about an hour a day keeping Mr. Newman up to date on the status of important jobs and discussing key problem areas with him. During the evenings, he spent several hours a week reading magazines such as *Purchasing, Factory,* and *Newsweek.*

In the normal course of business, Alan received only two reports on a periodic basis. One was a daily and weekly summary of the status of important jobs in the shops, and the other was a one-sheet report showing the amount of both direct and indirect labor dollars spent throughout the plant each week. He frequently advised Mr. Newman on the content of these reports in addition to other matters of importance. While Alan was responsible for the overall management of the company's manufacturing departments, he had relied heavily on Frank Madison, the plant superintendent, for the day-to-day supervision of the various departments.

Mr. Madison had been with the company since the early 1940's and had advanced through the company's fabricating shop until he became plant superintendent in early 1954, replacing the former superintendent, who had resigned. A quiet man, he seldom offered information unless asked, and occasionally seemed to have trouble expressing his ideas to others. Nevertheless, he had become thoroughly familiar with the technical aspects of his job and had frequently demonstrated what was described by Alan as an "amazing knowledge of what it should cost to get a given job done." He particularly enjoyed playing chess and had been Crampton's city champion for a number of years. Alan and Frank Madison together had made a number of changes in company procedures during 1958. Some of the major changes effected were revisions in the company's cost collection system and the introduction of a formal set of company rules and regulations.

The company's cost collection had been refined somewhat during the year. In reviewing several of the company's recent jobs, Alan had noticed a number of wide differences between estimates and actual costs. In some instances, actual costs exceeded estimates by as much as 300 to 400 percent. Alan had been unable, however, to determine the causes of these variations. Consequently, he and Frank Madison had revised the cost collection procedure to provide for the breakdown of direct labor into the various operations such as cutting, fitting, and welding. The revised method required workers to punch in and out on a time clock each time they changed from one operation to another. Under the previous method, it had been necessary to punch in and out only at the start and close of each day. No other procedural changes were made in the company's cost system, although Alan had wondered whether it was desirable for all manufacturing departments to carry the same burden rate.

In addition to refinements in the company's cost system, two other changes had been made. All company time clocks, previously set to indicate intervals of .1 hour, were reset to .01 hour, and a new set of rules and regulations was posted in the shop. Prior to the purchase of the company by Mr. Newman, a general set of company rules and regulations had been posted in the shop for a number of years. In talking with Frank Madison, however, Alan discovered that little or no enforcement of these rules had been carried out while Mr. Dillon, senior, was president of the company. Feeling that shop discipline was far too lax, Alan and Frank Madison had made minor revisions to the existing rules, attached a set of specific disciplinary actions for cases of violations, and posted them at prominent points in the plant. While no major violations had occurred since the posting of the new rules, there had been a significant number of minor infractions, principally tardiness.

"I guess the men didn't like those rules at all," Alan said. "They had been so used to coming in late that it was a real surprise to them when Frank started handing out warning slips. There still is a lot of squawking about it, but I think the lateness problem has been licked.

The basic problem is that the Dillons pretty much let these men have their own way and treated them like a bunch of children. Now we come in and have to try and get things back on a businesslike basis again. The men are bound to object, but we've just got to do it."

During October, 1958, Alan and Frank Madison had met with representatives of the union for the annual wage negotiation to discuss an across-the-board, 10-cents-an-hour wage increase demanded by the union. Both Alan and Frank Madison believed that such a request was not justified by the facts and argued strongly against any increase. To support the company's case, Alan had prepared a number of graphs and charts, showing the company's wage rates, the national cost-of-living index, and the wage rates for other firms in the area. Negotiations were carried on for some time, and finally the union agreed to postpone their demands until 1959. "That was pretty typical of the union," Alan explained. "They didn't really want a wage increase, and I don't think they expected us to give them one, but this is the only fabricating plant in the area that has a union, and they sure don't want to lose this foothold!"

"Those charts of Mr. Green's were nice and fancy all right," recalled Norman West, president of the union, "but they don't help us when we go to the grocery store." Norman had been with the company for 10 years and had held the position of union president for over a year. "The men generally think the new management is trying to do a good job," he continued, "but we have a lot of trouble with Mr. Madison. The old supervisor used to handle discipline on a personal basis, but all Madison does is keep handing us warning slips for rule violations.

"Mr. Newman seems like a very smart man, but we don't see nearly as much of him as we did of Mr. Dillon. The old gentleman was very interested in his own pet jobs, and he'd come right down into the shop to see how they were coming along. Now, Mr. Newman's a lot different. He's what you'd call a financial man, I guess, and we don't see him down in the shop so often. Some of the men feel that he is finally doing what a president should do—namely, looking after the company instead of looking after his own pet engineering jobs. Maybe they're right, but we'll probably never get to know him the way we did Mr. Dillon. At any rate, things sure are different around here now. There's one thing about this company's presidents," he continued, "and that's the fact that in all the years I've been here, neither Mr. Dillon or Mr. Newman have ever had much to do with the union. Mr. Burke used to handle it before, and now Mr. Green and Mr.

Madison represent the company, but Mr. Newman has never come. The men know this, but I'm not sure how they feel about it."

Plans for the Future

No immediate changes in the company's existing policies were contemplated. "There doesn't seem to be any immediate need for changing our operations radically in the future," explained Mr. Newman. "We still have to tighten up our organization some more and make our production operations more efficient, but the potentials in all three of our major fields look promising to me, so why should we do anything drastic? The company is really quite stable as it is, and we're in a strong financial position. Last year our sales took a big drop, but we still showed a small profit and paid some dividends. I think we're in pretty good shape, although I have been a bit concerned about the low level of work in the production shop."

No formal long-range plans had been formulated for the company, as Mr. Newman preferred to maintain a flexible operating policy and was skeptical of the value of definitive projections. "I'm not at all sold on the idea of fancy plans and projections," he explained. "A company's situation can change radically in such a short time that intricate forecasts of sales and profits just seem like a waste of time. I never have placed much faith in the two- or three-year projections of sales and earnings that a number of the investment advisory services always make on the big companies. Conditions have generally changed so fast that most of these figures have been 'way off anyway."

Mr. Newman mentioned that he recently had heard rumors that Mr. Dillon, senior, was trying to raise money to form a competing company. Details were obscure, but it appeared that the sum involved was in the neighborhood of $300,000. It was thought that the total employment would probably be about 40 persons. Mr. Newman had also heard from an equipment supplier that the Dillons had been asking for prices on a large crane. If true, this information would tend to indicate that the proposed company would be engaged in plate fabrication of some sort rather than in structural steel work.

In the event that Mr. Dillon was successful in raising the funds necessary for the formation of a small competing company, Mr. Newman thought it probable that both James Dillon and William Burke would leave their jobs with Dillon Fabricating and join the new company. The prospect of this increased competition had caused Alan Green to devote a considerable amount of thought to the company's position in its several lines of business, and in November, 1958, he was considering what recommendations, if any, he should make to Mr. Newman on how the company's competitive position might be strengthened over the next several years.

He realized that a number of small companies had been able to increase profits substantially by emphasizing the most profitable segments of their business, but he was uncertain whether this policy would be applicable to the Dillon Fabricating Company because of its well-established position in a number of fields. Furthermore, he was not exactly sure which of the company's several types of activity were likely to prove the most attractive from a long-run standpoint. "I'm not really sure where we go from here," he explained. "Do we keep on competing in all the fields we're in now, or should we start to specialize? For instance, what should we do about those commodities? Chuck Cooper tells me that we're having a tough time on price with some of the local dealers, but he thinks it may just be temporary. There must be a couple of thousand square feet there that we could use to spread out our fabricating work. Maybe we could build a shed in the yard and put it out there.

"Actually, though, in spite of all the problems, this is the sort of job I've looked forward to. I am really in charge of production and have been given a pretty free hand with the shops. Also, Mr. Newman has just offered me a chance to buy 200 shares of the company's stock at $20 a share. This should be a very profitable operation some day, but it will take a lot of work to get things really straightened out and running smoothly. Probably one of my biggest worries right now is to decide just which problems are the most important and what should be done about them."

2. TECNIFAX CORPORATION (A)*
Responding to a Competitor's Price Change

Tecnifax began operations January 1, 1949, having been established to manufacture and sell diazotype reproduction paper. In 1952, Tecnifax sales were $2.5 million. From 1950 through 1952, total annual production of the industry had increased by 220 percent. During the first week of January, 1953, the management of Tecnifax learned that the largest company in the industry was cutting the prices of its various types of diazo paper by 9 to 16 percent. In the past, the prices of Tecnifax products had been pegged at approximately the same level as the prices of this competitor. The Tecnifax management had to decide whether to change the prices of its own products.

Industry

Diazotype reproduction processes, sometimes called whiteprinting, were developed in Europe after World War I as direct competitors to the blueprint process for making prints of technical drawings and for related purposes. The inherent simplicity of the process, its positive-printing characteristics, the fact that images are reproduced as dark lines on white paper, and the speed with which prints can be produced gave the process rapid acceptance. It was widely used to reproduce engineering drawings, office forms, invoices, reports, and letters. In 1952, use of diazotype paper exceeded that of blueprint paper, although more blueprint was being used than ever before. The estimated industry production of diazo products for the years 1949 through 1952 is given in Exhibit 2–1.

In making diazo prints, an exposing step is followed by a developing step. In the exposing step, the original drawing or letter covers the coated diazo paper as exposure to ultraviolet light takes place. The ultraviolet light is supplied by a high-pressure mercury-vapor tube within the exposing equipment; the master drawing is between the lamp and the sensitized paper. The original drawing must be on translucent paper, and the image must be opaque to ultraviolet light. The ultraviolet light passes through the translucent paper to strike the

Exhibit 2–1

TECNIFAX CORPORATION (A)

INDUSTRY PRODUCTION OF BLUEPRINT AND DIAZOTYPE PAPER
(in thousands of tons)

Year	Blueprint Paper	Diazotype Paper
1949	10.0	4.2
1950	11.5	6.5
1951	11.9	11.1
1952	13.2	13.6

SOURCE: National Association of Blueprint and Diazotype Coaters.

underlying coated paper, except where prevented by the opaque lines of the original. The diazo paper is coated with certain coal-tar chemicals, called the diazo and the coupler. The diazo is decomposed where it is struck by the ultraviolet light. That portion which later constitutes the image is not affected, since it lies beneath the opaque lines of the original. The diazo paper is then developed by exposure to a hot, moist ammonia atmosphere. That part of the diazo which has not been decomposed by the ultraviolet radiation reacts with the coupler to give a colored diazo dye, and thus an image.

In another type of diazo process, the coupler (instead of being a part of the coated paper) is applied in a thin film to the sensitized paper after exposure has taken place. The coupler reacts with that part of the diazo coating which has been protected from the ultraviolet light by being beneath the opaque lines of the original drawing. The reaction takes place without exposure to an ammonia atmosphere. This is called the moist process. Although the dry process was said to be more versatile and to result in better prints, the moist process was sometimes preferred for those situations in which it was difficult to get rid of ammonia fumes. In 1952, the moist process accounted for approximately one-third of total diazo sales, a somewhat smaller market share than in earlier years. The Charles Bruning Company, a large manufacturer of drafting and office equipment and supplies, dominated the moist field.

The dry diazo segment of the industry included five major firms. Of these, Ozalid, a division of General Aniline and Film Corporation, was the largest, with an estimated share of about 60 percent of the dry diazo market. This was a decrease from its estimated market share of over 70 percent in the late 1940's. Other major competitors, in addition to Tecnifax, were manufacturers of engineering equipment and supplies, such as Dietzgen, Frederick Post, and Keuffel & Esser. The equipment used for exposing and developing the paper was manufactured principally by Ozalid, with two smaller companies also producing machines. The Bruning Company manufactured the equipment for exposing paper in the moist process. In 1953, Tecnifax did not manufacture equipment.

A high level of research activity was conducted by most of the companies in the industry. Recent developments had included the coating of new materials (such as cellulose acetate film and plastic-coated papers), the introduction of new colors, and the discovery of better ways to maintain product shelf life.

Tecnifax Background

The company president, Joe W. Coffman, had had a varied background since graduating from Arkansas Cumberland College in 1923. He was the first director of visual education for the Atlanta school system, and later was a producer of scientific and educational films and a consultant in the motion picture industry. In 1929, he went with Consolidated Film Industries, Inc., a company which had acquired many smaller firms at depression prices. Mr. Coffman advanced to executive vice-president of the parent company, and served as chief executive officer of various of the subsidiary firms, one of which was Columbia Phonograph Company. During this time, he developed a basic business philosophy holding that a company should serve equitably the interests of stockholders, employees, customers, vendors, and the general public. In 1943, Mr. Coffman left Consolidated Films to become a vice-president of General Aniline and Film Corporation, as general manager of the Ozalid Division. As a foreign-owned corporation, General Aniline was controlled by the alien property custodian. At that time, the Ozalid Division was the primary supplier of dry developing diazo paper to American industry. During the next five years, Ozalid sales increased by approximately 300 percent. Subsequently, Mr. Coffman objected to certain developments and left the company May 1, 1948.

After investigating several other employment opportunities, he decided to accept an offer of financial backing to establish a new company to manufacture and sell diazo-sensitized materials. After discussions with the senior member of a firm that made a practice of investing in small enterprises, an agreement was reached in October, 1948, which provided that the company was to be established as a wholly owned subsidiary of another company owned by the same firm.

Provision was made that the Tecnifax stock would be transferred to the parent investment firm when operations became profitable. It was understood that Mr. Coffman, as president and treasurer, would be in complete charge, although the stockholders would maintain a close and active interest.

Tecnifax started operations January 1, 1949, using a portion of the plant of Plastic Coatings, Inc. This company was a manufacturer of plastic-coated paper and was also owned by the parent investment company. It was located in Holyoke, Massachusetts, a center of the paper manufacturing industry. Originally, the diazo coating of the paper was done by Plastic Coatings to Tecnifax specifications. Within 10 months, this policy was changed to one under which Tecnifax rented the equipment and did its own manufacturing. On the first day of operations, Mr. Coffman was the only employee. However, several executives and salesmen soon left Ozalid to work for their old boss at Tecnifax. Eventually, about 20 people came to Tecnifax from Ozalid.

Losses were shown the first year on total sales of $87,000. However, operations were profitable by April, 1950, and for all months thereafter. The growth in sales for the years 1949 through 1952 is shown in Exhibit 2–2.

Plant Acquisition

As sales expanded, Tecnifax had rented office and warehouse space in various other buildings in Holyoke. However, in the spring of 1952, the opportunity arose to purchase a well-constructed group of buildings, of heavy mill construction, located on the Holyoke waterpower canal system. The mill had been built and occupied for many years by the American Thread Company, which was moving to the South. Although the building was sixty-four years old, Tecnifax considered it the best manufacturing property in Holyoke; it had been well kept up. There were five floors in the main building; the total area of all buildings was 250,000 square feet. It was estimated that Tecnifax sales of $25 million per year could be supported in these facilities. Tecnifax offered $100,000 for the real estate and waterpower rights, 25 percent of the amount asked. The offer was accepted.

After acquiring the plant, Tecnifax made a number of changes: new floor covering, improved lighting, air conditioning, conversion of the former engine room into modern offices, landscaping, and leveling of two unneeded warehouses to make parking space. Since all the floor space was not needed, two floors were rented for a total rental of $15,000 per year.

Exhibit 2–2

TECNIFAX CORPORATION (A)

TECNIFAX NET SALES FOR 1949 THROUGH 1952

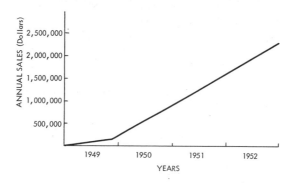

Production

The first step in the manufacturing of diazotype paper was coating the paper with diazo-sensitizing solution. This was done by two aqueous sensitizing machines, each 120 feet long and consisting of a wet and dry end. At the wet end, paper on rolls (6,000 yards or more in length) was guided by rollers to solution trays, where coating rollers revolving in the solution made contact with the paper, applying the sensitizer. After then passing an air knife, which controlled the amount of solution remaining on the paper, the web of paper passed to the drying channel, where excess moisture was removed.

Nine-hundred-pound rolls of the sensitized paper were then taken by elevator to the converting department, one floor below. There, the rolls were cut into large sheets, which were counted, checked for defects, trimmed to exact size, and wrapped in polyethylene-coated, brown kraft paper. Except for the checking step, these functions were performed by automatic equipment. After the wrapping table, the packages received the Tecnifax maroon and yellow label, which described the size, number, and kind of sheets in each package. Some paper was sold as rolls of various lengths (10 to 300 yards). Rewinding machines wound and measured these rolls.

The coating department was largely automatic. The converting and shipping departments involved considerable handling of the product. Since the coated material was sensitive to ultraviolet light, no operations were performed in sunlight, and the departments were lighted by incandescent lamps. The giant aqueous sensitizing machines, as well as certain other equipment, had been designed by Tecnifax engineers and built in Tecnifax shops. The Tecnifax management considered its manufacturing equipment, all of which had been recently built, to be at least as efficient as any in the industry.

All major producers devoted attention to quality control. Tecnifax quality control personnel checked raw materials, coating solutions, and the print characteristics of coated rolls. Workers took samples from every roll as it was being sensitized. These samples were sent by pneumatic tubes to the quality control print room where they were checked against standards for such printing characteristics as print speed, density, smoothness, and color. An intercom system made it possible for the quality control technicians to maintain continuous communication with the sensitizing department, so that machine conditions could be rapidly changed if necessary.

Management believed that, in purchasing, the company should show consideration for suppliers. A policy had been developed whereby, in the purchasing of paper, the suppliers would make the same percentage of profit on their sales to Tecnifax as Tecnifax did on its total sales. To facilitate this policy, both Tecnifax and the suppliers of paper made the needed financial information mutually available. This approach to purchasing had resulted in Tecnifax's obtaining a reduction in the price of paper purchased of from 5 to 10 percent. Management hastened to add that its relations with suppliers were excellent.

The Tecnifax council, an employee-elected organization, was responsible for social activities, the company newspaper, plant cleanliness, the parking lot, etc. Once a month, the president sat with the council to explain company policy, including financial data, the competitive situation, and production plans and problems. In 1953, there was no union; the council did not concern itself with wage rates.

Finance

All voting stock was owned by the investment firm with which Mr. Coffman made the initial agreement for launching the enterprise. Mr. Coffman and Mr. Hamilton (the vice-president and director of sales) had purchase agreements to buy nonvoting common stock. As the company had expanded, additional needs for funds had been met by equity investment by the original investors, by loans from other companies owned by these investors, and by loans from a Holyoke bank. No dividends had been paid. Various weekly and monthly reports were sent to the stockholders.

Sales

Tecnifax had moved vigorously to offer an expanded line of coated papers, in a greater variety of colors, sizes, and types of paper than had been available before. These Tecnifax innovations spurred other companies also to expand their lines, although the Tecnifax line was the broadest in the industry in all years after 1949. Tecnifax products were sold nationally through eight company-owned branches, and through eight distributors where the volume was not sufficient to support a branch. The distributors accounted for about 12 percent of Tecnifax sales. Normally, they were large blueprinters who offered blueprinting and whiteprinting services and sold a broad line of engineering and office supplies. They received a discount from list of 40 percent, and could offer discounts, as they saw fit, to their customers. Of the other companies in the industry, Ozalid sold mainly through branches, and the other companies sold largely through distributors.

There were 22 Tecnifax salesmen, from one to three being attached to each branch. In their selling, the salesmen tried to go through the purchasing agents to talk directly with the chief draftsman or office manager who would be working with the paper. The cost of the coated paper itself was small compared to the time that went into making the drawings or the letters which were reproduced. The salesmen felt that the broad line of Tecnifax products and the careful attention of the salesmen to individual problems would result in the users' specifying the Tecnifax brand to the purchasing agents. The salesmen normally did not take orders, but rather acted as technical consultants in the use of coated materials. Orders were sent by customers directly to branches. Standard items were inventoried at the branches, and could be shipped on the day the order was received.

The company sales management prided itself on the service provided customers. If competitive products were better for particular uses, salesmen were told to tell this to the customer. It was not considered unusual for a salesman to make a rush delivery in his car in order to keep a customer from running out of sensitized paper. Salesmen were paid a base salary plus a commission on all material sold. The Tecnifax compensation for salesmen was the highest in the industry. Management stated that they had needed good salesmen to get started, and they had paid to get them. Some salesmen made over $20,000 per year. Sensitized paper normally had a shelf life of four months to a year. Any paper with which customers were dissatisfied could be returned. The company motto was "It's easy to do business with Tecnifax."

In 1952, according to Mr. Coffman, the policy of the company was to have its prices similar to those of Ozalid. Historically, most companies in the industry had followed the lead of Ozalid in price changes, normally being about 5 percent below Ozalid's prices. The most vigorous price competition had been that provided by "garage coaters"—small companies that sold on a regional basis with prices as much as 10 to 30 percent lower than Tecnifax. Industry practice was to grant continuing discounts, based upon quantity. A discount was assigned to a particular customer according to the estimated volume of his annual purchases. The discount was applied even if his purchases fluctuated from month to month, although it was changed if it appeared that there was a permanent change in his needs for coated materials. The discounts ranged from 10 percent off list for purchases of $50 to $150 per month to 30 percent on purchases of over $1,000 per month. Although Tecnifax did not do so, some companies gave a 2 percent cash discount.

During the first week of January, 1953, Tecnifax learned that telegrams had been received by their principal customers stating the following:

Production economies due to greatly increased volume force substantial immediate reduction list price Ozalid sensitized papers. Your usual discount still applies. This unusual against-trend reduction offers you opportunity to obtain quality and reduced cost, doing business with the industry leader and originator of Ozalid process.   —OZALID

Within a week, the new price list was available, indicating price cuts of from 9 to 16 percent on various items. After an inspection of these prices, the management of Tecnifax came to the conclusion that the changes had been aimed to hit the principal items of the Tecnifax line, particularly those on which the competition of Tecnifax had been troublesome. To the best of management's knowledge, the Tecnifax manufacturing costs were as low as any in the industry. The company also considered its expenditures for administration, research, engineering, maintenance, and selling to be reasonable and comparable to those of other companies in the industry. These costs, as a percentage of sales, are given for 1952 in Exhibit 2–3. Management did not believe that any conceivable increase in the production speed of the coating machines could justify more than a 5 percent cost decrease.

Exhibit 2–3

TECNIFAX CORPORATION (A)

OPERATING STATEMENT FOR 1952
(in percentages)

Net sales		100.0%
Cost of goods sold		67.9
Gross profit		32.1%
Selling and administrative expenses:		
Administration and research	6.1%	
Engineering and maintenance	3.7	
Selling expense	13.8	23.6
Net operating profit		8.5%
Taxes		5.2
Net Profit after Taxes		3.3%

Information from the company's branch offices indicated that the other major producers in the dry diazo field were falling in line with the new Ozalid prices. These companies had been selling at about 5 percent below the Ozalid and Tecnifax prices; they were now cutting their prices again in order to match the new Ozalid prices. In order to estimate the effect of the prospective prices on Tecnifax profits, management recalculated the December operating statement for the company, substituting the proposed prices for those actually charged. The recalculation revealed a $400 loss, rather than the typical 1952 profit before taxes of $16,700. From this, it was estimated that the company would just about "break even" at the new price level.

Some of the sales executives estimated that sales volume might drop by 30 percent if the price cuts were not followed. This estimate was based upon an examination of the customer list and the resulting conclusion that there was a tight relationship, bound by service, with about 70 percent of the customers. It was thought that the other 30 percent bought primarily on a price basis. Because a high percentage of the cost of goods sold represented variable costs, it was estimated that a small profit could be shown at this lower sales volume.

At the meeting called to determine Tecnifax policy in regard to this price change, there was considerable discussion. One point of view was represented by an executive who emphasized that profits before taxes in 1952 had been only 8.5 percent of sales. He said, "If we match these prices, we'll be selling our products at a loss. It is suicidal to follow the lower prices now offered by others in the industry. We have competed successfully in the past despite slightly higher prices. The cost of diazotype paper is small compared to its importance. By continuing to emphasize service and a broad product line, we can maintain at least the greater part of our sales volume, *and* operate at a profit."

A second executive countered, "We have spent four years in building up our market position, and we just acquired this plant in order to support a larger sales volume. Our relationships with our customers are our most important asset, and we should not jeopardize them by refusing to recognize that conditions change. If we do not lower our prices, every company in the industry can undersell us. Let us recognize the fact that industry conditions change and that a company can only compete if it is flexible."

It was thought that a decision should be made within a few days, since many branches had reported that they were receiving telephone calls from customers who were wondering what action the company was going to take.

3. TECNIFAX CORPORATION (B)*
Development of a Marketing Program for Specialized Products

In 1951, Tecnifax began to manufacture diazo-sensitized film for use in color-proofing in the lithographic industry. Within a few years, a larger market developed in the use of diazo-sensitized film for making projectuals (slides) for use with overhead projectors and projection screens. By 1959, annual sales of this product exceeded $1 million. The primary means of promotion since 1954 had been semiannual "seminar-workshops in visual communication," sponsored by the company to promote the general cause of visual communication, and to instruct present and potential consumers in the use of Tecnifax and other visual communication techniques.

It was the practice of the management of Tecnifax to challenge existing policies as a means of determining whether changes might be advisable. In accordance with this policy, in 1959 management was examining the entire marketing program for coated film.

Background

As discussed in Tecnifax Corporation (A), the company started operations on January 1, 1949, in Holyoke, Massachusetts. The principal product was diazo-sensitized paper for use in reproducing technical drawings, letters, and office forms. In January, 1953, as recorded in Tecnifax Corporation (A), the company faced its greatest crisis when the dominant company in the industry cut its prices by 9 to 16 percent for various products. Sales volume increased in the following years, with the company emphasizing service and quality in its selling efforts. In 1959, net sales exceeded $7.3 million.

Coated Film

The Ozalid Division of General Aniline and Film had been the first company to diazo-sensitize sheets of cellulose acetate film, beginning in the middle 1940's. As with diazo-sensitized paper, an original

* Copyright © 1961 by the President and Fellows of Harvard College.

image could be reproduced by exposing and developing sheets of clear, coated plastic. The film was processed in the same ammonia-developing diazotype equipment used for processing diazo-sensitized paper. When this slide was used with an overhead projector, the image could be projected on a large viewing screen. Various colors could be used, but a separate and differently sensitized sheet of the film was required for each color. Multiple color pictures could be projected by overlaying several sheets. The composite result, mounted on heavy cardboard mounts, could be projected by hinging the separate color films so that each could be separately and sequentially "dropped" in register, to complete the total effect desired. These visual assemblies were referred to as projectuals, rather than slides, since they did not slide into the projector, but were laid on it.

Mr. Coffman had headed the Ozalid Division at the time the product was introduced. Originally, diazo film was sold to lithographers, who could see how a finished lithograph would look by making up "proofs" with the diazo film. They could, therefore, correct errors in color separation and show prospective customers the approximate printed result without first going to the time and expense of making the lithographic plates. Ozalid sales volume on diazo film did not develop rapidly. When Mr. Coffman left Ozalid, the new management of the division announced that the product would be dropped because it was not profitable. The lithographic firms using the film for proofing protested so strongly that the product was kept in the Ozalid line, but the price was doubled.

A year later, representatives of the lithographic industry approached Tecnifax, and asked it to make the product. The Tecnifax laboratories developed a newly formulated line of Diazochrome film, which the company began to sell in 1951. At that time, overhead projectors were coming into increasing use in visual communication, particularly for military training. The company developed a number of techniques for using projectuals (slides made with diazo film) with these projectors.

Methods were perfected whereby drawings, photographs, typing, graphs, and diagrams could be reproduced as 10" x 10" diazo projectuals, for screen presentation. Speakers could write directly on the projectuals, permitting them to add information as the audience watched. Furthermore, through the use of overlays, several colors could be superimposed, giving multiple color effects, and/or permitting new information to be introduced.

In 1954, at the request of the United States Navy, Tecnifax conducted a seminar-workshop on the use of diazotype materials and machines. Twenty-five navy men attended the seminar-workshop, which was of three days' duration. Tecnifax repeated the seminar for other navy groups and personnel from other military services, presenting six seminars within a period of a few months. Deciding that the seminar-workshop provided an excellent way to secure potential consumer interest in visual communication and in the use of diazo film, the Tecnifax management expanded the format and adopted the policy of major seminar-workshops on a semiannual basis. Thereafter, industrial, educational, and nonmilitary governmental personnel, as well as military personnel, were invited to participate.

The Seminar

Attendance at the seminars steadily increased until it exceeded 660 in the fall of 1959. The Sixteenth Seminar for Visual Communication, held October 20–22, 1959, included people from 38 states and several foreign countries. Industry, the armed forces, educational institutions, and federal and state governments were represented. Because of seating limitations, it was necessary to refuse some late requests for invitations; these applicants were told they would receive invitations to the following spring seminar.

Tecnifax made no charge for the seminar, and provided complimentary lunches, coffee breaks, and chartered bus service from the hotels to the plant. The participants paid for their own transportation to Holyoke, their lodging, and food. It was estimated that, on the average, the total expenses of each participant (including salary, transportation, and living expenses) were not less than $300 for the seminar. The Tecnifax traffic department secured reservations and made available free transportation at the airports and railroad stations. Shortly before the seminars, each participant received a booklet (describing the program) and information relating to his hotel reservation. The opening session was at 9 A.M. on Tuesday morning in the Holyoke Municipal War Memorial Auditorium. As each participant arrived, he received a briefcase of supplies and informational material. The welcoming address was followed by several speeches of general communication interest, some of which involved the use of projectuals with the overhead projector. At noon, everyone went to the Tecnifax plant for lunch and the workshop sessions.

From Tuesday noon until Thursday noon, the delegates attended 14 different workshops, each located on the third or fourth floor of the Tecnifax plant. For these workshops, the participants were assigned to groups of about 45, with the groups divided according to experience in visual communication techniques. As a member of his group, each person attended all 14 workshops, each of which lasted one hour. The workshop subjects included: a lecture-demonstration on the technology of the diazotype processes, practical laboratory work in creating and producing projectuals, and demonstrations of techniques for using polarized light with projectuals for simulating motion. The emphasis was on using diazo film; standard diazo papers received only passing mention. Some of the workshops were conducted by other companies in visual communication; these collaborators included Eastman Kodak Company, Polaroid Corporation, and Chart-Pak, Inc.

The participants varied widely in age and experience. Some were draftsmen or commercial artists who expected to be making the slides. Some were teachers, supervisors of visual education, or directors of company training programs. Half of the Tecnifax sales force, and even officers of competing firms, were present. At one seminar, all directors of the industry trade association were present, permitting a meeting of the board of directors to be held in the Tecnifax plant after the last session of the seminar. Many organizations sent people each year in order to keep informed of the latest developments in the field.

The participants seemed to infect one another with enthusiasm for visual communication. The conversation at the coffee breaks, the luncheons, and the hotels often centered on experiences in using overhead projectors and the diazofilm. About 40 percent of the people were from organizations that had not yet used these techniques; these people often buttonholed other participants and questioned them about their experiences. An open house was held at the plant each evening, in which the participants could get additional experience in the laboratories or question the workshop lecturers in greater detail. Several hundred people returned after supper for these evening sessions.

Ozalid, a competitor, had obtained from Tecnifax permission to demonstrate one of its new products at the evening meetings. The Tecnifax management always tried to avoid anything that might be construed as advertising for Tecnifax. In fact, the Tecnifax salesmen were housed in a motel separate from the other participants and were forbidden to do any selling during the seminar. Nevertheless, Tecnifax received considerable word-of-mouth advertising in the coffee-break conversations. In one case, a training supervisor for a large midwestern food chain (a man who had no previous contact with the industry) listened intently while two armed forces representatives talked about the rapid service they had received from Tecnifax salesmen. In addition, the participants became particularly familiar with the Tecnifax products.

On Thursday afternoon, everyone again assembled in the auditorium. Potential uses of diazo projectuals were illustrated by several presentations. One presentation was a "Speech Without Words," in which the "speaker" used only projectuals and background music in presenting, quite effectively, his ideas on the challenge of the Atomic Age. At 5 P.M., the seminar-workshop ended, and the participants received certificates of completion and left for their homes. Several weeks later a package of materials used in the seminar-workshops and descriptive literature relating to it were sent to the participants at their business addresses.

The average out-of-pocket costs to Tecnifax of each of the more recent seminar-workshops were slightly more than $25,000. This included materials, chartered buses, food, and overtime pay. Other costs were hard to estimate, since records were not kept of the total time spent on the project by members of the organization. Estimates of the number of man-days spent on each seminar ranged from 450 to 650. It was stated that the exact costs were not known, and that the precise benefits deriving from the seminar were difficult to determine.

Other Elements of the Marketing Program

The use of diazo film required overhead projectors and viewing screens; Tecnifax sold, but did not manufacture, these items. The company also rented them to prospective customers; the rental payments were deducted from the purchase price if the machine was later bought. If a customer needed a projector and a screen for a presentation in a distant city and had trouble obtaining one, the Tecnifax salesman would call various people in the city until the equipment was obtained. Tecnifax lost money on the rental service, but made a net margin, after allocation of sales and administrative expenses, of approximately 15 percent on the equipment sold. The sales of projectors since 1956 are given in Exhibit 3–1.

Tecnifax had dominated the diazo film market since the early 1950's. Ozalid and Frederick Post both competed vigorously, but it was estimated that Tecnifax had maintained a market share of approximately 75 percent. Although vigorous price competition had

Exhibit 3–1

TECNIFAX CORPORATION (B)

	1956	1957	1958	1959*
Tecnifax sales of diazo film	$668,000	$760,000	$899,000	$1,008,000
Tecnifax sales of overhead projectors .	$ 18,900	$ 29,500	$ 88,600	$ 278,000

* Estimate based upon 10-month sales.

occurred in the diazo paper field, the other companies in the industry had apparently followed the lead of Tecnifax in pricing diazo film. The profit margin on this film was higher than on diazo paper. Tecnifax had been a leader in introducing new products. In 1959, the Tecnifax line consisted of 22 different kinds of diazo film. There were 11 colors, and several of them were available on films of different thickness and surface characteristics. This was a considerably broader line than that of any competitor.

All Tecnifax salesmen sold diazo film as well as diazo-coated paper. Originally, an incentive compensation plan was established to encourage salesmen to promote diazo film. Under this plan, each salesman had a monthly goal, which was a three-month moving average of his sales of diazo film. If he surpassed the goal, he received a 10 percent commission on all sales of diazo film for the month. If he did not reach the goal, he received the customary 5 percent commission on all diazo film sold. In the two years the plan was in effect, it was found that only one salesman appeared to actively promote the product, and he slacked off periodically in order to lower his quota. The plan was eliminated.

It was thought that the special compensation plan was unsuccessful in motivating salesmen because in every sales territory there were great opportunities to expand sales of diazo paper, and because the introduction of the new concept of using diazo film in visual communication was a slow process. Therefore, most salesmen felt that their time could be used more profitably to themselves in developing new markets for diazo paper.

As an alternative, one salesman was designated as a "visual communication missionary" in 1957. He was to devote his entire time toward interesting prospective New England area customers in diazo film and the overhead projector. He was then to service the accounts he obtained. By 1959, he accounted directly for approximately 5 percent of the total company sales of diazo film and overhead projectors. A second missionary salesman was named in August, 1959, to develop visual communication sales in the Cleveland area. These missionary salesmen called on military, governmental, industrial, and educational institutions. Sometimes, however, they were asked by other Tecnifax salesmen to demonstrate the use of diazo film to customers who already purchased diazo paper from Tecnifax. In such cases, the missionary salesman received credit for selling the overhead projector, and the other Tecnifax salesman received the film account. Sometimes, the missionary salesmen sold film to companies that purchased diazo paper from other suppliers. In these cases, the missionary salesmen continued to service these accounts.

The missionary salesmen were paid on a straight salary basis. Although their salaries were less than the salary plus commission they would receive if they were selling diazo paper, both missionary salesmen thought this was compensated for by the bright future for diazo film. Bennett Schultz, who had been a missionary salesman for two years, was enthusiastic both about the film and the seminar. He said, "If I can get a prospective customer to the seminar, it's only a matter of time until I can close the sale. When people come to the seminar, they see the potential uses; they learn to use the materials; they gain confidence in the results; and they talk to dozens of others who have used the projectuals in visual communication."

Distributors received a 40 percent discount on diazo film. However, less than 5 percent of all diazo film sales were through distributors. Of the remaining 95 percent of total sales, Mr. Schultz (the missionary salesman) accounted for 5 percent, and the other company salesmen, operating out of the branches, accounted for the remainder.

Advertising expenditures specifically for diazo film were about $5,500 in 1959. This included expenditures for sales literature and for advertising in various business magazines. Inquiries resulting from the magazine advertising were referred to the salesmen in the appropriate areas. The actual advertisements were straightforward descriptions of the product. Mr. Coffman said, "If we were selling pretty girls, there would be good reason for having them in our advertisements. However, we're selling diazo film and paper. There is no point in our spending advertising money to insult the intelligence of the readers of our advertisements." Tecnifax representatives, particularly the missionary salesmen, also gave frequent group lecture-demonstrations, using diazo film projectuals, in the major branches. The competing firms relied heavily on local demonstrations to interest prospective customers; these often were conducted in hotel suites.

Tecnifax had also established a laboratory to develop new ways to use diazo film in visual communication, and to train customers in the techniques of projectual production. This was called the Visucom Laboratory. Since its inception in early 1958, it had trained approximately 500 people in projectual preparation. Draftsmen and artists attended three-to-five-day sessions which were similar to the seminars, except that they were somewhat more slanted toward practical laboratory work. This training was supervised by 10 members of the Tecnifax ·staff who were associated with the laboratory. These same men had developed a number of new techniques for using projectuals. These included various uses of polarized light and the use of photography with diazo film. The research laboratory investigated the basic chemistry of diazo reactions, developed new products, and worked to improve present products and manufacturing processes.

Mr. Coffman, the president, and Mr. Hamilton, the vice-president, also personally promoted the use of visual techniques to solve communication problems. It was estimated that each of them gave more than 50 talks per year, covering the broad field of communication, to various interested groups. These talks, or presentations, provided opportunities to demonstrate the use of overhead projectors and diazo film projectuals.

In 1959, it was estimated that 80 percent of total company sales of diazo film were to government agencies. On this business, prices were negotiated with the General Services Administration. Any government agency could purchase at the General Services Administration price, and the agency would also receive the same quantity discount as a civilian customer. The General Services Administration negotiations did not guarantee Tecnifax any particular volume of sales. Other suppliers had also negotiated with General Services Administration. Tecnifax had to compete with these companies to sell to the various government agencies. In many cases, despite a higher price, Tecnifax was given increasingly large orders because of its broad line of product and excellent service.

In 1959, Tecnifax sold diazo film but did not offer a slide-making service. Purchasers used the film to make their own projectuals. However, management was considering the production of finished projectuals for use in schools. The company would commission a skilled teacher to plan a set of projectuals for use in teaching a certain subject, such as algebra. Tecnifax would then make the finished slides, and sell them through its sales force to interested schools. Many teachers interested in using projectuals did not have the time or the skill to make them.

The cost for a school or company to begin using diazo film was estimated as follows:

Projector . . . . . $395 and up
Screen . . . . . . 92 and up
Introductory kit . . 198.50

(Kit includes the printer ($156.50), the ammonia developer ($32.50), a special staple gun ($12.00), 50 sheets of film, 10 mounts for the film, an exposing device, and various other items.)

Also available were lettering kits, marking pens, and chart-making tape, all of which Tecnifax sold, but did not manufacture. Additional film could be purchased for $21.90 per 100 sheets (8½" x 11").

Although sales had grown rapidly, management thought the industry was still in its infancy. They foresaw the time when most schools and industrial training programs in the country might use overhead projectors and diazo film projectuals.

Mr. Coffman thought it was very important that the marketing efforts of Tecnifax be devoted to building continuing relationships. He said, "To build this business to its potential dimensions, we must have the continuing support of our customers. We can obtain such support only by giving the customer full value for every penny he spends with us. Unless we do this, we have no right to accept his money."

On its film, the company had a profitable product, the sales of which had expanded rapidly as new uses were discovered and as consumers were educated to use the product. The company was, at present, the leader in this field. Management thought that diazo film was in the early stages of development and that a large expansion of industry sales would certainly occur. The company was eager, through the review and development of current policies and through plans for the future, to take advantage as completely as possible of the potentials existing in diazo film and in products that might grow therefrom.

4. QUALITY CARBON, INC.*

Finding the Cause of Operating Losses and Taking Action

"We've got to decide what to sell and then do a better job of selling it," said William Ashton, vice-president of Quality Carbon, Inc. The company manufactured carbon paper and typewriter ribbons. It had been established 40 years earlier, in 1919, by James Ashton (William Ashton's father) and three other men. Since 1951, annual sales had fluctuated between $300,000 and $584,000, with profits before taxes averaging about 3 percent of net sales. In November of 1959, it appeared that sales of $560,000 and a loss of about $20,000 would be shown for the year. William Ashton said that he realized the company had many problems, and he wondered which were most important. In particular, he wondered what could be done to return the company to profitable operations.

History

In 1919, James Ashton and Frank Charles, employees of the High-Top Carbon Company, of Patterson, New Jersey, left that company to establish an independent firm in Camden, New Jersey, to manufacture carbon paper and typewriter ribbons. Thomas Conrad, a chemist, joined them and became president of the new organization. These three men, in conjunction with John Miller, an independent investor, furnished slightly under $10,000 and received all the common stock. Friends of the founders furnished $50,000 and received 8 percent nonvoting cumulative preferred stock. Sales gradually increased as the company offered products to meet particular customer specifications or underpriced more established firms. Profits were not sufficient to pay dividends on the preferred stock until the 1930's. Early operations were conducted in a fourth-floor loft, but in 1933 the company moved to a building of concrete block construction, located in a residential section of Camden.

Of the founders, Mr. Conrad, the chemist, owned a majority of the common stock and served as president. He was variously described as "making all the decisions" or "contributing nothing but hot air." Mr. Charles was vice-president of manufacturing, and James Ashton was vice-president in charge of sales. Mr. Ashton had his office in New York City, but conferred frequently with the other two executives. Mr. Miller, the independent investor, did not participate actively in management.

Exhibit 4–1

QUALITY CARBON, INC.

ANNUAL SALES, 1945–1959
PROFITS AFTER TAXES, 1956–1959

Year	Gross Sales	Net Profits after Taxes
1945	$513,000	na
1946	422,000	na
1947	360,000	na
1948	254,000	na
1949	340,000	na
1950	310,000	na
1951	504,000	na
1952	478,000	na
1953	456,000	na
1954	398,000	na
1955	443,000	na
1956	538,000	$18,500
1957	564,000	7,100
1958	584,000	8,300
1959*	540,000	(20,000)

na—not available.
* Estimated.

In 1954, Mr. Conrad died. Some of his stock was purchased by James Ashton, who thereby gained majority control and became president. Mr. Ashton continued his participation in sales activities and kept his office in New York. He commuted one day a week to Camden to discuss matters with Frank Charles and to look over the financial records. In 1955, Jeffrey Charles, the son of Frank Charles, graduated from college and began to work full time for the company in manufacturing. He had worked for the company during vacations for a number of years. In 1957, William Ashton, the son of James Ashton, began working for the company as a salesman. He had received a chemical engineering degree in 1950 and had worked for seven years as a salesman for a large chemical company. In early 1959, both Jeffrey Charles and William Ashton were named vice-presidents. In September, 1959, Frank Charles retired and moved to California; his son Jeffrey took charge of the maufacturing operations.

The company sales for the 15 years ending 1959 are given in Exhibit 4–1. Profits for 1956–59 are also given. The compensation of the company officers had varied through the years, according to the profitability of operations. In recent years, the combined salaries of Frank Charles and James Ashton had totaled about $24,000 per year.

Products

"There probably isn't any one man in this company who knows how many products we sell," said William Ashton. Carbon paper was sold in three finishes, three weights of paper, and seven different brands. (Brands represented different quality and price levels, and all seven of these brands were owned by the company.) There were also special orders of carbon paper manufactured to meet the particular specifications of the government or large industrial users; this was called contract business. Additional combinations were created as salesmen agreed to modify existing numbers in order to meet the desires of particular customers. "In a study we conducted last spring," William Ashton commented, "we found that 88 different numbers of carbon paper were shipped in one month. Many of the salesmen probably didn't even know we had some of these numbers."

Typewriter ribbons were a second category of Quality Carbon business. Ribbons were sold in eight fabrics, three standard widths, and ten black inks (each of which could be varied in intensity). In addition, each brand of typewriter usually required a particular spool on which the ribbon was wound. It was observed that there were probably thousands of possible combinations.

A relatively new product, first sold in 1954, was "one-time carbon paper." It was used in carbon interleaved forms and was so called because it was used only once and then was thrown away. This poorer quality paper sold for about one-tenth the price of reusable carbon paper. It was sold on rolls to printers who made the forms. Another sales category consisted of resale items, which were purchased from other producers and resold. The major item was a particular kind of carbon paper used in hectograph machines. Other resale items were special kinds of carbon paper and typewriter ribbons; the volume of these products was minor.

"The problem of knowing our product line is a difficult one," said William Ashton. "The company came into existence and developed by offering to meet the particular needs of customers. Although the salesmen are now told to go easy on accepting special orders, most of them are in the habit of accepting all orders. The result is that we may end up with 10 different numbers of carbon paper that are practically the same, although each requires separate production." There was no extra charge for special orders.

Sales

The company's customers were classified as contract, consumer, and dealer. Contract customers were federal, state, and municipal governments and certain large industrial users. They established particular

Exhibit 4–2

QUALITY CARBON, INC.

COMPARATIVE BALANCE SHEETS

	December 31, 1957	December 31, 1958	October 21, 1959
ASSETS			
Current Assets:			
Cash	$ 3,385	$ 11,871	$ 2,052
Accounts and notes receivable, net ..	60,826	55,372	53,424
Inventory	114,500	84,661	93,980*
Total Current Assets	$178,711	$151,904	$149,456
Fixed Assets:			
Gross value, at cost	$102,781	$103,006	$105,640
Less: Reserve for depreciation ...	63,170	69,202	74,202
Net Value	$ 39,611	$ 33,804	$ 31,438
Other assets	239	1,956	2,592
Total Assets	$218,561	$187,664	$183,486
LIABILITIES AND CAPITAL			
Current Liabilities:			
Accounts payable	$ 48,310	$ 17,814	$ 33,510
Notes payable	21,936	17,948	20,944
Accrued payroll	3,481	2,650	—
Accrued taxes and expenses	4,604	3,617	5,430
Accrued income taxes	3,708	4,500	250
Total Current Liabilities	$ 82,039	$ 46,529	$ 60,134
Mortgage payable	26,188	23,621	21,381
Coupons outstanding	3,668	3,368	4,173
Total Liabilities	$111,895	$ 73,518	$ 85,688
Capital			
Common stock, no par	$ 6,830	$ 6,830	$ 6,830
Preferred stock, $100 par	50,000	50,000	50,000
Earned surplus	76,929	84,409	68,060
Treasury stock	(27,093)	(27,093)	(27,093)
Total Capital	$106,666	$114,146	$ 97,797
Total Liabilities and Capital ..	$218,561	$187,664	$183,485

* Estimated.

specifications, and bids were awarded on a price basis. Traditionally, about 50 percent of the total sales of the Quality Carbon company had been to contract customers; in 1959 this percentage had declined, due to the loss of a $60,000 per year contract for supplying carbon paper to the state of Pennsylvania. It was stated that Quality Carbon salesmen had to provide relatively little service to contract buyers.

Consumer sales were sales of standard items made directly to industrial users. Considerable service was required of the salesman as he

Exhibit 4–3

QUALITY CARBON, INC.

COMPARATIVE OPERATING STATEMENTS

	Year Ending Dec. 31, 1957	Year Ending Dec. 31, 1958	10 Months Ending Oct. 31, 1959
Net sales	$561,168	$579,604	$449,923
Cost of sales	456,989	467,182	373,536
Gross profit	$104,179	$112,422	$ 76,387
Other income	4,412	3,700	3,671
Gross income	$108,591	$116,122	$ 80,058
Selling and administrative expenses	97,879	103,334	96,571
Profit (loss) before taxes	$10,712	$ 12,788	$(16,513)
Provision for income taxes	3,571	4,500	250
Net Profit (Loss)	$ 7,141	$ 8,288	$(16,763)

called on the purchasing agent to determine whether adequate stocks were on hand and whether there were any problems in the use of the product. In attempting to obtain a new account, the salesman tried to talk to the typists, since it was said that if the office girls didn't like the brand, the purchasing agent would not buy it. Sales were also made to about 300 dealers located mainly in New Jersey and eastern Pennsylvania. These dealers included typewriter repairmen, stationers, and dealers in office supplies. The dealers received a 50 percent discount and carried only the Quality Carbon line. William Ashton said, "The most successful dealers go out after business and provide very good service for local users. However, for some reason they don't sell carbon paper as well as typewriter ribbon."

It was stated that there was rarely a conflict between Quality Carbon salesmen and dealers in competing for the same customer. If the dealers were energetic, the salesmen helped them. If the dealers only sat in their stores and waited for customers, the Quality Carbon salesmen did what they could to sell accounts in the same area.

In 1959, there were seven salesmen—three in New York City and four in New Jersey. Since the company had no dealers in New York

City, the three salesmen there sold directly to consumers. The four New Jersey salesmen sold all products, both to dealers and consumers. The president of the company, James Ashton, handled all of the contract accounts, in addition to selling to some consumers.

The New York salesmen were paid a straight commission, which varied from 3 percent for one-time carbon paper sales to 30 percent for sales to consumers. The income of these men averaged from $60 to $70 per week; all of them had been with the company for many years. Four salesmen were selling in various parts of New Jersey, two of whom had started during 1959. One man received $150 per week plus 8 cents per mile; a second received $75 per week plus $30 per week expenses; a third received a straight commission plus expenses plus part of his rent; William Ashton received $125 per week plus $30 per week expenses.

It was explained that the different methods of compensation had come about as each salesman bargained with James Ashton over his salary terms. The quality of selling was described by William Ashton as poor; the most common faults were lack of knowledge of the products and discouragement from the frequent customer complaints. (These complaints were described as a fixture in the industry.)

In addition to the salesmen, the company had what was termed a "valuable relationship" with an independent agent who handled all export business. This man had a flair for merchandising and many personal contacts. Due to his efforts, export business had grown rapidly during the past few years. He received a 5 percent commission and handled all contacts with foreign agents. James Ashton accounted personally for approximately 50 percent of total company sales, including virtually all sales to contract customers. His personal contacts, built up during a lifetime in the industry, were said to be an important factor in the maintenance of some of these accounts. Other accounts, particularly those of contract customers, supposedly were less dependent on his friendship.

In early 1959, William Ashton had sent a questionnaire to the salesmen, asking them what they would like to know. The emphatic response was, "More about the products." He then organized a sales meeting, in which he talked about sales techniques, markets, and the products. Although he thought the meeting was well received, he had been unable to organize any more meetings because of lack of time.

It was estimated that each salesman served from 200 to 500 accounts, some of which required weekly service and some of which sent in orders every year or so. One problem was the small size of many orders. A high percentage of orders were for less than $5.00, and some

Exhibit 4–4

QUALITY CARBON, INC.

SALES BY CATEGORY FOR FIVE MONTHS ENDING
MAY 31, 1959

Category	*Sales for Five Months*
Consumer	$34,511
Dealers	60,959
Contract	80,108
One-time	45,727
Resale	8,206

Sales of typewriter ribbons for five months ending May 31, 1959, totaled $104,310. Ribbons were sold to consumers, dealers, and contract customers.

were for less than $1.00. The dealers were described as particularly apt to call up the company and ask that "two green ribbons be sent over."

"We have to underprice the big companies," said William Ashton. "We price about 10 percent lower than the big boys on most of our standard items." Quantity discounts were traditional on sales to consumers, ranging up to 40 percent of list price for orders of 100 boxes of carbon paper or 50 dozen ribbons. Quality Carbon salesmen often emphasized this argument in approaching new customers, saying, "You have six or eight different kinds of typewriters in your office, and you buy the ribbons for each from the respective manufacturers. We sell guaranteed ribbons for all machines. Why not buy all your ribbons from us and get a quantity discount?" Bids on the contract business were made by James Ashton, who estimated direct costs and sometimes the overhead in arriving at a bid. No records were kept on the actual costs of individual orders. Contract business was described as increasingly competitive, with prices below what they had been 30 years earlier.

There was a wide range in the price of Quality Carbon products. For instance, a standard carbon paper made to government specifications was sold to the government at 50 cents per 100-sheet box. A high-quality carbon paper was sold through dealers to the public at $5.00 per 100-sheet box. Books of sales coupons of various denominations were offered to all consumers and were purchased by some. A book of coupons which sold for $10 would entitle the purchaser to $11.50 worth of Quality Carbon products. The coupons (which were similar to lunch tickets) had been adopted to permit customers to enjoy quantity discounts without having to stock a large quantity of products which might go stale. (The characteristics of both typewriter ribbons and carbon paper changed as the product aged.) James

Ashton had instituted the coupons as a promotional device some years before. However, the coupons never accounted for more than 1 percent of total Quality Carbon sales.

The company had previously done some advertising in office magazines. The results had been described as disappointing, since few inquiries had resulted. In early 1959, William Ashton experimented with direct mail advertising. He obtained a list of typewriter repairmen in the eastern United States. To these repairmen he sent a letter, telling them that Quality Carbon would teach them how to sell typewriter ribbons. There were 1,000 replies, and to these men he sent information about typewriter ribbons in general, and the Quality Carbon line in particular. He also notified the Quality Carbon salesmen that repairmen in their respective areas had answered the letter. Some of the salesmen visited the repairmen and began to sell typewriter ribbons to them; others did not. About 100 typewriter repairmen thereby became dealers for Quality Carbon ribbons; the majority of them were serviced by mail. By November, 1959, Quality Carbon sales to these dealers averaged from $500 to $1,000 per month.

The boxes for the carbon paper and ribbons were designed in the 1920's and used for over 30 years. In 1958 and 1959, most of the boxes were redesigned by an advertising agency and by William Ashton. The redesigned boxes, in addition to being more modern in appearance, cost only about two-thirds as much as the old boxes.

Competition

It was estimated that about 80 companies manufactured carbon paper or typewriter ribbons. A few of the companies were large, such as International Business Machines and Sperry Rand. However, most of the companies were small, family-owned concerns. Many of the companies specialized, both in products and in channels of distribution. For instance, some companies sold only ribbons solely through dealers; other companies might sell only carbon paper solely through their own sales force. Financial records of a publicly owned competitor, Old Town Corporation, are given in Exhibit 4–5.

Accounting

The president received monthly operating statements from the company's public accountant. Records of total sales of six categories were kept: contract, consumer, dealer, resale, one-time, and export.

Exhibit 4–5

QUALITY CARBON, INC.

Sales and net profits for 1954–58 of Old Town Corporation, a manufacturer of carbon paper, inked ribbons, and other office supplies. These products were sold through retail branches in New York City and 9 principal cities, through 980 dealers elsewhere in the United States, and through dealers in 35 countries.

Year	Net Sales	Net Profit after Taxes
1954	$6,387,958	$150,175
1955	7,444,566	18,073
1956	7,017,282	(327,938)
1957	5,857,534	131,103
1958	5,590,233	153,875

SOURCE: Standard & Poor's Corporation, *Standard Corporation Records.*

However, since costs were not accumulated by category, the actual profit for each was not known. The monthly operating statement was based on an estimated cost of goods sold. Physical counts of inventory were taken in July and December, and each count normally resulted in an adjustment to cost of goods sold of several thousand dollars for the six-month period. For many years, management had thought that contract business provided a low margin. However, losses shown in 1959, when contract business was down and other sales were up, caused them to wonder. "One of our biggest problems," said William Ashton, "is that we don't know which lines we're making a profit on. All of us would like to have more cost information. However, our line is so complex that it would probably cost a fortune to get it."

Production

The company's manufacturing plant was a two-story concrete block building, of 12,000 square feet, located in a residential section of Camden. Carbon paper manufacturing involved coating long rolls of paper with ink, cutting the rolls into sheets, and packaging the sheets. Typewriter ribbons were produced by inking rolls of fabric, of various widths, on special machines. The ribbons were then put on spools and packed. One-time paper was coated with ink on special coating machines; it was normally sold on rolls.

Manufacturing operations had been supervised by Jeffrey Charles since the retirement of his father, Frank Charles, in August, 1959. Frank Charles had worked actively in all phases of manufacturing, including scheduling, purchasing, formulating, testing, and personnel work. Although Jeffrey Charles had worked closely with his father, he was not used to making all decisions and "keeping his finger in all operations." He had lost 10 pounds in the three months since he took over.

There were 36 employees in the factory, two-thirds of whom were women. One foreman supervised the ribbon department, which included seven workers. This man had 23 years' experience in manufacturing typewriter ribbons with a large competitor; he was described as very competent. A second foreman supervised both the carbon paper manufacturing and the packaging department. Jeffrey Charles directly supervised the one-time manufacturing and the formulation of inks; he also personally did all scheduling and testing, and most of the purchasing.

The workers received an average wage of $1.35 per hour. Only the operators of the equipment that coated the carbon paper were considered skilled workers. There was no union, and a large number of the workers had been with the company for many years. There were few layoffs, and it was noted that manufacturing labor expense was regarded, more or less, as a fixed expense. In purchasing, Frank Charles had been eager to obtain quantity discounts. He often bought several years' supply of an item if he could get a 10 percent discount. In 1959, it was discovered that the company had enough orange cardboard, used to box one brand of carbon paper, to last for seven years. In late 1959, old inventory (mostly carbon paper) valued at about $1,200 had been thrown out. Twenty thousand pounds of old machinery had also been sold as scrap.

It was stated that management considered it desirable to take all purchase discounts, even if occasional short-term borrowing was required to do this. However, the cash balance was often low. The bookkeeper, who sent out the checks, had to decide whether to take the discount or to contact James Ashton, so that borrowing might be arranged. Since James Ashton was normally in New York, the bookkeeper did not bother him, with the result that the discount often was not taken.

The quality of raw materials was not checked, but the company had a policy of purchasing only from reputable suppliers who guaranteed the quality of their products. On finished goods, both the ribbons and carbon paper were tested on a typewriter by Jeffrey Charles. For ribbons, one sample was checked from the beginning and end of each run. For carbon paper, one sample was tested from each run, and another sample was filed for future testing in case there should be complaints. The testing involved actually typing with the carbon paper or ribbon and comparing the results visually with standards which had been prepared from their own standard carbon paper or ribbon. The company also had obtained a visual reflectometer, a device for measuring brightness. It was being used to check the orders of one contract customer who used the same device for checking incoming shipments. It was hoped that the reflectometer could be used more extensively in quality control in the future. It was stated that quality control had been much more of a problem in the past; some material had been shipped to customers which did not meet specifications. However, William Ashton said, "I don't think we're losing any business now because of quality."

Most of the manufacturing equipment was old, having been built in the 1930's in the company's machine shop. Nevertheless, management did not think it was significantly slower or more expensive to operate than that owned by competitors. It was estimated that there was enough equipment to support a sales expansion of perhaps 50 percent without having to go to two shifts. The only problem would be that of finding the space to store the inventory.

One major problem in their carbon paper manufacturing was that of small special orders. It was known that large orders (which were ordinarily for contract customers) could be run more cheaply than small ones, with the economies being primarily in the coating operation. Paper was fed into the coating machines on long rolls which, depending on the paper weight, could be coated in one and one-half to two hours. Since the inks were different for each number, the coating machine had to be cleaned whenever a different number was run. This cleaning required about 30 minutes. One roll made about 300 boxes of carbon paper. For a large order, a number of rolls could be run consecutively. Jeffrey Charles tried to schedule orders so that no runs would be for less than one roll. However, sometimes it was necessary to run fractional rolls for special or rush orders. With fractional rolls, there was often material wastage also.

Management thought its manufacturing costs as low as any in the industry, except with regard to short runs. William Ashton said, "A large manufacturer who sells a lot of one number can set up his coating machines for that number and coat roll after roll without stopping." No records had been kept of the average length run at Quality Carbon.

Finance

In 1959, 52 percent of the common stock was owned by James Ashton; Jeffrey Charles, John Miller, and the estate of the late Thomas Conrad owned the remainder. In regard to the 8 percent cumulative preferred stock, the company was 11 years in arrears on dividends. This was primarily due to losses in the early years of operations. In certain years during the last two decades, double dividends had been paid to these stockholders. There had never been a dividend on the common stock. In 1954, $30,000 had been borrowed from a Camden bank to finance the purchase of equipment to manufacture one-time carbon paper. The loan was secured by a mortgage on the building. James Ashton, as treasurer, handled almost all financial matters for the company.

Management

James Ashton was deeply involved in sales activities, spending most of his time in the New York sales office. He was described as being thoroughly familiar with the industry, knowing many other men in competitive companies who also had spent a lifetime in the industry. Some people in the company seemed to feel that he was reluctant to make changes and that the company was "just drifting." He was sixty-three years old, but still worked hard and appeared to be in good health. He had no plans for retirement. William Ashton estimated that 80 percent of his own time was spent selling, and the remainder was divided between advertising and general management problems. Jeffrey Charles described his typical day as involving one hour in scheduling, one hour in testing and quality control, and six hours in general supervision.

The board of directors, made up of James Ashton, William Ashton, Jeffrey Charles, and John Miller, met annually to satisfy legal requirements. No decisions, other than those called for by legal requirements, were made at the meetings of the board.

Conclusion

The loss for the first 10 months of operations in 1959 totaled over $16,000. William Ashton attributed this loss to three factors:

1. A high percentage of unprofitable small orders.
2. The loss of several valuable contracts; in particular, one with the state of Pennsylvania for $60,000 worth of carbon paper per year.

3. Added advertising expenses and the cost of two new salesmen who were not yet paying for themselves.

William Ashton was worried. He said, "The industry is becoming more competitive. We have to become more efficient in order to compete. As I see it, we have at least three major problem areas:

1. We should consolidate our line, dropping some numbers we now sell. Only, how can we do this? What numbers should we drop and how can we keep from losing customers in doing it?
2. We should have more definite organization. We should define areas of responsibility and get people to make decisions.
3. We should do a better job of selling, and, in particular, control our salesmen better. Above all, we need a concept of marketing—perhaps a combination of direct mail, direct selling, good packaging, and good service."

He added, "There may be other problems I don't see."

5. STEEL EXTRUSION, INCORPORATED (A)*
Developing and Exploiting a New Process

Steel Extrusion, Incorporated, had been formed in late 1958, in order to develop tooling and automation equipment for use in cold extrusion of steel. During 1959, the only employee was James Addison, a brilliant young inventor who had formerly worked in the cold extrusion research group of the Hercules Automobile Corporation. Although there was only one employee, a building had been built to house the development work. By December, 1959, almost $100,000 had been spent by Steel Extrusion for equipment and various development expenses. Mr. Addison thought the development work had progressed to the point where the equipment could soon be used in the cold extrusion of steel. At this time, the company received from New Castle Press, a large manufacturer of industrial presses, a proposal that an exclusive arrangement be made between the two companies. The board of directors of Steel Extrusion was meeting in the new plant in order to discuss the offer. The offer brought to a focus a number of other questions which had been discussed, but on which no decisions had been made.

Cold Extrusion Process

The process of cold extrusion (sometimes called chipless machining or impact extrusion), consisted of applying great pressure on a material, so that plastic flow resulted and the material took the shape of a die. The force was exerted by a press,[1] and the material was at room temperature when the process began. Cold extrusion had been used extensively for various nonferrous metals. However, despite a great deal of research effort by many of the largest companies in the country, the process had not yet been widely applied to steel.

---

[1] A press is a device for exerting large forces, sometimes up to several thousand tons. The press discussed in this case consisted of a ram, powered by mechanical means, which moved toward a stationary table. The material to be pressed was held between the ram and the table.

The Germans had been the first to cold extrude steel, when they made shells by that process during World War II. Pressures from 150,000 to 500,000 pounds per square inch were exerted on slugs of steel; these slugs had previously been coated with a zinc phosphate and soap solution, which provided lubrication for the processing. From slug to finished part might require from one to half-a-dozen extrusion steps, each of which was performed with a different die.

The greatest opportunities for cost savings with the process seemed to be in the forming of cup-shaped parts. These parts were often made on automatic screw machines which, starting with a bar of the desired outer diameter, cut out that center portion of the bar not needed in the finished part. Four advantages of cold extrusion were often mentioned:

1. Lower-cost steel could be used, since the steel did not have to be extensively machined.
2. Less steel was wasted, since almost all the metal in the slug was used in the finished part.
3. Close tolerances and a smooth surface finish could be obtained in the extrusion.
4. Better physical characteristics often resulted, since the metal flow followed the contours of the part.

One observer estimated the value of parts manufactured by cold extrusion in America during 1959 at from $6 to $10 million. This same man estimated the potential annual market for products so manufactured at $2 to $3 billion. Research was expensive, since a large investment was required for the press and tooling. Some of the technical problems had involved learning how the metal flowed plastically, designing tools that maintained tolerances without failing, and developing automated equipment. Because of the investment required, the process was looked on as most suitable for the mass production industries.

Background

James Addison, a tall, intense young man of about thirty-five, had been working in the cold extrusion research group of the Hercules Automobile Corporation for several years. Although he had developed several other processes which had been adopted by the company, he said he felt frustrated because of the slow progress of the cold extrusion research group. It seemed to him that the large organization was smothering his productivity with standard procedures, committee decisions, etc. While still working for the company, he went out in search of investors who would support his independent research in the field of cold extrusion.

One of the men to whom Addison talked was a public accountant in Chicago, who, being impressed by Addison's ability and desire, acquainted a number of his friends with Addison's situation. A group of eight businessmen agreed to finance Addison's development work, but they insisted that someone with business experience be obtained to manage the new enterprise. The brother-in-law of one of the investors was Bradley Cook, who was general manager of the Precision Tool Company, a job-order machine shop on the outskirts of Chicago (see Precision Tool case). Mr. Cook had the desired background of metallurgy and business management. He was informed of the venture and agreed to serve as president of the new company on a part-time basis, as long as operations could be conducted close to the Precision Tool plant so that he might continue as general manager of that company. Mr. Cook became an investor in the new company.

In December, 1958, James Addison quit his job with the automobile company and became the only full-time employee of Steel Extrusion. The nine investors committed $85,000, and James Addison received $15,000 worth of common stock in return for his personal note for that amount. This note was to be repaid from the profits of the company, with 10 percent of the profits before taxes each year being used to pay off the note. James Addison's salary was $1,000 per month. Bradley Cook received no salary, but was to receive 10 percent of the profits before taxes (up to $10,000 per year), as compensation.

The stockholders planned to have the corporation taxed as a partnership during the early years when losses or small profits were anticipated.[2] An executive committee, made up of Bradley Cook, James Addison, and one of the other investors, met weekly during the first six months of the company's existence. The committed funds were callable in 20 percent increments at the discretion of the executive committee.

After investigating a number of available buildings in downtown Chicago, the executive committee had a building constructed to its specifications in a new industrial development about five miles from

---

[2] Sections 1371 through 1377 of the Internal Revenue Code of 1954 provide that, under certain conditions, a small business corporation may elect to be taxed as a partnership. If taxed as a partnership, that proportion of the losses or gains of the company represented by a stockholder's proportion of stock owned would appear directly on his personal income tax return. One of the principal requirements is that the corporation may not have more than 10 stockholders.

the Precision Tool plant. The building had a 25-foot headroom and heavy floor construction, both needed for the press. It was built by a contractor who then leased it to Steel Extrusion. A $10,000 deposit was required of the company; they had the option to purchase the building and adjoining land at any time after the first six months of occupancy. Under the agreement, the base cost of the building was fixed at $100,000; the purchase price for the building was established at $93,000 at the end of the first six months of occupancy, $89,000 at the end of two years, and various decreasing amounts for subsequent years.

The building was of concrete block construction and contained 10,000 square feet. There were no partitions except for a small room in one corner, containing James Addison's desk and drawing board. A secondhand press and the equipment which James Addison had designed were in the center of the floor. About 75 percent of the building was unused; James Addison's voice echoed when he explained the equipment to visitors.

A manufacturer's representative was retained to investigate the opportunities for extruding steel parts on a subcontract basis for companies in the Chicago area. This man talked to various large manufacturers and obtained specifications on parts that could be made by cold extrusion. James Addison estimated the cost of manufacturing these parts by extrusion, and tentative bids were submitted. Since these bids were lower than the cost of manufacturing the parts by conventional processes, there was great interest in Steel Extrusion. Bradley Cook said that they had talked to these prospective customers, even though development of the Steel Extrusion equipment was not yet completed, in order to stir up interest and in order to get a feel for the market. In December, 1959, the manufacturer's representative claimed that if the tooling and automation equipment were ready, he could accept enough orders immediately to keep several presses busy.

Progress during the First Year

By December, 1959, one year after starting operations, James Addison thought the major technical problems had been solved. He had made considerable progress since February, 1959, shortly after the corporation had been founded, when he had demonstrated to the stockholders' satisfaction his ability to design the tooling to manufacture a particular part. At that time, he had satisfactorily produced a particular bushing from tooling he had designed. It was produced on a used 250-ton press, which the company had bought for $7,000. The equipment with which he produced the part was relatively crude, and he subsequently directed his efforts toward developing safety devices, repair features, automation equipment, and a shear to prepare the metal slugs. He spent the remainder of 1959 in developing this equipment, and subsequently submitted applications for four patents.

In the process, as it existed in December, 1959, steel bars were fed to a shear which cut off slugs of the desired size. Since almost all the metal in the slug was used in the finished part, it was important that each slug contain the same amount of metal. It was difficult to accomplish this, since the diameter of the bar stock varied. James Addison's equipment measured the diameter of the bar, compensated for changing diameters, and held the bar in a 4-ton grip as the shear cleanly cut the slug from the bar. James Addison had designed a special device that increased the force and the speed of the shear at the bottom of the cut; this permitted a clean cut, with no jagged edges. This automatic equipment, which was thought to be patentable, could shear 80 slugs per minute. Competitive techniques involved the slower and more costly sawing of the slugs. The slugs were then coated with the zinc phosphate and soap lubricant that facilitated the extrusion. It was important that this coating be uniform, and nine different tanks were normally used to clean and coat the material. James Addison thought he could reduce the number of tanks to two by incorporating certain ideas of his own.

The slugs were to be fed automatically to the press, where steel fingers would position them in the dies. Since most parts were made by several successive extrudings, the tooling was being designed so that as many as eight dies could be placed in the same press. The metal fingers would automatically move the part from one die to the next until the completed part was moved from the last die to the container for finished parts. The dies of tungsten carbide had great compressive strength, but very little resistance to shear forces. Thus, if the alignment of the dies were not perfect on every stroke of the press, the dies might snap. Addison had spent a great deal of time in perfecting the mechanism that would ensure automatic alignment.

Addison described the Steel Extrusion press, with its associated tooling and automation, as "the most complicated press in the world." However, he maintained that it was vastly superior to the equipment presently sold by the leading company in the field of cold extrusion tooling. Addison said that in order to produce a particular part an investment of $140,000 in the equipment of this competitor, exclusive of the press, would be required; the resulting production rate would be 50 parts per minute. By comparison, the Steel Extrusion equipment would cost $70,000, exclusive of the press, and would produce 100 parts per minute.

He had incorporated safety shields into the equipment, so that the operator would not be harmed if parts broke under the tremendous pressure. Those parts that would have to be replaced because of wear were designed so that replacement would be foolproof; that is, the parts would go in only the "right" way.

Emphasis had been placed on the development of universal equipment which could be used for a variety of similar parts. Addison said that with the substitution of different dies a number of different parts could be made on the development prototype equipment. He had also attempted to make the equipment compact, saying, "In a factory, space is money. Any competitor's machine would occupy several times the space of this one."

As development had progressed, James Addison had often reconsidered parts he had designed earlier and decided that he could make them better. However, instead of going back to redesign such parts at those times, he had concentrated on completing a working model. He hoped, on his second prototype, to design the equipment so that any perishable part could be replaced in two minutes. He also hoped to utilize more standard parts, so that the cost of the equipment could be lessened. He planned to improve the appearance of the machine, saying, "If a machine looks good, the operator will take pride in it and will keep it clean and maintain it."

The changes that James Addison hoped to make in the equipment would be incorporated into a second, prototype model. This model might be designed to meet the needs of a particular customer who would then buy it on a guaranteed basis. There was also the possibility that the second prototype model would be retained by Steel Extrusion, which would use it in conjunction with the first model for manufacturing purposes.

The tooling had been manufactured by the Precision Tool Company. This had been a natural relationship, since Bradley Cook was the general manager of Precision Tool, as well as the president of Steel Extrusion. When tooling had been needed immediately, Bradley Cook had seen to it that the order was rushed through the Precision Tool plant. In addition, employees from the Precision Tool plant had come down to the Steel Extrusion building whenever James Addison needed assistance.

The shear had been used to make slugs; the press had been used to produce extrusions; and the automation equipment had been operated at various times. However, the equipment had never been operated all together. In December, 1959, Bradley Cook and James Addison thought that only a few minor problems needed to be worked out before the unit could be operated automatically. They expected this to take only a few weeks and to cost no more than a few thousand dollars. Although they were confident that the important known technical problems had been solved, they still worried. Bradley Cook said, "I sometimes lie awake nights wondering about the problems we haven't discovered yet." Nevertheless, he had confidence that James Addison could handle any problems that might arise.

James Addison thought his success in apparently solving problems which large research organizations had been wrestling with for years was due to his approach. He said, "I challenge everything. I assume that I can design a part that will be better than that which already exists. I go ahead and design it and then challenge the expert to show me why it won't work. I have accomplished more in the past year, with very little help, than I could have done in three years with seven assistants at Hercules. There are sections in the research organization at Hercules whose chief function it is to see that nothing new is done. There are very few standard parts in this prototype model; as we needed parts, I designed them. At Hercules, there would have been staff meetings and weeks of deliberation to discuss every departure from standard design. Each research group had a vested interest in the parts it designed. For instance, the hydraulic department resented anyone's changes in their equipment."

The company's manufacturer's representative had talked to a number of large manufacturing companies and had learned that there were many parts, now being made by hot forging or automatic screw machines, which could be made by cold extrusion. The volume of these parts ranged from a few thousand to several million parts per year.

The management had not yet decided whether Steel Extrusion, Incorporated, would be primarily a subcontractor, manufacturing parts by cold extrusion, or a supplier of the equipment used in cold extrusion. Whichever decision was made, it was important to know the present cost of manufacturing parts that could be made by cold extrusion. In most cases, it was possible to determine these present costs rather accurately. The costs of steel, the wage rates, and the operating characteristics of the automatic screw machines were well known.

The direct cost of manufacturing parts by cold extrusion could also be estimated with considerable accuracy, Bradley Cook thought. The development work done during 1959 had indicated that material costs could be estimated quite closely; there was somewhat greater uncertainty in regard to direct labor costs, but the margin of error was not thought to be great. For many parts, it appeared that the savings in direct costs might range from 20 percent to 50 percent if cold extrusion were used.

The overhead costs for Steel Extrusion were difficult to estimate and were, in Bradley Cook's opinion, the largest potential source of error in estimating future manufacturing costs for the company. He pointed out that Steel Extrusion did not yet have an organization and that the future overhead costs would depend on how large an organization was needed. They would also depend on the number of presses Steel Extrusion would install in its plant. These factors would, of course, be influenced by whether the company was primarily a subcontractor or primarily a supplier of equipment.

The investment required for equipment to extrude a particular part was difficult to determine. Mr. Addison thought the incorporation of standard parts would permit substantial savings (as compared to the prototype model), although the magnitude of such savings was not certain. The investment in tooling and automation equipment which a company would have to make would range from about $35,000 to over $200,000. The cost of the tooling and equipment would be a function of the size of the press and the characteristics of the part being manufactured. The cost of the press would depend on its size, complexity, and whether it was secondhand or new. In general, the cost of the press would range from about $7,000 to over $1 million. At any rate, it was estimated that, for the manufacture of many parts, Steel Extrusion could promise a payback time of less than one year on the total investment in press and equipment to the company making the investment.

The Future

The $85,000 originally committed by the investors had been spent by the fall of 1959; an additional investment of 20 percent of the amount originally pledged was requested of each investor. This increased the total amount invested to $102,000; in December, 1959, the cash balance was about $7,000. Many of the investors were wealthy men. It was estimated that another $50,000 to $100,000 could be obtained from the group at the present stage of development.

Certain outsiders had expressed an interest in investing in the venture, and the original investors had discussed among themselves the advisability of permitting them to do so and the terms under which such investment would take place. Some stockholders felt strongly that the original investors had committed their money at a time when the risk was very high, and that any new investors should have to pay a higher price per share than the original investors had paid. Others agreed with this argument in principle, but felt that the actual price per share to be paid by new investors would be determined by bargaining and that the company would have to "get what it could." Bradley Cook felt that the primary issue in forecasting the company's growth was, "How fast can we raise money?" He hoped that the development costs to finish perfecting the equipment would not exceed a few thousand dollars.

If only tooling were sold, it was anticipated that Precision Tool would do the manufacturing on a subcontract basis. Thus, financing the tooling could be handled by Precision Tool, which would give Steel Extrusion generous terms of sale. If Steel Extrusion were to manufacture parts on a subcontract basis, substantial investments in presses, tooling, and other equipment would be needed. There was a high probability that the company could get a contract for the manufacture of a particular bushing for an automobile manufacturer. It was estimated that Steel Extrusion would have to install about $200,000 worth of presses and tooling in order to meet this contract. Mr. Cook thought the presses could be bought on extended terms, which would remove some of the immediate need for cash. He thought this particular contract might be lucrative enough for the payback time on the investment, including the presses, to be about eight months.

Management had been extensively considering what the company should sell. Tooling could be sold to manufacturers, who could use it either with presses they already had or with presses they could buy from press manufacturing companies. In the second case, Steel Extrusion would provide technical advice in the selection of a press. The tooling and other equipment would be manufactured on a subcontract basis by Precision Tool and would be sold and guaranteed by Steel Extrusion. James Addison would supervise its installation and the training of the operators.

The management was uncertain as to just how important it would be to offer a package which would include the press, tooling, and all related equipment. Some people thought prospective purchasers would have a strong preference for a guaranteed package which had been designed throughout to do the job. Others thought the company could compete successfully by selling only its patented tooling and its know-how.

Management was also strongly considering having the company manufacture parts on a subcontract basis. Bradley Cook thought the capital goods business was so cyclical that the company ought not to rely wholly on it. However, he saw problems in getting established as a manufacturer. He said, "Many companies might hesitate to rely on a new company with a new process as the primary supplier of an important part."

The possibility of serving both as an equipment supplier and a subcontractor was being considered. They would sell a manufacturer the tooling necessary to produce 60 to 70 percent of the producer's requirements for a particular part; Steel Extrusion would then receive a contract to manufacture the remaining needed parts. The management thought such an arrangement would be agreeable to many large companies. Mr. Cook said, "A large company does not like to have only one source of supply, even if it is itself. Because of possible strikes or fires, they would be happy to have us permanently supply a portion of their needs." They had already talked to three different companies interested in such an arrangement.

He also thought a dual contract would permit Steel Extrusion to use its manufacturing facilities as a pilot plant. Improvements could be tried out under production conditions. In addition, the manufacturing facilities could be used to demonstrate the successful operation of the equipment, both to prospective new customers and to customers who had purchased tooling and who might be having manufacturing difficulties in using it. Manufacturing on a subcontract basis looked more profitable to Mr. Cook than did selling tooling as of December, 1959. However, as cold extrusion equipment became more widely owned and as the techniques became more widely known, he thought that manufacturing might become relatively less profitable.

In December, 1959, management recognized that the whole process was probably in too early a stage of development for issues of this nature to be settled with any certainty. It was thought that Steel Extrusion might be primarily a producer of capital equipment for this process, perhaps arranging for the purchase of presses. Then plans might be made for an eventual spin-off of an enterprise in the Chicago area for the manufacture of parts using this process. This might be followed by similar expansion by division through setting up similar companies in other cities. At any rate, the present problems of the company required the immediate attention of management, and it was thought that decisions of such a long-range nature might be deferred. However, management thought that present decisions should not preclude such long-run possibilities.

During the first year of operations, most of the business decisions had been made by Bradley Cook, who had been spending one to two hours per day on Steel Extrusion affairs. When the development work was completed and orders began to come in, he thought the company would need a larger organization. He saw as one of his chief duties the training of such an organization. He said, "You don't build up a business yourself. You build an organization, and it builds the business."

In December, 1959, much of management's thinking about the problems of the company was brought to a focus by an offer from the New Castle Press Company. The New Castle Press Company, one of the largest manufacturers of industrial presses in the country, had proposed the following relationship between the two companies:

1. New Castle would purchase tooling and automation equipment for the cold extrusion process from Steel Extrusion at competitive prices.
2. The nationwide sales force of New Castle would then sell packaged units of New Castle presses and Steel Extrusion tooling.
3. The market for tooling would be handled completely by New Castle. If Steel Extrusion found companies that wanted tooling, they would refer them to New Castle. Steel Extrusion would not sell tooling to any other company.
4. Steel Extrusion would be free to manufacture, using the cold extrusion process. If New Castle salesmen found companies that wanted extruding done on a subcontract basis, they would refer them to Steel Extrusion.
5. New Castle would provide Steel Extrusion with presses to use in its manufacturing operations. Steel Extrusion would purchase these presses from New Castle, receiving very long terms of payment.

New Castle Press had only limited experience with cold extrusion of steel. One of their major competitors had developed tooling for use in cold extrusion and had been selling package units to certain large manufacturers. This competitor's equipment was that of which James Addison had been speaking when he said, "Ours will do twice as much and require only half the investment."

On the Wednesday evening after the offer had been received, the board of directors, consisting of all 10 stockholders, met in the almost empty building which housed the prototype model of the press. Bradley Cook opened the meeting and suggested that several questions might be considered:

1. Should they accept the general terms of the New Castle offer?
2. What specific terms, if any, should they strive to have changed?
3. What alternatives to accepting this offer should they investigate?
4. What other questions should they consider at this time in regard to the company's sales policy, financing, and organization?

The building was semidark and the big press cast its shadow over the meeting table. One of the directors remarked to James Addison that the decisions to be made that night might determine the entire future of the company.

6. STEEL EXTRUSION, INCORPORATED (B)*
Building a Company around a New Process

Steel Extrusion, Incorporated had been formed in late 1958 to allow James Addison, an inventive young engineer, to proceed with the development of tooling and automation equipment for use in the impact extrusion of small steel parts. Its establishment was the culmination of an 18-month effort by Mr. Addison to arrange suitable financing for the company, a task which was doubly difficult because of the newness of the process and the need for large capital equipment expenditures. Initially, Mr. Addison had been the only full-time employee. By April, 1962, the investors had contributed about $340,000 to Steel Extrusion, most of which had been used in the program of developing and debugging the impact extrusion process. At that time it had two extrusion presses, seven full-time employees, and sales of about $20,000 per month. The company expected to show its first monthly profits in April or May, 1962.

This event would help mark a significant turning point in the development of Steel Extrusion. The company was changing from one predominantly involved in development activities to one which placed more and more emphasis on production. Mr. Addison and Mr. Cook, president of Steel Extrusion, knew that this change would be accompanied by a new series of problems and issues with which they would have to deal. In April of 1962 they knew they should take action in a number of areas; however, they disagreed somewhat about the priority of certain issues. Therefore, they planned to fully analyze their company's current situation and develop a coordinated plan of action including all areas of activity.

Cold Forming Process [1]

As explained in Steel Extrusion, Incorporated (A), the process of cold forming steel parts consisted of applying great pressure on an

---

* Copyright © 1962 by the President and Fellows of Harvard College.

[1] This process has also been referred to as cold extrusion, cold forging, impact extrusion, and chipless machining.

unheated steel slug so that a plastic flow resulted, allowing the metal to assume the shape of the die cavity into which it was being forced by the external pressure.

Description of Presses

The pressure was applied by large presses of the type used for stamping and drawing operations. Such a press consisted of a large upright frame, a fixed platform to which the bottom halves of the cold forming dies were secured, and a sliding platform to which the punches were attached and which moved vertically within the press frame to apply the necessary pressure. Energy was supplied by an electric motor which drove a large flywheel, both of which were usually mounted at the top of the frame. Various types of mechanical linkages, driving through a heavy clutch, transferred the energy stored in the flywheel to the sliding platform and thence to the cold forming punches.

All parts of such a press had to be extremely heavy to withstand the great pressures and the jolting caused by an impact extrusion or stamping operation, and generally were designed with safety factors of two or three to one. Cold forming of steel required a pressure of about 100 tons per square inch. The parts that Steel Extrusion produced usually had cross sectional areas of between 1 square inch and 4 square inches and weighed between ¼ pound and 1 pound. Steel Extrusion's 400-ton press, designed to exert pressure of 400 tons on each stroke of the press at the rate of 70 strokes per minute, stood approximately 16 feet tall and measured about 6 feet square at its base. Despite its rugged construction, it shook visibly on each stroke and, when operating, made so much noise that two men standing close to it had to shout to make themselves heard.

Description of Process

The process of cold forming a steel part began with cold-rolled round bar stock. This stock was cut into small pieces, or slugs, each of which contained exactly the amount of metal needed in the finished pieces. At Steel Extrusion, this cutting operation was done on an automatic shear. The shearing operation hardened the slugs of steel because of the phenomenon known as strain hardening, or work hardening, which takes place in many metals when they are subjected to severe impacts or are cut or bent. (The working causes a distortion of the molecular structure of the metal, which results in this hardening process.) Impacts such as those imposed by the shear or the cold forming presses made the slugs harder, more brittle, and more resistant to plastic flow than they should be for easy cold forming. Therefore, the slugs were annealed, or heat-treated, in order to relieve the internal stresses that caused the hardening and to allow the metal to become once again soft enough to extrude. Steel Extrusion sent its slugs to another firm, Arron Corporation, to have them annealed. After heat-treating the slugs, Arron also performed the function of coating them with zinc phosphate and soap. This coating acted as a lubricant during the cold forming process.

When Steel Extrusion was ready to run a given part, the annealed and coated slugs for that part, which were transported and stored in 55-gallon drums or wooden tote boxes, were dumped into large bins alongside a press. Endless metal belts carried the slugs to small hoppers mounted high on the press, from which they rolled down gravity-feed chutes into the first position on the press table. Here, mechanical fingers on the automatic transfer mechanism would reach out, move one slug into the first die cavity, and release it. (As will be explained in more detail below, Steel Extrusion had multiple-punch presses on which three separate dies could be used simultaneously.) The press would take a stroke in which the punch would force the slug into the die cavity, an automatic ejector would lift the shaped part out of the die as the punch was raised again, and the automatic transfer mechanism, which was mechanically coordinated with the movement of the press itself, would again reach out and move the part. When finished, the part was mechanically kicked off the die platform, down another gravity-feed chute, and into a shipping container.

Finishing Operations

Usually, additional operations had to be performed on the parts before they were truly "finished." These operations included drilling and tapping any holes needed, taking finish cuts on the pieces with metal-cutting equipment, centerless grinding to obtain smooth finishes, and, for some parts, plating with chromium or copper.

Of these operations, the one most consistently performed was taking a finish cut on the ends of a part because it was difficult to achieve perfect extrusion to the extremes of the die cavities. These and other finish cuts were usually made on automatic chucking machines, an automatic lathe that operated in the same general manner as an automatic screw machine but took individual work pieces rather than bar stock into its chuck. Most automatic screw machines could be readily converted to "chuckers," a fact which allowed a manufacturer replacing screw machine parts with cold formed parts to continue to use many of his old machines. However, because of the small amount of metal removed in this finishing operation, a machine rigged as a chucker could often perform the necessary operations on a part that had already been cold formed in about one-tenth the time the same piece of equipment, working as a screw machine making the part from bar stock, would take.

Multiple-Punch Presses

Although many cold forming presses in use in the country were of the single-punch type—having only one die and one punch on the press—Steel Extrusion used multiple-punch units. Its 400-ton press had positions for three separate sets of dies and punches. The automation had been designed so that its action could be readily changed. The company could have separate slugs fed to each of the positions simultaneously, giving the press an output of three pieces per stroke, or have one piece transferred along from one position to the next, allowing one piece to be "hit" three times in three progressive dies before reaching its final shape.

This second arrangement was particularly important in forming pieces in which some of the metal had to be moved a considerable distance or where the shape was quite complex. As mentioned above, a severe impact tends to work-harden a piece of steel. Normally, this phenomenon would mean that a piece that had to be formed in three hits would have to be annealed prior to each one so that the steel would flow easily. However, there is a time element at work-hardening, so that if successive hits could be timed less than one second apart the hardening which took place between each impact was minimal. There was, of course, a limit to the number of successive hits that could be made in this manner. This limit was usually two or three, depending on the alloy being used, the shape of the part, and certain other factors. The most complex part being produced by Steel Extrusion in early 1962 took three hits, and was annealed and coated with lubricant prior to the first and third hits. This time element in work hardening was one requirement which had to be met by the automatic transfer sytem. If the press was stopped, allowing a piece to sit for a longer period of time after being subjected to one hit, it was advisable to remove it. Otherwise, there existed a danger of overstressing and damaging the tooling.

Tooling (Dies and Punches)

The design of the dies and punches for a part was also of major importance in obtaining successful extrusion. Mr. Addison stated that the ability to design effective tooling [2] and efficient automatic transfer equipment (described above) was the fundamental competitive strength of Steel Extrusion. Although he knew that many others were working in the field, and several technical papers had been written on the process, he felt that his firm had a degree of competence in tooling and automation design which few, if any, others had.

Most of Steel Extrusion's tooling (dies, punches, etc.), had been made of one of the high-speed steel (tool steel) alloys prior to 1962. By April, 1962, however, the company was having many of these items made of more costly but much harder tungsten carbide. The difference in price was on the order of 2 or 3 to 1, but Mr. Addison thought the average life of the harder metal would approach 10 times that of high-speed steel.

The tooling for impact extrusion consisted, in general, of a die cavity and a punch shaped specifically for the job at hand, along with "backup tooling" which could be used for many different jobs. The first class of tooling, called "perishable details" by the company, was the most likely to fail, and within this class the punches in general lasted only one-fifth to one-tenth as long as the cavity dies. The second class, the backup tooling, consisted of the items that supported, guided, and contained the perishable details or working tooling. The extremely high pressures to which the steel slugs were subjected necessitated careful support of the dies and punches. The supporting parts were designed to transfer the forces of impact extrusion from the punches and dies to the tool platforms of the press in such a way that the working tooling would not fail.

Care in the design and fabrication of all tooling for impact extrusion was particularly important, because much of it would be subjected to forces close to its ultimate strength. In many cases it was impossible to provide dies or punches with the "traditional" safety margins of 100 percent or more without making them much too

---

[2] Tooling, as used in this case, refers to the dies, punches, etc., used in impact extrusion.

ponderous. Because of the space limitations of the press platforms, Steel Extrusion, using multiple-punch presses, often had to work even closer to ultimate metal strengths than did firms using single-punch presses.

Mr. Addison pointed out that under these conditions tool life was difficult to predict. The slightest flaw or impurity in the metal, the smallest variation in the stress relieving process used could make a significant difference in tool life. For example, the longest-lived punch for one item made in quantity by Steel Extrusion lasted for 50,000 pieces; the one with the next longest life lasted only for 10,000. Subsequent analysis of the metal in these punches and even in ones which had had shorter lives failed to show any differences. Mr. Addison was trying, in April, 1962, a policy of removing all punches after 7,500 strokes to anneal them, but he did not yet know how much difference this would make in their lives. (Punch changes took about five to ten minutes.)

Despite the experience gained by Steel Extrusion and by others in the field, there was still a great deal of uncertainty about tool design, tool life, etc., in early 1962. Because of the empirical nature of almost all the practical knowledge in the field, Steel Extrusion with its two years of production experience had, in the opinion of its officers, a decided advantage over the many companies which had only recently entered the field of cold forming.

Company Background

Until the spring of 1960, Steel Extrusion was occupied with the development of the cold forming process. This activity is described in Steel Extrusion, Incorporated (A).

Beginning Production—1960

After turning down the offer from New Castle Press Company (described in the first case), Steel Extrusion continued its work to perfect a fully automatic impact extrusion press. By April of 1960, Mr. Addison felt that he had a system which would soon be ready for an initial production run. The company had received, through the efforts of one of its stockholders who was also a manufacturers' representative, an open order to supply a small cylindrical part for the Alpha Corporation, a local maker of bicycles. Steel Extrusion could begin producing on this order as soon as the press was ready, subject, of course, to Alpha's requirements, which were tied to the model year of the bicycle industry.

However, the prospect of a steel strike was present in April, 1960. The investors who had backed the company financially since 1958 and who, along with Mr. Addison, made up the board of directors for Steel Extrusion were reluctant to make the additional financial commitment necessary to stockpile a great quantity of steel at that time. Although Mr. Addison was confident that production could soon be started, the system had not yet worked under production conditions. Therefore, the decision was made to gamble on a short steel strike.

By the time the press was actually ready for production runs, the strike was in progress and steel was virtually impossible for a new customer to obtain. The strike lasted so long that by the time steel was again available the pre-Christmas inventory buildup by the Alpha Corporation had been completed. Also, most of the automobile manufacturers and their major subcontractors, who as a group represented the largest source of potential business for Steel Extrusion, had already committed themselves to other suppliers for their full model-year requirements. Not until late 1960 did Steel Extrusion finally begin volume production. The company's monthly sales volume since November, 1960, is given in Exhibit 6–1.

Exhibit 6–1

STEEL EXTRUSION INCORPORATED (B)

Sales Records

	Sales	Gross Loss*	Net Loss
November, 1960–February, 1961	$15,879	$26,206	$29,214
November, 1960–February, 1961 at monthly rate	3,970	6,552	7,304
1961–March	1,384	8,383	9,273
April	5,497	5,545	6,685
May	5,825	4,082	4,977
June	4,999	5,833	7,752
July	4,949	(83)†	1,162
August	14,161	2,501	4,269
September	6,911	6,445	7,548
October	7,110	10,375	12,048
November	11,927	2,370	4,161
December	8,268	2,810	4,607
1962–January	10,178	2,977	3,929
February	19,580	1,987	4,481

* Gross loss is the loss from manufacturing. including manufacturing overhead but before selling and administrative expenses.
† Profit.

Recent Activity

During the 16-month period up to February, 1962, Steel Extrusion worked on a total of four major jobs. Although these were bona fide production orders, they were used by Mr. Addison and his associates to gain experience, to shake down the equipment, and to improve its performance. The volume involved in these contracts was only a small fraction of the company's theoretical capacity, but Steel Extrusion chose not to go after other business until it had the chance to walk through its first production runs. During this period, Steel Extrusion experimented with various improvements in the design of the automatic transfer equipment, with different alloys and heat treating methods for dies and punches which might improve their lives, and with attempts to cold form parts with different shapes and sizes.

The interest in impact extrusion among several large firms in the greater Chicago area (which included such industrial complexes as those in Gary, South Bend, and Detroit) aided Steel Extrusion in its experimentation program. For example, the Beta Corporation, a major supplier for the automotive and aviation industries, said, "You can go through our screw machine division and try to make any part which you think you can save money on." Although its go-slow policy dictated a cautious approach to such offers, Steel Extrusion had made prototype runs on several additional parts for Beta Corporation and for some other firms. Mr. Cook, who handled most of the negotiations with potential customers, usually tried to get the customer to pay for experimental tooling and for the raw material used. On some occasions, Mr. Cook had been successful. Contributions of this nature are listed as Tool Sales on the company's income statements. Mr. Addison expected some of these prototype runs to become production orders in the near future.

In this area, as in that of production contracts, Steel Extrusion had chosen to proceed slowly. It had concentrated on only a few customers and had picked only the most promising items to experiment with. However, Mr. Cook reported that he was encouraged by the reception he was currently receiving from the company's few customers. Engineers and production executives of these firms had become openly enthusiastic about the cost savings possible from impact extrusion, whereas initially they had voiced skepticism and exhibited reluctance to try the new process. Both Mr. Addison and Mr. Cook were confident that other firms would readily see the advantages of cold forming after the potential cost savings were pointed out to them.

Experimental Work

Steel Extrusion's reputation had led it to be asked to experiment with some exceptionally difficult jobs. For example, the Component Parts Division of Atlas Automotive, Inc., had asked both the Atlas Technical Division and Steel Extrusion to experiment with impact extrusion of beryllium. This rare metal, which is extremely light but lacks the ductility of steel or aluminum, was used for missile parts and in nuclear reactors. The Component Parts Division needed a certain beryllium part in quantity and knew that if it could be cold formed rather than machined significant savings in material would result. Mr. Addison immediately went to work on the problem, and as Mr. Cook sat in the office of the division general manager with several cold formed beryllium parts in his hand, the Technical Division telephoned to say that it had completed its study and was forwarding a full report saying that cold forming of beryllium was impossible. This experiment, however, had not led to a production order.

Another such request came from the owner of a local machine shop that previously had worked with Steel Extrusion on several orders. He was then doing work for a company making missile components. This company needed a small plunger (shaped something like a double ended auto engine valve) made of titanium. (Titanium is a relatively light but strong metal often used for jet engine parts. It is considered somewhat more difficult to work than stainless steel.) The machine shop owner asked if Steel Extrusion could make the part by cold forming, pointing out that this would reduce material costs about 40–50 percent below what they would be if made on screw machines. (Titanium costs about $7.00 per pound, and the piece in question would weigh about 1 pound completed.) Mr. Addison stated in this case that if the missile component manufacturer could supply some sample slugs of titanium, Steel Extrusion would begin to experiment with cold forming it.

This experimentation with new configurations, new metals, and new methods took a great deal of Mr. Addison's time. Even though the company's total production volume was small, there were still bugs in the process. For example, the chutes which fed slugs to the first press station had been fabricated out of stock chute sections, sheet metal, and C-clamps. Because these admittedly temporary chutes were rough, slugs often jammed in them, requiring the press operator to stop the operation every 10 to 20 strokes to clear a chute. The first of a new set of custom-made chutes which were expected to eliminate this problem were delivered in early April, 1962. Lack of time had prevented earlier action by Mr. Addison.

Transfer Mechanism Problem

Another problem associated with Steel Extrusion's cold forming process was related to the performance of the automatic transfer mechanism. Mr. Addison had still not been able to develop a solution to this problem. He stated that he could develop safety devices which would automatically stop the press if the transfer mechanism failed to pick up a piece or did not release it at the next station. However, he could not be certain that the piece, once released by the transfer mechanism, remained in position. This was extremely important, because if the piece were not centered in the die when hit by the punch, the unsymmetrical load could easily break the punch and/or crack the die and might cause cracking of the press frame or damage to the mechanical linkages.

The vibration of the press and the speed at which the automatic transfer mechanism worked made it a very real possibility that the slug might move after it was released. As of April, 1962, Mr. Addison had not yet solved this problem, so the press had to be run at the slow rate of 28–30 strokes per minute to allow the operator to conduct a visual check on the position of the pieces prior to each stroke.[3] Mr. Addison had found that faster rates of speed were impractical because the operator could not then perform this inspection properly. Even at 28–30 strokes per minutes, the operator's eyes grew tired easily, and he often began stopping the press every few strokes to check more carefully on the position of one of the slugs.

This program of walking through a relatively few production orders while conducting a great deal of experimental work had, of course, been expensive. The company had yet to show an operating profit, although it expected to begin doing so in April or May of 1962. Furthermore, the company used large and expensive equipment and costly tooling, which required significant capital expenditures. Steel Extrusion's financial statements are included as Exhibits 6–2, 6–3,

---

[3] The press had a quick-acting power clutch, allowing the operator to disconnect the punch platform from the flywheel almost instantaneously, and an air brake which was simultaneously engaged to the platform.

Exhibit 6–2

STEEL EXTRUSION INCORPORATED (B)
INCOME STATEMENT
12 Months to October 31, 1961

Sales:

Tools	$ 23,941	
Parts	42,774	$ 66,715

Costs:

Start-up	$ 9,428	
Direct labor	6,224	
Material	12,671	
Outside costs	6,176	
Perishable details	2,011	
	$ 36,510	
Manufacturing expenses	100,066	136,576
Selling and administrative		8,661
Other expenses (est.)		4,980
Net Loss		$ 83,502

Exhibit 6–3

STEEL EXTRUSION INCORPORATED (B)
INCOME STATEMENT

	November, 1961	December, 1961	January, 1962	February, 1962	4 Months to February, 1962
Sales, parts	$ 8,148	$ 8,268	$ 4,740	$ 19,580	$ 40,736
Prime costs:					
Labor	713	642	315	1,032	2,702
Material	2,568	2,353	1,328	5,527	11,776
Outside costs	968	686	451	2,814	4,919
Perishable details	—	331	—	1,142	1,473
Total prime costs	$ 4,249	$ 4,012	$ 2,094	$ 10,513	$ 20,870
Prime margin	$ 3,899	$ 4,256	$ 2,646	$ 9,065	$ 19,866
Manufacturing overhead	6,614	6,804	9,902	10,922	34,242
Gross profit (loss)	$(2,715)	$(2,548)	$(7,656)	$(1,857)	$(14,376)
Selling and administrative expense	1,133	816	711	1,459	4,119
Operating profit (loss)	$(3,848)	$(3,364)	$(7,967)	$(3,316)	$(18,495)
Sales, tools	$ 3,779	$ —	$ 5,438	$ —	$ 9,217
Less: Start-up costs	3,434	262	759	130	4,585
Gross profit (loss), tools ..	$ 345	$(262)	$ 4,679	$(130)	$ 4,632
Total profit (loss)	$(3,503)	$(3,626)	$(3,288)	$(3,446)	$(13,863)
Other income (expense)	(658)	(981)	(641)	(1,035)	(3,315)
Net Profit (Loss)	$(4,161)	$(4,607)	$(3,929)	$(4,481)	$(17,178)

Exhibit 6–4

STEEL EXTRUSION INCORPORATED (B)

BALANCE SHEETS

	October, 1960	October, 1961	February, 1962
Current Assets:			
Cash	$ 5,824	$ 7,441	$ 5,253
Accounts receivable	15,025	5,033	16,286
Inventory	240	19,349	35,817
Prepayments	1,060	4,147	4,065
Total	$ 22,149	$ 35,970	$ 61,421
Other Assets:			
Deposits, etc.	10,000	10,000	11,140
Notes receivable, officer's	27,000	27,000	27,000
Property and Equipment:			
Machinery and equipment	25,743	90,624	97,140
Dies	3,751	22,950	22,950
Office equipment	103	103	103
Leasehold improvements	3,161	3,311	3,633
Less: Depreciation	(8,917)	(40,658)	(47,815)
Organization costs (net)	1,221	814	679
Total Assets	$ 84,211	$ 156,241	$ 176,251
Current Liabilities:			
Notes payable	$ —	$ 83,808	$ 19,799
Accounts payable	14,127	19,004	18,923
Accruals	76	3,455	5,808
Total	$ 14,203	$ 106,267	$ 44,530
Long-term debt	$ —	$ 63,468	$ 162,393
Common stock	180,000	180,000	180,000
Retained earnings	(109,992)	(193,494)	(210,672)
Total Liabilities and Capital	$ 84,211	$ 156,241	$ 176,251

and 6–4. Exhibit 6–5 includes some representative cost figures on some of the company's jobs.

Production Policy

In December of 1960, Steel Extrusion had received an offer, described in the Steel Extrusion, Incorporated (A) case, from New Castle Press Company, a large press manufacturer. New Castle had asked Steel Extrusion to concentrate on the manufacture of tooling for impact extrusion presses, which would be sold, along with New Castle presses, by the New Castle sales force. At that time, the investors in Steel Extrusion had decided to decline this offer and focus their company's attention on subcontract extrusion work. This policy was still in force in April, 1962. At that time, Steel Extrusion was operating

Exhibit 6–5

STEEL EXTRUSION INCORPORATED (B)
SELECTED JOB COST DATA

| | Job A | | Job B | | Job C | | Job D | |
	First* Month	Last† Month	First* Month	Last† Month	First* Month	Last† Month	First* Month	Last† Month
Sales (number of pieces)	497	72,624	10,192	38,621	47,215	19,015	55,098	36,190
Sales price (per piece)	$.165	$.165	$.137	$.137	$.073	$.073	$.063	$.063
Costs (per piece):								
Labor	.028	.008	.014	.008	.012	.014	.015	.004
Material	.034	.045	.045	.042	.017	.017	.020	.019
Outside costs ...	.059	.030	.018	.011	.021	.026	.010	.004
Perishable details	—	.016	—	—	—	—	(.002)	—
Total direct costs	.121	.099	.077	.061	.050	.057	.043	.027
Gross Profit‡	$.044	$.066	$.060	$.076	$.023	$.016	$.020	$.036

* The first month for which cost breakdowns were available, in all cases a month in the summer of 1961.
† The last month for which cost breakdown was available, either February, 1962, or the last month prior to that when the job was run.
‡ This item corresponds to the prime margin item on the company's income statements. It represents contribution to fixed costs.

on a two-shift basis, using the new large press for production runs and the older 250-ton press to do experimental work and to handle prototype runs. The smaller press was not automated and had to be loaded by hand.

Production Volume

The company's present contracts occupied the 400-ton press full time, although its theoretical capacity (70 strokes per minute or 4,200 per hour) was several times actual production. The need to operate at reduced rates, the high amount of downtime caused by bugs and the need for frequent tool changes, all of which have been mentioned above, limited production severely. Actual output on a "good" two-shift day was currently about 7,500 pieces, or at an average rate of about 470 per hour. Mr. Addison was hopeful of reaching the rate of 10,000 per day (625 per hour) during April. (During one recent seven-hour period, the large automated press had produced 4,900 pieces.) He expected that production would be raised to an average rate of 1,000 per hour within a few months. (This rate would still leave a good allowance for downtime.) These increases would be made possible by the continuous improvements being made in the feeder system (e.g., new chutes for the slugs) and by use of harder alloys for dies and punches in order to lengthen their lives.

New Presses

In January of 1962, the company had decided to order another 400-ton press. This machine was expected to be delivered in July, 1962, and would be the same size as the present large press, allowing tooling to be interchanged between them. This new press would cost about $80,000 and would require automatic transfer equipment and permanent tooling expected to cost an additional $30,000. The capacity would be similar to that of the present press. Mr. Addison stated that Steel Extrusion should be operating at a solid profit with the addition of this unit. Mr. Addison had also tried to purchase a small, single-punch 150-ton press at the same time. He had argued that such a unit could be used exclusively for hand-fed prototype runs, allowing the 250-ton triple-punch press to be automated and utilized for production runs. However, the investors had vetoed this plan.

Heat-Treating and Coating Line

There was a certain amount of disagreement among some of the founders of Steel Extrusion about the future production policy of the company. For example, Mr. Addison felt that the company should next acquire its own heat-treating and coating line, so that it would not have to send the steel slugs an outside contractor to have them annealed and coated with lubricant. Mr. Cook, however, did not think this plan would represent the most profitable way of spending the company's money.

Mr. Addison argued as follows: "We will have three presses after delivery of the new 400-ton unit. Assuming that all of them, including the present 250-ton press, are automated, they each should produce about 1,000 pieces per hour. The average weight per piece is about three-quarters of a pound, giving us a total production of 2,250 pounds per hour, or, on a two-shift basis, about 36,000 pounds per day. Using the present outside contractor for heat-treating and coating, it takes about six days between the time the bar stock is first sheared into slugs and the time the finished units are ready to ship. The steel we use costs us about nine to ten cents per pound. Therefore, the raw material cost component of our in-process inventory will be about

$20,000. Heat-treating and coating costs us three cents per pound, and since at any time at least half our inventory will be treated and coated, this will add some $3,000 to the value of inventory. These two costs alone will give inventory a direct value of $23,000 without even considering the labor component. With our own treating and coating line, we would need only a three-day in-process inventory. The money that would be released by this inventory reduction would amount to something more than $11,500, more than enough to cover the down payment on our own line. Therefore, because having our own facility would also be more convenient, I think we should get one."

The estimated costs of the line were $60,000 for the heat-treating furnace and $25,000 for the coating line. The down payments would be 10–15 percent. An addition to the building would be required to house the facility, but an addition was planned eventually in any case. Mr. Addison thought that if any addition were built at this time the company should have about 14,000 square feet added. The present building occupied 8,000 square feet and was leased to Steel Extrusion for $660 per month. Since the present rent payments were for both the building and the entire lot of land on which it was built, Mr. Addison expected that rent on any addition would be at a lower rate than the current payment.

Mr. Cook, on the other hand, felt that Steel Extrusion should get additional presses before spending money on the heat-treating–coating line. He was not sure that Mr. Addison's assumptions about production volume were entirely valid, and he felt that the company would get a greater return on investment from presses. He also pointed to Steel Extrusion's excellent relationship with Arron Company, which had been doing the heat-treating and coating on a subcontract basis. Arron was also a job extrusion shop but was rarely competitive with Steel Extrusion, because Arron concentrated on small, high-volume parts of the type that could be completely formed with one hit, rather than the multiple-hit, lower-volume items Steel Extrusion preferred. Arron had occasionally referred potential customers to Steel Extrusion when Arron had not been able to do their job. Mr. Cook wondered if this friendly relationship would change if he stopped using Arron for heat-treating and coating.

Although both men felt that some further analysis of the available figures should be done before a decision was made, they knew that this issue should be resolved before too long, as it would affect the nature of the company's business. On the one hand, Steel Extrusion would concentrate on design of tooling and the operation of presses;

on the other, it would operate a more thoroughly integrated cold extrusion plant which, with the addition of automatic chucking machines, grinders, and others, would perform the entire process of converting bar stock into completely finished parts. (Chuckers, grinders, drill presses, etc., to handle the company's proposed volume might cost about $50,000.) Because of the extremely high capital cost of presses and of the heat-treating–coating line, any significant move in either direction would tend to foreclose the company's opportunity to move in the other, at least in the short term. Both Mr. Addison and Mr. Cook recognized the importance of being fully cognizant of the long-range implications which either move would hold for Steel Extrusion.

Personnel

In 1962, the key man in the Steel Extrusion operation was still Mr. Addison. (See Steel Extrusion, Incorporated (A) for additional background information on Addison and Cook.) Mr. Addison had had the initial idea for the company and had originally been its only employee. Prior to formation of Steel Extrusion, he had been a member of the impact extrusion research group of the Hercules Automobile Corporation. In the period from 1958 to 1962, he had been completely responsible for the design, development, purchase or manufacture, assembly and operation of all the impact extrusion equipment in use at the Steel Extrusion plant. In 1962, he spent substantially all his time overseeing production and doing the required engineering work of the company. Most of these efforts were in such activities as determining whether a "new" part could be extruded, how it should be made, designing the tooling and automation, and dealing with suppliers of dies, punches, etc.

Mr. Cook, president of Steel Extrusion, had continued in his primary position as general manager of Precision Tool Company, a machine shop specializing in precision tool and die work on the outskirts of Chicago. He had been brought into the investor group before the company was founded to provide business guidance. Mr. Cook stated that he spent about 20–30 hours per week working on Steel Extrusion problems, handling a major portion of the sales and customer service activities as well as acting as the company's business manager, treasurer, and chief executive. Mr. Cook was also active in several other small firms in the Chicago area. He drew no salary from Steel Extrusion.

Joel Revere, one of the original investing group, acted as a sales agent for Steel Extrusion. He was an independent manufacturers' representative, selling the products and services of noncompetitive firms to the various large companies in the Chicago area. Mr. Revere had built up, over the period of several years in which he had been a manufacturers' representative, a number of contacts within the local manufacturing community. Many of these men were with companies that might also be potential customers for impact extrusion parts. Mr. Revere had been instrumental in helping Steel Extrusion obtain some of its current jobs. He also had an assistant who helped to service some of the company's accounts. He had an agreement with Steel Extrusion whereby he received a commission of 5 percent of all sales made by the company up to $25,000 per year, and 3 percent of all sales above $25,000.

The foreman of the shop was a young man named Jim Bolton. His background had included some experience with electrical wiring, hydraulic systems, press operation, and machine shop practice—the areas of ability Mr. Addison felt were of most importance to Steel Extrusion. He had been with Steel Extrusion for about one and one-half years and had assisted in the final phases of the preproduction work with the cold forming press. Jim was well liked by the other men in the shop and seemed to be effective as a leader. He was being given more and more responsibility for "getting jobs done" as time went on, thereby relieving Mr. Addison of many of the details of the production operations and supplier relations.

Steel Extrusion had five other employees. Three, including one who had just been hired in early April, worked on the day shift. Two men handled the second shift alone. This number of people was about the minimum that would support the company's operation. Whenever a press was operating, one man was needed at its control station to maintain continuous visual check on the operation of the transfer mechanism. Part of a second man's time was required for helping with tool changes, filling the raw-material hoppers, and removing full boxes of finished parts. One such helper was expected to be able to service up to three presses. Other "part-time" jobs in the shop at its present level of production were those of operating the shear, hand-feeding prototype runs through the small press, and performing general housekeeping activities. Because common sense and mechanical aptitude were more important than extensive past training in a production employee, Mr. Addison foresaw no problems in acquiring more men.

All bookkeeping and secretarial work for Steel Extrusion was done free of charge at Precision Tool Company. In the past, the amount of this work had been relatively small, but recently the volume had been increasing and was taking a substantial portion of several girls' time. Precision Tool could not justify supplying it free now that it was no longer just a spare-time job for a girl who was already on the payroll. Mr. Cook felt that it was time for Steel Extrusion to make provision for someone to handle the bookkeeping and secretarial functions and also to relieve Mr. Addison of some routine activities, such as expediting and coordinating work with suppliers, which he was currently performing. Possibly both a man and a woman would be needed.

As soon as any office personnel, other than one person, were added to the firm, a new office would be needed. The present office was a 10-by-10-foot glassed-off corner of the plant which housed a desk, drawing board, filing cabinets, and tables. When the presses were running, it offered virtually no insulation from the high noise level in the plant. Mr. Addison felt that an office addition should be built in front of the present building to provide more and quieter working spaces.

Sales and Competition

As mentioned earlier, Steel Extrusion had made the decision to concentrate on the cold forming of parts as a subcontractor to the large manufacturing firms in its area, such as automobile companies, airframe manufacturers, heavy machinery builders, and large appliance firms. Despite the growing interest in impact extrusion throughout the metalworking fields, Mr. Cook knew of no company directly competitive with Steel Extrusion.

Most of the cold forming machines in existence were owned by large manufacturing firms. The first companies to get into the field had been a few manufacturers located in the East. After World War II, several of the German engineers who had participated in the development of the process in Germany during the war came to this country. They helped these eastern firms to construct impact extrusion presses for the production of large items of the 15–20-pound size, such as gun shells. These presses, with capacities of 1,000 tons or more, were single-punch units and operated at rates of about 15 strokes per minute. Two or three firms in 1962 were still operating these large presses, both for proprietary products and subcontract work. However, their size made them noncompetitive with Steel Extrusion.

Major Manufacturers

All three of the major automobile firms had become interested in the savings possible with cold extrusion, and to varying extents they were experimenting with the process. These companies, along with the many relatively large firms that supplied them with metal component parts (e.g., starter motors, generators, spark plugs, bearings), represented a major portion of the potential market for cold formed items. Two of the three major automobile companies were known to possess their own impact extrusion presses and to be cold forming a small number of parts for their 1962 model-year cars. Trade rumors and several recent specific occurrences seemed to indicate that they would continue to expand their in-shop extrusion capacity.

The activities of many of the country's larger manufacturing concerns in the cold forming field were well known, since many of these firms wrote articles for trade journals, explaining their experiences. The process was still new enough in 1962 to make good copy for the many journals read by executives in the metalworking industries. Most of these articles were quite enthusiastic about the savings being realized.

For example, *Iron Age*, in its January 21, 1960 issue, described an impact extrusion operation then being used by J. H. Williams & Company, of Buffalo, New York, to manufacture sockets for socket wrenches. J. H. Williams & Company claimed that it was realizing material savings of between 40 and 60 percent over identical parts made on automatic screw machines. It was also stated that the cold formed sockets were stronger than machined parts because the grain of the metal conformed with the shape of the part, rather than being parallel to the center line of the original bar stock as would be the case in a machined piece.

A second example of a specific impact extrusion application was described in the June 1, 1961 issue of *Automotive Industries*. Molloy Industries, Inc., of Detroit, was cold forming stainless steel propeller shafts and drive shafts for Evinrude outboard motors. Another *Iron Age* article, published in its June 22, 1961 issue, described an impact extrusion line being operated by a General Motors Corporation division. The Saginaw Steering Gear Division was cold forming ball joint housings for Cadillac and Buick automobiles on a 1,000-ton press operated at the rate of 26 strokes per minute. These were only a few of the trade journal articles on impact extrusion published in 1960, 1961, and 1962. In addition to descriptions of specific applications, they included several technical papers on particular aspects of the field, such as metallurgical, lubrication, die design, and automation problems.[4]

Press Manufacturers

At least one large press manufacturer was selling complete impact extrusion systems, including the press, tooling, and automatic feeder units. The press capacities offered ranged from 100 to 5,000 tons. The fastest production rate listed in the company's brochure was 3,400 per hour, achieved by a 500-ton press producing a bearing race which measured about 1 by ¾ inch. The officers of Steel Extrusion did not know how many of these units had actually been sold. Most of the installations with which they were familiar had been built by using one of the standard model presses available from many large machine manufacturers and incorporating custom designed tooling and automation. Steel Extrusion's installations were of this second type.

Arron Company

A few firms with impact extrusion presses did perform subcontract work, but of a type that differed from Steel Extrusion's. Chief among these was Arron Company, of Chicago, described above, which sought very high-volume (100,000 pieces per month or more) orders that could be run on single-punch presses using low-cost tooling. (A typical punch for Arron might cost $2.00 or $3.00, according to Mr. Addison.) Arron could stand a high rate of tool failure with this policy, because tool changes could be made quite quickly on the type of presses it used. On a multiple-punch press, not only were tool changes more complicated, but a single failure would stop three or more spindles rather than just one. These differences in manufacturing policy tended to limit the competition between the two firms. Only once had they submitted competitive bids on the same job, and this was because the customer specifically requested both to do so. On this quote, clearly more suited to the Steel Extrusion manufacturing operation, Arron's quote was several times that which Mr. Addison submitted.

Both Mr. Cook and Mr. Addison said "There is more than enough

---

[4] Examples of such articles can be found in the following trade magazine issues: *Wire & Wire Products*: October, 1960; November, 1960; December, 1960. *Iron & Steel Institute*: November, 1959; July, 1960. *Engineering*: October 21, 1960; December 29, 1961. *Research*: December, 1961.

business in this field for everyone. Arron is turning down more work than they are taking. One of our biggest problems is keeping our customers happy with our present output—we have more orders on the books for the next few months than we will be able to fill. We try our best not to compete with Arron or any other extruder. The important thing now is to develop the industry, to compete with other methods of production, such as screw machines or hot forging, and to try to put off the day when we will get harmful competition within our own field."

Sales Policy

Mr. Cook felt that the reasons for the lack of competition in the job extrusion field were that the process was still experimental in nature and the high cost of the necessary equipment. These same factors had also kept Steel Extrusion from instigating a major sales effort. Instead, Steel Extrusion had established a close working relationship with a few large firms, located in its geographic area, which used a high volume of screw machine parts. From the many items used by these companies, Steel Extrusion had chosen a few particularly suited to cold forming. As described above, it had used these first jobs to work the bugs out of its manufacturing process.

The company had done no advertising and did not even have a descriptive brochure. Addison and Cook explained that they feared any advertising would elicit such a volume of requests for quotes that answering them would take all Mr. Addison's time. Furthermore, they would have to turn down many jobs because of their limited capacity and the relatively small size of their present presses. They felt that this could do serious damage to Steel Extrusion's reputation.

In addition to these factors, they saw no positive reason for any promotional efforts. They stated that more work could easily be obtained from their present customers as soon as Steel Extrusion developed greater capacity. They considered their sales problem to be one of choosing the right jobs to work on and the right companies to cultivate rather than merely getting orders.

Market Estimates

Mr. Cook estimated that there was currently an annual volume of about $2 billion worth of impact extrusion work available. In support of his estimate he pointed to an *Iron Age* article showing United

States cold forming steel consumption increasing from virtually nothing in 1950 to 8,000 tons in 1959. Consumption in 1959 was felt to be only a minor fraction of the potential in this field. Mr. Cook stated that impact extrusion could take over 20–30 percent of the volume of parts currently made on screw machines, 10–15 percent of hot forgings, and 5 percent of castings. Various statistics on the dollar volume of these industries are included as Exhibit 6–6. Mr. Cook estimated that the average sales value of cold formed parts would be approximately 25 cents per pound.

Exhibit 6–6

INDUSTRY STATISTICS FROM 1958 CENSUS OF MANUFACTURES

Area	Iron and Steel Foundries	Iron and Steel Forgings	Screw Machine Products	Bolts, Nuts, Washers and Rivets
New England				
Value added by manufacture	10.4	29.0	39.1	70.8
Value of shipments	16.0	58.8	62.7	119.4
Middle Atlantic				
Value added by manufacture	112.0	50.8	40.7	111.0
Value of shipments	176.8	104.1	67.1	184.9
East North Central				
Value added by manufacture	170.0	209.3	131.3	244.4
Value of shipments	259.6	456.6	234.0	442.2
West North Central				
Value added by manufacture	26.0	—	12.6	4.4
Value of shipments	39.2	—	19.8	7.7
South Atlantic				
Value added by manufacture	7.1	—	1.9	10.6
Value of shipments	na	—	3.9	18.3
East South Central				
Value added by manufacture	5.1	—	0.8	8.9
Value of shipments	9.2	—	1.3	17.7
West South Central				
Value added by manufacture	18.1	—	1.7	2.6
Value of shipments	na	—	3.3	7.4
Mountain				
Value added by manufacture	3.7	—	—	—
Value of shipments	6.5	—	—	—
Pacific				
Value added by manufacture	37.7	13.6	—	72.4*
Value of shipments	na	35.6	—	na
Total United States				
Value added by manufacture	383.9	310.1	250.0	504.7
Value of shipments	596.3	670.9	425.1	880.3

* No breakdown available between type of output.

NOTE: States included in areas are as follows: New England: Me., N.H., Vt., Mass., R.I., Conn. Middle Atlantic: N.Y., Pa., N.J. South Atlantic: Del., Md., D.C., W.Va., Va., N.C., S.C., Ga., Fla. East North Central: Ohio, Mich., Wis., Ind., Ill. West North Central: N.D., S.D., Neb., Kan., Minn., Iowa, Mo. East South Central: Ky., Tenn., Ala., Miss. West South Central: Ark., La., Okla., Tex. Mountain: Mont., Idaho, Wyo., Nev., Utah, Colo., Ark., N.M. Pacific: Wash., Ore., Calif.

Selling Problems

A once-significant problem connected with selling impact extrusion had been, according to Mr. Cook, that of overcoming the resistance which seems to spring up in reaction to any entirely new process or method. This resistance was, in early 1962, much less apparent than it had originally been. Mr. Cook explained that the average engineer or production executive, once he has recommended manufacture by one method (usually the traditional one), then becomes committed to it. His vested interest in this method stems from his unwillingness to admit that he may have been wrong. However, Mr. Cook reported that recently the trade publicity given to impact extrusion had helped it to become an accepted manufacturing method, and the savings possible with the process had been proven in many cases. As of early 1962, a few firms were said to be embracing impact extrusion wholeheartedly, and many others were at least willing to listen to Steel Extrusion's story. Mr. Cook stated that once he was able to cold form a given part and show the potential material savings, which were often in the order of 50 percent, the customer companies found it hard to ignore the facts.

Pricing

One facet that continued to be a problem, however, was the reluctance of prospective customers, most of whom already had their own screw machine divisions, to include a fair allocation for burden in the costs used for comparative analysis. "We already have those screw machines," they said, "we might as well continue to use them unless you can supply us at less than our present direct costs." This reaction on the part of customers had led Steel Extrusion to price its parts at a level slightly below the direct costs of identical screw machine parts. Mr. Cook felt that this price was often only a fraction of the true cost such items would have if made on screw machines. As an example he cited one part made by Steel Extrusion that was priced at 18 cents, whereas just the material cost of the same piece made on a screw machine had amounted to 17 cents. A friend of Mr. Cook had strongly indicated that he felt Steel Extrusion was grossly underpricing the parts it produced. "After all," this man argued, "you have a significant investment in presses, automation, and tooling as well as in engineering and development time on the part of your people. You should be pricing at a level high enough to allow recovery of these expenditures." Mr. Cook, however, felt that as long as he was competing for parts that had been designed for screw machine production, and primarily against captive screw machine shops of large companies, he had to continue to price on the basis of his customers' direct costs. Furthermore, he felt that Steel Extrusion could still be profitable on this basis.

Both Mr. Cook and Mr. Addison were confident that this area of sales resistance, as well as the remaining "resistance to change" among some customers, would tend to decline naturally with time. "No one can ignore savings like this for long. Our job is one of customer education, and our present operating policy—concentrating on a few manufacturers with whom we can establish close working relationships—is ideally suited to overcoming these areas of resistance at a minimum of cost to us."

Financial Aspects

As of April, 1962, the original nine investors and Mr. Addison were still the only stockholders in the company. They had contributed a total of $342,000, the most recent capital contributions being in the form of long-term debt. These men, who were by and large encouraged by the recent progress of the company, had indicated their willingness to contribute further to cover the 10 percent down payment for the 400-ton press on order. Both Mr. Cook and Mr. Addison expected that the net cash outflow from operations, which had recently been running between $2,000 and $3,000 per month, would soon cease. In fact, they hoped to show a profit in April or May.

The investors had been willing to continue their support of Steel Extrusion's development program, notwithstanding the size of the investment which had been required, because of their faith in the ultimate potential of the company. They knew that the financial statements did not yet reflect this potential, and they did not wish to give up any of the company's stock until the operating figures were such that it could be sold at a high price. Furthermore, Steel Extrusion had elected to be taxed as a partnership, which allowed the investors to charge their pro rata portion of the company's losses against their own income. This meant, however, that Steel Extrusion would have no tax loss carry-forward to offset against its own initial earnings.

Notwithstanding the willingness of the present investor group to continue their support of the company, Mr. Cook knew their resources were not infinite. If the company were to continue to expand, it would have to broaden its investor base to get needed capital. Also, the original investors wanted the company to move toward eventual public ownership so that a market could be established for their stock. Therefore, Addison and Cook both recognized that they should be thinking of acquiring new investors and preparing Steel Extrusion for a trip to the capital markets.

Mr. Addison felt that this trip should be undertaken during the summer of 1962. He wanted to use the funds that would then be raised to finance an expansion program. He was confident that the job of debugging Steel Extrusion's cold forming process was largely completed. Mr. Addison wanted to see the company add a heat-treating and coating line, several more intermediate-sized presses in the 400–500 ton range, at least one large press with a capacity of about 1,000 tons, and several smaller units for prototype runs and production runs of very small pieces. Addition of these units would, of course, require an addition to the plant and the employment of more people.

Mr. Cook, although recognizing the need to plan for additional capital, felt that the actual move should be deferred until the following year. He argued that with the installation of the second 400-ton press Steel Extrusion would be able to show solid profits. He expected sales to reach a level of at least $500,000, and probably $750,000, by year-end, and he stated that these levels could be obtained by the company's present staff plus only one or two additional press operators. "At that time, Steel Extrusion will have an extremely interesting income statement, allowing it to get its new funds on a very favorable basis."

Future Policies

As of April, 1962, Steel Extrusion's production policy was that the company should concentrate on the cold forming of parts in the ¼-pound to 1¼-pound size range, which required several hits to complete, and for which cold forming offered substantial savings over machining. Steel Extrusion performed only the shearing and the actual impact extrusion of the parts it produced, subcontracting the heat-treating and coating functions and either subcontracting the necessary finish machining on the parts or delivering them to the customers unfinished.

Steel Extrusion's sales policy was one of concentrating its attention on a very few large customers who were using a substantial volume of screw machine parts of the type and in the size range most appropriate for production by cold forming. It had, in April, 1962, three active customers for whom it was making a total of four different parts. It was also working closely with each of these customers to find other parts that could be cold formed profitably and would produce direct savings for the customer.

The separate but related questions of whether Steel Extrusion should continue to follow these two policies in the future, or should modify or completely discard one or both of them, were of major concern to Cook and Addison in April, 1962. Notwithstanding the advantages of the policies Steel Extrusion was following in April, 1962, Cook and Addison were aware of certain dangers that existed in the program. Many of the advantages seemed to stem from the fact that Steel Extrusion's program was quite specific, allowing the company to concentrate both its technical and financial resources on developing competence in a small segment of the total process of manufacturing parts by impact extrusion and on the specific needs of a few large but cooperative customers. However, this same specialization generated the dangers which Steel Extrusion saw in its program.

Although Steel Extrusion's specialization made it less vulnerable to competition in its own small area of competence, this made it more vulnerable in other ways. Each of its few customers had substantial leverage with Steel Extrusion. The loss of one customer or even one order might be quite serious. In April, the company faced just such an event. One item, which accounted for about 25 percent of its current volume, was sold to a large manufacturer who, in turn, used it in a component supplied to an even larger corporation. Both Steel Extrusion and the component manufacturer had tooled up on the basis of the ultimate customer's statements that it intended to purchase its total requirements for the component—a very substantial volume—from the component manufacturer for at least five years. In April, about six months after the start of production, the ultimate customer announced that it had changed its mind and would itself begin manufacturing the total requirements for the components within a year. This not only meant the loss of one of Steel Extrusion's largest jobs but also threatened to place the company in an embarrassing position. Mr. Cook thought the ultimate customer in this case would wish to continue using cold formed parts to make the component and might ask to purchase them from Steel Extrusion. Because of the company's established relationship with the component manufacturer, which used a substantial volume of parts that could be cold formed, Mr. Cook felt that he might have to turn down any request made by the ultimate customer, even though that firm also had substantial potential for cold formed items, and Steel Extrusion had been hoping to gain it as a direct customer for some time.

Mr. Cook knew that situations similar to this one tended to occur relatively frequently within the heavy machinery and automobile industries, which represented a major part of Steel Extrusion's market. He also knew that some of the large firms in these industries might purchase cold formed parts initially but then install their own equipment once their volume began to reach a higher level. Cook and Addison both knew that as Steel Extrusion added more presses to its own plant the existence of these dangers would become more important to their company. They were both aware that many local machine shops lived a feast-or-famine existence because most of their business was in overflow work from the large companies.

Addison and Cook wished to always remain aware of the long-range implications of Steel Extrusion's sales and production policies. They realized that the cost of the capital equipment needed to expand production under any policy was such that the company would be committed to its chosen direction for a number of years. However, they knew that it was time for definite action in order to firmly establish their company's position as an important factor in the impact extrusion field.

Future Action

Mr. Cook and Mr. Addison agreed that to do this the following actions might be desirable, at least in some circumstances, but did not fully agree as to which moves should be made first. Nor were the other investors in complete agreement on these points. (The order in which these various moves open to Steel Extrusion are listed does not necessarily represent the opinion of either Mr. Cook or Mr. Addison.)

1. Install a heat-treating and coating line.
2. Install automatic chucking machines, grinders, drills, and/or a plating line.
3. Purchase a 1,000-ton press.
4. Purchase several more 400–600-ton presses.
5. Purchase several small 100–200-ton presses for prototype work.
6. Build a plant addition and/or office addition.
7. "Conveyorize" the plant to provide fully automatic material flow.
8. Prepare a descriptive brochure.
9. Begin an advertising campaign.
10. Employ a full-time sales engineer who could include in his duties

such activities as contacting engineers in order to have cold formed parts designed into new parts and assemblies.

11. Raise outside funds to allow a full-scale expansion, either by a private placement or a public offering.

12. Employ a full-time business manager.

In summary, both Mr. Cook and Mr. Addison realized that they had brought this enterprise along to a point where continued development of the business depended on the making of constructive decisions. Once made, many current decisions would constitute long-range commitments for the company. The two men knew that they could not do everything at once, and that in some areas the data they had to work with were less complete than might be desired because of the newness both of their company and the industry. However, they felt that they should develop a coordinated program of future action which could be presented to the investors within the next few months.

7. PREMIUM PRODUCTS, INCORPORATED*
Problems in Product Line, Distribution, and Organizational Development

Premium Products, Inc., was established in 1949 in Norwood, Pennsylvania, and initially manufactured thin, pressure-sensitive tapes to replace the hand-drawn lines on organization charts. These tapes were applied to a white plastic grid board which formed the background for various types of charts and diagrams. Line and bar charts and diagrams could be constructed rapidly and accurately by simple applications of tape lines on the plastic board. In the case of a misplaced line, the tape in question could easily be pulled off the plastic sheet and replaced. The company had experienced substantial growth, and by early 1958 was producing close to 2,000 different products centering around the application of pressure-sensitive tapes in drafting, data presentation, and chart preparation. In 1958, the company owned a modern plant in Plainview, Ohio, a small town close to Akron. Sales in 1957 approximated $500,000. Exhibits 7–1 and 7–2 give selected financial data on the company.

In mid-1958, Philip Marshall, president of Premium Products, was faced with the problem of determining the company policy on future growth. As he saw it, growth could be accomplished by expanding the present product line, by concentrating on the development of new markets, or by a combination of both methods. He was also concerned over the realization that some young members of the management team felt the company was losing the aggressive spirit which had made it successful in the past. He was of the opinion that this feeling was possibly contributing to the somewhat restless spirit he had noticed in some of the younger men. Since his background had been in personnel before joining Premium Products, Mr. Marshall realized that the problems of future company growth and of providing a stimulating atmosphere for the younger members of the management team were closely intertwined, and that any decisions he might make would have to face squarely up to these problems.

Exhibit 7–1

PREMIUM PRODUCTS, INCORPORATED

OPERATING AND FINANCIAL STATISTICS—BY YEARS

As of Dec. 31	WORKING CAPITAL				
	Net Working Capital	Current Assets	Current Liabilities	Inventories	Accounts Receivable Net
1950	$(2,346)	$ 8,965	$11,312	$ 3,209	$ 1,677
1951	2,886	12,977	10,091	6,855	2,468
1952	10,605	17,518	6,912	9,963	6,594
1953	7,235	20,125	12,891	8,790	8,068
1954	14,959	29,943	14,107	12,534	14,998
1955	29,518	52,220	22,702	20,596	29,042
1956	14,747	97,550	82,803	29,822	37,197
1957	54,418	120,226	65,808	44,310	58,819

	FIXED ASSETS						
		Cost		Reserve for Depreciation			
	Total	Land and Building	Machinery and Equipment	Total	Building	Machinery and Equipment	Net
1950	$ 359	$ —	$ 359	$ 46	$ —	$ 46	$ 313
1951	3,946	—	3,946	394	—	394	3,552
1952	7,000	—	7,000	1,390	—	1,390	5,610
1953	8,506	—	8,506	2,929	—	2,929	5,577
1954	10,198	—	10,198	4,525	—	4,525	5,673
1955	21,904	—	21,904	8,140	—	8,140	13,764
1956	141,546	83,505	58,041	10,518	—	10,518	131,028
1957	187,087	100,636	86,451	23,322	3,645	19,677	163,765

	LIABILITIES						
	Total Liabilities	Total Current Liabilities	Notes Payable Banks	Notes Payable Stockholders	Accounts Payable	Accruals for Taxes, etc.	Mortgage Payable —
1950 ..	$ 11,312	$11,312	$ —	$ 9,246	$ 1,099	$ 967	$ —
1951 ..	10,091	10,091	—	6,620	1,330	2,141	—
1952 ..	6,912	6,912	—	—	2,397	4,515	—
1953 ..	12,891	12,891	2,630	4,821	1,768	3,672	—
1954 ..	14,107	14,107	—	4,821	4,793	4,493	—
1955 ..	22,702	22,702	—	—	12,825	9,877	—
1956 ..	133,119	82,803	21,914	—	43,866	17,023	5,031
1957 ..	171,206	65,808	17,513	15,339*	17,557	15,381	105,398

	NET WORTH					
	Total Net Worth	Capital† Stock	Capital Surplus	Subscribed Stock	Treasury Stock	Earned Surplus
1950	$ (744)	$ 1,183	$12,990	$ —	$ —	$(14,642)
1951	8,810	1,429	18,486	—	(44)	(11,061)
1952	17,546	1,429	18,486	—	(44)	(2,325)
1953	13,203	1,429	18,486	—	(44)	(6,668)
1954	25,274	1,578	22,904	—	(9)	801
1955	43,867	23,667	8,914	—	—	11,286
1956	96,763	35,706	32,269	11,256	(1,446)	18,978
1957	121,621	43,236	61,087	—	(1,819)	19,117

* Due within one year.
† Par value $10 until 1955, when a 4-for-1 split was effected, which reduced the par value to $2.50/share.

Exhibit 7–2

PREMIUM PRODUCTS, INCORPORATED

OPERATING AND FINANCIAL STATISTICS—BY YEARS

		SALES	
Year Ended		Distribution of Sales	
Dec. 31	Net Sales	% Commercial	% Government
1950	$ 15,493	72	28
1951	88,198	32	68
1952	134,766	46	54
1953	116,910	88	12
1954	155,937	85	15
1955	215,119	88	12
1956	319,045	90	10
1957	461,017	91	9

		EARNINGS	
	Gross	Income and Franchise Taxes	Net	Dividends Paid
1950	$(14,489)	$ —	$(14,489)	$ —
1951	3,582	—	3,582	—
1952	9,126	391	8,735	—
1953	(4,312)	30	(4,342)	—
1954	8,144	721	7,423	—
1955	18,698	6,438	12,260	1,775
1956	23,412	8,544	14,868	3,277*
1957	11,616	4,771	6,845†	6,706

* Excluding stock dividend of 10 percent.
† After nonrecurring expenses of $10,000.

The company was formed in 1949 by Frank Childs and Ralph Irving as the result of Mr. Childs' idea of using opaque pressure-sensitive tapes and plastic sheets to replace the laborious job of drawing dark ink lines on organization charts. Mr. Childs had been in the personnel field with a well-known national concern and was well aware of the time and expense involved in drawing organization charts by hand. Mr. Irving, who was Mr. Childs' neighbor in Norwood, had been with a large office equipment company for many years and in 1949 was sales manager for the Eastern division. In addition to his sales background, he possessed an inventive, mechanical mind and enjoyed tinkering with new ideas.

The two men worked on the problem in their spare time, until in the fall of 1949 they felt they had developed a satisfactory method. So great was the potential they saw for this sort of a product that they decided to organize a corporation to promote the method. Mr. Childs left his job to devote his entire time to the new company.

Shortly after the incorporation in 1949, Mr. Childs was talking with one of his friends, Philip Marshall, about the company's prospects. Mr. Marshall had been employed by a large manufacturing concern for over twenty-five years and was experienced in the fields of personnel and accounting. As time passed, Mr. Marshall had formulated a desire to join a smaller concern and invest both his funds and time in its operations. So strong was this desire that Mr. Marshall had left his job in 1949 and had been searching for a suitable small company. Prior to discussing Premium Products, Inc., with Mr. Childs, he had investigated over twenty small concerns. Mr. Marshall was impressed with the company's potential, and after a thorough investigation a suitable arrangement was negotiated whereby Mr. Marshall joined the company in an executive capacity and became a stockholder. Mr. Marshall became general manager in 1950 and president in 1951, when Mr. Childs accepted an important position elsewhere. He purchased a sizable block of stock and had periodically added to his holdings to the point where he soon became the largest, but not controlling, stockholder of the company. Mr. Childs and Mr. Irving retained their stock interest in the company.

Within a few years, the company had rapidly broadened its line to include pressure-sensitive materials for use in the plant and office layout fields as well as expanding the uses of its original product to include much of the scope of the visual aids field. Printed, adhesive-backed templates were designed to scale and could be easily attached to or removed from the plastic boards to build up a plant layout diagram in a short length of time. Templates were scaled ¼ inch to the foot and included desks, chairs, tables, machines, cabinets and various types of office equipment. If changes were required in a given layout situation, all templates and standard tapes (which represented walls) could be easily removed from the plastic board and relocated in alternative arrangements.

In addition to plant and office layout work, applications were being developed in the visual aids field, which involved the construction of many types of charts, exhibits, and drawings through the use of adhesive-backed tapes and plastic background boards. It was generally thought that the use of tapes in these applications was far less time-consuming than the traditional pen-and-ink method, due both to the relatively short time required for initial application and the ease of making changes in existing charts or layouts.

The line was further broadened in 1954 to include transparent planning boards and grids. These were thin, transparent plastic sheets on which lines had been printed, and they were particularly adapted for use as a base for tape charts and layout diagrams which required duplication of the original by reproduction processes using a light source. Work flow and data processing symbols, curved tapes, transparent colored tapes, and many other types of printed tapes were added to the line in 1956. The company in 1957 acquired the assets of a manufacturer of printed shading materials. These shading materials were used extensively in both artwork and chart-making, and consisted of thin plastic sheets printed with varying shades of colors or designs on one side, with an adhesive bonding agent on the reverse side. By 1958, the line had been expanded further and included easels, printed tapes for use as newspaper and advertising borders, and various devices to simplify the application of the entire tape line.

New applications for tapes were constantly being sought. One of the applications that had developed most rapidly, in Mr. Marshall's opinion, was the use of tape in engineering drawing, whereby a draftsman could draw lines with tape faster and more accurately than with ink and be provided with a ready means for correcting errors. "We have been doing much work in this area," explained Mr. Marshall. "Our pioneering is resulting in increasing acceptance of the tape method of drafting. I don't know how much we sell in this area now, but I feel this will be a large and profitable field for us."

In addition to the standard items, the company carried a group of kits containing a selection of the company's products. If a customer desired a special type or size of tape or a special kit, the company would quote a price for the special order and handle it on a custom basis.

Sales were originally made through a series of manufacturers' agents, but by 1953 a program had been started to shift the distribution to a series of geographically separated dealers. The change was made because management felt that agents were not especially well equipped for the selling job, which was considered to be one of education and demonstration. There was also a desire voiced by many customers that the ability to buy a product locally was of some importance. The dealers were chosen from among art materials dealers and engineering supply houses, for it was believed that the products and services sold by these outlets were most nearly comparable to Premium's products.

Aggressive promotion of the new distribution system succeeded in obtaining over 30 dealers in the first year, 1953—a figure that had grown to nearly 160 by 1958. The distribution of dealers was based mainly on area population, with the result that in 1958 the heaviest areas of concentration were the East and Midwest. In addition to dealers within the continental United States, in 1958 the company was represented by several Canadian dealers and one Hawaiian dealer.

Dealers were of three types: art materials dealers, who carried several lines of artists' supplies such as paints, brushes, and easels; engineering supply houses, which carried a broad line of drafting instruments, T-squares, rulers, slide rules, etc.; and large reproduction on blueprint houses, which had their own engineering supply department and sold a line of products similar to the independent engineering supply houses. In every instance, a basic consideration was that the dealer had outside salesmen who would demonstrate the product.

Dealers were initially given exclusive representation for Premium Products within a large geographical area. The growth of the company and of the dealer networks, however, soon required that more than one dealer be assigned to a territory. Despite this reduction in sales areas, few dealers in 1958 could not look back on a steadily increasing volume of sales of Premium products. Dealers were allowed discounts from list price based on industry practice, and carried a stock of the faster-moving items.

The company had maintained a policy of not competing with its dealers. On orders that came directly to the plant, Premium contacted the appropriate dealer, who filled the order from his stock if possible. In the event he did not carry the item, he so informed Premium, who shipped from their own stock and credited the dealer with the sale. Sales volume of dealers in 1957 ran anywhere from $2,000 to $80,000, with the average sales per dealer running about $4,000.

The company operated in leased quarters in Norwood until 1956, when a new plant was opened in Plainview, a small town on the outskirts of Akron, Ohio. One-third of the employees elected to make the move from Norwood to Plainview. The plant was of one-story construction, attractively designed, and adequate land was available for future expansion. Acquisition of the plant entailed purchase of a considerable amount of machinery, which greatly increased the production capacity of the company.

Competition in 1958 consisted of some smaller firms, mostly in the East, and a small company on the West Coast. In the opinion of management, however, these firms presented no real competitive threat because their distribution systems were felt to be inadequate and the quality of their products was considered to be inferior to that of Premium. During late 1957 and early 1958, Premium was approached several times by representatives of a large drafting supply manufacturer, who, noting the success of Premium Products, was anxious to enter the field. "Basically, the situation boiled down to a choice of two alternatives," said Mr. Marshall. "Either we produced products for this company for resale under their own label, or it was obvious that they would go into direct competition with us."

Mr. Marshall said it was unlikely that the large company would move directly into competition on the production level, but rather that they would probably seek to make a comparable agreement with one of Premium's competitors. Under the larger company's proposal, sales would be made direct to the larger company at the same discount granted to dealers, plus an additional discount about equivalent to Premium's advertising and promotion expense.

In the event he accepted the proposal of the large drafting supply manufacturer, he was concerned about the effect on his dealers, who would be placed in competition with the hundreds of this company's outlets practically overnight. He further realized such an alliance would increase his inventory requirements and production problems. On the other hand, he could visualize a substantial amount of competition coming from this source if the offer was not accepted in some form. The threatened competition from large firms in the drafting supply field had not come as a complete surprise to Premium, however, and the company's strategy for meeting this form of competition had been to devote almost 10 percent of sales to advertising for the express purpose of establishing the reputation of Premium as the leader in its field. Strict control over product quality had also been stressed, and management felt that users of these products realized the superiority of Premium's merchandise.

Diversification into new fields was planned for the future, and in 1958 development work was being pressed on several items. Work had been done on developing a close-tolerance, die-cut terminal pattern for use in drawing printed circuits, and in 1958 management was considering an additional investment of $10–$15 thousand in new machinery, which would allow production to be started on a limited scale.

Drafting for printed circuity required the hand-drawing of a large number of small, round terminal shapes, and was an extremely time-consuming process. With the development of a standard line of die-cut, adhesive-backed terminal patterns, it was visualized that a great deal of printed circuit drafting, then done by handwork with pen and ink, could be done by using combinations of terminal patterns and standard tapes placed on a plastic grid board. Two smaller competitors—one in the Midwest and one on the West Coast—were doing similar work and had recently commenced production. Initial market reaction was thought to be favorable. Management realized that the field offered a large potential market, but was postponing the expenditures pending further investigation.

One weakness of the Premium line in 1958, in the opinion of management, was the lack of a suitable means of lettering. Lines, bars, circles, and other shapes could be easily handled by relatively simple applications of Premium tapes. Lettering, however, was possible only by typing or drawing on pressure-sensitive paper to be affixed to the charts or by using ready-made letters produced by others. Although development of a lettering system would increase scheduling difficulties and create an additional inventory burden, Mr. Marshall and Mr. White felt it was imperative that such a system be developed and, further, that success in this field would provide a significant competitive advantage over competing products and permit Premium to keep its leadership in the industry.

In addition to the work on printed circuit patterns and lettering, work was continually being done on additions to the standard tape line. Management expected Premium's sales to grow 15 to 20 percent per year and indicated that the biggest growth over the next 10 years would probably come from products not being produced in 1958. The dividing line between new products and additions to the standard line was rather thin in 1958, due to the nature of the tape line. For instance, a colored tape with white diagonal stripes was produced in four widths and four colors, including black. Whether or not a fifth color or size should be considered a new item or an addition to the present line was somewhat open to question. The variety of patterns, colors, and widths had grown rapidly over the last few years, and in 1958 over 2,000 combinations were being produced. Ideas for new variations were constantly being uncovered, and the decisions to produce such products were generally decided upon jointly by the heads of the production and sales departments.

In 1958, production was under the direction of Lee Clark, who had joined the company in 1951 at the age of twenty-eight. Mr. Clark had been in sales with another company, but on joining Premium Products had shown such aptitude in the new production process that he soon was placed in charge of the entire production operation. In 1958, he was the vice-president in charge of production and headed a department of some 25–30 people. He was admired and respected throughout the company for his drive and enthusiasm for new ideas.

The vice-president and sales manager in 1958 was Harold White, who joined the company in 1955 at the age of thirty-three. Mr. White had been employed by a large, well-known office equipment firm, where in his first year he had gained membership in that company's sales club for outstanding performance. Since joining Premium, he had been instrumental in broadening the dealer network and was respected throughout the company for his natural sales ability. On the wall behind his desk hung the following passage:

> On the plains of hesitation
> bleach the bones of countless millions
> who, at the dawn of victory,
> sat down to rest,
> and resting died. . . .

Ideas for many new products came from the sales department. In many instances, a large customer might want a new shade or size of an item already in production. This request would be relayed to Mr. White, who would then confer with Mr. Clark, verbally indicating his sales estimates for the proposed new item. There was often disagreement between these two concerning the advisability of producing and stocking a new item. Mr. Clark would typically question the validity of Mr. White's estimates and point out the difficulty and high costs of producing items of questionable sales potential, while Mr. White would constantly emphasize the dangers of not supplying the customer's needs and the desirability of offering a full line. At times, these disagreements had become quite heated, and occasionally Mr. Marshall was called on to make the decision. Generally, however, Mr. Marshall left these matters entirely to Mr. White and Mr. Clark, feeling that such decisions were properly their function. He was concerned, however, that perhaps he should begin to play a more active role in these matters in an attempt to reduce the apparent friction between the production and sales departments.

Mr. Clark stated his position in this way:

Not only is the line too complex, but we are adding even more products to it every day. The sales department's estimates of new product potential are often highly optimistic, and many new items have fallen into the slow-moving category after the initial order. We have been so busy adding new items to the line that I don't honestly believe there is any one item which has been fully exploited to its potential. There are a lot of fat-margin items that are not being pushed. I would guess that about half of our sales and about two-thirds of our profit are in the 300 most popular items; yet, we have over 2,000 items in our line today.

Our inventory is not moving fast enough to suit me. We have so many items that I have two people who do nothing but keep up to date with our perpetual inventory cards.[1] Sales of many items are sporadic and, in my opinion, too small to justify retention; yet, I keep hearing that we must offer a complete line. All this means to me is short, costly runs and lost profits in items we should be pushing and developing. I wonder how much worse off we would be today if we hadn't been selling everything to everybody for the last few years.

I guess it boils down to how you want to run a business. Do you sell a little of everything, letting all the items move mostly on their own momentum, or do you concentrate on the more profitable items and plan your line accordingly? I realize we must carry certain items, but I think we have gone too far. To my way of thinking, there never will be any single item that will please everyone, but we should be more selective. I'd have to check the records to be sure, but it seems to me that we've added about 500 items in the last year or so. Sometimes, I feel we are little better than a job shop.

Frankly, I'm worried about our dealers, too. We are throwing so many different items at them that they must have a hard time keeping up with them all. They also have to carry a bigger inventory, and the addition of a lot of new items may cause them to cut down on orders of our good items. In fact, I think there is some evidence that this is happening right now.

Mr. Clark also felt that the emphasis on providing a great number of items was taking time and money which could be put to better use in entering new fields. "We have spent so much time worrying about the great number of items we carry that we have lost ground to competition on new products. We have stalled our work on die-cut printed circuits, and now our competitors are in production."

Mr. White, on the other hand, was of the opinion that the recent additions to the line had been entirely justified. He recalled that one of the major problems he had faced on joining the company in 1955 was a growing dissatisfaction caused by the limited scope of the tape line. He explained that several of the company's good customers had complained that while the line was excellent as far as it went, it did not even start to meet all their requirements.

"You hear this enough and you soon become satisfied that more variations are called for," he stated. "We tried to handle new requests on a special order basis at first, but this didn't work out due to the expense and inconvenience involved. We finally decided that

---

[1] The production control office maintained perpetual inventory cards which showed the current physical inventory and the sales of each item.

we'd have to consider each item as a potential new addition to our line if we kept getting a series of special requests for it."

Mr. White explained that he would first formulate a sales estimate for a given new item and would then approach Mr. Clark with the idea of adding it to the line. After some discussion of the investment requirements, probable costs, and sales break-even required, the two men would decide on the advisability of adding the item to the product line on a permanent catalog basis. "We don't always agree, either," he added. "At times, Lee has thought we were adding too many items and claimed that we were not doing the job on the ones we had, but I maintained that we must continue to meet our field requirements and satisfy our customers. I've pushed pretty hard on this and have succeeded in adding considerably to our line in the last few years. Of course, I'm not always right, and some of the items I spoke for haven't lived up to my expectations, but I honestly feel that if I can make correct decisions 75 percent of the time in this game, I'm doing a good job."

Mr. White received reports of monthly unit sales for each item in the line, which he used for control purposes. These reports could be easily converted to dollar sales by item by insertion and extension of unit prices, and could be broken down by salesman, states, or region. He felt this information was useful in showing how each item was moving and used these reports as a basis for administrative review of the sales pattern for the company's various product lines. The company did not have a cost accounting system in 1958, but Mr. White thought a simple system might be installed which could provide more specific data on the profitability of the various items and product groups.

Generally, however, Mr. White was satisfied with the progress of the product line and summed up his feelings with the statement, "As a result of broadening our line over the past few years we have been able to satisfy about 80 or 90 percent of our customers with stock items. About 10 percent have asked for special items. In addition, we have opened new vistas in the uses for our products."

While Mr. Clark and Mr. White did not always agree on matters of product policy, they were in close accord on the subject of top management's willingness to exploit new fields through aggressive and prompt action.

In speaking of the top management, Mr. Clark indicated that he had much respect for the group, but that he felt at times the board of directors unnecessarily delayed action on new ideas the company should exploit immediately. At other times, he indicated, the board sometimes made decisions that would not have been made if the impact on operations had been realized. "I live with operating problems every day," stated Mr. Clark, "and as a result of this I can anticipate the effects of many decisions an outsider could not. Perhaps the board is a little too far removed from operations."

In speaking further on what he saw as a lack of aggressive action on the part of top management, Mr. Clark summed up his position, saying, "Granted, as a company grows in size it needs more working capital, and we are not entirely free from financial strain now, but it seems to me that basically what this company lacks today is a little of what might be called the gambling instinct."

"I somehow feel that we aren't moving forward as fast as we once did," he added. "I know I can feel this in my job. This business runs in cycles. For a while, you are rushing around like mad trying to get out something new, and then there are times when business as usual is the order of the day. At present, we're in one of those low points, and I find the routine is getting me down a bit. Frankly, I'm never happier than when I'm working on some new thing, wrapped up in hectic work and trying to answer three phones at once."

Mr. White's feelings closely paralleled those of Mr. Clark on this subject, and he expressed his views in this way: "Now that we've started to really meet the demands of our customers, I think it's time to reassess our position. We've got to decide what fields we want to exploit and really start emphasizing these. It seems to me that lately we've failed to move fast enough and take the risks necessary to get into new markets. I'm thinking here of the die-cut terminal patterns and our lettering, but there are other instances. I feel we need two more salesmen to handle our present sales volume. I've given lots of thought to this and have pointed it out to Mr. Marshall several times, but I still haven't got my men, even though they would pay for themselves in well under a year. I'd like to turn over some of our new products to one of our three salesmen and let him run with the ball, but we are so busy now, we don't have any time for it.

"I believe much of our success in the past has been dependent on our ability to run with the ball while the big companies were still thinking about it. Lately, we've been trying to act too big. We cogitate too much, rehash ideas too long, and have started to slow down in our aggressive risk-taking capacity. It's pretty painful to wake up and find that someone else has gone and beaten us to the punch."

The board of directors was composed of Mr. Marshall; Mr. Irving, who advised the company on new products on a part-time basis; Stewart Quinn, of Quinn and Associates, a well-known consulting firm; and Leonard Eagle, the company counsel. Frank Childs, one of the founders, was not a member of the board because his home was on the Pacific coast, but he occasionally attended meetings in an advisory capacity. Mr. Marshall acted as chairman. In 1958, members of the board held a substantial amount of the common stock of the company.

Ownership of the common stock in 1958 was divided roughly as follows: 70 percent was owned by Mr. Marshall, Mr. Childs, and Mr. Irving (or their families); another 20 percent was divided among Mr. Quinn, Mr. Eagle, Mr. White, and Mr. Clark; and the remaining 10 percent was split among some 60 small investors, who included friends, local residents, and employees. Mr. Marshall held the largest block, which amounted to about 40 percent of the total. Mr. White and Mr. Clark owned a nominal amount, or about 1 percent each.

Mr. Marshall was of the opinion that it was a questionable practice to offer employees company stock, for he felt it was not wise for an employee to have his salary and savings tied up with the same company. Before agreeing to permit an employee to purchase stock, Mr. Marshall had personally talked with each man, advising him to buy only if he had other savings and could afford to invest in a stock for which there was no immediate market. "I wanted everybody to go into this with their eyes wide open. I actually tried to discourage them from buying stock."

Mr. Marshall had always favored a board on which the majority of the members were not actual members of operating management. Principally, he was of the opinion that an "outside" board, due to its greater objectivity and scope of experience, was far more effective in guiding the company than was an inside board with its limited outlook. Mr. Marshall realized that there were some advantages in bringing Mr. Clark and Mr. White on the board, but did not feel he could safely do this until another outside member could be found to balance the new, inside members. He had been looking for a new outside member since early 1957. Exhibit 7–3 gives a memorandum, written to the board by Mr. Marshall in 1957, which resulted in adoption of the resolution to raise the membership from four to seven.

Mr. Marshall viewed membership on the board as only one of several methods he was using to try to bring Mr. Clark and Mr. White

Exhibit 7–3

PREMIUM PRODUCTS, INCORPORATED

Proposal

To increase the board of directors of Premium Products, Inc., from four to seven members, of which four will be "outside" directors and three "inside."

Structure of the Board [1]

There should be a majority of outside directors who do not depend on the company for their principal livelihood. The board should include also the principal operating executives, comprising the president, vice-president in charge of production, and vice-president in charge of sales, who make up the "operating committee."

Present board members have a broad general business background, with certain specific areas of greatest specialization. They are as follows:

Name	Area of Specialization
*Leonard J. Eagle, attorney Baker, Cross, Able, & Daniels New York, New York	Legal
*Steward P. Quinn Quinn & Associates Cleveland, Ohio	Human relations, organization, finance
*Ralph S. Irving, retired (formerly with Royal McBee) Plainview, Ohio	Sales, invention
Philip N. Marshall, president Premium Products, Incorporated Plainview, Ohio	Personnel, organization, finance, accounting

How Can Outside Directors Serve the Company?

1. In policy-making.
    a. Decide objectives and niche of the company (products, markets, distribution methods, sources of supply, should we produce or purchase for resale, etc.).
    b. Plan the future of the company—where is the business heading?
    c. Protect the interests of the minority stockholders.
    d. Assure management development and succession.

---

[1] Mr. Marshall explained that most of this memorandum was adapted from *The Board of Directors in a Small Corporation*, by Myles Mace. (Boston, Mass., Harvard Business School, 1948.)

* Present outside directors

Exhibit 7–3—Continued

2. In providing an opportunity for advice and counsel as requested by management in the solution of day-to-day operating problems for which management and not the board members must be held primarily responsible.
3. In reviewing the progress of the company.
4. In setting compensation for principal operating executives, including basic salaries, profit-sharing plans, and bonuses.

What Qualifications Should an Outside Director Have?

1. Honesty and integrity, with firmness, stability, and judgment in the determination of underlying issues.
2. An awareness and intimate understanding of the problems of small business.
3. Willingness to devote the necessary time regularly to the affairs of the company, as opposed to sporadic interest.
4. Financial stability, including a willingness to invest in qualifying shares and, although *not a basic requirement*, ability to invest or to interest potential investors.
5. Primary interest in the field of merchandising, production, or engineering to round out the scope of the present board.
6. Ability to teach or coach the management to be better administrators (assumes willingness of management to listen).
7. (Desirable, but not necessary) knowledge of printing, paper products, plastics, office equipment, electronics, retail distribution, drafting materials and supplies, reproduction methods, graphic presentation, plant layout.

What Incentives to Serve Does the Company Offer to a Director?

1. An opportunity to participate in and influence the progress of a growing business through discussion with stimulating associates.
2. An opportunity to contribute to the growth of the industrial community.
3. An opportunity to invest in a business, the growth of which he can influence.
4. Retainer (should not be a significant factor, currently $400 per annum, plus expenses).

How Much Time Must a Director Devote to the Company?

1. Attendance at four meetings each year (generally held on Saturday), with special meetings if circumstances require.
2. Study and analysis of operating reports, quarterly audits, budgets, trends.
3. Review of policy recommendations of management.

Exhibit 7-3—Continued

Where Can We Find Candidates for Directorship?

1. Educators in the field of business or economics.
2. Presidents of successful small companies with national distribution.
3. Retired business executives.
4. Retired armed forces personnel.
5. Business consultants.

Where Might We Get Names of Prospective Candidates?

1. National associations such as the American Management Association, National Association of Manufacturers, National Federation of Sales Executives, related industry trade organizations, and similar organizations.
2. Bank presidents.
3. Secretaries of local chambers of commerce.
4. Deans of colleges and universities.
5. Editors of related business publications.

Competitors or customers and dealers should not be considered. The man selected should be within 125 miles of Plainview, preferably closer.

into the top level, policy-making area of the company. He felt that it was necessary to offer a number of things to a promising member of management to retain the man. "First of all, you must pay a base salary that is competitive. When a man has demonstrated ability for top management thinking, I'd like to bring him in on a special management incentive bonus, perhaps tied to profits. This is, of course, above and beyond any company-wide plan that might be in effect. Perhaps the most important factor is that you give the man the feeling he is growing individually and that he is an active participant in the entire company operation. This entails letting the man know you trust him, and even means he should be allowed to make some of his own mistakes without interference from above.

"I have attempted to foster this feeling by letting the younger department heads assume hiring and firing responsibility over their own employees. Of course, I have to pass on all wages and salaries to maintain the balance within the company.

"One of the toughest problems you must face in administration is that the growth of a company implies the narrowing of each individual's area of responsibility, especially at the top. What with specialization and the natural spreading of responsibility that comes with growth, the scope of a man's responsibility must narrow, even though the job itself gets bigger and more complex. One of the hardest things for our young men to realize is that from now on their rate of growth will probably be at a slower pace," he added. "I can appreciate their frustrations, but it seems to me that it's inevitable."

As he reflected for a moment, it seemed to Mr. Marshall that the problem of retaining and stimulating young men was really quite basic and, in fact, bore directly on his objectives for the company. "I get a great personal satisfaction out of seeing men develop," he stated, "and I guess that it's one of my objectives to see that the men in this company do just that. I want to build a healthy, stable organization. In 1957, we had a very distasteful experience. We had overestimated the projected size of our volume and had built up our staff accordingly. When the business didn't materialize, we just had to let some people go. I don't want that to happen again here.

"Of course, one of our objectives is also to make a profit, and an above average one, too. You see this chart here? I call it my inspiration chart. It portrays sales growth of 15–20 percent a year compounded. There is a very delicate balance you must consider when you think of growth. I want to see the company grow as fast as necessary to maintain the challenge to the men, but not so fast as to go broke for lack of adequate working capital. You must strike a very delicate balance in maintaining both the challenge to the young men and a healthy growth picture for the company as a whole. The way I feel now, I'd like to keep on working here for a good many more years. I'm sixty now, but fully intend to keep working and not retire at sixty-five. Of course, there's always the danger of one's losing his sharpness and becoming less willing to take the risks he would have taken when he was younger. This will happen to me someday, and what's worse, I may not realize it. I only hope I can hear the bell when it rings."

Mr. Marshall was aware that there was a certain feeling between Mr. Clark and Mr. White that he and the board were too slow in moving on some matters. "I realize that they may feel we are a bit conservative at times, but I always remind them that we haven't done too badly in the past, and that we're making progress. It seems to me that the record speaks for itself."

As he considered the position of the company in July, 1958, Mr. Marshall realized that he was faced with several situations requiring the decisions of top management. One issue to be considered was the means of maintaining the challenge for the younger members of the management team, and specifically whether or not Mr. Clark and

Mr. White should be elected to the board of directors. Although he firmly believed that another outside director would first have to be found so as to maintain the outside balance on the board, Mr. Marshall felt that this question was important enough to bring before the board at its next meeting.

Mr. Marshall was also of the opinion that the attention of management should be focused on evaluation of the company's potential earning power and what specific means might be employed to achieve this goal. He also believed that it was imperative that he and Mr. Clark and Mr. White constantly discuss means by which the future earning power of the company could be further increased by greater emphasis on established items, as well as by the addition of new products.

8. THERMAL DYNAMICS CORPORATION (A)*

Deciding whether to Undertake a Development Project

The Thermal Dynamics Corporation specialized in finding industrial applications for plasma technology.[1] The company had investigated a wide range of applications in which extremely high temperatures were useful, and had manufactured a general-purpose plasma torch which was sold to research laboratories interested in investigating plasma. The company was located in Lebanon, New Hampshire, about five miles from the campus of Dartmouth College. In 1959, total sales were about $420,000.

In December, 1959, the management of TDC was considering whether to undertake a new development project. It would involve trying to develop a device which would utilize plasma for industrial cutting purposes; the product would probably be called a plasma flame cutter.

Company Background

The founder of the company was James Browning who, by arrangement with the Thayer School of Engineering at Dartmouth College, divided his attention between his work as professor of mechanical engineering at the Thayer School and as an executive of the Thermal Dynamics Corporation. In 1955, he and several other engineers organized Combustion Products Research, a consulting firm which specialized in investigating problems associated with combustion and high temperatures. In 1956, the consulting firm received a contract to investigate the application of plasma technology to metallizing, a process by means of which materials with high melting points could

---

* Copyright © 1962 by the President and Fellows of Harvard College.

[1] Plasma—a substance in which the individual atoms have been broken down into ions and free electrons. This condition is brought about by the application of extremely high energy levels to a substance and in the TDC investigations was brought about by temperatures from 5,000° to 60,000°F. Further technical information is given in Appendix 8–A.

be sprayed. Thereafter, Mr. Browning and his associates became increasingly involved in investigating applications of plasma.

In January, 1958, Combustion Products Research ceased to exist as an active business organization, and the Thermal Dynamics Corporation was formed to concentrate on applications of plasma technology. The new company had total personnel of 12, including 4 engineers, and total capitalization of $1,000. James Browning was president of the company, and divided his time between administrative duties and laboratory work.

TDC had several research contracts which provided all the company's revenue during the first six months of 1958. However, during this same period TDC developed its first product, a general-purpose plasma torch with certain accessory equipment. This product was offered to the market in August, 1958. During the next 15 months, TDC sold about 45 of these torches, almost all of them to research and development laboratories. These laboratories used the torches for experiments in welding, cutting, and spraying as well as more basic research into the nature of plasma.

Sales of the company for 1958 and 1959 were as follows:

Year	General-Purpose Torches	Research Contracts	Total
1958	$ 20,000	$50,000	$ 70,000
1959 (estimated)	395,000	25,000	420,000

TDC's sponsored research had primarily been directed at gathering information relating to the particular applications of plasma technology—for example, learning the techniques to form titanium in particular shapes and thicknesses by plasma-spraying. The terms of these contracts normally did not require TDC to surrender any proprietary rights, in that TDC as well as the sponsoring company could use the research findings.

TDC had never had either a separate sales force or manufacturing representatives. Management believed that the company did not have enough sales to support its own sales force. However, management also thought that whoever was representing TDC in a sales capacity should be well informed on the latest developments in plasma technology. In their opinion, manufacturers' representatives would not have the technical background, the motivation, or the close association with the laboratory that would be necessary.

Therefore, in selling the general-purpose torch, the first step in the sales procedure was to generate interest through articles in trade magazines and through papers presented at meetings of technical societies. Typically, each such article generated a considerable number of inquiries, mostly in the form of letters to TDC. The company then sent these prospective customers promotional literature, describing the torch, and invited them to visit the TDC plant to see a demonstration of the torch. In some cases, a TDC engineer would visit several interested companies to answer questions about the plasma torch and to learn more about the prospective customers' specific interests in regard to plasma research.

Many prospective customers also visited the TDC plant; in 1958 and 1959, about 50 percent of those who visited the TDC plant purchased general-purpose torches. A general-purpose torch and the needed accessory equipment sold for about $7,500 to $12,000, depending chiefly on the capacity of the power supply. The accessories included a control console which automatically regulated the flows of electricity, stabilizing gas, and cooling water. There were also the pumps and heat exchanger for the cooling water, and the power supply which converted alternating current to the direct current required for the plasma torch; the power supply accounted for 50 to 75 percent of the total cost of the plasma torch package.

TDC's production activities were largely subcontracted. The company had seven or eight general-purpose machine tools, on which were produced several components of the control console used with the general-purpose torch. The power supplies were produced to TDC's specifications by a large manufacturer of electrical equipment; these were shipped directly from the manufacturer's plant to the customer. The torches were produced by another company, which shipped them to the TDC plant for assembling, adjusting, and testing. The control console was assembled in the TDC plant, from both purchased components and parts manufactured by TDC.

One problem associated with TDC's small sales volume, and mentioned several times by management, was the high cost incurred because many components could not be purchased in volume. Another cost problem, even more important in management's opinion, was the lack of production engineering in the general-purpose torch. One executive estimated that the manufacturing cost of the torch could be cut by 75 percent just by simplification and substitution of standard parts and less expensive materials.

TDC also offered a spraying service. In spraying, powder was fed into the high-velocity plasma stream, and was then impacted in a molten state onto a part to be coated, forming a high-density, well-bonded coating. A great many materials could be sprayed, including tungsten, platinum, titanium, and various carbides and borides.

Use of plasma in spraying applications had been investigated for several years by Mr. Browning and his associates on a contract-research basis. In December, 1959, TDC management was planning to offer a service, beginning in early 1960, in which TDC would spray materials on a contract basis. Management thought that such a service might enjoy a very rapid growth in sales, perhaps becoming a very significant part of the total business. From its initial capitalization of $1,000 in January, 1958, the company's growth had been financed entirely from internally generated funds. The general-purpose torch was a high-margin product, and all profits had been retained within the company. In 1959, profits before taxes were estimated at about $110,000. The company had not done any long-term borrowing, although management was not averse to doing so if growth made it necessary.

Mr. Browning had served both as president and chairman of the board until the fall of 1959, at which time he turned over the presidency to Merle Thorpe, an engineer in his early thirties, who had joined the company in 1956 after working several years for a competitor. Mr. Thorpe had taken part of his engineering work under Professor Browning at the Thayer School. Mr. Browning said he was spending about 60 percent of his own time on laboratory work, about 30 percent on teaching, and about 10 percent on administrative duties. Mr. Browning described himself as more an engineer than an administrator and seemed glad that he had been able to pass the administrative duties to Mr. Thorpe, who apparently was both a competent and enthusiastic manager.

Mr. Browning owned 60 percent of the outstanding stock; Mr. Thorpe owned 30 percent; and two TDC technicians owned the remaining 10 percent. In speaking of growth, Mr. Browning said, "We could stabilize at this point, concentrate on certain applications of plasma technology, and have a nice comfortable business. However, we do not choose to do this. We prefer to grow as fast as possible, consistent with minimizing risk."

Mr. Thorpe, the president, emphasized that an outstanding characteristic of the company was growth. He said, "We talk about how things used to be done, and we are referring to only six months ago."

TDC had had no difficulty in attracting competent engineers; in fact, a number of visiting sales engineers had asked management to consider them when additional engineers were hired. Management thought the company's location (in the heart of the New Hampshire ski country) was an incentive for many people, possibly with a special appeal for graduates of Dartmouth College or the Thayer School of Engineering. Another incentive was the broad scope of problems a TDC engineer encountered; this apparently was the reason why two engineers had left more specialized jobs at Bell Laboratories to come to TDC.

Origination of the Idea for a Plasma Cutter

Mr. Browning had been interested in the problems of industrial cutting for a number of years. He had used the general-purpose plasma torch for cutting experiments, but did not believe that it could be used as a commercially practical cutter, inasmuch as its power capacity was too low, its electrode usage was too high, and it lacked the reliability needed for sustained operation. TDC had conducted some sponsored research in the fall of 1959 to accumulate systematic data in regard to the cutting capabilities of the plasma torch. This information included cutting speeds, metal thicknesses, and operating costs. The sponsor of this research was a large processor of scrap who was interested in learning whether the application of plasma technology to its cutting problems would be more economical than the mechanical shears and oxyacetylene torches it was using.

This research, which was paid for by the scrap processor on a cost-reimbursable basis, cost about $5,000. The findings confirmed Mr. Browning's opinion that the general-purpose torch was not a commercially practical cutting tool. However, the data indicated that plasma cutting might be an economical way of cutting a great variety of materials. It was known that the cutting speed, cleanness of cut, and thickness of cut were all functions of the electrical power of the torch. The general-purpose torch, with which the experiments were conducted, carried maximum power of 100 kw. Extrapolating from the data gathered in the experiments, TDC engineers concluded that a torch with a power capacity of 200 kw. might be an economical cutting tool—one which would offer substantial cost savings over oxyacetylene cutting torches. Mr. Browning was not sure that a plasma cutting torch with the desired characteristics could be developed; however, if it could be achieved, he estimated that the resulting cutting costs might be less than 50 percent of the equivalent costs using oxyacetylene equipment.

In December, 1959, Mr. Browning was considering whether to undertake the development of a plasma cutter. Mr. Browning devoted over half of his time to laboratory research. At that time, having finished certain other projects, he wondered whether he should concentrate his attention on the development of a practical plasma cutter.

The chief technical objective that Mr. Browning thought necessary to achieve was a higher power capacity—200 kw. rather than the 100 kw. capacity of the general-purpose torch. In doing this, he thought it might be possible to utilize the body of the general-purpose torch (called the F–40 torch body); however, it would probably be necessary to change the basic kind of gas flow from linear flow to a whirling "vortex" flow. The life of the general-purpose electrode was about 10 to 30 hours; since a new electrode cost about $22, he thought it highly desirable to experiment with various materials, shapes, and cooling systems, in an attempt to increase this electrode life.

In speaking of the technical problems involved, Mr. Browning emphasized the empiricism of their approaches to problems encountered in finding commercial applications for plasma technology. Minor changes in the dimensions, shape, or material of an interior component of the general-purpose torch could markedly change the performance or reliability of the torch in an almost unpredictable manner. He said, "I made no estimate of the time it would take to develop a practical plasma cutter, because I wasn't even sure it could be done." He added, "Invention and the investigation of new concepts do not lend themselves to planning."

A project to develop a practical plasma cutter, if undertaken, would probably occupy about 50 to 60 percent of James Browning's time (which was about the maximum he thought he could devote to laboratory work). Probably, it would also require at least half the time of one laboratory technician and of a machinist who would produce the equipment for testing. If the initial investigations were successful, Mr. Browning thought it probable that additional company personnel would be added to the project to assist in testing, engineering design, and market development. As previously mentioned, Mr. Browning did not think it possible to predict the amount of time or effort it would take to achieve a practical plasma cutter.

Mr. Browning thought there was absolutely no doubt of the need for a practical plasma cutter. He cited the growing use of materials such as graphite, aluminum, copper, and stainless steel, none of which could be cut efficiently with oxyacetylene torches.[2] He considered the company's earlier research, sponsored by the scrap processor, which indicated that a plasma cutter might offer substantial savings in operating costs over oxyacetylene cutting methods. Mr. Browning had always been interested in industrial cutting problems, and his earlier consulting work had included investigations of gasoline and oxyacetylene torches. This experience, plus his conversations with the scrap processor, gave him what he considered a good feel for the market for industrial cutting equipment. He estimated that between 4,000 and 7,000 machine-driven oxyacetylene installations were used for cutting in the country, and that the number of hand-held oxyacetylene torches was probably in the hundreds of thousands. He did not estimate the potential market for a plasma cutter, although he felt it might run to thousands of units per year (with a total dollar value of several million). However, he was confident that TDC could sell at least several hundred plasma cutters per year, and that that volume would be sufficient to make the product a successful addition to the line.

A Competitive Product

Several years earlier, the Ajax Company, a division of a large chemical company, had developed a plasma cutting torch which it sold to companies wishing to cut materials such as aluminum, titanium, and tungsten, which could not be cut with oxyacetylene torches. Ajax did not promote the torch for ordinary cutting of mild steel, and concentrated on those applications in which only plasma cutting could do the job. The price of the Ajax torch and associated equipment was about $5,000 to $6,000; the purchaser paid a use royalty of about $2,000 at the time of purchase.

Technically, the Ajax cutting torch differed from the proposed TDC plasma cutter in several ways. Its maximum power capacity was slightly over 100 kw., which imposed, in the opinion of TDC's management, severe restrictions on cutting speed, thickness, and quality of cut. The method of stabilization used in the Ajax torch was called wall stabilization. According to the Ajax patents, in this method of stabilization "the plasma gas, rather than constricting the arc, be-

---

[2] Copper and aluminum conducted heat away from the cutting area too rapidly to permit efficient cutting. Stainless steels formed chromium oxides with melting points above the 5,600°F. maximum temperature of the oxyacetylene flame.

comes an integral part of the arc stream, filling the nozzle from wall to wall." The extent to which wall stabilization actually differed from gas-sheath stabilization and vortex stabilization—the methods used by TDC—was open to question, since there was a very limited scientific understanding of the actual mechanics involved. According to the TDC management, the Ajax torch also was difficult to adjust and involved a time-consuming and delicate process by which the electrode was centered.

The performance characteristics and operating costs of the Ajax cutting torch were roughly known by the TDC management. The operating costs, which ranged up to 10 cents per foot for 2-inch thick, mild steel, were, in the opinion of TDC's management, excessively high. This was primarily because the Ajax torch used argon gas (costing about 10 cents per cubic foot). Mr. Browning estimated that Ajax had sold about 200 torches over the last few years, almost all of them for cutting uses in which oxyacetylene torches were not suitable. TDC thought Ajax looked on its cutting torch mainly as a gas user and sold it primarily because it provided customers for Ajax's argon and hydrogen.

Ajax's sales of plasma cutting torches and the gases to be used with these torches appeared to be very small compared to its sales of oxyacetylene equipment and associated gases. Total sales of oxygen and acetylene for both welding and cutting uses were estimated at over $1 billion for 1959; it was estimated that Ajax accounted for a substantial part of these sales. TDC executives thought that Ajax's strong commitment to the oxyacetylene market was the reason Ajax had not promoted its plasma cutting torch for any uses in which it would compete with oxyacetylene torches. This was in direct contrast to James Browning's point of view; he thought it was entirely possible that the plasma cutter eventually would completely replace the use of oxyacetylene torches for cutting purposes. In the oxyacetylene field, TDC had no established position that would be disrupted.

A Point of Decision

As Mr. Browning considered whether to undertake this development project, he also considered his own personal interests. He thought the technical problems would be scientifically interesting. He said he had always taken pride in solving problems such as this in which his scientific training could be brought to bear practical fruit. He also thought it particularly important that any engineer within the company should be free to investigate problems he found particularly interesting. He applied this philosophy in managing the engineering effort of the firm, and he considered it important, of course, in his own choice of a project.

Another factor considered by Mr. Browning was the $100,000 in cash which TDC had in the bank. He did not think he could foresee the exact development costs of the new product, and he made no prediction as to the funds required to manufacture and market the new product. However, he knew that if his initial investigations were successful, TDC would have to make additional financial commitments in order to exploit his findings. He thought that the company's $100,000 in cash, plus its continuing stream of income resulting from sales of the general-purpose torch, would permit TDC to take advantage of the information resulting from his initial investigations.

The decision would be made by James Browning. Despite the factors favoring such a project, he did not consider the decision an easy one. The company was growing rapidly, and there were other possible applications of his time. There was a need for improvement of the general-purpose torch in order to decrease its manufacturing cost and improve its reliability. There was a need for adapting the torch to such specific applications as testing rocket nose cones, which would probably involve accumulation of test data and development of accessory equipment.

Apart from his work with TDC, Mr. Browning had developed another product, a sandblaster utilizing a rocket burner which appeared to be several times more effective in cleaning than conventional, compressed-air sandblasting equipment. Mr. Browning wondered whether he should spend some time investigating the prospects for this product. He knew that some additional development time would be needed to perfect the product.

Another alternative considered by Mr. Browning was to devote more time to administrative duties within the company, perhaps advising other TDC engineers and supervising the coordination of various projects. No one within the company filled the position of chief engineer or research director, and this situation was reflected in the fact that there had been some duplication of projects.

These alternatives all appeared highly promising to James Browning, although it was difficult to estimate the relative value of his time if applied to the different alternatives. In December, 1959, the proposed TDC plasma cutter was only an idea. As Mr. Browning considered the various factors pertinent to the decision, he wondered whether he should undertake the project, choose one of the other alternative uses of his time, or seek additional information before making a decision.

APPENDIX 8-A

Plasma Technology

Definition of Plasma. Plasma is a state of matter in which all or part of the atoms have broken down into ions and free electrons. It should be distinguished from blood plasma, which is a completely different substance. Plasma is sometimes referred to as a fourth state of matter.

True plasmas, in which all electrons are stripped from the atomic nuclei, exist only at extreme temperatures, far above the maximum temperature of 60,000°F. encountered in the TDC investigations. A plasma cutter achieving temperatures between 5,000°F. and 60,000°F. would produce a partial plasma, in which some of the atoms would separate into free electrons and positive ions.

The Plasma Torch. A plasma torch is a device for producing plasma. Its operation involves having an electric arc jump from one electrode to another through a confining space. A plasma-forming gas is constricted to flow through the same passage. That portion of the gas which comes in contact with the arc is heated to a very high temperature. The gas, which is partially ionized and therefore a plasma, is then ejected from the nozzle of the torch.

The peripheral gas—that not touching the arc itself—is relatively cool and has a higher velocity than the ionized gas within the arc. In this way, the walls of the torch are protected from the intense heat of the arc and plasma (although it is still necessary to cool the walls with water). The peripheral gas is less ionized than the gas within the arc; it therefore is less conductive. This phenomenon, coupled with the relatively higher speed of the peripheral gas, tends to constrict, or squeeze, the arc, further increasing the temperature of the plasma. The arc is therefore carried down the torch, while being kept in the center of the chamber, away from the walls of the torch.

Plasma torches are either of the nontransferred-arc or transferred-arc type. In the first, the arc begins and ends within the torch. The Thermal Dynamics general-purpose torch was of this sort. In this torch, the anode is the wall of the torch. After the arc has traveled some distance toward the nozzle, it breaks through the stabilizing gas to impinge on the wall in an umbrella pattern. It does not damage the torch wall, because it has already given up most of its energy to the gas and it strikes the wall over a broad area.

The transferred-arc type of plasma torch involves an arc which leaves the torch in order to impinge on a workpiece; the workpiece must be a conducting material, since it serves as an electrode. Because of the longer contact with the arc, more gas heating occurs, and temperatures as high as 60,000°F. are possible. The plasma cutter was to utilize a transferred arc. The cutting process occurs as the metal is melted at the point of contact with the arc and hot plasma. The molten metal is then blown away by the plasma and hot gases, which emerge from the torch at speeds of up to 40,000 feet per second.

There are various kinds of stabilization, including gas sheath, vortex, wall, and magnetic. This appendix deals with gas sheath stabilization, which was used in the TDC general-purpose torch, and with vortex stabilization, to be used in the TDC plasma cutter.

In gas sheath stabilization, the injected gas moves in a parallel relationship to the arc within the torch. The arc is constricted by a sheath of gas, much thicker than the arc diameter. The high velocity of the gas prevents the arc from grounding on the nearest point of the nozzle; the arc is thus carried down the nozzle until the gases in the surrounding sheath become sufficiently heated and ionized to permit the arc to ground against the nozzle wall (assuming that it is a nontransferred-arc torch).

In vortex stabilization, the stabilizing gas is swirled into the chamber to produce an intense vortex. The arc travels within the low-velocity core of this vortex out the nozzle to impinge on the workpiece (assuming this is a transferred-arc torch). Vortex stabilization apparently permits a longer arc than other methods of stabilization and is more suitable for higher power inputs. Thermal Dynamics engineers considered it a less reliable method of stabilization because it was newer and had not been tested as extensively.

A number of other critical factors in plasma torch design will be only mentioned. These include electrode shape, electrode positioning, kind of stabilizing gas, nozzle design, power requirements, and materials of construction.

SIMPLIFIED DRAWING OF
PLASMA CUTTER

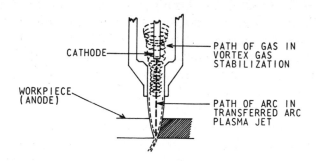

CATHODE ——

PATH OF GAS IN
VORTEX GAS
STABILIZATION

WORKPIECE
(ANODE)

PATH OF ARC IN
TRANSFERRED ARC
PLASMA JET

GENERAL PURPOSE
PLASMA TORCH

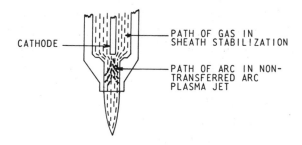

CATHODE ——

PATH OF GAS IN
SHEATH STABILIZATION

PATH OF ARC IN NON-
TRANSFERRED ARC
PLASMA JET

9. THERMAL DYNAMICS CORPORATION (B)*
Deciding about Product Characteristics

After deciding to undertake the development of a plasma cutting torch, Mr. Browning spent some 25 to 30 hours per week working on the project. Initially, his efforts were concentrated on trying to achieve a gas stabilization pattern in which the gas whirled at high speeds around the electric arc. This pattern differed from that of the TDC general-purpose torch in which the gas traveled in a straight path through the torch, parallel to the arc.[1] Mr. Browning had very limited experience with swirl, or vortex, stabilization, but he thought it would be necessary in order to carry a high current through the torch and out to the workpiece without shorting against the wall of the torch. Mr. Browning said his approach to investigating vortex stabilization was largely empirical, since it was difficult to predict the results of varying the shape of the gas inlet slots, the diameter of the nozzle, or the amount of power.

Assisting Mr. Browning were two men who were putting in half time on the project—a technician who performed the laboratory work and a skilled machinist who built various parts to James Browning's specifications. This machinist was a key man in the company's product development efforts. He could take rough drawings and convert them into finished parts, and because of his close familiarity with the laboratory problems of using plasma he could interpret, make his own decisions as to details, and often contribute useful suggestions relating to product design. He worked exclusively with the company's engineers and did not construct any parts for production models. Often, he had parts ready for laboratory testing within a few hours after receiving the sketch.

In March, 1960, the project approached a second point of evaluation in which a decision was necessary. Mr. Browning had been successful in achieving a form of vortex stabilization which promised to make possible a plasma cutter with a power capacity of 200 kw. How-

---

[1] See drawing in Thermal. Dynamics Corporation (A), Appendix 8–A.

139

ever, the decision had not yet been made as to whether the new plasma cutter would adopt the torch body used with the general-purpose torch or whether the plasma cutter would be incorporated into a completely redesigned torch body, one developed specifically for the new product.

The general-purpose torch body was a cylindrical nylon tube which housed various components, including those that regulated the stabilizing gas flow, the electrode, and the nozzle which shaped the pattern of the plasma as it emerged from the torch. These components were the essential heart of a plasma torch and were to be considerably different in the plasma cutter from those in the general-purpose torch. Mr. Browning's investigations of vortex stabilization had been directed primarily at developing certain of these new components. It was technically possible for the plasma cutter to be housed in the body of the general-purpose torch. This body was more than a cylindrical casting. It included the electrical leads and the inlets for stabilizing gas and cooling water. The dimensions of the body had been carefully developed by extensive testing in order to provide maximum product life and to minimize problems of heat transfer and electrical shorting. James Browning thought the cutting performance of a plasma cutter (speed, thickness of metal cut, and quality of cut) would be about the same, regardless of which alternative was followed.

The general-purpose torch was a research tool, and its torch body was bulky and expensive. It was too heavy to be used as a hand-held plasma cutter, which would limit its use to machine-driven installations. It was versatile and could be used with various attachments and components to do spraying, cutting, or welding; this was an important attribute for a laboratory tool, but was not a particularly useful characteristic (in management's opinion) for an industrial plasma cutter.

One significant factor pointing toward a completely new design was the high cost of the F–40 torch body. It had never been designed with production economies in mind, and management estimated that its manufacturing cost could be decreased from about $350 to about $75, just by the substitution of standard parts and simplification.

A factor favoring the use of the F–40 torch body was its reliability. It had been used for almost two years, and the bugs in it had been discovered and corrected through appropriate changes in dimensions and materials. Management felt that any new design would have reliability problems which would not be discovered except through extensive testing, and perhaps not until the product was placed on the market—such things as corroding parts, leaking seals, and faulty electrical connections. Overcoming these problems would require scarce engineering time, would delay the introduction of the product to the market, and perhaps would result in dissatisfied customers who found bugs in the new product.

In regard to timing, Mr. Browning estimated that a decision to design a new torch body would delay introduction of the new product by six months to a year. Management did not consider speed of development to be of primary importance, since no specific customers were clamoring for the new product. However, management desired to have the product on the market and contributing to the company's profit as soon as possible. TDC also feared that other companies, recognizing the need for a practical plasma cutter, might develop one and beat TDC to the market.

If the old F–40 torch body were chosen for the new product at this time, management anticipated that at some future time TDC would develop a second generation of plasma cutters. This second-generation product would incorporate various changes resulting from what TDC learned in testing, producing, and marketing the first generation of plasma cutters. The second generation of the new product would also be incorporated in a lightweight, inexpensive torch body designed specifically for use in industrial cutting. A lightweight plasma cutter could be used as a hand-held tool, which, in management's opinion, would tremendously expand the potential market for the new product.

A Point of Decision

Mr. Browning believed that investigation of vortex stabilization had proceeded to the point at which a decision would have to be made as to whether the plasma cutter would be incorporated in the old F–40 torch body or in a new torch body specifically designed for the new product. Mr. Browning and Mr. Thorpe considered the above-mentioned factors as they pondered the decision.

10. THERMAL DYNAMICS CORPORATION (C)*
Deciding about Major Additional Commitments to a Project

Mr. Browning and Mr. Thorpe decided to utilize the old F–40 torch body in developing the plasma cutter. They also decided to undertake development of an inexpensive, light, hand-held torch body at some undetermined time in the future.

Further Development

Technical development continued under James Browning's supervision. He concentrated his attention on the internal geometry of the plasma cutter in order to perfect the pattern of gas stabilization flow and in order to increase electrode life. A major task at this stage of development was overcoming problems of reliability, associated with the fact that materials were forced to operate under extreme conditions. Substantial progress was being made in this area. In James Browning's opinion, the project was approaching the point at which the major technical problems had been solved, and subsequent development effort should be devoted more toward further improvements in reliability and toward gathering cost and performance information.

Mr. Browning was not too interested in that kind of work and did not think it was the best use of his talents. He said, "I'm more an inventor than an engineer." He felt that if the plasma cutter were to be carried to market introduction, it would be necessary to assign a competent man, with both engineering and executive capabilities, to have complete charge of final development, market planning, and all activities connected with the new product. Those men in the TDC organization who had such capabilities were completely tied up with other responsibilities and, in the opinion of Mr. Browning and Mr. Thorpe, could not be freed to concentrate on this project.

In addition, no one in the TDC organization had experience in marketing a relatively large-volume product, as the plasma cutter was expected to be. Management also thought it desirable to add to the TDC organization someone with experience and contacts in the oxy-acetylene equipment field. Mr. Thorpe recalled a man he had met several years earlier—George Klasson, who had extensive experience in sales and engineering in this field. Mr. Thorpe thought it might be possible to bring this man to TDC to supervise the plasma cutter program. Management did not investigate any other man for the job, because Mr. Klasson seemed to meet the requirements so admirably. These factors brought management to a reevaluation of the outlook for the plasma cutter and resulted in what was later referred to by Mr. Browning as "the most significant decision" in the development of the plasma cutter.

The decision facing management was not just whether to hire an additional engineer-executive. As management saw it, it was a decision as to whether to devote a major percentage of the company's resources to the project. If the plasma cutter were to be introduced to the market within the next year, the level of effort devoted to the project would have to be increased. The nature of Mr. Browning's early development work on the plasma cutter had been such that he and his two part-time assistants could investigate the problem adequately; little would have been gained by putting additional personnel on the project. However, if Mr. Klasson were hired and the new product were carried to market introduction, there would be hundreds of minor problems to be solved. Different activities associated with the project could be carried on simultaneously, such as arranging for promotional literature, working with the subcontractors on production problems, and assembling detailed cost and performance data.

If the project were to be continued, management anticipated that Mr. Klasson might be hired to supervise it. He would require the full time of the company's most competent research machinist, the full time of a laboratory technician, and the full time of a man to assist in engineering design. It was anticipated that experienced men would be placed on the project and that additional men would be hired and trained to take over their duties. In addition, Mr. Browning did not plan to drop the project suddenly; he would assist Mr. Klasson until he was on his feet, and he would continue to some extent his own laboratory investigations of certain technical problems associated with the plasma cutter, principally concerned with alterna-

tive approaches to electrode design. Therefore, Mr. Browning estimated that a decision to hire Mr. Klasson would involve a commitment to spend from $5,000 to $7,000 per month on the new product.

In evaluating the technical factors bearing on the decision, Mr.
Browning thought the major technical uncertainties had been diminished to such a degree that there was no question that a practical
plasma cutter could be achieved. He thought the problem of electrode life merited additional attention, but that the plasma cutter
could be introduced to the market without major advances in this
area. Improvement of reliability and appearance, the development of
accessory equipment such as a control console and the mechanism
which would guide the plasma cutter, and the gathering of cost and
performance data appeared to be the principal technical tasks remaining. Because of his awareness of the multitude of technical bugs
that might arise, Mr. Browning hesitated to estimate the time necessary to achieve these objectives.

Another factor bearing on the decision was the company's financial
position. In March, 1960, the company's cash balance in the bank
was about $100,000—all accumulated from retained earnings of the
previous two years. Sales of the general-purpose torch were proceeding at the rate of about $80,000 per month. This product, which was
TDC's chief revenue producer and which carried a high profit margin,
was supporting the company's other development work. If sales stayed
at the level of $80,000 per month, management estimated that the
company could support development of the plasma cutter (even at
the proposed rate of $5,000 to $7,000 per month) without drawing
down the cash balance of $100,000.

In management's opinion, the greatest risk associated with a decision to expand development on the plasma cutter was whether the
sales of the general-purpose torch would hold up. In March, 1960,
the short-term sales outlook was shaky, primarily because of a general
downturn in business, and management knew that, "when business
gets bad, expenditures for research equipment are among the first to
suffer." If sales dropped drastically, perhaps to $30,000 per month, the
drain on the company's cash balance would be rapid, and the $100,-
000 would be exhausted within a few months. Management was
concerned that a double-barreled combination of added product development expenditures and a possible downturn in business might
bring TDC to the point where it would not be able to complete development of the plasma cutter or might be forced to introduce it to
the market before testing was completed. TDC had not taken any

specific steps during the three months preceding March, 1960, to gain additional information about the market. Nothing had happened to shake management's opinion that there was a large market for a practical plasma cutter.

A Point of Decision

Mr. Browning and Mr. Thorpe considered these factors in discussing whether to hire Mr. Klasson to supervise the plasma cutter project. Management realized that it did not have a great deal of information it would like to have, including studies of possible channels of distribution and methods of promotion, laboratory data on the economics of cutting with the new product, and a more thorough study of the patent picture. However, gathering this information would be one of the primary responsibilities of the new executive, if he were hired.

If management decided to hire Mr. Klasson and to provide him with the assistance it thought he would need, this would mean a commitment of about 10 to 15 percent of the company's total personnel to this one product development project. Management wondered: Should Mr. Klasson be hired? Should the present level of effort be continued under Mr. Browning's supervision? Should the project be dropped? Should the decision be delayed until more information is obtained?

11. THERMAL DYNAMICS CORPORATION (D)*
Marketing a New Product

Mr. Browning and Mr. Thorpe decided to hire Mr. Klasson to supervise the plasma cutter project; the decision was made with the expectation that at least three other men would be assigned on a full-time basis to work on the project under Mr. Klasson's supervision. The board of directors approved the decision; all members said they realized this meant a major commitment.

Final Development

Mr. Klasson accepted the offer and joined TDC in April, 1960. Since he had no background in plasma technology, he initially worked very closely with Mr. Browning. As he learned more about plasma and the plasma cutter, he relied less on Mr. Browning and assumed more responsibility for all phases of the plasma cutter project. This was in accordance with Mr. Thorpe's general policy of giving a man an area of responsibility and letting him carry the ball.

Mr. Klasson assumed responsibility for the further technical development of the new product, and under his supervision a new concept of electrode design was developed which increased electrode life from about 10–30 hours to over 50 hours. The tungsten electrodes used in the old design cost about $22 each, while those used in the new design cost about $3.00 each.

Development work also involved what George Klasson called a "thousand little problems," many of them involving slight changes in the internal geometry of the plasma cutter. In June, 1960, Mr. Klasson drew up a schedule to assist in planning the various activities associated with the development of the new product. These included the following:

1. Design and manufacture of the handle.
2. Selection and ordering of the carriage for the torch.
3. Selection and ordering of the exhaust system.

4. Selection and ordering of the face shield and gloves.
5. Selection or design of a coolant circulator.
6. Design and manufacture of the control console.
7. Selection of a power supply.
8. Selection and ordering of packaging.
9. Consultation with public health officials in regard to possible health hazards.
10. Design and printing of promotional material.
11. Writing and printing of an instruction booklet.

For each activity, Mr. Klasson estimated the number of months needed and indicated on a graph the start and completion of each task, with particular attention to when each item would be ready for shipment. He had no desire to delay introduction because a particular activity, such as writing the instruction booklet, had not been started in time. The responsibility for all these activities rested with Mr. Klasson, who had three men working full time with him on the project.

Machine-driven oxyacetylene installations included equipment for holding the cutting torch and moving it across the material to be cut. Often, there was also equipment (called a pantograph) which would permit a number of cutting torches to cut a particular shape simultaneously, reproducing a master shape. TDC was designing the plasma cutter so that it could be installed on this existing equipment. However, a problem was presented in that existing equipment had been designed with the relatively slow cutting speeds of oxyacetylene torches in mind. The plasma cutter was able to cut mild steel much faster, but was limited to some extent by the speed of existing devices which moved a cutting torch across the material to be cut. TDC planned to approach manufacturers of this accessory equipment in order to persuade them to manufacture special high-speed equipment.

During the summer of 1960, the Ajax Corporation (which had been selling a plasma torch for cutting purposes) offered to license TDC to use all Ajax patents which applied to plasma technology. Ajax indicated that it considered certain of its patents to be basic and implied that the TDC general-purpose torch infringed on these patents. Ajax asked for royalties which, in the opinion of TDC's management, were completely unreasonable.

Mr. Browning had known that Ajax had applied for over 30 patents pertaining to plasma technology. Most of these were still pending, so he had had no opportunity to become familiar with them. However, the patents which Ajax claimed to be basic had been issued several years earlier, and Mr. Browning was familiar with these. Both Mr. Browning and TDC's patent counsel had studied these Ajax patents at the time they were issued. They applied to what Ajax called "wall stabilization," which was similar to the gas sheath stabilization and vortex stabilization that TDC utilized.

According to Mr. Browning, the essential question was whether gas sheath stabilization was a form of wall stabilization. He said, "The patents are complex and can only be interpreted by one intimate with the field." TDC had applied for patents on gas sheath stabilization, but these were still pending. The problem was further complicated by the fact that the theoretical understanding of the mechanism of gas stabilization was poor and was the continuing subject of investigation by various individuals interested in the field.

Mr. Browning and TDC's patent attorney jointly studied the patents for several days; they included in their study certain patents which had been recently issued to other companies active in the field. They concluded that TDC was not infringing on the Ajax patents, and Mr. Browning made the decision to reject the Ajax offer and to proceed without interruption to the development of the plasma cutter. He was aware that Ajax might choose to involve TDC in long and costly legal proceedings, but he thought TDC's patent position was sound. Another factor, although one not heavily weighting his decision, involved the possible antitrust implications of a large company such as Ajax trying to stamp out a company with only 45 personnel.

In November, 1960, TDC was issued a patent on gas sheath stabilization. Management thought that issuance of this patent considerably reduced the probability of patent infringement proceedings. In August of 1960, Mr. Klasson and Mr. Thorpe froze the design of the plasma cutter. The decision had been postponed for some weeks while certain variables of electrode design were being investigated. Despite the fact that the continuing experimentation was leading to greater understanding of the electrode design, they finally decided on a particular design so that components might be ordered and market introduction might take place several months hence without further delay.

During the fall of 1960, laboratory work with the plasma cutter centered on the gathering of performance and cost data which could be used in promotional literature and in advising prospective customers as to how the plasma cutter could be used to solve their particular problems. Data on the performance and operating costs of the TDC

SOURCE: Thermal Dynamics Corporation.

Exhibit 11-1

THERMAL DYNAMICS CORPORATION (D)

COMPARATIVE COST AND PERFORMANCE DATA—CUTTING MILD STEEL PLATE

Plate* Thickness Inches	TDC Plasma Cutting Speed† Inches/Minute	TDC Cutter Cutting Cost‡ Cents/Foot	Oxyacetylene Torch Cutting Speed Inches/Minute	Oxyacetylene Torch Cutting Cost‡ Cents/Foot	Ajax Plasma Torch§ Cutting Speed Inches/Minute	Ajax Torch§ Cutting Cost‡ Cents/Foot
¼	525	.23¢/ft.	26	2.00¢/ft.	525	.83¢/ft.
½	200	.65	22	2.60	—	—
¾	100	1.75	20	3.05	100	6.11
1	80	2.07	18	3.90	—	—
1½	50	—	16	—	—	—
2	40	3.10	13	5.15	40	10.93
3	20	—	10	—	—	—

* Material cut is ordinary mild steel.
† Cutting speeds given are not maximum but are limited by speed of traveling mechanism and available power.
‡ Cutting costs do not include overhead and amortization of equipment involved. Neither do they include replacement costs of electrode and nozzle for plasma torch.
Assumed costs were the following: oxygen, 0.50 cent/cu. ft.; natural gas, 0.08 cent/cu. ft.; nitrogen, 1.38 cents/cu. ft.; hydrogen, 2.00 cents/cu.ft.; power, 1.05 cents/kw.-hr.; labor, $2.00/hr.
§ It is assumed that cutting speed, power consumption, and gas consumption are the same for the plasma torch as for the TDC plasma cutter. (In fact, cutting speed of the torch is probably considerably less because of lower power capacity.) The plasma torch uses a mixture of 65 percent argon and 35 percent hydrogen for stabilizing gas.
Assumed cost of argon: 10.00 cents/cu. ft.
Investment costs might be as follows: oxyacetylene unit, $100; plasma cutter and associated equipment, $8,000; plasma torch and associated equipment, and use license, $8,000.

plasma cutter, the Ajax torch, and oxyacetylene torches are given in Exhibit 11–1, p. 149.

In early December, 1960, TDC made arrangements to sell plasma cutters to three different companies on a trial basis. If, after 45 days' use in the field, the companies were satisfied with the performance of the new product, they would pay TDC for the machines. (TDC would have preferred outright sale of the plasma cutters, but the prospective customers insisted on trial purchases because the product was new and unproved.) TDC anticipated keeping in close touch with these customers in order to learn of any problems arising from the use of the product in the field.

Mr. Klasson was also taking steps to ensure that health hazards or rumors of health hazards might not interfere with the development of the market for the new product. He knew that an operator would have to wear an apron, a mask, and protective gloves when operating the equipment. He knew there was a danger that toxic gases might be formed as a by-product, necessitating an exhaust system. He was not sure whether there was any danger of ear damage from the shrill screams of the equipment or of inhalation of suspended metal particles. Accordingly, Mr. Klasson had arranged for several representatives of the U.S. Department of Public Health to visit the TDC plant for several days in order to test for possible health hazards and to make suggestions regarding such hazards. Mr. Browning said it would not be necessary for TDC to obtain any sort of underwriter's approval on the plasma cutter.

Management was not greatly concerned over promotion of the new product. Arrangements had been made for articles describing the product to appear in several technical journals in the late autumn of 1960; a picture of the plasma cutter in action would be the cover picture for two of these magazines. Securing this publicity had not been difficult, apparently due to the novelty of the product and the close relationship cultivated by management with the editors of various journals. Past experience had indicated that the publication of the articles would be followed by a deluge of letters inquiring about the new product.

TDC had prepared several pamphlets describing the company and the plasma cutter; these would be sent, along with a card requesting more information, to any prospective customer inquiring by mail about the plasma cutter. Subsequent follow-up would depend on the method of distribution which TDC chose for the product.

This decision about channels of distribution was viewed by management as of particular importance in determining whether the "invention" became a significant "innovation." Management was considering five alternative methods of distribution:

1. To develop TDC's own sales force.
2. To establish an exclusive sales arrangement with a large company which produced and sold gases such as nitrogen and hydrogen.
3. To establish an exclusive sales arrangement with a large company which produced and sold electrical power supplies.
4. To establish nonexclusive arrangements with a large number of welding supply distributors.
5. To establish geographically exclusive sales arrangements with a number of manufacturers' representatives around the country.

One factor bearing on this decision was the overall size of the market. Management was particularly concerned that the demand for plasma cutters might grow so explosively that TDC would be unable to supply the market. Unsatisfied demand might cause other companies to enter the field; TDC might then find itself at a disadvantage in competing with large, well-financed companies having strong sales forces.

TDC was planning in terms of selling $1 million worth of plasma cutters (not including power supplies) in 1961. With the aid of extensive subcontracting, Mr. Browning thought it might be possible to supply several times that volume of plasma cutters to the market if needed. Management hesitated to estimate the total potential market for plasma cutters, but thought it might someday total many millions of dollars annually.

Plasma technology was developing rapidly, and Thermal Dynamics, Ajax, and Western were rapidly tying up a number of possible technical approaches to various problems through patent applications. Management thought that if potential competitors did not enter the field within the next year or so, they might never do so because of the lead that TDC would have built up in technical know-how and market acceptance. Appendix 11–A gives additional information regarding competing companies and cutting techniques.

This concern with meeting the demands of what might grow quickly into a very large market caused management to favor alternatives 2 and 3, in which established sales organizations could be enlisted to the TDC cause almost overnight.

A second factor, which management considered vital, was the importance of training salesmen in plasma technology and keeping them in touch with the anticipated rapid technical advance in the field.

Management wondered whether a sales organization with other products to sell would have the time or the interest to keep informed and to instruct potential customers in the use of the plasma cutters.

Producers of both gas and electrical equipment would find the plasma cutter complementary to their lines. A TDC plasma cutter would use between four and five dollars' worth of hydrogen and nitrogen gas for each hour of operation. (However, there was some possibility that future technical development might result in practical air- or water-stabilized plasma cutters, both of which would offer large cost savings to users but little incentive for promotion by companies which sold industrial gases.) The plasma cutter would also be attractive to producers of electrical power supplies inasmuch as about 50 to 75 percent of the total price of a plasma cutter and accessory equipment ($7,500 to $12,000) was accounted for by the power supply.

Thermal Dynamics had been in contact with a large producer of electrical equipment which had indicated a definite interest in handling the plasma cutter. This company's welding supply division had over 1,000 salesmen. This company produced the power supply that TDC offered with its general-purpose torch. The details of the proposed agreement had not been worked out, but would include the following features:

1. The electrical company would receive a discount from list price of about 35 percent on the plasma cutter.
2. The agreement would be for three years and could be discontinued by either party on 60 days' notice.
3. List prices on the plasma cutter would be set by Thermal Dynamics.
4. TDC would have the responsibility for training the salesmen, although the electrical company would pay the salaries and expenses of the salesmen while they were attending whatever "schools" TDC might set up to instruct them.

Some of the alternative methods of distribution looked intriguing, but management had not had the time to investigate them fully. In addition, TDC did not want to stir up the industry by making inquiries among a number of possible channels of distribution.

A Point of Decision

Management considered this decision to be of paramount importance, not only in bringing about the widespread use of the new plasma cutter, but also in its long-run implications for the distribution of other products the company might develop. Management wondered whether the proposed agreement with the electrical manufacturer should be accepted, or whether a decision should be deferred until additional information bearing on alternative methods of distribution could be obtained.

APPENDIX 11–A

The Competitive Picture

Since the potential applications of plasma technology were so widespread, a number of organizations were engaged in research and development in this area. These included various agencies of the federal government, a number of universities, several nonprofit research institutes, and such companies as General Electric, General Dynamics, and Avco Corporation. Most of the effort had been directed toward research into the basic nature of plasma or toward development in regard to particular applications with which TDC had not been concerned, such as chemical synthesis or magnetohydrodynamics. Besides TDC, two companies [1] were offering plasma hardware to the market— the Ajax Company, a division of a large chemical company, and the Western Corporation, a small West Coast company.

Apparently, Ajax had been promoting its cutting torch only for cutting nonferrous materials. Mr. Browning estimated that Ajax had sold about 200 to 250 of these torches since the product was first introduced in 1958. Estimated cutting costs for this torch are given in Exhibit 11–1. It had a considerably higher cutting cost than the TDC plasma cutter, and was not economically competitive with oxyacetylene torches for cutting mild steel. (The Ajax torch used relatively expensive argon gas and had a relatively slow cutting speed because its power capacity was only about 100 kw.)

The Western Corporation offered a nontransferred-arc torch to the market. The product was not suitable for cutting, but had been used for spraying and as a general-purpose research tool. Apparently, the company had sold the product through manufacturing representatives. Mr. Browning understood that this method had not been very

---

[1] The names of these companies have been disguised.

successful, because these representatives were not sufficiently knowl-edgeable in plasma technology.

Thermal Dynamics, in developing the plasma cutter, had moved into competition with a number of other cutting methods, including shearing, sawing, and oxyacetylene burning. For ferrous material, oxy-acetylene cutting was the most important of these methods by far. With this method, a preheat flame using oxygen and acetylene brought the edge of the steel up to a temperature of about 1,400–1,600°F. When this temperature was reached, a stream of pure oxy-gen under pressure was directed on the heated metal, producing a severing cut from the oxidation of the iron as well as the erosion of unoxidized molten metal.

Mr. Browning estimated that there were 4,000 to 7,000 machine-driven oxyacetylene cutting installations in the country and that the number of hand-held oxyacetylene torches was in the hundreds of thousands. Ajax was one of the numerous companies supplying gases and oxyacetylene cutting equipment to this industry.

In regard to mechanical cutting methods, Thermal Dynamics re-ported that a limited amount of testing had indicated that plasma cutting was considerably more economical than sawing for all thick-nesses of material. However, for straight cuts, mechanical shearing was apparently less costly for thicknesses up to one-half inch; for thicker materials, plasma cutting had a cost advantage.

12. LIQUID METALS, INC. (A) *

Planning the Organization of a Growing Technical Company

One of the major products of Liquid Metals, Inc., was an electro-dynamic pump capable of pumping liquid metals at temperatures of up to 2,400°F. without having any moving parts or seals in contact with the metal being handled. This pump was one of several highly technical products developed by the founders and majority stockholders of Liquid Metals, Inc., Mr. and Mrs. Gordon R. Findlay.

In November of 1961, this company had about completed what might be considered the first phase of its life; it had developed lines of liquid metals handling equipment and of inert gas repurification and recovery equipment, along with a high degree of technical competence in these areas. Sales were running at an annual rate of about $200,000. Now the market was beginning to provide a substantial increase in demand for its products, and the Findlays were concerned with the job of acquiring and training the group of men that would be needed if their company was to participate in serving these developing needs.

General Background

In 1961, the products sold by Liquid Metals, Inc., were divided into two general categories—components for liquid metal handling systems and equipment for the recovery and repurification of used inert gas. Although these areas appear to be quite different, they are similar in their technology and often overlap in their fields of application. As of 1961, most of the company's activities had been in the design and development of this equipment and in prototype production; no volume manufacturing of any item had yet taken place.

Liquid Metals, Inc., had been incorporated in 1958 as the successor to Findlay Science Engineering Company, a proprietorship which had been owned by Mrs. Findlay. This predecessor company, which had been operated jointly by both Findlays, had been engaged in development work on some of the firm's products for about 10 years.

Mr. Findlay became chairman and president of Liquid Metals, Inc., while Mrs. Findlay held the position of treasurer and was also a director. Both were full-time employees of the firm, and together they held about 75 percent of its stock. Their combined salaries were about $27,000.

Both Findlays had degrees from Massachusetts Institute of Technology. As undergraduates, Mr. Findlay had studied chemistry and mechanical engineering, while Mrs. Findlay majored in chemical engineering. At the graduate level, she continued to work in the chemical engineering area, concentrating on automobile-engine combustion problems, and he studied in the fields of organic chemistry and chemical engineering.

The Liquid Metals, Inc., plant was located in Westford, Massachusetts, on a 28-acre piece of property owned by Mrs. Findlay. This site, close to the new "outer belt" highway around Boston, was about 30 miles northwest of the city. The plant itself was a two-story, cinder block building which had been built as a chicken coop, had been utilized as a factory by another firm, and was being used to store hay when the Findlays purchased it. It had a total of 3,000 square feet of floor space. The ground floor was used for manufacturing, while the second served as office and engineering space. In November, construction was being started on an addition which would add about 4,500 square feet to the manufacturing floor space, and plans were being drawn up for another new building which would have about 12,000 square feet of space. The Findlays were doing much of the engineering and contracting work for these new buildings themselves. They expected the first addition to be ready for use in February, 1962.

Liquid Metals, Inc., had 17 full-time employees and 4 who worked on a part-time basis. Sales in the year ending June 30, 1961, had been $101,000, yielding a profit of $500. That had been the first annual profit shown by the firm's books. In November, Mr. Findlay estimated that sales were running at an annual rate of about $200,000. The company had a $175,000 backlog of firm orders. Financial data are given in Exhibits 12–1 and 12–2.

Development of Product Lines

Mr. and Mrs. Findlay began development work on liquid metal systems in 1948 in the basement of their home. Much of the work was done by Mrs. Findlay, as Mr. Findlay took a full-time engineer-

Exhibit 12-1

LIQUID METALS, INC. (A)

COMPARATIVE BALANCE SHEETS*

	May 31, 1960	June 30, 1961	Sept. 30, 1961
Current Assets:			
Cash	$ 3,272	$ 395	$ 7,871
Accounts receivable, net	16,666	53,996	43,654
Inventories	34,661†	23,300‡	36,594
Prepayments and deposits	2,496	5,679	4,503
Total Current Assets	$57,095	$ 83,370	$ 92,622
Fixed Assets, Net:			
Machinery	$13,613	$ 8,789	$ 14,001
Laboratory equipment	1,160	609	559
Office equipment	2,456	1,661	2,170
Leasehold improvements	—	869	2,225
Company projects in process	—	—	5,183
Total Fixed Assets	$17,228	$ 11,928	$ 24,138
Deferred Charges:			
Product development and proposal engineering costs	$ —	$ 24,621	$ 25,094
Patent development, net	1,577	1,373	1,348
Total Deferred Charges	$ 1,577	$ 25,994	$ 26,442
Total Assets	$75,900	$121,292	$143,202
Current Liabilities:			
Accounts payable, trade	$20,682	$ 21,119	$ 27,642
Accounts payable, other	9,694	8,288	7,433
Notes payable, bank	25,832	14,647	17,797
Notes payable, other	12,992	7,087	12,400
Accruals	2,438	3,222	2,350
Advances from officers	21,600	6,407	10,183
Total Current Liabilities	$93,238	$ 60,770	$ 77,805
Long-Term Debt:			
To stockholders	$ —	$ 1,975	$ 1,975
Other	—	9,000	—
Total Term Debt	—	$ 10,975	$ 1,975
Capital:			
Stock and capital surplus	$67,500	$142,713	$145,688
Retained earnings (deficit)	(84,838)	(93,166)	(82,266)
Total Capital	$17,338	$ 49,547	$ 63,422
Total Liabilities	$75,900	$121,292	$143,202

May not be additive due to rounding.

* These statements have been summarized from detailed company financial statements prepared as follows: May 31, 1960—prepared by the company for its prospectus (see case); June 30, 1961—prepared by accounting firm as part of year-end statements; September 30, 1961—prepared by accounting firm as part of quarterly statements. Various notes to the financial statements which were not considered essential to the case have been left out. Figures have been rounded by the case writer.

† Purchased raw materials and components, $10,749; manufactured components, parts and assemblies, $23,912.

‡ Raw materials, $4,209; component parts, $13,478; work in process, $5,613.

Exhibit 12–2

LIQUID METALS, INC. (A)

STATEMENTS OF PROFIT AND LOSS*

	Year Ending June 30, 1959	11 Months Ending May 31, 1960	Year Ending June 30, 1961	3 Months Ending September 30, 1961
Sales	$ 73,247	$ 77,221	$100,104	$41,094
Cost of goods sold	74,742	57,218	80,954	19,786
Gross profit	$ (1,495)	$ 20,003	$ 19,150	$21,308
General, selling and administrative	42,214	59,104	15,475	10,175
Income from operations	$(43,708)	$(39,101)	$ 3,674	$11,133
Other income (expense), net	—	—	(3,460)	(232)
Net income before special items	$(43,708)	$(39,101)	$ 215	$10,901
Special items	—	—	268	—
Net income	$(43,708)	$(39,101)	$ 483	$10,901

* These statements have been summarized from detailed company financial statements prepared as follows: May 31, 1960—prepared by the company for its prospectus (see case); June 30, 1961—prepared by accounting firm as part of year-end statements; September 30, 1961—prepared by accounting firm as part of quarterly statements. Various notes to the financial statements which were not considered essential to the case have been left out. Figures have been rounded by the case writer.

ing position with a large research firm in order to provide for their living expenses and to finance their product development activities. He continued to work in the evening and on weekends on liquid metal handling products. By 1954, they had perfected the electrodynamic liquid metal pump, and in the latter part of that year began production of prototype models. These were highly successful and extremely reliable on test loop applications in the nuclear aircraft program. Several of them have been in almost continuous operation since 1955.

A description of the pump and the principles of its operation is included as Appendix 12–A. By 1961, Liquid Metals, Inc., had made pumps to handle metals at temperatures of 2,400°F. and to develop pressures of 2,000 p.s.i. at capacities ranging from a fraction of a gallon to several hundred gallons per minute. The price of a "typical" pump was about $10,000, although prices varied widely depending on size, materials used, etc.

The immediate market for such pumps was in the nuclear energy field, particularly in the various programs involving the development of nuclear power plants which would use liquid metal heat transfer systems. The two such major programs in 1954–55 were those involved with the development of the nuclear aircraft and the sodium-cooled reactor of the type used in the U.S.S. "Seawolf." In 1956, however, a curtailment of the nuclear aircraft program and a stretch-out of the liquid metal-cooled power breeder reactor programs seriously reduced the demand for liquid metal pumps and other system components. The sales prospects for the company, which had looked good, suddenly dropped to almost nothing. Several men who had been employed in anticipation of higher production volume had to be laid off. The Findlays realized that the market for liquid metals handling equipment for nuclear applications was, at that time, still five or ten years off, and that a broader product line was necessary to support their company in the interim.

In early 1957, the firm began work on a line of equipment for purifying the inert gases, argon and helium. Mr. Findlay had had some previous experience in this field and, as stated above, the technologies involved tended to overlap those of the liquid metals field. Two types of purifiers were developed—one utilizing liquid metals to remove the impurities in the gases, and the other using cartridges of metals such as titanium or zirconium which, when heated, acted as getters of impurities.

Argon or helium is used to provide an inert atmosphere in which highly sensitive or reactive metals can be welded or otherwise worked. Such metals are fabricated inside chambers called dry boxes, or glove boxes. These chambers have windows and gastight gloves, allowing a man to handle items placed inside the box. To shield the sensitive metals from the oxygen in the air, the boxes are filled with an inert gas after all necessary equipment has been sealed inside. Inert gases are used, rather than vacuums, because the problems of handling the equipment inside are simpler when no pressure difference exists between the inside of the box and the atmosphere, and because it is easier to maintain a high-purity environment with inert gas than with a vacuum.

Examples of industries that use inert atmospheres are: the electronics field, for purifying gas used in growing silicon crystals for diodes and transistors; the metals field, for use in systems for handling reactive or powdered metals; and the nuclear field, in connection with the helium-cooled reactor program.

Initially, sales of Liquid Metals purifiers went slowly. However, in 1959 and 1960 the line was expanded to include recovery equipment and dry boxes, rounding out the items needed to make a complete system for the continuous reuse of inert gases. Normally, after the gas in a dry box had become contaminated, or when the box had to be opened to remove a workpiece, the inert gases were merely vented into the atmosphere. The Liquid Metals, Inc., system allowed these gases to be recovered, repurified, and recycled, and proved capable of processing gases to yield a higher level of purity than that of the normal gas originally supplied by the gas manufacturer. Soon, repurification system sales began to increase. Many more companies needed inert atmospheres, as sensitive metals were being used in more industries. In addition, the government put pressure on some of its suppliers who used large volumes of inert gas to purchase recycling equipment. This was done both to reduce the costs of certain cost-plus-fixed-fee contracts (helium costs 8–10 cents per cubic foot) and to prevent permanent loss of a natural resource. (Helium, when vented into the air, quickly dissipates and tends to rise to the top of the atmosphere. This makes it economically unfeasible to recover in any significant quantities.)

Initially, the inert gas manufacturers were hostile to repurification systems, but the Findlays convinced the large industrial gas companies that Liquid Metals equipment would increase rather than decrease the markets for gas. Many companies had manufacturing processes that did not require use of inert gases, but in which their use would be desirable if it were less expensive. The utilization of repurification equipment made it economically feasible for many such companies to begin using inert gases. Sales of inert gas repurification systems reached a level of about $50,000 in 1961, representing half the firm's dollar volume for that year.

During the period from 1955 to 1961, even though they looked to other areas for immediate sales support, the Findlays retained their faith in the ultimate future of the liquid metals field. They continued the development work both in liquid metals technology and in customer education. The line of liquid metals handling equipment was broadened to include all the components and instrumentation associated with liquid metals loops, or systems. These included such items as electromagnetic flowmeters, special valves, pressure indicators, leak detectors, and heat exchangers.

The Findlays also worked to establish Liquid Metals, Inc., as the acknowledged focal point of information about liquid metals technology. Mr. Findlay gave information freely to anyone wishing it, in the belief that such action would encourage the use of liquid metals and, therefore, Liquid Metals equipment. Occasionally, this policy had been questioned by friends and even employees. These people had argued that Mr. Findlay should charge consulting fees for the information and help he gave to others. However, the Findlays stated that they wanted to sell products, not services. They found that, because Mr. Findlay did give assistance freely, others working in the field began to make a habit of contacting him regularly to discuss their projects. As a result, he had a broad knowledge of what was going on in the liquid metals field, and by 1961 the company was looked on throughout the field as an important center of information about it.

Mr. Findlay stated in the fall of 1961 that he felt this past activity was beginning to pay off. Interest in the technology of handling liquid metals was again increasing for both commercial and government applications, especially in connection with nuclear and ion-propulsion systems for spacecraft and cooling systems for space stations. He felt that his firm would be asked to participate extensively in future programs, both in manufacturing equipment it had already designed and in developing the new products which would continue to be needed. Liquid Metals, Inc., had a number of new liquid metals proposals outstanding in late 1961—many with the National Aeronautics and Space Agency (NASA)—and Mr. Findlay felt that several of these, with a dollar value of about $200,000–$300,000, would soon be accepted and that another, worth $500,000, might be. In November, 1961, the firm already had an order backlog of about $175,-000, almost 90 percent of which was in the liquid metals area; the remainder was for inert gas systems.

Production

The company's production facilities included a few general-purpose machine tools, welding equipment for the special metals with which it worked (e.g., stainless steel, columbium, tantalum), and test equipment. On production items—i.e., those items for which prototype units had already been built and tested—most of the ordinary machining work and some of the routine welding were subcontracted to machine shops in its area. Liquid Metals, itself, however, did all special welding, all assembly work, and all testing. The testing process was considered the most important function in the manufacture of Liquid Metals equipment. It was extremely important that the company make sure that no piece of equipment contained flaws that might leak or fail under the severe conditions present in liquid metals systems.

In November, the production force numbered 11 full-time men and several who worked part time on a second shift, up from only three full-time and two part-time men as recently as June. Most of these men were highly skilled mechanics, machinists, or welders, and most of them had worked for the firm on a part-time basis before they were employed permanently. The Findlays had made a policy of this practice. They tried to hire men whose abilities were known to one of their other employees or themselves, but they felt there was no substitute for actual observation of a man working in their shop. By asking a prospective employee to moonlight or work part time for them, the Findlays could evaluate him, and he could evaluate the company, before he had left his previous job. The Findlays felt that this method of hiring had worked quite well for them in the past, but were not sure how practical it would be as the company grew larger.

The shop was run by a foreman who had been hired in the early spring of 1961. A graduate of Wentworth Institute, he had previously been employed as a maintenance mechanic, and he had a good working knowledge of machining, machinery, both power and light wiring, and diesel operation. (The company has its own diesel-electric plant.) In addition to the normal duties of a shop foreman, he handled the purchasing of all shop supplies and recently had begun doing some of the production scheduling work.

Purchasing

Until September of 1961, an ex-lab technician, Jim Price, who had worked with Mr. Findlay at MIT, had handled raw material purchasing and production scheduling. However, he had left the firm because, as he put it, he could no longer stand the pressure of his job. The Findlays reported that Jim was competent in handling the detail work of his position but was not aggressive enough to be happy working for a firm such as Liquid Metals, Inc. Jim had stated that although he enjoyed the work the severe time pressures under which he had to perform made him nervous and uncomfortable. He had left a previous job for the same reason. When asked to expand on what they meant by "necessary aggressiveness," the Findlays stated that this requirement stemmed from the fact that at Liquid Metals, Inc., everyone, and particularly they themselves, had many more things to do than time in which to do them. As an illustration, they spoke of the job which Jim Price had recently left, and which, in late November, they were seeking to refill.

The purchasing position at Liquid Metals, Inc., included much more than the clerical functions of inviting bids, preparing purchase orders, and handling the paper work of the purchasing activity. The man filling this job was often given only a set of blueprints or engineering drawings and the performance specifications of the item with which to work. He had to prepare material lists, draw up material and component specifications, decide what to make, buy, or subcontract, select suppliers, let purchase orders, and take care of all expediting, checking, and other follow-up work. In Jim Price's case, these functions had been only part of his job, as he had also handled much of the production scheduling and costing work of the company.

With this much scope to his activities, Jim Price was not expected to make all the necessary decisions without help from Mr. Findlay. However, the man in this position was expected to do as much as he could on any particular order before getting help. Because Mr. Findlay was always busy and usually on the run, the man holding the job had to be "aggressive" in getting Mr. Findlay to take the time to make the needed decisions so that the purchasing work could continue. Jim had not been aggressive and, in addition, had been reluctant to make many borderline decisions he should have made himself. As a result, work piled up on Jim's desk, since the processing of new bids and orders halted until Mr. Findlay happened to have some time to spare, or until the pressure of an approaching deadline made Mr. Findlay check up on the status of an order.

The Findlays stated that this type of situation existed with many jobs at Liquid Metals—both in the management and engineering areas. They saw no way of changing things as long as the firm continued to work in highly technical areas and to grow as rapidly as it was now. They felt that this situation was one that they and other employees would have to continue to live with for some time to come. Therefore, they wanted aggressive men who would be willing to take a great deal of initiative, continually and voluntarily expand their areas of responsibility as they gained in experience and ability, and get tough with Mr. Findlay or other busy employees when important decisions had to be made.

Financial Aspects

Financially, Liquid Metals, Inc., and its predecessor had had to "run lean," as Mrs. Findlay put it. Although in mid-1960 the company had experienced a serious working capital shortage, Mr. Findlay felt that as of November, 1961, the firm was in a reasonably comfortable financial condition.

The Findlays had purposely tried to go as far as possible on their small initial capital, internally generated funds, and available credit. The severe cash squeeze in 1960 had come when an increase in orders had raised working capital requirements to a higher level than their bank was willing to supply. To solve this financial crisis, the Findlays attempted to sell stock in their firm under the intrastate offering exemption of the securities regulations. In June, 1960, they drew up a prospectus offering 20,000 shares at $6.00 per share. This block would have represented about 25 percent of the total shares that would have been outstanding had the stock been placed.

Although Mr. Findlay spent a great deal of time visiting a number of venture capital firms, investment bankers, and private investors, he was unable to sell the stock. One of the private investors he had contacted stated that, while Mr. Findlay was obviously enthusiastic about his company's future, he (the investor) just couldn't understand what Liquid Metals, Inc., was doing. In retrospect, Mr. Findlay thought his failure to interest professional investors had probably been due to the extremely technical nature of the company's work and the highly specialized nature of its markets. However, two men who were familiar with the technology made small investments in the company in the fall of 1960, and these funds, together with a liberal extension of trade credit by several of the firm's suppliers, allowed Liquid Metals, Inc., to weather that particular financial crisis.

By December, 1961, Mr. Findlay believed that the growth of the company, its position in the liquid metal industry, and the development of the market itself were such that further equity capital could be raised relatively quickly if it became necessary to get additional funds. The recent increases in sales and in the level of the company's order backlog, neither of which were present a year previously, would support the Findlays' expectations for the growth of their markets. He thought the 1961 profit and an expected good profit for 1962 would vouch for the earning power of the company.

Also, Liquid Metals, Inc., had recently established relations with a large Boston bank, which had indicated that a working capital loan would probably be available when required. Mr. Findlay stated that the financial condition of Liquid Metals, Inc., was certainly far sounder, from a bank's point of view, in late 1961 than it had been a year earlier.

Management

In November, 1961, the management team of Liquid Metals, Inc., consisted of Mr. and Mrs. Findlay. Mr. Findlay took charge of sales, finance, production, engineering, and research, doing most of the selling and research himself. Mrs. Findlay oversaw purchasing, accounting, and legal work, dealt with the majority of the personnel problems that arose, and did a great deal of engineering computation work. Mr. Findlay handled most of the outside contacts and was often required to spend considerable time at customers' facilities giving technical assistance. Mrs. Findlay ran the office and plant on these occasions.

Neither of the Findlays had had any formal business training. The firm subscribed to a number of helpful business publications, including the Prentice-Hall management letter series, and it had had the assistance of its bankers, accountants, and legal counsel; but most of the Findlays' business abilities had been learned by the trial-and-error method.

Two of these trials, and errors, had occurred when on separate occasions the firm hired men to be business managers. Both moves to employ men with business ability had been made in an attempt to lighten the work load the Findlays were carrying so that they could spend more time on engineering and sales work—the areas where they felt they were most valuable. This time would have to come from that which they were then spending on minor business details and office management.

The first man they hired as a business manager had previously been in a middle management capacity at a large manufacturing firm. He had joined Liquid Metals, Inc., during the summer of 1960. The Findlays had, somewhat reluctantly, heeded his request that they not talk with his former employer, relying on the fact that he was a director of their local bank. However, they subsequently learned that he not only misrepresented his previous position and salary, but also was deliberately doing things to jeopardize Liquid Metals' reputation. He was, therefore, discharged.

The second business manager, employed in July, 1961, was an officer who had been a top member of a procurement group of one of the military services. This man had visited the firm off and on for almost a year prior to July, 1961, helping them with some of their financial planning and record-keeping problems. His references were favorable. However, he too failed to perform satisfactorily, largely because of an inability to grasp the technical aspects of his work, and was let go only 45 days after being permanently hired.

The Findlays later gave two main reasons for his failure. The first was that he tried to turn the company into a nine-to-five operation. The Findlays, who often worked 18 hours a day themselves and occasionally slept in the office to save commuting time to their home, did not feel that Liquid Metals, Inc., could be run on anything other than a round-the-clock basis at this stage of its development. The second, and more important, reason this ex-military officer didn't work out was that he proved unable to handle the detail work he was hired to perform (e.g., making out material lists from engineering drawings and discussing with subcontractors the details of the operations to be performed). Mr. Findlay felt that his satisfactory record with the military had been real, but that he had been in a position where he had to make policy decisions based on data generated by others. He, himself, apparently was unable to generate the data needed for a decision. Mr. Findlay stated, "We didn't need another policy-maker, we needed men who could handle the detail part of the management function."

To assist the Findlays in their many jobs, the company had employed both an engineer and an accountant during the summer of 1961. The accountant had been obtained as a result of a help-wanted ad in several local newspapers, after the part-time bookkeeper had had to leave to devote her full time to her husband's growing business. Although initially employed as a bookkeeper, the new man had been doing an excellent job, and in November the Findlays were grooming him to assume the controllership function for the company. The engineer was also doing a good job in his special area. Liquid Metals, Inc., used two additional design engineers on a part-time basis to take ideas and concepts from Mr. Findlay and turn them into engineering drawings. Both of these men, who spent 20–30 hours per week on Liquid Metals, Inc., work, had been associated with the firm in this manner for several years.

One manufacturer's representative had been handling sales of the company's inert gas systems in the New England area since the spring of 1961. This man had become familiar with these products during the previous year when he had been associated with the company on a half-time basis. Since he sold several other lines to the type of industrial customer who used inert gas systems, he had asked the Findlays if he could take on the Liquid Metals gas repurification line.

Mr. Findlay, thinking that the use of representatives for the gas line might be a way of giving him more time to spend on the more technical liquid metals area, had allowed the representative to begin selling gas systems. It seemed worthwhile to try out this approach to sales with a friend in a local area to help to determine whether it would work for all gas system sales. In the fall of 1961, Mr. Findlay stated that it was still too early to be certain as to whether or not the approach would work. He was somewhat dissatisfied with the results to date and with the fact that the representative's work had been primarily in getting leads for Mr. Findlay, who then had to determine the customers' needs and close the sales. However, the Findlays still felt that a manufacturers' representative sales organization might be desirable for certain products, and they hoped that with further experience the New England representative might become more effective.

The Findlays realized that the present sharp increase in demand for their company's products and services made it imperative that they get a broader management team to help operate the firm. They felt that as soon as possible they should add men to help in the purchasing, production control, and inside sales areas. They would also quickly need several more full-time engineers and a number of production people.

To fill both engineering and business positions, they wanted men who had a broad field of interest. They wanted ambitious men who might be able to take top management positions in divisions or subsidiary companies as Liquid Metals grew. The engineers would have to be interested in, and knowledgeable about, business matters, and the businessmen should be familiar with the technical aspects of the company's work. In other words, the Findlays felt that every member of the management and engineering teams should be able to talk to and understand everyone else.

These requirements were based on both short-term needs and long-range plans of the firm. Immediately, men were needed to do the many jobs that would have to be done in the rapidly expanding company. The Findlays did not feel they could conduct extensive training programs for new men; employees would have to learn their jobs largely by themselves, and rapidly begin contributing to the operation of the business. They would quickly have to gain an understanding of all aspects of the company and its technologies.

In the longer term, the men employed at this time would need breadth of interest and ability because of the Findlays' plans for growth and expansion. They felt that Liquid Metals, Inc., should remain a small development-type company, restricting its work to research and prototype production and keeping an atmosphere conducive to creative engineering work. However, they knew that the significant profits tended to be in volume production rather than in research and development work. Since they did not feel that the volume shop could be compatible with the creative one, they were tentatively planning to establish divisions or subsidiaries to assume responsibility for manufacturing and selling items for which a volume market developed. They felt that the gas repurification line might be the first to be split off. The managers and engineers brought into Liquid Metals, Inc., to meet the needs of the current expansion would be placed in charge of these production units as they were spun off from the core company.

With these needs and plans, the Findlays would demand from every new employee a high level of competence and a willingness to work hard, and they recognized that such men would be difficult to find. They also felt strongly that a man should be willing to accept the full risk of changing jobs if he were to come with them. They were not willing to write long-term employment contracts; they expected a man to have enough faith in his abilities, and in the future of Liquid Metals, Inc., to join them on a trial basis at first. In addition, it was obvious that Liquid Metals, Inc., could not at this time offer large salaries to attract good men, although its salary scale was not disproportionately low. The Findlays were never willing to give large pay increases (over the man's former salary) to new people and had turned down prospective employees who had demanded this treatment.

However, the Findlays felt that they did offer sufficient inducements to get the type of people they wanted. A management stock option plan had been established, and any man who proved capable of contributing to the company would be given options under it after working with the firm for a while. However, the Findlays were not certain as to the type or extent of ownership participation which would have to be offered to attract and hold competent men. Also, as mentioned previously, the Findlays were thinking of a policy of expansion by division which would allow competent young men to be given significant responsibilities as the organization grew. They were confident that Liquid Metals, Inc., would experience a rapid and profitable growth which would allow any man joining their firm now to progress virtually as far as his abilities would allow him to go.

Positions to Be Filled

In their thinking about building a broader management team, the Findlays had several specific jobs in mind. These were purchasing, production scheduling and control, and inside sales. They also felt that another good design engineer should be added soon to help back up Mr. Findlay. The firm would not add all these people at once, Mrs. Findlay said, "We haven't got enough money to fill all the jobs. It takes at least six months to train a new man to the point where he is really pulling his own weight. It costs money to support a man for this time, and we also need funds to get established in our new building, and to buy a new welder, one or two new lathes, a Bridgeport milling head, a grinder, and other production equipment. Also, we can't allow the company to get top-heavy with overhead people. However, we should be preparing to fill the positions as soon as our sales will support them. Right now, it's the space and production equipment shortage that is holding us up."

The Findlays felt that probably filling the purchasing and production control positions should come first, but they had no firm priority list in mind. The addition of any one of the men would free up some of Mr. Findlay's time and would therefore be helpful. If they found an excellent prospect for any one job they would probably hire him, and they felt that none of the positions should be filled just for the sake of filling it, unless a good man could be found. All three of the management positions to be filled would demand men with enough background in engineering to fully understand the products and processes of Liquid Metals, Inc. A description of the purchasing job requirements has been given above.

The production control and scheduling position seemed to call for a man of capabilities similar to those of the purchaser. The scheduler would be expected to be responsible for the estimating on new proposals. He personally would have to determine the delivery date the company could promise, and, working with the purchaser, would collect the data needed to price the proposal. The scheduler would also schedule all production, purchasing, and subcontracted work. This would require intimate knowledge of the shop load and backlog, machine and assembly times, lead times for purchased material and component delivery, production engineering and drafting times, the capability and reliability of each of the machine shops that might do subcontract work, and the time needed for testing and debugging all products. The scheduler would be expected to develop and maintain accurate production flow diagrams and schedules, and to keep records sufficient to allow the company to rapidly spot engineering or production delays, take immediate corrective action, and to evaluate performance on each job in order to allow both internal improvement and more accurate estimating and scheduling on subsequent orders.

The inside salesman's function would consist primarily of backing up Mr. Findlay when he was selling in the field and of being the initial contact for all customers contacting the company. He would have to know enough about the firm's capabilities, products, backlog, and prices to handle all preliminary contacts with, and questions by, either the engineers or purchasing agents of prospective customers. He would be expected to be familiar with both gas repurification and liquid metals handling processes and with potential customers' own operations so that he could, with experience, assume more and more of the responsibility for providing help to customer engineers in accordance with the Findlays' policy of giving information freely to these people. The inside salesman would also be expected to maintain records of correspondence and telephone calls with customers and keep appropriate sales records. He should be a man with the basic ability to develop into a sales manager who could supervise either company salesmen or manufacturers' representatives who might be added in the future.

The engineer who might be added would have to be a man able to do much of the same sort of farsighted design and engineering work performed by Mr. Findlay, and would have to have the capacity to grow with the company in the same way that the new management people would be expected to.

In addition to these salaried employees, Liquid Metals, Inc., would need to hire immediately, as space became available, more shop people to operate new machines, perform assembly and testing work, etc., in order to keep up with the company's sales volume growth. In discussing ways of finding and evaluating suitable people for the various management positions which were open, Mr. and Mrs. Findlay made various comments about some of the possible methods.

They did not feel that man-wanted ads in trade or technical journals would be a desirable approach. Although Liquid Metals, Inc., used help-wanted ads in local newspapers when it needed a bookkeeper, and through these ads had found a man with whom they were quite pleased, the Findlays felt that the people they were now seeking were of a different type. Their requirements in a prospective bookkeeper had been relatively standard and easy to define, and there were people suitable in the local area. On the other hand, the qualities of a man to fill one of the new management positions or the engineering job were far more difficult to define. Mr. Findlay stated that he did not have the time to analyze and interview the deluge of applicants that would come from most trade journal ads. Furthermore, he said, most of the replies would be from professional jobhoppers rather than from the sort of man Liquid Metals wanted. He added that newspaper advertising would be similarly unsuitable in this case.

Mr. Findlay's comments about employment agencies were generally favorable. Liquid Metals, Inc., had developed a continuing relationship with one agency in Boston. This relationship had come about after the firm had contacted Mr. Findlay in the spring of 1961, looking for positions in which to place some men on its roster. He expressed interest in seeing résumés, transcripts, and references, but was at first disappointed in that the agency often did not send complete data and was slow in answering requests for information. However, as the agency apparently began to realize more fully what Mr. Findlay expected of it, it began to do a much better job for him. Through it, the company had recently acquired an engineer with whom Mr. Findlay was satisfied so far. Although the agency fee appeared high at first glance—10 percent of the first year's salary—Mr. Findlay felt this to be well worth the screening job the agency was now doing for him. He thought this or another agency might be able to help in his search for new people. He stated that the agency had listings of men in the middle management range, but that Liquid Metals, Inc., had no experience with this type of person from any agency.

Liquid Metals, Inc., had never contacted any university alumni placement office. Mr. Findlay stated that he did not know how they worked, but that this might be a way of finding men. However, he added, "I'm not sure how good the people who go back to their college looking for a job would be. I know I'd never ask MIT to find me a job, and I wonder if the type of person we need here would do this."

Mr. Findlay felt that a good potential source of people was Liquid Metals' customer and supplier companies. He knew people in several such firms who had become mildly dissatisfied with their jobs and future prospects, and several who had expressed an interest in joining Liquid Metals, Inc. These people were familiar with the company's products and with the problems of liquid metals and/or gas repurification systems. Mr. Findlay stated that if he approached any of these men he would have to be extremely careful. No customer or supplier would be expected to like having its people pirated. Furthermore, many of these men were extremely valuable to Liquid Metals, Inc., in their present positions.

The Findlays had been thinking for some time about beginning to build a management and engineering team. However, it was not until recently that there had been any pressure to do so rapidly. In November, a combination of factors, including the sharp increase in sales and orders, the pending completion of the plant addition and purchase of new equipment, and the departure of Jim Price, created the need to add such people immediately. The Findlays had several questions in mind as they considered this need. Were the jobs they had in mind the right ones to try to fill? Should they establish any definite priority in filling them? What specific qualities and abilities should they look for in prospective employees for each position? What was the most efficient way to locate likely prospects? How should they go about evaluating these men? And, finally, what should they offer to these men, and how should they train them?

APPENDIX 12–A

Description of the Liquid Metals, Inc., Electrodynamic Pump

The electrodynamic pump developed by the Findlays for handling liquid metals utilizes the same principle employed in an eddy brake. In an eddy brake, a stationary magnetic field is applied to stop a moving copper disk. In the electrodynamic pump, a magnetic field is mechanically moved in order to drag a liquid metal.

The pump consists of two main parts. The first is a pump tube, shaped to form a nearly closed circle with radial entrance and exit projections. The second essential component is a magnetic circuit having opposed pole pairs arranged so as to pass a magnetic flux through the tube walls and the liquid metal contained therein.

The pole pairs are mechanically rotated around the outside of the tube loop so that the lines of magnetic force between the pole pairs move relative to the liquid metal in the pump tube. This movement indirectly sets up eddy currents in the liquid metal around the pole projections. This electric current flowing in the liquid metal interacts with the lines of magnetic flux and produces in the metal a force which tries to make the metal flow at the same rate as that at which the poles are moving. Although fluid friction prevents the liquid metal from actually attaining this rate, the principles involved are such that any slippage caused by a restriction of the flow of the liquid metal causes, in turn, an increase in the eddy currents making the metal move. This factor makes the electrodynamic pump a relatively efficient device.

The Liquid Metals, Inc., electrodynamic pump incorporates the following features:[1]

Zero leakage: there are no seals or stuffing boxes in the liquid metal-carrying part of the pump.

The pump will operate equally well in either direction: reversing the drive motor reverses the direction of liquid flow.

The complete range of output pressures is controlled by adjusting the small direct current which produces the magnetic flux between poles.

Pressure heads to 500 p.s.i. are readily obtainable.

Flow capacity is limited only by the tube cross-sectional area and the rate of rotation of the poles; hydraulic losses are minimal.

Complete isolation of the magnetic circuit from the pump cell (i.e., from the tube section containing the liquid metal) enables the LM Pump to operate at very high liquid metal temperatures: 1,650°F. is the upper limit for standard LM Pump Cells, while special LM Cells are available, at extra cost, for higher operating temperatures.

The rotation of the magnetic structure automatically produces forced convection cooling of the magnetic field coils.

The inherent mechanical simplicity of the LM Pump insures dependability in service.

Heat loss from the high-temperature liquid metal is minimized in the LM Pump because of the good thermal isolation of the pump cell from the rest of the pump.

---

[1] Quoted from a brochure prepared by the company in 1960.

13. HENDERSON AND JOHNSON, INC. *

Reexamining Major Policies

Henderson and Johnson, Inc., of Gloucester, Massachusetts, manufactured and sold paint—primarily marine paint. Of total sales amounting to $425,401 in 1960, marine paints accounted for 92 percent, while most of the remainder consisted of interior and exterior house paints. In Gloucester, the company operated its own paint manufacturing plant, which employed 11 men, and its paint store, which sold to local fishermen, pleasure boat owners, and homeowners. Approximately 22 percent of the company's total sales were made through this store, and the remainder through wholesalers and retailers in scattered sections of the eastern and Gulf coasts. Sales to retailers were made by Henderson and Johnson direct in some areas and through wholesalers in other areas. In some areas, these sales to wholesalers and to retailers were solicited for Henderson and Johnson by manufacturers' representatives; in other areas, they were not.

The company had a record of profitability and sales growth under the management of its president and owner, James N. Abbott, Jr., but in late 1960 sales had begun to show what Mr. Abbott considered to be an adverse trend. Sales in recent months had been lower than those of the corresponding months of the preceding year. Mr. Abbott had for some time concerned himself with problems of building sales and also with developing improved products for the company. He had not considered these problems urgent. However, because of constantly increasing sales in previous years, a drop of $26,522 in sales for 1960 prompted him to appraise the overall course the company was taking.

History

Henderson and Johnson had been founded during the late 1800's by two men who left another, and still older, Gloucester paint company, Tarr and Wonson, Ltd. Mr. Abbott had acquired Henderson and Johnson, Inc., in 1947. He had later also acquired Tarr and Wonson, Ltd., in 1953, and had made it part of Henderson and Johnson.

In 1960, both companies were owned by Mr. Abbott, and though legally they were separate corporations, they worked together; Tarr and Wonson was the manufacturing company, and Henderson and Johnson was the selling company. Financial statements for the two companies are presented in Exhibits 13–1, 13–2, and 13–3. Industry data appear in Exhibits 13–4 through 13–9.

Exhibit 13–1

HENDERSON AND JOHNSON, INC.

COMBINED* FINANCIAL STATEMENTS OF HENDERSON AND JOHNSON AND TARR AND WONSON

	1956	*1957*	*1958*	*1959*	*1960*
INCOME STATEMENTS					
Net income	$332,371	$350,800	$405,319	$448,220	$421,698
Cost of sales	204,938	219,416	251,640	265,684	247,952
Total selling expenses	53,638	64,681	80,102	81,366	77,923
Total general and administrative ..	42,921	44,166	52,516	65,606	62,152
Net profit	30,874	22,537	21,061	35,564	33,671
Other income	2,422	1,863	3,034	180	835
Federal income taxes	1,292	8,159	6,695	10,723	10,351
Profit after Taxes	$ 32,004	$ 16,241	$ 17,400	$ 25,021	$ 24,155
BALANCE SHEETS					
Current Assets:					
Cash........................	$ 12,809	$ 22,699	$ 34,797	$ 19,180	$ 50,908
Accounts receivable	50,212	28,227	51,848	49,637	42,810
Inventory	66,670	72,466	74,472	90,167	87,848
Prepaid expenses	738	786	1,531	2,556	2,778
Life insurance cash value	1,414	1,717	2,022	2,330	2,641
Total Current Assets	$131,843	$125,895	$164,670	$163,870	$186,985
Securities investments	7,000	21,063	—	29,413	27,615
Net Fixed Assets	66,338	65,270	69,011	67,974	65,521
Trademarks and formulae	10,000	10,000	10,000	10,000	10,000
Other assets	—	2,240	175	4,658	3,053
Total Assets..............	$215,181	$224,468	$243,856	$275,917	$293,174
Current Liabilities:					
Accounts payable	$ 14,895	$ 9,296	$ 12,443	$ 16,297	$ 15,515
Notes payable	1,000	1,600	3,800	4,500	3,800
Accrued expenses	6,105	9,356	11,322	17,187	16,888
Total Current Liabilities	$ 22,000	$ 20,252	$ 27,565	$ 37,984	$ 35,203
Term loan payable	9,000	6,400	15,200	18,000	15,200
Stockholders' Equity:					
Stock outstanding:					
Preferred, 6% cumulative	$ 26,000	$ 23,400	$ 13,200	$ 9,000	$ 9,000
Common	112,000	112,000	112,000	112,000	112,000
Surplus	46,181	62,415	75,891	98,933	120,771
Total Liabilities	$215,181	$224,468	$243,856	$275,917	$293,174

* Combined from Exhibits 13–2 and 13–3 for convenience. Actually, the company did not use comparative or combined statements.

Exhibit 13–2

HENDERSON AND JOHNSON, INC.

COMPARATIVE INCOME STATEMENTS
(Not Including Tarr and Wonson)

	1956	1957	1958	1959	1960
Gross sales*	$236,918	$242,924	$399,322	$426,103	$404,559
Returns and allowances ...	1,698	1,770	2,743	3,325	3,335
Net sales	$235,220	$241,154	$396,579	$422,778	$401,224
Cost of paint	181,266	183,030	301,641	315,172	299,912
Cost of merchandise	4,244	5,626	8,188	7,523	6,743
Freight-in	120	82	182	223	104
Cost of goods sold	$185,630	$188,738	$310,011	$322,918	$306,759
Freight-out	3	69	391	436	50
Advertising	3,737	2,490	11,528	10,116	8,752
Boat show expenses	1,065	794	2,770	2,030	1,872
Commissions	8,053	7,426	13,741	15,268	16,075
Sales salaries	65	1,360	4,240	4,320	2,800
Travel	1,238	1,170	2,483	1,906	1,062
Store salaries	6,347	7,578	9,135	9,668	9,011
Other selling expense	2,589	5,407	6,170	5,875	8,200
Total Selling Expenses.......	$ 23,097	$ 26,294	$ 50,458	$ 49,619	$ 47,822
Officer's salary	7,500	7,500	10,800	10,800	10,800
Office salaries	8,113	8,577	8,941	9,395	9,721
Taxes	2,049	1,860	2,622	3,302	3,243
Interest	91	—	—	138	—
Pensions and profit sharing	—	—	—	2,028	1,387
Insurance	373	409	496	606	1,179
Travel	1,432	1,759	1,489	1,954	1,150
Other general and adminis- trative	3,828	4,007	4,876	5,559	4,496
Total General and Adminis- trative	$ 23,386	$ 24,112	$ 29,224	$ 33,782	$ 31,976
Profit on sales	3,107	2,010	6,886	16,459	14,667
Other income	2,422	1,863	3,034	180	835
Profit before taxes	$ 5,529	$ 3,873	$ 9,920	$ 16,639	$ 15,502
Federal income tax	1,292	937	2,442	4,992	4,650
Profit after Taxes	$ 4,237	$ 2,936	$ 7,478	$ 11,647	$ 10,852

* Tarr and Wonson billings for 1956 and 1957 not included.

Tarr and Wonson had been founded in 1863 by two Gloucester ship painters who, by trial and error, had developed a special paint which could be used on the bottom of a ship to prevent the fouling normally caused by marine growth. The company prospered, selling its antifouling paints to local fishermen, who found them very effective in preventing the growth of barnacles and other sea life on the bottoms of their boats during the long months at sea.

Exhibit 13–3

HENDERSON AND JOHNSON, INC.

COMPARATIVE INCOME STATEMENTS FOR TARR AND WONSON, LTD.
(Excluding Henderson and Johnson)

	1956	1957	1958	1959	1960
Sales—Henderson and Johnson	$181,737	$189,061	$295,677	$317,095	$304,568
Net sales—trade*	97,151	109,646	8,740	25,442	20,474
Net income	$278,888	$298,707	$304,417	$342,537	$325,042
Material cost	153,876	167,373	177,974	193,596	183,700
Freight-in	1,356	1,361	1,536	1,657	1,690
Direct labor	24,388	26,847	31,827	37,429	34,855
Supervision	8,524	9,133	9,725	9,990	9,683
Laboratory	2,154	3,461	3,006	2,186	2,302
Utilities	5,343	4,976	5,604	4,984	4,860
Supplies and repairs	2,353	3,356	4,279	6,221	3,845
Depreciation	3,051	3,232	3,355	3,798	4,826
Total Manufacturing Expenses	$201,045	$219,739	$237,306	$259,861	$245,761
Freight-out	19,158	21,050	26,567	27,407	27,098
Advertising	5,846	9,517	552	309	67
Boat show expense	988	2,545	19	292	147
Commissions	1,735	1,892	182	1,534	1,130
Sales salaries	1,232	500	—	—	—
Travel	1,469	1,937	1,639	1,545	1,620
Other selling expense	113	946	685	660	39
Total Selling Expenses	$ 30,541	$ 38,387	$ 29,644	$ 31,747	$ 30,101
Officer's salary	7,500	7,500	10,800	10,800	10,800
Taxes	5,479	5,224	4,900	5,475	5,170
Interest	956	771	1,289	1,602	1,736
Pensions and profit-sharing	—	—	—	5,415	3,570
Insurance	3,704	4,235	4,230	5,651	6,068
Other general and administrative	1,896	2,324	2,071	2,879	2,832
Total General and Administrative	$ 19,535	$ 20,054	$ 23,292	$ 31,824	$ 30,176
Net profit	$ 27,767	$ 20,527	$ 14,175	$ 19,105	$ 19,004
Federal income tax	—	7,222	4,253	5,731	5,701
Profit after Taxes	$ 27,767	$ 13,305	$ 9,922	$ 13,374	$ 13,303

* Figures for 1956 and 1957 are for sales under Tarr and Wonson label billed by Tarr and Wonson. After 1957, these were sold to and billed by Henderson and Johnson.

Later, two other men, Walter Henderson and Louis Johnson, who had worked for Tarr and Wonson, left the company to set up their own enterprise across the bay, using a waterfront shack and a few wooden barrels to mix and deliver paints in competition with Tarr and Wonson. Both companies grew and expanded the variety of paints they offered, and by the end of World War II, each had reached annual sales of about $100,000. However, by this time the original owners had become quite old, and management of Tarr and

Exhibit 13–4

HENDERSON AND JOHNSON, INC.

TOTAL SALES OF PAINT, VARNISH, AND LACQUER BY ALL UNITED STATES COMPANIES

Year	Annual Sales ($1,000)	Month	Monthly Sales 1959	1960
1947	$1,193,741	July	$162,700	$156,400
1948	1,207,281	August	153,000	167,100
1949	1,106,949	September	149,600	150,900
1950	1,326,744	October	139,600	140,700
1951	1,399,087	November	117,300	127,000
1952	1,340,759	December	116,200	—
1953	1,402,733			
1954	1,360,884			
1955	1,563,982			
1956	1,580,460			
1957	1,603,800			
1958	1,629,300			
1959	1,727,400			

SOURCES: Bureau of the Census, United States Department of Commerce; *Oil, Paint & Drug Reporter.*

Exhibit 13–5

HENDERSON AND JOHNSON, INC.

QUANTITY AND VALUE OF PAINTS AND VARNISHES SHIPPED BY ALL PRODUCERS IN THE UNITED STATES

	Total Production (1,000 Gallons) 1947	1954	1958
Trade sales:			
Exterior		112,832	131,143
Interior		156,920	155,410
Other		13,134	19,328
Marine paints:			
Ship bottom	2,387	2,058 ⎫	9,849
Other	7,855	6,047 ⎬	
Industrial finishes		279,177	240,064
Other		10,080	14,106
Paints, varnishes, lacquers, japans, and enamels, total . . .		580,248	569,960

SOURCE: Bureau of the Census, United States Department of Commerce.

Wonson had passed to third- and fourth-generation heirs. Walter Henderson, who by then had acquired full ownership of Henderson and Johnson, became interested in selling his company and offered it to James Abbott for $15,000 down and $15,000 per year up to a total of $60,000.

Exhibit 13–6

HENDERSON AND JOHNSON, INC.

DATA ON UNITED STATES PAINT, VARNISH, AND LACQUER COMPANIES IN 1959

	Median	Upper Quartile	Lower Quartile
Current assets to current debt (times)	2.95	5.60	2.14
Net profits on net sales (%)	3.59	5.32	1.11
Net profits on tangible net worth (%)	9.91	16.17	3.95
Net profits on working capital (%)	15.50	31.81	7.28
Net sales to tangible net worth (times)	2.69	4.44	2.20
Net sales to net working capital (times) . . .	4.95	7.30	3.87
Collection period (days)	36	23	49
Net sales to inventory (times)	6.1	8.6	4.9
Fixed assets to tangible net worth (%)	31.8	21.7	46.8
Current debt to tangible net worth (%) . . .	29.6	17.0	45.9
Total debt to tangible net worth (%)	43.9	33.9	94.6
Inventory to net working capital (%)	67.1	48.6	90.6
Current debt to inventory (%)	80.3	48.2	107.7
Funded debts to net working capital (%) .	17.6	5.3	31.6

SOURCE: "14 Important Ratios in 36 Manufacturing Lines," *Dun's Review*, December, 1960, p. 58.

Mr. Abbott had studied economics at the University of Pennsylvania, from which he graduated with a B.S. in 1934. Following his graduation, he did statistical work for the government and, for a while, taught accounting and statistics at the Wharton School of the University of Pennsylvania. During World War II, he served in the navy, and after the war he joined his father's boat repair yard in Gloucester. "Walter Henderson's company looked like a good buy to me," said Mr. Abbott. "It was making money, though I wasn't sure how much; it had a sizable inventory, and it had $14,000 in the bank. There were no accounts payable, because Mr. Henderson had paid the bills as they came in.

"Walter Henderson left the day I moved into the company, and since I didn't know anything about making paint, I told everybody to continue what they were doing until I learned what we should be doing. Then I started learning about paint. Raw material suppliers were very helpful in knowing about the processes and explaining them to me. They also sent specialists to help me learn how to improve our operations and products. To try out new ideas, I set up a small experimental paint laboratory, in which I spent most of my own time during the early days.

"One day a man with a thick German accent dropped in and an-

Exhibit 13–7

HENDERSON AND JOHNSON, INC.

NATIONAL REGIONAL STATISTICS

Region	1947		1954			1958		
	Number Employees	($1,000) Value Added by Manufacture	Number Employees	($1,000) Value Added by Manufacture	Establishments with 20 or More Employees	Number Employees	($1,000) Value Added by Manufacture	Establishments with 20 or More Employees
Paints and varnishes—total ...	53,412	$469,584	56,580	$642,656	552	56,941	$734,039	577
New England	2,541	17,331	2,472	23,478	26	2,217	26,736	29
Middle Atlantic	17,253	148,694	17,033	191,622	156	16,021	199,119	159
East North Central	19,417	172,416	20,111	236,278	164	19,791	262,753	164
West North Central	3,254	32,181	3,953	49,167	40	3,826	53,365	42
South Atlantic	n.a.	n.a.	2,671	26,256	37	3,607	44,662	52
East South Central	2,123	n.a.	2,113	25,137	24	2,097	28,051	21
West South Central	n.a.	n.a.	2,015	20,976	25	2,489	31,274	31
West	5,426	52,127	6,209	69,739	80	6,893	88,079	79

SOURCE: Bureau of the Census, United States Department of Commerce.

Exhibit 13–8

HENDERSON AND JOHNSON, INC.

TYPES OF BOATS IN USE IN 1959 IN THE U.S.

	Number	*Gross Tons*
Motor boats over 16 feet	541,000	
Inboard motor boats	319,000	
Large cruisers	4,000	
Outboard boats	3,940,000	
Sailboats	496,000	
Rowboats, dinghies, canoes, etc.	2,500,000	
U.S. Great Lakes (1,000 gross tons and over) ..	364	2,418,400
U.S. merchant fleet (1,000 gross tons and over):		
Privately owned	1,023	9,519,000
Government owned	1,973	14,517,000

SOURCES: Boating Industry and U.S. Maritime Commission.

Exhibit 13–9

HENDERSON AND JOHNSON, INC.

RECREATIONAL BOATS IN USE IN THE U.S.

Year

1947	2,440,000
1952	4,333,000
1956	6,686,000
1957	7,071,000
1958	7,330,000
1959	7,785,000

SOURCE: Boating Industry.

nounced that he was a plant layout expert and consultant. He asked how many gallons per employee per hour my plant produced, and I told him I didn't know. He asked me to guess, and after some figuring I said maybe 2½ gallons. He said in that case I needed him. I asked the price, and he said $500. I offered $200 to start and the remainder if the savings justified it. He accepted, and by making some simple improvements raised output from an actual figure of 1½ gallons per employee per hour up to 4."

In 1953, Mr. Abbott learned that Tarr and Wonson, the old competitor across the harbor, was in serious difficulty and could be bought. Although Tarr and Wonson's sales were around $60,000, the company was suffering continual losses, due to antiquated and inefficient production methods, which had built a deficit of $117,000 against equity of $120,000. Mr. Abbott decided to buy the company for its sales and its physical assets, which had been depreciated to well below their estimated market value, and was able to do so for a cash payment of $682, which was paid to the company for 682 shares of treasury stock—controlling interest in the 1,200-share total. He later bought out most of the remaining minority stockholders.

On January 24, 1954, just as the purchase of Tarr and Wonson was concluded, a fire started in the Henderson and Johnson plant and burned it to the ground. Fortunately, however, much of the paint-making machinery and some raw materials were salvageable. Mr. Abbott had the obsolete Tarr and Wonson plant machinery and fixtures removed, including gaslights which had been used for illumination until only a year or two before, and replaced the old equipment with salvaged equipment from the Henderson and Johnson plant, plus some new equipment. By mid-February, the plant had resumed partial production, and by mid-March full production had been resumed. Not an order was lost.

All sales to Tarr and Wonson customers were continued under the Tarr and Wonson label, and invoiced by Tarr and Wonson, until 1958. In 1958, all paints with the exception of some antifouling paint were put under the Henderson and Johnson brand—the only brand advertised by the company—and invoiced by Henderson and Johnson. This change, according to Mr. Abbott, had no perceptible effect on sales to Tarr and Wonson customers. On some antifouling paint, however, the Tarr and Wonson label was retained because it was the only brand that some customers would accept in antifouling paint. In 1960, approximately the same amount of antifouling paint was sold under the Henderson and Johnson label as under the Tarr and Wonson label. Paint sold under both labels was of identical composition.

Products

Products of Henderson and Johnson fell into two broad categories —marine paint and house paint. Marine paint included antifouling paint, anticorrosive paint, and hull and topside paint. House paint, which was part of an industry classification known as trade sales, included interior paints and exterior paints. Each of these types of paint differed significantly from the others in its physical composition, characteristics such as speed of drying and hardness, and in its applications. A breakdown of the company's sales by categories appears as Exhibit 13–10.

As indicated in Exhibit 13–10, 92.2 percent of the company's sales in 1960 were of marine paint, and 30.1 percent of marine paint sales

Exhibit 13-10

HENDERSON AND JOHNSON, INC.

Product Analysis for the Company

	1954	1955	1956	1957	1958	1959	1960
Annual production (gallons)	68,323	67,018	79,587	78,660	95,147	93,329	85,771
Marine finishes (percent total production)	85.3%	88.4%	91.1%	89.0%	92.0%	93.9%	92.2%
Antifouling (percent of marine)	40.3	40.2	29.5	31.0	28.9	28.9	30.1
Hull and topside	48.5	45.9	50.5	48.2	45.4	51.9	53.1
Anticorrosive	1.8	1.9	2.0	3.2	1.6	1.6	1.0
Workboat*	2.6	6.1	11.5	10.2	17.0	12.1	11.4
Preservatives†	3.9	3.6	3.5	3.5	3.4	2.6	1.8
Miscellaneous	2.9	2.3	3.0	3.9	3.7	2.9	2.6
Total Marine	100%	100%	100%	100%	100%	100%	100%
Trade sales (percent total production)	9.5%	10.3%	6.7%	9.8%	6.3%	5.3%	6.8%
Interior (percent trade sales)	22.4	21.4	25.2	32.5	26.9	37.9	30.3
Exterior	64.2	71.6	67.6	55.7	64.1	52.1	63.5
Pliolite‡	13.4	7.0	7.2	11.8	9.0	10.0	6.2
Total Trade Sales	100%	100%	100%	100%	100%	100%	100%
Special orders§ (percent total production)	5.2%	1.3%	2.2%	1.2%	1.7%	0.8%	1.0%

* Workboat included paint sold on consignment to ship chandlers, who usually sold to owners of commercial vessels such as steamships and banana boats. Included in this category were all types of marine paint.

† Preservatives were applied to wood, ropes, nets, and canvas to prevent attack by insects, fungus, and mildew.

‡ Pliolite was a rubber-based compound mainly for use on cement surfaces—surfaces such as interior and exterior floors and swimming pools.

§ Special orders included compositions not normally carried in the company's standard line but made to customer order.

consisted of antifouling paint. Practically all antifouling paints contained the same active ingredient originally used by Tarr and Wonson—cuprous oxide. It had not been known how the antifouling effect was produced by cuprous oxide until 1945, when a navy research team explained the process. Cuprous oxide reacted with the water that came in contact with it and released copper ions, which, in turn, killed any marine microorganisms coming into close contact with the painted surface. Thus, nothing could grow on the painted surface. As the cuprous oxide reacted with the water, it was used up; so in order that the antifouling effect continue, it was necessary that more cuprous oxide continually present itself to the water. To accomplish this renewal of cuprous oxide at the water interface, two approaches had been developed and were in use.

The approach favored by Henderson and Johnson was known as that of the soluble matrix. In Henderson and Johnson antifouling paint, the vehicle, or binder, in which the cuprous oxide was mixed was, to a certain slight degree, soluble in water. As the paint was contacted by water, it slowly dissolved away, thus continually exposing a new and fresh layer of cuprous oxide to become ionized and ward off growth.

The other approach used what was known as the continuous contact principle. In this approach, the binder that held the cuprous oxide was not soluble in water, and it therefore remained intact while the cuprous oxide was eaten away. So that fresh cuprous oxide would be exposed as the outer particles of it dissolved away, a very high concentration of cuprous oxide was put in the binder. Then, as one particle of cuprous oxide was used up, another particle jammed closely behind or beside it became exposed so it could react, and the water thus ate its way from one particle to another, producing a honeycomb in the insoluble matrix as it advanced. Inevitably, however, some particles completely surrounded with insoluble binder never became exposed by the water and were thus wasted.

Both approaches, according to Mr. Abbott, had their advantages and drawbacks. Soluble matrix paint used less cuprous oxide and therefore cost less. Also, it left no honeycomb to be scraped away before repainting. The continuous contact approach, however, permitted use of vinyl and other plastics in the binder, which made the paint less susceptible to erosion caused by movement through the water at high speeds. Paints using this approach had effective lives of up to two years and could withstand a substantial amount of abuse.

For these reasons, they were bought by the navy and steamship lines, usually, according to Mr. Abbott, in large quantities from the four or five largest paint companies. These users always sandblasted their hulls clean before repainting, so that a remnant of insoluble honeycomb was not a significant disadvantage.

Henderson and Johnson sold several grades of antifouling paint. The top grade sold for $26 per gallon, was suitable for boats of any speed, and had an effective life up to 12 months. The cheapest, which accounted for two-thirds of all anti-fouling paint sold by the company in 1960, was priced at $10 per gallon and was recommended for low speed boats, such as local fishing boats whose top speed was about 10 knots. It provided antifouling protection for one fouling season in northern waters, which usually ran from April through August, or for a shorter period in warmer southern waters. Many who used this grade, such as local fishermen, usually pulled their boats out of the water at least once per year and always repainted them on these occasions.

Above the waterline, a variety of paints were used, including hull paints, varnishes, deck paints, and engine enamels, depending on the particular applications. Generally, the requirements of these hull and topside paints were that they be fast-drying and form a hard surface with high resistance to atmospheric exposure. In the case of iron or steel surfaces, the application of antifouling paint on the hull and topside paint was preceded by a coat of anticorrosive paint, the function of which was to prevent rusting.

Other than marine paints, the only products manufactured by Henderson and Johnson were house paints. Interior house paints were in many cases similar to hull and topside paints in being fast-drying and in forming a hard, abrasion-resistant surface. Others were especially suited to use on plaster surfaces. Interior enamels did not require the weathering resistance of hull and topside paints, and they could generally be more brittle, but they also often were required to form a more glossy surface.

Exterior house paints were specialized according to the material of which the exterior of the house was made, whether stucco, shingles, or clapboards. Clapboards, for instance, because of their high degree of expansion and contraction with atmospheric temperature changes, required a relatively elastic paint. Linseed oil, because it dried slowly, was not desirable as a binder for interior paints, but it was excellent for use on clapboards because it formed an elastic surface.

In all, Mr. Abbott estimated that the company might mix in the course of a year as many as 150 different formulae in the marine paint category, 50 in the house paint category, and perhaps another 50 on special orders which were mixed to customer specifications. Many house paint formulae were mixed as white, either to be sold as white or to be colored later according to customer request by adding pigment to individual cans. By stocking capsules of pigments separately from the paint, the company managed to offer a total of 189 different colors to customers from a relatively small inventory of paint composed of a few base formulae.

Sales

Henderson and Johnson sold through several channels, as mentioned earlier, including its own Gloucester store, plus wholesalers and retailers in more distant geographical areas. In 1960, the company had selling agreements with five manufacturers' representatives who were given commissions on all sales to their respective geographical

Exhibit 13–11

HENDERSON AND JOHNSON, INC.

Geographical Sales Record for 1959

Area	Number of Representatives	1959 Sales
Florida	1	$148,000
Gloucester store	0	108,200
Other New England	1	101,700
Gulf states	0	50,000
Puerto Rico	0	15,500
Carolinas	1	11,300
New York metropolitan area	0	10,500
Foreign export	0	6,000
Pennsylvania	1	300
Maryland, Delaware, Washington, D.C. ...	1	0
		$451,500

areas. In some areas where the company did not have manufacturers' representatives, some Henderson and Johnson customers continued to send in their orders without being solicited to do so. Most of the company's sales were made in the New England, Florida, and Gulf areas. There were several stretches on the Gulf and eastern coasts in which no sales were made, and practically no sales were made to either the West Coast or the inland marine markets. The geographical sales breakdown during 1959 is shown in Exhibit 13–11.

Prices and discounts of Henderson and Johnson were typical for the industry. Retailers, such as marine supply stores, hardware stores, ship chandlers, marine railways, and boatyards, were given 50 percent off list and typically sold at somewhat under list. Wholesalers were given 50 percent and 20 percent off list. On sales to wholesalers in a representative's area, the representative was given a 10 percent commission on the wholesaler's net cost. If, in an area where the company was not represented by a wholesaler, a representative was able to sell to a retailer direct, he was given 20 percent of the retailer's cost, which was more than twice his normal commission per gallon on sales to wholesalers. Mr. Abbott hoped this policy would encourage expansion of sales in new areas by getting more retailers to carry Henderson and Johnson paints. "Trying to interest a wholesaler in carrying your paint is like trying to push on a string," he said. "The wholesaler carries hundreds of marine items and doesn't care which of them the retailers buy, just so they buy. So I think the only way to get a wholesaler to carry out paints is to have some retail accounts to offer him." In accordance with this philosophy, Mr. Abbott had prepared written in-

structions for representatives, a copy of which appears as Exhibit
13–12.

Exhibit 13–12

HENDERSON AND JOHNSON, INC.

INSTRUCTIONS FOR REPRESENTATIVES

April 7, 1960

AREAS WHERE DISTRIBUTION IS SPOTTY OR ABSENT

1. Survey the territory carefully and thoughtfully to map the natural
    marketing centers where a jobber should be located, but do not at-
    tempt to set up jobber yet.
2. Work hard to promote dealer and user accounts in the area. We
    will cooperate by making direct shipments wherever necessary, and
    will even stretch the rules on freight allowance during this develop-
    ment period if we have to. This is hard work, but there are compen-
    sations. Remember your commission is double on these 50 percent
    accounts, and they are a surefire way to get a good distributor. Watch
    these accounts carefully to make sure no one steals them during this
    development period.
3. Now pick out your distributor, one who is sales-minded and with
    good credit. Show him the orders you have filled for the dealers, and
    he'll be interested. The more dealers and users you have set up the
    more interested he will be in taking on the line. Caution: watch out
    for distributors who already have a competitive line of marine paint.
    He may agree to take on our line by placing an order and later trying
    to switch your accounts, but even this would be difficult for him if you
    keep contact with the dealer. Best plan is to get a distributor without
    another line, or one who will agree to drop the competitive line. But
    remember you are in the top bargaining position if you have the dealer
    and user accounts. After your distributor is established, proceed as
    below.

AREAS WHERE DISTRIBUTION IS ESTABLISHED

4. Do you want to be popular with your distributors? Then don't go
    to them asking for orders. Instead, *bring* them orders. Bring them
    orders from established dealers and users, and bring them new dealer
    and user accounts; 95 percent of your effort should be at the dealer
    and user level. The distributor will then *have* to give you an order to
    keep up his stock.
5. Look over distributor stock and see that it is sufficient to fill the
    orders you brought in. Check constantly with dealers and users to see
    that all the stock they ordered from the distributor was received. *A
    distributor constantly out of stock will lose your dealer accounts.* Re-
    port to the factory those distributors without sufficient stock to give
    prompt and complete service to their accounts. Check with factory
    and change distributors if necessary.

Exhibit 13–12—Continued

6.　Go out and visit dealers and users by yourself and also with jobbers' salesman. The salesman is selling hundreds of materials—you are selling paint. Give it the emphasis the salesman can't give it. Know the line. Read articles on how to paint boats, etc. Study thoroughly the thumbnail descriptions of each item in our price list so you know what we've got and what it's for. Tell them about people they may know who use and like our products. Help dealer arrange stock in attractive display in prominent position in the store. See that dealer has signs prominently displayed outside or in window as well as inside. Tell factory about any new colors or items we don't have in our line and for which there is an apparent demand. Estimate whether demand is local or general. Also tell factory about any unusually good compliments on our products, or any justified complaints.

7.　The jobber is basically a warehouseman, never count on him as a salesman. *The selling is done by the manufacturers' representative at the dealer and user level.* The final measure of the representative's effectiveness is sales, and these can come *only* through dealer and user accounts. Keep a record of such accounts opened by you. Are they still active and happy? They are the ones who in the end will determine the amount of commissions. How many have you opened?

When Mr. Abbott bought Henderson and Johnson in 1946, $60,000 of the company's sales were coming from accounts in the Gulf area. However, the representative who had obtained these accounts many years earlier showed no evidence of active attempts to expand sales further, and therefore he was dropped by Mr. Abbott in 1957. Without direct sales representation in the area, sales declined to $55,000 in 1958, $50,000 in 1959, and then rose to $53,000 in 1960.

Between 1946 and 1953, total sales grew from $106,000 to $206,000. Half of the total increase took place in Florida, due to the efforts of one representative. "He didn't look it," said Mr. Abbott, "but he could sell anything. He was seedy and unprepossessing, but a real old-time drummer, a spellbinder. He would call on boatyards and retail stores and make customers of them. I don't know how he accomplished this, except that he had a natural sales personality. When he had secured several of these retailers as customers in an area, he would offer a local wholesaler all of them as accounts if the distributor would agree to stock our paints."

Mr. Abbott had found it necessary to discontinue this Florida representative during 1959, because the man had become unacceptable personally to several customers. Two other Florida representatives had been appointed, based on recommendations of some of the larger distributors. The company's other three representatives had been taken on during 1959 as a result of their own initiative in contacting Henderson and Johnson.

A full-time salesman had been hired by the company in 1957 to solicit accounts in the New England area. However, Mr. Abbott concluded that the sales made by this man did not warrant the expense of retaining him. The salesman was released in 1960. Attempts by Mr. Abbott to obtain representatives in new areas had not met with success. Some representatives indicated an unwillingness to join Henderson and Johnson, because the company maintained a policy of not paying a representative his commission until a customer paid the account from which the commission was generated.

Through the company's own store in Gloucester were made not only marine paint sales, but also nearly all of the company's house paint sales. Mr. Abbott, who liked to work in the store and talk with customers, estimated that the store accounted for perhaps 10 percent of the total house paint sales in Gloucester, selling mostly to amateurs who liked to paint their own houses.

He also estimated that the store accounted for over 90 percent of local marine paint sales, practically all of which were made to fishermen and pleasure boat owners. In discussing consumer preference, Mr. Abbott didn't emphasize brand preference, but he thought habit and convenience played a large part in the average boat owner's decision about which paint to buy. He believed most Gloucester fishermen used Henderson and Johnson paints because they were equal to other brands in quality and price and were available locally for quick delivery in any desired quantity.

He suspected that paint users in other geographical areas bought Henderson and Johnson marine paints either out of habit or else because they were the only paints available from some dealers. He thought that coastal marine paint users, who accounted for 98 percent of the company's marine paint sales, used the paint primarily for maintenance work on a wide variety of boat types, but he was not sure. He did not know how sales were divided among different types of users, but he estimated that roughly 60 percent of total sales went to pleasure boat owners and 60 percent of Gloucester marine paint sales went to fishing boat owners.

There were, he knew, vast paint markets which Henderson and Johnson had not touched. Among these were marine paints used by the navy and steamship lines. The navy bought in quantities of from

10,000 to 100,000 gallons on a competitive bid basis. Mr. Abbott had not actively sought sales to this market, because he thought the high volumes and low margins involved made it inadvisable for Henderson and Johnson to do so. Original-equipment makers in the marine industry, as well as other users of industrial finishes, including makers of appliances, toys, autos, and machinery, composed another market to which the company had done no selling. These users generally required paints especially suited to their products and to the fast-drying requirements of mass production. Mr. Abbott believed the company could develop the paints required by these users, but he questioned the wisdom of attempting to enter these specialized markets where he understood that relationships between paint suppliers and users were typically quite strong and prices very competitive. He knew there were many of these specialized markets, although he had not made any systematic examination of them.

Marine markets, both coastal and inland, seemed to him to offer the most promise for sales expansion. Each year he received several letters from inland boat owners inquiring whether a paint was available to prevent fouling in fresh water. He did not know how effective cuprous oxide paint was in fresh water, though he knew it often did not work in fresh water. Nor did he know whether there might be a better fresh-water antifouling paint available. He had not heard of one. Development of such a paint might, he thought, be an effective way of expanding marine paint sales to inland markets. But he believed the key problem of expanding sales would still be that of obtaining effective manufacturers' representatives.

"We have never spent much on promotion," said Mr. Abbott. "Perhaps we should, but it's hard to see how to go about it most effectively. We tried magazine advertising a few times, and are currently doing so, but it is hard to attribute any specific benefits to any specific advertisement or magazine. Our distribution is limited to certain coastal areas, but media aimed at boat owners generally are not. We have tried promotion by displays in boat shows at Boston, Chicago, New York, and Miami. They are quite expensive, but I think the New York show is worthwhile because it's so large.

"It's hard for anyone to build sales volume in this business. Several large house paint companies have been trying to take advantage of the boom in pleasure boating by diversifying into the sale of marine paints, but without much success. House paints go through different channels, such as hardware and wallpaper stores, while marine paints go through marine supply houses and ship chandlers. To expand from one type of sales to another, a company needs a different distribution system. The only way I can see to develop new sales is to get more manufacturers' representatives to sell among the boatyards and retail marine supply stores, and then use those new accounts to induce more distributors to carry our paints. This system is what worked for us in Florida. The trouble is, we can't seem to get it to work in other areas."

Production

Mr. Abbott had typically not concerned himself with day-to-day operations of the plant, which was located across the harbor from the Gloucester store and office. Plant operations were under the direction of the general manager, Winship Pierce, who spent most of his time conducting experiments in the paint laboratory. Arthur Wonson, the plant foreman, made out production schedules, supervised the men, and performed regular quality control checks in the paint laboratory.

Since early 1954, all paint production had been performed in the Tarr and Wonson plant, which was located on a narrow spit of land surrounded on three sides by water. The plant was built partly out over the water, and it had been proven possible to catch lobsters from the windows. There was no room for expansion.

Raw materials were delivered by truck and moved to the upper floors where the mixing process began. From there, they fed by gravity to successively lower floors as they were ground, strained, filtered, canned, packed in boxes, and stacked in finished goods inventory. A diagrammatic description of the process appears as Exhibit 13–13. All movement of materials was performed by the men in the plant under the supervision of the foreman, Arthur Wonson. Fifty-pound bags of pigments were moved and emptied into mixers by hand. Vats, each containing 100 gallons of paint, were pushed on rolling platforms from the final mixing process to an area where the paint was poured through a cheesecloth strainer stretched across the top of a tub from which cans were individually filled through a hand-operated spigot. The filled cans were then placed in cartons, which were moved on pushcarts to rooms where the men unloaded them and piled them in stacks, ready for shipment.

There were three separate sets of mixing vats, so that it was possible to produce a wide variety of paints with a minimum of time required for cleaning equipment. One set, used only for white paints,

Exhibit 13–13

HENDERSON AND JOHNSON, INC.

PAINT PRODUCTION AT TARR AND WONSON

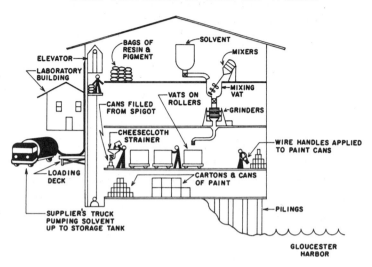

had to be kept absolutely free of any contaminating colors. A second set was used only for bottom paints, because they contained the active ingredient cuprous oxide, which was undesirable in other paints. The third set was used for mixing paints of various other types and colors. By judiciously scheduling the change of production from one color to another, it was possible to follow a sequence that required no cleaning of equipment. For instance, in the change from yellow to green, the presence of slight amounts of yellow in the green did not produce a noticeable change in the color of green. Similarly, the change could then proceed to blue, and so forth. The final color in the sequence was battleship gray, which then could be worked back to the lighter colors.

Occasionally, a sequence would be interrupted for a rush order and the equipment was cleaned, a procedure which took about two man-hours; but such occurrences were infrequent, generally not happening more than two or three times per year. The normal weekly schedule was prepared in advance, depending on the needs of the finished goods inventory for which maximum and minimum quantities had been established, and also taking into consideration the number of current orders on hand. A record of plant production output is included in Exhibit 13–14.

Exhibit 13-14

HENDERSON AND JOHNSON, INC.

PRODUCTION OUTPUT RECORD AT TARR AND WONSON

	1957*					1958					1959					1960				
	Payroll	Production	Man-hours	Cost per Gal.	Gals. per Man-hour	Payroll	Production	Man-hours	Cost per Gal.	Gals. per Man-hour	Payroll	Production	Man-hours	Cost per Gal.	Gals. per Man-hour	Payroll	Production	Man-hours	Cost per Gal.	Gals. per Man-hour
Jan.	$ 2,277.	5,479.	1,186.	$0.42	4.62	$ 3,168.	7,735.	1,609.	$0.41	4.81	$ 4,457.	8,641.	2,049.	$0.52	4.22	$ 2,890.	6,812.	1,331.	$0.42	5.12
Feb.	2,218.	5,785.	1,171.	0.38	4.93	2,416.	5,616.	1,182.	0.43	4.75	3,589.	8,559.	1,630.	0.42	5.25	2,985.	8,175.	1,346.	0.36	6.07
Mar.	3,407.	9,206.	1,677.	0.37	5.42	2,660.	7,136.	1,291.	0.32	5.53	3,711.	8,202.	1,676.	0.45	4.90	3,308.	9,145.	1,506.	0.36	6.07
	7,902.	20,470.	4,084.	0.38	5.08	8,244.	20,487.	4,082.	0.42	5.02										
Apr.	3,209.	12,026.	1,517.	0.27	7.93	2,920.	8,655.	1,325.	0.34	6.53	3,773.	9,711.	1,717.	0.39	5.65	4,116.	8,198.	1,863.	0.50	4.40
May	3,542.	7,510.	1,718.	0.47	4.37	4,365.	10,331.	1,915.	0.42	5.39	4,735.	10,663.	2,122.	0.44	5.02	3,603.	9,615.	1,561.	0.37	6.16
June	2,444.	6,870.	1,220.	0.35	5.63	3,422.	8,915.	1,518.	0.38	5.87	3,642.	9,098.	1,628.	0.40	5.59	3,331.	8,518.	1,477.	0.39	5.77
	9,195.	26,406.	4,455.	0.31	5.93	10,707.	27,901.	4,758.	0.39	5.86										
Three Days Fire Cleanup																				
July	2,141.	6,002.	1,086.	0.36	5.52	2,822.	6,968.	1,139.	0.40	6.11	3,917.	8,361.	1,820.	0.47	4.37	4,093.	6,979.	1,838.	0.59	3.74
Aug.	3,027.	6,415.	1,533.	0.47	4.18	3,144.	6,852.	1,415.	0.46	4.84	2,919.	7,013.	1,402.	0.42	5.00	3,002.	4,726.	1,348.	0.63	3.51
Sept.	2,312.	4,800.	1,171.	0.48	4.10	2,561.	7,640.	1,216.	0.34	6.28	2,922.	5,587.	1,416.	0.52	3.94	3,697.	4,134.	1,695.	0.89	2.44
Oct.	2,239.	4,837.	1,138.	0.46	4.25	3,321.	6,411.	1,581.	0.52	4.06	3,404.	4,972.	1,633.	0.68	3.05	2,804.	5,906.	1,276.	0.48	4.63
Nov.	2,860.	4,264.	1,473.	0.67	2.90	3,257.	8,713.	1,562.	0.37	5.58	2,660.	5,788.	1,273.	0.46	4.55	2,967.	7,002.	1,362.	0.42	5.13
Dec.	2,953.	5,466.	1,528.	0.54	3.58	3,489.	10,175.	1,647.	0.34	6.18	3,940.	6,734.	1,909.	0.59	3.53	3,689.	6,561.	1,699.	0.56	3.86
Total	$32,629.	78,660.	16,418.	0.41	4.73	$37,545.	95,147.	17,400.	0.39	5.47	$43,669.	93,329.	20,275.	0.47	4.61	$40,485.	85,771.	18,302.	0.47	4.69

* 1957 includes payroll taxes.

The Paint Laboratory

The small paint laboratory that had been set up by Mr. Abbott in 1948 was used for quality control checks and for product development, most of which had been aimed at improving antifouling paint. Arthur Wonson usually spent 15 minutes checking a sample of each 100 gallons to make sure that such properties as viscosity, drying time, opacity, gloss, and color were what they should be. "There is generally not much difference between the qualities of the better paints of different companies," said Mr. Abbott. "If one company develops significant product advantages, the others are pretty quick to catch up. It is important though, to keep a close check on quality, because one bad batch of paint can do a lot of harm to the reputation of a company."

Product development work was aimed both toward improving products and toward cutting costs. Most of this research was performed by the technical manager, Winship Pierce. He had worked over thirty years in the paint industry, and was quite active in the New England Society for Paint Technology, of which he had once been president. He was assisted by a local high school science teacher, who contributed about 600 hours per year, and on occasion by Mr. Abbott, who took a strong interest in the laboratory. "Suppliers are always offering new materials for us to try," said Mr. Abbott, "and we like to test those that appear to offer the most promise. We are careful to thoroughly test anything new for from 6 to 24 months before putting it on the market."

The largest portion of product development work at Henderson and Johnson had been aimed at developing a more effective marine antifouling paint. There were two main drawbacks to the soluble matrix antifouling paints then being made by the company. One was that they were more susceptible than insoluble matrix paints to erosion caused by rapid motion of a boat through water. For this reason, the navy and steamship lines generally preferred insoluble matrix paints which lasted longer.

A second shortcoming was that the cuprous oxide did not react with the water at a continuous rate throughout the life of the paint. In order to produce the antifouling effect of killing organisms which tried to cling to the hull, it was necessary that a certain minimum amount of cuprous oxide react with the seawater per unit of time. But in the existing soluble matrix paints, the rate of reaction of the cuprous oxide varied over the life of the paint, being from two to three times the required minimum for approximately the first third of the paint's life, and being less than the required minimum for approximately another third of the total time a layer of the paint still covered the bottom. This departure from the ideal level reaction rate caused what Mr. Abbott believed was a significant amount of waste. When the reaction was above the minimum required, an unnecessary amount of cuprous oxide was given off to the seawater. That the rate dropped below requirements while there was still one-third of the paint left meant the fraction of paint left was wasted and also that the boat had to be repainted sooner than would otherwise be necessary.

Consequently, the aim of research on bottom paints conducted in the Henderson and Johnson laboratory was to find a composition that would result in a reaction of the cuprous oxide which was just above the minimum required rate and which was constant over time until the paint was all gone. At the same time, the improved paint should be resistant to erosion, even at the highest boat speeds. Mr. Abbott thought it quite possible that such a paint could be developed, and that the company which succeeded in doing so would enjoy a great marketing advantage. Yet he knew of no other companies that had made significant progress on the problem.

"Our experimental approach has been mainly one of simply trying many different combinations in the paint composition," he said. "We developed what we call an accelerated leeching-rate apparatus, and with it we have tested over 2,000 different formulae. In this device we immerse a specimen of dried paint in a chemical solution that simulates in one day the same reaction as would occur from 100 days' immersion in seawater. Then we measure the amount of cuprous oxide that has gone into solution by the amount of change in color of the solution to determine the rate at which the reaction has occurred. Formulae which show promise under accelerated leeching are further tested by actual exposure in Florida waters. A commercial testing laboratory in Florida immerses the test specimens and reports to us monthly.

"We've been conducting these experiments now for several years and have tested thousands of specimens. We have been able to upgrade our bottom paints to some extent, but we haven't yet found the big technological advance we're seeking. Of course, neither has anyone else. I've talked to some of the big chemical companies, telling them what I wanted, but not what I wanted it for. None of them had an answer. They have all been looking for paint composition that will last longer, not for paints that will slowly dissolve. I suspect that the failures they have experienced in their research would be of more interest to us than their successes."

Future Plans

"I'm not sure just where we should go from here," he continued. "We seem to face a number of problems and possibilities. Our sales have me quite concerned. Should we try to engage more manufacturers' representatives, and if so, how? Should we advertise more, and if so, what media should we use to reach our geographically scattered markets? How else can we meet our increasing competition? There were hardly any paint manufacturers in Florida before the war. Now there must be hundreds. The southern states of Florida, Louisiana, and Texas account for nearly 50 percent of our sales, but local producers springing up in those areas have obvious advantages over us for giving quick delivery and so far as freight charges are concerned.

"Maybe we should hire a full-time sales manager. But would the resultant volume increase support such a move? I'm afraid we might continue a certain tendency we have shown in the past to experience some increased sales without a corresponding increase in profits. It seems to me that we were profiting just about as much a couple of years ago as now, but then we weren't working so hard. Another alternative might be to hire a commercial laboratory to accelerate our product development. I recently discussed the possibility of developing a constant leeching-rate antifouling paint. The chief chemist thought it could be done, but he said he could not predict how much time it would take or what the total cost would be. He thought the best basis of payment would be for us to hire them at their standard rate of $18 per chemist hour. That way, we could terminate the arrangement at any time if the results appeared to be unpromising.

"Perhaps we should hire them to work on an antifouling paint to be used in fresh water. Development of such a paint might be a good way for us to enter the inland marine market. One problem is, though, that I don't know what the areas of fouling are inland, or exactly what kind of fouling occurs in them. I suspect that different kinds of fouling occur in different areas, and that in some fouling is no problem at all. Even if we did know what kind of fouling occurred in a certain area, it would be a problem to test samples in that area under controlled conditions. We found in the past that boat owners aren't interested enough to do a careful testing job, painting test samples on their boats, keeping track of the type of exposure, reporting at intervals, and so forth.

"Finally, I have been considering the advisability of engaging a management consultant to help in working out some of these problems. But before seeking such a man, it might be well to decide exactly what problems he should work on and what answers he should look for. Then, of course, the problem would be how to go about finding the right management consultant.

"Which problem to concentrate on, what action to take, what help to hire—these are all questions that seem to be demanding answers now. Fortunately, we are not in trouble financially or losing money at present. But I suspect we may be unless good answers are developed to these questions soon. Personally, I don't care how big a volume we reach in this company, but I'd like to see us operate efficiently and make a healthy level of profit. On the other hand, maybe we should just sit tight while the profits continue and then close up when they stop. Or maybe I should look for an opportunity to sell out to one of those house paint companies that have been trying to enter the marine paint market."

14. BURKE CANDY COMPANY*

Placing a Value on a Minority
Shareholder's Stock

In October, 1949, after a dispute between stockholders of the Burke Candy Company, A. K. Martin, a St. Louis businessman, agreed to act as chairman of a committee to establish a value for 1,000 shares of the common stock. At the time, there were 10,000 shares of common stock outstanding; these were owned by various descendants of Jeremiah Burke, who founded the company in 1860. A majority of the shares were held by three grandsons of Jeremiah Burke, each of whom was active in the management of the company. The board of directors of the company included the grandsons, the company's lawyer, and a commercial banker.

A cousin, Mrs. Richard Wilson, who owned 1,000 shares, over a period of time had expressed sharp dissatisfaction with the policies and results of the majority's management. After protracted discussion, the majority stockholders agreed to buy Mrs. Wilson's shares at "a fair price." However, the ideas of the management group and Mrs. Wilson and her lawyer as to "fair value" were very different. Finally, each group agreed to the appointment of a three-man committee to establish the value of the shares. Each group named one man to the committee, and the two nominees together had selected Mr. Martin as the third member and chairman of the committee.

Realizing that his views as to the value of the stock might well prove decisive, Mr. Martin undertook an inquiry into the affairs and financial status of the company. He learned that the Burke Candy Company had long operated as a general-line house, that is, it manufactured a wide variety of candies with no one type of candy predominating. While most candy houses had started in this way, by 1948 most confectionery manufacturers had specialized in one or more lines, so that general-line houses accounted for only some 11 percent of total industry sales. Burke products included: five- and ten-cent specialty items, such as packages of mints and caramels; package

---

  * Reproduced from *Case Problems in Finance* by Robert F. Vandell and Alan B. Coleman (4th ed.; Homewood, Ill.: Richard D. Irwin, Inc., 1962) by permission of the publisher and of the President and Fellows of Harvard College.

goods chiefly in the less-than-one-dollar-per-pound retail category; bulk goods, such as hard "Christmas candy" and unpackaged chocolates; penny goods, such as small marshmallow eggs; and candy bars. The company was generally acknowledged as the first American manufacturer of one of the popular types of chocolate bars. This candy was first marketed about 1900 in the form of large blocks which the retailer cut apart to sell. The Burke company then furnished the retailer with small glassine bags in each box of blocks so the retailer could cut the bar from the block and slip it into a bag as he gave it to the customer. A change in manufacturing was next introduced so that each bar was a separate piece of candy. This was enthusiastically received, so the company then decided to wrap each bar separately and label each wrapper Burke's Best-Bet Bar.

Despite its early success with the Best-Bet Bar, the company did not go along with a general tendency in the industry toward specialization in bar goods or other types of candy, and sales of Best-Bet Bar did not grow relative to competitive products. During World War II, however, the company did sell large quantities of Best-Bet Bar and other bar items to the army and navy for sale in PX's and ships' stores. As military demand fell off, postwar sales returned to the prewar pattern of wide distribuiton among product lines.

Like most candy manufacturers, Burke owned no retail outlets. The company's products were marketed through brokers and by the company's own sales force. Direct sales effort was concentrated in Missouri and adjoining states, and primarily on candy and tobacco jobbers, and on grocery, variety, and drug chains. Sales through brokers were primarily made to candy jobbers. In an effort to compensate for declining military sales, the sales manager in 1946 and 1947 had expended substantial amounts in national magazines and in trade paper advertising and other efforts to gain national distribution through brokers. Almost half of 1948 sales had been through brokers, many in distant areas. One broker in Texas had been particularly effective in producing volume. On the other hand, the advertising expense involved had been substantial, and the company was forced to absorb almost all the freight in order to compete successfully in distant states. Further, the brokers, who operated on a 5 percent commission, appeared to concentrate their efforts on standard product items which were easy to sell but carried a very low margin to the manufacturer.

In general, competition among manufacturing confectioners was keen, except during World War II when sugar rationing limited production and demand was strong. Competition was particularly keen in unbranded candies, and with the exception of its candy bars, most of the Burke products were either unbranded or the brand meant very little to buyers. Two other candy manufacturers located in St. Louis competed directly with the company in the metropolitan area, and manufacturers in Chicago and Indianapolis also competed strongly in the St. Louis market area.

Reviewing the financial records of the company, Mr. Martin found that operations had been profitable during the 1920's. Severe competition had developed during the 1930's, and recurring losses were suffered owing to declining sales and an apparent tendency to change too slowly with the times. The company had entered the depression in strong financial condition, however, and had successfully withstood the drain of cash from the company caused by unprofitable operations. Operations proved profitable in 1939, and the development of a sellers' market during World War II contributed to very profitable years. Management officials pointed out, however, that the lack of profits during prewar years had given the company an unfavorably low base of "normal" earnings for purposes of excess profits taxation. Consequently, Burke's excess profits taxes were higher than those of its competitors with similar earnings *before* taxes. As is indicated in Exhibit 14–2, postwar operations were also profitable until 1948.

Mr. Martin talked at length with the management regarding the large losses suffered in 1948 and in the first eight months of 1949. The management explained that a large portion of the losses in 1948 had resulted from a very sharp and unexpected decline in the market prices for chocolate, sugar, and other major raw materials. The cost of raw materials accounted for almost 80 percent of total cost of sales, and the purchasing officer had made heavy forward commitments at fixed prices during 1947 and early 1948. At the same time that the market prices of these commodities were falling rapidly, a decline in the company's own physical volume of sales set in. For competitive reasons, it was necessary to reduce the company's selling prices substantially. Further, management at first had diagnosed the decline in sales as a temporary development. Consequently, appropriate retrenchment measures were not taken for some months after sales declined.

By August of 1949, a number of steps had been taken to remedy the situation, and operations in August were profitable for the first time in many months. Purchasing methods had been revised so as to minimize the risks of further inventory price decline. Also, steps had been taken to strengthen the management of the company through employment of a young and aggressive man with an excellent educational background who had been highly successful during a business career of some 10 years. This man, the son of one of the majority stockholders, had been established as executive vice-president and given substantial responsibilities for the overall direction of the company. In addition, major changes had been made in the company's sales methods and personnel. The sales force had been strengthened, and major efforts had been made to improve the company's sales effort in the home St. Louis area.

In addition, painstaking analysis had been made of the profitability of various product items and lines. As a result, a number of unprofitable items were dropped, and sales effort was shifted to particularly promising and profitable items. New product development was also being pushed aggressively. In general, management officials were convinced that the new policies were well advised and would produce results.

In the summer of 1948, the board of directors voted to suspend the dividend payments. It was then that Mrs. Wilson, whose only income from the company was in the form of dividends, expressed particular concern and had sought the advice of her lawyer, L. K. Eagle, regarding her investment. Dividend payments since 1938 are shown in Exhibit 14–2. Since the stock was held only by members of the Burke family, and all transfers had been among various members of the family, no market existed for the shares of the company. Investigation showed that there was no active market in the shares of any confectionery manufacturing company of comparable size and nature in the Midwest, so that no closely comparable market quotations were available as guides to the value of the Burke stock.

Acting in anticipation of difficulty in arriving at a satisfactory valuation, Roger Burke, the new executive vice-president of the company, in September requested the Midwestern Company, local investment bankers, to undertake an appraisal of the value of the stock. Largely on the basis of the summary data given in Exhibits 14–1 and 14–2, along with personal discussion of the firm's affairs and policies with its officers, the Midwestern Company had arrived at a maximum valuation of $12 per share. Their report took the form of a letter, attached as Exhibit 14–3.

Mr. Martin talked at some length with officials of the Burke Company regarding the financial statements as of August 31, shown in Exhibits 14–1 and 14–2. He first sought to establish the validity of the book value of the stock as shown on the balance sheet. He was told that the accounts receivable consisted entirely of receivables from

Exhibit 14–1

BURKE CANDY COMPANY

BALANCE SHEET, AUGUST 31, 1949

Assets:

Cash		$ 13,396
Accounts receivable, net		32,673
Inventory:		
Raw materials	$101,665	
Candies in process	13,833	
Finished candies	84,209	
Packaging materials	32,002	
Other supplies	8,183	239,892
Prepaid expenses		25,606
U.S. bonds		145,172
Total Current Assets		$456,739
Factory building and land, net		61,868
Annex building and land, net		182,914
Equipment, net		200,072
Total Assets		$901,593

Liabilities:

Accounts payable, trade and commissions		$ 51,944
Notes payable, bank		75,000
Accrued expenses		28,080
Total Current Liabilities		$155,024
Common stock ($11.50 par)................		115,000
Reserve for contingencies		65,856
Paid-in surplus		562,092
Earned surplus January 1, 1949	$ 14,060	
Plus tax refund to company	108,844	
Less: Loss since January 1, 1949	119,283	
Earned surplus August 31, 1949		3,621
Net worth August 31, 1949		$746,569
Total Liabilities		$901,593

the trade for merchandise sold. The amount of receivables shown was net of a reserve for bad debts of $30,000. This reserve had been accumulated over several years and was considered more than ample to cover expected bad debt losses. The raw material inventory consisted primarily of cornstarch and syrup, chocolate, sugar, and nuts. Mr. Martin satisfied himself that the company maintained accurate inventory records and that the material concerned was in good physical condition. Inventories were valued at the lower of cost or market. Prepaid expenses consisted largely of prepaid insurance premiums. Company officials explained that the large investment in United States bonds represented a temporary investment of funds earmarked to pay for machinery soon to be ordered. This machinery was needed to modernize several of the company's manufacturing operations, and

Exhibit 14–2

BURKE CANDY COMPANY

SELECTED DATA

	Net Sales	Net Profit or (Loss) before Taxes	Net Profit or (Loss) after Taxes	Dividends
1938	$ 975,714	$(38,934)	$(38,934)	—
1939	930,942	(27,493)	(27,493)	—
1940	956,425	(25,647)	(25,647)	—
1941	1,175,383	27,007	27,007	—
1942	1,423,455	136,456	86,027	$23,000
1943	1,679,869	220,755	76,002	34,500
1944	1,917,260	193,343	45,169	40,250
1945	1,914,799	216,427	61,464	40,250
1946	2,073,594	201,531	89,915	46,000
1947	2,636,122	316,302	143,802	80,500
1948	1,769,103	(212,806)	(117,791)	23,000
1949—8 months	700,495	(119,283)	(119,283)*	—

	Net Profit or (Loss) after Taxes as Percentage of Net Sales		Net Profit or (Loss) after Taxes as Percentage of Net Worth	
	Industry†	Burke	Industry†	Burke
1938	1.5%	(3.9)%	3.8%	(5.5)%
1939	2.1	(3.0)	5.9	(4.0)
1940	2.2	(2.7)	6.5	(4.0)
1941	2.8	2.3	8.6	4.0
1942	4.1	6.1	15.8	11.5
1943	4.7	4.5	16.0	9.7
1944	5.2	2.4	20.1	5.8
1945	2.9	3.2	13.5	7.5
1946	7.9	4.4	11.8	9.7
1947	7.0	5.5	19.2	15.7
1948	6.5	(12.0)*	13.9	(28.1)*

Comparison of Selected Ratios, 1948

	Industry†	Burke
Turnover of net worth	2.68	2.34
Turnover of working capital	5.32	4.92
Average collection period	15 days	15 days
Current ratio	3.48	2.50
Fixed assets to net worth	41.5%	58.6%
Total debt to net worth	35.8%	27.6%

* Before tax refund credit, which can be carried back against 1947 earnings.
† Figures are the median figures reported by 45 firms.

management believed that the machines would pay for themselves in a few years by lowering costs.

In the opinion of the company officials, the fixed assets of the company were very conservatively valued. Operations were carried on in a multistory concrete building, which with an annex building occupied

Exhibit 14–3

BURKE CANDY COMPANY

LETTER FROM THE MIDWESTERN COMPANY

September 20, 1949

MR. ROGER BURKE
Burke Candy Company
203 West Illinois Street
ST. LOUIS 6, MISSOURI

DEAR MR. BURKE

We have made an examination of the Burke Candy Company based principally on financial statements furnished us by you, and other information which you have given us; and we have also examined the markets of stocks and financial statements of other companies in similar lines of business, so as to arrive at an opinion as to a fair value for the stock of the Burke Candy Company.

As I told you over the phone today, this is a very difficult question for us to answer, principally because the pattern of sales and earnings of your company does not justify its comparison with the history of the other companies with which you compete. These other companies in general have profits for most of the years, if not all the years, under review; while your company has made money only during the war and the first year or two after war, and during 1948 and the first eight months of 1949 has lost a substantial amount of money. The stock of the Burke Candy Company, therefore, could not be valued on the same basis as the other stocks, being intrinsically more speculative.

The speculative aspects of the stock are increased by the fact that your company is now evidently changing its type of business and has not yet indicated any earnings possibilities from the new type of business. In addition, the changeover requires a relatively substantial capital expenditure which has depleted and will probably continue to deplete your working capital position.

The company has some real estate holdings which might be used as a source of additional working capital if sold; but you have not indicated any such intention, and therefore I assume that the company will have to get along for capital expenditures and current operations on its present working capital position, augmented by profits in the future, if any.

As I told you, there is usually no relationship between market value and book value when valuing common stocks; in fact, any study of such relationship leads to such wide disparities that the only conclusion from such a study can be that there is no connection between market value and book value.

I believe the only likely buyer of stock of your company would be some person familiar with the type of business you are in, who would be willing to buy control at a sacrifice price and take over management of the company in the hope of making operations profitable and, therefore, of making himself a substantial profit by entering into the management. I do not

Exhibit 14-3—Continued

believe it would be possible to sell the stock to investors in this area, because the company's record does not justify such an offering.

We are of the opinion that the stock of the Burke Candy Company, based largely on the previous comments, is not worth over $12 per share.

I am sure that you will appreciate that the comments made above are not in any way a reflection on the management of the company, but are made from the point of view of an outsider looking at the figures and the company's course of business in an effort to arrive at an impartial valuation of the stock.

Very truly yours,
THE MIDWESTERN COMPANY
(Signed) JOHN K. GRIMES, *Vice-President*

an entire city block in the center of an industrial area. Advanced construction ideas had been incorporated in the construction of the main building in 1909, and the building was considered in excellent condition and entirely adequate for the needs of the company. With the land it stood on, the annex building—carried in the balance sheet at $182,914 (net of the reserve for depreciation)—was also of concrete construction and of multipurpose type. This building had housed certain operations of the company discontinued in 1938. At that time, the building was leased to a bakery company that was expanding its operations. When the 10-year lease expired in 1948, a shortage of factory buildings in the area existed, and the company was able to lease the 84,000-square-foot building for one year at 55 cents a square foot, or $46,200. The lessee assumed all costs of the building except property taxes, which were about $10,000 a year. In September, 1949, it was expected that a 5-year lease would be signed at about 45 cents a square foot per annum, or $37,800 before taxes.

The multistory building in which the operations of the company were conducted provided a total floor area of 133,400 square feet. Current construction costs of similar type buildings were approximately $8.00 a square foot. The management believed that with an unhurried sale of the main building, they could realize approximately $3.50 a square foot, or approximately $466,900, for the building. The newer annex building was thought to have a normal resale value of about $4.50 a square foot.

The equipment of the company was considered fairly efficient, although much of it had been in use for many years. It was believed that depreciation rates had been appropriate, so that balance sheet values represented reasonable values from accounting point of view.

When Mr. Martin raised the question of realizable values in the event the company was liquidated, the officials of the company appeared reluctant to discuss the subject. They commented that many of the 175 employees of the company had been with the concern for many years, that they had faith in the business, and that management had no intention of terminating the business. Finally, they did agree to discuss the value in liquidation of each major asset. It was believed that the net value of receivables could be collected completely, with perhaps a 10 percent excess of collections over the amount shown net of the unusually large reserve. The liquidating value of the inventory was regarded as hinging on the speed of liquidation. It was felt that in an unhurried liquidation the inventory could be completely worked off at between 60 and 80 percent of its book value. Much of the value of prepaid expenses would be lost in liquidation; so that an estimate of 25 percent was given as the realizable value. The value of the fixed assets in liquidation was regarded as particularly problematical. If a willing buyer were available, as indicated above, the two buildings probably could be sold at approximately $3.50 and $4.50 per square foot. If no buyer were anxious to have the space for immediate use, distress sale could be expected to attract buyers only at a very much lower price. Currently, the market for industrial real estate in the area was active, and it was thought that a willing buyer could be found within a few months.

The value of the equipment in liquidation was highly uncertain. It was thought of most value to a candy manufacturer who would take over the entire plant. In 1947, the company had received and rejected informal inquiries from two large manufacturers regarding the possibility of sale of the company to them for operation as a branch plant. No inquiries had been received since that time. Much of the equipment would be next to valueless in a hurried liquidation, and the total proceeds from equipment in such circumstances would probably be no more than 30 percent of the book value.

15. ADCOLE CORPORATION*
Evaluating the Financial Routes Open
to a Small Manufacturing Enterprise

Adcole Corporation was established in 1957, with capital of $25,000 and a staff of seven people, to design and assemble technically advanced electronic equipment and systems. From the time of its establishment to the fall of 1961, $24,000 in contributed capital and 20 more employees had been added. For the fiscal year ending in June of 1961, sales had been $360,000, yielding profits of $7,000. Total assets had grown to $180,000 and net worth to $65,000. During this period, Adcole's devices had been on about thirty of the country's space shots, and the firm had developed an excellent reputation for its ability to design and assemble highly complex electronic circuitry for space-age applications.

Although Adcole's financial condition in the fall of 1961 was quite comfortable in terms of present sales, its management team felt that additional contributed capital would be needed if the firm was to grow as planned. Therefore, in October of 1961, these men drew up a descriptive document, "A Profile of Adcole Corporation." The profile was given to a number of individuals connected with the financial community who expressed interest in the company, but no active moves were made to begin serious negotiations in any direction. By January, 1962, the officers of Adcole Corporation had received comments on their profile from a wide variety of financial sources. They felt that it was now time to begin actively seeking additional funds and wondered which of the many routes open to them should be chosen for concentrated effort.

The Company

Background on the company is given in "A Profile of Adcole Corporation," reproduced as Appendix 15–A. In January, 1962, Mr. Cole, president of Adcole Corporation, estimated that sales and profits

---

were running quite close to the levels projected in the pro forma statements and that nothing had happened in the prior six months to make him question the forecasts presented in the profile.

The Profile

In the fall of 1961, the management team of Adcole Corporation realized that in many ways their company was moving into phase two of its development. As they stated in the profile, they knew that undertaking proprietary research and development activities, along with the increases in working capital and fixed assets required by any growing firm, would create a cash need in excess of the amount which could be expected to be generated internally. They felt that, although the funds then available would be adequate for some time, it would be well to begin laying the groundwork for a trip to the money markets. Adcole had never experienced a serious cash bind, and its officers did not want it to do so in the future. As the first move in the preparation process, they wrote the profile reproduced as Appendix 15–A.

This document was intended to provide a description of the company—its people and products, its potential, and its needs—complete enough so that a prospective investor or underwriter could, on reading it, make an intelligent decision as to whether he wished to conduct a more thorough analysis of the company. Mr. Cole knew that various investors had different ideas as to what sort of situation constituted an attractive deal. He felt that investors, on reading the profile, should be able to make the decision as to whether or not this general situation might be attractive. If it clearly would not be, he did not want them to have to spend more of their own and the company's time finding this out.

The amount of additional paid-in capital mentioned in the profile and used in its pro forma statements was $250,000. Adcole's officers recognized that the company did not actually require the full amount immediately, and Mr. Cole stated that, in fact, they had had to stretch a bit to find immediate uses for it in the pro forma financial statements of the profile. However, when the profile was prepared they were considering the possibility of an underwritten public issue to be made under Regulation A of the Securities Act of 1933, and they knew that any smaller amount would be extremely difficult to sell. Furthermore, the full $250,000 would soon be needed if the company grew at the planned rate.

Which Financial Route?

Mr. Cole stated that the company was not firmly committed to this amount of capital nor to any specific method of getting it. Although the officers of Adcole Corporation wished to gain public ownership for their company eventually, they felt that they should consider every reasonable source of funds for their immediate needs in order to proceed along the financial route which would be in the company's best long-term interests. The three main routes they saw open were: (1) the public offering, (2) the private placement, and (3) merger with another company. Although public offerings and mergers were fairly limited routes, a private placement could be made to anyone from the professionals, such as SBIC's and venture capital firms, to the casual investor who might only rarely speculate on a situation such as this.

In order to evaluate these possibilities, Adcole made available its profile to a number of people interested in the firm. These included friends and acquaintances connected with the financial world, prospective investors who approached the firm directly, and various others who had some knowledge of the money markets. It was hoped that these men's comments would provide the Adcole management team with enough background to make an intelligent decision as to which financial route to follow.

Although the Adcole management team was open to any reasonable suggestion regarding capital sources, its members did have several specific thoughts in mind as they approached this decision. These were based on their experience both with Adcole and in their previous positions. They wished to place their stock in "investors' hands." If a public issue were made, they did not want the wide fluctuations in the stock price that seemed to come when traders became active in any security. They felt that such gyrations would have an unfavorable influence on both Adcole's suppliers and customers. They would like to see a slow, steady rise in their stock if the firm went public.

Furthermore, they stated, the need to find true investors was as great with a private placement as with a public issue. Private individuals who would not be prepared to stand by the company through rough times could be a serious problem, as could people who would try to run the company, even though they were not familiar with the technology involved or the details of the operating problems. Mr. Cole also saw a danger in placing securities in the hands of people who would take sporadic interest in the company. Such people, he said, might be off in Europe when you want some advice or may have insufficient knowledge of the company's operation to exercise intelligent judgment in times of crisis. Finally, the officers of Adcole felt that on the basis of their projections a fair price for the present stock would be $100 per share, or about one-third of the equity for $250,000. However, they knew they should consider more than the immediate price per share in evaluating the various possibilities open to them.

During the fall of 1961, the members of Adcole's management team had received comments from men connected with many of the sources of funds listed previously. These comments included both general thoughts about the advantages and disadvantages of various financial routes for Adcole and rough estimates of the financial packages which their sources might be willing to offer. These comments are given separately in subsequent cases.

In mid-January they decided that it was time to make a decision regarding Adcole's financial future. They wanted to be able to conduct negotiations in an orderly fashion without being under the pressure of a severe cash shortage (which could develop if they delayed too long). They felt that they should consider the advantages and disadvantages of each possible financial route and decide which one they should actively seek to follow.

APPENDIX 15–A
A Profile * of Adcole Corporation
October 15, 1961

History

Adcole Corporation commenced operations during July, 1957 with capital of $25,000 and a staff of five engineers and two other employees. Since the start, $24,000 in capital, ten engineers and ten other employees have been added. For the year ending June 30, 1958, sales amounted to $55,000 with about a $20,000 loss; second year sales were $144,000 with an $11,000 profit; third year sales were $187,000 with a $13,000 profit; fourth year sales were $360,000 with a $7,000 profit.

Staff

The most important asset of Adcole Corporation is its technical staff. A. D. Cole, president, Chester G. Kuczun, Dr. Maurice A. Meyer, vice presidents, and Dr. Robert M. Fano, consultant, are electronic engineers with many years of responsible engineering experience and high professional standing. Before starting the new company, three of these men were employed by Laboratory for Electronics, Inc. Mr. Cole was a founder of that company and was for ten years vice president in charge of engineering and production. Mr. Kuczun was manager of the section which developed instruments for commercial sale. Dr. Meyer was chief engineer and the developer of a Doppler navigator system for aircraft which led to multimillion dollar contracts. Dr. Fano is Professor of Electrical Engineering at M.I.T. Since early 1958, Mr. Cole has served as a member of the Weapons Systems Evaluation Group in the Office of the Secretary of Defense.

Since the inception of company activities, a number of highly competent engineers have been added to the staff. Résumés of the engineers are included in the appendix. The present personnel complement is:

---

* The profile has been reproduced in its entirety except for résumés. Three have been included as examples, but eight have been omitted to save space.

Engineers 15
Technicians 6
Draftsmen 3
Administrative 2
Sales 1

       Total 27

Long-Term Plans

The management of a new company starting business in the electronics field has two main choices; to attempt to sell services or to attempt to sell products. An organization selling services requires little initial capital and incurs relatively small risk; but profit in terms of percentage of sales is small. An organization starting with the goal of early sales of proprietary products requires relatively large capital to finance product development, tooling, sales promotion, etc., and incurs a relatively large risk; but the profit may be quite significantly larger.

In the long run, a company must have substantial sales of proprietary products to provide an attractive margin of profit and stability for its business activities. Although there are eminently successful companies dealing almost exclusively in services such as Stone and Webster and Arthur D. Little, they are few in number. The management of this company proposes to achieve the long-term objective of a sizable business in proprietary products by engaging first in the sale of services. The following paragraphs will explain this in some detail.

Phase 1

In this first phase engineering work is sought on a contract basis. Almost any type of work may be acceptable provided it is honest and can be done at a profit. To obtain such work the main need is for a highly competent technical staff. Every effort is made to build a good reputation and establish the basis for a continuing flow of work from the government and other sources. As early as practicable in this phase some areas of the electronic field should be selected for concentration. The surest way to continue to get work is to develop the capacity for doing something that is in reasonable demand better than most anybody else. For a small company this can be achieved only by some specialization.

Phase 2

After a competent organization of at least modest size has been established and is selling its services on a profitable basis, attention should be given to the development of proprietary products. Generally at this point the engineering work for others will have developed or partially developed some items that can be sold. These may have a limited market but may be attractive, nevertheless, because little or no development cost is required. The income from the business will begin to support a modest effort on new product development. Much of this kind of activity constitutes a reimbursable cost on government contracts. Management should be on the alert for new product opportunities. The best climate for originating these ideas is within a competent organization busy on engineering work. At some time in this phase, provided the capital is available, it may become desirable to expand the product development activity beyond that supportable from current income. Such an investment may well be desirable provided the new product prospects indicate adequate potential; however, at no time should such an investment be so large as to represent a crippling blow to success should the prospects fail to materialize in part or in full. Fundamental to this method of operation is the theory that an active, competent engineering organization will inevitably generate fine new products. Since successful new products will simply move the company from a position that is good to one that is better, there is no justification for taking large risks.

Phase 3

This phase is reached when the company is doing a large volume of profitable business with 50 percent or more in proprietary products. Income from the operation must provide enough margin to provide for expending five to ten percent of the gross on research and development. Management must maintain a high order of technical ability in the staff, keep the company abreast of the advancing technology, and remain alert to new opportunities.

In practice there is no clean-cut line of demarcation between the three phases set forth above. Adcole Corporation has achieved a degree of success in the first phase and is to some extent into phase two. At this time it is still desirable to increase the volume of contract work and to enlarge the technical staff. Particularly desirable is the addition to the staff of young men who have outstanding competence in some of the areas of recent development in electronics. Substantial effort is being devoted to these ends.

Subsequent sections of this document will cover some examples of proprietary products which are of the type described as early activities of phase two. Several of these have promise of providing a sound base for further progress in product development.

Accomplishments and Future Prospects

The company's operations logically fall into several product lines. Annual sales and profit forecasts for these product lines are given in the Appendix, and are summarized below:

| (Thousands of dollars) | | | | | | |
| | 1961 | | 1962 | | 1966 | |
Present Line	Sales	Profit*	Sales	Profit*	Sales	Profit*
Space instrumentation .	280	16	405	31	1,405	114
Test equipment	80	10	180	22	600	85
New product lines	—	(15)	110	5	400	25
Total above	360	11	695	58	2,415	224

* Income from operations before Federal Income Taxes.

A discussion of each of these product lines is given below.

Space Instrumentation

The company has devoted a major portion of its effort since its founding to designing and building highly specialized instrumentation for rocket and satellite space probes. To date this work has been primarily for the U.S. Air Force and has been unusually successful. Most of this instrumentation has been tailor-made for this particular experiment and involves knowledge of miniaturization and space environments as well as a broad background in electronic circuit design which is not generally found in other companies particularly of size comparable to Adcole Corporation.

The company's reputation of experience and success in this field is rapidly spreading to other government agencies concerned with the investigation of space. New contracts have recently been received from different groups within the Air Force and inquiries have been received from the Naval Research Laboratory, Smithsonian Astrophysical Observatory, the National Aeronautics and Space Administration and other organizations. The company is currently bidding for the development of a special purpose radar to indicate distance and velocity on approaching the moon with two of the five companies who are seeking the prime contract on the Apollo moon shot program. This work alone would be well in excess of a million dollars. McGraw-Hill forecasts over 150 percent increase in expenditures for space electronics in the next four years and Adcole Corporation confidently expects to obtain an increasing share of this rapidly expanding business.

Most of the work to date has been on research and development type contracts on a cost-plus-fixed-fee basis. This type of contract does not provide a high profit margin but can lead to the development of proprietary products which can be sold on a fixed-price basis with considerably higher profit. The company has already developed the following proprietary products which it expects to represent an increasing percentage of the sales in this product line in future years with a corresponding increase in profit margin.

Radiation potential analyzer—A new type of sensing device for measuring solar radiation and ion and electron distributions in space, knowledge of which is used to determine the nature of the environment for space vehicles, to further define the forces governing weather and communications, and for additional applications which are classified.

Solar aspect system—Optical-electronic devices for use in rockets and satellites to measure the orientation of the vehicle carrying them with respect to the sun. Many rocket and satellite experiments require such a device.

Electronic commutators—A device used in rockets and satellites to sequentially switch a number of outputs to the radio transmitter in the vehicle thereby greatly reducing the number of radio channels required for relaying information to a ground station.

Test Equipment

Electronic test equipment may be roughly divided into two groups: special purpose, which is designed for a specific application and is frequently quite complex and sold to relatively few companies; and general purpose, such as oscilloscopes, voltmeters, etc., which is sold to a much broader market, although individual units are usually much less expensive.

Adcole Corporation has been involved only with special purpose test equipment up to the present time and has actively pursued this business for only a little over a year. Most of the test equipment which has been built by the company has been used for testing gyroscopes used in inertial guidance systems of intermediate range and intercontinental ballistic missiles. Specifically, most of the sales have been of equipment called a Digital Data Recording System which serves to measure the drift or error of the gyro and present a printed or punched-tape record of this drift. Adcole is the only manufacturer of this equipment in the country. Users of this equipment include M.I.T. Instrumentation Laboratory, Bendix Aviation, A. C. Spark Plug, Lockheed Aircraft, U.S. Air Force, United Aircraft, and Minneapolis-Honeywell.

Digital data recording systems represent a relatively small portion of the electronic equipment used in testing gyros. The company has very recently entered the larger market with encouraging results. Close contact is maintained with the M.I.T. Instrumentation Laboratory (located across the street), the leading center in the country for the

development of advanced gyros and testing techniques. This association is invaluable in the inertial field.

The future outlook for electronic gyro test equipment is very promising. An increasing number of guided missiles are using interial guidance systems. These include the Atlas, Minuteman, Titan, Polaris,
Jupiter and Thor missiles. As the state of the art of gyro performance
is advanced, testing requires not only a greater amount but also more
complex electronic test equipment.

The company has made various other types of special test equipment which includes a tracking system simulator. The first unit was
sold to Radio Corporation of America. This unit is used in the laboratory to provide artificial stars with suitable motion to test star
tracking and navigation systems which play an important role in missiles, space ships, and airplanes. This is typical of the type of special
test equipment which Adcole is well qualified to build.

The company has a number of ideas, and has done some preliminary research work, on several general purpose laboratory instruments. These include a digital impedance meter, a programmable signal generator, and a digital precision phase shifter. A definite need
exists for all of these instruments and the company has the technical
ability to develop them. However, a broader capital structure is required before an undertaking of this scope can be actively pursued.
A substantial increase in manufacturing facilities and marketing organization will ultimately be required. No sales are forecast for general purpose instruments until 1964 and only a very modest amount
for 1966.

Profit margins on test equipment are substantially higher than on
research and development contracts. Digital Data Recording Systems
have profit margins from 20 to 30 percent. Lower margins in 1961
reflect a portion of the initial development costs which have now
been largely recovered. Other special purpose test equipment generally have slightly lower profit margins because there is more competi-
tition. General purpose test equipment, however, frequently has margins in excess of 30 percent which reflects the greater risk involved.

New Product Lines

A significant amount of work has been spent on new product lines
which has not resulted in any sales to date. By far the greatest amount
of work has been in the area of medical electronics. Most of this
has been on several types of electronic heart pacers. One type may

be used for emergency treatment of cardiac arrest in lieu of heart massage. This consists of an external unit a little larger than a pack of cigarettes which is connected to two electrodes in the form of hypodermic needles which are inserted through the chest wall into the heart. This is a simple procedure which can be performed by any doctor. Several units of this type have been used successfully on a number of occasions at the Children's Hospital and another hospital in Boston for the past year.

Another type of heart pacer has been developed. This type is completely implanted in the patient and is used in those cases where the patient has permanent heart block or Stokes-Adams disease. With this disease, the person has attacks where the heart fails to receive a signal to provide an adequate pulse rate. The implantable pulser is about the size of a book of matches, contains a battery which will last approximately five years, and has a number of unique features. It has been accepted by the Children's Hospital for implanting in human patients.

The company is currently negotiating with a leading instrument company for the sale of rights to manufacture and market these heart pacers. These units would complement their existing line of medical electronics and the company is quite interested in them.

A number of members of the company's technical staff have extensive background in various types of radar which, in certain areas, is probably unequalled by any other company in this country. The company currently has a contract for $70,000 with Raytheon Company for certain equipment used in a radar application. A proposal has been submitted to the Marine Corps and other agencies for a unique radar landing system for aircraft which has generated quite a bit of interest. A variation on the airplane Doppler radar navigation system, with which Adcole Corporation personnel have extensive experience is being developed for boats. The feasibility of an underwater Doppler navigation system has been established. When a complete working unit is developed, the company plans to sell the invention to a company with a line of marine electronics.

Sales Staff

The problem of effectively reaching the prospective customers with the necessarily limited resources available to do so is a major challenge to most small electronic companies. A good beginning has been made with the recent addition of Harry Lowell, an experienced marketing engineer, to the staff. Even more recently, the sales effort has been augmented by retaining the services of a group of sales representatives, Continental Consultants, Inc. This organization maintains a staff of sales engineers and offices in Washington, Philadelphia, Ft. Monmouth, N.J., Dayton, Ohio, Rome, New York, Los Angeles, and Boston. They are expected to be of considerable help in obtaining new business, especially government research and development work.

Financing

Although the company is able to comfortably sustain its present level of operations, the lack of financial resources of greater magnitude does impose certain undesirable limitations. Principal limitation is the fact that any new steps or additions must be limited to modest ones that will provide a return in a short period of time. In order to make rapid progress the company must increase both its capabilities and its sales efforts. A rapid increase in these, although highly desirable in the long run, would require an investment which would take some time to recover or at least such a risk would be involved. Development and introduction to the market of new products also requires an investment and an extended period for recovery.

The company would like to add approximately $250,000 to its capital. The pro forma balance sheet shown in the Appendix gives the projected use of this capital. In the fiscal year ending June 30, 1962, fixed assets are increased by $26,000 which will be required for high altitude simulation and testing equipment, more electronic laboratory equipment, and for additional machine and sheet metal tools. Working capital is increased by $194,000 of which $33,000 is expected to be obtained from retained earnings. Approximately $63,000 is planned for new product development in the fiscal year ending June 30, 1962. This amount is required for the development of additional gyro test equipment, completion of the development work on heart pacers, and continuation of research on other new products.

Physical Facilities

The company rents 6,000 square feet of office and laboratory space at an annual cost of $7,800. About 1,500 square feet of this is rented to Massachusetts Institute of Technology, Instrumentation Laboratory for $3,900 per year. This space will be adequate for an increase of perhaps 50 percent in size of the staff. When this area becomes inadequate, new rental space will be sought in the same general area. No purchase of real estate is contemplated.

The laboratory is well equipped with small tools and electronic equipment. The company owns about $25,000 worth of laboratory and office equipment.

Present Capital Structure

The company has 10,000 shares of common stock authorized at no par value. Of these, 6,321 shares have been issued. Paid in capital is $49,105.

A. D. Cole	4,950 shares
Chester G. Kuczun	445 shares
Mrs. Eva McGee	401 shares
Robert M. Fano	250 shares
Harry N. Lowell	25 shares
Maurice A. Meyer	250 shares
Total	6,321 shares

Board of Directors

The Directors of the Corporation are A. D. Cole, Chester G. Kuczun, Robert S. Hills, Robert Fano, and Maurice A. Meyer. A. D. Cole is President and Treasurer and Mrs. Winifred Lee is Clerk.

Forecasts

Various forecasts or pro formas have been prepared. Details are contained in the following material. Factors of major significances are presented in graphical form.

CONDENSED BALANCE SHEET AT 6/30/61 AND PRO FORMA THROUGH 6/30/66
(000 omitted)

	Year End 6/30/61	Year End 6/30/62	Year End 6/30/63	Year End 6/30/64	Year End 6/30/65	Yea 6/.
ASSETS						
Current Assets:						
Cash (1)	15	30	32	38	44	
Accounts receivable (2)	67	120	190	270	300	
Inventory (3)	56	130	240	300	400	
Prepaid expenses...........	3	—	—	—	—	
Total Current Assets	141	280	462	608	744	
Life Insurance—Cash Value....	3	3	4	5	6	
Fixed Assets (4)..............	24	50	70	80	90	
Product Development Costs (5)..	12	75	75	75	75	
Total	180	408	611	768	915	1
LIABILITIES AND NET WORTH						
Current Liabilities:						
Notes payable (6)	11	—	130	185	210	
Accounts payable (7)	66	35	55	80	100	
Accrued liabilities (8)	24	25	30	35	45	
Advanced payment........	14	—	—	—	—	
Total Current Liabilities ..	115	60	215	300	355	
Net Worth:						
Capital stock	49	299	299	299	299	
Earned surplus	16	49	97	169	261	
	65	348	396	468	560	
Total	180	408	611	768	915	1

(1) Cash is arbitrarily kept relatively low. The amounts shown are adequate since enough collateral exists for im short-term borrowing.

(2) This figure is based on an average of receivables of nearly two months. This conservative projection includes all for hold-backs on government contracts.

(3) This includes parts, work in process, and finished goods. The increase in inventory as a percent of sales refle increased sales of proprietary items which must be kept in stock.

(4) This figure covers laboratory equipment, machine tools, and office and laboratory furniture. Using the depre allowance to buy new equipment will make it adequate. No purchase of real estate is contemplated.

(5) In general, product development costs for a new product line are capitalized and charged off against sales in years while costs of improving existing products are expensed in the year they occur. The increase in the fiscal year 6/30/62 is based on the need to conclude research on several promising new product developments quickly. In suc years new product developments are capitalized at a rate equal to the write-off of prior development costs.

(6) This is short-term borrowing against receivables from a bank. Excess collateral is available since banks curren 80 percent of receivables.

(7) Payable within 45 days of billing.

(8) Includes employee income tax withheld, accrued payroll, accrued vacation, and other accrued taxes.

SALES AND PROFIT FORECAST—1961–1966

	1961		1962		1963	
	Sales	Profit	Sales	Profit	Sales	Profit
Space instrumentation	280	16	405	31	645	48
Test equipment	80	10	180	22	310	31
New product lines	—	(15)	110	5	170	10
Total sales and profit before taxes	360	11	695	58	1,125	89
Federal income tax		4		25		41
Net income		7		33		48

	1964		1965		1966	
	Sales	Profit	Sales	Profit	Sales	Profit
Space instrumentation	995	75	1,225	93	1,405	114
Test equipment	400	50	520	67	600	85
New product lines	230	13	290	19	400	25
Total sales and profit before taxes	1,625	138	2,035	179	2,415	224
Federal income tax		66		87		111
Net income		72		92		113

ADCOLE CORPORATION

SUMMARY OF OPERATIONS FOR THE FOUR YEARS
May 20, 1957 (Date of Incorporation) to June, 1961

	For the Fiscal Year Ending June 30			
	1958	1959	1960	1961
Gross income	$55,336	$143,000	$187,466	$359,719
Costs and expenses	76,763	132,503	172,573	352,703
Income from operations	($21,427)	$ 11,397	$ 14,893	$ 7,016
Other income, net	1,174	3,076	3,927	4,077
Net income (loss) before Federal income taxes	($20,253)	$ 14,473	$ 18,820	$ 11,093
Federal income taxes applicable to above income	—	3,700	6,000	3,600
Net income (loss) before special credit ...	($20,253)	$ 10,773	$ 12,820	$ 7,493
Special Credit—Federal income tax reduction from carry-forward of 1958 operating loss	—	3,700	1,500	—
Net income (loss) including the Federal income tax reduction from carry-forward of 1958 operating loss	($20,253)	$ 14,473	$ 14,320	$ 7,493

ADCOLE CORPORATION

Balance Sheet—June 30, 1961

ASSETS

Current Assets:

Cash		$ 14,791
Accounts receivable		67,434
Unbilled expenditures and accrued fees on cost reimbursement contracts		52,110
Costs incurred on fixed-price contracts plus estimated profits thereon		4,064
Prepaid expenses		2,745
Total Current Assets		$141,144

Cash Surrender Value of Officer's Life Insurance (face amount $100,000)		3,064
Equipment, at cost:		
Laboratory equipment and tools	$21,330	
Office furniture and equipment	5,474	
Leasehold improvements	495	
	$27,299	
Less—Accumulated depreciation	3,149	24,150
Product development costs		11,448
		$179,806

LIABILITIES

Current Liabilities:

Unsecured note payable in equal monthly installments to April, 1964 (bank loan)		$ 10,720
Accounts payable		65,796
Advances received on contract in progress		14,000
Accrued Liabilities:		
Payroll and vacation pay		13,524
Taxes, other than Federal income tax		2,528
Federal income tax		8,100
Total Current Liabilities		$114,668

Stockholders' Investment:		
Common Stock, no par value		
Authorized—10,000 shares		
Issued and outstanding—6,321 shares	$49,105	
Retained Earnings	16,033	65,138
		$179,806

ADCOLE CORPORATION

Profit and Loss Statement
Fiscal Year Ending June 30, 1961

Gross income	$359,719.00
Costs and expenses	352,703.00
Income from operations	$ 7,016.00
Other income, net	4,077.00
Net income (loss) before Federal income taxes	$ 11,093.00
Federal income taxes applicable to above income	3,600.00
Net income (loss) before special credit	$ 7,493.00
Special credit—Federal income tax reduction from carry-forward of 1958 operating loss	—
Net income (loss) including the Federal income tax reduction from carry-forward of 1958 operating loss	$ 7,493.00

PER SHARE BOOK VALUE—ADCOLE CORP.

Pro Forma

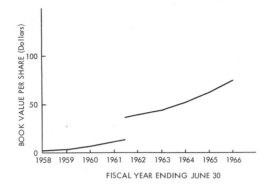

NET WORTH—ADCOLE CORP.

Pro Forma

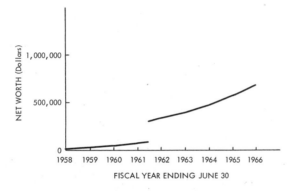

PER SHARE EARNINGS—ADCOLE CORP.

Pro Forma

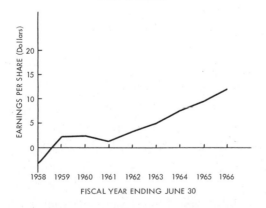

NET PROFIT—ADCOLE CORP.

PRO FORMA

FISCAL YEAR ENDING JUNE 30

GROSS BUSINESS—ADCOLE CORP.

PRO FORMA

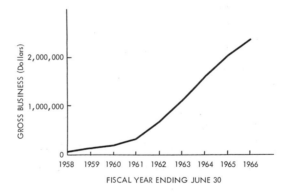

FISCAL YEAR ENDING JUNE 30

Addision D. Cole—President and Treasurer

Personal Data:
    Birth Date: 1–29–1919
    Address: 22 Robinhood Road
                    Natick, Massachusetts

Education:
    B.S. in Electrical Engineering, 1941, University of Washington, Seattle,
    Washington.

Experience:
    1941–1942   Bonneville Power Administration, Portland, Oregon

1942–1945	Mass. Institute of Technology Radiation Laboratory

Was employed as a development engineer. Later became project engineer on various airborne radars. Served a period of a year as a consultant to the National Defense Research Committee. Spent most of the period in England as an advisor to top officials in the Air Ministry of Aircraft Production.

1945–1946	Cole, Holdam and McGrath

This was a consulting firm. Little activity, as this was shortly abandoned to start an electronics company.

1946–1957	Laboratory for Electronics, Inc.

Was one of the founders of the company with the position of vice president. Originally was in charge of engineering and active in engineering sales. Later was in charge of production as well. During the ten years the company grew from nothing to a total force of 800 doing about $7,000,000 annually. A very good engineering reputation was achieved, particularly in the fields of radar, moving target indicators, ultrasonic delay lines, and Doppler navigators.

1957—Present	Adcole Corporation

Consultant Weapons System Evaluation Group, Washington, D.C.

Chester G. Kuczun—Vice President and Chief Engineer

Personal Data:
Birth Date:	2–20–1920
Address:	Sunrise Road
	Boxford, Massachusetts

Education:
B.S. in Electrical Engineering, 1942, Massachusetts Institute of Technology.

Experience:
1942–1945	Air Force: Florida, Australia, New Guinea

Commanding Officer of early warning radar platoon. Three years overseas.

1945–1946	Watson Labs., Ft. Monmouth, N.J.

Officer in charge of IFF Branch. Navigation Laboratory— responsible for the development of all Air Force Ground IFF equipments.

1946–1947   Belmont Radio Corporation, Chicago, Illinois
Assisted in the design of the company's first television receiver. Worked on K-band RF systems and test equipment for airborne radar systems.

1946–1957   Laboratory for Electronics, Inc.
Project engineer in charge of a team of engineers, designers, draftsmen, and technicians. Responsible for the design and development of equipment, the preparation of manufacturing information, production engineering, and production liaison. Had considerable experience with sales, contract administration, customer relations, and field engineering.
Responsible for the following types of equipment:
Laboratory Instruments
Electronic Data Processing Machines
Various radar equipments

1957–Present   Adcole Corporation

Maurice A. Meyer—Vice President

Personal Data:
Birth Date: 3–15–1918
Address: 19 Sherwood Road
Natick, Massachusetts

Education:
B.S. in Electrical Engineering, 1939, Massachusetts Institute of Technology. M.S. in Applied Mathematics, 1947, Massachusetts Institute of Technology. Ph.D. in Engineering Science and Applied Physics, 1952, Harvard University.

Experience:
1939–1940   Fada Radio Company—junior engineer

1940–1942   Aircraft Radio Laboratory, Wright Field, Dayton, Ohio
Did development on blind landing systems. Set up first Microwave ILS Experimental System.

1942–1946   U.S. Signal Corps
Participated in airborne radar operation and as Officer in Charge of ground radar reporting stations. In 1945 assigned as army representative to the Combined Research Group at the Naval Research Laboratory and participated in the development of the Mark V IFF system.

1947–1960   Laboratory for Electronics, Inc.
Served first as project manager on the development of special receiver and computing circuitry for Height Find-

ing Radar. Appointed Associate Chief Engineer in 1952, Director of Engineering in 1955, and Director of Advanced Development in 1959. Is one of the foremost authorities in the country in the field of Doppler radar. Responsible for the development of the following equipment:

    Helicopter Navigation Systems

    Doppler Navigation System for P–105 Fighter Aircraft

1960–Present   Adcole Corporation

16. HANLEY, HOLMES*
AND COMPANY
Evaluating a Private Placement through
a Brokerage House

Adcole Corporation's financial condition in the fall of 1961 was quite comfortable in terms of present sales but its management team felt that additional contributed capital would be necessary if the firm was to follow its planned pattern of growth. Therefore, Adcole's officers had prepared a descriptive note on their company and had circulated it among various men connected with the financial community. From the comments of these men, they planned to determine which financial route should be followed by Adcole. One of the sets of comments they had received was that of Anthony Deets, research director of the Boston office of a nationwide brokerage firm, Hanley, Holmes and Company.[1]

Background—Mr. Deets

Mr. Deets' firm was a relatively large and respected brokerage firm which had offices in most major cities and partners on the important securities exchanges. Its business was primarily that of a broker and adviser for its clients; however, the firm did occasionally attempt to place an issue privately. These private issues usually consisted of securities of small "growth companies." They were generally placed with one or a few individuals who, in addition to their activities in widely traded securities, occasionally invested in more speculative small situations such as Adcole.

Mr. Deets, as Hanley, Holmes' research director, was often the man who found and evaluated these small situations. He knew most of the men among the firm's clients who were looking for such opportunities and often made the choice of the man or men to whom a given attractive situation should be presented. Mr. Deets usually made the

---

[1] General background material on the company and its need for additional capital is given in Case 15, Adcole Corporation. Included as an appendix to that case is the descriptive note, "A Profile of Adcole Corporation," which served as the context within which Mr. Deets made his comments.

necessary introductions and often assisted to a limited extent in the negotiations. When appropriate, Hanley, Holmes received a portion of the securities involved as a finder's fee, and often Mr. Deets or another member of the firm continued to advise the small company on financial matters after the placement. Mr. Deets also performed or directed various research and analysis activities in connection with the securities of large companies, and he acted as customers' man on a small number of clients' accounts.

General Comments

Mr. Deets felt that Adcole's situation at this time was such that a private placement would be more suitable for the company than a public offering. He stated that the price per share which Adcole could get would probably be significantly higher in a public offering than in a private placement. However, he felt that other factors made the public sale a less desirable financial route for the company at this time. Mr. Deets suggested that Adcole consider placement with either a group of private investors or a good SBIC. The following paragraphs present a summary of the reasons he gave for this recommendation.

Adcole has only a four-year life. Its profits history, although relatively consistent, has been slight. It lacks the sort of long, solid record that would make it attractive to a good, established underwriting house. Furthermore, the proposed size of the issue is so small that traditional commission rates would not begin to pay for a larger underwriting firm's costs of analyzing, preparing, and placing the issue. Therefore, for a public offering Adcole would probably have to go to a small new firm willing to accept issues of Regulation A size in order to help get itself established.

Although most of these new small Reg. A houses are every bit as honest as the larger underwriting firms, there are several potential disadvantages to a company in becoming associated with one. Because the house is new, its personnel often lack experience in analyzing and pricing new issues. The house usually has not had time to develop a good marketing organization or a large following of investor clients. Furthermore, the small new firm often lacks sufficient contacts in the financial community and abilities in the public information area to enable it to generate, among other investment houses, a significant interest in a new issue. All these factors tend to increase the chances that the new issue will go badly, i.e., suffer a price decline shortly after the date of issue.

Other potential dangers stemming from these factors lie in the type of stockholders likely to be gained by the company. Most new small underwriting houses lack the large, stable group of customers which larger ones have. This fact means that the small firm will have much less control over the type of stockholders the company gets when it goes public. The small house may be unable to achieve a satisfactory regional distribution. It also may place a disproportionately large number of the offered securities in the hands of traders.

If the price of a new issue gets a fast run-up in the aftermarket before the company's sales or earnings justify the high price, there is apt to be a subsequent harsh price decline from the top. If a large number of shares are traded at or near the top, the new shareholders may well prove to be a disgruntled lot at subsequent stockholders' meetings.

If an issue goes badly, it will be proportionately more difficult for the company to raise money in the public markets in the future. The company's public image is at stake in any offering, and particularly so when it goes with a new underwriting house. The possibility that the new small firm may not grow as rapidly as the company which it takes public may put the officers of the company in a difficult position by forcing them to seek another underwriter for subsequent issues. Such a position might be particularly disadvantageous if the public image created by the prior issue was less than desirable.

With prospects for future financing as well as present stockholder relations being so strongly tied to the market performance of the new issue, many managers of smaller companies fall into the trap of beginning to pay more attention to the price of their stock than to the operations of their company. Again, this danger is particularly strong when there is no real substance in the company's records to support an artificially high market price.

Finally, there is an obvious danger to the company's reputation if the new small underwriting firm is a bucket shop [2] or is obviously manipulating the market price to realize a profit on options or warrants it may have acquired.

If one of the reasons for going public is to gain a real market for its securities, the company may be deluding itself in thinking that this can be accomplished by a Regulation A-sized issue. An issue of $250,000 worth of securities priced at $5.00 per share represents only 50,000 shares. If each new stockholder made a $250 investment (only 50 shares), there would be only 1,000 stockholders. The market in a case such as this would be quite thin—probably inactive and/or highly volatile. This would make it very difficult for the underwriter to get any brokerage house to make a market [3] in the security, and it would mean that, even though the com-

---

[2] Originally, the term bucket shop was used to refer to an operator who accepted a client's money without actually executing the client's order. The bucket shop gambled that the client would be wrong, thereby allowing it to buy (or sell) more advantageously and keep the difference as profit. This operation is now illegal and almost extinct. Today, many people use the term bucket shop to refer to small underwriting firms of questionable repute which tend to market new issues on the basis of glamour or artificial puffing rather than solid earnings or profit records.

[3] Whenever a securities dealer, investment banker, or syndicate manager names a price at which he will buy a given security, and another price at which he will sell it, he is thereby making a market in that security. The fact that a market for an unlisted or over-the-counter security is maintained by one or several firms provides liquidity to the investor in that security. The value in having a number of houses making a market

pany was "public," the real value in terms of preparing the market for a larger future issue would probably be relatively insignificant.

In summing up his remarks on a public issue, Mr. Deets said: "A small company should remember that it's much easier to grow up with a small family than with a big one." He stated that, although the price per share from private sources would probably be less than would be obtained through a public issue, the company would receive the benefits of the private sources' interest, business assistance, and good offices in connection with future financing moves.

When asked about the wisdom of shopping around to find the best deal for the company, Mr. Deets warned, "the merchandise can very easily become shopworn." He felt that, although there can be a wide variation in the initial ball-park estimates made by different people, all investors of any given type will come down to about the same final package because, "after all, everyone is going to be evaluating the deal on the same set of facts." He did not advise shopping either among underwriting firms or among professional capital firms such as SIBC's or venture capital companies, pointing out that often these sources would not consider a deal unless they knew they had exclusive rights to it if they should like it. However, Mr. Deets thought that some shopping could be done in the preliminary stages of investigation with casual investors or finders. But, he stated, even these people would want assurance of having first refusal before putting any significant time into analyzing a firm.

Estimated Financial Package

When asked to give a general or ball-park idea of the financial package Adcole might be offered by private financial sources, Mr. Deets made it clear that he could only estimate in a general way at this time. Any final offer would have to be made on the basis of a much more thorough analysis than could be done with only the profile to go on, and after meeting the men concerned and seeing the operation. (However, he did state that the profile seemed to be well prepared and complete enough to send to prospective private investors in order to sound out their interest.)

---

lies in that with several men assigning values to the securities the price is likely to more accurately reflect the strength of the company than would be the case if only one man set the daily prices. If only the original underwriting house maintains the market, the price is immediately suspect, particularly when the underwriter holds warrants or options, and more so in view of recent criticism of several over-the-counter underwriters by the SEC and other securities dealers.

Mr. Deets felt that a financial package fair to both the company and to the investors might consist of the following:

1. Stock representing 25 percent of the equity of the firm for $50,000.
2. Convertible debentures for a second $50,000. These debentures would carry a reasonable rate of interest and be convertible into the number of shares that would represent an additional 20 percent of the stock outstanding after conversion. (This, with the stock purchased outright, would give the investor, after conversion, 40 percent of the equity.)
3. Giving the company a call on an additional amount of money (probably about $100,000) to be provided when needed on a straight loan basis.

Mr. Deets stated that while this plan would not give Adcole the projected $250,000 immediately, he did not think they actually needed this much and felt that the proposed schedule of investment on an as-needed basis was more suitable at this time. "If you don't need money, don't get it," he said, pointing out that the return on investment on unused funds would be pretty poor in relation to what the small, speculative company would have to pay for them. These funds could probably be put up by one or several of Hanley, Holmes' investor-clients within one to three months of the time they were first approached. They could then be expected to take an active interest in the company and to provide business assistance when needed.

On the basis of this information, Mr. Cole and the other members of Adcole's management team were trying to decide, in January of 1962, whether they should choose the route of the private placement for their current financial support. More specifically they wondered whether they should ask Mr. Deets to contact some of Hanley, Holmes' investor-clients in search of these funds.

17. MACEDONEAN SECURITIES, INC.*

Consideration of a Public Stock Issue

Adcole Corporation's financial condition in the fall of 1961 was quite comfortable in terms of present sales but its management team felt that additional contributed capital would be necessary if the firm was to follow its planned pattern of growth. Therefore, Adcole's officers had prepared a descriptive note on their company and had circulated it among various men connected with the financial community. From the comments of these men, they planned to determine which financial route should be followed by Adcole. Because they wanted to have eventually a public market for their stock, Adcole's officers wanted to look carefully at the possibility of having a public issue to obtain the currently needed funds. They were very glad to get the comments of Eugene Lord, of Macedonean Securities, Inc.[1]

Background—Macedonean Securities, Inc.

Macedonean Securities, Inc., was a small and relatively new underwriting house located in New York City. It had been founded in the spring of 1961 by Emil Kay, formerly the new-issue manager of a well-known major underwriting firm. (Before talking with Mr. Lord, the officers of Adcole Corporation had inquired from several men in the New York financial community about Mr. Kay's reputation. They had been told that his abilities were highly regarded and that he was considered to be a thoroughly honest and reputable man.)

Macedonean had handled five issues prior to January, 1962, all of which had been brought out under Regulation A of the securities laws.[2] A reading of the prospectuses involved indicated that these five

---

[1] General background material on the company and its need for additional capital is given in Case 15, Adcole Corporation. Included as an appendix to that case is the descriptive note, "A Profile of Adcole Corporation," which served as the context within which Mr. Lord made his comments.

[2] Regulation A allows companies seeking not more than $300,000 to use a short form of registration with the SEC. This is often less expensive and takes less time than the full registration prescribed by the Securities Act of 1933. Under Regulation A, the company escapes some of the requirements of full registration. For example, an offering circular is used rather than a full prospectus, no red-herring prospectus is required (or

situations were extremely speculative, but with one exception the securities had acted well in the aftermarkets. All but the exception had risen to a modest premium soon after being sold, none of these had dropped sharply at any point, and all were selling at or above issue price in January, 1962.

The exception was a firm named Aerospace Electronics Labs, which was issued at $4.50 per share but "got away from us," as Mr. Lord put it. "You know how new issues were going back in June, 1961—AEL jumped from issue price to $14 within a couple of weeks. Now that the market has reacted from those wild months, AEL has suffered along with all the others that skyrocketed." Aerospace Electronic Labs was quoted at $1.50 bid in mid-January of 1962.

Mr. Lord stated that he had become associated with Macedonean in the summer of 1961, and was acting as the firm's New England new-issue manager. This was not a full-time job but supplemented his own small management consulting business.

Going Public

Mr. Lord stressed to the officers of Adcole Corporation the many general advantages of going public at an early age of the corporate life. His comments are summarized below.

One of the most obvious basic advantages is that a public market is created for the securities of the company. This can be beneficial to the company and to its current stockholders in a number of ways. A value will be placed on the company for estate-valuation purposes, eliminating the possibility that the government will demand an audit of the company's records in case one of the stockholders dies. Also, the fact that a market exists for the stock means that a deceased stockholder's executor can sell a portion of his holdings, if funds are needed to pay estate or inheritance taxes, without putting the company in the position of having to redeem the stock at a time that could be embarrassing from a cash standpoint.

Furthermore, that a public market for the stock of a company exists will make it far easier for the firm to merge or to acquire other organizations. A merger candidate will tend to be more willing to accept stock for his company if the stock is traded publicly than he will if no market exists for the securities. People tend to shy away from becoming enmeshed in

allowed), and financial statements need not be certified by independent public accountants. Regulation A holds certain disadvantages for the underwriter. For example, since there is no red herring the underwriter is barred from talking about a pending issue until it clears SEC, and the underwriter is prohibited from selling any warrants he receives in a Regulation A underwriting for 13 months.

A red herring is a preliminary prospectus which does not give the issue price but can be used to acquaint the financial community with the company involved.

illiquid situations unless they have firm control over them. In addition, the market price placed on the stock eliminates many of the valuation problems that might otherwise arise.

An established public market will make it easier for the company to raise money in the future. The first time anyone "goes out," he will pay more for the new money than he thinks he should, but once his company has public ownership it becomes much easier to raise additional funds. The first issue must bear all the costs of initial public information efforts and selling expenses. Furthermore, the company must pay for the risk that the underwriter takes in marketing any new issue. It is far better for the company to incur these costs on a small public issue at an early stage of its life than to wait until later when the dollar amounts involved could be much greater.

In addition to these benefits accruing from the establishment of a public market for a company's securities, other distinct advantages are associated with going public. The company escapes the problems of dealing with one major investor who, with a large amount of money in the situation, is likely to be quite demanding of executive time and may expect to participate in management decisions. This could be particularly troublesome if the company's activities are highly technical and difficult for the ordinary investor to fully understand. With a public issue to raise funds, however, the company gains a broad base of stockholders. An underwriting house like Macedonean, which has a large customer organization, can widely distribute shares of an issue and prevent any concentration which would challenge management's control of the company. Since all the investors who buy the new issue know it is a speculative purchase, they will not tend to bother management so long as the company continues to grow and to issue good news to support a healthy and rising market for the stock.

The broad stock distribution and resultant wide interest in the company which comes with a public issue is also beneficial in terms of customer relations. One of the major problems for many small firms is that of getting their name and their field of special competence known by potential customers. A publicly traded security and the attending attention given to the company helps to get its name around both within and outside the financial world, for most executives today own some stock and read the financial sections of papers and business magazines. An analysis of the company and a buy recommendation from a financial writer can help to produce product sales as well as to strengthen the market price of the stock.

Macedonean's Activities after the Issue

Mr. Lord stated emphatically that Macedonean Securities, Inc., was not the type of underwriting house that merely sold an issue and forgot it. He felt that when dealing with a smaller business the underwriter had a continuing responsibility to the company—not only to help management spend the new funds wisely but to be of general financial assistance to the firm.

Macedonean would, of course, make a market for the new security and could get three or four other brokerage firms to maintain markets. Macedonean would take the responsibility for guiding the company's financial public information program. This would include insuring publication of interesting news releases in financial sections of daily newspapers and in various financial journals. Macedonean would also work to interest financial analysts and columnists in the company and in making buy recommendations for its stock.

In addition to giving continuing support to the stock in the public market, Macedonean would assist the company with its internal financial problems. Macedonean would ask to put a representative on the company's board of directors, and this man would closely follow the firm's progress. He would act as general financial counsel and would be able to call on other Macedonean staff members to provide specific advice when necessary. Macedonean's numerous contacts in investment, banking, and consulting circles also put its staff members in an ideal position to recommend outside professional help if such should be required.

If the company wished to grow by acquisition or merger, Macedonean would help find, evaluate, and negotiate with appropriate candidates. Mr. Lord stated that its professional contacts, mentioned above, and its relationships with many other small companies were invaluable in this area. Macedonean had already arranged several mergers for some of the companies it had underwritten.

In summary, Mr. Lord said: "It is our policy to assist our companies in every possible way and to help them develop into sound businesses. We, of course, hope to grow with them."

Mr. Lord's Proposal

Mr. Lord had been sent a copy of the Adcole profile prior to meeting with the company's officers in late January. He had, therefore, been able to develop a ball-park proposal based on the data and projections given in the profile. He stated, however, that his comments were not an offer but only an estimate of what Macedonean would offer if a thorough analysis of the company supported his initial impressions.

"First," said Mr. Lord, "the company's name should be changed to something like Adcole Electronics or Adcole Aerospace." He explained that with a new small issue few investors bother to read the prospectus thoroughly and that the company's name should be descriptive enough to tell the prospective investor what business it is in. "Last fall," he said, "we brought out a small company called Winton Corporation, which makes magnetron tubes for military radar and radar cooking ranges. The issue price was $3.00 per share. Looking back on that issue, we now feel that we could have priced it one or one and a half points higher if it had been named Winton Microwave. It's now selling for about $5.00"

When asked whether the name electronics might not be pretty well worn out, a comment which Adcole had received from several other people, Mr. Lord agreed and stated that another equally descriptive term might be better. He said that the actual name to be used should be management's decision, but he offered to discuss specific suggestions with the Adcole people after they had thought about their own wishes. Mr. Lord stated that Macedonean would want to place a man on the Adcole board and would ask the company to hire a business manager. When asked about his reasons for the second request, and the specific duties he contemplated for this man, he commented as follows: [3]

You men are all engineers and, from your résumés, extremely competent ones. You shouldn't have to spend all your time worrying about business details. The addition of a competent business manager would strengthen your organization and allow you more time for engineering work. Macedonean would ask you to use the business manager in good faith in those areas where he was more experienced, but we would make no specific requirements. You would, of course, have the final word in choosing the man for this job.

Mr. Lord added that this was probably an unusual request to be made by an underwriting house. "The bucket shops would only want to get your stock out so they could play with it. This request is in line with our policy of working with our clients to help them develop sound organizations. In that same vein, we would want first refusal on all future financing done by Adcole."

Mr. Lord then suggested that the company be recapitalized to 250,000 shares of stock. Present stockholders would be given 100,000 shares pro rata, and 100,000 shares would be sold to the public at $1.50 per share on a best efforts, all-or-none basis [4] and as a Regulation A issue. This sale would net to the company $135,000 allowing Macedonean a 10 percent underwriting commission. Adcole would be asked to reimburse Macedonean for $25,000 of its legal, accounting, and promotional expenses. Mr. Lord stressed that this allowance

[3] Mr. Lord's comments are summarized.
[4] Explained below.

would cover not only the many direct costs of the issue but also the expenses connected with the continuing financial public relations program which Macedonean would conduct. It would not be required to account for these expenses. Macedonean would also ask for options to purchase 20,000 shares at 10 cents per share. There would be no restrictions on the disposition of the remaining 30,000 authorized shares. He estimated that the issue could be completed in about four months from the time Adcole decided to proceed.

When asked about the exact meaning of best efforts, all or none, Mr. Lord stated that this type of arrangement was normal for small situations such as Adcole. Macedonean would use its best efforts to sell the entire issue to the public, but if the entire issue could not be sold within 90 days, all moneys collected from subscribers would be returned in full. Mr. Lord stressed that Macedonean would never accept the issue if it were not sure the entire amount could be sold, but it could not reasonably be expected to make a firm commitment when dealing with such a speculative firm as Adcole Corporation.

Mr. Lord further explained that he chose $150,000 as the amount for the issue because he felt that was all the company really needed at this time. "It's better to start off with a small amount and keep 50 percent of the company. When more money is needed, you can probably get the additional $100,000 for as little as 5 percent of your stock." He stated that his suggested issue price was placed at the very low $1.50 level to emphasize that the company was highly speculative. "This price says that and will help keep out the unwary people who might be bothersome if the company doesn't meet its projections. Also, at that figure there is little chance that the price will go down very far even if you have some bad news."

Mr. Lord explained that he arrived at the price by looking at the projections. "With 200,000 shares outstanding, your projected 1962 earnings will be 16 cents per share. At 15 times earnings—a reasonable figure for a situation like this—the stock price would be $2.40. However, because that $33,000 profit is still uncertain, we have to lower the times–earnings ratio. That's why I suggest $1.50. It's too bad you weren't in this position last June. You could have gone out at $2.00 per share then, but the new-issue market has since turned down."

The discussion then turned to earnings and to the fact that the sales and earnings figures from Adcole's first half of fiscal 1962 had been up to the projected rate of growth. (Adcole's fiscal year ends on June 30.) Mr. Lord stated that he had assumed this was the case and would expect the company to include good six-month financial statements in its prospectus. "Still," he said, "you can't include projections in the prospectus, so you are asking the public to buy a real speculative deal. However, if you can wait until audited statements are available for the full fiscal year of 1962, you will be in a much sounder situation. If you could show $50,000 in earnings for this year, we could value the company at $700,000. That shouldn't be too hard in a company like Adcole. Your accountant can raise or lower your stated earnings tremendously just by the way he treats R&D expenditures and inventory valuation. I notice he has already capitalized some of your development costs.

"If we wait until year-end statements are ready, we could get an issue out in the early fall of 1962. Assuming the $50,000 earnings level, we could probably sell 25 percent of the company for $175,000 or 50 percent for $350,000. Either way, I would issue 100,000 shares to the public; any lower number would be insufficient to get an active market. At that point I would probably suggest a full registration instead of a Regulation A deal. You'll be more solid then, and we might as well emphasize that by taking advantage of the prestige which the long form provides."

Mr. Lord said that if Adcole chose to wait and go public in the fall, Macedonean's fees would be appropriately lower to reflect the fact that the stock would be less speculative. Mr. Lord estimated that on an issue of 100,000 shares at $3.50 per share they might ask for underwriting commissions of 10 percent with the same $25,000 expense allowance needed with the smaller immediate issue, and that the warrants requested would be for 20,000 shares but at the issue price of $3.50 per share.

The officers of Adcole Corporation, in considering Mr. Lord's comments, realized that others from the financial community had argued against going public. However, they were impressed with some of Mr. Lord's comments, and they appreciated his willingness to give them a detailed estimated financial package and the reasons for his specific suggestions. They felt that they should seriously consider the advantages and disadvantages of having a public issue to get the needed funds for their company.

In late January of 1962, the members of Adcole's management team realized that they should soon make a decision about the financial route best for their company. They were wondering whether a direct public offering would be more appropriate than getting private capital, whether they should decide to deal with Macedonean Securities, Inc., and if so whether they should register for an issue in the spring or take Mr. Lord's second suggestion of going public in the fall after fiscal year-end statements would be available.

18. DIVERSIFIED VENTURES, INC. *

Evaluation of One Type of Venture Capital Firm as a Source of Funds

Adcole Corporation's financial condition in the fall of 1961 was quite comfortable in terms of present sales but its management team felt that additional contributed capital would be necessary if the firm was to follow its planned pattern of growth. Therefore, Adcole's officers had prepared a descriptive note on their company and had circulated it among various men connected with the financial community. From the comments of these men, they planned to determine which financial route should be followed by Adcole. One of the sets of comments they had received came from Thomas Rainie and Robert Conklin, the founders and officers of Diversified Ventures, Inc.[1]

Background—Diversified Ventures, Inc.

Diversified Ventures (Diven) had been founded as a venture capital firm in 1959. In addition to its two officers, it had only one employee, a secretary, and it occupied a small office in an old building located in the middle of a heavily industrialized area close to New York City.

Rainie and Conklin both had M.B.A. degrees and some business experience prior to establishing Diven. Mr. Conklin had graduated in the early fifties and subsequently had worked in the treasurer's office of a large New Jersey electronics firm. Mr. Rainie had received his M.B.A. degree a few years later and had spent several years working with various small enterprises in the northern New Jersey area. He had been a member of the operating management of one company and in a consulting capacity with several others.

Diven's first ventures had been small and risky situations requiring investments of $15,000 to $20,000. As the firm developed, however,

---

* Copyright © 1962 by the President and Fellows of Harvard College.

[1] General background material on the company and its need for additional capital as given in Case 15, Adcole Corporation. Included as an appendix to that case is the descriptive note, "A Profile of Adcole Corporation," which served as the context within which Rainie and Conklin made their comments.

240

it began to seek larger opportunities, and in January, 1962, was working on one which would need $4.5 million. In its three years of operation it had looked at a number of investment opportunities and had actually gone into six different situations, including both real estate deals and small manufacturing companies. It currently had several more under consideration. Diven did not operate in the same way as most venture capital firms. Rather than selling shares in Diven to get a large cash account and then seeking investments, the owners of Diven found and evaluated the investment situations first, and then approached the particular sources of funds they thought would be most suited for each deal.

Mr. Conklin stated that their method of operation offered several advantages. First, it was easier to sell a specific attractive situation to a prospective investor than to convince him to contribute to a common pot from which the officers of the venture capital firm would make unknown investments in the future. When each situation was treated as a separate deal, it could be set up in the specific framework most suitable for that situation; i.e., one investment might be set up as a limited partnership, another to allow the investors to purchase shares in a company directly, and still another might be made strictly by Diven with borrowed funds. Each situation could be taken to the type of investor most suitable for the company and, specifically, to investors who could be expected, on the basis of past experience, to find it attractive.

Secondly, the Diven method of operation placed some of the burden of evaluation on the investor. The investor always made the final decision about whether his money would be used for any particular deal. Conklin and Rainie still had to gather and verify the important facts and do the legwork connected with developing a sound financial package to propose to investors. However, they felt that their stopping short of making the actual investment decision eliminated many of the stockholder relations headaches which they might otherwise have. Although they might be criticized if they had overlooked any important facts in writing a proposal, they could not be accused of making a "poor" investment decision. Furthermore, they said that because they had to be able to answer the very searching questions of knowledgeable investors, they were impelled to conduct extremely thorough analyses of all prospective situations.

Diven never sent out a proposal to an investor without first talking with him to see whether he might be interested. If so, a written presentation was made, often individually prepared as a letter, with the necessary supporting material, so that Rainie or Conklin could tailor it to the particular desires of the prospective investor. Although Diven's activities were in some ways similar to those of a finder, Mr. Rainie stressed that he and Mr. Conklin went far beyond the functions of many finders. They took the responsibility for looking after each of the investments they helped to make. One of the two men usually sat on the board of directors of each company Diven had sponsored, and sometimes one or both of them might become officers of the firm. On one occasion, Mr. Conklin had become a full-time and fully paid financial officer of a company, but usually the work done by the two men for their invested companies was of the free consulting type.

Diven was compensated for its services in connection with finding investors for companies by being given a portion of each new issue. In the past, the amount had varied with the details of the situation and had ranged from 0 to 50 percent of the total securities involved in the investment. Also, in addition to compensation for various services to these companies, Diven had earned fees for consulting work done with other firms in need of financial advice. In the various situations with which Diven had been associated, Conklin and Rainie had in some cases acted strictly as advisers to companies, in other cases as agents for investors, and in still others their efforts consisted primarily of getting two parties together without truly representing either one. In the cases where they had not represented the company in negotiations, they often "shifted seats to the company's side of the table" after an investment was made in the belief that usually at that time the best interests of company and investor were one and the same.

Mr. Rainie stated that as long as all parties always knew where Diven stood, the two men could often be helpful to several groups in a situation at the same time. "However," he added, "we always have to be completely honest and aboveboard."

General Comments

When asked to comment on Adcole's situation and its need for funds, Mr. Conklin stated that it was impossible to recommend a specific "correct" program for the company without meeting the people involved and learning more about the business. He said that Diven makes it a policy not to approach any situation with preconceptions of any sort, preferring to allow the most suitable program to evolve over time as the parties get to know each other and their respective needs.

However, on the basis of the profile, Mr. Conklin did say that Adcole shouldn't go public at this time. He felt this way not just because of Adcole's small size but also because of its lack of maturity. "A company should have stabilized enough so that sales and profits are consistent from quarter to quarter before it sells stock publicly, otherwise its stock prices will tend to fluctuate radically." Mr. Conklin doubted that Adcole's management could keep absolute control if it tried to raise the needed funds through a public issue.

Conklin and Rainie felt that Adcole's idea of trying to determine which financial route was best suited for its needs was a sound approach to financing. They stated that it was not so important to predetermine the specific person or financial firm as it was to be certain that the type of investor Adcole chose would be best for the company. Their comments seemed to indicate that they felt Adcole should seek the advice of an experienced person to help in making their choice instead of, or in addition to, the present program of talking with actual sources. They stated that Diven could act in such an advisory capacity because it was not committed to any one type of financial source and had experience with almost all.

The officers of Diven pointed out that shopping around could easily hurt the company's chances of getting capital, because there was so much overlap and consultation between various sources. No one, they said, could make an intelligent decision about either the price per share or about the mechanics of the issue (i.e., type of securities, timing of the purchase, negative provisions, etc.) until a detailed study of the company was made, and no one would commit time for such an evaluation unless he was sure of getting the deal if he liked it.

Conklin and Rainie were also asked about a question that had come up as a result of previous comments by other men from the financial community. Should Adcole raise a large sum of money, some of which could not be used immediately, or should they raise only as much as they need now? Could the company plan on going back to the same well again? Diven's officers replied that the important point in this area was that the company specify what it was planning to do with the new funds, and make sure that it raised enough money to do that job. "As long as it is making solid progress, the company can return to the same source of funds, and Diven, if it were working with the company, would expect and wish it to do so.

However, the firm should not allow itself to be caught without enough money to complete the program it promised to finish with that amount. Companies should plan ahead so that they can go out for more financial support when they are in an attractive position."

The officers of Diven did not feel that Adcole's position, as presented by the profile, was so attractive as it might be. They stated that essentially all Adcole had to offer to an investor now was a group of people—although admittedly an impressive group—and some ideas, which might or might not pay off. "It is now only another small engineering firm doing specialized R&D work with little commercial potential. It has no major product and virtually no plant. They are asking for pure R&D money to be spent on projects which are not clearly specified, which may or may not yield products, and which probably could be undertaken equally well by other groups of competent engineers."

Mr. Conklin also observed that, from his point of view, Adcole's profile would be a much more effective selling tool if it put more emphasis on the various items already developed by the company, explaining the products and estimating their potential markets, sales volume, profitableness, etc. However, notwithstanding his reservations, Mr. Conklin stated that he would be interested in considering an investment in Adcole if its officers were to decide that "we [the officers of Diven] are people who can do something for them."

Estimated Financial Package

Conklin and Rainie were reluctant to commit themselves to any specific estimate of a financial package that might be suitable or fair for Adcole and for prospective investors. Again, they expressed the importance of meeting the men at Adcole and working out with them the most appropriate deal. However, they thought that if the profile projections were supported by a careful analysis Diven might offer to arrange financing that would provide Adcole with its $250,000. Diven would want for the investors about 50 percent of the equity for $100,000 and would make a 5-year loan of an additional $150,000. The loan would carry with it various negative provisions restricting the uses to which the funds could be put to specified product areas and specific development programs. Diven would expect to closely watch the expenditure of its funds to make certain that their use would result in tangible product lines, and in significant sales and profits.

In January, 1962, the officers of Adcole Corporation were considering the comments of Conklin and Rainie. They wondered whether this type of venture capital firm would be a good source of funds for their company and, specifically, whether they should ask Diven to undertake a more extensive analysis of their situation and make them an offer.

19. HERCULES CAPITAL CORPORATION*
Evaluation of an SBIC as a Source of Capital

Adcole Corporation's financial condition in the fall of 1961 was quite comfortable in terms of present sales but its management team felt that additional contributed capital would be necessary if the firm was to follow its planned pattern of growth. Therefore, Adcole's officers had prepared a descriptive note on their company and had circulated it among various men connected with the financial community. From the comments of these men, they planned to determine which financial route should be followed by Adcole. One of these sets of comments came from John Baker, a staff member of Hercules Capital Corporation.[1]

Background—Hercules Capital Corporation

Hercules Capital Corporation, a small business investment company (SBIC) licensed under the Small Business Investment Act of 1958, was one of the first such firms to sell its stock publicly, and in 1961 it was one of the largest SBIC's in the country. (Appendix 19–A presents general background on the SBIC program.) Its head offices were located in New York City, and it maintained a regional office in Boston. Hercules' total capital was about $12 million, of which approximately half had been invested as of the end of 1961. Roughly 50 percent of Hercules' investments had been in firms in or connected with the electronics industry; the rest were spread among a wide variety of small growing companies in other industries. In all, 13 different firms were represented in the Hercules portfolio.

Hercules had used almost every investment instrument open to the SBIC's. It tried to tailor the type of security asked of each company to that firm's particular situation. In its portfolio, Hercules held subordinated debentures (with and without detachable warrants), sub-

---

[1] General background material on the company and its need for additional capital is given in Case 15, Adcole Corporation. Included as an appendix to that case is the descriptive note, "A Profile of Adcole Corporation," which served as the context within which Mr. Baker made his comments.

ordinated notes, convertible subordinated debentures, and common stock. In all cases, Hercules held common stock, warrants, and/or instruments convertible into stock. In some cases, it held only common stock, while in others it held a combination of debt and equity (or instruments convertible into equity). Some of its investments were fully paid up, while in other situations Hercules had invested an initial sum and committed itself to additional investments based on expected future requirements. Hercules' policy was to make all loans at a 6 percent rate (although the Small Business Act of 1958 permitted much higher interest charges). It adjusted for the relative risk of each situation in the negotiation of the amount of its equity position or of the conversion price. The percentage of equity which Hercules held in its invested companies (or would hold after taking down all commitments, exercising all warrants, and converting all convertible debt) ranged from a low of 2 percent to a high of almost 70 percent. The average was about 30 percent. Its smallest investment (including commitments) was $63 thousand; its largest was $975 thousand.

Mr. Baker had graduated from Harvard Business School in 1960. He joined Hercules after spending a year in the financial department of a New York consulting firm. Mr. Baker was assigned to the Boston office of Hercules Capital Corporation, as one of several staff members evaluating and negotiating with New England companies that presented attractive investment opportunities.

What Hercules Had to Offer

Mr. Baker stated that when Hercules Capital Corporation made an investment in a small business it stood ready to provide much more than money for the client company. He felt that the capital contribution was only one part of a Hercules investment in a business; the inputs of time and advice constituted a major portion of what Hercules could do for its clients.

Hercules, unlike some SBIC's, did not demand that its clients sign a management consulting contract as a prerequisite to getting funds. It did ask that the firm be represented on the client's board of directors, and its experience had been that most companies called on Hercules for advice and assistance whenever it was needed. Much of this advice was given for no charge by the Hercules staff member on the board, or by one of his associates if the problem required specialized knowledge in an area with which the board member was not thoroughly familiar. Hercules also had management contracts with some of its clients.

In addition to the obvious area of financial planning, accounting, and control, Hercules had a number of men experienced in sales and production. One of the members of the Boston staff had previously been a manufacturer's representative, selling various electronic components in New England, and several New York staff members had held positions in the marketing area before joining Hercules. Others on the staff had managed small businesses in the course of their careers.

Hercules also assisted its client in the personnel area. The firm was continually being approached by capable men seeking positions in growing small companies, and, in addition, Hercules learned of other able men in business and technical fields in the course of its normal operations. If a company wanted to fill a particular post, Hercules could find and suggest several qualified men to the client company's management, and Hercules made a practice of sending to each of its clients summary résumés of the better men who approached it looking for positions. Hercules conducted an initial screening of all these people.

Mr. Baker said that Hercules would not invest in any company which, in the opinion of the staff, could not stand on its own two feet and be a success. However, he felt that the assistance and advice that Hercules could give would help its client companies grow bigger and faster than they would without Hercules' participation.

Estimated Financial Package for Adcole

Mr. Baker stated that he felt Hercules would certainly be interested in looking into Adcole Corporation. He stated that its staff seemed especially strong and, assuming that investigation yielded evidence to support the estimates given in the profile, the company's sales and profit projections seemed quite attractive. Mr. Baker's only immediate qualification was that Adcole's sales were virtually all either directly or indirectly to the government, whereas he would prefer to see some income from commercial sources to provide a better balance in the company's work.

Although he voiced the obvious reservations about making a dollar estimate only on the basis of the profile, Mr. Baker stated that he felt the projected sales and earnings figures indicated that 30–40 percent of the equity in Adcole would be a fair price for $250 thousand. The actual financial instruments that Hercules would want would probably be 6 percent subordinated debentures convertible into the appropriate amount of stock, although, as noted above, a variety of financial vehicles were possible.

In January of 1962, the officers of Adcole Corporation were considering the comments made by Mr. Baker. They asked themselves if an SBIC might be the most appropriate source of capital for Adcole at this time and, specifically, whether they should concentrate on obtaining their financial support from Hercules Capital Corporation.

ADDENDUM TO HERCULES
CAPITAL CORPORATION

Not long after Adcole's officers talked with Mr. Baker of Hercules Capital Corporation, and before they took any further action on their search for financial support, one of the members of their management team attended a symposium on financing new ventures. This symposium was sponsored by one of the Boston universities as part of a running program of lectures on various business problems. Mr. Baker spoke at this symposium, presenting the point of view of Hercules Capital Corporation.

The officers of Adcole Corporation were quite interested in several points made by Mr. Baker, particularly as some of them seemed to apply to their own search for funds. Mr. Baker's comments are summarized below.

When a man seeks financing, the first thing he should have is a significantly greater knowledge of his subject—his business—than anyone else. He should be an expert in his field before he asks others to invest in him: there is nothing so disquieting to a prospective investor as finding out that he (the investor) knows as much or more than the person seeking funds in that man's area of competence. Hercules looks for both knowledge and experience in his field when considering a prospective client.

In addition to knowledge and experience in his field, the man (or company) that seeks financing should have a unique competence to sell. He should have a new product or a novel service idea, rather than only a plan to produce what others are already producing. Each new proposal is in competition with every other for funds. It is hard to convince most investors to finance a company with a me-too proposal, when these investors have completely new ideas coming to them continuously. The actual process of going out after funds is as difficult to generalize about as any other business process. "The statements given below are only one man's [Mr. Baker's] impressions, albeit based on a fair amount of observation. There are many other views."

The first step in going out after money is to find out what sources of capital are available and what they are like. There are advantages and disadvantages to every type of source, and the company should be aware of these. The company may wish to talk with people working in the financial world and/or call on professional help from men such as business school professors who are familiar with the various types of sources of capital available.

Next, with a rough idea of the types of people the company wishes to approach, its officers and management should translate their ideas into dollars—the language of investors. They should prepare a proposal or prospectus that describes their company—its plant, people, and products—its market, its plans, and its finances—both historical and projected. A well-conceived and imaginatively prepared proposal is extremely valuable in a company's quest for funds. "Every man with money to invest has a wide variety of proposals continuously crossing his desk. Yours must be able to catch his eye."

However, preparation of the proposal should not consist only of writing an effective sales tool to use in talking with prospective investors, it should also involve a critical analysis of the company, its cash needs, and its plans. The projections of the proposal should be realistic enough to be readily defended under examination but not so conservative that they are unappealing to the prospective investor.

The company should not allow itself to be trapped into believing all its own blue-sky. In working out its needs and their timing, the company should be completely realistic and honest with itself. In this area, as well as that of learning about the various sources available, the company would probably also do well to get professional advice. The average executive of a typical small company goes out after risk capital only once or twice in a lifetime. This infrequent exposure to the financial world often does not provide him with the ability to design an attractive financial prospectus or present it to prospective investors. Just as the managers of a small company would call on an experienced lawyer to help them draw up their wills, they should seek a man with financial experience to help them in preparing their company's prospectus.

All this preparatory work should be done by the company well in advance of the time it will actually need the funds to be raised. Investors tend to move slowly. Even Hercules, with its trained, full-time staff, usually takes two months or more to evaluate, negotiate, and close an attractive deal. Furthermore, evidence of good foresight and planning at this stage can not help but impress the potential investor more than a distress, or ill-prepared, situation.

When the executives of the small company are ready to go out seeing people with money, they probably still will not know for certain what sources of funds will be best for them, even though they should have a general idea of what types of sources might be best. For example, they may know that a private placement is most appropriate, but not which source of private capital (individual, SBIC, etc.) would be best.

They should determine the several types of sources that seem most appropriate to their needs, and should determine, perhaps again with professional assistance, the two or three best or most likely institutions or individuals of each type. Then, the company executives should visit each person—starting with the least likely source among the group in order to gain experience before going to the people who seem most appropriate—to get a more specific idea of what each source has to offer.

The company should not be overly concerned with price per share at this point; actually, the final prices arrived at by almost all investors (of the same general type) will probably be very close. "I don't really know what accounts for this similarity. I don't believe it's just that everyone looks at the same set of facts, because different people will draw different conclusions from identical facts. However, it has been my observation that final offers from different people will usually be quite close." The company executives should concern themselves with the qualitative aspects of the prospective investor. What can he do for them beyond providing money? Hercules, for example, has on its staff experts in every functional area of business who can offer advice when the company needs it. It is particularly strong in the technical sales area. If an extensive consulting job is required, Hercules can arrange for a qualified independent consultant. By virtue of its contacts and reputation, Hercules can help a company to get proper bank accommodation, to go public at a later date, or to find qualified businessmen or engineers to round out the company's staff.

A second question, particularly important for the company, is: Are these men with whom we will be happy, with whom we can work well for the next several years? Will they understand our problems? Can we appreciate theirs? Can we live with them? On the basis of these conversations, the company executives should choose the one specific source of funds that seems most appropriate for the company. If necessary, they can call on some people a second or third time, but once the choice has been made they should stop shopping around and concentrate on this one source until they have either concluded a deal or reached an obvious impasse. "They should not burn their other bridges, however—merely cease crossing them." This choice will usually have to be made before prices or percentages are mentioned.

Even at this stage, the executives of the company should not get too specific too soon. They should try to learn as much about the investor as possible. He, in turn, will wish to thoroughly analyze the company. He will consider the individuals involved, the product, the market, and the company's financial plan. Obviously, a thorough proposal that includes all the important facts and appropriate references will not only cut down the amount of time the investor takes to arrive at a decision but also will probably help to convince the investor that the management team which prepared it is made up of able and competent men. "I would rather see Grade A individuals with a Grade B product than vice-versa."

The investor will also want to know how he can expect to get out of the situation with a profit, and preferably a capital gains profit. This could be accomplished by such moves as going public or merging at a future date. He will expect no definite agreement on this subject but will look for indications that the opportunity will develop and that the company will take it.

"Once the investor starts talking dollars or percents, he has taken the bait; now the company just has to reel him in." As negotiations proceed, the company executives should concentrate on the most important details first. They should be flexible—have in mind a range of acceptable deals rather than one firm package. As the deal begins to take shape, the company should continue to look critically at the quality of the package in terms of the company's needs and other background information. The further along the negotiations get, the harder it becomes for the company to withdraw graciously.

The officers of Adcole Corporation were glad to have this additional information on Mr. Baker's point of view, since they were considering Hercules as a possible source of capital. However, they recognized that some of his comments suggested tactics somewhat different from those they were following, and they wondered whether in light of his opinions they should modify their own program for getting financial support.

APPENDIX 19–A

Small Business Investment Companies[1]

In 1958, the Congress passed a law, "The Small Business Investment Act of 1958," which provided for the establishment of a new type of private financial institution. These institutions, to be called small business investment companies (SBIC's), were expected to fill

---

[1] The reader should be aware that this appendix was designed to provide general background for the case on Hercules Capital Corporation. It is by no means all-inclusive. Also, the SBI Act is being continuously amended, and the SBA is rapidly changing the many regulations under which SBIC's operate in attempts to improve the benefits open to bona fide small businesses while closing unforeseen loopholes in the laws and regulations. Therefore, many of the specific restrictions and provisions given in this appendix may have been changed to some extent since it was written.

a particular gap which Congress considered to exist in the country's financial structure. This gap was in the area of long-term financial support for small companies.

The SBA was charged with the responsibility of administering the SBIC program. A new SBIC must obtain a license from the SBA, and the SBA can revoke this license if the SBIC is not operating in accordance with the provisions of the act. To stimulate the formation and operation of SBIC's, the Congress provided to them and their stockholders a number of special inducements. The two most important types of inducements were the tax advantages and the opportunity to leverage the private funds involved. The major provisions of the act (as amended up to September, 1961) are as follows in these two areas.

1. Except in certain circumstances, an SBIC would be exempt from the personal holding company taxes. (The exceptions to this exemption were (a) if the SBIC became inactive and (b) if an SBIC stockholder also owned 5 percent or more of the stock in a company financed by that SBIC.

2. As long as an SBIC was actively engaged in operations under the act, it would not be subject to the accumulated earnings tax.

3. An SBIC would get ordinary loss treatment for tax purposes on any debenture or stock received on conversion of a debenture that went bad, and it would be entitled to carry these losses forward or backward to offset ordinary income in other years.

4. An SBIC would be allowed a tax deduction equal to 100 percent of dividends it received, rather than the normal 85 percent credit, with certain minor limitations relating to public utility and foreign securities.

5. An SBIC shareholder (original or subsequent) would be taxed on all gains realized from future sale of his SBIC stock at capital gains rates, but could treat all losses as offsets to ordinary income.

6. A publicly held and registered SBIC could distribute all income and/or capital gains in any year to its shareholders without paying any taxes on these funds, and the shareholder would be taxed on the capital gains that were passed through at personal capital gains rates. (This is a result of the Regulated Investment Company Act of 1940, which applies to publicly held SBIC's registered under it.)

7. The SBA would contribute half of the initial capitalization of a new SBIC, up to a maximum contribution of $400,000, by purchasing 5 percent debentures in the SBIC. These matching funds were subject to the limitation that they would be provided only if private funds are not available at reasonable rates. In practice, this limitation had rarely been enforced as of the end of 1961, but by early 1962 the SBA was requiring disclosures on the part of SBIC owners to prove an inability to provide needed funds.

8. An SBIC could borrow from the government an amount equal to 50 percent of its capital and surplus up to a maximum of $4 million, subject again to the provision that private funds were not available at reasonable rates.
9. An SBIC could incur total indebtedness up to four times its paid-in capital and surplus from whatever sources might be available.
10. A bank could invest in SBIC equity securities up to 2 percent of the bank's capital and surplus.

The SBI Act as amended placed certain restrictions on the operations of SBIC's. The important provisions may be summarized as follows.

1. The minimum capitalization of an SBIC was $300,000, of which at least $150,000 must have been provided by private sources.
2. An SBIC could invest not more than 20 percent of its capital and surplus in any one client company up to a maximum dollar amount of $500,000. The $500,000 ceiling was imposed in the 1961 amendments and did not affect previous SBIC investments in excess of that amount. Under certain conditions, the SBA could still approve larger investments by a single SBIC, and several SBIC's were allowed to participate to make a collective investment in excess of their individual limitations. In early 1962, the SBA was also permitting SBIC's to use a formula whereby they could invest 50 percent of their uncommitted funds in situations over $500,000 without specific approval.
3. An SBIC could not charge interest rates on its loans in excess of 15 percent (or less if so restricted by state laws).
4. SBIC investments had to be long term. In general, they had to be for a minimum of five years, with repayment or sinking fund payments not in excess of 20 percent per year.
5. An SBIC was restricted to investments in small United States business. "Small" was defined by the act in terms somewhat similar to the terms applicable to the SBA itself. In general (and with certain exceptions), these criteria were (a) the company could not dominate its field, (b) assets could not exceed $5 million or net worth $2.5 million, (c) average net income for the preceding two years could not exceed $250,000 after taxes. In addition, certain areas of business were expressly prohibited. Examples of these were: agriculture, relenders, single-project businesses, bare-land speculations, and activities contrary to the public interest. The SBA could, however, make individual exceptions to these limits.

SBIC's were allowed to make outright loans to client companies, to purchase equity, and to purchase debt-equity or near-equity packages such as convertible instruments and warrants. If it desired, the SBIC was allowed to ask for collateral for its loans. In practice, although some SBIC's tended to favor certain types of instruments, almost every legal type of deal was being used by SBIC's in 1961.

The SBIC's were allowed to perform management or engineering consulting services and to charge for these services. They could also establish consulting subsidiaries. These services could be sold to both client companies and nonclients (although some restrictions were placed on nonclient consulting, including the same size restrictions applicable to financing by an SBIC). SBIC staff members were prohibited from being operating members of a client's management team or employees of a client. They could, however, sit on a client's board of directors. Many large SBIC's considered that their consulting abilities were definite assets to their clients, although some people had criticized certain SBIC's for insisting on a continuous consulting contract as a condition of financing a small company.

As of October 31, 1961, the SBA had received 774 proposals for SBIC licenses. A total of 407 licenses had been granted. The 407 licenses had total initial capital of about $145 million, of which $50 million represented SBA commitments. The SBA estimated that in October, 1961, the total SBIC funds available, including the additional funds raised by many SBIC's to supplement their initial capital, amounted to about $395 million. About half of this amount had been invested in some 2,000 small businesses.

Different men in the financial field and in the small business area tended to disagree about the value of the SBIC program and the various provisions and restrictions of the SBI Act as amended and implemented. However, although some men felt that additional changes should be made in the laws and regulations to improve the program from the point of view of small business and/or the public good, most also felt that, in general, the SBIC's were helping to fill the need for risk capital for small businesses.

20. JOHN BUCKLEY*
Evaluating and Financing Small Companies

"My job is to bring together small growth companies in need of funds and investors seeking long-term growth opportunities," said John Buckley. Mr. Buckley was retained by the underwriting firm of Wilson, Clark and Mathews to find and evaluate small growing manufacturing firms in need of equity capital. He attempted to arrange financing that would be mutually advantageous to investors, the underwriting firm, and the company. During the 12 years he had spent in this kind of work, Mr. Buckley had formed definite opinions as to the best ways of approaching, evaluating, and financing small manufacturing companies.

Mr. Buckley's Background

Mr. Buckley studied for two years at an eastern men's college before entering the Naval Intelligence Service during World War II. While in the navy he took law courses at night. Returning to college after the war, he participated in the establishment of a building materials company which operated during his last two years in college. He then entered the Harvard Business School, and while earning his M.B.A. degree he served as an investment adviser to several trust accounts.

On graduation in 1948, Mr. Buckley joined the Golden Gate Investment Company, a San Francisco underwriting firm, as vice-president with duties in investment counseling, portfolio management, and investigation of special opportunities. During the next nine years, he investigated hundreds of opportunities to arrange equity financing for small companies. Of the 11 firms for which he actually arranged such financing, he said that only one proved to be disappointing to investors. Even that one, however, is still in operation and may yet realize on its potential.

From 1956 to 1958, he was with the United States government, doing a top-priority study of national survival under conditions of nuclear warfare. In 1959, he was retained as a consultant by Wilson,

Clark and Mathews, a prominent Los Angeles underwriting firm. In this new position, he investigated equity investment opportunities in small firms; he received a retainer and also a special fee associated with each venture for which financing was actually arranged. As indicated below, it was Mr. Buckley's policy to limit his investigation to small companies manufacturing highly technical products which were in the early stages of growth.

Method of Operation

Mr. Buckley employed the following procedure in order to enable investors to achieve the largest capital gains:

1. Select an industry that was entering into a period of dynamic growth.
2. Make an intensive survey of all companies (located within the section of the country under consideration) which were active in that industry.
3. Screen this group, by means of a preliminary checklist, to weed out the obviously unsuitable or unattractive situations.
4. Accumulate detailed information on the remaining potential candidates, and seek the confidential opinions of competent authorities concerning these companies.
5. Screen again to select the most promising situations, and make personal contact with the chief executives of those firms.
6. In those cases where preliminary interviews and plant inspection tours led to a mutual interest in the possibility of new financing, Mr. Buckley would assign a team to study the corporate structure in detail from the technical, legal, marketing, and financial angles.
7. The few really attractive situations that survived all the above steps would then receive a specific proposal from Mr. Buckley.
8. When the proposal had been accepted and the new money provided, the board of directors would ordinarily be expanded and strengthened to provide a more diversified orientation at the top management level. In some cases, Mr. Buckley himself would be asked to serve on the board.
9. After the new funds had been absorbed, careful consideration would subsequently be given to establishing and maintaining an active over-the-counter market for the stock and to the possibility of a large-scale public offering later at an advanced price level.

Corporate Needs and Investor Incentives

"The most effective way to accumulate funds under today's tax structure is through long-term capital gains. However, stock market prices are so high in the so-called growth securities (in relation both to book value and earnings) that the best way to achieve these capital gains is to find closely held companies with long-term growth opportunities and get in early," said Mr. Buckley.

He went on to say that the investors who put money in these companies got, initially, neither security of principal, nor high yields, nor safety through diversified product lines. They were buying potential. Mr. Buckley said he did not want speculators—in-and-outers who would trade the stock before a record of earnings was established. Instead, he wanted investors—people who would invest sizable amounts —at least $5,000—and who would then hold the stock for several years. He also sought investors who could benefit the company in other ways, through contacts, prestige, technical knowledge, or business acumen.

The companies for which he sought to arrange financing often faced the dilemma of needing large amounts of capital to finance growth, yet being unable to pay high fixed charges and having owners who were unwilling to relinquish control. Among such nonbankable companies, Mr. Buckley limited his efforts to small manufacturing concerns based upon advanced technology, which had reached that point of maturity in which reorders had begun to come in from customers. He felt that the presence of reorders, as an indication of product reliability and market acceptance, tended to considerably reduce the risk associated with the venture.

He recalled wryly that he had not always adhered to this policy and that, at an earlier stage of his career, he had helped to arrange the financing of a company being formed to introduce a "revolutionary" new consumer product. Market tests using products manufactured in the laboratory had been quite promising. However, the company was unable to achieve necessary quality under actual manufacturing conditions, and the product was unsuccessful. Those who had invested in this venture were disappointed at the resulting low profits and low price of the stock. This company, however, is still in operation.

The investment firm of Wilson, Clark and Mathews had connections with a number of investors interested in long-term growth opportunities. It was Mr. Buckley's job to find the proper companies and to arrange mutually satisfactory financing. "A cardinal principle is to seek and not to be sought," said Mr. Buckley. He believed that of the many companies which needed financing, only a small percentage offered the capital appreciation possibilities he sought. For this reason, he neither advertised nor used calling cards, fearing that if he did so he would be inundated by small businessmen needing money. He much preferred to conduct his own investigations and then approach the likely prospects.

He started by obtaining, usually from a chamber of commerce, a list of all the manufacturing companies in an area. From this list of 300 to 400 companies, he eliminated all except small companies manufacturing products based upon advanced technology and operating in an industry he had selected as offering growth opportunities. Then he inquired among lawyers, auditors, bankers, sales engineers, scientists, and professors for information and opinion about these companies.

Mr. Buckley required several independent favorable recommendations about a company before considering it further. Then, upon the basis of a Dun and Bradstreet investigation of these firms, he cut his list down to 10 or 20 companies. He would work only with audited statements. He then arranged personal interviews with the chief executives of these companies. He did not want to enter these initial meetings as a stranger, but preferred to be introduced through some common acquaintance. In the initial interview, he looked for affirmative answers to the following questions:

1. Was there a need for funds to finance growth?
2. Were there one or more products with commercial application (as distinguished from government applications)?
3. Was there capable management in depth?
4. Was there a semiproven record of earnings, and were customers reordering?
5. Was the company at that stage of growth in which it had only recently been founded, yet had a going-concern value?
6. Were there the competitive features (patent protection, order backlog, recognized leadership in a particular field)?
7. Did the company have a clean record (free from federal investigations, corporate litigations, stockholder suits, etc.)?

Mr. Buckley said that in the important areas of evaluating a member of management he sought such characteristics as confidence in himself, command of his field, and clear convictions with respect to personal and corporate objectives.

In developing a financing plan, Mr. Buckley had to balance the needs of the company, the prospective investors, and the underwriting firm. The owners of the company usually wanted to retain control and avoid heavy fixed charges. Prospective investors wanted a price that would put them in on the ground floor and allow capital appreciation as the company grew. The underwriting firm was concerned with marketability, with underwriting commissions and risks, and with a reputation for being associated with attractive issues. He frequently employed a nonvoting common stock which participated fully in earnings and placed a minority on the board, but which left actual control in the hands of management.

Mr. Buckley said, "The price should normally be near book value, since that is a recognized indication of relative value in the early stages of company growth. There is rarely a long record of earnings; more often there is only a promise of future growth." Most of the issues he had promoted in the past had substantially increased in price within several years after introduction. He felt that a successful refinancing served the best interests of investors, the company, and especially the country as a whole, since advanced technology bears an important relation to national survival. A specific instance of Mr. Buckley's activities is given in Pacific Electronics, Inc., Case 21.

Exhibit 20–1

JOHN   BUCKLEY

Performance Record of Several Issues Developed by Mr. Buckley

1. A scientific instruments company:
   Placed privately in 1948 @ $80/sh.
   Split 40 for 1 in 1951.
   Issued 5 percent stock dividends in 1952, 1956, 1957, and 1958.
   Split 2 for 1 in 1959.
   Over-the-counter market established in 1957.
   1959 price range: Low, 6½; High, 11.
2. A food processing company:
   Public issue in 1949 @ $3/sh. of Class A stock (nonvoting but with prior claim in liquidation over Class B), with the underwriters receiving a bonus of Class B (voting) stock at 5¢/sh.
   Merged with another company in 1959, receiving one share of new stock for each ten shares of Class A. Class B declared valueless.
   1959 price of new stock: Low, 2½; High, 5½.
3. A private investment trust:
   Offered in 1950 @ $10/sh.
   Stock dividends (over and above cash payments) totaled about 120 percent on original issue by 1959.
   1959 price range: Low, 15; High, 17½.
4. An electronics manufacturing company:
   4–6 percent convertible debentures issued in 1951 (4 percent regular interest, plus 2 percent contingent interest if earned). Investor received one bond plus one share of stock as a bonus for each $1,000 invested.
   Stock was split 15 for 1 in 1955.

Exhibit 20–1—Continued

Debentures were called by the company in 1958, at which time *all* outstanding debentures were converted into stock on a $4.17 basis. An over-the-counter market was promptly established @ 5¼.
1959 price range: Low, 5; High, 16.
5. A real estate development company:
7 percent convertible debentures issued in 1952, with each purchaser of a $1,000 bond receiving a bonus of 10 shares of common stock.
By 1956, all bonds had been called serially, so that investors exercised the option of receiving all their money back (plus a premium for the early call) while retaining their bonus stock, or of converting their bonds into stock @ $11.11/sh.
Fair value of stock in 1959, $40/sh. (issue still privately held).
6. An aerodynamics research company:
Private placement of common stock in May 1959, @ $112/sh. on highly selective basis.
A stock restriction requires that investors intending to sell must offer their stock first to the company.
Fair value estimate in late 1959 is $180/sh.

21. PACIFIC ELECTRONICS, INC. *
Appraisal of a Specific Financing Plan

Pacific Electronics, Inc., was founded in 1951 to do research, development, and custom manufacturing in electronics. Sales grew from $6,200 in 1952 to $375,000 in 1958; management expected that annual sales would reach $1.6 million by 1963.

Joseph Phillips, president and one of the principal stockholders, realized that a shortage of cash was limiting the company's ability to bid on new contracts and that this shortage was threatening to stifle company growth. In April, 1959, he was considering a proposal to issue a limited-voting common stock, the sale of which would provide $256,500 to the company. The plan had been proposed by John Buckley, who was associated with the underwriting firm of Wilson, Clark and Mathews.

Industry

The electronics industry had enjoyed spectacular growth, in part because of the large-scale application of electronics to modern weapons. It was estimated that industry sales would reach $7.9 billion in 1959; this contrasted with industry sales of $3.3 billion in 1950.

Exhibit 21–1

PACIFIC ELECTRONICS, INC.

ANNUAL INDUSTRY SALES OF ELECTRONICS PRODUCTS
INCLUDING RADIO AND TV

(In Millions of Dollars)

1947	$1,750
1950	3,300
1952	5,490
1955	6,200
1957	7,000
1958	6,900
1959	7,900 (estimated)

SOURCE: *Standard & Poor's Industry Survey*, March 5, 1959.

---

* Copyright © 1960 by the President and Fellows of Harvard College.

Annual sales of the industry for certain years are shown in Exhibit 21–1.

The federal government was the largest buyer of electronic products, with military uses accounting for 58 percent of industry sales in 1958. Sales of individual companies were thus greatly dependent on decisions of the federal government relating to defense spending. In 1959, prices of many electronics stocks hit new highs as investors indicated confidence that industry growth would continue.

History

The company started in 1951 as the part-time activity of 20 engineers then on the staff of the Electronics Laboratory of Western University, located in University City, California. Early work consisted of consulting in the evenings; this continued until 1955, when six members of the group withdrew from the Electronics Laboratory to devote their full time to the company. During the next few years, the company designed and began to manufacture specialized electronic test equipment. It also undertook a number of research and development projects involving missile guidance and radar.

As the company's reputation grew, sales expanded from $6,200 in 1952 to $375,000 in 1958. Personnel increased from one full-time employee in April, 1955, to 60 employees in 1957. The company changed location several times, with space increasing from 1,000 square feet to 20,000 square feet.

Operations were profitable in all years except 1951, 1953, and 1958. The 1958 deficit of $1,600 was caused primarily by the cutback in defense orders at that time. Pacific had moved to larger quarters and had expanded the staff to 60 in anticipation of a number of new contracts. When several orders were canceled and other prospective orders failed to materialize, it was necessary to release 20 men, 10 of them graduate engineers. Financial data for the years 1951 to 1959 are given in Exhibits 21–2 and 21–3.

Sales

Defense spending increased in 1959, and, by February, Pacific Electronics had a $225,000 backlog, the largest in company history; sales were being made at the annual rate of almost $600,000. Management felt that this growth in sales would continue, and plans were being made upon the basis of the following sales predictions:

Exhibit 21-2

PACIFIC ELECTRONICS, INC.

STATEMENTS OF INCOME FOR THE YEARS ENDING SEPTEMBER 30, 1951 THROUGH 1958 AND FOR THE SIX MONTHS ENDING MARCH 31, 1959

	1951	1952	1953	1954	1955	1956	1957	1958	(six months) 1959
Net sales	$1,740	$6,200	$10,293	$23,843	$41,412	$147,382	$358,995	$374,961	$294,876
Cost of sales	1,425	3,730	6,865	18,361	24,727	112,355	298,475	322,135	256,350
Gross margin	$ 315	$2,470	$ 3,428	$ 5,482	$16,685	$ 35,027	$ 60,520	$ 52,826	$ 38,526
Operating expenses	533	2,352	3,532	4,705	15,437	29,585	38,197	54,423	27,565
Income (loss) before federal income taxes	$ (218)	$ 118	$ (104)	$ 777	$ 1,248	$ 5,442	$ 22,323	$ (1,597)	$ 10,961
Provision for federal income taxes					401	1,802	7,370		3,368
Net income	$ (218)	$ 118	$ (104)	$ 777	$ 847	$ 3,640	$ 14,953	$ (1,597)	$ 7,593
Refundable federal income taxes									9,608
Net Income Plus Refundable Federal Income Tax	$ (218)	$ 118	$ (104)	$ 777	$ 847	$ 3,640	$ 14,953	$ (1,597)	$ 17,201

Year	Annual Sales
1959	$ 540,000
1960	675,000
1961	900,000
1962	1,200,000
1963	1,600,000

In 1959, about 80 percent of sales was contract research and development work; the remainder was divided between consulting and manufacturing. It was sometimes difficult to draw a distinction between manufacturing and development, since development often involved the production of prototypes. The production of units subsequent to the prototypes was usually defined as manufacturing. It was anticipated that manufacturing would account for an increasing percentage of total sales in the future.

The company was both a prime and subcontractor; subcontracting accounted for over half the total sales. Contracts were on the basis of both fixed-price and cost-plus-fixed-fee. The percentages of each were expected to change as follows:

	1958	1959	1960
Fixed price	20%	50%	60%
Cost + fixed fee	80	50	40

Government defense contracts accounted for 85 percent of total sales in 1958. The cost-plus-fixed-fee government contracts provided reimbursement of costs, as stipulated in the Armed Services Procurement Regulations, plus profit in the form of a fixed amount. The profit rarely exceeded 10 percent of total costs. Other government contracts were on a fixed-price basis in that a price was established for each unit. Some of these were redeterminable, with profits seldom going above 10 percent. On other fixed-price contracts, the price was fixed regardless of cost. Mr. Phillips considered fixed-price contracts without provision for redetermination more desirable for work in areas in which the company was experienced, because savings due to improved methods could then contribute to increased profits.

Most sales resulted from successful bidding for contracts. The company employed three methods to learn about and solicit business. One method was to read about new projects in trade journals. Unfortunately, this source was of limited value, because most of the contracts had already been awarded by the time news articles appeared. The second method, and the one which had proved most valuable in the past, was through personal contact with others in the industry. On an informal basis, on such occasions as meetings of technical socie-

Exhibit 21–3

PACIFIC ELECTRONICS, INC.

BALANCE SHEETS AS OF SEPTEMBER 30, 1951, THROUGH 1958
AND AS OF MARCH 31, 1951

	1951	1952	1953	1954	1955	1956	1957	1958	(March 31) 1959
ASSETS									
Current Assets:									
Cash	$1,101	$ 632	$ 543	$ 585	$ 4,225	$13,205	$ 14,473	$ 22,639	$ 15,990
Accounts receivable	550	467	2,017	1,189	9,176	34,266	54,910	63,111	120,753
Inventories	398	4,368	13,142	7,500	3,628	10,048	34,562	66,201	35,925
Refundable federal income taxes (Note A)									9,607
Prepaid expenses					320	1,009	3,238	3,921	3,788
Total Current Assets	$2,049	$5,467	$15,702	$ 9,274	$17,349	$58,528	$107,183	$155,872	$186,063
Cash value of life insurance							356	2,053	2,053
Fixed assets, including leasehold improvements, net of depreciation			2,020	1,856	3,032	5,279	15,551	12,769	11,998
Deferred charges (Note B)								30,394	30,394
Total Assets	$2,049	$5,467	$17,722	$11,130	$20,381	$63,807	$123,090	$201,088	$230,508

Exhibit 21-3—Continued

LIABILITIES AND STOCKHOLDERS' EQUITY

	1951	1952	1953	1954	1955	1956	1957	1958	(March 31) 1959
Current Liabilities:									
Accounts payable	$ 155	$ 47	$ 6,357	$ 2,023	$ 757	$ 1,466	$ 3,765	$ 35,122	$ 27,023
Notes payable: Banks, demand			3,000	1,200	4,971	27,300	45,196	97,797	114,356
Salaries and wages payable	835		1,870	1,037		4,533	6,140	4,676	1,315
Payroll taxes payable	247	362	649	247	2,312	3,276	8,733	4,376	7,141
Estimated federal income tax liability						1,841	7,390		3,367
Total Current Liabilities	$1,237	$ 409	$11,876	$ 4,507	$ 8,040	$38,416	$ 71,227	$141,971	$153,202
Stockholders' Equity:									
Common stock, $1.00 par value (Note C)	$ 687	$3,439	$ 4,034	$ 4,034	$ 7,281	$13,469	$ 21,118	$ 26,698	$ 27,286
Capital in excess of par value	343	1,719	2,016	2,016	3,640	6,862	10,732	14,003	14,403
Retained earnings	(218)	(100)	(204)	573	1,420	5,060	20,013	18,416	35,617
Total Stockholders' Equity	$ 812	$5,058	$ 5,846	$ 6,623	$12,341	$25,391	$ 51,863	$ 59,117	$ 77,306
Total Liabilities and Stockholders' Equity	$2,049	$5,467	$17,722	$11,130	$20,381	$63,807	$123,090	$201,088	$230,508

NOTE A: The company has adopted the policy, effective with its 1958 tax return, of deducting development costs on its federal income tax returns in the year in which incurred. The refundable federal income taxes ($9,607) represent the estimated refund due the company under the carryback provisions of the Internal Revenue Code in deducting development costs, discussed in Note B, for tax purposes and are a nonrecurring source of income.

NOTE B: The company has capitalized certain development costs which were incurred in the development on new commercial products. Tax benefits of the amortization of development costs of $30,394 have been realized as indicated in Note A.

The company plans to amortize approximately $18,000 of these development costs for the year ended September 30, 1959.

NOTE C: Of the 100,000 shares of common stock authorized, 27,286 shares were outstanding as of March 31, 1959. There were also outstanding options with respect to 2,280 shares at $2.61 per share, 550 shares at $2.46 per share, 400 shares at $1.89 per share, and 26,600 shares at $1.50 per share. Options as to 5,450 shares expire by September 30, 1959; 90 percent of these options are with respect to shares at $1.50 per share. The remaining options expire by September 30, 1960. Of the outstanding options, 85 percent have been granted to the four officers who hold slightly over 50 percent of the outstanding common stock.

ties, company executives learned of projects in which the company might be interested. Sometimes, because of its reputation, the company was asked to bid on certain projects. A third method, and one which Pacific was using increasingly, was to contact certain technical groups and purchasing agents within the government. Until 1959, this had been done on a limited scale by company officers; however, in early 1959 the company engaged two sales representatives to do some of this contact work.

One representative worked with air force procurement at Wright-Patterson Field in Dayton, Ohio. His job was to inform the government of Pacific's abilities in fields in which research was contemplated and to inform Pacific of possible opportunities to submit bids. He received a $500-per-month retainer fee and also represented another company. In four months, his work had not resulted in any contracts, but air force procurement had formally requested Pacific to bid on 12 projects. No formal requests had ever been received before.

The other man had started to represent Pacific in March, 1959. He was located in Washington and had contacts with higher levels of government procurement. He devoted only a small portion of his time to Pacific's interests and received a fee of $100 per month. Several requests to bid on projects had been received as a result of his efforts, although no contracts had resulted. A full-time salesman was to be hired in mid-1959. By 1963, management expected that there would be two full-time salesmen in addition to the two men on retainer in Dayton and Washington.

From 3 to 30 companies competed with Pacific in bidding on each project. They varied in size from companies even smaller than Pacific to Minneapolis–Honeywell, with some competitors very similar to Pacific. Management felt that demonstrated capability was more important than low price in successfully competing for bids.

Production and Physical Plant

In 1959, about 10 percent of total sales represented custom manufacturing; this work was done by trained technicians. Although it was thought that manufacturing was more profitable than research and development contracts, management had decided on a basic policy of manufacturing only when the company had some unique advantage over competition, such as that arising from the development of a product. Mr. Phillips thought the company did not have the facilities or know-how to compete effectively in manufacturing, solely on the basis of manufacturing skill. He wondered if Pacific might someday profitably purchase a company with manufacturing experience. In 1958, the company moved to the fourth floor of a large building, on the outskirts of University City, which contained 20,000 square feet of floor space. This space was considered adequate to support annual sales of $1.2 million. Mr. Phillips had been told that an additional 20,000 square feet on the third floor of the same building could be leased when needed.

Personnel

An outside observer had commented that the outstanding asset of Pacific Electronics was brains. In 1959, there were 18 graduate engineers, 6 with masters' degrees, working for the company. In addition, several members of the faculty of Western University, who were outstanding in their specialized fields, were associated with the company as consultants. There was a great shortage of engineers in the field, and the company considered its close contact with Western University to have been an advantage in attracting outstanding young graduate engineers from that school.

Certain nontechnical members of the organization had also come from Western University. The company controller had been assistant accounting officer of the university; the treasurer, whose association with the company was part time, was the business manager of the electronics laboratory of the university. A member of the local financial community had commented that he was impressed by Mr. Phillips' understanding of business management, by the company's reputation for technical competence, and by the fact that management did not appear to be a one-man show.

Finance

Mr. Phillips thought the company needed $200,000 to $300,000 immediately in long-term capital. Of immediate concern was the financing of two $150,000 contracts on which the company would start work in late summer 1959; these contracts provided for the development and installation of electronic test equipment. Each would require expenditures of about $70,000 for materials. Pacific would be unable to bill for these projects until the equipment was delivered, installed, and tested, which was expected to be about four months after the start of the projects. However, testing and final clearance for payment was sometimes delayed.

The Metropolitan National Bank had indicated it was willing to increase Pacific's line of credit from $115,000 to $200,000 to help finance these projects, if the bank had assurance that Pacific would obtain additional equity capital. Management planned to use about $25,000 of the new capital for certain items of new equipment; the remainder would be invested in working capital. Mr. Phillips indicated that initially about $100,000 to $150,000 of materials would be purchased, and the remaining money would be used to reduce the bank loan and accounts payable. As sales expanded, it was thought that the line of credit with Metropolitan Bank might build up to as high as $250,000. Mr. Phillips thought this new capital would support total annual sales of almost $2 million.

In considering kinds of financing, Mr. Phillips did not think the company could afford heavy fixed charges. He felt that the rapid growth forecast for the company would mean a great demand for funds in the years ahead, and that the company therefore would not be in a position either to amortize a term loan or to pay interest charges. A second point of concern was control of the company. Four men, all active in the management of the company, owned slightly over 50 percent of the stock. Ownership of the remaining stock was divided among 38 people, all of whom were either present or former employees, directors, or officers of the company. These men had worked hard and had seen the company grow from a part-time venture to its present size. After these efforts, they did not want outsiders to take over the management of the firm. As Mr. Phillips said, "We would like to keep running our own show."

The executives of Pacific Electronics were not certain whether any plan of financing could be arranged which would provide $200,000 to $300,000 of long-term capital, would not impose heavy fixed charges on the company, and would permit the present owners to retain control. However, all members of the Pacific management felt that action would have to be taken soon; financial worries were distracting executives from the engineering projects on which they were working.

There was also the possibility of a merger. Because of the specialized experience and knowledge of the men in the organization, Pacific Electronics was attractive to certain larger, better financed companies. Mr. Phillips had talked to several companies, and it was rumored that the board of directors of one company had authorized an offer. Although such a possibility offered relief from financial worries, the

Pacific management was concerned over possible loss of identity within the larger organization.

It was at this time, in March, 1959, that Mr. Phillips was introduced to John Buckley, who was associated with the underwriting firm of Wilson, Clark and Mathews. Mr. Buckley had helped to arrange equity financing for a number of other small manufacturing firms in the past. During the next few weeks, except as he was limited by restrictions concerning the release of classified information, Mr. Buckley made an intensive study of Pacific operations. His investigation included products, customers, margins, and the relation between the timing of expenditures and receipts for particular contracts. He then sought to develop a plan of financing which would meet the needs of the company and also be attractive to customers of Wilson, Clark and Mathews who were interested in capital gains.

After formulating a plan, Mr. Buckley arranged to present it to the board of directors of Pacific Electronics. He invited Mr. Phillips and the other directors to dinner in a conference room of a downtown hotel. After the directors were well fed, Mr. Buckley went to a blackboard, which he had had placed in the front of the room, and presented the following plan:

1. 100,000 shares of Class A common stock with limited voting rights would be authorized and offered for sale to the public through Wilson, Clark and Mathews. Total authorized stock would then consist of 100,000 shares of Class A stock and 100,000 shares of Class B stock, the presently existing common, both of par value $1.00.
2. The offering price to the public would be $3.00 per share; the underwriters would receive 30 cents per share sold plus 1 share for each 19 shares sold. Thus, if the entire 100,000 shares were issued, 95,000 shares would be sold to the public, with a commission of 30 cents per share; this would provide $256,500 to the company. The underwriters would then receive a commission of $28,500 plus 5,000 shares, for which they would make no payment in cash.
3. There was to be a firm underwriting of 80,000 shares, of which the underwriters would receive 4,000 shares and agree to purchase 76,000 shares for cash. The remaining 2,000 shares were on a best efforts basis, with the underwriters to receive 1 share for each 19 shares sold to the public plus 30 cents for each share sold to the public.
4. The board of directors was to be increased from five to nine members, with three members being elected by the holders of Class A stock. This is a nonvoting stock except for the right to elect these directors and the provision relating to authorization of additional stock (item 6).
5. The Class A stock and Class B stock would participate in ordinary dividends, share for share as though one class; and in any distribution

made in liquidation on the basis that the Class A stock should first receive $3.00 per share, the Class B stock should then receive $3.00 per share, and any further distribution "should be divided equally between the two classes of stock."

6. Except as approved by a majority of Class A stock, no stock senior to it or on a parity with it, and no increase in Class B stock beyond 100,-000 shares should be authorized.

7. The outstanding options to purchase 29,830 shares of stock at prices ranging from $1.50 per share to $2.61 per share may be exercised. No further options shall be granted to purchase Class B stock for less than the book value at the time the options are granted.

Mr. Buckley proposed that the offering be made under Regulation A of the Securities Act of 1933. The provisions of this regulation are given in the appendix.

After Mr. Buckley had presented his proposal and answered questions, he withdrew and the Pacific directors discussed the offer.

One executive said, "There's something wrong here; it's too good to be true. These investors would be putting more money into the company than we have. They must be crazy to acquire such a stake in the company's future and not want control."

Another director pointed out that many listed electronic stocks sold at several times book value. Therefore, he felt that Pacific should also receive several times book value for any new common stock issued, and he urged rejection of the offer.

Mr. Myer, the treasurer, then spoke. "Unless we get substantial amounts of new funds immediately, we'll be unable to bid on several attractive projects that are being considered. We need money badly and we need it now; we're not in a position to haggle or to turn down an offer like this."

After further discussion, it was evident that other directors were waiting for Mr. Phillips to express an opinion.

APPENDIX 21–A

Regulation A of the Securities Act of 1933

Under Regulation A of the Securities Act of 1933, exemption from registration is provided for small public offerings in which the amount the public pays does not exceed $300,000. This exemption is not automatic but is available only if certain conditions are met. These include the filing of a notification with the SEC, and the filing and use of an offering circular containing basic information about the company, its financial condition, properties, officers and directors, the underwriter, and the security itself. The offering circular must be delivered to each prospective purchaser at or before the time any written offer to sell the security is made.

Ordinary registration of public offerings under the Securities Act of 1933 requires the disclosure of considerably more information about the company than issuance of securities under Regulation A.

22. VENCAP, INC.*

Establishing a Venture Capital Firm

Actually, I don't know if we are going to make it or not. For the past three years a group of us has been trying to build $5,000 and an idea into a company with somewhere between $5 and $10 million of capital. As I write this article, we are just approaching the point where we expect either to take off at high speed, or fall on our faces and have to begin all over again. Your guess is as good as mine as to how it will turn out.

Our enterprise is VenCap, Inc., a closed-end investment company organized in 1955 to produce capital appreciation for its stockholders by furnishing equity capital to individuals and small firms with promising new ideas, processes, and products. Right now, after at least one failure, we have two projects going which could take us around the corner. They were selected from literally hundreds of possibilities that have been presented to us, ranging from novel toothpicks to $400,000 machines.

But I am getting ahead of my story. Let me give you the background.

Back in early 1955 a group of about 20 B-School students who were graduating that June and planning to settle in the Boston area got together several times to see if they couldn't form an investment club. Some of us were particularly interested in making venture capital investments in new enterprises; others wanted to participate actively in the management of lively new companies. So we worked out a format which would combine the two objectives by providing a limited amount of "starting capital" and some management know-how.

We figured that off-beat new ideas need this kind of boost in their early stages. So our money was to go for market testing of new products, the investigation of the commercial feasibility of unusual ideas, and the initial investment for production equipment required for really promising opportunities. Furthermore, we reasoned, very few small firms that are just getting started can afford a balanced, full-time management. Consequently, we decided that we would offer help, either on a limited basis by supplying representation on a Board of Directors, or on a larger scale through direct assistance by VenCap personnel. In short, we agreed that we would provide management assistance whenever and wherever desirable and possible in order to improve the company's chance for success and shorten its development period.

We Get Our First Shock

Little did we imagine what *that* idea was going to involve!

At any rate, having settled on our objectives, we turned to the problem of capital. At this point we got our first shock: we could only raise about $5,000 between us, and that kind of money wasn't going very far.

But by this time we had become enthusiastic about the idea and its potential, so we determined to incorporate and seek outside money to supplement our own limited resources. A study of various SEC regulations revealed that we would be classified as an investment company and, thus, be subject to the "Investment Company Act of 1940." We believed that we could operate under this regulation by obtaining certain exemptions, but this meant conforming to two basic requirements: we had to hold our capitalization down to $100,000 and sell all our stock to residents of Massachusetts.

Undismayed by these limitations, we went ahead with our plans, which called for starting with slightly less than $100,000, establishing a successful operating record, and later relinquishing our SEC exemptions and marketing a substantial stock issue.

VenCap, Inc., was organized as a Massachusetts corporation in September, 1955, with an authorized 4,500 shares of no par value common stock. The long and detailed application for the exemptions was prepared and filed with the SEC, and in December, 1955, the agency issued an order granting our request.

We began our preparations and launched a Massachusetts public offering at $20 per share in February, 1956. Then began a long series of promotional activities, telephone calls, letters, evening meetings with potential stockholders, and what not. It's not easy to sell stock in an idea, but by June some 180 investors had taken up the entire issue.

Our total company organization expenses, plus the cost of issuing, distributing, and selling the stock came to less than $2,000—a very modest sum indeed for such an undertaking. Needless to say, the low figure was made possible only by many hours of uncompensated evening and weekend effort, since all the participants held regular full-time jobs.

Before actually launching VenCap's program, we decided to strengthen the Board of Directors by adding some people of more experience. So we enlisted the assistance of some mature and well-regarded men who joined those of the original group on the Board—Vernon Bahr '55, Chairman of the Board; Francis E. Baker, Jr. '55, President; Jerome S. Augustine '52, Treasurer; William H. White '55, Clerk; and William R. Haney '55, Director.

They Said "It Can't Be Done"

During the whole process, people constantly told us that VenCap was doomed to failure. Come to think of it, some still are. After all, we are warned, we have a relatively small capitalization, our personnel are inexperienced, and the risks involved in financing new enterprises are high indeed. But we thought then—and we think now—that the potential gains in comparison to the risks make Vencap a worthwhile venture. Furthermore, we maintain that success is never the result of a statistical average, but rather of individual talent and judgment.

In selling the stock, we said frankly that this was a high-risk security. In addition, we assured our stockholders and potential stockholders that they would be given the first opportunity to make direct investments in any promising companies which we might establish, or in attractive situations where VenCap did not supply the entire initial capital requirements. Up to now we have not sought outside funds, but we expect that direct investments by stockholders participating on a joint venture basis will eventually become an important aspect of our operations. As a matter of fact, for many of our stockholders this possibility of direct investment supplies the most appealing reason for participation in our company. With the financial foundation laid, active VenCap operations were started in July, 1956. Bill White assumed responsibility for the preparation of all financial reports and records; Jerry Augustine, Frank Baker, and I became the full-time (but unsalaried) operating nucleus of the firm. A small office was opened and, with the assistance of other VenCap directors, we began a concentrated search for intriguing investment opportunities.

Originally we expected to work half time for VenCap and the other half on consulting or research activities which would generate some income for us. But we had to abandon this idea very quickly because locating and evaluating potential new enterprises proved to be a most time-consuming task.

We had no idea that there were so many people with projects looking for money! During our organization period alone, we turned up nearly 100 possibilities which were carefully reviewed. Though none of them worked out, they did serve to guide us to sources for other leads.

Our first step was to prepare a small brochure outlining our proposed investment activities in order to help introduce us to the investment community. We then made personal calls on bank loan officers throughout the area, met with personnel from state and area development groups, the federal Small Business Administration, investment brokerage houses, business brokers, and loan companies. We sent a mailing to many corporation and patent attorneys, and made follow-up calls on any who expressed an interest.

All these activities certainly opened the floodgates! Almost all of the ideas that came pouring through were completely unsuitable for us; only about ten in every one hundred even merited our serious consideration. Of these, only about one in ten seemed worthy of a detailed investigation. And, again, only one in ten passed through this fine screening. In short, we figure that our "promising opportunity ratio" is about one out of every thousand possibilities that are offered to us.

The Pot of Gold and the Rainbow

But these percentages don't worry the inventors. Almost without exception, they all are convinced that if they could just get adequate financing, their idea would make at least a million dollars.

I wish I had the space to describe even a handful of the items we have looked at and the people who have presented them to us. I'll never forget the morning I came into the office to find an enormously fat man sitting on our bench holding a little paper umbrella over his head—or the highly secretive inventor who spent what seemed like ages telling us about the potential of his idea and inquiring into our methods before he would break down and let us know what he had in mind. (Turned out to be a drying frame for bras—we weren't interested!)

Then there was the man who came in carrying an enormous arm-load of drawings, pictures, sketches, blueprints, and so forth, and asked, "Do you have a few minutes to look over my invention?" Looked to us more like a few hours or years! And what about the fellow who appeared at the door with a large suitcase in each hand? "I brought a small model along to show you the machine in operation," he said. And behind him we could see two of his husky associates struggling under the weight of an enormous trunk.

Well, we've been offered a device which measures—and records—the amount of liquor poured from bottles (very helpful when dealing with your wife's relatives); a gold mine in the West; a firm to process trash fish into fish oil and ground fish meal; ultraviolet microscopes; radiant heating equipment; a housing development for retired couples; and an automatic window-cleaning machine.

Many of the situations have been highly interesting. One man had a system which would feed the sound for drive-in theaters into car radios in order to improve its quality. Another possibility was a new kind of rubber for use in spin-casting of jewelry; still a third person created a special kind of oil to be used in breaking in automobile engines.

And so it goes—some good, some strictly from Rube Goldberg; some developed by experienced, well-trained inventors, some by out-and-out promoters and dreamers. A few of the potential entrepreneurs appeared to be shysters; others had devoted many years and all of their personal funds to the development of their ideas.

Sorting the sheep from the goats—and making sure that we ourselves didn't fall into either category—was a tough job indeed. To help in the investigation and evaluation of potential investment, we have been able to obtain valuable guidance from many experienced businessmen and scientists. As a matter of fact, we are constantly surprised by the extent of uncompensated advice and assistance which is available for evaluating a product or starting a new enterprise. Many people, apparently, have a real interest in small business, and will gladly devote some time and effort to assist a new enterprise.

From this host of possibilities we picked out three situations that appeared promising. But our first one let us down miserably, and, as I have said, we have yet to find out what the other two will do.

We started off on our first venture in the fall of 1956 with two garden novelty items which we hoped would be the foundation of a company for marketing promising new consumer products. One was a plastic and metal drinking fountain for children which could be attached to any standard threaded outdoor faucet; the other was a novel dispenser for water-soluble fertilizers. It seemed to us that these two items were naturals. Housewives, we figured, would be delighted with the prospect of keeping muddy feet out of their kitchens by providing facilities for a drink outside, and do-it-yourself fans certainly would welcome this new means of keeping their gardens and lawns well nourished.

So we did all the "right" things. We checked the products with many people who had had experience in this line, and they were all enthusiastic. We showed models at hardware trade shows, called on department stores and catalogue houses, talked to potential consumers. It seemed foolproof.

All in all, these two items apparently met our need for novelties which could be manufactured easily, would support administrative and distribution costs, and would return a good profit to our stockholders.

To get the project under way, we established a wholly-owned subsidiary which was designed to serve as a vehicle for marketing the products, and invested $25,000. The promoters already had tool and die facilities for building plastic molds and the other equipment required.

We hired a sales manager who had extensive experience in marketing novelty products and soon had achieved national distribution through 20 manufacturers' representatives. Within four months from the date we went into production, our sales to the trade exceeded $200,000. The drinking fountain was carried by nearly every major hardware wholesaler and department store in the country; Sears Roebuck and many small mail-order houses had taken it on; and trade channels were well stocked. We began counting our chickens: according to our expectations, first-year sales could run over $1 million with profits hitting a figure of over $100,000.

Everything was set, and we were on our way.

It Should Have Worked Out

Then suddenly something happened. The consumer didn't behave as he was supposed to at all. "What an interesting product," he said, as he walked past the items on the dealers' shelves. But he never stopped to put down his money, so we had no reorders from the trade, and the retailers were hip-deep in drinking fountains and fertilizers.

Happily, we saw the trend quickly enough to salvage two-thirds of our investment by cutting back production and personnel and unloading all remaining inventory. Eventually the production equipment was sold, and we emerged with wounded pride, but without disastrous losses.

We took our second plunge in early 1957. This time we decided to finance a new company which had developed a spring-activated starter for small gasoline engines. Since our device has a reasonable cost and is much easier to operate than the usual rope-pull equipment on such products as outboards and power lawn mowers, we think the potential market is excellent. Sales of power mowers total about four million units in the United States each year, and the figure on outboards runs to hundreds of thousands.

Of course, people have been trying to develop such a starter for a long time. But our inventor has struck on a new angle which seems to have licked the major problems which had interfered in the past, and we are very hopeful.

Our funds supported testing and further development of the starter, and made it possible to obtain increased patent protection. Our management efforts were devoted to finding out exactly how the manufacturers wanted the starter to perform and look, and what were the best methods to sell the starter in volume to lawn mower manufacturers and retail garden equipment outlets.

We decided that the best sales approach was to license the device to one of the three major small gasoline engine manufacturers. So we concluded a favorable exclusive licensing arrangement with the manufacturer which we believed was best suited to the job of producing and selling the starters. The agreement was signed, sealed, and delivered this winter, and the starter company itself is currently inactive awaiting royalty income from starter sales.

If these sales come up to our expectations, we should receive a very substantial return on our original investment—and thus far everything looks fine. But we can't help remembering the drinking fountain and the fertilizer dispenser—so we are keeping our fingers crossed.

We Get into Electronics

Last spring, as our third venture, we financed a new and highly specialized electronics company which was established in conjunction with experienced technical people. The company is called Microsonics, Inc., and designs and produces ultrasonic solid delay lines. These devices are intricate electronic components which are used to store or delay electrical signals for a precise interval of time—measured in millionths of a second. They are used primarily in advanced radar systems, electronic counter-measures, and in certain electronic testing equipment.

Preliminary production difficulties in this field, where manufacture is part art and part science, have slowed us up, so Microsonics is not as far along as we thought it would be by this time. But we seem to have overcome the initial road blocks and have completed a number of difficult projects. The sales potential looks increasingly favorable to us—but you can never tell!

So we are still at the stage of holding our breaths on this one, too—especially in view of the fact that the company is going to need some additional financing for working capital in the next few months. We hope that by July it will be strong enough to seek outside financing; in the meantime, we will supply as much help as we can. But if it isn't able to go out on its own for money by the summer—well, we'll have a new set of problems to deal with.

In the face of these two embryonic operations, VenCap is cutting back on overhead and holding off on any future investments temporarily. The company is balanced on a knife edge, and the next year or so should tell the story.

If you see a spring starter or an ultrasonic solid delay line on the market, talk it up, won't you? And how about buying half a dozen?

Exhibit 22–1

OFFERING CIRCULAR

VenCap, Inc.

Organized September 9, 1955
as a Massachusetts Corporation

A "VENTURE" or "RISK CAPITAL" Enterprise

**4330 Shares of no par value COMMON STOCK
Price $20.00 per Share**

THESE SECURITIES ARE OFFERED PURSUANT TO AN EXEMPTION FROM REGISTRATION WITH THE SECURITIES AND EXCHANGE COMMISSION. THE COMMISSION DOES NOT PASS UPON THE MERITS OF ANY SECURITIES NOR DOES IT PASS UPON THE ACCURACY OR COMPLETENESS OF ANY OFFERING CIRCULAR OR OTHER SELLING LITERATURE.

	Offering Price	Underwriting Discounts and Commissions[1]	Net Proceeds to Issuer[2]
Total[3]	$86,600.00	none	$86,600.00
Per Share	20.00	none	20.00

[1] The shares are offered directly by the Company itself.

[2] Before deduction of expenses of the Company, estimated at $1500.

[3] Assuming that all shares offered hereby are sold.

THIS OFFERING AVAILABLE TO MASSACHUSETTS RESIDENTS ONLY

The date of this Offering Circular is February 16, 1956

Exhibit 22–1—Continued

VENCAP, INC.

**100 Memorial Drive
Cambridge, Mass.**

TABLE OF CONTENTS

No person has been authorized to give any information or to make any representations other than those contained in this Offering Circular and, if given or made, such information or representations must not be relied upon as having been authorized by the Company. This Offering Circular does not constitute an offer to sell Common Shares to anyone who is not a resident of Massachusetts.

Exhibit 22–1—Continued

OBJECTIVES OF THE COMPANY

The founders of VenCap, Inc. believe that many investment opportunities exist in small and growing enterprises with promising products, processes and market positions. In our Nation's rapidly changing and highly specialized technology, many new products and processes are being generated by small firms and individuals not affiliated with large organizations. Also, frequently small firms with superior, although not new, products enjoy market positions that could be further developed. VenCap, Inc. was established to provide a medium through which individual investors may participate in such venture capital opportunities.

VenCap, Inc. proposes to furnish capital to individuals and small firms with promising ideas, processes and products. It is the belief of the founders of the Company that the location and selection of these promising venture capital possibilities will be facilitated by the unusual personnel resources of VenCap, Inc. All of its officers and directors have had extensive business training, and most are young and in a position to apply their knowledge and abilities to the difficult task of judging men and ideas.

The venture capital opportunities in which the Company invests should have a good prospect of producing long-term capital appreciation. VenCap, Inc., by providing a diversification over a number of such enterprises, expects to constitute a medium of investing in such situations at a minimized risk. Further, by investing in these enterprises at an early stage in their growth, VenCap, Inc. extends to its shareholders the possibility of unusual growth of capital.

Within the limits of sound business practice, VenCap, Inc. expects to regularly distribute to its shareholders information on the enterprises in which it has made investments. It is expected that through this information Company shareholders will have the added opportunity of making private commitments in promising opportunities in the event that the Company is not interested, for portfolio reasons, in supplying all the capital needed for a particular enterprise.

3

Exhibit 22–1—Continued

POLICIES

It is a fundamental policy of the Company that its principal and primary activities will consist of investigation, research and analysis with respect to new or existing enterprises, processes or products, and of furnishing capital to or purchasing securities of other companies primarily and principally engaged in the conduct or development of new enterprises, processes or products, or the development of existing processes or products. The Company reserves freedom, however, to hold cash uninvested, to invest for limited periods in Government Bonds, or to invest in other securities if, in the opinion of its Directors, such a policy be prudent at any time.

The Company does not propose to issue securities senior to the shares of Common Stock offered hereby; however, the Company reserves the right to borrow money for its corporate purposes on short term paper or bank loans authorized by its Board of Directors and deemed by the Board to be reasonably necessary or advisable in connection with the profitable operation of the Company's business, and to pledge or mortgage any of the Company's assets to secure same.

There is no particular industry or group of industries in which the Company intends or proposes to concentrate its investments or expenditures. It may develop in the early life of the Company that its investments or expenditures will be concentrated in one particular industry or group of industries. However, the Company will not invest more than 50% of its capital and surplus in the securities of any one company or enterprise, nor more than 75% of its capital and surplus in any two companies or enterprises.

The Company has no fixed policies with respect to acquiring control of the companies in which it invests. It is anticipated that in some instances the Company will have control of companies or enterprises in which it invests, and it may form and thereafter control subsidiaries for the purpose of facilitating the policies of the Company.

The Company has no fixed policies as to the type of securities in which it will invest its assets, but it is expected that the Company will invest primarily in common stocks and securities convertible into common stocks. The Company intends to select for its investment portfolio securities which, in the opinion of the Directors, may be retained profitably on a long-term basis. However, the Company reserves freedom of action with respect to porfolio turnover as it is expected that the Company in buying securities will contemplate the probability that they will ultimately be sold and in particular instances may be sold at a relatively early date.

The Company does not propose to engage in the general business of purchasing securities with a view to distribution thereof and accordingly does not intend to engage in the general business of underwriting securities issued by other persons. The Company will not invest in securities issued by any other investment companies.

The Company does not intend to engage in the business of purchasing and selling real estate or commodities or commodity contracts, and does not intend to engage directly in

Exhibit 22–1—Continued

manufacturing or merchandising. The Company does not propose to engage in the business of making loans to other persons other than loans or advances to promote the commercial development of such articles, processes, business enterprises or endeavors as the Board of Directors deems to embrace possibilities of ultimate gain or profit to the Company.

In addition, the Company is subject to restrictions under the provisions of the Investment Company Act of 1940, particularly with respect to transactions with certain affiliated persons and underwriters, borrowing money, restrictions on the creation of cross-ownership or circular ownership of shares between any issuer and the Company, and restrictions on changing investment policies without the consent of shareholders. The Company is not permitted to issue any of its securities (1) for services; or (2) for property other than cash or securities except as a dividend or distribution to its security holders or in connection with a reorganization. Moreover, the Company may not sell any common stock of which it is the issuer at a price below the current net asset value of such stock except in accordance with certain provisions of the Act.

THE COMPANY

Introductory Statement

Boston and its suburban towns are dotted with laboratories and workshops which are unknown at this time to investors. A number of these small concerns are potential contributors to the Nation's economic and scientific growth, but ideas are lying dormant in their workshops because of lack of capital and management skills. These many untapped sources of ideas and developments offer significant opportunities for the profitable placement of venture capital.

Due in part to the proximity to great educational centers and to well-known research organizations, and in part to the pioneering and enterprising nature of Massachusetts investors, Massachusetts is an area in which new developments, new ideas and new processes have flourished. However, the profitable placement of capital needed by the more promising laboratories and workshops is a job requiring considerable time and a high degree of professional judgment and training. The establishment of a medium through which investors could participate in such venture capital projects was discussed from time to time by several businessmen living and working in the Boston area. Out of these discussions came the idea of forming VenCap, Inc.

History

In early 1955, a proposal was advanced calling for the establishment of a corporation whose function would be to seek out new ideas, processes and products, and to furnish capital necessary for the successful development of these ideas, processes and products. In March of 1955, a meeting was held and a resolution was drawn recognizing a common desire to organize the proposed corporation and to assist in its development. The persons participating in these organizational efforts have received no remuneration from any source for such participation (with the exception of Norman P. Singer, Director and General Counsel, who received $200.00 for certain legal services), nor will they receive any remuneration therefor from the Company, although certain of the persons will be directors and officers of the Company and for their services in such capacities may receive remuneration from the Company.

Exhibit 22–1—Continued

On September 9, 1955, the Company was organized as a business corporation under the laws of the Commonwealth of Massachusetts. The Company's charter powers have been designed to enable the Company, from the standpoint of Massachusetts Business Corporation Law, to function in the manner above indicated under the caption "Introductory Statement." The Company, under the Investment Company Act of 1940, is classified as a closed-end, non-diversified investment company of the management type.

Although a number of new ideas, processes and products have been investigated by the Company, no investments or investment commitments have been made as of the date of this Offering Circular.

Status Under Investment Company Act of 1940

In September, 1955, the Company filed an application for an order of the Securities and Exchange Commission for exemption from certain provisions of the Investment Company Act of 1940. In an amendment to the application, the Company agreed that it would accept and be subject to any specified provisions of the Act that the Commission deemed necessary or appropriate.

The Commission, having considered the matter, issued its order dated December 14, 1955, granting an exemption which provides in substance that: (1) the Company is exempted from Section 7 and thus not required to register under Section 8 of the Act, (2) the Company may make a public offering of securities without compliance with minimum net worth stipulations contained in Section 14 of the Act, (3) the Company is permitted to purchase securities of which it is the issuer, and (4) the Company is not required to file with the Commission many of the documents and reports set forth in Section 30 of the Act.

The Company, so long as it retains the above-mentioned exemption under the Act, may not sell securities in excess of the aggregate sum of $100,000; may sell its securities only to residents of Massachusetts; and must at all times maintain its classification as a closed-end investment company.

However, all provisions of the Act, except those specifically exempted, apply to the Company and to all other persons in their transactions and relations with the Company as though the Company were a registered investment company.

MANAGEMENT

The business and affairs of the Company are managed by the officers and a Board of Directors. The Directors and officers of the Company, and the present principal occupation of each, are as follows:

Name and Address	Position and Offices with Company	Present Principal Occupation
Jerome S. Augustine 10 Post Office Square Boston, Massachusetts	Director	Associate of Scudder, Stevens and Clark, Investment Counsel

Exhibit 22–1—Continued

Name and Address	Position and Offices with Company	Present Principal Occupation
Vernon A. Bahr Harvard Business School Soldiers Field Boston, Massachusetts	Director and Chairman of the Board	Member of the Faculty, Harvard Graduate School of Business Administration
Francis E. Baker, Jr. 26 Mt. Vernon St. Boston, Massachusetts	Director, Clerk and Treasurer	Business Research
Harry L. Barrett, Jr. 21 Main St. Durham, New Hampshire	Director	Business Research
John M. Frey 808 Commonwealth Ave. Boston, Massachusetts	Director	Assistant to the President, Cadillac Automobile Co. of Boston
Kingston L. Howard 40 Ames St. Cambridge, Massachusetts ·	Director and President	Assistant to the Sales Manager, Brigham's Inc.
Norman P. Singer 31 Chase St. Newton, Massachusetts	Director and General Counsel	Lawyer
Gordon L. Wahls 40 Ames St. Cambridge, Massachusetts	Director	Assistant to the General Manager, Brigham's, Inc.
William H. White Kendall Mills Walpole, Massachusetts	Director	Staff Accountant, Kendall Mills Finishing Division, The Kendall Company

Seven of the nine Directors—Messrs. Augustine, Bahr, Baker, Frey, Howard, Wahls and White—are graduates of the Harvard Graduate School of Business Administration. Norman P. Singer is a graduate of the Harvard Law School. Harry L. Barrett, Jr., holds a Ph.D. in Economics from Harvard University and is a graduate of Northeastern University School of Law. He was formerly an assistant professor at the University of New Hampshire. Gordon L. Wahls is currently a member of the faculty of Boston University.

Each of the nine Directors, with the exception of Harry L. Barrett, Jr., owns directly 10 shares of the Company's Common Stock. Harry L. Barrett, Jr., has a beneficial interest

Exhibit 22–1—Continued

in 10 shares. The sum of all shares mentioned above is 90, or approximately 60% of the outstanding shares of the Company.

The officers and Directors have agreed that, for the Company's first full fiscal year, they will serve without remuneration from the Company. However, officers and Directors may provide personal services to individuals and concerns in which the Company invests and for such services may receive remuneration directly from such individuals or concerns.

CAPITALIZATION

The capitalization of the Company consists of a single class of Common Stock with no par value, of which 4500 shares are authorized. There are now 151 shares issued and outstanding.

Each share is entitled to one vote for the election of directors and all other matters and to participate equally in the assets of the Company in the event of liquidation. Upon issuance, the shares offered hereby will be fully paid and nonassessable.

The holders of Common Stock are entitled to receive such dividends as may from time to time be declared by the Board of Directors of the Company. There is no provision in the charter or other instrument of organization or in any contract, undertaking or other instrument which restricts or limits the payment of dividends, or sources from which dividends may be declared or paid on the Common Stock. Nevertheless, any payment wholly or partly from any source other than net income must be accompanied by a statement disclosing the source or sources of such payment.

The Common Stock is not subject to call for redemption, but does have a restriction on the transferability thereof to the effect that no sale or transfer of shares shall be made to any person unless such shares shall have first been offered in accordance with the transfer restriction to the Company. [1]

The 151 shares of Common Stock presently outstanding were issued for cash, in the amount of $20.00 per share, to members of the Company's Board of Directors and to other persons who participated in the formation of the Company.

---

[1] **Restriction on transfer:** No sale or transfer of shares of stock of this corporation shall be made to any person unless such shares have first been offered for sale as hereinafter described. Such offer shall first be made in writing to the corporation and shall state the price at which the offeror is willing to sell and shall name an arbitrator. Within thirty days thereafter, the corporation, acting by its Board of Directors, may reject said offer or it may accept said offer at the price named or it may request to have such shares appraised by arbitration, in which event it shall name an arbitrator, and the two so named shall choose a third arbitrator. The arbitrators shall appraise the shares, the decision of a majority of the arbitrators to be binding. If any arbitrator shall neglect or refuse to appear at any meeting appointed by the arbitrators, a majority may act in the absence of such arbitrator. If the corporation shall choose to purchase said shares at the appraised value the offeror shall, upon payment or tender to him of such appraised value, transfer and assign such shares to the corporation. If the corporation rejects said offer or fails to take action on it within thirty days after it is made, or if the corporation fails to make payment or tender of the offered or appraised price within ten days after acceptance or appraisal, the offeror shall then be free to sell or transfer such shares to any person whatsoever, provided that if such shares have not been sold or transferred at the expiration of six months next succeeding the date of offer to the corporation, the offeror shall again hold the shares subject to restrictions of sale and transfer herein contained. The expenses of the arbitrators are to be borne equally by the parties.

Exhibit 22–1—Continued

TERMS OF OFFERING

The Company itself is offering hereby 4330 shares of its no par value Common Stock for cash at the rate of $20.00 per share. Each subscription for shares shall be evidenced by a subscription agreement substantially in the form of the one herein set forth under the caption of "Form of Subscription." The Company reserves the right, in its discretion, to reject any order or subscription, in whole or in part for the purchase of any of the Common Stock. If a subscription received by the Company is cancelled for any reason, the subscriber shall be relieved and discharged of any obligation of any kind to the Company and the Company shall likewise be relieved and discharged of any obligation of any kind to such subscriber.

The Company does not intend to make or authorize any concessions, commissions or variations in price as to the Common Stock offered hereby.

Correspondence relating to this offering should be addressed to Francis E. Baker, Jr., Treasurer; VenCap, Inc.; 100 Memorial Drive; Cambridge 42, Massachusetts. A convenient form of subscription is contained on the back page of this Offering Circular.

ESTIMATED EXPENSES OF OFFERING

The Company estimates that its expenses in connection with the issuance, distribution and sale of the 4330 shares will be approximately as follows:

Broker and Salesmen registration	$100.
Federal Original Issue Tax	130.
Mailing Expenses	270.
Printing	500.
Legal Expenses	100.
Miscellaneous, including travel, telephone and various out-of-pocket expenses	400.
TOTAL	$1,500.

APPLICATION OF PROCEEDS

After sale of the 4330 shares offered hereby, the net proceeds to the Company from such sale (after deduction of the expenses of offering estimated at $1500) will aggregate approximately $85,100. Such proceeds will enable the Company to make investments in such projects now under consideration as the Directors may approve and in such future projects as may be approved by the Directors. The Company reserves the right, however, to use the proceeds for such purposes as the Board of Directors, in its discetion, shall determine.

There are no requirements as to the amount of capital that must be paid in before the Company actually begins making investments. The Company anticipates that some investments may be made before sale of all the 4330 shares offered hereby.

Numerous projects have been called to the attention of the Company and the Company has under active consideration at the present time a variety of new ideas, processes and prod-

Exhibit 22–1—Continued

ucts. The Company does not intend to consider only those projects which are submitted to it, but is actively searching for promising developments. The form of investment in each of the projects will be determined by the needs of the project commensurate with ultimate capital appreciation for the shareholders of the Company.

An indication of the type of projects now being considered by the Company can be gained from the following brief listing:

participation in the development and licensing of a unique new method for animating advertising through the use of polarized light;

participation with a group of highly experienced electronic engineers desiring to establish a specialized research and development company;

participation in a company which by virtue of a new process manufactures and sells Continental pastries in a compact frozen form;

participation in the establishment of a company for the distribution and sale of a new and patented fungicide;

participation in a small company which manufactures and installs industrial deodorant systems based on a new chemical formula;

participation in the establishment of a company to license or to distribute and sell a new and patented machine tool component;

assistance in the development of an unusual method of lighting Christmas tree ornaments without the use of wires;

establishment of a firm to manufacture and market a new type of shoe polish which can be applied from an aerosol container;

assistance to an individual who has developed and patented a unique combination shutter and awning;

assistance to a small company with a patented line holder for use in building construction;

participation in a concern specializing in the integration of materials handling systems with automation systems;

participation in a firm controlling a patented keyboard which greatly reduces typing time;

participation in a company which has developed a hypodermic pain inhibitor;

participation in a company which has developed a new method of electro-heating;

participation in a company producing a new type of battery corrosion arrester;

participation in a boat manufacturing company which has an unusual manufacturing process and unique designs;

participation in a company which manufactures novelty products from wood waste; and

participation in a small electronics company engaged in developing and manufacturing specialized industrial products.

Exhibit 22–1—Continued

The Company contemplates that the investment in nearly any one of the above listed possible projects would be within the $15,000 to $30,000 range. No Director or officer of the Company now has an interest in any of these projects.

The above listing of possible projects does not constitute a representation that the Company intends to make investments in any of these projects. The projects are listed merely to provide an indication of the types of projects the Company is currently evaluating.

ADDITIONAL INFORMATION

The Company has not contacted any Underwriters for the purpose of soliciting their purchase of the Common Stock offered hereby or their assistance in the sale of the offering.

The First National Bank of Boston has been appointed Custodian of all securities and funds of the Company. This institution will perform no management or policy making functions for the Company. Company personnel having access to securities and funds are required to be bonded in such reasonable amount as the Board of Directors shall determine.

Reports showing the financial condition of the Company will be sent to all shareholders at least semi-annually, and will contain the usual and customary financial statements and a list of securities owned by the Company. Financial statements will be certified at least annually by independent public accountants.

Since income from dividends and interest is not a primary objective of the Company, it is anticipated that such income may not initially be sufficient to cover the operating costs of the Company.

Further information concerning the shares offered hereby and concerning the Company is to be found in the "Application for Exemption from Section 7 (a) of the Investment Company Act of 1940, Requested by VenCap, Inc., Under the Provisions of Section 6 (d) of Said Act" on file with the Securities and Exchange Commission, Washington, D.C. The application may be inspected by anyone at the office of the Commission without charge and copies of all or any part of it may be obtained upon payment of the Commission's charge for copying.

The Company itself will perform the functions of a Transfer Agent and a Registrar for its Common Stock.

Exhibit 22–1—Continued

FINANCIAL STATEMENTS

VENCAP, INC.
Balance Sheet
December 31, 1955

Assets		Liabilities & Net Worth	
Current Assets:		Net Worth:	
Cash	$2,575.79	Capital Stock—No Par Value:	
Subscriptions Receivable	340.00	Authorized, 4500 Shares;	
		Issued, 151 Shares	$3,020.00
Total Current Assets	$2,915.79	Subscribed but not Issued,	
		17 Shares	340.00
Organization Expense	444.21		
	$3,360.00		$3,360.00

Statement of Receipts and Disbursements
Through December 31, 1955

Net Cash Receipts		$3,020.00
Less Disbursements:		
Legal	$200.00	
Secretarial Services	73.39	
Printing	64.05	
Massachusetts Corporate Registration Fee	50.00	
Envelopes and Mimeographing	19.83	
Minute Book and Corporate Seal	18.50	
Telephone, Postage, Miscellaneous	18.44	444.21
Cash Balance		$2,575.79

14

Exhibit 22–1—Continued

FORM OF SUBSCRIPTION

Subscription to Common Stock

Dated _____, 1956

VenCap, Inc.
100 Memorial Drive
Cambridge 42, Massachusetts

Dear Sirs:

I hereby subscribe for _____ shares of the Common Stock of VenCap, Inc., a corporation organized under the laws of the Commonwealth of Massachusetts, and agree to pay therefor the sum of $20.00 per share, payable as follows:

This agreement is entered into with the understanding that the stock of VenCap, Inc. is composed solely of no-par common stock of the kind hereinabove subscribed for, and with the further understanding that the voting power at all stockholders' meetings is lodged in the holders of this stock.

It is agreed that no stock is to be issued under this agreement until the amount of this subscription is paid in full in cash, and any payment becoming due on the stock hereinabove subscribed for, or any note given therefor, not paid within 15 days after due, shall at the option of the Company cause this subscription to become null and void.

I understand and agree that this subscription is subject to rejection or acceptance by the Company and if accepted, such acceptance and the sale and delivery of said shares shall be deemed to take place in Massachusetts.

In case of my death before the subscription price is fully paid, the Company will refund the full amount paid by me to my legal representative, provided a request therefor, together with notice and proof of death, is given the Company within six months of date of death.

This subscription contains the entire agreement between the Company and myself. No agent or representative of the Company or any other person has any power to change or alter the terms of this subscription.

Receipt of a copy of the Offering Circular, dated February 16, 1956, relating to said shares is hereby acknowledged.

All payments will be made payable to VenCap, Inc.

Very truly yours,

Telephones:
TRowbridge 6-2200
ELiot 4-4362

_____
(Name of Subscriber)

_____
(Address)

15

Exhibit 22–2

VENCAP, INC.

January 25, 1957

To the Stockholders:

VenCap, Inc. now is more than one year old as a corporation, but only seven months have passed since operations were commenced on a full-time basis. During these months your company has investigated many situations in its search for attractive venture capital investment opportunities. By December 31, 1956, funds were invested in one situation.

The investment criteria maintained by your Board of Directors are rigorous. It is expected that only a very small percentage of all situations investigated will be deemed suitable for investment of your company's funds. Consequently, favorable results take considerable time, and expenses of investigation may be high, but the potential for ultimate profits is improved. The risks have been large, and will continue to be large, but the officers and directors of your company believe that these risks are justifiable in relation to the profit potential.

In October, your company established a wholly-owned subsidiary—Consumer Products, Inc.—and obligated a total of $25,000 to this subsidiary. Moreover, at the end of 1956, your directors were seriously considering several other promising situations for investment. You will be given further information regarding these situations via newsletters.

Although VenCap, Inc. is a young company, it radiates a spirit of confidence and determination—better prepared now than at the time of its formation for the challenging tasks and opportunities which lie ahead.

Francis E. Baker, Jr.   Vernon A. Bahr
President   *Chairman*

Exhibit 22–3

VENCAP, INC.

August 19, 1957

To the Stockholders:

As a venture capital investment company, the objectives of VenCap, Inc. have been to develop capital appreciation through investing in growth situations and, further, to assist the maximum development of profit potential in each investment by providing operational assistance when required. Since the time of the last report to stockholders, your company has continued its search for attractive venture capital opportunities and has made two additional investments. In January 1957, $5,000 was invested in the common stock of the Radian Corporation. In March, VenCap, Inc. participated in the establishment of Microsonics, Inc. and obligated a total of $30,000 to this new company.

Exhibit 22–3—Continued

At the present time your company is in the process of liquidating its investment in Consumer Products, Inc. Operations of this wholly-owned subsidiary did not live up to expectations, and your Board of Directors deems it advisable to sell the fixed assets of the subsidiary rather than continue operations. Pending consummation of such a sale your directors have established a reserve for loss covering this VenCap investment.

During the past six months the management of your company has utilized most of its time working in and with the concerns in which VenCap has invested. New companies typically have numerous problems in becoming established and in getting operations underway on a satisfactory basis. Consequently, your directors felt that management's time during this period could be more profitably spent assisting the growth of investments already made rather than concentrating on new investment possibilities.

The current VenCap investments have reached a stage where their requirements for operational assistance are reduced. The primary emphasis of VenCap is now once again on selecting attractive venture capital situations for investment of VenCap's funds along with those of stockholders who desire to participate on a joint-venture basis. Efforts are being concentrated on locating and evaluating venture capital opportunities in the $50,000 to $200,000 range of proposed investment. The assistance of stockholders in informing the company of such possible investment opportunities is earnestly desired.

FRANCIS E. BAKER, JR.   VERNON A. BAHR
President   *Chairman*

Exhibit 22–4

VENCAP, INC.

February 12, 1958

TO THE STOCKHOLDERS:

Although venture capital investments involve substantial risks, and results take time, there are possibilities for unusual capital growth. In its investments VenCap, Inc. foregoes immediate returns in the hope of substantial capital appreciation once an enterprise has successfully gone through its growing pains.

SUMMARY OF INVESTMENTS

During the last six months of 1957 your company approved an agreement to sell most of the assets of its wholly-owned subsidiary, Consumer Products, Inc. Nevertheless, your Board of Directors has established a reserve for loss covering the outstanding portion of this VenCap investment.

The Radian Corporation has successfully concluded a licensing agreement on its major development, the spring starter. Your directors feel that the profit prospects for this investment are quite favorable.

Exhibit 22–4—*Continued*

Since its establishment in March of 1957, Microsonics, Inc. has had some operating difficulties. However, operations became profitable in January 1958, and prospects point to further expansion in sales and profits.

PRESENT PROGRAM OF ACTION

Microsonics, Inc., if it continues to make progress, probably will require additional funds during the first six months of 1958. The most likely source for such funds is VenCap, so your directors believe it prudent to conserve VenCap liquid assets at present, in view of the limited capitalization of your company. Consequently, VenCap overhead expenses have been curtailed and new investment operations reduced temporarily.

Of course, your company is still searching for additional attractive investment opportunities. We look forward to the continuing support of stockholders and other friends in this activity.

FRANCIS E. BAKER, JR.   VERNON A. BAHR
President   *Chairman*

Exhibit 22–5

VENCAP, INC.

August 11, 1958

TO THE STOCKHOLDERS:

VenCap overhead expenses and new investment operations were substantially reduced during the first six months of 1958. This was done in order to conserve capital pending further developments in the VenCap subsidiaries. Your company's management has been engaged during this period in assisting subsidiary operations. VenCap overhead expenditures are expected to remain at a minimal level during the second six months of 1958; nevertheless management is actively continuing to investigate new investment possibilities.

Developments in Microsonics, Inc. have been especially encouraging. This VenCap subsidiary now has a book value in excess of your company's investment. Further, its earnings potential appears favorable. Order backlog for the remainder of 1958 is the highest in the company's history.

The Radian Corporation has been advised, by the exclusive licensee for its patented spring starter, that the starter is now tooled for production and will be introduced to the original equipment manufacturers' market during late August. Your directors feel that the profit prospects for this subsidiary are encouraging.

We regret that Jerome S. Augustine had to resign in May from his positions as treasurer and a director of VenCap, Inc. He has been an integral part of your company's management since its inception. Mr. Augustine believed it necessary to terminate his active role in VenCap, Inc., because he made other employment commitments in the investment field. Hans H. Estin was elected by the VenCap Board of Directors to fill the position of

Exhibit 22–5—Continued

treasurer, until the next annual meeting of the stockholders. Mr. Estin has been a director of your company since 1956, and is intimately acquainted with its activities. We are pleased that he has consented to undertake the important role of treasurer.

Because of the relatively low interest rate being paid on short-term notes, your Board of Directors has decided to invest VenCap funds not immediately required for venture capital investments in securities of good quality and ready marketability. Your directors believe that this type of investment offers not only better return than short-term notes, but also the possibility of capital appreciation. An investment committee (consisting of Lloyd B. Waring, Hans H. Estin and Vernon A. Bahr) was established in early July and such investments are being made at the present time.

FRANCIS E. BAKER, JR.   VERNON A. BAHR
President   *Chairman*

Exhibit 22–6

VENCAP, INC.

February 24, 1959

TO THE STOCKHOLDERS:

The past year has been an interesting one for your company. It started with a period of anxiety because of difficulties being experienced in the various subsidiary companies financed by VenCap. And the year closed with your company having a considerably larger net worth than at any other time during its two and one-half years of operations.

During the year, company expenses and investigation of new investment possibilities were kept at a low level. Your directors' efforts were concentrated upon assisting the further development and growth of VenCap's two active investments. The future of one of these, The Radian Corporation, does not appear promising at the present time. However, the other—Microsonics, Inc.—had steady increases in sales volume and a good profit pattern.

After considerable study and thought, your Board of Directors decided to offer for sale the common stock of Microsonics held by VenCap. A sale of this stock was accomplished on January 20, 1959. Your directors are pleased that this profitable sale was concluded.

The low level of VenCap's activities during 1958, and the profitable sale of its stock in Microsonics, focused attention upon another problem—namely, to determine a plan of action for the most worth while future use of VenCap's assets. The individuals previously active in the day-to-day management of your company had made outside commitments during 1958 and early 1959 . . . and were not in a position to terminate these commitments and again devote full time to VenCap. Your directors feel that capable full-time management is essential if a venture capital investment company such as VenCap is to have a reasonable chance for success.

Exhibit 22–6—Continued

Therefore, your Board of Directors has decided to present and recommend to VenCap stockholders a plan of liquidation and dissolution of the company. If the plan is approved by stockholders, your directors have stated their intention to distribute as soon as possible the maximum prudent amount of VenCap's current liquid assets (probably about $19.00 per share). Thereafter, the remaining assets of your company will be distributed as soon as they can be converted on reasonable terms into cash. This latter distribution may require from one to three years.

During the past year, the directors have devoted considerable time and effort on behalf of your company. I wish to take this opportunity to thank them for these sincere efforts and their wise counsel. I am also grateful for the continuing loyalty of VenCap stockholders.

VERNON A. BAHR
Chairman

Exhibit 22–7

VENCAP, INC.

BALANCE SHEET
December 31, 1956

ASSETS

Investments:

Commercial paper—at cost which approximated market .	$64,381.35	
Wholly-owned subsidiary—at cost and fair value as determined by directors:		
Common Stock	500.00	
Notes receivable	16,202.25	$81,083.60
Cash		3,752.75
Interest accrued		297.92
Miscellaneous accounts receivable and prepaid expenses		556.27
Furniture and fixtures—at cost	$ 688.00	
Less allowance for depreciation	66.50	621.50
Organization expenses and expense on capital shares, less amortization		1,822.32
Total Assets		$88,134.36

LIABILITIES AND CAPITAL

Liabilities:

Trade accounts payable		$ 494.17
Pay roll taxes and taxes withheld from pay rolls		136.71
State taxes		54.06
Total Liabilities		$ 684.94
Capital:		
Common Stock without par value:		
Authorized, issued, and outstanding—4,500 shares—Note	$90,000.00	
Surplus—deficit*	2,550.58*	87,449.42
		$88,134.36

NOTE: During the year ended December 31, 1956, 4,349 shares of Common Stock were sold for an aggregate cash consideration of $86,980.00. The net asset value per share of the outstanding Common Stock was $19.43.

Exhibit 22–8

VENCAP, INC.

STATEMENT OF INCOME AND EXPENSES AND SURPLUS-DEFICIT *
Year Ended December 31, 1956

Income:

Interest earned		$1,472.32
Miscellaneous		19.41
		$1,491.73

Expenses:

Office salaries	$737.78	
Printing and postage	589.83	
Travel	486.32	
Telephone	466.29	
General	427.50	
Rent	290.13	
Provision for amortization	274.74	
Accountants' fee	200.00	
State and other taxes	189.26	
Office supplies	154.91	
Electricity	72.12	
Periodicals and pamphlets	70.12	
Provision for depreciation	42.98	
Insurance	40.33	4,042.31
Net Loss and Surplus—Deficit* December 31, 1956		$2,550.58*

Exhibit 22–9

VENCAP, INC.

INVESTMENTS
December 31, 1956

	Principal Amount or Shares	Cost
Commercial Paper		
Commercial Credit Company, $3\frac{3}{8}\%$ due 1/2/57	$10,000.00	$ 9,914.69
Commercial Credit Company, $3\frac{3}{8}\%$ due 1/7/57	10,000.00	9,915.62
Commercial Credit Company, $3\frac{3}{8}\%$ due 4/1/57	30,000.00	29,744.06
Commercial Investment Trust, Incorporated, 3% due 2/4/57	10,000.00	9,849.17
General Motors Acceptance Corporation, $3\frac{3}{8}\%$ due 2/27/57	5,000.00	4,957.81
Total Commercial Paper		$64,381.35
Wholly-Owned Subsidiary		
Consumer Products, Inc.		
Common Stock	500	500.00
Notes receivable	$16,202.25	16,202.25
Total Investments		$81,083.60

Purchases and sales of investment securities, other than Government securities, during the year ended December 31, 1956, aggregated $215,060.34 and $133,976.74, respectively.

Exhibit 22–10

VENCAP, INC.

BALANCE SHEET
December 31, 1957

ASSETS

Investments:		
Short-term notes—at cost and approximate market ...		$19,880.20
Other investments—at cost	$52,000.00	
Less reserve for loss—Note	17,000.00	35,000.00
Total Investments		$54,880.20
Cash		2,071.60
Interest accrued		53.44
Accounts receivable from affiliated companies		4,083.40
Prepaid expenses and utility deposits		173.24
Furniture and fixtures—at cost, less allowance of $167.40 for depreciation		445.66
Organization expenses and expense on capital shares, less amortization		1,402.92
		$63,110.46

LIABILITIES AND CAPITAL

Liabilities:		
Accounts payable		$ 172.06
Pay roll taxes, taxes withheld from pay rolls, and state excise tax		267.55
Total Liabilities		$ 439.61
Capital:		
Common Stock without par value:		
Authorized and outstanding—4,500 shares—paid in	$90,000.00	
Earned surplus—deficit*	10,329.15*	
Provision for loss on investments—Note	17,000.00*	62,670.85
		$63,110.46

NOTE: During the year the product rights and producing assets of a wholly-owned subsidiary were sold under an agreement which provided, among other things, that the entire contract is dependent on the satisfactory performance of certain of the assets to September 16, 1958. The subsidiary has realized a substantial portion of the sales price and from such proceeds has liquidated $8,000.00 of its 6 percent subordinated notes payable to the company. In the event the assets fail to perform as specified in the agreement the entire amount of $8,000.00 will have to be refunded and the reserve for loss on investments increased by a similar amount.

The net asset value per share of the outstanding Common Stock was $13.93.

Exhibit 22–11

VENCAP, INC.

STATEMENT OF INCOME AND SURPLUS-DEFICIT *

Year ended December 31, 1957

Interest earned on:

Short-term notes	$ 847.25
Other investments	1,471.99
	$ 2,319.24
Miscellaneous income	243.00
	$ 2,562.24

Expenses:

Management services—officers	$4,500.00	
Office salaries	1,883.29	
Professional services	720.00	
Rent	559.00	
Telephone	499.12	
Office supplies, etc.	434.84	
Amortization	419.40	
Insurance	355.32	
Printing and postage	314.06	
Travel	234.33	
Pay roll taxes	98.86	
Periodicals and pamphlets	85.90	
Depreciation	81.63	
State fees	70.00	
State excise tax	45.94	
Electricity	24.78	
General	14.34	10,340.81
Net Loss*		$ 7,778.57*
Earned surplus—deficit* at January 1, 1957		2,550.58*
Earned Surplus—Deficit* at December 31, 1957		$10,329.15*
Provision for loss on investments		$17,000.00

INVESTMENTS

December 31, 1957

	Principal Amount or Shares	Cost	Value
SHORT-TERM NOTES			
General Motors Acceptance Corporation, 3½%, due 1/3/58	$10,000.00	$ 9,970.83	$ 9,970.83
General Motors Acceptance Corporation, 3½%, due 3/4/58	10,000.00	9,909.37	9,909.37
		$19,880.20	$19,880.20—A

OTHER INVESTMENTS

Consumer Products, Inc.:			
Common Stock (100%)	500	500.00	—0— —B
6% subordinated notes receivable	$16,500.00	16,500.00	—0— —B
Microsonics, Inc.:			
Common Stock (90.9%)	1,001	6,000.00	$ 6,000.00—C
6% debentures	$24,000.00	$24,000.00	24,000.00—C
The Radian Corporation:			
Common Stock (40%)	67	$ 5,000.00	$ 5,000.00—C
Total Investments.................		$71,880.20	$54,880.20

A—At cost which approximated market.
B—After deduction of reserve for loss in the amount of $17,000.00.
C—At fair value as determined by directors.

Purchases and redemptions of investments during the year ended December 31, 1957, aggregated $117,704.87 and $126,908.27, respectively.

Exhibit 22–12

VENCAP, INC.

BALANCE SHEET
December 31, 1958

ASSETS

Investments—at market or fair value as determined by directors (cost $76,830.91):			
Common Stocks		$20,175.00	
Affiliates		99,545.12	$119,720.12
Cash			2,173.76
Due from affiliated companies			564.33
Deposits, dividends receivable, etc.			180.42
Furniture and fixtures—at cost, less allowance of $270.38 for depreciation			342.68
Organization expenses and expense on capital shares, less amortization			983.52
			$123,964.83

LIABILITIES AND CAPITAL

Liabilities:			
Trade and other accounts payable			$ 144.40
Estimated federal income taxes—Note			11,000.00
Total Liabilities			$ 11,144.40
Capital:			
Common Stock without par value:			
Authorized and outstanding—4,500 shares —paid in		$90,000.00	
Earned-surplus deficit*		10,657.27*	
Accumulated realized gain on investments		1,588.49	
		$80,931.22	
Unrealized appreciation of investments ..	$42,889.21		
Less estimated federal income taxes—Note	11,000.00	31,889.21	
Net assets applicable to outstanding Common Stock (equivalent to $25.07 a share)			112,820.43
			$123,964.83

NOTE: The Company has not qualified as a regulated investment company for federal income tax purposes. The estimated liability for federal income taxes at December 31, 1958 has been computed in accordance with applicable provisions of the Internal Revenue Code.

Exhibit 22–13

VENCAP, INC.

STATEMENT OF INCOME AND EARNED-SURPLUS DEFICIT *
Year Ended December 31, 1958

Income:

Interest		$1,811.12
Dividends		316.49
Miscellaneous		4.00
		$ 2,131.61

Expenses:

Telephone	$440.83	
Amortization	419.40	
Insurance	347.74	
Rent	255.00	
Professional services	250.00	
Miscellaneous	206.44	
Printing and postage	169.06	
Travel	126.55	
Depreciation	102.98	
Office supplies	66.73	
State excise tax	50.00	
State fees	25.00	2,459.73
Net Loss		$ 328.12
Earned-surplus deficit* at January 1, 1958		10,329.15*
Earned-Surplus Deficit* at December 31, 1958		$10,657.27*

STATEMENT OF REALIZED GAINS ON INVESTMENTS
Year Ended December 31, 1958

Aggregate proceeds from sales of investments	$29,841.32
Aggregate cost based on specific security sold	28,252.83
Realized Gain and Balance of Accumulated Realized Gain on Investments at December 31, 1958	$ 1,588.49

STATEMENTS OF UNREALIZED APPRECIATION OF INVESTMENTS
Year Ended December 31, 1958

Unrealized appreciation of investments:

At December 31, 1958	$42,889.21
At January 1, 1958	—
Increase in Unrealized Appreciation of Investments	$42,889.21

Exhibit 22–14

VENCAP, INC.

INVESTMENTS
December 31, 1958

	Principal Amount or Shares	Cost	Value
COMMON STOCK			
Chrysler Corp.	200	$10,725.79	$ 10,250.00—A
Great Plains Development Co. of Canada	100	1,825.00	2,050.00—A
New York, Chicago & St. Louis Railroad Co.	100	3,235.00	3,187.50—A
Upjohn Co.	100	4,500.00	4,687.50—B
Total Common Stocks		$20,285.79	$ 20,175.00
AFFILIATES			
Consumer Products, Inc.:			
Common Stock (100%)	500	$ 500.00	$ —
6% subordinated notes receivable ..	$16,500.00	16,500.00	2,000.00
Microsonics, Inc. (Note):			
Common Stock (90.9%)	1,001	6,000.00	69,000.00
6% subordinated debentures	$24,000.00	24,000.00	24,000.00
The Radian Corporation:			
Common Stock (40%)	67	5,000.00	—
6% advances	$ 4,545.12	4,545.12	4,545.12
Total affiliates		$56,545.12	$ 99,545.12—C
Total Investments		$76,830.91	$119,720.12

A—Value based on quoted closing market price.
B—Value based on quoted closing bid price.
C—At fair value as determined by directors.

NOTE: On January 20, 1959 the company sold its holdings in Common Stock of Microsonics, Inc., for $75,000.00 in cash. In connection with the sale the company agreed to a modification of the terms of the 6% subordinated debentures issued by Microsonics, Inc., whereby they may be called and redeemed in full at a discounted price of $18,000.00 on or before January 1, 1960 and at a discounted price of $22,000.00 on or before January 1, 1961. Provision for the discount that may be taken in 1959 has been made by reducing the value of the Common Stock holdings.

Purchases and sales and redemptions of investments during the year ended December 31, 1958 aggregated $87,992.35 and $83,041.64, respectively.

Exhibit 22–15

VENCAP, INC.

NOW . . . a SELF-MIXING FERTILIZING UNIT

★ No concentrate to mix or bucket to carry
★ Never a moment lost in "spraying"
★ Spreads ANY WATER-SOLUBLE plant food
★ Eliminates danger of burning lawns

ferta-mix
TRADEMARK

EASIEST METHOD KNOWN FOR FEEDING MODERN LAWNS and GARDENS

FERTA-MIX . . . amazing modern gardening aid . . . *automatically* and *correctly* apportions the amount of plant food needed for lawns and gardens *directly* through garden hose to sprinklers, soakers, etc. No mixing, no bother. Exclusive agitating action does all the work. FERTA-MIX needs no special fertilizer either. One cup of *any water-soluble* plant food placed in the transparent mixing chamber feeds approximately 1,000 square feet of lawn in 10 to 15 minutes, spreading fertilizer uniformly over the watering area.

● *Mixer:* transparent unbreakable Tenite
● *Cap:* red plastic, screw-on type
● *Easy-on Connectors:* strong, nickel-plated brass
● *Size:* (approx.) width, 3¼ in. depth, 7½ in.

NO CLOGGING NO CLEANING

ALSO Handy for washing cars, windows, houses. Sprays insecticides.

Retail **$3.95**

Dealer Discount Less 40%

1. Attached to faucet
2. Between lengths of hose
3. On lawn sprinkler
4. Attached to spray nozzle

FERTA-MIX GIVES YOU ALL THESE *SELLING* ADVANTAGES:

No special mix needed; no outside utensils
Automatic; no tiresome tramping around the lawn
Unconditionally guaranteed against defective material and workmanship

FEEDS THRU SPRINKLER

EYE-CATCHING PACKAGE with INFORMATION . . . INDIVIDUALLY BOXED
FREE MAT ADS

For details, write:

Printed in U.S.A.

CONSUMER PRODUCTS, INC., 84 State Street, Boston, Mass., Phone: CApitol 7-7570

Exhibit 22–16

VENCAP, INC.

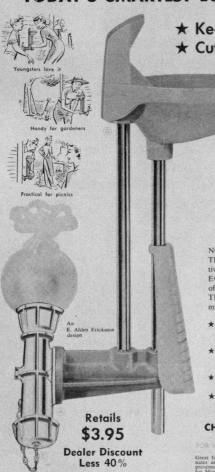

23. GEOCHRON LABORATORIES, INC. *

Getting a Company Started

Geochron Laboratories, Inc., was incorporated in June, 1960, for the purpose of offering a commercial service to persons and firms interested in determining the ages of rocks and minerals. The company's four founders were Robert Lemer, Marc Altman, and Richard Freedman, all members of the class of 1960 at the Harvard Business School, and Harold Krueger, a graduate geologist employed by MIT until June, 1960, as research assistant in the department of geology and geophysics.

The company had grown out of preliminary discussions among the four men which culminated in a report written by Mr. Freedman, also a graduate geologist, for a second-year course in new businesses at the Harvard Business School. The report had examined the feasibility of commercially exploiting a rock-dating technique known as potassium-argon isotope analysis. This technique was based on the well-established fact that a particular radioactive type of potassium, K^{40}, decays, with a half-life of approximately 1.3 billion years, into Ar^{40}, an isotope of the inert gas argon. By measuring the ratios of the amounts of the two isotopes, where the initial amount of K^{40} was known and the radiogenic (decay product) argon had been sealed in, it was possible to estimate with comparatively great precision the age of the rock in which the isotopes were contained. Estimates could be made of ages in the range of 1 million to 4.5 billion years.

The technique used by Geochron was not the only means of rock-dating available to the geologist, but other known methods appeared to have greater limitations. Dating through fossil analysis was less precise, and had the further disadvantage that fossils were not always found where they might be most helpful. Other isotopic analyses in existence made use of the decay series involving uranium lead, rubidium strontium, and thorium lead; but these required the presence of rarely occurring elements, whereas potassium was one of the more commonly occurring elements. Carbon dating had been a great help to scientists, but its use was limited by the fact that it measured only ages less than some 70,000 years. The gap between 70,000 and one million years, the approximate period of the Ice Ages, was not capable of accurate estimation by K–Ar or other existing methods. The founders of Geochron felt confident, given this state of dating technology, that K–Ar dating provided three significant advantages which would make it an especially salable service: (1) it was precise by existing standards, (2) it had wide geographic applicability, and (3) it spanned a large period of geologic history.

When Geochron was formed, Mr. Lemer became president; Mr. Krueger, vice-president and technical director; Mr. Freedman, vice-president and geologist; and Mr. Altman, treasurer. They felt that their service would be of primary interest to geologists employed in academic establishments, oil or mining firms, or government service. Little present competition was thought to exist. While there were laboratories performing K–Ar dating, there were perhaps less than 20 in the Western Hemisphere, and these were principally government and university installations. Several of the largest oil companies had the facilities, but they were not interested in selling the service. The great majority of oil companies were not set up to perform the analyses. Only one potential commercial competitor, Isotopes, Inc., existed, but it was not considered to be a serious threat.

Concerning potential competition, Mr. Lemer was aware that neither the process nor the apparatus was patentable. He also knew that the separation equipment, flame spectrophotometer, mass spectrometer, and other necessary laboratory hardware could be acquired for less than $70,000. Technically trained people were not so easily found, although several schools (MIT among them) had been training scientists in geochronology since 1955. In any case, an exclusive option on the services of Mr. Krueger had been obtained by the company. He had acquired considerable experience in geochronology at the University of Minnesota and at MIT, training under several of the leading geochronologists in the country.

In the spring of 1960, before forming the company, the principals made their first effort to measure the market for commercial K–Ar dating. Already aware that there were essentially no laboratories available for routine commercial service, they decided on a mail survey of geologists as the fastest and least expensive means of assessing market potential. A questionnaire was constructed and mailed with a covering letter (Exhibit 23–1) to 500 geologists early in March, 1960. In selecting their sample, the founders drew largely from people who had been members of the Geological Society of America for at least five years. The principals realized that the true universe of geologists

Exhibit 23–1

GEOCHRON LABORATORIES, INC.

Letter and Accompanying Mail Questionnaire

24 Blackstone Street
Cambridge 39, Massachusetts

February 29, 1960

Dr. John Smith
Mammoth Oil Company
Tulsa, Oklahoma

Dear Dr. Smith:

In recognition of the growing importance of age determinations in geological research, we plan to establish a commercial geochronological laboratory. The laboratory staff is presently associated with one of the major research centers in the country, and has been active in the field of geochronology for a number of years.

Commencing in the fall of 1960, we shall be equipped for potassium-argon age determinations. Accuracy ranges from plus or minus 1 percent for Precambrian rocks, to plus or minus 2½ percent for Early Tertiary specimens. We expect that this information should be useful to university researchers, governmental surveys, mining companies, and oil companies.

As potassium-argon age determinations have been heretofore unavailable to most geologists, it is difficult for us to determine the laboratory size needed to provide adequate service. For this reason, it would be very helpful if you would fill out and return the enclosed questionnaire, even if you have no use for the facilities.

It is nearly impossible for us to compile a complete list of geologists with interest in age determinations. Therefore, our survey would be much more complete if you would pass on the extra questionnaire to an interested colleague.

Procurement of this information is the best way we can think of to determine and fill your requirements. Thank you for your cooperation.

Yours very truly,

(Signed)
Robert J. Lemer

Enclosure

Exhibit 23–1—Continued

GEOCHRON LABORATORIES, INC.

Potassium-Argon Survey*

This questionnaire is designed only to help us to determine your requirements. This is not a commitment on your part; we just want your best guesses. If you prefer to write us a note or letter rather than filling out this form, that would be equally helpful. You need not give your name unless you wish to.

1. Name _____

   Address _____

   _____

   Specialty _____
   (Petrology, Sedimentation, etc.)

2. The exact cost per determination will depend very largely on the scale of operations that proves possible. We expect, however, that the charge will probably exceed $300, but will certainly be less than $600. Do you think you would utilize this service for potassium-argon age determinations?

   Yes _____ No _____ Probably _____

   As a rough estimate, how many determinations do you think you might

   require per year? _____

3. Are there any other age-determination methods you would like to have available? Other uses of isotope analyses? Would you like us to provide a consulting service as well as the raw data?

4. Any additional comments, criticisms, or questions would be appreciated. Please use the reverse side if required.

   * Prepared by Geochron Laboratories, Inc.

was far larger than the 5,000-member GSA, with perhaps 35,000 in the U.S.A. alone and over 100,000 in the world. At the time, however, Mr. Lemer, who assumed responsibility for preliminary market analysis, was a student at the Harvard Business School, and his survey was severely limited by time and financial restraints.

Of the 210 respondents to the questionnaire, 41 percent indicated that they would utilize the proposed service at the quoted price of $300 to $600. This range had been chosen after a cursory estimate of operating costs indicated that, with an operation of 200 to 300 determinations per year, prices within this span would yield a profit. (The break-even point at an average price of $350 per determination would be less than 200 units annually, figuring monthly costs to be about $5,000. Above 200 units, marginal profit would rise sharply, since most of the costs were thought to be fixed.)

The respondents who indicated that they would utilize the age determination service estimated an average annual requirement of 2.5 determinations, or a total of 225 per year from the 87 who responded affirmatively. If questionnaires mailed to 500 geologists indicated an expected volume of 225 per year, how many requests for determination might be forthcoming from the entire universe of geologists? It was thought that the first year might produce 750, with succeeding annual increments of 750 not unreasonable to expect, though clearly a wide range of possible demand levels existed.

With these encouraging thoughts in mind, it was decided that Geochron would purchase equipment, at a cost of approximately $35,000, which would afford a sample-analyzing capacity of about 400 per year. The price schedule would be $350 for raw (unseparated) rock and $300 for purified samples. On June 8, 1960, the firm was incorporated with one million common shares (no par) authorized, and arrangements for the acquisition of laboratory equipment were initiated. Shortly after incorporation, most of the original list of 500 geologists was approached again, this time through the mailing of Technical Bulletin No. 1 and a covering letter. The bulletin described the laboratory as it would be in the fall, introduced its principal staff members, and provided information of a technical nature about the analyses that would be performed. Also, Mr. Freedman made plans to visit academic geologists and technical employees of oil and mining companies in an attempt to develop familiarity with Geochron's services throughout the geological profession. He expected as well to attend professional and trade conventions where he would discuss age determinations and provide literature on the company.

Financing

Shortly after incorporation, the four principals as a group loaned the corporation approximately $1,000 to cover out-of-pocket expenses. They had expected that substantial financial backing would be forthcoming by the fall of 1960 from one of several private investors who had evinced strong interest in Geochron. As the summer wore on, however, it became apparent that no backing could be expected from these sources, so the principals accelerated their solicitations (which had begun on a modest scale in January) of Boston investment houses and SBIC's. Receiving little encouragement and no definite offers, they began to pound pavements in New York City, first utilizing personal contacts and later working on references and cold-call prospects. September came and went, and still no funds. Mr. Lemer realized that most of Geochron's anticipated business would occur in the fall, after geologists had returned from their summer explorations, and without capital to purchase equipment Geochron would have to turn away business.

One day late in September, a Canadian friend of Mr. Freedman's got in touch with him in Cambridge. The friend had received one of the 300 publicity folders (Exhibit 23–2) which the company had distributed to a wide range of personal contacts in the United States and Canada. He suggested that the Geochron management contact one of the smaller brokerage firms, Globus, Inc., of New York. When Mr. Freedman hesitated, mentioning the immediacy of the company's cash needs, the Canadian source remarked that Morton Globus could often make a decision to commit funds to a company in as little as three hours' time.

An appointment with Mr. Globus was arranged, and within three hours he had agreed in principle to underwrite a public issue of Geochron common stock in the amount of $150,000. Since preparations for the public offering would undoubtedly require several months' time, both the officers and Morton Globus agreed to seek out sources of temporary funds. These creditors could then be repaid out of proceeds from the public issue. One private investor advanced the company $5,000 cash in return for a promissory note due July 31, 1961, or convertible into 8,000 shares of common stock at the time of public issue.

Also, Globus, Inc., and some of its officers and associates took a $30,000 convertible promissory note on the same terms. At the time of issue of the two notes, mid-October, 1960, the company sold to the private investor 2,000 common stock purchase warrants, and to the holders of the $30,000 note 60,000 warrants. These warrants were purchased at 2½ cents apiece, and each warrant entitled its holder to buy one share of Geochron common stock at $1.00 until October, 1965. With these proceeds, the company was able by the end of October to make progress payments of $15,000 on laboratory equipment under construction, and to defray its general expenses.

On February 16, 1961, Globus, Inc., and Ross, Lyon & Co., Inc., offered to the public, under a long-form registration, 150,000 shares of Geochron common stock at $1.00 per share. Proceeds to the com-

Exhibit 23–2

GEOCHRON LABORATORIES, INC.

PUBLICITY FOLDER

POTASSIUM – ARGON

AGE DETERMINATIONS

GEOCHRON'S MASS SPECTROMETER
USED FOR VERY PRECISE ARGON MEASUREMENTS.

Geochron Laboratories, Inc.

24 Blackstone Street, Cambridge 39, Mass., U.S.A.

Exhibit 23–2—Continued

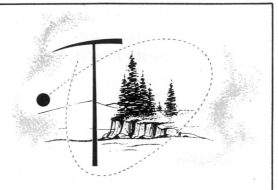

Here, in a few pages, we have tried to outline some of the most important aspects of geological age determinations by the potassium-argon method. Geochron is happy to make this service generally available for the first time.

Naturally, in a brief booklet, we cannot anticipate the specific problems our readers may have. Our technical staff welcomes the opportunity of corresponding with members of the geological profession concerning particular problems or applications of interest to them.

Please contact either:

H. W. KRUEGER, *Technical Director*

R. O. FREEDMAN, *Geologist*

GEOCHRON LABORATORIES, INC.
24 Blackstone Street, Cambridge 39, Mass., U.S.A.

CONTENTS PAGE

2

Exhibit 23–2—Continued

WHAT ARE
POTASSIUM-ARGON AGES?

The potassium-argon method of age determination is based on the radioactive decay of K^{40} to Ar^{40}. K^{40} has a half-life of approximately 1.3 billion years, enabling a wide range of geologically useful ages to be measured by potassium-argon analysis. Ages from less than 1 million to over 4,500 million years have been measured by this technique. As a result of recent advances, incorporated in our facilities, even younger materials may be dated, although with reduced precision. Thus, virtually the entire geologic time-scale is encompassed.

The analysis of a sample for potassium and radiogenic argon determines the parent-to-daughter ratio. This, plus the known decay constants for K^{40}, allows the calculation of the time elapsed since formation of the potassium-bearing sample.

Recently, technological advances have made possible the extremely precise measurements necessary in this work. For example, our mass spectrometer enables us to measure argon content with a precision of a few parts per billion.

APPLICATIONS

Uses of age data in regional studies or mapping programs, structural studies in complex areas, and localized petrological studies are fairly self-evident.

Less widely known, but no less important, are applications to petroleum geology, mining geology, mineral exploration, and economic geology.

Tuffs, bentonites, and volcanic ash-falls in general provide excellent material for the petroleum and stratigraphic geologist, when in sedimentary sequences. They are ideal from the standpoint of representing a single instant in time. Even where recognized as important key-beds, most such units remain to be dated. Many other strata may be dated directly, by means of their glauconite content.

3

Exhibit 23–2—Continued

Under certain structural conditions, the dating of crystalline rocks (e.g. dikes, sills, basement complexes) may help solve difficult stratigraphic problems. Dating of detrital sedimentary grains may help determine the source(s) from which they were derived.

Applications to economic and mining geology range from delineating metallogenetic epochs on a possibly continent-wide scale to solving age relationships in the vein systems of a single mine. In between, geochronology provides a key to recognizing metallogenetic provinces. It thus becomes possible to direct mine development or mineral exploration programs with more efficiency (and less money) than otherwise would be the case.

MATERIALS SUITABLE
FOR ANALYSIS

Any potassium-bearing mineral is potentially suitable for K-Ar age determinations. In actual practice, certain materials have proven superior to others. The list below discusses those of particular interest and widest applicability.

Neither grain size nor percentage of potassium-bearing mineral normally affects the reliability of an age determination. For example, a volcanic ash with $\frac{1}{2}\%$ very fine-grained biotite is just as suitable as a pegmatite with 25% very coarse grained sheets of biotite. An exception is the case of a few extremely fine-grained rocks where mineral separation may pose a problem.

MICAS: Biotite, Muscovie, Phlogopite, and Lepidolite. These minerals retain all of their radiogenic argon, and have become the standard for K-Ar age determinations. Naturally, where the mica is of metamorphic origin, the age determined reflects the date of latest recrystallization of the rock rather than that of original emplacement or deposition.

4

Exhibit 23-2—Continued

GLAUCONITE: The most widespread and reliable of sedimentary minerals suitable for age determinations. Glauconites have proven useful throughout the age range 1 million to 1600 million years.

AMPHIBOLES: Hornblende and soda amphiboles have recently been proven suitable for age determinations in a large number of cases, notwithstanding their low potassium content. Much of the interest in amphiboles stems from their apparent ability to withstand considerable thermal metamorphism without argon loss.

PYROXENES: Although presently unproven, pyroxenes have aroused considerable interest from the standpoint of suffering small argon loss under thermal metamorphism. This lab is interested in cooperating with researchers in investigating the pyroxene group further.

FELDSPARS: The feldspars as a group are not good minerals for age determinations, with the important exception of sanidine.

OTHERS: A great many other potassium minerals are suitable under particular conditions or have potential as age indicators. These include leucite, sylvite, and other with essential potassium, plus a host of minerals with minor potassium content.

In addition, certain unseparated materials may be dated directly; slates, phyllites, and young fine-grained volcanics have proven especially useful.

If in doubt as to the suitability of a sample, please correspond with our Technical Director. Better still, submit the sample for free examination.

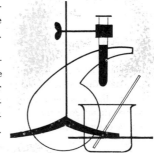

5

SAMPLE REQUIREMENTS:

Prepared Mineral Separate:

Send 10 or more grams of clean mineral, if possible. The *minimum* size ranges from 2 grams for an ancient, potassium-rich sample to 10 grams for a young, potassium-poor sample. If prepared samples of mineral separates are sent, they should meet high standards of purity.

Unprepared (Whole Rock) Samples:

An unseparated rock sample (hand specimen, core, chips) should generally be large enough to yield the quantities of mineral separate noted above. Usually, to obtain 10 grams of pure mineral, we find that we need a sample containing about 30 grams of the mineral. A hand specimen or equivalent quantity generally suffices; however, if you have 5 or 10 lbs., send it along.

We do not return unused material unless asked to do so; however, it is kept on file, available to the sender on request.

SHIPPING

Air freight, railway express or parcel post (securely packed!) is recommended. Where time is of little importance, rail or ocean freight is satisfactory. Samples from abroad should be clearly labeled, "Scientific Specimens — No Commercial Value".

6

Exhibit 23–2—Continued

LABORATORY FACILITIES

Sample preparation facilities include complete comminution equipment, magnetic separators, heavy liquid equipment, and petrographic equipment for control of separations.

The argon extraction systems are patterned after the best features of those at the University of Minnesota and at M.I.T. The systems are all directly connected to the mass spectrometer, although otherwise completely independent. A 'continuous' spike system, similar to that in use at M.I.T., serves each system.

Mass spectrometric analyses are made on an instrument patterned after that designed by J. H. Reynolds of the University of California. This is the most sophisticated instrumentation available for the purpose, and, indeed, ranks among the most sensitive of measuring devices known to man. Its capability to analyze extremely minute quantities of argon enables us to determine the age of very young or potassium deficient specimens.

Rigorous quality control is exercised throughout the operation. The Ar^{38} spike is repeatedly calibrated by two independent methods; mass spectrometric analyses are fractionation and discrimination corrected. Regularly scheduled standard samples, and random replicate analyses of routine samples ensure constant precision levels. Potassium analyses, determined by means of a flame spectrophotometer, are regularly repeated gravimetrically. The overall analytical error of the age determination is thus held to less than 2%.

●

We welcome the opportunity

of answering any questions you may have

7

Exhibit 23–2—Continued

CHARGES

(All Prices in U. S. Dollars)

Age Determinations

Complete Potassium-Argon age
determination, on unprepared sample : **$350**

Complete K-Ar age determination on
prepared sample (pure mineral separate) : **$300**

Separate Services Available

Mineral Separation & Purification (an
overage is charged when technician's
work exceeds 15 hours)........................ : **$ 60**

Potassium Analysis .... : **$ 40**

Argon extraction, mass spectrometric
analysis, and reduction of data to
Ar^{40} content, or age .... : **$275**

Analysis of received pure argon sample
for Ar^{36}, Ar^{38}, and Ar^{40}.................. : **$125**

Fees Arranged:

For consulting service, and analysis of other alkali metals.

Delivery

Generally, we return results within 30 days of receipt of
specimen. In cases of extreme urgency, a priority service
can be arranged.

Geochron Laboratories, Inc.

24 BLACKSTONE STREET, CAMBRIDGE 39, MASS.
Telephone TRowbridge 6-3691

8

pany were $105,000. The issue was oversubscribed. At the same time, the four founders as a group received 70,000 shares at 1 cent per share, in return for $700 of the $1,000 they had originally loaned to the company. The other $300 was repaid to them in cash. Just prior to the public issue, the four founders had authorized themselves options to purchase 17,500 shares apiece at $1.10 per share over the five subsequent years. Thus, if all options and warrants were exercised, the number of common shares outstanding after the public issue would be:

Founders	70,000	18.0%
Founders, option plan	70,000	18.0
Globus, Inc., et al.	30,000	7.7
Globus, Inc., et al., warrants	60,000	15.4
The public	150,000	38.4
Private investor	8,000	2.0
Private investor, warrants	2,000	0.5
Totals	390,000	100.0%

Later Developments

Shortly after the successful public issue, the four founders sat down to take stock of their progress. A source of extreme disappointment had been the sales volume; during the eight months from July, 1960, through February, 1961, only eight requests for age determinations had been received, and all were still being processed. The management believed that the low level of orders stemmed primarily from the forced absence of advertising due to lack of capital. Since the issuance of Technical Bulletin No. 1, shortly after incorporation, no mailings had been sent to potential customers; consequently, the anticipated inflow of fall orders had failed to materialize. Also, no personal visits to conventions or to the geologists of potentially large customers had been made by Mr. Freedman, again because of financial limitations. Since the principals found themselves, in March of 1961, with equipment affording an annual capacity of about 400 determinations, for which they had paid $35,000, they felt compelled to spare no reasonable expense necessary to generate a substantial level of orders.

Accordingly they began advertising in various technical journals and trade publications. A large-scale direct-mail effort was begun, including a covering letter, a pamphlet describing the laboratory, and the offer of a complete bibliography of geochronology on return of a reply card. This mailing was sent to 5,000 geologists, of whom 10 percent were foreign. In April, 1,000 pamphlets and 2,000 wallet-size plastic geological time scales were distributed at a petroleum geologists' convention. In May, a second direct-mail promotion was sent to the same 5,000 geologists who had received the first mailing. This time, a letter, an information sheet on the subject of sample requirements for K–Ar age determinations, and a small cloth bag for use in collecting samples were enclosed. Also, Mr. Freedman made several sales calls on large firms in the eastern sections of the United States and Canada.

By the fall of 1961 it became obvious, in the words of Mr. Lemer, that, ". . . development of demand for our age determination services, as indicated by rock samples received, has been slower than expected. It seems likely that demand for a service as advanced and complex as ours will take longer to develop than was originally anticipated." Only 41 requests for determinations had been received from February, the time of the public offering, through November, 1961. Consequently, the six-month report to stockholders, arriving in December, announced the resignation of Messrs. Lemer and Freedman. Though Mr. Altman retained the title of treasurer, he accepted full-time employment elsewhere. The company had shown an operating loss of $33,000 on no sales in its first year, and a loss of $31,000 on sales of $7,300 for the first six months of its second year.

The Current Situation

In the second half of its second year of operation, the company began to show signs of improvement. Requests for determinations averaged eight per month during the six months ending May 31, 1962, and the company showed a loss of only about $3,000 during that period. Though there was a two-year deficit of some $67,000, the working capital position was far from desperate. There were net current assets of about $75,000, of which $70,000 was cash, as of May, 1962. Since Lemer and Freedman had relinquished their options to all except 2,500 shares apiece under the company option plan, potential dilution had been reduced by 30,000 shares to 360,000 shares. As of May, 278,100 shares were outstanding and the remaining 81,900 were reserved for potential conversion of warrants and options. The stock was quoted over the counter at about 25 cents per share in October, 1962. It had traded at a price as high as $7.00 per share shortly after the public offering date. Recent balance sheets for the company appear as Exhibits 23–3 through 23–6.

In the summer of 1962, Mr. Krueger, the only founder remaining

Exhibit 23–3

GEOCHRON LABORATORIES, INC.

BALANCE SHEET, OCTOBER 31, 1960

Assets:

Cash	$19,470.20	
Progress payments for laboratory equipment under construction	15,000.00	
Leasehold improvements	666.66	
Organization expenses	801.65	
Administrative and general expenses	2,478.77	
Telephone deposit	60.00	
Total Assets		$38,477.28

Liabilities:

6% unsecured convertible notes	$35,000.00	
Unsecured loans from officers	654.59	
Accrued officers' salaries	240.00	
Accrued interest	87.50	
Accounts payable	245.19	
Total Liabilities		$36,227.28

Capital:

70,000 Common shares issued and outstanding	$ 700.00	
Additional paid-in capital	1,550.00	
Total Capital		$ 2,250.00
Total Liabilities and Capital		$38,477.28

Exhibit 23–4

GEOCHRON LABORATORIES, INC.

BALANCE SHEET, MAY 31, 1961

ASSETS

Current Assets:

Cash	$ 21,715	
Marketable securities, at cost (which approximates market value)	64,931	
Advances to employees	947	
Prepaid expenses	847	
Total Current Assets		$ 88,440

Property and Equipment, at Cost:

Laboratory equipment	$ 34,753	
Furniture and fixtures	1,067	
Leasehold improvements	2,013	
	$37,923	
Less: Accumulated depreciation and amortization	4,227	33,696
Organization expense, less amortization of $262		2,877
Total Assets		$125,013

Exhibit 23–4—Continued

LIABILITIES

Current Liabilities:

Accounts payable	$ 2,055	
Accrued taxes	917	
Total Current Liabilities		$ 2,972

Stockholders' Investment:

Common stock, 1 cent par value; 1,000,000 shares authorized, 267,100 shares issued and outstanding	$ 2,671	
Additional amounts paid in on common stock	152,475	
Retained earnings (deficit)	(33,105)	122,041
Total Liabilities		$125,013

Exhibit 23–5

GEOCHRON LABORATORIES, INC.

BALANCE SHEET, NOVEMBER 30, 1961

ASSETS

Current Assets:

Cash	$ 20,477.77	
Marketable securities at cost, approximate resale value	49,706.00	
Accounts receivable	2,303.70	
Accrued interest	256.54	
Deposits	161.80	
Prepayments	491.54	
Total Current Assets		$ 73,397.35

Property and Equipment, at Cost:

Laboratory equipment	$ 33,943.44	
Furniture and fixtures	1,376.80	
Leasehold improvements	2,102.79	
	$ 37,423.03	
Less: Accumulated depreciation and amortization	10,604.47	26,818.56
Organization expense, less amortization of $575.43		2,563.42
Total Assets		$102,779.33

LIABILITIES

Current Liabilities:

Accounts payable	$ 238.14	
Accrued taxes	874.38	
Total Current Liabilities		$ 1,112.52

Stockholders' Investment:

Common stock, 1 cent par value; 1,000,000 shares authorized, 278,100 issued and outstanding	$ 2,781.00	
Additional amounts paid in on common stock	163,365.44	
Retained earnings (deficit)	(64,479.63)	101,666.81
Total Liabilities		$102,779.33

Exhibit 23–6

GEOCHRON LABORATORIES, INC.

Balance Sheet, May 31, 1962

ASSETS

Current Assets:

Cash	$ 9,797	
Deposits in savings banks, including accrued interest of $567	60,767	
Accounts receivable	6,014	
Prepaid expenses	987	$ 77,565

Property and Equipment, at Cost:

Laboratory equipment	$ 34,452	
Furniture and fixtures	1,630	
Leasehold improvements	2,103	
	$ 38,105	
Less: Accumulated depreciation and amortization	16,815	21,370
Organization expense, less amortization of $889		2,250
Total Assets		$101,185

LIABILITIES

Current Liabilities:

Accounts payable	$ 734	
Accrued liabilities	2,029	
Total Current Liabilities		$ 2,763

Stockholders' Investment:

Common stock, 1 cent par value; 1,000,000 shares authorized, 278,100 shares outstanding	$ 2,781	
Additional amounts paid in on common stock	163,365	
Retained earnings (deficit)	(67,724)	98,422
Total Liabilities		$101,185

with the company on a full-time basis, hired a technician to help him in performing K–Ar analyses, raising to three the number of employees. Requests for determinations were still sporadic; the company had received 29 such requests in June, 8 in July, and 1 in August. Mr. Krueger emphasized that the company was operating profitably at that time, with cash expenses averaging less than $2,500 per month. His long-term objective was to gradually build up the company's reputation, primarily through word of mouth from satisfied customers, to the point where it could generate a reasonable return for the common stockholders. He recognized that a carefully managed program of corporate acquisitions might also improve the firm's profit picture.

24. SPRAY CHEMICAL CORPORATION*
Finding and Buying a Business

Early in March, 1959, Bruce Jordan and Neil Jeffries met with their attorney, George Abramson, to consider a recent crisis in their aerosol packaging business. One of their largest customers had filed suit against them that afternoon, claiming damages in a dispute over a contract concerning rights to an aerosol shoeshine formulation.

Background

Bruce Jordan, president and treasurer of Spray Chemical Corporation, of Lawrence, Massachusetts, had attended Harvard Business School after graduation from Harvard University in 1956. While in college, Jordan first had become interested in business as a career. In 1954, in partnership with a college roommate, he had bought a truckload of antifreeze in New York and sold it to individuals at far below retailers' prices. That spring, prior to vacation, he and his roommate paid cash for all the refrigerators they could buy on campus and stored them in a garage they rented in Concord, Massachusetts. During the summer, they purchased a carload of secondhand refrigerators from a remodeled apartment house in New Jersey. In the fall, Jordan and his roommate divided $2,000 as their profit on sales made to incoming college students.

Decision to Enter Small Business on Graduation

During his two years at Harvard Business School, Jordan did a considerable amount of thinking about his career. In his earlier business experiences, he had found a great source of satisfaction in small situations in which his efforts had been the prime factor. He took placement interviews during his second year and supplemented these with letters to local firms. After turning down all the offers from compa-

---

nies that had interviewed him, Jordan decided to concentrate his efforts on locating a small company with which he could satisfy the following criteria:

1. Maximum equity from money invested.
2. Investment in a growing industry.
3. Opportunity to use his abilities.
4. Trust in the management of the company.
5. Security for his investment.

Search for the Right Opportunity

Jordan looked on the task of finding a small enterprise as a full-time job and waited until after graduation to launch his campaign. His first step, after finding few leads from college and business school sources, was to talk with several older businessmen who were friends of his family. Harry Aldrich, senior vice-president of the Merchants Federal Bank, suggested that Jordan consult William Sprague, of Sprague Associates, business brokers, and Peter Baldwin, a young credit analyst in his bank.

Jordan found Mr. Sprague, who maintained a small office in the downtown financial district of Boston, very helpful in recommending possible opportunities for investment. He told Jordan that his specialty was negotiating the sale or merger of privately-held companies. His leads came mostly from bank officers like Aldrich, who recommended Sprague Associates to clients who wanted to buy or sell businesses. Sprague kept a list of companies that had come to his attention and devoted his time to soliciting his customers—that is, clients with money they wanted to invest in a business. Jordan received leads to five companies from Sprague in return for an agreement that he would approach these companies through Sprague Associates. In this way, Sprague assured his company of the traditional 5 percent broker's fee, which would be paid to them by the seller.

When Jordan met Baldwin for lunch early in June, he outlined his objectives and said that Aldrich had suggested a meeting. Baldwin agreed to help. Baldwin had graduated from Harvard Business School in 1954 and had gone to work in the credit department of the Merchants Federal Bank. His function had been to analyze loan requests of hundreds of companies in the New England area, and he had become a specialist in the electronics companies which had grown up in Cambridge, Massachusetts, and spread to Route 128, outside Boston. Baldwin gave Jordan the names of several small electronics firms that needed money and management assistance.

Baldwin, in addition, recommended lawyers as an excellent source of new business leads and suggested that Jordan call on the firm of Abramson and Abramson. George Abramson, one of the partners, had been one of Jordan's classmates at Harvard and after law school had joined his father's firm. Since the firm specialized in trial work, George Abramson was able to tell Jordan of two bankruptcy actions the firm was handling. He suggested that Jordan's combined management training and funds for investment would have maximum leverage in rebuilding these bankrupt companies. They made data on these companies available to Jordan that afternoon.

Other sources of leads for investment turned up as Jordan followed through on his investigations of the companies recommended by Sprague, Baldwin, and Abramson. Consultants, certified public accountants, the Small Business Administration, and local chambers of commerce were other sources of leads which Jordan also investigated. Newspaper advertisements in the *Wall Street Journal, New York Times, Boston Herald,* and other papers were sources which Jordan recognized as potential aids in his campaign. While he saw many attractive ads in these papers, he did not follow up any of them. He believed that evaluation of these ads would be tremendously time-consuming and that the companies concerned would be advertising only as a last resort. Banks, brokers, venture capitalists, and others would have declined assistance in such instances.

Screening the Leads

Jordan soon began to get the leads he had hoped for. Exhibit 24–1 outlines some of the companies to which Jordan was directed during a two-week period in July. He quickly learned that his problem was to follow up and analyze the many opportunities that came to his attention. Jordan found that his job of screening really began with an evaluation of a company's financial condition. In many instances, records were incomplete or misleading. Therefore, he made a point of going to the source data and working up a rough net quick asset position by tabulating cash, accounts receivable, inventory, and accounts payable. In many instances, he found doubtful receivables, as well as overvalued inventory, and incomplete listings of accounts payable.

Exhibit 24–1

SPRAY CHEMICAL CORPORATION

PARTIAL LIST OF OPPORTUNITIES FOR INVESTMENT
EVALUATED BY BRUCE JORDAN IN JULY, 1958

Situation	Source of Lead	Location	Result of Evaluation
1. Bakery wanted money and assistant to president	Investment banker	Boston	Industry works nights and Sundays. Money needed for promotion where risk seemed high. Jordan believed it would be hard to get along with the president.
2. Howard Johnson's restaurant franchise	Friend who had been very successful in the business	New England	Jordan learned that several prime franchises were available, but did not feel he would really be in his own business under a franchise arrangement.
3. Sandpaper manufacturing business	Peter Baldwin	Lowell	An inventor wanted to start a business, with administrative help, which would sell a special sanding device he had developed. Jordan believed there was too much competition in the area from such established companies as Norton and Bay State Abrasives.
4. Spray Chemical Corporation	Harvard Business School Alumni Placement Office	Lawrence	Jordan's choice for investment and management of a new enterprise.
5. Gear Manufacturing Company	Harry Aldrich	Rhode Island	Jordan found three technical men who owned some special machinery to manufacture precision gears. They wanted money to buy more equipment. Jordan knew he would have little say in the management of this highly technical operation.
6. Compass Manufacturing Company	Classmate	Boston	This was a family company with many relatives of the owner on the payroll. They were interested in having him join the firm as general manager, but did not wish to share the equity.
7. Sardine canning factory	Maine Area Development Council	Portland	This lead came as a result of correspondence to the Maine Chamber of Commerce. Jordan traveled to Portland but quickly learned that the industry was plagued by overcapacity.
8. Motel	George Abramson	Maine	This was a run-down property with a very short season. The trip north was a "complete waste of time."

Spray Chemical Corporation

One of the companies suggested to Jordan was the Spray Chemical Corporation, of Lawrence, Massachusetts, northwest of Boston. It had been organized in 1956 and was engaged in contract packaging of aerosol products. Jordan made an investigation of the aerosol industry and could see the increasing use of aerosol dispensers. Spray Chemical owned packaging equipment, which it had installed in a rented wooden building. Sales had grown steadily from December, 1957, to June, 1958. See Exhibit 24–2, which gives sales figures for December, 1957, to February, 1959.

Jordan was greatly attracted to Frederick Scarelli, president of Spray Chemical Corporation, and saw in him a potential partner who could provide the sales representation required to keep Spray Chemical in continued operation. In their initial conversations, Scarelli said he was willing to have Jordan buy an equity in his company and take complete control of the office and factory so that he could concentrate on sales. Jordan learned that Scarelli had worked through Suffolk University Law School by selling for Smart Distributors, Inc., an aerosol packager in Cambridge. In 1956, after graduation, Scarelli had formed the Spray Chemical Corporation. Scarelli's cousin, who had a chemical training, worked nights as production engineer to supervise the maintenance of packaging machinery and formulation of the products.

Exhibit 24–2

SPRAY CHEMICAL CORPORATION

SALES, DECEMBER, 1957 TO FEBRUARY, 1959

December, 1957	$ 1,549
January, 1958	1,299
February	2,096
March	3,356
April	8,781
May	8,024
June	10,023
July	8,588
August	5,527
September	13,472
October	5,987
November	5,997
December	17,556
January, 1959	4,010
February	1,438
Total Sales	$97,703

Jordan believed that the opportunities with Spray Chemical had all the elements necessary to satisfy him, and on July 26 he made a preliminary offer to participate in the business. The details were to be worked out after he had had time to review the company's finances. Jordan believed that his estimate of the value of the company should not depend on earnings or book value, but should take into consideration the fact that the business was a going concern in a growth industry.

As he looked into the financial records that Scarelli showed him, Jordan found that they were inconsistent and inaccurate; the figures on the balance sheet, for example, conflicted with figures on the corresponding income statement. He also uncovered three conflicting sets of balance sheets for the same date. One had been prepared by an accountant, one by an SBA administrator prior to a $20,000 loan, and the other prepared by Scarelli. Jordan began the process of reconciling the figures. It took him many hours just to correct the cash account balance by working back through the checkbook stubs and bank statements. He found that an error of $1,000 had been made by the secretary. He also found that many accounts receivable were slow and from poor credit customers. Furthermore, the inventory consisted of several thousand dollars' worth of obsolete cans, valves, and boxes. Examples of balance sheets and operating statements for dates before and after Jordan's affiliation with Spray Chemical are given in Exhibits 24–3 and 24–4.

In examining the expense accounts, Jordan found that the company had been losing money and operating inefficiently. After this examination, Jordan knew Spray Chemical was in serious financial trouble, but he believed that with his capital the company could be made profitable. He was prepared to fix terms that would give him an equity as well as security for his investment. Jordan and Abramson had made a careful study of the terms of the $20,000 loan from the SBA and found that the security for this loan was limited to fixed assets. (See Exhibit 24–5.) Therefore, at that time no accounts receivable or inventory were pledged. Jordan had observed the production operations of the business during this period and knew he could improve the production system. Fred Scarelli, he had learned, had little knowledge of operating a business. Also, Jordan's investigation into the trend of the aerosol industry showed that sales of contract packages had been on a sharp upward trend. Jordan felt he could rely on this factor to put the business back on its feet.

Exhibit 24–3

SPRAY CHEMICAL CORPORATION

COMPARATIVE BALANCE SHEETS

Source	1/10/58 SBA Application	4/30/58 Fred Scarelli	5/23/58 Friend of Jordan	7/31/58 Bruce Jordan	2/28/59 Bruce Jordan
Current Assets:					
Cash....................	$ 534.62	$ 501.00	$ 1,509.11	$ 1,203.58d	$ 62.86
Accounts receivable......	5,625.39	4,100.00	3,724.22	8,959.88	6,281.01
Inventory	13,008.16	13,200.00	15,192.49	14,764.00	18,555.97
Deposits and other	250.00	566.80	250.00	566.80	—
Prepaid interest	946.40	—	—	—	—
Total Current Assets	$20,364.57	$18,367.80	$20,655.82	$23,087.10	$24,899.84
Fixed Assets:					
Machinery and equipment	$26,753.56	$26,754.00	$26,754.00	$26,754.00	$29,454.00
Accumulated depreciation	975.00	1,168.85	1,406.07	1,837.79	3,578.65
Total	$25,778.56	$25,585.15	$25,347.93	$24,916.21	$25,875.35
Factory improvements ...	$ 1,847.50	$ 1,848.00	$ 1,848.00	$ 1,848.00	$ 2,128.51
Accumulated depreciation	0	92.40	110.63	138.60	265.12
Total	$ 1,847.50	$ 1,755.60	$ 1,737.37	$ 1,709.40	$ 1,863.39
Furniture and fixtures ...	—	$ 738.00	—	$ 738.00	$ 856.00
Accumulated depreciation	—	100.00	—	118.45	173.32
Total	—	$ 638.00	—	$ 619.55	$ 682.68
Office equipment	$ 1,511.17	$ 773.17	$ 1,511.17	$ 773.17	$ 511.70
Accumulated depreciation	84.00	77.32	192.30	94.90	92.10
Total	$ 1,427.17	$ 695.85	$ 1,318.87	$ 678.27	$ 419.60
Automobile.............	$ 2,200.00	$ 2,200.00	$ 2,200.00	$ 2,200.00	—
Accumulated depreciation	400.00	500.00	950.00	610.01	—
Total	$ 1,800.00	$ 1,700.00	$ 1,250.00	$ 1,589.99	—
Total Fixed Assets...	$30,853.23	$30,374.60	$29,654.17	$29,513.42	$28,841.02
Total Assets	$51,217.80	$48,742.40	$50,309.99	$52,600.52	$53,740.86
Current Liabilities:					
Accounts payable	$ 9,954.02	$ 5,000.00	$17,470.03	$24,223.32	$12,477.83
Taxes payable.........	1,105.22	388.69	1,657.21	2,340.94	1,044.69
Total Current Liabilities	$11,059.24	$ 5,388.69	$19,127.24	$26,564.26	$15,522.52
Notes payable	16,979.25	25,503.78	26,071.00	25,503.78	54,604.63
Total Liabilities ...	$28,038.49	$30,892.47	$45,198.24	$52,068.04	$68,127.15
Net worth	23,179.31	17,849.93	5,111.75	532.48	14,386.29d
Total Liabilities and Net Worth	$51,217.80	$48,742.40	$50,309.99	$52,600.52	$53,740.86

d deficit.

Exhibit 24-4

SPRAY CHEMICAL CORPORATION

OPERATING STATEMENTS PREPARED BY BRUCE JORDAN

	Three Months to 7/31/58		Six Months to 10/31/58	
Gross sales		$26,636.17		$51,582.68
Discounts		99.32	$ 142.61	
Sales returns and allowances			1,053.85	1,196.46
Net sales		$26,536.85		$50,386.22
Cost of goods sold:				
Beginning inventory, April 30, 1958	$13,200.00		$13,200.00	
Materials purchased	18,980.00		49,848.19	
Freight inward	844.94		1,683.45	
Labor	3,404.53		5,303.00	
Cost of goods delivered	$36,429.47		$70,034.64	
Ending inventory	14,764.00		13,241.44	
Cost of Goods Sold		21,665.47		56,793.20
Gross margin		$ 4,871.38		$ 6,406.98[d]
Expenses:				
Manufacturing expense:				
Supplies expense	$ 316.15		$ 563.81	
Factory insurance expense	489.54		793.59	
Rubbish and cleaning	21.37		21.37	
Depreciation, machinery and equipment	668.94		1,337.88	
Depreciation, factory improvements	46.20		92.40	
Depreciation, motor vehicles	110.01		220.02	
Rent	1,275.23		1,943.96	
Maintenance and repairs	224.08		260.06	
Heat, light and power	498.50		793.65	
Massachusetts payroll tax expense	—		224.32	
Total Manufacturing Expense		$3,650.02		$ 6,251.06

Exhibit 24–4—Continued

	Three Months to 7/31/58		Six Months to 10/31/58	
Expenses—continued				
General and administrative expense:				
Officers' salaries	$ 900.00		$ 1,650.00	
Office salaries and expense	1,195.00		2,245.00	
Shipping expense	127.78		411.20	
Auto expense	314.05		932.51	
Telephone expense	529.68		1,100.46	
Entertainment	145.26		334.63	
Commissions	606.56		656.78	
Legal and accounting expense	454.70		930.14	
Insurance expense, general	90.00		133.60	
Advertising expense	486.50		971.50	
Bank charges	15.36		42.77	
Interest expense	198.71		542.26	
Miscellaneous expense	11.00		1,368.59	
Depreciation, office furniture	18.45		40.84	
Depreciation, office equipment	17.58		36.93	
Travel	23.80		23.80	
Bad debt expense	—		51.80	
Freight outward	—		121.12	
Total General and Administrative Expense	$ 5,134.43		$11,593.93	
Total Expenses		8,784.45		17,844.99
Unadjusted net operating loss		$ 3,913.07[d]		$24,251.97[d]
Accounts payable, April 30, 1958			$ 5,000.00	
Less: Accounts payable, October 31, 1958			12,432.52	
Adjustment for accounts payable				7,432.52[d]
Loss for Period				$31,684.49[d]

[d] deficit.

Exhibit 24–5

SPRAY CHEMICAL CORPORATION

Loan Agreement with Small Business Administration

This Administration is authorized (pursuant to Section 207(a) of the Small Business Act of 1953, as amended) to enter into a Participation Agreement on SBA Form 136 with Lawrence National Bank, Lawrence, Massachusetts (hereinafter call "Bank"), for the purchase from Bank through the Regional Office of this Administration at Boston, Massachusetts, of an immediate participation of 75% of the Loan to be made by Bank to Spray Chemical Co., Inc., Lawrence, Massachusetts (hereinafter called "Borrower"), on Borrower's Application dated February 11, 1958, and Bank's letter dated January 20, 1958, Docket No. L-302, 612-BOS. The Participation Agreement is to be executed in behalf of this Administration by the Regional Director of said Regional Office, and the Loan is to be in the amount and disbursed subject to the conditions (in addition to the conditions set forth in the Participation Agreement and the written instructions, if any, of Regional Director to Bank) as follows:

1. Amount: $20,000.
2. Note Payable:
   a. *Five* (5) years from date of Note, with interest at the rate of six (6%) per annum, and installments, including principal and interest, each in the amount of $387, payable monthly, beginning one month from date of Note, and the balance of principal and interest payable five (5) years from date of Note; with the further provision that each said installment shall be applied first to interest accrued to the date of receipt of said installment, and the balance, if any, to principal.
3. Collateral:
   a. First Mortgage of all machinery, equipment (including automotive equipment), fixtures and furniture now owned and hereafter acquired by Borrower including, but not limited to machinery, equipment (including automotive equipment), fixtures and furniture referred to in Borrower's financial statement and fully described in a Schedule prepared and made a part of Borrower's Application and stated therein to have a total net book value of $30,854 as of December 21, 1957.
   b. Assignment of Life Insurance on the life of Frederick Scarelli in the amount of $20,000.
   c. Guaranty on SBA Form 148A of Frederick Scarelli, President and Treasurer, and his wife.
4. Use of Proceeds of Loan:
   a. Approximately $11,055 for debt payment as follows:

First National Bank of Boston	$9,604
Commercial Credit Corp.	518
Lowell Trust	74
Remington Rand Corp.	359
L. A. Black Co., Inc.	500

   b. Balance solely for operating expenses of Borrower.

Exhibit 24–5—Continued

5. Total annual compensation of the following officer of Borrower to be limited to the amount set opposite his name:

Frederick Scarelli, Pres. & Treas. $3,000

6. Fixed asset limitation of $2,000.

7. Prior to first disbursement on account of the loan, Borrower shall submit evidence, satisfactory to Bank and Regional Director that its obligation due L. A. Black Company, Inc., in the approximate amount of $1,672 has been re-written on terms substantially as follows:

(a) 3 (three) year maturity.

(b) Interest rate not exceeding 6%.

(c) Monthly payments not to exceed $51 on account of principal and interest.

(d) Subordination of lien to Small Business Administration liens.

8. Prior to first disbursement on account of the loan, Borrower shall submit evidence, satisfactory to Bank and Regional Director, that its obligation due L. A. Black Co., Inc., in the approximate amount of $424 has been re-written, on terms substantially as follows:

(a) 2 (two) year maturity.

(b) Interest rate not exceeding 6%.

(c) Monthly payments not to exceed $19, on account of principal and interest.

(d) Subordination of lien to Small Business Administration liens.

9. Agreement of Borrower, satisfactory to Bank, that it will submit quarterly financial statements.

10. Prior to each disbursement on account of the Loan, Bank shall be in receipt of evidence satisfactory to it in its sole discretion, that there has been no adverse change since the date of the Application, or since any of the preceding disbursements, in the financial or any other condition of Borrower, which would warrant withholding or not making any such disbursement or any further disbursement.

11. Such other conditions not inconsistent with the provisions of this Authorization or of the Participation Agreement as may be imposed by Bank and Regional Director.

12. Disbursement of the Loan shall be made in the discretion of Bank in accordance with the provisions of this Authorization and the Participation Agreement, provided that no disbursement shall be made after a date four months from the date hereof.

The foregoing Authorization is issued pursuant to the approval of the Loan Application by the Small Business Administration on _____, 19___.

WENDELL B. BARNES, *Administrator*

by _____

BERNARD F. O'NEIL, *Chief*
Financial Assistance Division
Small Business Administration

Negotiation for Terms

By mid-August, Jordan had completed his evaluation of Spray Chemical and was prepared to make an offer for participation in the equity. But before making an offer, he reviewed his own financial position. Exhibit 24–6 gives figures for his net worth position as of June 30, 1958, and February 28, 1959. He wanted to maintain a reserve at first but, if necessary, was willing to commit all his securities. On August 20, he became a stockholder and creditor of Spray Chemical under the following conditions:

1. He bought 5 percent of Spray Chemical common stock from Scarelli for $1,250. Scarelli previously owned 100 percent.
2. He received an interest-bearing note from the company for a $10,000 loan.

Exhibit 24–6

SPRAY CHEMICAL CORPORATION

Bruce Jordan's Net Worth Position

		June 30, 1958	February 28, 1959
Cash in bank		$ 2,000.00	$ 273.65
	Closing		
30 shares Armco Steel	50¼	1,507.50	
40 shares Bethlehem Steel	41¾	1,670.00	
30 shares General Electric	60	1,800.00	
30 shares Halliburton Oil	61	1,830.00	
120 shares Pure Oil	37¾	4,530.00	
51 shares Texas Company	71⅜	3,640.13	
50 shares Union Pacific R.R.	29⅜	1,468.75	
78 shares Spray Chemical Corp.			0
$30,000 Note due from Spray Chemical Corp.			24,836.98*
Automobile		750.00	750.00
Total Assets		$19,196.38	$25,860.63
Debts:			
Loan, brother			500.00
Loan, wife's savings account pledged			2,500.00
Loan, father			17,000.00
Loan, Lawrence Trust			1,000.00
Chattel mortgage, labeling machine			1,700.00
Beneficial Finance Co., "fly now, pay later"			400.00
Total Liabilities			$23,100.00
Net Worth		$19,196.38	$ 2,760.63

* Notes secured by following 2/28/59.

Accounts receivable	$ 6,281.01
Inventory	18,555.97
	$24,836.98

3. His note was secured by all inventory and accounts receivable (25,000 estimated value) and would pay semiannual interest at 6 percent. If the company failed to meet the interest payments, he could take control of the company and liquidate his security.
4. He received a bonus of 5 percent of the stock for making the $10,000 loan.
5. Spray Chemical gave him an option on 15 percent of the common stock, good for one year on conversion of $5,000 of his note.
6. He became consignee of all checks as the assistant treasurer of the corporation.

A Second Look

In reviewing the events that followed this investment in Spray Chemical Corporation, Jordan later told a case writer:

There were a great many things I found out after making this deal with Scarelli. In the first place, about $5,000 worth of accounts payable showed up which I had not counted on. They had been using a card system to record payables, and the additional debts just were not recorded. Some of this I attribute to the mistakes of the secretary, but most of the $5,000 was tucked away in the back of a desk drawer. The next thing which hurt was my discovery that the federal withholding and social security taxes had never been paid, although they had been withheld from wages of employees. This created another $2,500 liability I had not counted on. In addition, there were some small things that had been hidden from me. The company car that was on the books for $1,700 had been driven around without any oil and was worth only the salvage value of $50. Boy, I have really learned not to trust other peoples' statements. If I were doing this again, I would talk to everyone until I was satisfied that everything was fully recorded and truthfully represented. However, in spite of my mistakes here, I think my premise was sound—buy cheaply into a company not selling on earnings ratios where your talents will be useful in increasing the going business value.

A Second Investment

In mid-September, as the result of the pressures of creditors for payment of their debts, Jordan estimated that another $20,000 was needed for working capital to buy material, improve equipment, and carry several substantial accounts receivable which were slow in meeting their payments. Jordan borrowed $10,000 from his father and added his $10,000 of reserve from his securities. He received $20,000 in notes from the corporation, plus a stock bonus of 10 percent. At this point, Jordan had tied up $31,250 in cash for a 20 percent ownership with an option on an additional 15 percent and notes for $30,000.

Jordan's New Role

In September, Jordan became vice-president of Spray Chemical Corporation. He believed at the time that his responsibilities would be concentrated in the areas of production and finance. However, in retrospect, Jordan later said, "Looking back I can see my role. I was doing everything. I was handling sales (although I didn't know it at the time), production, purchasing, finance—everything!"

Jordan faced the problem of dealing with creditors soon after the investment of his $20,000. The accounts payable totaled $26,612 and consisted of about 100 accounts. The company's two telephone circuits were continually jammed by creditors seeking payments. Jordan, who took these calls, told each of them who he was, how he planned to put the company back on its feet and then asked to be allowed to settle the debt over a period of a year by small monthly payments. He was able to show his good faith by pointing out that he had not been drawing any salary. He found most creditors willing to go along with this plan as long as they were kept informed. He made it a policy to call his creditors whenever he could see that Spray Chemical's cash position would not allow the corporation to meet the scheduled monthly payment.

According to Jordan, production was another area where Spray Chemical appeared to have been running inefficiently.[1] He recommended and initiated some changes, adding a conveyor belt and an automatic labeling machine. With the new production line, he was

---

[1] Labor costs and overhead were the two important factors in the cost of aerosol contract packaging, since the purchase price of cans and gas varied only when large quantities were purchased.

Spray Chemical was able to keep its filling equipment in production a maximum of 15 percent of the time because of changes in setup, breakdowns, shortages of materials, lack of backlog, and the frequent downtime when all the labor was required in the capping, labeling, packaging, and shipping operations.

Overhead was about $800 a month above variable costs and owners' salaries. All pricing was done on the basis of labor, materials, overhead, and profit. The overhead and profit figures were added to the other costs on the following basis:

Order Size	Cents Added to Labor and Materials
1 to 1,000 cans	6 to 20
1,000–5,000	5
5,000–20,000	3
over 20,000	2

The filling equipment would fill from 15 to 35 cans a minute, depending on can size. Jordan estimated the average filling rate at 22 cans a minute.

able to save the expense of four hourly workers out of the seven individuals who had been required to achieve a continuous flow of production, and to eliminate much of the costly double handling that had been required. He bought the machines on his own account for $1,700, financing the purchase with a chattel mortgage. Spray Chemical leased this equipment from him at a rental sufficient to pay the monthly interest and principal charges on the mortgage.

A Crisis in Management

In October, Scarelli was involved in an automobile accident and called Jordan to say that he would be laid up for a few weeks because of a broken collarbone. During this period, the sales activity of Spray Chemical came to a halt except for the contact which Jordan had with customers by telephone. When Scarelli did get back on his feet, he made frequent visits to the office to sign checks, but no new orders came to the company from his activities. About the time that Jordan was going to ask Scarelli for a redoubled sales effort, he had a telephone conversation which went as follows:

JORDAN: Good morning, Spray Chemical.
VOICE: Is Fred there?
JORDAN: No, I'm sorry, may I take a message?
VOICE: No message, thanks. I was trying to find him. He was supposed to meet me here at the bowling alley this noon.
JORDAN: Well, I'm sure he'll be there if he has an appointment.
VOICE: No, he's probably still asleep, since he was up with me here until one o'clock.

Several days after this conversation, Jordan saw a newspaper article in the local paper which named Scarelli as promoter and financial backer of a new bowling alley. This news came as a serious blow to Jordan, for his suspicions of the last weeks were confirmed—Scarelli had left Spray Chemical entirely in Jordan's hands. Since production was now running efficiently, sales were the crucial factor in keeping operations in the black. One of the vital factors in Jordan's analysis of the going value of Spray Chemical had been the sales ability of Scarelli. Now, Jordan himself was faced with the problem of finding customers.

A Change in Management

One of Jordan's first actions after learning of Scarelli's bowling alley promotion was to call a classmate at the business school, Neil Jeffries, who had just returned from a honeymoon trip to Europe. Jeffries had been active in the New Enterprises Club while at Harvard and, in Jordan's mind, was an excellent prospect for a sales-oriented partner in Spray Chemical. Jeffries had been married early in the summer of 1958 and had traveled to Europe with his bride to investigate products in Scandinavia for potential items to import into the United States. He had $10,000 which he planned to use in financing an enterprise. Jordan's call reached Jeffries the day before he had planned to begin looking for a promising new enterprise.

Jordan and Jeffries discussed the future of the aerosol industry and the many problems Spray Chemical was facing. Jeffries was not anxious to invest in a company with so many unknowns, and he told Jordan that he would prefer to work at Spray Chemical for a month at no salary to become more familiar with its problems and potentials before he made a decision. Jordan was anxious to have Scarelli leave the company and promised Jeffries a substantial equity in the business if he should decide to continue with it.

Jordan planned to force a showdown with Scarelli and ask him to sell out his interest or devote his full time to Spray Chemical activities. As the weeks passed and Jordan tried to find out Scarelli's intentions, several other items turned up in early October which gave Jordan the evidence he needed to force a showdown. First, Jordan was told by Spray Chemical's banker that Scarelli had borrowed $3,000 in the company's name. These funds had been invested in the bowling alley. Second, Jordan learned that Scarelli had pledged some unauthorized common stock for collateral to a bank loan which went to the bowling alley, and, finally, Jordan doubted that Scarelli had paid sufficient income taxes on his earnings from Spray Chemical. Using this information as leverage in bargaining with Scarelli, Jordan was able to make a settlement with him. For $15,000, Scarelli agreed to sell Jordan his stock in Spray Chemical and give a release from any and all claims for salary, loans, and commissions.

Jordan borrowed $7,000 from relatives to make a down payment to Scarelli, and Jeffries agreed to buy a 48 percent interest in Spray Chemical for $8,000. Jordan did not pay this full amount to Scarelli. A portion was held in escrow by Abramson until a thorough investigation could be made to see that all debts and other liabilities incurred by Spray Chemical through Scarelli's actions had been discovered. Jordan found personal loans had been made to the company by Scarelli's cousin and another individual to the amount of $1,700. He also learned that Scarelli had accepted an advance against delivery of merchandise and had not deposited the $500 with Spray Chemical. When the investigation was complete, Jordan and Jeffries found that the escrow deposit would just cover the added liabilities, and it was returned to the corporation.

Shine-Up and Rapid-Shine

During the reorganization of ownership in Spray Chemical, and while Scarelli was still president, Jeffries devoted his full time to selling packaging contracts. He called on companies and individuals in many fields, but found it hard to take packaging business away from competitors. Reliability, financial strength, facilities for formulation, testing, and quick delivery were more important than the price concessions Jeffries could make because of Spray Chemical's low overhead. In November, Jeffries turned to a project that he and Jordan had developed after a visit to a competitor's plant. He had seen elaborate production and testing equipment for quality control, but little research laboratory equipment. They decided to offer special services for formulations of new products to new customers. Since neither of them was a chemist, they relied heavily on assistance from their suppliers, the major chemical firms. *Modern Packaging*, a trade journal, also supplied the industry with many new ideas and formulations, and Jordan and Jeffries found they were able to translate this information into new products for several of their customers.

Shine-Up was a product developed in this manner. Jeffries told E. F. Greenspoon, a customer with a national distribution organization, about a product which, when sprayed from a small can, was very effective as a shoeshine. After being tested, this product was ordered from Spray Chemical in large quantities. Spray Chemical thus was suddenly confronted with production problems, and went on a three-shift-a-day, seven-day-a-week drive to meet the orders for Shine-Up.

After two weeks, Greenspoon told Jeffries that he had sold his rights to Shine-Up to Edward McCormack, and that McCormack wanted to clarify his rights to the formula. Subsequently, McCormack and his lawyer went to Lawrence with a contract which stated that Spray Chemical would not produce the Shine-Up formulation for anyone else during the 1958–59 season. Jordan and Jeffries agreed to sign the contract because of the large volume of sales they expected from Shine-Up. They believed that they could "get out of it some way" if it was necessary, but did not expect any adverse developments. Unknown to Jordan and Jeffries, however, Scarelli had accepted an order for the same formulation from the Crawford Company, one of the firm's largest customers. The product was to be called Rapid-Shine. Labels and promotional literature had been produced at Crawford's expense. Jordan tried, but was unable to get a release from his contract with McCormack so that he could fill this order.

Early in January, Herbert Berenson called to introduce himself as the new owner of Shine-Up. A group he headed had taken over national promotion of the product, and he wanted to become acquainted with the production facilities. During the ensuing meeting, in exchange for a price reduction on volume orders of Shine-Up, Berenson gave Jordan a verbal release from the contract with McCormack. After this release, Spray Chemical began to deliver small quantities of Rapid-Shine to the Crawford Corporation.

After several weeks, competition between these two products began to be felt in the marketplace. Rapid-Shine dropped its price for a 6-ounce can from $1.49 to 98 cents. Soon after this move, Shine-Up increased the size of its can from 6 ounces to 12 ounces and priced the new size at 98 cents to meet the growing competition from Rapid-Shine. At this point, Berenson called Jordan and made it very clear that he was unhappy about the business Spray Chemical was doing with Rapid-Shine. He said, "I am taking a licking from the Crawford Corporation on a product that was all mine when I took over from McCormack. Unless you straighten out this mess very quickly, you will find yourself in hot water with my lawyer."

While these events were developing, Jordan went on a 10-day wedding trip on the fly-now, pay-later plan. During his absence, several thousand cans of light [2] Shine-Up and Rapid-Shine were shipped out. This was the first serious production problem which had developed at Spray Chemical, and the testing steps which Jordan later established to detect such deficiencies enabled the company to avoid serious losses. Mr. Berenson, however, told Jordan that he was very upset with the lack of quality control on Shine-Up. He threatened to not pay his bill, which amounted to $4,000 at the end of February, and in a surprise move, filed suit against the corporation. He claimed damages on the basis of his contract, which gave him exclusive right to the shoe-shine formulation during the 1958–59 season.

---

[2] Cans were light when filling machinery failed to load the required amount of concentrate.

25. J. R. SANFORD
CORPORATION (A) *
Deciding whether to Purchase a Company

In August, 1958, Richard Trent, a member of the small business consulting firm of Baker and Trent, Inc., was wondering whether to make an offer to purchase the J. R. Sanford Corporation. The Sanford company was a leading producer of certain kinds of automatic paper-handling equipment for use in offices and printing shops; net sales were about $400,000 in 1957. However, the company was near bankruptcy, and Mr. Trent had been asked if he wished to make a purchase offer.

Mr. Trent's Background

After graduation from high school in 1936, Mr. Trent spent the next six years with a Boston utility company, working his way up from office boy to assistant to the vice-president. From 1942 to 1945, he served in the army. He then completed the undergraduate course at Harvard in three years and followed that by attending the Harvard Business School. From 1950 to 1952, he was in the planning department of a large West Coast aircraft manufacturer, and from 1952 to 1955 he served on special assignments with National Metals, Inc., a small manufacturing firm. He left the company in 1955 to establish a business consulting firm with Arthur Baker, who had formerly held administrative positions in several small firms. During the next three years, Baker and Trent provided business consulting services for many small businesses and also acted as brokers in finding buyers for certain firms.

Although Mr. Trent had earned a living from consulting, he had found the experience to be frustrating. One problem was the difficulty in getting businessmen to recognize problems and to take corrective action. He said, "Many men acquire or found a business for noneconomic reasons, related more to a way of life than making a

---

profit. They do not think in terms of improving their return on investment, but rather in terms of maintaining a comfortable existence. If the consultant makes a suggestion, such as the development of specific accounting data bearing on one of the firm's problems, the manager may reject the advice, more because he dislikes working with figures than because he has thought through the suggestion.

"Another problem is that many managers of small businesses think a consulting firm is a nonprofit institution. Consulting is like medicine in that the patient may decide in retrospect that his recovery was so easy the doctor or consultant couldn't have done much and wasn't worth the fee. They have an emotional resistance to paying fees of $100 per day, which are needed to ensure the consultant a reasonable return after providing for business expenses. A consultant cannot afford to get a reputation as a man who has to sue to collect, so he is foredoomed to failure." Because of these difficulties, Mr. Trent was considering leaving the consulting field when, in November, 1957, Baker and Trent was asked to advise the J. R. Sanford company, located in Middletown, Massachusetts.

History of the Sanford Company

The company was founded by J. R. Sanford, in Middletown, Massachusetts, in 1949. Mr. Sanford, an engineer, designed the paper-handling equipment which the company had been selling since that time.

The company's products included collating machines and machine-making carbon snap-out forms. Collating machines arranged sheets of paper in a designated order as part of the process of making booklets or of assembling office papers. With a folding device attached, the collator could assemble flat sheets of paper into complete booklets of up to 64 pages. The Sanford machines were automatic and, depending on the size, could collate from 18,000 to 72,000 sheets per hour. The price of these machines ranged from $4,000 to $16,000 apiece. Forms-making machines were used to glue sheets of paper together along one edge with little spots of glue. Carbon interleaved business forms were a typical product of this process. The price of these machines ranged from $1,100 to $2,800.

There were two principal competitors in the collating machine market. One was the Thompson Equipment Company, a manufacturer of printing equipment and supplies. Thompson Equipment sales totaled $35 million in 1956, which was the last year for which data were available at the time Mr. Trent came to consult with Sanford in 1957. The other principal competitor, American Office Equipment, Inc.,

Exhibit 25–1

J. R. SANFORD CORPORATION (A)

COMPARATIVE PERFORMANCE DATA FOR COLLATORS*
AS DETERMINED BY SANFORD MANAGEMENT

Company	Price†	Speed (Sheets per Hour)	Size (Floor Space in Sq. Ft.)
American Office Equipment ...	$5,700	5,000	12.4
Thompson Equipment*	$4,700 to $6,900	16,000	25.0
Sanford*	$3,800 to $4,500	18,000	4.9

* Four-station machine without folding attachment.
† Depends upon the sheet sizes.
SOURCE: Dealer bulletin prepared by the Sanford company in 1957.

specialized in office supplies and equipment, and had sales of $70 million in 1956. For both companies, sales of collating machines were only a small percentage of total company sales. Competition in the forms-making machine market came from several very small companies, each of which accounted for only a small fraction of industry sales.

Industry sales of automatic forms-making machines were estimated at $300,000 for 1956, of which Sanford accounted for about 80 percent. Sanford sales of collating machines totaled about $160,000 in 1956, which was about 20 percent of the industry total. Both markets were expected to grow with the increased tendency toward automated office procedures; it was expected that the collating market would grow more rapidly.

Net sales of the Sanford company climbed from $205,000 in 1949 to $535,000 by 1951. The Sanford management believed its machines to be more economical, more compact, and faster than competitive machines. Comparative performance data for collators as prepared by the Sanford management in 1957 are given in Exhibit 25–1. However, sales dropped after 1951, and were $403,000 in 1956. Losses occurred in all years after 1953. Available financial data for the years 1949 through 1956 are given in Exhibits 25–2 and 25–3.

The Situation

In attempting to assist the Sanford company, Mr. Trent investigated various company activities. He found that all products were marketed through a network of 140 United States dealers and through two company-owned sales offices in Chicago and New York. The deal-

Exhibit 25–2

J. R. SANFORD CORPORATION (A)

INCOME STATEMENTS FOR YEARS ENDING DECEMBER 31, 1949–56

	1949	1950	1951	1952	1953	1954	1955	1956
Gross sales	$220,760		$608,111		$515,438	na	na	$453,418
Less: Dealer and cash discounts	15,774		73,023		55,128	na	na	49,565
Net sales	$204,986		$535,088		$460,310	$365,667	$415,993	$403,853
Beginning inventory*	$ 33,672		na		$ 69,626	na	na	$ 87,170
Purchases	66,982	M	na	M	139,397	na	na	123,502
Direct labor	na		na		33,983	na	na	43,118
Manufacturing overhead	na	I	na	I	77,361	na	na	131,301
Total	$100,654	S	na	S	$320,367	na	na	$385,089
Less: Ending inventory*	10,989		na		72,089	na	na	97,737
Cost of Goods Sold	$ 89,665		$247,086		$248,278	$240,837	$312,562	$287,352
Gross margin	$115,321	S	$288,002	S	$212,032	$124,850	$103,431	$116,501
General and administrative expenses	na		na		na	na	na	$102,641
Selling and shipping expenses	na	I	na	I	na	na	na	38,103
Total	$ 70,775		$255,706		$159,649	$160,102	$131,023	$140,744
Net operating profit	$ 44,546	N	$ 32,296	N	$ 52,383	$ (35,253)	$ (27,593)	$ (24,243)
Other income	—		7,685		—	495	—	314
Total	$ 44,546	G	$ 39,981	G	$ 52,383	$ (34,758)	$ (27,593)	$ (23,929)
Less: Interest	na		na		na	na	na	2,299
Net profit (loss) before taxes	$ 44,546		$ 39,981		$ 52,383	$ (34,758)	$ (27,593)	$ (26,228)
Less: Taxes	14,116		12,755		20,597	(9,255)	(9,627)	na
Net Profit (Loss) after Taxes	$ 30,430		$ 27,226		$ 31,786	$ (25,503)	$ (17,965)	$ (26,228)

* Inventories include only material and direct labor.

These income statements were available to Mr. Trent at the time he was asked to advise the Sanford company in November, 1957.

na—not available.

J. R. SANFORD CORPORATION (A)

Balance Sheets as of December 31, 1949–56

	1949	1950	1951	1952	1953	1954	1955	1956
Assets:								
Cash		$ 16,204	$ 1,353		$ 8,103	$ 2,719	$ 1,128	$ 2,390
Accounts receivable		102,698	43,193		79,384	42,205	55,574	38,667
Inventory*		17,538	54,629		72,089	76,937	87,170	97,737
Total		$136,450	$ 99,175		$159,576	$121,861	$143,872	$138,794
Machinery and equipment (net)	M	na	na	M	na	na	na	na
Furniture and fixtures (net)		na	na		na	na	na	na
Total	I	$ 14,765	$ 46,500	I	$ 53,516	$ 64,194	$ 65,134	$ 61,292
Reserve (finance company)						—	$ 1,795	$ 4,328
Deposits	S	$ 9,656	$ 9,918		$ 4,860	$ 34,423	4,346	—
Other				S	2,719		24,715	5,303
Total		$ 9,656	$ 9,918		$ 7,579	$ 34,423	$ 30,856	$ 9,631
Total Assets	S	$160,861	$155,593	S	$220,671	$220,478	$239,861	$209,717
Liabilities and Capital:								
Accounts payable	I	$ 22,523	$ 21,164	I	$ 37,714	$ 52,923	$ 85,159	$ 85,380
Notes payable	N			N	1,200	6,144	18,706	8,184
Accrued payroll and expense		736	1,012		3,526	6,221	4,887	6,678
Withholding taxes payable						†	†	†
Customers' deposits	G			G	—	4,466	13,293	10,815
Taxes accrued		47,792	16,380		25,508	23,504	6,075	15,228
Total		$ 71,051	$ 38,556		$ 67,948	$ 93,258	$128,120	$126,285
Long-term note							$ 2,486	$ 408
Capital stock outstanding		$ 46,390	$ 46,390		$ 46,390	$ 46,390	$ 46,390	$ 46,390
Retained earnings		43,419	70,646		106,333	80,829	62,864	36,635
Total		$ 89,809	$117,036		$152,723	$127,219	$109,255	$ 83,025
Total Liabilities and Capital		$160,861	$155,592		$220,671	$220,478	$239,861	$209,717

* Inventories include only materials and direct labor.
† Included in taxes accrued.
These balance sheets were available to Mr. Trent in November, 1957.

na—not available.

ers received a 25 percent discount from list price, and were expected to install and service the machines as well as train the operators. All dealers also handled other items of printing and office equipment. Dealerships were not exclusive; for example, in Los Angeles there were seven dealers.

Mr. Sanford also personally arranged direct sales to any customers who answered the company's advertisements in trade magazines; dealers were not given a commission on these sales. In 1957, about 50 percent of total sales were made in this way. This created a problem in that dealers were reluctant to service machines they had not sold. In Mr. Trent's opinion, this practice was disrupting the morale of the dealers and converting them into mere order takers.

The company was housed in a modern building containing 20,000 square feet of floor space, which was being used at about 50 percent of capacity in 1957. The building was owned by a separate corporation which was wholly owned by Mr. Sanford; rent was $1,100 per month and did not include heat, taxes, or insurance. In November, 1957, there were 25 employees in the Middletown plant, two of whom, in addition to Mr. Sanford, served in an executive capacity. However, it appeared to Mr. Trent that most decisions in all areas of company activity were being made by Mr. Sanford.

There were also eight engineers in a research and development laboratory located in Chicago; the cost of maintaining this laboratory was approximately $50,000 per year. In the income statement, this was charged in part to manufacturing overhead. Few improvements or developments had come out of this laboratory, apparently due in part to a rapid turnover in technical personnel. Mr. Trent thought this turnover was due to personal differences between Mr. Sanford and the technical men involved.

Production involved machining of certain parts, assembling, painting, and buffing. The operations performed were typical of many machine shops and, in Mr. Trent's opinion, did not require any special skills. The equipment included lathes, drill presses, and assembly benches—all in excellent condition. Mr. Trent thought there was enough equipment to produce for annual sales of about $1 million.

Mr. Sanford owned 90 percent of the stock. The remaining 10 percent of the stock was owned by Ralph Beller, who did general administrative work. Although records were incomplete, it appeared that Mr. Sanford was drawing a salary of about $50,000 per year and was also charging about $50,000 per year in personal expenses to the company. Loans on accounts receivable and equipment totaling about

$13,000 had been obtained from a local finance company at interest rates of 18 percent per year.

Apparently, records were not kept in a consistent manner, and some transactions were not even recorded. There was no knowledge of product costs, and it appeared that the financial statements had not been prepared with sufficient care to be reliable. Such records as had been prepared had not been preserved systematically, so that, as can be seen in Exhibits 25–2 to 25–5, some of the balance sheets and income statements were missing entirely.

After his investigation, Mr. Trent made a number of suggestions designed to improve the management of the company. However, Mr. Sanford did not follow the suggestions; Baker and Trent therefore

Exhibit 25–4

J. R. SANFORD CORPORATION (A)

INCOME STATEMENTS FOR YEAR ENDING DECEMBER 31, 1957, AND FOR SIX MONTHS ENDING JULY 30, 1958

	1957	1958 (*unaudited*)
Gross sales	$453,041	$199,076
Less: Dealer and cash discounts	49,468	29,338
Net sales	$403,573	$169,738
Beginning inventory*	$ 97,737	$ 81,586
Purchases	127,954	38,088
Direct labor	32,356	12,752
Manufacturing overhead	122,752	44,784
Total	$380,799	$177,210
Less: Ending inventory*	81,586	59,124
Cost of Goods Sold	$299,213	$118,086
Gross margin	$104,360	$ 51,652
General and administrative expense	$113,092	$ 67,710
Selling and shipping expense	29,770	9,440
Research and development	—	2,082
Total	$142,862	$ 79,232
Net operating profit	$ (38,502)	$ (27,580)
Other income	1,469	—
Total	$ (37,033)	$ (27,580)
Less: Interest	1,847	2,647
Net profit (loss) before taxes	$ (38,880)	$ (30,227)
Less: Taxes	—	—
Net Profit (Loss) after Taxes	$ (38,880)	$ (30,227)

* Inventories include only material and direct labor.
  In addition to earlier financial statements, these were available to Mr. Trent in July, 1958.

Exhibit 25–5

J. R. SANFORD CORPORATION (A)

BALANCE SHEETS AS OF DECEMBER 31, 1957, AND JULY 30, 1958

	1957	1958 (unaudited)
Assets:		
Cash	$ 576	$ 2,094
Accounts receivable	38,628	38,523
Inventory*	81,586	59,124
Total	$120,790	$ 99,741
Machinery and equipment (net)	na	na
Furniture and fixtures (net)	na	na
Total	$ 58,143	$ 48,321
Reserve (finance company)	$ 6,425	$ 5,923
Deposits	—	825
Other	6,557	13,932
Total	$ 12,982	$ 20,680
Total Assets	$191,915	$168,742
Liabilities and Capital:		
Accounts payable	$ 89,471	$ 72,821
Notes payable	11,981	23,093
Accrued payroll and expenses	4,080	3,749
Customers' deposits	10,192	4,664
Taxes accrued	20,772	9,867
Total	$136,496	$114,194
Long-term note	$ 1,275	$ 7,297
Capital stock outstanding	$ 46,390	$ 46,390
Donated surplus	10,000	33,333
Retained earnings	(2,246)	(32,472)
Total	$ 54,144	$ 47,251
Total Liabilities and Capital	$191,915	$168,742

* Inventories include only materials and direct labor.
In addition to earlier financial statements, these were available to Mr. Trent in July, 1958.

na—not available.

broke off the association. Eight months later, in late July, 1958, Mr. Trent received a distress telephone call from Mr. Sanford.

Mr. Trent arrived to discover that the company's position had deteriorated considerably. Records indicated there had been a net loss of $38,000 for 1957. Financial data for 1957 and the first six months of 1958 are given in Exhibits 25–4 and 25–5. From a consideration of liabilities and assets, Mr. Trent estimated that the company would have a negative net worth of $30,000 if liquidated at that time. Two signatures were already on a bankruptcy petition. Back payroll taxes had not been paid for two years. It appeared that Mr. Sanford might be liable personally for certain of the company's debts, in which case he might lose his home, his car, and the building.

Mr. Trent told him that he could have aided him eight months or even six months before, but that it was now too late. Mr. Sanford replied by offering to sell his share of the company to Mr. Trent. He pointed out that since the financial situation was so urgent, a decision would have to be made within 24 hours.

The Decision

Mr. Trent did not have time to secure an audit of the company's records. He was aware that errors or misrepresentations might exist in the records. He made a personal examination of the inventory and decided that it was undervalued and was probably worth at least twice the $59,000 listed on the balance sheet. Although his previous association with the company as a consultant had been brief, he was aware that a number of improvements could be made in the management of the company. It also appeared to him that the company's products were well designed and superior to competitive products.

Although Mr. Trent had no personal funds that he could invest, he knew of a friend from whom he could secure a long-term loan for $10,000. He had about decided that consulting with small businesses was a dead-end street. He had seen the poor management practices of many managers of small enterprises, including a lack of knowledge of costs and an inability to think in economic terms. It might be easier, he thought, to compete against small businessmen than to advise them.

Mr. Trent realized that, except for his judgment based upon inspection of the inventory, he had little evidence of assets. He was not at all sure the financial statements showed all the liabilities. He was not so familiar as he would wish to be with customer relations and with attitudes of customers and dealers toward the company. Nevertheless, he realized that he would have to give Mr. Sanford an answer the next day.

26. J. R. SANFORD CORPORATION (B)*
Attempts to Improve Profitability

In late July, 1958, Richard Trent had been asked if he wished to make a purchase offer for the J. R. Sanford Company. As indicated in Sanford (A), he had only 24 hours to make the decision because of impending bankruptcy. He made an offer for Mr. Sanford's shares, 90 percent of the shares outstanding; the offer was accepted.

The company was a leading producer of collators and carbon snap-out forms-making machines;[1] sales had totaled $245,000 in 1958. In August, 1959, reflecting on his 12 months with the company, Mr. Trent thought he had achieved substantial progress toward making operations profitable. However, he realized that there were still many problems to be faced and decisions to be made.

Background

Mr. Trent had been a member of the business consulting firm of Baker and Trent when he was offered the opportunity to purchase from J. R. Sanford the Sanford company, located in Middletown, Massachusetts. Although the company had been profitable for the first five years after its establishment in 1949 and was a leading producer of certain kinds of paper-handling equipment, losses had occurred in all years after 1953. Mr. Trent purchased Mr. Sanford's shares for $2.00 in July, 1958. At that time, two creditors had already signed a bankruptcy petition.

Finance

A shortage of cash was Mr. Trent's most pressing problem. There were over 300 creditors, some of whose accounts had been outstanding for over three years. Back payroll taxes, totaling $5,600, had not been paid. It appeared to Mr. Trent that if the company were liqui-

---

[1] Collating machines are used to arrange sheets of paper in a designated order; forms-making machines are used to fasten sheets of paper together with spots of glue. The machines are described more fully in Sanford (A).

dated liabilities would exceed assets by about $25,000. Total cash was about $2,000.

Mr. Trent secured a personal loan of $10,000 from a friend. He either contacted personally or wrote to each of the firm's 300 creditors, telling them of the company's financial plight and saying that they would probably receive no more than 10 cents on the dollar in the event of liquidation. He then included a token payment in evidence of his sincerity, and proposed a schedule for the repayment of each debt. Mr. Trent visited the office of the District Director of Internal Revenue, taking along the keys to the plant. He told them that he could not pay the $5,600 at that time, and said that if they wanted to be responsible for putting 16 men out of work, he would leave the keys with them. The department consented to a schedule of repayments.

He had been with the company less than a week when a truck arrived with an $8,000 collator which was being returned. It had been sold on a trial basis; however, there was no mention of this fact in the company records. The former owner of Sanford had discounted the account receivable with a local finance company, and Mr. Trent was forced to redeem the pledged receivable for $5,000, the amount originally loaned; this took most of his remaining cash.

About 10 percent of accounts receivable had to be charged off to bad debts. Terms of sale were 1 percent 10/net 30, although the company rarely received payment within 30 days. It was also discovered that the company, under the former management, had taken $3,500 in deposits for equipment promised, but not yet designed. It was necessary to set up a schedule for the repayment of these customer deposits.

In succeeding months, the company continued to be hard-pressed financially, although loans totaling $45,000 were obtained from the Metropolitan National Bank of Boston in November and December, 1958. At the time Mr. Trent purchased the company, in August, 1958, loans from a Middletown finance company totaled about $30,000. These were secured by accounts receivable and inventory, and carried an interest rate of 18 percent. The loans obtained from the Metropolitan National Bank were used in part to repay the finance company; some of the bank loans were secured by equipment, and others were secured by inventory and accounts receivable. The interest rate on the bank loans was 6 percent. Mr. Trent, in speaking later of his success in obtaining these bank loans, said that the bank had made the loans because of confidence in the Sanford products and management.

The company had continued to occupy a modern building in Middletown owned by Mr. Sanford, the founder and former owner of the company. However, in October the rent was increased from $1,100 to $2,100 per month by Mr. Sanford. The company was using only 50 percent of the building's 20,000 square feet of floor space, and Mr. Trent estimated the company's break-even sales volume in these quarters was $47,000 per month. Mr. Trent said that with the higher rent he couldn't afford to stay; yet with his lack of funds he couldn't afford to move.

In December, 1958, Mr. Trent arranged to move the company to Ridgefield, Massachusetts, 40 miles from Middletown. The Ridgefield Development Corporation made the company an unsecured loan of $25,000 and also agreed to construct for the company a building with 10,000 square feet of floor space in a new industrial park near the city. The building was to be leased to Sanford for 86 cents per square foot per year, with taxes and insurance not included. It was expected that the building would be finished by September, 1959, and in the meantime the company was established in an old building in Ridgefield. In Mr. Trent's opinion, an important consideration of this arrangement was that he was not required to personally endorse the loan to the company.

Financial data for 1958 and the first six months of 1959 are given in Exhibits 26–1 and 26–2. Mr. Trent considered the records maintained prior to his acquisition to be unreliable. He thought that inventory had been undervalued, that certain charges had not been allocated in a consistent manner, and that some company transactions had not even been recorded. He had an auditor come in to put the accounts on a more systematic basis, and he asked him to check the existing inventory with special care. Existing inventory had been valued to include only materials and labor; it was revalued to include also manufacturing overhead. Mr. Trent had believed that the inventory was worth at least $118,000 at the time he purchased the company. When the auditor told him that the inventory would perhaps run higher than that amount, Mr. Trent asked him to keep it as low as he could, consistent with his responsibilities. It came to $120,000, even after throwing out a certain amount of inventory that was judged worthless. Complete audited statements were not available until December 31, 1958.

Mr. Trent instituted the practice of making cash flow forecasts, of using pro forma statements, and of gathering information relating to production costs. He said that the company would not really be able

Exhibit 26–1

J. R. SANFORD CORPORATION (B)

BALANCE SHEETS AS OF JUNE 30, 1958, DECEMBER 31, 1958, AND JUNE 30, 1959

	6/30/58 (unaudited)	12/31/58	6/30/59
Current Assets:			
Cash	$ 2,094	$ 1,988	$ 3,158
Accounts receivable	38,523	31,315	31,455
Inventory*	59,124	113,410	103,896
	$ 99,741	$146,713	$138,509
Fixed Assets:			
Machinery and equipment (net)	na	$ 31,362	na
Furniture and fixtures (net)	na	6,552	na
	$ 48,321	$ 37,914	$ 31,850
Other Assets:			
Reserve (finance company)	$ 5,923	$ 4,811	$ 4,731
Deposits	825	1,455	(79)
Other	13,932	128	274
	$ 20,680	$ 6,394	$ 4,926
Total Assets	$168,742	$191,021	$175,285
Current Liabilities:			
Accounts payable	$ 72,821	$ 54,603	$ 42,389
Notes payable, due within 1 year	23,093	30,035	9,752
Accrued payroll and expenses	3,749	12,597	3,000
Withholding taxes payable	†	5,848	1,463
Customers' deposits	4,664	3,200	2,950
Taxes accrued	9,867	2,396	2,770
	$114,194	$108,679	$ 62,324
Notes payable, long term	$ 7,297	$ 20,278	$ 46,361
Net Worth:			
Capital stock outstanding	$ 46,390	$ 46,390	$ 46,390
Donated surplus	33,333	33,333	33,333
Retained earnings	(32,472)	(17,659)	(13,123)
	$ 47,251	$ 62,064	$ 66,600
Total Liabilities and Capital	$168,742	$191,021	$175,285

* Inventory for June 30, 1958, includes only material and labor; at later dates inventory also includes manufacturing overhead.
† For June 30, 1958, taxes accrued includes withholding taxes payable.

na—not available.

Exhibit 26–2

J. R. SANFORD CORPORATION (B)

INCOME STATEMENTS FOR SIX-MONTH PERIODS ENDING JUNE 30, 1958, AND JUNE 30, 1959, AND FOR THE YEAR ENDING DECEMBER 31, 1958

	Six Months Ending 6/30/58 (unaudited)	Year Ending 12/31/58	Six Months Ending 6/30/59
Gross sales	$199,076	$295,738	na
Less: Dealer and cash discounts	29,338	50,966	na
Net sales	$169,738	$244,772	$111,831
Beginning inventory	$ 81,586*	$ 81,586*	$113,410
Purchases	38,088	49,272	24,168
Direct labor	12,752	22,918	10,330
Manufacturing overhead	44,784	65,253	19,809
Total	$177,210	$219,029	$167,717
Less: Ending inventory	59,124*	113,410	103,896
Cost of goods sold	$118,086	$105,619	$ 63,820
Gross margin	$ 51,652	$139,153	$ 48,010
General and administrative expense	$ 67,710	$ 61,355	$ 18,663
Selling and shipping expense	9,440	53,884	18,983
Research and development	2,082	20,430	3,584
Total	$ 79,232	$135,669	$ 41,230
Net operating profit	$ (27,580)	$ 3,485	$ 6,780
Other income	—	408	2,060†
Total income	$ (27,580)	$ 3,893	$ 8,840
Less: Other expenses			
Interest	$ 2,647	$ 6,586	$ 1,565
Other	—	11,719‡	2,739
Total	$ 2,647	$ 18,305	$ 4,304
Net profit (loss) before taxes	$ (30,227)	$ (14,412)	$ 4,536
Less: Taxes	—	401	na
Net Profit (Loss) after Taxes	$ (30,227)	$ (14,813)	na

* Inventories include only material and labor.
† Includes bad debts recovered totaling $1,701.
‡ Includes moving expenses, bad debt loss, and loss on sale of fixed assets.

na—not available.

to determine the cost of manufacturing individual items until a history of costs had been assembled in the new plant in Ridgefield.

Sales

In June, 1959, sales were at an annual rate of $300,000. About 95 percent of this represented United States sales; the remainder was overseas. The breakdown by product line was estimated as follows:

	Estimated 1959 Sales	Estimated Market Share
Collators	$100,000	20%
Forms-making machines..........	$200,000	80%

The principal competitors in the collator market were American Office Equipment, a manufacturer of office equipment and supplies, with 1957 sales of $90 million; and Thompson Equipment, a manufacturer of printing equipment and supplies, with 1957 sales of $51 million. The competitors in the forms-making machine market were very small, and none of them accounted for a significant share of the market.

Sanford products were distributed by 139 dealers throughout the United States and by 8 overseas dealers. Mr. Trent had secured a manufacturers' representative who was familiar with exporting problems to distribute to the 8 overseas dealers and to obtain other overseas dealers. The company sold directly to the 139 United States dealers. At the time Mr. Trent bought control of the company, there were also company-owned sales offices in Chicago and New York, accounting for annual sales of $20,000 and $80,000, respectively. Mr. Trent thought the sales volume did not justify maintaining these offices and discontinued them in August, 1958. The former manager of the New York office established his own dealership, handling only Sanford products. The dealers sold, installed, and serviced the machines. In addition, they trained the operators who would use them. They received a 25 percent discount and did not normally carry inventory.

Under the old management, about 50 percent of sales had been made through the dealer organization and about 50 percent directly to customers. Mr. Trent thought this arrangement had angered dealers, particularly when customers contacted dealers to service machines they had not sold. He therefore adopted a basic policy that sales would be made only through the dealer organization. He sent letters to all dealers, informing them of this decision.

The dealers sold complementary items of printing and office equipment. Each dealer normally had three or four salesmen who worked on a 10 percent commission. In Mr. Trent's opinion, these salesmen were poorly trained and often knew less about the product than the prospective customer. In an effort to improve their knowledge of Sanford products, Mr. Trent had been sending monthly Fact Bulletins to his dealers' salesmen. These bulletins were concerned with potential markets and with competitive advantages of Sanford machines. Dealerships had been awarded on a nonexclusive basis; for sample, in Los

Angeles there were seven dealers. Mr. Trent estimated that 60 percent of his dealers sold less than $5,000 worth of Sanford products per year.

Mr. Trent hoped to establish company-owned sales offices in major cities. American Office Equipment sold through a company-owned dealer organization, although Thompson Equipment sold through an organization of independent dealers. In support of his plan, Mr. Trent cited the New York dealer who had formerly headed the company-owned outlet in that city. This dealer sold nothing but Sanford equipment, and his salesmen were quite familiar with the products. In June, 1959, this dealer's sales were at the annual rate of $100,000, which was one-third of total company sales. It was also Mr. Trent's plan to have these company-owned sales offices train and supervise a network of dealers in outlying areas. "The way it is now," he said, "I can't begin to keep in touch with 139 dealers."

These offices, he figured, would each require an investment of $15,000. He thought that annual break-even sales volume for each office would be about $100,000 and that there were 10 or 15 cities with the potential to support such a volume. To man these offices, Mr. Trent planned "to find the best men competition has and hire them." He expected to have to offer them substantial increases in pay, perhaps 50 percent more than the $8,000 per year he thought these men then averaged. He thought this method would eliminate the need for extensive training, would decrease the number of costly mistakes newcomers would make, and would give him experienced salesmen with ready-made contacts.

In June, 1959, about $600 per month was being spent for advertisements in the *Graphic Arts Monthly*. An additional $400 per month was being spent on brochures for dealers, newsletters to dealers, and sales travel expenses. About 50 inquiries per month resulted from the advertisements, and these were referred to dealers in the appropriate areas. The previous Sanford management had spent about $10,000 per year on advertising but had not referred the inquiries to dealers; the Sanford management had sold directly to those customers. Since there were multiple dealerships in many cities, a problem arose in regard to Mr. Trent's decision to refer inquiries to dealers. This was the question of whether inquiries should be referred to all dealers in a given area. Mr. Trent thought that advertising was effective and hoped that when he had more funds he could increase advertising expenditures to $2,500 per month.

On November 1, 1958, prices were increased 10 percent on all products. This increase had been announced several months before and had resulted in a number of pending sales being closed before that date. Even after the change, the Sanford collators, priced from $4,200 to $5,000 for a four-station model, were about 5 percent cheaper than similar competitive models, according to Mr. Trent. In regard to pricing, he said, "From our standpoint, it is very important that prices be stable. We lack the financial resources to be able to stand a price war."

Product Development

Mr. Trent said the Sanford collator had been chosen over several competitive machines in a test conducted by purchasing officials of the state of Ohio. This confirmed Mr. Trent's belief that Sanford collators were faster, smaller, less expensive, and more versatile than competitive machines.

Under the former ownership, there had been a research and development laboratory in Chicago, employing eight engineers. However, because this installation was costing about $50,000 per year and had not resulted in many substantial developments, Mr. Trent discontinued it in August, 1958. He retained one engineer and had him work first on certain problems that were disrupting production. Then he sent him into the field to talk to dealers and customers in order that he might learn about servicing and operating problems.

In Mr. Trent's opinion, the Sanford machines could be redesigned so as to cut manufacturing costs while maintaining performance. He pointed out that heavy gauge metal was used throughout the machines, even on the covers, and that heavier gears than needed were used in many places. "We could cut the cost of Sanford machines by 50 percent with better engineering," said Mr. Trent. "This saving could then be passed on to consumers to give us a real competitive advantage." On another occasion he remarked that Sanford should strive to keep its machines just slightly better than competitive machines. He was afraid that if the performance advantage of Sanford machines became too great, competitors would be spurred to major redesign efforts. He felt that Sanford did not yet have the financial or human resources to match such competitive action.

Production

Much of the equipment from the Middletown plant had been put into storage until the new Ridgefield building was finished; in the interim, only assembly work was performed in the Sanford plant, with other work being subcontracted. It was anticipated that the same manufacturing functions would be performed in the new Ridgefield plant as had been done in Middletown; these would include manufacturing of nonstandard parts, assembling, and painting.

In the past, the Sanford machines had always been constructed by hand, with no semblance of a production line. Mr. Trent said that he could cut costs considerably by producing machines in lots of 10 and by purchasing raw materials and standard parts in larger lots. However, he bemoaned the fact that sufficient volume to do this had not developed and that even if it did he did not have the financial resources to take advantage of the opportunity.

Inventory reduction had been a major source of funds during Mr. Trent's first year with the company. In August, 1959, inventory levels were uneven; the level of certain parts was so low that Sanford had to rely on prompt delivery by suppliers in order to maintain steady production. In July, 1959, despite a backlog of orders totaling $38,000, Sanford shipments totaled only $12,000—this compared with average monthly shipments in 1959 of over $18,000. The reason for this decreased production was a shortage of certain key parts, caused when a supplier was unable to make delivery because of vacations.

Personnel

When the Sanford company moved to Ridgefield from Middletown, a distance of about forty miles, six members of the old organization came along. They included Mr. Trent, the executives in charge of production and sales, one engineer, one man whose experience was in inventory control and purchasing, and one lady in the office. By June, 1959, Sanford had hired 11 Ridgefield workers, mostly for production. As soon as the company moved into new quarters, it was anticipated that five more production workers would be hired.

Mr. Trent said, "We lack many of the staff people we would like to have. However, we have to hold down the overhead, and so we depend on people's knowing several jobs. Even now, with our organization of 17, we could probably support annual sales of $900,000 without hiring any more staff or management people." Mr. Sanford, the former owner, had made all important decisions in all areas of company operations. Mr. Trent was trying to get the sales and production executives to take more responsibility now, although he was finding this to be difficult because of their lack of experience in making decisions.

Size and Attitude toward Growth

In considering Sanford's position in the industry, Mr. Trent thought that certain advantages accrued to a small company competing with larger companies. One advantage was flexibility and speed. He said, "I can make changes in our products this afternoon if I think it necessary." He also thought that a greater sense of teamwork existed within the smaller company. He said, "Our people know that the future of their jobs is closely tied to company profits. Everyone works hard and tries to contribute ideas that will make the company successful."

He also saw disadvantages to being small. He thought it was difficult for a small company to obtain and support an adequate distribution organization. He pointed out that the sales expenses of Sanford had to be carried by only two lines, whereas the sales expenses of a larger company could be absorbed by a number of lines. Mr. Trent also thought the small company suffered because it was unable to maintain an adequate staff. Specialists in such fields as accounting, market research, and production control could not be added to the organization until annual sales reached at least $1 million.

He thought perhaps the most serious disadvantage to being small was that internally generated funds were rarely sufficient to support adequate efforts to improve present products and to develop new ones. He said, "In fields based upon technology, competitors will be developing new and better products. If you don't do the same, your company will die." In accordance with this evaluation, Mr. Trent felt that Sanford must adopt a basic policy of growth, and, in fact, it was his hope that sales could be expanded by 200 to 300 percent each year.

Objectives and Future Financing

As he thought about the considerations that had led him to purchase the company, Mr. Trent realized that he had had two alternatives in mind.

1. Build the company up so that it could be sold profitably within one to three years.
2. Improve the profitability of the company and strive to acquire control

of, or to establish working relationships with, a number of other small companies. He would then devote his time to supervising a central group of staff services such as accounting and market research. He would be a member of the board of directors of each of these small companies and might or might not be an officer in each.

At the end of one year, Mr. Trent thought he could look back on some solid achievements. During the first six months of 1959, sales had been $112,000 and profits $4,300; during the corresponding period of 1958, under the former management, sales had been $170,000, and a loss of $30,000 had been shown. In August, 1959, there was a backlog of orders totaling $30,000; one year earlier the backlog had been zero.

He also considered the following to have been substantive accomplishments:

1. The financial statements were put on a systematic basis, with some assurance that all existing liabilities were recognized.
2. The impending actions of the holders of accounts payable were postponed.
3. The company was moved physically to a new plant, built for its use, and with space available for expansion.
4. Relations with the dealer organization were improved.

Despite these developments, Mr. Trent thought the company's progress had reached a critical point. He was not sure whether continued development could be achieved without substantial equity investment. He thought a shortage of funds was limiting profitability through restricting advertising and product development efforts, and through causing manufacturing and purchasing inefficiencies. Because of this lack of funds, he was afraid that subsequent periods might not be so profitable as the first six months of 1959.

Inadequate funds also caused Mr. Trent to fear for the very future of the company. Despite a reduction in accounts payable by almost $30,000 in the past year, there were still over 200 creditors, some of whose accounts had been outstanding since 1955. At the time Mr. Trent bought the company in 1958, he had persuaded the creditors to refrain from bankruptcy proceedings so that he might have an opportunity to make the company profitable and thus repay them in full. He was afraid that some of these creditors might again become impatient, take court action, and "start a snowball rolling" which would end in involuntary bankruptcy for Sanford. Mr. Trent thought the company needed $100,000 in new capital, the money to be used to repay creditors, to expand inventory, and to increase advertising and research activity.

In considering possible sources of funds, Mr. Trent did not think Sanford could generate enough funds internally unless profitability could be improved. And, he lamented, "this cannot be done until more funds are obtained." He questioned to what extent additional equity investment could be obtained prior to the showing of the added earnings which would probably result from such investment. He realized that he had possibly been too optimistic as to what could be accomplished in one year and that he was now possibly too pessimistic about the future. In any event, the alternatives, as he saw them now, were:

1. Sell the equity interest and invest the proceeds in other situations.
2. Bring the company along for one or two years more and then sell it.
3. Issue equity financing with the expectation that he will remain.

27. THE BRIDGETON

BROADCASTING CORPORATION*
Employees Consider Purchasing a Company

On a Friday morning in June, 1953, Robert Moore entered the office of Raymond Ordway, general manager of radio station WDBA in Bridgeton, Connecticut. Before Mr. Moore had an opportunity to give notice that he was leaving his four-month-old job as a time salesman, Mr. Ordway told him to close the door because he wanted to talk. "Bob, how would you like to buy my 50 percent interest in WDBA? I want to get into a TV station in a larger city than Bridgeton, and I'm ready to sell out. The price is $15,000."

Taken by surprise, Mr. Moore did not mention his plans to leave and asked for two weeks in which to make a decision. He also asked Mr. Ordway for the latest balance sheet and income statements, and was given the statements reproduced as Exhibits 27–1 and 27–2. These were the first actual figures on station operation that he had seen, and they confirmed his belief that WDBA was in serious financial difficulty.

After Mr. Moore had left Mr. Ordway's office, he telephoned the vice-president of a large aircraft manufacturing company in New Jersey to ask for two more weeks in which to make a decision on the job he had been offered. The vice-president, whom Mr. Moore had met in his previous job, had called him a week earlier and offered him the position of assistant to the president at a salary of $7,000 per year. Mr. Moore's assignment would be that of coordinator of the activities of the eight plants operated by the rapidly expanding company. After considering the opportunity for a week and comparing it with his position at WDBA, he had decided to accept it. He felt that Mr. Ordway's unexpected offer to sell out, however, presented an entirely new opportunity to be compared with the aircraft company's offer.

Robert Moore

After his graduation from a prominent graduate school of business administration in 1951, Mr. Moore spent several months in Europe visiting with his father, an executive of a large oil company. Return-

Exhibit 27-1

BRIDGETON BROADCASTING CORPORATION

PROFIT AND LOSS STATEMENTS*

	Fiscal Year Ending May 31, 1951	Fiscal Year Ending May 31, 1952	For the Month of April, 1953	June 1, 1952, to April 30, 1953
Time sales revenue:				
Local programs	$23,263.68	$20,090.42	$1,282.78	$12,410.12
Local announcements	31,040.71	39,445.08	2,321.19	34,897.20
National and regional programs	1,198.05	55.00	—	45.00
National and regional announcements	831.00	4,580.30	992.80	9,985.39
Network	—	2,659.03	—	1,994.36
Total Time Sales Revenue	$56,333.44	$66,829.83	$4,596.77	$59,332.07
Incidental broadcasting revenue:				
Sale of talent	$ 2,940.85	$ 3,220.44	$ 265.86	$ 2,777.30
Sale of wire facilities	—	—	—	35.65
Sale of records and transcriptions	45.25	16.50	38.40	74.00
Cash discounts earned	5.54	20.26	—	8.78
Total Revenue	$59,325.08	$70,087.03	$4,901.03	$62,227.80
Direct expenses:				
Agency commissions	$ 532.22	$ 1,413.02	$ 183.05	$ 2,374.29
Cost of talent sold	3,080.37	3,073.93	254.98	2,643.35
Cost of wire facilities	—	—	—	47.04
Cost of records and transcriptions	23.58	20.90	—	—
Other commercial program costs	3,092.47	2,537.12	438.03	1,970.30
	6,728.64	7,044.97		7,034.98
Gross Profit on Sales	$52,596.44	$63,042.06	$4,463.00	$55,192.82

Exhibit 27-1—Continued

	Fiscal Year Ending May 31, 1951	Fiscal Year Ending May 31, 1952	For the Month of April, 1953	June 1, 1952, to April 30, 1953
Technical department expenses:				
Salaries	$6,139.27	$ 7,764.59	$ 635.51	$ 7,060.01
Power and light	921.55	998.79	85.15	919.68
Fuel	90.06	111.99	—	85.94
M & R technical equipment	277.67	330.82	41.07	253.06
Tubes	33.41	74.13	3.60	132.58
Transmitter lines	109.09	95.00	7.95	87.50
Outside engineering expense	122.74	70.10	—	50.25
Other tech. dept. expense	32.98 $ 7,726.77	30.35 $ 9,475.77	5.26 $ 778.54	23.81 $ 8,612.83
Program department expenses:				
Salaries	$8,060.18	$11,910.46	$1,211.70	$13,440.74
M & R studio nontechnical equipment	10.15	167.93	—	200.77
Music, records and transcriptions	2,120.44	342.99	40.12	323.59
News service	1,790.68	2,060.42	170.55	2,042.50
Royalty and license fees	1,845.36	2,369.46	180.90	2,049.50
Other program department expense	347.67 $14,174.48	53.42 $16,904.08	34.05 $1,637.32	149.80 $18,206.90
Sales department expenses:				
Sales commissions, local	$6,840.04	$ 8,626.48	$1,019.30	$ 6,692.57
Sales commissions, station				
Sales representative	356.88	393.39	—	396.70
Advertising	305.70	196.16	26.80	258.74
Sales promotion expense	588.25	430.63	13.48	49.48
Other sales department expense	21.22 $ 8,122.09	216.47 $ 9,863.13	— $1,059.58	1,775.45 $ 9,172.94
Total Technical, Program, and Sales Expense	$30,013.34	$36,243.58	$3,475.44	$35,992.67
Gross before General and Administrative Expense	$22,583.10	$26,798.48	$ 987.56	$19,200.15

Exhibit 27-1—Continued

General and administrative expense:	Fiscal Year Ending May 31, 1951	Fiscal Year Ending May 31, 1952	For the Month of April, 1953	June 1, 1952, to April 30, 1953
M & R office equipment	$ 84.66	$ 72.99	$ 32.90	$ 40.58
Salaries	9,655.42	10,316.34	846.28	9,420.80
Rent	2,105.60	2,778.36	236.18	2,609.41
Light and heat	468.76	541.64	40.26	480.82
Travel	391.24	117.06	27.55	273.65
Telephone and telegraph	1,263.39	1,118.69	134.27	1,359.56
Dues	619.00	512.00	100.91	860.84
Stationery and supplies	421.83	447.14	19.83	181.04
Postage	265.16	208.94	48.31	174.63
Entertainment	110.45	89.43	4.67	111.37
Freight and express	173.48	10.43	4.21	18.85
Depreciation of L.H. improvement	1,534.01	2,132.03	180.12	1,981.34
Amortization of L.H. improvement	287.77	350.33	31.45	346.05
Bad debts	581.14	690.83	51.97	572.60
Insurance	635.00	526.30	45.37	505.30
Legal and auditing	1,278.00	279.00	77.05	494.97
Collection expense	—	.93	—	170.85
Real estate taxes	—	124.60	10.38	114.26
State unemployment compensation taxes	969.50	748.44	120.35	813.35
State income or franchise tax	31.63	205.07	195.98	195.98
FCAB taxes	631.30	487.58	67.05	499.05
FUC taxes	134.26	206.51	13.37	200.64
Other taxes	35.00	11.00	—	16.45
Interest	615.76	576.20	33.40	423.85
Other general and administrative expenses	94.45	223.34	43.42	270.73
Amortization of franchise	926.33	1,111.62	92.63	1,018.96
Donations	38.00	55.00	27.42	27.42
Directors' fees	—	—	87.75	789.76
	$23,351.14	$23,941.80	$ 2,573.08	$23,973.11
Profit or (Loss) for the Period	($768.04)	$ 2,856.68	($ 1,585.52)	($ 4,772.96)

* Statements prepared by a public accountant.

Exhibit 27–2. BRIDGETON BROADCASTING CORPORATION

Assets and Liabilities

ASSETS	May 31, 1951		May 31, 1952		April 30, 1953	
Current Assets:						
Cash, Bridgeton National Bank	$ 1,738.52		$ 1,595.17		$ (6.20)	
Petty cash fund	27.00	$ 1,765.52	27.00	$ 1,622.17	27.42	$ 21.22
Accounts receivable, trade	$ 9,084.00		$ 9,484.53		$ 8,060.54	
Accounts receivable, other	1,909.37		279.59		37.18	
	$10,993.37		$ 9,764.12		$ 8,097.72	
Less: Reserve for bad debts	504.56	10,488.81	1,185.48	8,578.64	1,060.63	7,037.09
Total Current Assets		$12,254.33		$10,200.81		$ 7,058.31
Fixed Assets:						
Building	$ 1,891.89		$ 1,891.87		$ 1,891.87	
Leasehold improvements	3,478.74		3,528.10		3,720.06	
Transmitter equipment	8,224.83		8,285.25		8,285.10	
Radiating system	4,509.84		4,509.84		4,509.84	
Studio technical equipment	4,543.92		4,556.26		5,004.23	
Studio furniture and fixtures	731.63		797.00		863.26	
Office furniture and fixtures	1,350.12		1,350.42		1,613.44	
	$24,730.97		$24,918.74		$25,887.80	
Less: Reserve for depreciation	1,821.79		4,528.77		6,824.17	
Total Fixed Assets		22,909.18		20,389.97		19,063.63
Prepaid and Deferred Charges:						
Prepaid insurance	$ 394.35		$ 623.49		$ 567.04	
Cash advances	60.00		—		—	
Prepaid rent (transmitter site)	88.00		88.00		110.00	
Prepaid interest	477.65		175.65		28.77	
Total prepaid and deferred charges		1,020.00		887.14		705.81
Other Assets:						
Goodwill	$ 6,334.42		$ 6,334.42		$ 6,334.42	
Organization expense	103.86		103.86		103.86	
Franchise	10,189.92		9,078.30		8,059.34	
Total Other Assets		16,628.20		15,516.58		14,497.62

Exhibit 27–2—Continued

	May 31, 1951	May 31, 1952	April 30, 1953
LIABILITIES			
Current Liabilities:			
Accounts payable	$ 4,158.87	$ 2,314.59	$ 4,809.67
Accrued FOAB taxes	146.35	109.84	133.72
Accrued FUC taxes	49.83	160.04	41.42
Accrued state UC taxes	182.34	130.86	120.35
Accrued withholding taxes	688.30	380.87	547.46
Accrued real estate taxes		124.60	114.26
Accrued interest	164.15	164.15	467.87
Accrued royalties and license fees	335.43	727.94	1,582.38
Accrued rent	110.00	196.00	181.69
Accrued wages	766.10	730.51	633.09
Accrued agency commissions	58.26	180.62	375.24
Total Current Liabilities	$ 6,659.63	$ 5,220.02	$ 9,007.15
Other Liabilities:			
Notes payable, C.I.T. Corp.	$ 9,706.22	$ 5,707.15	$ 2,169.68
Notes payable, Bridgeton National Bank	1,713.90	342.50	
Notes payable, Coleman Ordway*	5,500.00	5,500.00	5,500.00
Notes payable, W. D. Pease			670.00
Total Other Liabilities	16,920.12	11,549.65	8,339.68
Capital:			
Capital stock common, $10 par value	30,000.00	30,000.00	30,000.00
Surplus†		(2,631.85)	(1,248.50)
Profit (loss) for the period	(768.04)	2,856.68	(4,772.96)
Total Liabilities and Capital	$52,811.71	$46,994.50	$41,325.37

* Loan made to corporation by Raymond Ordway's father. Interest at 5 percent. Due and payable on December 31, 1955.
† Surplus as of May 31, 1952, is adjusted to show loss of $1,863.81 by embezzlement. Surplus as of April 30, 1953, is adjusted to show further loss of $1,473.33 by embezzlement.

ing to New York in November, he secured a position with a recently formed consulting firm through the recommendation of one of his professors. His principal job was to write reports dealing with the government contract work done by the firm's clients. Mr. Moore became unhappy with what he was doing and found it difficult to get along with his immediate superior. In December, 1952, he resigned and began looking for another position. In graduate school, Mr. Moore had formed an inclination to look to small business for a career, since he felt that a small company would put his education to work the most rapidly. He characterized himself as an independent person who would be more happy operating a business of his own rather than working for others.

Having decided that some sales experience would be of value to an independent businessman, Mr. Moore spent six weeks reading the help-wanted advertisements in the *New York Times*, looking for an interesting sales opportunity. In February, 1953, he noticed an ad for a time salesman by radio station WDBA in Bridgeton, Connecticut. Consulting a map, he discovered that Bridgeton was a city of approximately 43,000 people, located some 50 miles from New York City. Since college days, when he had become involved in organizing a student program over the local radio station, Mr. Moore had been interested in the radio-television industry. He had written to the major networks to inquire about a position as a time salesman, but had decided that it would be impossible for him and his wife to live on the $65 per week salary offered. What interested Mr. Moore in the WDBA advertisement was that it was an out-of-town concern advertising in the New York paper. To Mr. Moore, a small concern going that far afield for a salesman meant that "something might be going on." He called WDBA immediately and arranged for an appointment with the general manager that evening.

First Impressions

Mr. Moore and his wife arrived in Bridgeton on a cold and bleak February night, and found it to be a depressing-looking industrial city with very little to distinguish it from many New England towns that had felt the effects of economic change. Raymond Ordway, general manager of WDBA, met the Moores in the doorway of the five-and-ten-cent store on Main Street and brought them up to the fourth floor offices and studios of the station. Mr. Moore's first impression of his prospective employer and the station were anything but encouraging. Mr. Ordway was about thirty-five years old, short, and stout, dressed in flamboyant clothes topped off with a black homburg hat, and was smoking a large cigar. The station, which consisted of two small broadcasting studios and one office with six desks, was painted a much-faded pink and blue.

When Mr. Moore noted the lack of activity in the station, he was informed that WDBA was a music and news station, licensed to operate from sunrise to sunset. During the course of the next three hours, Mr. Moore learned the following facts. WDBA was a 1,000-watt independent station operated by the Bridgeton Broadcasting Corporation, which was controlled by Raymond Ordway. The corporation had been formed in 1950 by Mr. Ordway, who had received financial assistance from his wealthy father and three other stockholders. The station reached an audience of over 150,000 people, located principally in Bridgeton and the nearby town of Dunster, which had a population of 24,000. Besides the morning and afternoon music and news programs there were two one-hour foreign language programs on Sunday mornings. The station depended primarily for its revenue on the sale of spot announcements to local merchants (see Exhibit 27–3). Competition came from a network station in Bridgeton, WQTW, which operated from 6 A.M. to 12 midnight. In addition, three large New York City radio stations and two New York television stations could be received in Bridgeton. Besides Mr. Ordway, WDBA employed 10 people: a chief engineer and his assistant, a program director, two announcers, two salesmen, a bookkeeper, a copywriter, and Mr. Ordway's wife, who served as secretary.

Although Mr. Moore's first impressions had been anything but reassuring, he was heartened by the fact that Mr. Ordway did not balk when he said he needed $100 per week to live. After discussing the opportunity with his wife, Mr. Moore decided to take the job. He reasoned that it would, at least, provide a living for a while and give him the sales experience he wanted in what he considered an interesting industry. He went to work the following Monday, and by March 1 had moved to Bridgeton.

Second Impressions

Mr. Moore had not been working many weeks when he became convinced that WDBA faced some serious problems. The foremost problem in his mind was Mr. Ordway himself. He discovered that Mr. Ordway was known by few people in Bridgeton, and those that

Exhibit 27–3

BRIDGETON BROADCASTING CORPORATION
Retail Rate Card

BROADCAST ADVERTISING RATES

No. Times	Discount	1 hr.	½ hr.	¼ hr.	10 min.	5 min.	1 min.*	30 sec.†	15 sec.‡
1	Net	$40.00	$24.00	$16.00	$12.00	$8.00	$4.00	$3.00	$2.00
13	2½%	39.00	23.30	15.60	11.70	7.80	3.90	2.93	1.95
26	5%	38.00	22.80	15.20	11.40	7.60	3.80	2.85	1.90
52	10%	36.00	21.60	14.40	10.80	7.20	3.60	2.70	1.80
104	15%	34.00	20.40	13.60	10.20	6.80	3.40	2.55	1.70
156	20%	32.00	19.20	12.80	9.60	6.40	3.20	2.40	1.60
260	25%	30.00	18.00	12.00	9.00	6.00	3.00	2.25	1.50
312	30%	28.00	16.80	11.20	8.40	5.60	2.80	2.10	1.40

* 1 minute or up to 125 words.
† 30 sec. or up to 60 words.
‡ 15 sec. or up to 30 words.

WEEKLY PROGRAM FREQUENCY RATES

	For 3 Programs per Week				*For 6 Programs per Week*		
	13 wks.	26 wks.	52 wks.		13 wks.	26 wks.	52 wks.
½ hr......	$64.80	$57.60	$50.40	½ hr......	$ 97.20	$82.80	$68.40
¼ hr......	43.20	38.40	33.60	¼ hr......	64.80	55.20	45.60
10 min....	32.40	28.80	25.20	10 min....	48.60	41.40	34.20
5 min....	21.20	19.20	16.80	5 min....	31.40	27.60	22.80

	For 5 Programs per Week				*For 7 Programs per Week*		
	13 wks.	26 wks.	52 wks.		13 wks.	26 wks.	52 wks.
½ hr......	$84.00	$72.00	$60.00	½ hr......	$109.20	$92.40	$75.60
¼ hr......	56.00	48.00	40.00	¼ hr......	72.80	61.60	50.40
10 min....	42.00	36.00	30.00	10 min....	54.60	48.20	37.80
5 min....	28.00	24.00	20.00	`5 min....	36.40	30.80	25.20

Special saturation packages, station option time:
 1 minute announcements, minimum of 25 to be used in one week's time or less, $2.50
 per announcement.
 30 second announcements, minimum of 25 to be used in one week's time or less, $2.00
 per announcement.
 15 second announcements, minimum of 20 to be used in one week's time or less, $1.25
 per announcement.

GENERAL INFORMATION

1. FREQUENCY—POWER—TIME
 Operating power 1000 watts, clear channel.
 Licensed to operate sunrise to sunset.

Exhibit 27–3—Continued

2. LENGTH OF COMMERCIAL COPY

Total Length of Broadcast

5 Minutes	.............1:15
10 Minutes	.............2:10
15 Minutes	.............3:00
30 Minutes	.............4:15
60 Minutes	.............7:00

3. NEWS SERVICE

World and national news by International News Service. Local news from WDBA newsroom.

4. MUSIC CLEARANCE

Complete licenses of BMI, ASCAP, and SESAC. Time rates include music copyright fees.

5. TALENT

Rates on request.

6. TRANSCRIPTION EQUIPMENT

Fully equipped for 33⅓, 45, and 78 rpm. Two sets of dual turntables.

7. REMOTE BROADCASTS

Charges for remote control pickups quoted on request.

8. SERVICE TO CLIENTS

Complete facilities of station program and advertising departments available at no extra cost.

9. POLITICAL

Regular rates apply. Payable in advance. 24-hour deadline on copy. Frequency rates allowed.

10. COMMISSIONS AND DISCOUNTS

a) Commissions to advertising agencies recognized by the station only, 15 percent.
b) Bills are rendered weekly. No cash discounts. Bills are due and payable when rendered.
c) Announcements and programs cannot be combined to earn larger discounts.
d) These rates are for convenient reference. They are not to be considered as an offer of facilities and are subject to change without notice. Time discounts on card rates apply to total number of broadcasts for the same sponsor in one year under original or renewed contracts.

11. COPY REQUIREMENTS

Program material and commercial copy subject to station approval. WDBA subscribes to the code of ethics of the National Association of Radio and Television Broadcasters.

knew him had little respect for him. The station personnel were frank to admit their dislike for their boss, and Mr. Moore soon shared it. Mr. Ordway spent most of his time in the office, discussing grandiose promotion schemes, but Mr. Moore never once observed him produce any actual business. In addition, Mrs. Ordway was hurting the already low morale by not performing any useful task so far as Mr. Moore could tell.

Near the end of April, Mr. Moore was invited to a meeting at the home of Jack Marsh, WDBA's program director and morning announcer. In attendance besides Moore and Marsh were Don Cummings, chief engineer and owner of 10 percent of the common stock, and Paul Flynn, the announcer for the afternoon music program. Mr. Moore had come to consider these three men as the only capable men in the organization. There was immediate agreement among the four men that WDBA was in trouble. Don Cummings reported that the tarpaper shack housing the transmitter, about two miles from the studio, was completely inadequate. The station's antenna was bent and unpainted. In addition, he noted that much of the equipment was run down, and a system of remote control of the transmitter from the studio was sorely needed. Mr. Moore reported that the situation was poor in his department also. His sales had reached a level where he was bringing in enough cash to pay his own salary. However, in his opinion, the salesman who was on a $25-per-week salary was not worth even that much. The other salesman, who worked on a 15 percent commission basis, was not producing nearly so much as he should.

From the other men, Mr. Moore secured the payroll data (shown in Exhibit 27–4) and some idea of operating costs. Since he knew that, at best, about 350 to 400 spot announcements were broadcast per week at an average of $2.50 each, he quickly reached the conclusion that WDBA was losing money. The other men told Mr. Moore that their solution to the problem was to have him take Mr. Ordway's place as general manager. Mr. Moore pointed out that neither he nor anyone else could move Mr. Ordway out of the situation, since he controlled the corporation. The meeting ended without a plan of action.

Exhibit 27–4

Estimates of Weekly Payroll

1. Chief engineer $75
2. Assistant engineer 42
3. Program director 75
4. Announcer 45
5. Announcer 45
6. General manager 125
7. Bookkeeper 50
8. Copywriter 40
9. Secretary 35
10. Salesman.......................... 100
11. Salesman.......................... 25
12. Salesman (commissions) 45–50

Appraising the New Opportunity

When Mr. Ordway made his offer to sell out, Mr. Moore rethought some of his analysis of the problems of WDBA. He still concluded that the basic reason for the present financial difficulty was Mr. Ordway's poor management. In his opinion, the programming was handled very effectively by Jack Marsh, and he had a high opinion of Don Cummings as an engineer. While some limited statistics on the market covered by WDBA were available (see Exhibits 27–5 and 27–6), Mr. Moore tended to use his own experience, gained in selling the market for four months, in appraising this factor. He had conducted an informal survey of listenership since his arrival in Bridgeton by peering through the windows of parked automobiles to see on which station the radio had been tuned. The frequency with which he heard WDBA programs from radios in small shops, garages, etc., convinced him that the station had a good audience in Bridgeton. A professional listenership survey of doubtful accuracy had placed WDBA first among all stations reaching Bridgeton in February, 1953.

Exhibit 27–5

BRIDGETON BROADCASTING CORPORATION

DATA SHEET

WDBA   BRIDGETON, CONNECTICUT

1000 W. Day Only

Network: Independent

Corporate name and address:

Bridgeton Broadcasting Corporation
450 Dean Street, Bridgeton, Connecticut

Personnel:

Raymond Ordway, General Manager

1950 data:	*Within 0.5 MV/M Contour*
Audience:	
Population	155,500
Households	43,430
Radio homes	42,710
Market 1949 sales:	
Total retail	$124,500,000
Food store	36,900,000
Drug store	4,060,000
Evaluation:	
Sales per capita	$800
Food per family	850

Exhibit 27–6

BRIDGETON BROADCASTING CORPORATION

INDUSTRIAL EMPLOYMENT FIGURES
Compiled by the Bridgeton Chamber of Commerce

The following figures give the total industrial employees and the number of industries in Bridgeton, Connecticut, in May and November.

May, 1935	7,151 employed,	90 firms
May, 1936	8,034 employed,	91 firms
November, 1936	8,871 employed,	93 firms
May, 1937	9,432 employed,	93 firms
November, 1937	8,449 employed,	94 firms
May, 1938	6,926 employed,	93 firms
November, 1938	7,859 employed,	89 firms
May, 1939	7,802 employed,	90 firms
November, 1939	8,606 employed,	89 firms
May, 1940	7,964 employed,	89 firms
November, 1940	8,927 employed,	88 firms
May, 1941	9,442 employed,	89 firms
November, 1941	10,373 employed,	89 firms
May, 1942	10,401 employed,	90 firms
November, 1942	10,498 employed,	90 firms
May, 1943	11,837 employed,	90 firms
November, 1943	11,945 employed,	96 firms
May, 1944	11,053 employed,	97 firms
November, 1944	11,445 employed,	96 firms
May, 1945	11,482 employed,	98 firms
November, 1945	9,878 employed,	107 firms
May, 1946	11,229 employed,	107 firms
November, 1946	12,659 employed,	111 firms
May, 1947	12,428 employed,	109 firms
November, 1947	13,238 employed,	109 firms
May, 1948	13,019 employed,	110 firms
November, 1948	13,087 employed,	104 firms
May, 1949	11,418 employed,	103 firms
November, 1949	11,355 employed,	102 firms
May, 1950	11,200 employed,	102 firms
November, 1950	13,896 employed,	104 firms
May, 1951	12,505 employed,	103 firms
November, 1951	12,206 employed,	102 firms
May, 1952	11,975 employed,	100 firms
November, 1952	12,064 employed,	99 firms
May, 1953	12,083 employed,	99 firms

However, WDBA did not even appear on a recent A. C. Nielsen rating of stations in the area.

In appraising the potential for increasing sales, Mr. Moore felt that with hard work it might be possible to more than double the current sales figure. The station could handle an average of 180 spot announcements and 15 5-minute news broadcasts per day without serious overcrowding. His own experience in selling time had convinced him that the other salesmen had been overlooking much of the potential business in the area. He discovered that WDBA had no accounts in the whole town of Dunster—only two miles away—and that many of Bridgeton's 600 merchants had never been approached. To reach the potential he thought existed, Mr. Moore realized that he would have to hire and train an entirely new sales force.

The Board of Directors

A week after he had made his offer, Mr. Ordway invited Mr. Moore to attend a special meeting of the board of directors of the Bridgeton Broadcasting Corporation, called for the purpose of offering his stock to the other stockholders and the corporation in accordance with a previous agreement. Besides Mr. Ordway and Mr. Cummings, the board consisted of the two remaining stockholders, each of whom held 20 percent of the stock. Mr. Moore had met both Mr. Manning, an employee of an electronics company, and Mr. Pease, a lawyer for the same company, on previous occasions. The offer of Mr. Ordway's stock was a formality, since the stockholders had declined their option informally and the corporation had no cash. During the meeting, Mr. Moore realized that it would be very difficult to persuade Mr. Ordway to lower his price, since he expressed the opinion that he would wait, if necessary, to find a buyer willing to pay what he was asking.

After the meeting, Mr. Pease engaged Mr. Moore in a conversation concerning Mr. Moore's possible purchase. Mr. Moore admitted to Mr. Pease that at that point he was still reluctant to commit $15,000 of personal funds to a business that was in poor financial condition. He pointed out that while his wife had an inheritance of $10,000 he did not want to touch it, and he had only $2,000 in the bank. The rest of the funds would have to be supplied by his father on a personal loan basis, and he would like to keep his requests for help from his father as reasonable as possible. Mr. Pease agreed with Mr. Moore's point of view and suggested that while he was not interested in buying a controlling interest because he was located too far away, he would be interested in buying one half of Mr. Ordway's stock. Mr. Pease said he was anxious to protect his present investment by getting some good management into WDBA, and he felt that Mr. Moore could do the job.

Mr. Moore returned home and wrote a letter to his father, who was returning from his overseas assignment the next day. In the letter, he outlined briefly the opportunity that had been presented to him and asked about the possibility of a loan if he should decide to buy. Exhibit 27–7 is his father's answer. Exhibit 27–8 is another letter from his father after he had been sent the financial statements shown in Exhibits 27–1 and 27–2. Exhibit 27–9 is a letter from Mr. Manning to Mr. Moore's father. Exhibit 27–10 is a letter from Mr. Pease to Mr. Moore's father, written at Mr. Manning's request.

Exhibit 27–7

THE BRIDGETON BROADCASTING CORPORATION

June 10, 1953

My Dear Bob:

As regards the proposed loan to cover a 25 percent purchase of stock in WDBA, I feel that I have not had available sufficient information to convince me that this is a sound financial investment. However, such an analysis is really your responsibility, and you can unquestionably gather together the necessary information and make the best resolution of these facts. If it is your wish that I make a loan as an expression of my confidence in you, the answer is definitely and unreservedly yes, assuming, of course, that I have the cash available. I think, however, that you should be reasonably sure in your own mind that you have resolved all the facts, and that your decision is not merely an expression of enthusiasm for a good cause.

Since this would be a loan on some businesslike terms, say for example, drawing a 4 percent interest, I think you should be reasonably sure that the investment will show sufficient earnings to pay the necessary interest and a reasonable amortization of the loan. This means that the net earnings should be at least 4 percent and preferably in the proximity of 10 percent; otherwise, the loan would become a burden and would result in a reduction in your income, which neither one of us would care to have happen.

The P&L history has been unfavorable. Current profits are nil, and it seems to me that there are plenty of obstacles ahead of reasonable earnings. Competition with TV is certainly a tough one, and my guess is that this will get tougher as community stations are established and colored pictures become a reality.

Competition from the large network radio chain may also become more severe as they may have to improve their programs, and possibly even reduce their rates to compete with TV.

Good salesmanship with a real program which has a large listener reception can probably improve the P&L. Reduction in operating costs or an increase in the rates to customers are other means of improving P&L, but I presume they are not too realistic. The past four months will have given you an opportunity to appraise the possibility of increasing the station's income. What are the actual facts on station income versus expense? Why should future earning prospects be any brighter? How much of an increase in business is necessary to show net earnings of say 5 to 10 percent? Unless you can see real prospects of improving the P&L outlook, I would pause

Exhibit 27–7—Continued

and give serious consideration before making any investment into such an enterprise.

In addition to the P&L outlook, you should perhaps make an analysis of the financial balance. Assets and liabilities should be within a reasonable proximity of one another, and it is presumed that your only assets are the physical plant, while your liability is the outstanding stock you are proposing to purchase. When convertible assets, such as the physical plant, represent only a small portion in comparison with the liabilities, then that old intangible, goodwill, becomes of questionable value, especially if earnings are low.

All these are questions which I am sure you have carefully weighed, and which will receive the benefit of your good judgment.

It is recognized that the financial appraisal is not the only one which needs to be considered. If this business suits your and Anne's ideas as regards the future outlook for happiness, if the location is all that you desire, if your associates are congenial and capable, and if you have the makings of a happy, enterprising business team, then perhaps this might be considered as an investment in experience and happiness. In resolving these factors, only you and Anne can make the appraisal, and I am sure that good, sound judgment will be applied in this analysis.

One other matter that needs to be carefully weighed is the organizational problem in which you, as general manager, are a minority stockholder. You must be sure that your relationship to the business is a sound one, not only for you but also for your other shareholders and your business associates. Your responsibility should be well defined, as should those of the board, so that the other stockholders and officers of the company do not indulge in station management, and that full responsibility is left on you, with your responsibility being directly to the shareholders. Let us raise some questions to make sure that the relationship is sound. If for any unforeseen reason the business should decline and another general manager is desired by the stockholders, this would probably mean your resignation, and in this case, what do you do with your shares? If, as we should expect, the business succeeds, and you should wish to sell out for a capital gain and possibly to obtain another opportunity at some other location, can you dispose of your shares at their market price, or must you return them to the other stockholders at par?

My only desire is to be of assistance. If I can help in any way in gathering, analyzing or resolving the facts, let me know and we'll get together. We could probably come up for a weekend if such a visit would be of assistance.

If you are satisfied with the outlook after weighing all of the many facets of this problem, I suggest that you let me have your report and analysis of the facts in a concise review, together with the amount of the loan, interest, etc. which you feel is desirable. There can then be a very prompt decision on my part, and you must keep in mind that my decision can only be a vote of confidence in you and a desire to help you find happiness, self-satisfaction and success in your business efforts. Believe me, I only want

Exhibit 27–7—Continued

to be of assistance, and you have my best wishes and fullest confidence in your outlook for happiness and success.

Sincerely, as ever,

/s/ DAD

Mr. ROBERT M. MOORE
450 Dean Street
BRIDGETON, CONNECTICUT

Exhibit 27–8

THE BRIDGETON BROADCASTING CORPORATION

June 17, 1953

DEAR BOB:

I have had an opportunity to study the well-prepared financial review which you presented for the Bridgeton Broadcasting Corporation, and offer the following comments for your consideration:

1. The balance sheet shows that the current cash position is too low, especially in view of the present low earnings. This could be improved by reducing the accounts receivable.
2. The reserve for bad debts may also be too low, and an effort to reduce the accounts receivable will probably permit a more reliable value under this account.
3. The items listed under other assets, including goodwill, organization expenses, and franchise, appear to be far too high when compared with the fixed assets. The real value of goodwill for a corporation which has shown no profit is probably close to zero. The franchise costs appear to be so high that it might even lead to a suspicion that some milking might have been in progress by previous officers. My offhand guess is that somebody has charged some personal expense under this item, and might have taken stock against this expense charge. I would suggest that your auditor break this item down to see:
   a) Who got the money;
   b) What was done to deserve this money;
   c) What needs to be done to avoid recurrences, assuming that this is an indication of undesirable business ethics.
   The charges under other assets are all indicative of inadequate management during the early stages of getting the business established, and they represent a considerable burden to future management that has to pay for previous inefficient results.
4. When reviewing the balance sheet, the basic question is: "What is the real worth of the company if it has to face reasonable liquidation?" My score is about as follows:

Exhibit 27–8—*Continued*

Current assets.................	$ 7,058.31	
Fixed assets	25,887.80	
Prepaid expenses	705.81	
Liquid Assets		$33,651.92
Current liabilities	9,007.15	
Other liabilities	8,339.68	
Liabilities		17,346.83
Real Worth		$16,305.09

In brief, the 3,000 shares of $10 par value stock are probably worth today, under reasonable liquidation, less than 50 cents on the dollar—not a very attractive stock for investment purposes.

5. The profit and loss statement appears to be self-explanatory.
6. The royalties and license fees appear to be high in comparison to the gross business, and should be negotiated downward if possible. It is suggested that these fees might better be based on net profits rather than gross business, and a payment of 10 percent on net profits would appear to be more reasonable for such an item.
7. Administration expense appears to be excessive but can probably be reduced after careful study. I have the feeling, however, that any reduction in administration expense will probably be offset by an increase in operating expenses, especially for salaries and wages, since it will soon be necessary to increase these costs if you are to maintain morale and build up a live organization.
8. Unless profits can be appreciably increased rather promptly, the stock is really unattractive from any point of view. The appraisal of the probability of improving profits can only be made by one who has experience with the business, a knowledge of the organization and its personnel, an outlook for such business in the community, and a knowledge of the competitive advertising forces which are at play. This appraisal must necessarily be yours, or that which you can obtain from your friends and advisers in whom you can place your confidence.
9. It seems to me that the real need is for an appreciably larger business volume. Assuming that the direct expense in obtaining new business is approximately 50 percent, it would appear to me that the sales revenue must be increased by approximately 50 percent before this could be considered an attractive business venture. Increased revenues of $30,000 per annum with an estimated net profit of $15,000 might allow a dividend of approximately 20 percent on the par value of the stock after establishing reasonable reserves for the amortization of the $5,500 debt, improving the cash position, and for capital expenditures which might be required for improving business efficiency. Such a dividend would allow you to pay interest and amortize your proposed loan in about six years. There appears to be little evidence to support any assumption that such an improved profit position can be attained, and I seriously doubt that anyone could accomplish it in even the most favorable circumstances in less than five years. I have a

Exhibit 27–8—Continued

feeling that this is a marginal business which, after careful management and hard work on the part of the entire organization, may continue to exist with a small profit during good times, and with real hardships when the going gets rough and advertising expenses are reduced.

I feel quite unqualified to appraise the outlook for developing this business into a sound venture, but it is my feeling that the odds are certainly not favorable for success. In my own conservative mind and with the lack of local background, I would invest no money in this business, but I recognize that you may feel that it is a worthwhile gamble.

I am willing to make the loan that you have suggested on the basis of my confidence in your judgment and ability. The terms of this loan can be negotiated between us to a satisfactory arrangement, and I suggest that you give me a personal note with interest at 4 percent per annum to be paid annually, with the note falling due in, say, 10 years. If these terms are not satisfactory, they can be adjusted.

There are certain aspects of this venture which must be carefully weighed if you are to protect yours and the company's best interests:

a) Let us be pessimistic and assume that your efforts will not be successful, and as a consequence a new manager is required. How does the company get a new manager and get you out of the business? I would suggest that in case of failure to produce reasonable profits after a period of several years, you may either offer to resign or a majority of the directors can request your resignation, in which case the other stockholders would be required to purchase your stock at par value.

b) Let us assume that your efforts are successful. What is the incentive for you to work hard, put the business on its feet, and at the same time involve a risk to your investment? It is suggested that you have the right to purchase a majority holding in the company within a period of, say, five years at par value, such majority stock to be obtained from, first, the stock which has not yet been issued, and then a pro rata share from the other stockholders.

c) It is also suggested that efforts be made to purchase stock now offered for sale at a more realistic value, say, at $6.00 or $7.00 a share instead of at par.

I regret that I cannot advise you to undertake an investment where the outlook is so pessimistic. The risk is high, the odds are against you, and you must appraise the chance for improving profitability. Recognize that this is a gamble, which means that you must be prepared mentally, morally and in every other way for a failure in this venture and to charge the loss against experience.

I know that you will make a sound decision, and you can be assured any decision that you make will receive my fullest blessing, my very best wishes, and the benefit of any assistance which I may be able to offer. I am only

Exhibit 27–8—Continued

sorry that the outlook based on your good financial analysis is not a bright one.

Perhaps we should get together for a final discussion before your final decision is made.

Sincerely, as ever,

/s/ DAD

MR. ROBERT MOORE
450 Dean Street
BRIDGETON, CONNECTICUT

Exhibit 27–9

THE BRIDGETON BROADCASTING CORPORATION

June 22, 1953

MR. JOHN F. MOORE
Room 2865
Colonial Building
NEW YORK 20, NEW YORK

DEAR MR. MOORE:

Bob has asked me to introduce myself to you and to give you a word picture of how the Bridgeton radio station situation appears from my point of view. In discussing the matter recently, Bob quoted to me a few excerpts from a letter you sent to him, and I can't help but feel, as I project myself ahead some fifteen years, that in a similar situation I would want to express to my son as careful and accurate an analysis of the facts available to me as you have.

There is no question, of course, that a detached and objective look at our balance sheet leaves considerable doubt in the mind of a prospective investor. On the other hand, there are certain aspects of the balance sheet which, when explained, cast a somewhat more optimistic light on the situation. For example, there are items such as accumulated directors' fees and travel expenses, items which we voted as proper expenses of the corporation some time ago but which have never been paid. Actually, this is a small, closed group, and if it appeared to be for the benefit of all of us to do so, we could wash these right out of the picture at any time. However, we are carrying them on the books in the hope that some time in the foreseeable future we may discharge these obligations as appropriate sums due the directors. As a matter of fact, Bob would share with Mr. Pease in the disbursement of directors' fees accumulated for Mr. Ordway. There are other items in the aggregate picture that reflect a rocky beginning which was our misfortune in the early days of our operation. We suffered a serious financial loss due to a delay in proceeding with construction and operation of the station, incurred as a result of FCC litigation prompted by the intervention of a New York City station relative to our operation. Although this

Exhibit 27–9—Continued

case was summarily dismissed in our favor three months later, we were, of course, not compensated for it. A further loss of serious magnitude to us was incurred through an embezzlement by one of our early employees. Our recovery in this case was only a fraction of the loss, and it was just one of those things.

Well, we were young and inexperienced and, although we've still a lot to learn, I do think we have had a few of the corners knocked off. In addition to coming through these early bitter experiences, we were from the start undercapitalized. We knew this before we began, but we were not discouraged. The fact is that in the relatively short time we have been operating, since February, 1950, we have successfully reduced our total original capital indebtedness which was in excess of $20,000 to a figure less than $8,000 at the present time. This has included the liquidation of a three-year note to C.I.T. Corporation, covering our technical equipment. This note will be completely discharged in another five months, and its original value was about $12,000. This, we think, is progress and indicates that a cold view of the balance sheet does not reveal the entire picture. It has been a blood, sweat, and tears proposition, true, but none of us has milked this corporation for one cent. We have all worked closely together toward a common goal and have sacrificed our own personal interests in attempting to attain the goal.

A word about Mr. Pease may be of interest to you. He is a lawyer, a man about thirty-five years of age, married, with three children, an exceptionally capable person, in my estimation, and a good personal friend. I have had considerable business dealings with him aside from Bridgeton, as he has been for several years a member of the legal staff of Randall Manufacturing Company by whom I am also employed. Our company has recently recognized his ability by promoting him to the position of assistant to the general manager of our radio and television division in St. Louis, one of the more hardheaded competitive business operations which we have. His decision to invest his own funds in the radio station was made after he had decided to accept the St. Louis position, and I think this in itself reflects not only his ultimate confidence in the operation, but also in his associates in the venture. I certainly accepted it in this light and look on it as a further challenge to my own efforts on behalf of the station, which are given to the fullest extent that my time will allow. I am going to ask Mr. Pease to write a few lines to you himself.

Don Cummings is a man of approximately thirty years of age, married, with family responsibilities also, having several young children. He and your son are the two of us who at least are making a living on the station and who are on the scene of operations. Don is a capable chief engineer and has saved us many dollars and headaches on the technical end of the operation. He is completely loyal, and whatever he lacks in business acumen he sincerely tries to make up with devotion to the cause. In other words, he is not in this for fun—it's his life's work and he takes it seriously.

As for myself, you might say that I was the promoter of the venture at its inception. My interest then, as now, was to acquire an interest in a small

Exhibit 27–9—Continued

business which over the years could return a small, but dependable, profit. I have not looked on this as a get-rich-quick scheme but as a measure of the type of security one might be able to fall back on if the need arose. I am employed by Randall Manufacturing Company on the staff of the general manager of the equipment divisions, with responsibilities as to management direction of our commercial endeavors. Although WDBA is a part-time venture for me, it is not a plaything because I cannot afford playthings. I, too, have family ties. We have five children and, like most others, I have to keep my nose to the grindstone.

I think you can see from the above that none of us is affluent, that we are in this with a view to making it a profitable business venture for all. We have given freely of our time and talents, such as they are. We are not going to jeopardize our investments or work of the past four years. We have made this perfectly clear to Bob Moore and, in placing in him the confidence we all have in his ability, we have had a clear understanding with him from the very beginning on several points. First of all, we do not expect miracles. We recognize not only his ability but also that he is relatively inexperienced in some phases of business management. He is humble enough to recognize these shortcomings too, and this fact merely strengthens our feeling that he will work hard to improve himself along these particular lines. It is a comfort to us that without interfering in any way his wife is providing excellent moral support to Bob during these difficult weeks, and I feel that she will continue to do so. We have also had it clearly understood among us that if it appears at any moment that the expedient thing to do is to unload, we will do so without prejudicing the original investment of any of us. I am completely confident that we can do this if it becomes necessary.

I hope you won't interpret this lengthy letter as an attempt to convince you that your analysis of the situation is not completely correct as far as it goes. It is merely an effort to provide some of the background and some of the personal highlights of this situation. I wish that it were possible for us to talk this over in person, because I would like to obtain your firsthand reactions myself. I am sincerely concerned with the whole matter, and while I am ultimately confident that the market exists for our station, I am certainly not unaware of the difficulties that an undercapitalized venture encounters at the hands of an unscrupulous competitor in a field in which radical economic changes are at least possible in future years. Nevertheless, I face the future with the confidence that proper management can make the station reasonably successful if sufficient time and dollars are available and that, at worst, a liquidation of our holdings is possible without substantial personal loss.

If there are any points you would care to discuss further with me, please do not hesitate to call on me. I hope that we may meet in the not too distant future.

Very truly yours,

/s/ William T. Manning, Jr.

Exhibit 27–10

THE BRIDGETON BROADCASTING CORPORATION

June 23, 1953

Mr. John F. Moore
Room 2865
Colonial Building
New York 20, New York

Dear Mr. Moore:

Bill Manning sent me a copy of his letter to you dated June 22. I am attempting to comply with Bill's request that I drop you a line in connection with the station.

I am assuming that Bill's letter arose from an objection of yours to Bob's prospective investment in Bridgeton, ignoring the source of whatever funds Bob will use. There is no doubt that as an investment the balance sheet and the operating statistics of Bridgeton present a very poor speculation. My decision to buy is based on the fact that the amount involved is not of major importance to me and that failure to purchase Ordway's stock would mean, substantially, the effective loss of my previous investment. It is also, however, based on my belief that this organization can be profitable and can pay off within a reasonable period the investment made by the stockholders, if it is well run.

I do not presume to advise you as to the advantages occurring to Bob, but I personally feel that he has a good opportunity, and that we are fortunate to have him. This station could obviously support a general manager at a reasonable salary, even if it never makes a nickel. This was the problem in connection with Ordway, since his majority interest is obviously attractive at a price of $15,000 to any one of the numerous radio station managers on the market. They could purchase the stock at $15,000, pay themselves a good salary, and live off the corporation without ever returning a penny to the stockholders. Obviously, Bob cannot do this since he will not control the corporation, but we certainly intend to see that his association is profitable to all of us.

The encouraging factor on operations, although it has been discouraging to the station managers, is the existence of the other radio station, WQTW. This station went into Bridgeton just before the war with a capitalization identical to ours. Even allowing for the wartime advertising splurge, their success was spectacular. Their gross income averaged in excess of $125,000 a year, and their gross expenditures something between $80,000 and $90,000. The station was sold a few years after the war for a gross price in excess of $225,000. This enormous capital load has made it necessary for their management to fight us tooth and nail ever since the arrival of our station in the market. However, what reports I am able to obtain indicate their inability to amortize and pay off their capital investment to the stockholders. Splitting the market between two stations has reduced their gross to someplace between $80,000 and $100,000, and our

Exhibit 27–10—Continued

gross to $60,000. I think the market has a greater potential, and we have managed to ensure ourselves the number one position in spite of our daytime-only operation. In fact, the daytime operation may be a blessing to us and a detriment to them in view of the impact of television, particularly in the evening hours.

The very success of WQTW demonstrates conclusively to me that our ability to capitalize on radio in Bridgeton, while not unlimited, certainly has ample opportunity for profit. My further objectives in Bridgeton were to diversify our operation into other allied lines as soon as we could accumulate some capital surplus. To be frank about it, I had expected to branch into television, and Ordway's failure to try to include the organization in his television picture was another reason for my decision to buy him out. I think that Bob should be able to put the station on its feet financially, to pay off the various investments, and to find associated businesses in Bridgeton which could offer diversification and opportunities for expansion at a profit to all of us.

Unfortunately, my move to St. Louis prevents my close contact with the station, but I think that its operation in the next few months will either demonstrate that we can make a go of this and other enterprises in Bridgeton, or that we should dispose of the property at cost or at some slight profit—something which I am sure we can do without too much difficulty.

If there is any further information I can give you, please feel free to write me, or if you ever get to St. Louis give me a call and let us have lunch together.

Very truly yours,

/s/ W. O. PEASE

28. TASK CORPORATION *

Policies of a Growing Firm with Many Technical Products

As of early 1961, Task Corporation was a company with 110 employees, 35 of whom were engineers or draftsmen, engaged in designing and making a variety of products, including force-sensing instrumentation, electric motors, pumps, blowers, and refrigeration equipment.

Task had been formed and incorporated in 1954 by a group of mechanical and aeronautical engineers with the objective of engaging both in research and development work and in the manufacture of proprietary products. The first work of the company had been in the development of wind tunnel test instrumentation, and in accord with the initial objective a line of products was subsequently developed. The number of different Task products had grown rapidly, and the company had also grown in terms of sales and the number of employees.

Profits had grown with the size of the company until the past two years. During 1959 and 1960, Task had shown little profit or had sustained losses which management attributed to two causes. One was a heavy product development effort which had yielded products expected to recoup with later profits the heavy expenses incurred to develop them. The other included certain unforeseeable adverse market developments for existing Task products.

Recent conversations with a large company that had expressed interest in acquiring Task had raised not only the possibility of merging but also issues as to how Task could best continue to operate independently. How best to manage an expanding variety of products and designing capabilities, how to most effectively direct the efforts of an increasing number of employees, and how to cope with ever-increasing needs for funds were issues which called for attention as the company continued to grow.

Although he was not personally inclined to favor the idea of Task's being absorbed by a larger company, the president of Task, Elmer Ward, thought that the probable effects on Task of such a merger should be carefully considered in developing a reply to the inquiry of the larger company. Against the possibility that no merger would take place, he thought it would be well to reconsider the overall operating policies of Task. In particular, he was concerned with problems involved in building a sales force for Task, with maintaining the flexibility and creativity of the company as it grew, and with satisfying demands for more capital that always seemed to accompany growth.

Background and Products

The initial philosophy of balancing research and development work against manufacture of proprietary products had been developed by Elmer Ward, based on his experience in the aircraft industry. Mr. Ward, a mechanical engineering graduate of Cal. Tech., had worked for several years as an instrumentation engineer with technical service firms that provided specialized engineering and research services for aircraft companies in the Los Angeles area. He had observed that aircraft companies drew for assistance on two types of smaller companies—those independent firms which provided engineering services and equipment useful during the design of new types of aircraft, and those which manufactured components used in production of aircraft.

It seemed to him that aircraft designs tended to be developed in generations. When aircraft production was in full swing, there was little need by the aircraft companies for outside engineering assistance, since the only engineering work to be done was that involved in minor modifications of the existing aircraft designs. However, during full production demand was high for the products of the outside firms which manufactured components used in production. At the same time, various advancements in science and the state of the art of designing aircraft would be accumulating, until the aircraft companies were prompted to incorporate these advancements in a new family of designs. Then, under market pressure to get these new designs developed and into production, the aircraft companies would start to draw heavily on the assistance of independent technical firms, while at the same time starting to cut back on production of the old designs. Thus, the demand by the large aircraft companies for outside technical services and research equipment would be high when the demand for outside manufacture of production components was low, and vice versa. He concluded that sole concentration in either of these cyclical activities was undesirable, but that it should be possible to develop a company which combined them in such a way as to satisfactorily level out the cycles.

The first job of Task Corporation involved engineering and fabrication of a device to be used in research and development work. During 1953, Mr. Ward had undertaken in his spare time to solve for another company some engineering problems associated with design of models to be used in wind tunnels for simulating real airplanes in flight. From measurements of such forces as lift and drag exerted on a model in a wind tunnel, aeronautical engineers predicted the characteristics of full-sized experimental aircraft designs. Before long, this part-time activity of Mr. Ward's had grown to the point where it seemed to justify establishment of a company, and in 1954 Mr. Ward and several other instrumentation engineers incorporated Task, initially to make wind tunnel models. At the same time, thought was given to development of products that Task could call its own and that might enjoy continuing demand.

As a step toward developing such products, the company carried out what Mr. Ward referred to as the "productization" of a certain test instrument known as a wind tunnel sting balance. This was a device for simultaneously supporting a model from behind and measuring the forces acting on the model under test in a wind tunnel. A high degree of structural strength was required to assure that the model would not be torn loose by the force of winds up to several hundred miles an hour, and thereby destroy itself and damage the tunnel. Strain gauges in the balance measured forces acting on the model, including linear forces and torques acting about three perpendicular axes. Skillful design and careful placement of strain gauges were required to assure that torques and forces could all be separately resolved in magnitude and direction.

Balances had been made and used for many years; often they were made by those who used them. Frequently, these attempts resulted in inferior equipment and sometimes in complete failure. Balances in use were, for the most part, in the opinion of Mr. Ward, less than satisfactory. It seemed to him that no design of the balances in use had employed the best combination of the latest improvements in devices and techniques which had been developed. He therefore proceeded to design what he considered to be a better type of wind tunnel balance.

After working out the basic design, Mr. Ward and other Task engineers visited potential customers and inquired about their requirements for balances. From a consensus of the requirements, a catalog was compiled, listing shapes, dimensions, and characteristics, to develop what Mr. Ward referred to as an "aura of standardization." The balances were further "productized" by advertisement through magazines and mailed brochures describing their construction, characteristics, and applications. Nevertheless, the balances were still largely custom items for a limited market, frequently being designed and manufactured individually. Also, their use was confined to research and development work. So management continued their search for other types of proprietary products for Task.

Because some engineers in Task had experience in the design of aerodynamic and hydrodynamic equipment, the company sought, and in 1956 succeeded in obtaining, a contract for the design and construction of a blower to be used in the aircraft industry. It was to be a very-high-performance device –powerful, but light in weight, consisting of a fan driven by an electric motor. It was decided to integrate design of the fan and that of the motor, and since none of the Task engineers was experienced in electric motor design, electrical engineering help was sought from the proprietor of a two-man company which made small electric motors used in wind tunnel models to simulate aircraft engines. With the help of this man, whose entire enterprise was shortly acquired by Task, the blower project was a success, and Task engineers learned and developed some novel and valuable techniques for designing electric motors.

Mr. Ward pointed out that extensive handbook information, available for many years, explained in detail how to design various types of electric motors. The traditional approach involved, first, working out the electrical design of the motor, the amount of iron in the magnetic circuit, the number of turns in the coils, and so forth, and then, second, adding devices to keep the motor sufficiently cool, such as large air spaces, heavy copper end turns on the coils, and fans to blow cooling air over the parts. In the approach used by Task engineers who, as mechanical engineers, were not familiar with electrical engineering traditions, the electrical and thermodynamic designs were developed together, rather than separately, and the result turned out to be motors that were both more compact and more efficient. By using improved construction materials developed subsequent to the traditional motor designing methods, it was found possible to improve still further on conventional designs.

These improved motor designing methods, which were kept secret by Task engineers who alone were skilled in applying them, enabled the company to build some outstandingly high-performance motors, including one which was air-cooled, weighed only 188 pounds, and was capable of continuously delivering 248 horsepower. To the best of the company's knowledge, this motor was the lightest in weight per horse-power that had ever been built. Soon a variety of other applications for lightweight, high-powered motors in the aircraft industry attracted Task's designing abilities, and the product line was broadened to include other blowers, pumps, fans, and, most recently, specialized lightweight refrigeration equipment.

Other products were also developed as a result of Task's interest and experience in force-measuring instrumentation. One was a stick force dynamometer, or device for measuring the force applied by the pilot to the control stick of an airplane. Another was a load cell, which measured forces and translated them into electrical signals. The flexure pivots developed could be used as strong, but essentially frictionless, flexible joints. The pivots were to be used for mounting rockets which were to be test fired on the ground and permitted to move within flexible constraints to test their engine and control systems.

Work had also been done by Task in the development of Schlieren systems. These were complex optical systems which made visible the shock waves produced in high-speed wind tunnels. Knowledge of the visual characteristics of the waves was useful in conducting experiments with compressible fluids. Mr. Ward considered this range of engineering and manufacturing activities to be in conformity with the company's strategy, which he had described in the 1958 annual report as follows:

Task Corporation was formed for the purpose of providing engineering services and fabrication facilities for the design, development, and production of aerodynamic research equipment, force-measuring instruments, and electromechanical energy-converting devices. The field of interest includes fluid mechanics (aerodynamics and hydrodynamics), solid mechanics, optics, and, in a supporting role, electronics.

Three general rules have been applied to the interpretation of this very broad field of interest:

1. All work undertaken by the company should ultimately result in the manufacture of hardware *which can be produced by the company.* The attitude expressed by this rule directs a majority of the effort to the development of proprietary products.
2. A balance must be maintained between research and development articles and production items, such that the alternating demands for these two basic types of products will not cause excessive work load fluctuations.
3. No commitments will be made to undertake work which is foreign to the accomplishments of established personnel.

Management was reasonably confident that it had a feel for the profitability of its various types of work. Experience with wind tunnel balances indicated that these were the most profitable items the company currently produced. Schlieren systems, which were made for use in wind tunnel experiments to render shock waves visible, had not been profitable. Motors, pumps, blowers, and refrigeration equipment had been very expensive to develop, and the expenses of developing them had, in the opinion of management, been responsible for most of the recent losses appearing on the financial statements. These losses had been further aggravated by several crashes of a new type airliner which was to use a Task blower. The crashes had depressed sales of the airliner, which, in turn, depressed sales of the Task blower. It was expected by management, however, that large production orders for the other recently developed Task products would soon earn the company a profit.

Sales

Management believed that ability to solve engineering design problems was mainly what Task had to sell to a new customer. Mr. Ward observed that selling sometimes required the discovery of customer problems which the customer himself had not even been aware of. In any event, the new customer with a problem had to be sold the idea that Task could develop a product to solve it.

Being thus tailor-made to solve particular customer problems, the products of Task might have a disadvantage of not being suitable for sale to broad markets. But offsetting this possible disadvantage was the company's expectation that its products might also enjoy what essentially amounted to monopoly positions in those narrow markets for which they had been especially designed. For example, Task had designed a $3\frac{1}{2}$ horsepower pump drive motor for supplying hydraulic oil to feather a certain type airplane propeller in case the normal hydraulic system failed. The propeller manufacturer had incorporated the Task unit in the overall engineering design of the propeller only after spending a substantial amount of time and money studying and testing it. The standard inventory of spare parts for users of the propeller specified inclusion of the Task unit and parts for it. Consequently, propeller users as well as the propeller manufacturer expected to use no other emergency feathering motor but Task's. Task's management expected that they would not be likely to change to the motor of any other company, even if the Task motor were copied identically and offered at a moderately lower price. It was expected that sales of this pump motor would be about 250 new units per year at $175 each.

Management estimated that approximately 90 percent of the company's sales either came to Task without being solicited or else were generated by the personal selling efforts of the president or a project engineer. Repeat sales tended to follow automatically in many cases, as discussed above. Most Task products were unique for their applications, so that customers had relatively little choice between sources. Task was, for instance, the only company in the country offering the convenience and economy of a relatively standard line of wind tunnel balances and wind tunnel model motors. By 1960, Task had sold a total of 140 balances, ranging in price from $12,000 to $55,000 each.

Sometimes, the services of Task in designing new products were sought without the necessity for solicitation. Mr. Ward believed that Task had attracted some customers simply because the company was outstanding in its ability to design and manufacture high performance electric motors. "I once made an offer to a prospective customer that he could either give us his motor problem, or he could give it to any other company and then show us the motor they came up with; and if we couldn't sketch out a better design in one hour, I would pay him a hundred dollars. I have noticed advertisements in trade publications by several of the larger electric motor companies, boasting that they use a computer to design their motors which is capable of evaluating several thousand designs in an hour to select the best design. But my hundred-dollar offer still holds. Our motor design methods permit us to optimize a design as we go along, and it also allows us to apply judgment about many more variables than the computer can possibly consider.

"We recently started making a tiny motor for a company which will use it in running a calculator. The calculator required a motor that was very small, but quite high powered. The calculator company had one prominent motor company make a motor for the need, but the most powerful motor they were able to make within the required size proved to be not powerful enough to run the machine. After seeking help from all the motor companies they knew and finding that none of them could do the job, the calculator company sent a scatter letter to all the companies they could find who might be able to help them. We happened to get one of their letters, undertook to solve the problem, and did. Our motor was within the required size limits and gave twice the required power."

In cases where sales had not come to Task unsolicited, they had for the most part been made personally by Mr. Ward. A substantial portion of his time was spent visiting present and prospective customers of Task, many of whom were among the aircraft and missile companies of the Los Angeles area. Each year, he also made four or five trips across the country and through the East, visiting potential customers. Such trips not only served to generate sales directly and to make other companies aware of the existence of Task, but Mr. Ward believed they also made Task more responsive to needs of the market. "I learn things like the fact that engineers now designing missiles plan to shift from alternating current equipment to direct current, which indicates that we should be making direct current motors in addition to our original line of alternating current motors," he said. "We recognize the fact that as a small company Task must be an industry follower, not creating the trends, but being guided by them. And since I make most of the product decisions for the company, it is important for me to be aware of the trends. Visiting in the field helps me maintain this awareness."

After learning the nature of a prospective customer's problem, the first step for Task was usually to develop an engineering proposal, which explained the approach to be taken in solving the problem and the expected cost. During 1960, Task submitted approximately 400 proposals, which cost an estimated $55,000 to prepare. In some cases, Mr. Ward had prepared the proposals himself. But, ordinarily, he would select one of the other engineers in the company, discuss the problem with him, and ask him to prepare the proposal. Bids on all proposals were developed by the president and by the director of manufacturing, Randy Winters, usually after the two of them had discussed the matter together. Mr. Winters commented that pricing often involved a considerable amount of guesswork, sometimes requiring that costs be estimated for products even before it had been possible to determine what those products would look like.

"Of course, not all our bids turned out to be profitable," commented Mr. Ward. "For instance, there is that case where we invested about $50,000 in the development of a blower for a new airliner. But then several of the planes crashed, and the airplane manufacturer was unable to sell as many planes as he had anticipated. We, in turn, suffered a drop in sales of our blower and were therefore unable to recover our development costs from the follow-on orders we had expected. In another case, we developed a special compressor for a ground support air-conditioning system. The company that was supposed to produce the rest of the unit proved unable to do so, and we undertook to make the entire unit. We succeeded, but not before the inevitable delay made us lose money on the job. Still another time, we developed a stick force dynamometer for a test aircraft which we thought would find a continuing market in later model aircraft control systems. But as it turned out, no new aircraft power control systems have been developed since."

Although sales had grown consistently since the company's inception, Mr. Ward thought the company should build a sales force. As the company grew, his own time had been subject to more demands, making it increasingly difficult for him to carry the selling load himself. Task had been fortunate in finding one man interested in selling whose background made him well suited for the job. In his previous employment, he had been with companies in the instrumentation business, the electric motor business, and the hydrodynamic equipment business, so that he had become familiar with the various types of products which Task made. At Task, he served as the in-house sales coordinator, handling customer relations and doing some sales solicitation in the local area. However, Task had not been able to find other potential salesmen whose experience qualified them so well as this man's to selling the variety of Task's services and products.

An attempt had also been made to develop sales through use of manufacturers' representatives. Several such representatives throughout the country had been obtained, but the sales had not followed. It was the opinion of management that the representatives, although they were engineers, did not have a sufficient understanding of the technical products and capabilities of Task.

"Another alternative might be to have our engineers each do more selling in his technical area," said Mr. Ward. "They all spend some time in the field now, dealing with customers to work out designs and handle problems. We could have the engineers take more of their time for calling on prospective customers, but that might be an expensive and inefficient way to sell. It takes a lot of missionary work just to get in the door where engineering problems can be discussed. More missionary work is later needed to keep the customer relationship alive. One of the large missile companies now buying from us learned from a study of its own purchasing activities that 90 percent of its purchases were made from vendors who called on them three times per week, and that if a given vendor decreased the number of his calls the company's purchases from him diminished accordingly.

"It seems likely that we will have more selling to do, and I can't go on increasing my own selling load indefinitely. I find that unless each of our customers gets visited every so often, they tend to assume that we have gone out of business. We put 13 advertising insertions in *Aviation Week* each year, but that alone doesn't seem to be enough to keep them convinced that we're still in business. The problem seems to arise from our wide variety of products plus our small size. We can't find more men qualified to sell our whole line, and yet we can't afford to develop a separate sales force for each type of product we make. If we narrow our scope too sharply, we run the risk not only of wasting part of our engineering and manufacturing abilities, but also of stifling the spirit we must have to do our best work."

Engineering and Manufacturing

When a proposal had been accepted by a customer, it became an engineering project, and Mr. Ward assigned it to an engineer for completion. Usually, he assigned it to the same engineer who had prepared the proposal, although sometimes he assigned projects to other engineers and sometimes he served as the project engineer himself. It then became the responsibility of this project engineer to work out a solution to the customer's problem, develop a preliminary design for the product, have drawings made by the draftsmen, make arrangements with outside vendors whose help would be needed in making various components of the product, and guide the prototype of the product through fabrication and assembly in the Task shop. The project engineer's responsibility for a given program generally ended once the prototype had been made and proven satisfactory, at which time the follow-on production run usually began.

"It is up to the project engineer to get the job done," commented Mr. Ward. "But we don't think of him as any kind of formal leader to do it. We don't endow him with official authority over anyone, and we don't set up any predetermined channels for him or anyone else to follow. He can go directly after help from anyone in the company capable of giving it to him, including me. He has to conduct himself with tact and keep on pushing or his product won't get made. For instance, he can't just turn a set of drawings over to the shop and expect them to be carried out, as is commonly done in the larger companies. Here, he must work closely with the machinist, explaining, keeping the machinist interested, checking on progress, and helping to work out shop problems, or his drawings will go to the bottom of the pile while the machinist works on other projects."

The shop of Task was equipped to provide the typical functions of a job shop, plus fabrication work on production runs, plus testing both for research and for quality control. Raw materials were bought in various states of prefabrication. Although no accounting distinction was made as to the stage of completion in which materials and parts were purchased, it was a policy of Task to have a substantial amount of the fabrication work which was involved in production runs performed by outside contractors. Management thought this was necessary in order to avoid additional capital drains which would be required to extend the manufacturing capabilities of Task, and that it was more economical because the outside subcontractors performed the work for a lower price than it would cost Task to do the work.

The shop was under the direction of Randy Winters, a graduate mechanical engineer who had been one of the original founders of the company. Mr. Winters had been placed in charge of the shop in 1955, when its personnel included a total of 15 men and its activities were confined mainly to projects in which only one or very few of each product were made. Prior to taking charge of the shop, Mr. Winters had been a project engineer, and he saw his first job as that of promoting cooperation between project engineers and shop personnel, because the engineers were having some difficulty getting their designs carried out in the shop.

"I had to discharge a couple of troublemakers in the shop who were being deliberately uncooperative," he said. "And I also had to educate the engineers to design things so they could be made in the shop. It's altogether too easy to design a part that looks great on paper but is almost impossible to machine. I also explained the need for care in designing right the first time, because it costs money to make things in the shop and the shop has no erasers with which to correct mistakes as the engineering department can. I began feeding jobs into the shop as far ahead as possible so there would be less strain when things began to move. The engineer, the shop foreman, the machinist, and I would get together and discuss jobs in advance so there would be agreement among us on how to solve the design and fabrication problems, which we could foresee. Once engineering and the shop were working on a job together, I mostly kept hands-off and just watched.

"This project method was the way the whole shop operated until 1959, and it is essentially still the way prototypes are handled. My main job then was to see that the shop kept rolling and to keep out systems that the get-organized people wanted to introduce. Some wanted detailed schedules telling who was to do what, when and how.

Others wanted fancy accounting systems. But I thought such systems would just bog us down. My approach was just to announce what we had to get done and tell the shop to get going on it. The only piece of paper in the shop was a time card.

"By 1960, however, we had found it necessary to formalize somewhat. Orders for greater numbers of our products which had started coming in 1959 required that we funnel larger runs of parts through the shop along with the individual prototype projects, and soon interference began arising between the two types of work. For instance, I might go into the shop looking for a bunch of parts needed in assembly on a motor order involving $10,000 worth of units per week and be told that the work had been suspended on those parts in order to run through a special project that the president had asked for in order to make a certain sale. To prevent this sort of confusion, we set up separate groups for certain types of production assembly, such as the armature-winding group, and we generally separated the paths followed by prototypes from those followed by production-run jobs.

"We also had to add more paper work, much of it in order to get onto the approved vendor lists of some big potential customers handling government contracts. These companies would generally send a man in to inspect each prospective supplier. He would want to see systems for assuring that quality would be carefully controlled and for assuring that changes requested by the customer would be incorporated in products. We started forms for initiating, authorizing, and checking changes to drawings or parts; production control forms, cost sheets, work orders, and so forth. We set up a quality control department to see that parts met specifications, that equipment in the shop was properly maintained, and that the accuracy of our measuring devices was traceable to the Bureau of Standards.

"I pulled out three men to take care of production control on large-run orders. They see to it that parts are made by vendors and by our shop as required for assembly, they keep track of stores, and they notify the assembly department when parts are on hand, ready to go. So far, each of these men and I have had to assume individual responsibility for assuring that certain orders are kept moving. We have found that for some reason an order will always fall behind unless some one person stays with it and pushes it. We haven't yet found a system that will run jobs through without a competent coordinator on each job.

"We have tried not to organize more than we absolutely had to. We avoided making any organizational charts or job descriptions, hopefully to prevent the occurrence of what every organization seems to strive for—that is, running downhill toward internal stability. Both our work load and our products are subject to so much variation that we can't afford to have people whose jobs are so well defined that they just do certain things in the way of work and then conclude they are all finished. So much of our work is on a custom-order basis that we have to be able to move people around. Some of our people who would normally be on salaries in most companies are on hourly wages here. If they were on salaries, they would be less willing to come in to work on Saturdays when the work load is up. Our way of operating is frustrating to many people when they first join us. We give them freedom they haven't been used to elsewhere, and they feel less secure. When we move them around, they get nervous. But if they can hang on for a while, they find out how much they can get done and then they begin to relax.

"In many engineering problems there is no orderly approach that

Exhibit 28–1

TASK CORPORATION

COMPARATIVE INCOME STATEMENTS
(Years Ending December 31)

	1955	1956	1957	1958	1959	1960
Sales	$262,381	$543,345	$870,149	$900,130	$986,712	$1,482,789
Expenses:						
Manufacturing labor	67,933	104,443	133,107 ⎫	282,774	384,593	489,099
Engineering labor ..	61,130	85,765	129,372 ⎭			
Outside purchases ..	13,706	60,924 ⎫	299,848	245,250	316,422	497,973
Outside services	27,004	135,356 ⎭				
Manufacturing over-						
head	52,874	73,078	97,849	136,838	186,242	283,681
Engineering overhead	14,196	31,755	58,000	91,457	104,771	160,507
General and adminis-						
trative	28,268	59,289	97,122	72,372	100,133	124,673
Sales expense	10,465	8,546		23,623	39,778	63,037
Interest	3,577	3,617	5,703	6,080	9,466	22,494
Inventory decrease .	2,909	(64,248)	220	(1,173)		(13,905)
Other expense and						
(income)	(167)	(260)	(2,000)		(90,843)	
Less: Deferred en-						
gineering ex-						
pense	(9,630)				(54,591)	(149,996)
Less: Plant im-						
provements ..	(17,735)*					
Total Expense .	$254,530	$498,265	$819,221	$857,221	$995,971	$1,477,563
Profit before tax	$ 7,851	$ 45,080	$ 50,928	$ 42,909	$ (9,259)	$ 5,226
Tax	2,348	14,963	20,983	17,000	(2,500)	1,500
Profit after Tax	$ 5,503	$ 30,117	$ 29,945	$ 25,909	$ (6,759)	$ 3,726

* Cost of testing equipment built in the Task shop for testing the company's own products.

will work, and it is impossible to plan so that everyone can just work along smoothly. The only time we get superior results is when we have to have them; and this usually happens at the last minute. This process may be uncomfortable, but we think it is relatively efficient because we generally get the answer we want the first time around, and we have solved a lot of problems that the big companies couldn't handle. Recently, we beat a big company that wanted six months and $50,000 for a certain type of motor. We built it in one month for $23,000. This big company was probably just like several of them that have the pressure so low they are virtually paralyzed. They have huge rooms full of engineers who can't get anything done. We sometimes wonder how they survive.

"But we face problems with our way of operating, too. For instance, one of our engineers recently finished up a project on which he had essentially been his own boss. We gave him another job on which there was an initial order for 750 motors with eventual follow-on orders expected to amount to from 5,000 to 7,000 more units. Naturally, on a quantity this great we wanted to do careful planning and keep close controls so as to minimize costs and maintain quality.

"I knew the job was about due for release, so I was looking for the blueprints to come through from the blueprint department. When they came through, it would be my signal to set up the planning, records, tooling lists, and so forth. Abruptly, I learned that 30 units were already under construction in the prototype shop. Who had released the prints? The project engineer. Where were my copies? He had crossed my name off the distribution list, assuming that he was still on his own to get the job done as he had been on the previous project. How can we avoid scrambles like this without straitjacketing ourselves in a lot of rigid formal procedures?"

The president, Elmer Ward, had also noticed difficulties in maintaining the company's informality as it grew. "People have repeatedly told us we should get organized," he said, "but we have been doing our best not to. We have observed an inverse relationship between the virility or ability to get hard jobs done well and on time, and extent of formal organization. The more formal we bocome, the harder it is to get work done. It's not a matter of sheer numbers of people, but rather one of obstacles to short circuits, to directness; the sort of obstacles that exist when A can't talk to B unless C is present.

"Another problem we haven't yet solved is how to get a job done without having someone constantly mother it. In some big companies I have visited, projects seem to be performed by groups in which no

Exhibit 28–2

TASK CORPORATION

COMPARATIVE BALANCE SHEETS

(Years Ending December 31)

	1954	1955	1956	1957	1958	1959	1960
Assets:							
Cash	$ 6,024	$ 1,611	$ 2,508	$ 18,650	$ 19,782	$ 1,746	$ 14,569
Accounts receivable	19,538	35,170	56,405	113,689	140,672	157,813	194,945
Inventory	21,448	18,819	85,491	86,428	139,004	212,463	226,368
Prepaid expenses	3,637	2,825	4,457	4,186	4,038	3,251	6,905
Anticipated tax refund	—	—	—	—	12,000	23,500	—
Total Current Assets	$50,647	$ 58,425	$148,861	$222,953	$315,496	$398,773	$442,787
Fixed assets	$16,105	$ 66,317	$105,102	$118,795	$131,058	$162,098	$206,138
Less: Depreciation	860	7,249	15,870	31,010	47,809	66,312	87,832
Net Fixed Assets	$15,245	$ 59,068	$ 89,232	$ 87,784	$ 83,249	$ 95,786	$118,306
Organization expense	$ 438	$ 438	$ 413	$ 413	$ 413	$	$
Patents	388	1,659	2,265	7,141	8,080	7,659	7,215
Deposits	435	414	4,518	3,985	3,985	5,040	7,392
Deferred development costs	—	9,630	—	—	—	33,591	169,160
Deferred debt expense	—	—	—	—	—	8,810	7,971
Total Other Assets	$ 1,261	$ 12,141	$ 7,196	$ 11,539	$ 12,478	$ 55,100	$191,738
Total Assets	$67,153	$129,634	$245,289	$322,276	$411,223	$549,659	$752,831

Exhibit 28–2—Continued

	1954	1955	1956	1957	1958	1959	1960
Liabilities:							
Accounts payable	$ 2,856	$ 6,167	$ 34,222	$ 28,167	$ 84,635	$119,121	$173,227
Notes payable, bank	24,000	26,739	30,004	66,281	135,908	20,000	181,144
Notes payable, other	16,000	6,600	5,900	3,400	—	20,000	20,000
Contracts payable	4,815	8,640	12,918	5,745	—	—	—
Accrued taxes	2,494	5,220	19,959	26,678	—	—	—
Accrued wages	4,072	7,601	13,371	19,023	—	—	—
Other accruals	539	2,787	16,116	4,482	40,303	19,136	23,332
Total Current Liabilities	$54,776	$ 63,754	$132,490	$153,776	$260,846	$178,257	$397,703
Long-term debt						$180,000	$160,000
Stock issued and outstanding	$12,000	$ 60,000	$ 88,300	$120,000*	$120,000*	$170,000	$170,000
Retained earnings	377	5,880	24,499	48,500	30,377	21,402	25,128
Total Net Worth	$12,377	$ 65,880	$112,799	$168,500	$150,377	$191,402	$195,128
Total Liabilities	$67,153	$129,634	$245,288	$322,277	$411,223	$549,659	$752,831

* 24,000 shares.

single person knows everything about the project. When I have a question, they just direct me to a group. But here we can't seem to work that way. Every one of our jobs seems to need a person who lives with it and knows its every detail, or else it gets left behind. It would be a help if we didn't have to work this way, because it is hard to find enough people to mother all the jobs that have to be done.

"I have found myself becoming separated from our projects more and more as we have expanded. I used to be intimately familiar with every job, but now there are some that I follow very little. Now I have to have a list on my wall which someone else keeps up-to-date for me so I can keep track of what work is going on, what our delivery schedule is, and how well we are keeping up with it.

"These problems seem to intensify as we grow, and we seem to be forced toward more organization, more paper work, more formality. So far our approach has been to fight a delaying tactic against organization. But the question is: How long will delaying tactics continue to preserve the virility of the company as it grows? Or is there a better approach than the one we are taking to accomplish this end?"

Future Plans

Forecasting for Task was performed by the controller, Ray Williams. A graduate in business administration and economics from the University of Southern California, Mr. Williams had spent several years in public accounting before joining Task in 1955. His forecasts, before they became final, were submitted to Elmer Ward, who looked them over and suggested any changes he thought appropriate. These changes had usually been minor. Copies of forecasts that had been prepared by Mr. Williams and approved by Mr. Ward in the late fall of 1960 appear as Exhibits 28–3, 28–4, and 28–5.

"My approach in making the forecasts," commented Mr. Williams, "consists mainly of extrapolating past trends and then adjusting them according to whatever special circumstances I can foresee on the horizon. Of course, I can't predict what new types of products we will become involved with in the future. We are operating in an area where new possibilities are opening up all the time, and when we see an area of promise, we tend to develop it and worry about the costs later. So it's hard to say what we'll be working on next, or how much we'll make or lose on it. It continually puzzles me as to where we are going next and how we are going to get there. If we had stuck to wind tunnel balances, we could have continued to be a very profitable 20-man operation. But there would have been little possibility for growth and no challenge. So we're glad we didn't."

As indicated in the forecasts, it was expected that the company would require external capital, for continued expansion, amounting to $500,000 in 1961. Stock issues had been sold several times in the past. Initially, the company's stock had been sold only to employees, their relatives, and friends. But in 1959, the need for capital had become so great that employees and their relatives could not provide it, and the company's bank had refused to increase the amount of its loans, recommending that public financing be sought.

As the result of inquiries toward this end, a certain large brokerage firm suggested private placement. Terms for such a placement were developed, and Task accepted the suggestion. Through the brokerage firm, 5,000 shares of Task common stock were sold at $10 per share, together with a 10-year note for $200,000, with warrants attached. The warrants provided that 37½ shares of common stock for every, $1,000 of the note could be bought for $12.50 per share at any time during the life of the note. A major share of the offering was bought by partners of the brokerage firm, two of whom subsequently became members of the Task board of directors.

Management expected that one way of meeting future capital needs might be to make a public offering. However, it had been observed that the low profit position of the company might make it difficult to raise additional capital by selling stock. Another possible method of meeting capital needs had recently come to the attention of management in the form of inquiries by a large company, Mammoth Industries, which was interested in the possibility of acquiring Task. Mammoth had asked Mr. Ward to propose terms on which a merger would be acceptable to Task.

Mammoth had several divisions, one of which manufactured mechanical and hydraulic machinery. This division had developed in its machinery several specialized electric motor requirements which only Task had been able to satisfy. As a result, the manager of the division had suggested to his superiors that it might be desirable for Mammoth to absorb Task and thus have the ability to satisfy its own needs for electric motors.

The managers of Mammoth had told Mr. Ward it was not possible to completely predict what action would be taken with Task once a merger was made. They did point out that Task was less than one-fourth as large as the smallest division of Mammoth, so it was not

Exhibit 28–3

TASK CORPORATION

GROSS INCOME
1956–1959 Actual
1960–1965 Projected

	1956	1957	1958	1959	1960	1961	1962	1963	1964	1965
Pumps	—	—	—	—	$ 10	$ 10	$ 15	$ 20	$ 30	$ 40
Blowers	—	—	—	—	(20)	20	30	40	50	60
AC motors	$10	$15	($55)	$10	100	100	110	130	150	170
DC motors	—	—	—	—	(50)	100	110	130	150	170
Refrigeration equipment	—	—	—	—	20	30	30	30	30	30
Air conditioning	—	—	—	—	(10)	40	50	70	100	125
Measuring systems	55	45	100	130	70	100	150	185	205	240
Optical systems	(15)	10	(20)	(25)	(5)	—	—	—	—	—
Test instrumentation	—	(15)	(25)	(20)	5	4	4	4	4	4
Miscellaneous	—	—	—	—	2	1	1	1	1	1
	$50	$55	$ 0	$95	$122	$405	$500	$610	$720	$840

NOTE: 000 omitted from each column (figures are in thousands).

Exhibit 28–4

TASK CORPORATION

PROJECTED INCOME STATEMENT

	Actual 1959	1960	1961	1962	Projected 1963	1964	1965	Total
Sales	$986,712	$1,400,000	$1,900,000	$2,500,000	$3,000,000	$3,500,000	$4,000,000	$17,286,712
Costs and expenses:								
Cost of sales	$919,465	$1,278,000	$1,500,000	$2,000,000	$2,390,000	$2,780,000	$3,160,000	$14,027,465
Selling expense	39,778	60,000	80,000	120,000	150,000	180,000	210,000	839,778
Research and development expense	27,262	60,000	90,000	120,000	150,000	180,000	210,000	837,262
Interest expense	9,466	22,000	30,000	10,000	10,000	10,000	20,000	111,466
	$995,971	$1,420,000	$1,700,000	$2,250,000	$2,700,000	$3,150,000	$3,600,000	$15,815,971
Income before federal income taxes	($ 9,259)	($ 20,000)	$ 200,000	$ 250,000	$ 300,000	$ 350,000	$ 400,000	$ 1,470,741
Provision for federal income taxes	(2,500)	—	98,500	124,500	150,500	176,500	202,500	750,000
Net income	($ 6,759)	($ 20,000)	$ 101,500	$ 125,500	$ 149,500	$ 173,500	$ 197,500	$ 720,741
Retained earnings at beginning of period	$ 28,161	21,402	$ 1,402	$ 102,902	$ 228,402	$ 377,902	$ 551,402	$ 28,161
Retained Earnings at End of Period	$ 21,402	$ 1,402	$ 102,902	$ 228,402	$ 377,902	$ 551,402	$ 748,902	$ 748,902

Exhibit 28–5

TASK CORPORATION

Projected Statement of Financial Position

	Actual 12/31/59	12/31/60	12/31/61	Projected 12/31/62	12/31/63	12/31/64	12/31/65
Current Assets:							
Cash	$ 1,746	$ 8,036	$139,036	$ 58,536	$ 24,036	$ 35,536	$ 33,036
Accounts receivable	181,313	200,000	250,000	350,000	400,000	450,000	500,000
Inventories	212,463	364,463	529,463	589,463	689,463	829,463	1,019,463
Prepaid expenses	3,251	3,251	3,251	3,251	3,251	3,251	3,251
Total Current Assets	$398,773	$575,750	$921,750	$1,001,250	$1,116,750	$1,318,250	$1,555,750
Current Liabilities:							
Notes payable, bank	$ 20,000	$200,000	—	—	—	$ 50,000	$ 100,000
Notes payable, current position of long-term debt	20,000	20,000	20,000	20,000	20,000	20,000	20,000
Accounts payable	119,121	170,000	100,000	100,000	100,000	100,000	100,000
Accrued expenses	19,136	19,136	117,636	143,636	169,636	195,636	221,636
Total Current Liabilities	$178,257	$409,136	$237,636	$ 263,636	$ 289,636	$ 365,636	$ 441,636
Net working capital	220,516	166,614	684,114	737,614	827,114	952,614	1,114,114
Fixed assets	$162,098	$200,000	$300,000	$ 400,000	$ 500,000	$ 600,000	$ 700,000
Less: Accumulated depreciation	66,312	90,312	126,312	174,312	234,312	306,312	390,312
	$ 95,786	$109,688	$173,688	$ 225,688	$ 265,688	$ 293,688	$ 309,688
Other assets	$ 55,100	$ 55,100	$ 55,100	$ 55,100	$ 55,100	$ 55,100	$ 55,100
Total forward	$371,402	$331,402	$912,902	$1,018,402	$1,147,902	$1,301,402	$1,478,902
Deduct: Long-term liability	180,000	160,000	140,000	120,000	100,000	80,000	60,000
Stockholders' Equity	$191,402	$171,402	$772,902	$ 898,402	$1,047,902	$1,221,402	$1,418,902
Represented by:							
Capital stock	$170,000	$170,000	$670,000	$ 670,000	$ 670,000	$ 670,000	$ 670,000
Retained earnings	21,402	1,402	102,902	228,402	377,902	551,402	748,902
	$191,402	$171,402	$772,902	$ 898,402	$1,047,902	$1,221,402	$1,418,902

likely that divisional status could be granted. Although the division of Mammoth which used Task motors was located several thousand miles from the Task plant in Southern California, it was thought likely that Task would not have to move. No firm statement had been made by Mammoth as to the degree of freedom Task would be allowed in undertaking new projects, or the extent to which the full breadth of the existing Task product line would be supported. But from conversations with the president of Mammoth, Mr. Ward surmised that Mammoth's interest in Task was confined almost entirely to abilities in the design and manufacture of electric motors.

Mr. Ward thought it would be well to analyze two broad courses for the company. One possible course was that of merger, and the main issues included what a merger could be expected to mean to Task and what terms Task would be willing to accept. The other course was that of continuing to operate independently, which raised the question of what operating policies should be followed if Task were to do so.

29. ELOX CORPORATION OF MICHIGAN (A)*

Development of Policies to Take Maximum Advantage of a Technical Lead

In early 1959, the management of the Elox Corporation of Michigan was engaged in a comprehensive review of the company's competitive position in the light of certain developments which had been occurring in the field of electrical discharge machining.

For the first few years following its incorporation in 1950, the company had enjoyed a virtual monopoly in the development and production of electrical discharge machine tools in the United States. Encouraged by the results Elox was achieving, however, several foreign companies had introduced competitive models in this country, and in early 1959 these firms were continuing their efforts to secure a larger portion of the American market for this equipment. It was also believed that some of the largest domestic machine tool manufacturers were making plans to introduce their own electrical discharge units in the near future.

These developments had caused management to reevaluate its existing position in view of the prospects of increased competition. The objective of this analysis was the formulation of policies which would permit the company to retain its dominant position in the field of electrical discharge machining in the face of anticipated future competition.

Essentially, the process of electrical discharge machining was a practical application of the phenomenon that two conductive materials are eroded if an electrical discharge occurs between them. For example, shorting of a spark plug to an auto engine block with a screwdriver causes a spark to jump across the gap, eroding both the block and the screwdriver. In commercial applications, an electrical current was connected both to the workpiece and the electrode, which were then brought in close proximity. The differences in electrical charges caused sparks to jump the gap between the electrode and the work-piece. These electric arcs, which occurred intermittently many times a second, virtually disintegrated the metal to be removed from the work-piece. The size and shape of the cut could be predetermined within narrow limits, as the shape of the cavity was essentially determined by the shape of the electrode.

Basic features of this equipment were an electronic power supply unit and a delicate mechanism which advanced the electrode toward the workpiece. Frequently, standard machine tools such as milling machines and grinders were converted to the electrical discharge process by the addition of such equipment. The advent of electrical spark machining permitted jobs hitherto impossible to be performed simply and economically as well as effecting substantial savings in a wide variety of other machining jobs involving intricate contours, extremely hard metals, and close tolerances.

The first commercial applications of electrical discharge machining (EDM) in this country were found in the extraction of broken cutting tools from expensive dies and production parts. The process was developed almost simultaneously by two Detroit companies, the McKechnie Machine Company and the Elox Corporation, during the early years of World War II.

Both McKechnie and Victor Harding, then the president of Elox, had been employed as engineers by large manufacturing companies in the area but had developed the process privately in their basement shops during leisure hours. Initial progress was slow for both companies, however, and in 1949 both McKechnie and Harding were contacted by John Larkins, Jr., a young electrical engineer who had become familiar with the process through use of several McKechnie units in a small machine shop he had established in Cleveland.

As a result of extensive subsequent discussions, the three companies were merged in 1950 under the name of the Elox Corporation of Michigan. Realizing the limitations of their size and available funds, McKechnie, Harding, and Larkins had decided to combine their efforts and expand the process into applications they felt could not be exploited if they were to remain in direct competition with one another. Accordingly, these three, plus two others active in the Elox Corporation, became the initial stockholders of the newly formed Elox Corporation of Michigan in 1950. Total employment in the new company numbered seven people at that time. Under the forceful leadership of Mr. Larkins, who had become president of the company, an ambitious program of research and development was initiated to explore the possibilities of broadening known applications for the process.

Standard machine tools, such as milling machines, grinders, and boring machines, were purchased from the larger manufacturers and converted to the Elox process by the addition of power supplies, tool feed mechanisms, and other specialized equipment. The production of completed Elox units, therefore, was basically an assembly operation for the company, as only the fabrication of the power supply circuitry was done by Elox; manufacture of the heavier items was subcontracted to other firms. This practice of buying all but the power supplies from outside suppliers and of assembling the various component parts into completed units had continued in effect and was still being followed in early 1959.

The company negotiated an agreement with the Cincinnati Milling Machine Company in 1952 under which Cincinnati contributed funds to further the development of the process in return for the right to purchase completed power supplies from Elox which could be used to convert Cincinnati machines to the electrical discharge process. It was understood that Cincinnati could then sell these converted units through its regular sales force under the name Elektrojet. These funds were used to improve the general design of the power supply circuitry and the electrode feed control mechanism, with the result that closer tolerances and a faster metal removal rate were obtained.

In the years from 1951 to 1953, further work was done to improve the process from an engineering standpoint. Meanwhile, substantial sums were being spent on sales promotion, market development, and the education of potential customers in the possibilities of the Elox process. In 1953, the company sold its first diesinking machine. The unit was developed by Elox in response to a particular customer's immediate problem and did not represent a sale of a standard model machine. As time progressed, however, standard machines were developed and sold, although special development-type jobs continued to be undertaken in response to specific customer inquiries.

Management soon realized that it was extremely important not only to sell machines but also to adequately instruct customers in their proper use. Instruction in the actual operation of the machines proved to be no particular problem, but it was learned that the savings anticipated from the process frequently were not being realized due to inefficient preparation of the electrodes by customers in the field.

A training school for customers was subsequently established in the company's plant at which operators were fully instructed in methods of economical electrode manufacture and efficient machine operation.

All direct expenses of the school were paid by Elox. Management was of the opinion that the most promising future customer was a present user who was able to exploit the possibilities of the process. Consequently, the company believed that funds devoted to this activity were well spent and would contribute substantially to the future growth of sales. In addition to the operator training school, the company had prepared a detailed set of handbooks on the operation and maintenance of Elox equipment which it distributed to customers, together with current engineering releases on new methods and applications developed through research at Elox.

In the period from 1956 to 1958, a more complete line of equipment was developed for the diemaking industry, including newly developed machines for the manufacture of forging and stamping dies. Continued research work revealed that the electrical discharge machining process, while it was capable of producing accurate work in many instances, had some practical limitations with regard to cutting speeds.[1] Realizing the desirability of improving the speed of metal removal, the company devoted a substantial sum of money to research on this problem.

In mid-1958, it was announced that an entirely new process had been developed. The new process, electrochemical machining, was essentially a companion process to electrical discharge machining, but relied on an electrochemical or electrolytic action on the workpiece rather than on a series of electrical discharges between electrode and workpiece. The process was essentially the reverse of electroplating, and used a basic electrochemical action coupled with an electrode to accurately machine a hole or cavity into a work block. A very sensitive servo feed system was used to advance the electrode into the work block as machining progressed, in a manner similar to EDM. Since substantially all the electrochemical machining took place at the area in closest proximity between electrode and work, an accurate reproduction of the electrode shape was formed in the work block.

Theoretically, there was no limit on the rate of metal removal in ECM such as occurred in EDM. As more current was used and the size of the electrode and workpiece increased, however, the accuracy obtainable became progressively less. While tolerances of ±.0005 inches were obtainable with EDM, typical tolerances with ECM were in the neighborhood of ±.015 inches. One further feature of ECM

---

[1] Cutting speed was essentially a function of the amount of current applied to the electrode and the workpiece. It was discovered that at currents over 100–150 amperes, heating of the coolant, electrode, and workpiece reached such proportions that the desired accuracy could not be maintained.

was that the costs of electrode preparation and the rate of electrode wear [2] were far lower than in EDM. The resultant lower electrode cost, when coupled with the higher rates of metal removal obtained, indicated that ECM might well find wide usage in production applications.

It was believed that the ECM process would essentially complement rather than replace EDM, and several applications were foreseen wherein cavities might be roughed out with ECM and finished with EDM. While no ECM machines had been manufactured for sale by the end of 1958, management believed that development had progressed to the point where the feasibility of the process had been proven. Further refinement and research work were considered necessary before units could be offered for sale by the company.

Actual and potential competition in both processes was expected to come from several sources. Existing competition came almost entirely from foreign sources, but it was believed that many of the large domestic machine tool manufacturers would be introducing competitive machines in the future. As of early 1959, foreign competition consisted of the Japax America Corporation, a subsidiary of one of Japan's largest machine tool companies, and three European companies.[3] While the machines of these companies operated on the same broad principle as Elox equipment, all incorporated the basic European type of circuitry, which was considered less advanced and inferior to the Elox design.[4]

---

[2] The very nature of the electrical discharge process caused an erosion both of the workpiece and of the electrode. Although most of the erosion took place in the workpiece, nevertheless sufficient wear occurred in the electrode so that the sinking of a deep cavity by EDM might require the use of more than one electrode to complete the job. In ECM, however, electrode wear was of substantially smaller proportions, and several cavities might be machined with only one electrode.

[3] The process was also said to have been developed by the Russians, but little was known about plans for the sale of equipment in world markets. Scattered reports, however, mentioned applications which were thought to indicate a highly advanced state of development of the art.

[4] Elox power supplies incorporated a design that used a large number of vacuum tubes, whereas foreign machines were equipped with power supplies designed around the European circuitry, which used various combinations of condensers and resistors to obtain the required electrical output.

In some applications requiring separate roughing and finishing cuts, Elox units were said to provide comparable surface finishes very much faster than equipment using foreign circuit designs.

While both types of design permitted comparable metal removal rates on the roughing cut, Elox units were believed to leave a cavity surface which could be three times less irregular and rough. Further, Elox equipment was said to be able to produce a comparable finish cut up to three times as fast as competitive units, assuming an identical roughing cut. Since the Elox roughing cut was three times faster, this meant it was possible to rough out a cavity in approximately the same time as European-circuit equipment, but perform the finishing cut in about one-ninth the time, assuming comparable quality and finishes.

Some newer models of the Japax machines claimed a metal removal rate several times faster than Elox equipment, but Elox engineers believed that such performance represented only a theoretical maximum figure which could not be sustained in normal operations. In addition, investigation had confirmed previous beliefs that the close tolerances obtained on Elox equipment could not be duplicated by the larger Japax units at the higher removal rates mentioned. In early 1959, it was known that Japax had established demonstration facilities on the West Coast and was actively seeking customers in the aircraft and missile producing areas there. No concrete information was available, however, on how successful these efforts were proving to be.

European equipment, on the other hand, compared favorably to Elox machines with regard to accuracy and tolerances obtainable, but suffered from the basic design disadvantages previously mentioned. The majority of these machines were also considerably smaller than Elox equipment and could not accommodate workpieces of the size handled by Elox machines. Although European units had been offered for sale in the United States for several years, they had not met with broad acceptance due to their small size and limited capabilities. It was believed, however, that these smaller models had sold well in some foreign markets where their small size and precision capabilities had proven of great value.

Two of the largest domestic machine tool manufacturers, the Ex-Cell-O Corporation and the Cincinnati Milling Machine Company, were also known to be active in this field. Neither company had aggressively marketed electrical discharge equipment, although Cincinnati had made some scattered sales of its Elektrojet machines. In contrast, Elox was known to have placed over 600 precision electrical discharge units throughout the country in the period from 1953–58. Both of these large companies, however, were doing private research on similar processes. Ex-Cell-O was known to be devoting active effort to developing its process, Method-X, while Cincinnati had recently established a separate electronics division to perform research on a similar line of equipment. The Cincinnati research and development staff consisted of approximately 150 men, although only a small portion of them were thought to be working on the development of electrical discharge machine tools.

It was not known how soon either or both of these companies would begin to aggressively market competitive equipment. When such a move did occur, it was considered likely that the new equipment would be sold by members of the regular sales forces of Ex-

Cell-O and Cincinnati in addition to their standard line of machine tools. Cincinnati Milling was known to have about 120 sales engineers and service personnel in various parts of the country in 1958.

In addition to Ex-Cell-O and Cincinnati, Elox management knew of the existence of several smaller domestic companies that had developed small electrical discharge machines. It was thought, however, that these companies were concentrating their efforts almost entirely in the tap removal field, and no indications were present of any attempts on the part of the smaller companies to introduce larger, more versatile machines.

The company was not aware of any direct competition in the ECM field. It was known, however, that a small firm, the Anocut Engineering Company, of Chicago, had developed an electrolytic grinding process which used somewhat the same basic principle. While existing machines had been limited strictly to grinding equipment, it was not considered impossible that this company might be working on development of cavity-sinking units.

In addition to competition from the sources noted above, an entirely different process for the machining of hard substances had been developed by the Raytheon Manufacturing Company, of Waltham, Massachusetts. "Impact grinding," as it was called, employed an electromechanical transducer to convert alternating electric current into mechanical vibration at 25,000 cycles per second, well above the range of the human ear. These vibrations were transmitted directly to a soft steel cutting tool. When an abrasive mixture was inserted between the cutting tool and the material to be cut, the cutting tool actuated the abrasive forcefully, thereby producing its own counterpart in the workpiece.

Impact grinding was not limited to work on a conductive material, but could perform complex jobs on plastics, glass, and ceramics, as well as on extremely hard metals. Tolerances claimed were closer than those produced by electrical discharge machining, but cutting rates were generally slower. In addition the size of the cavity produced was, by the very nature of the process, somewhat limited. A practical limit of about one square inch in cutting tool cross-section existed in early 1959. Despite the limitations of the process, impact grinding was believed to have a great number of potential applications where small, accurate, irregular shapes were required in extremely hard materials.

By 1959, Elox had been granted over 40 patents on various features of their EDM units, and several other patents were pending, including applications on some features of the new ECM equipment. Management believed the patent position to be exceptionally strong and cited as evidence the fact that no competitive units had been introduced which employed the essential features of the Elox tube circuitry, despite its apparent advantages. Although some of the basic patents had been received in the early 1940's and would expire within a few years, management believed that adequate protection would still be provided by the many patents rceived on improvements to the basic features of Elox equipment. As of 1959, the company had not found it necessary to enforce patent restrictions through litigation in the courts.

Despite the existing and potential competition from the several processes related to their own, the management of Elox believed that their biggest source of competition lay in the field of conventional machining methods. "Metals have been removed in the same basic way for almost 200 years," explained one of the company's officers, "and our biggest problem today is in overcoming the resistance to change. Despite the many advantages our equipment provides, only about one out of ten potential customers is sufficiently imaginative to be interested."

He believed that the reluctance to accept the Elox process stemmed mainly from two groups—the management of potential customers and labor unions. As a result of intensive selling and educational efforts on the part of the company, it was believed that by 1959 the process was beginning to be accepted on a broad basis at management levels in industry. Much less success had been experienced at the union and worker levels, however.

"This gets a bit discouraging at times," he continued. "There seems to be a feeling among the unions that widespread use of the process will result in substantial unemployment. Take the forging die industry for example. For years, these dies have been made by hand by skilled craftsmen. As labor rates have risen, the high cost of these dies has caused industry to consider other methods of metalworking, such as die casting and stamping, as replacements for forging. Despite the economies we have been able to effect in the manufacture of forging dies through use of the Elox process, progress has been surprisingly slow. There have even been scattered instances of workers deliberately trying to turn out inferior work on our machines just in hopes that the equipment would be removed. Actually, such attitudes and fears are unfounded. We honestly believe Elox can help groups like the forging die manufacturers regain much lost ground, but acceptance has been slow. People just don't stop to think that although Elox might mean fewer labor hours per die, the reduced costs might very well increase the number of dies sold so that total employment would actually rise.

"Basically, the problem is one of education," he continued, "but it's a very costly sort of job for a company our size to take on almost single-handed. As a matter of fact, it would be a lot easier if we had some domestic competition. Even though it would make us work harder to stay ahead, the cumulative effect of several companies actively pursuing sales would be of great benefit to everybody concerned."

Sales of Elox products were handled both by the company's own technical salesmen and by independent distributors spread throughout the country. In 1958, the company employed 16 salesmen and was represented by 12 distributors. Their efforts were supplemented by six service representatives—three in Detroit and one each located on the East Coast, in Chicago, and on the West Coast. Each salesman was assigned to a territory surrounding one of the large metalworking regions of the country and was expected to make calls on potential customers within this area. In regions where the estimated volume was not sufficient to justify the services of a full-time salesman, the company was represented by distributors.

Distributors were paid on a commission basis and received from 10 to 15 percent of list prices, depending on the particular model sold. In addition to handling sales of Elox products, distributors typically carried several other lines of conventional machine tools. Distributors' sales personnel were given periodic training in Elox equipment at the company's plant in Royal Oak, Michigan. Foreign sales were also handled by distributors. Scattered sales were made in Canada, Mexico, and various European countries, but foreign volume had never achieved great importance in the company's total sales picture, typically averaging somewhat under 5 percent of sales. There were no service personnel in foreign countries in 1958, and service was handled either by foreign distributors or through correspondence with the home office in Royal Oak.

Direct sales through company salesmen had typically accounted for the vast majority of domestic sales of Elox products, and it was believed that almost 85 percent of the company's total dollar volume came from this source, with the remaining 15 percent coming from distributors. The company's salesmen were given a thorough indoctrination and training period at the company's plant before being assigned to a territory. Management believed that this training was necessary in order that each salesman might be thoroughly familiar with the capabilities and limitations of the process and equipment.

Salesmen were paid a basic salary plus a small, graduated overriding commission on sales above an annual quota. Salaries of salesmen in 1958 ranged from approximately $600 per month to upward of $1,000 per month, plus expenses and car. Bonuses seldom exceeded $2,000–$3,000 per year. Although sales had risen over tenfold since the company's incorporation, management had not been entirely satisfied with the rate of sales growth, and in 1959 was considering a change from the existing method of compensation to a straight commission basis of about 10 percent on sales. If such a move were undertaken, salesmen would be expected to finance their own expenses and transportation.

The efforts of company salesmen, distributors, and service personnel were supplemented by a special demonstration staff, located at the plant in Royal Oak. This group was equipped with several machines and had been especially trained to demonstrate the company's products and processes on the actual problems of customers and potential customers. Two other demonstration facilities had been established in 1956—one in Chicago and one in New Jersey—but had been discontinued because of the expense involved.

Sales and research effort were devoted toward what were believed to represent the largest potential fields of application for the company's products and processes. Chief among these was the diemaking industry. In the opinion of management, the field of stamping and blanking dies was considered especially promising, as it encompassed a wide range of industrial uses, including applications in the aircraft, missile, and auto manufacturing industries.

Other potential high-volume fields included forging dies and die casting dies, and continued efforts were being made to develop further applications in these areas in 1959. Smaller markets, such as potential uses in the field of extrusion die manufacture were not considered of sufficient importance to be actively developed, as they were made up of only a few manufacturers and did not provide enough volume in 1959 to justify substantial investments of time and money. Management planned, however, to enter these markets at some unspecified time in the future.

The majority of sales in 1958 were made up of standard, general-purpose equipment applicable to a wide variety of uses; over 60 percent of sales fell in this category. These machines were offered for sale to all potential customers and were usually available within a short period of time. The remainder of the company's business was devoted to the development of specific applications for individual customers. Manufacture of these machines typically extended over longer periods of time, and substantial sums were often involved on such orders. While most of the standard equipment was priced in the approximate range of from $10,000–$30,000 per unit, special jobs often substantially exceeded this figure, with one order amounting to as much as $215,000.

Management planned an increasing emphasis on broadening the company's standard line of machines. It was thought that more and more of the company's volume would be represented by standard types, since many of the machines developed for special purposes were subsequently introduced as standard models. Despite plans for further emphasis on standard equipment, it was anticipated that continued work would be done on special applications, although such sales probably would represent a somewhat smaller portion of total sales than the 35–40 percent of 1958.

Total expenditures for marketing and research work had always been high at Elox, and it was estimated that an amount equal to almost 40 percent of total sales was being spent in these areas. Management believed that these heavy expenses were essential, however, in view of the constant need for industry education and the development of improved equipment.

There were some indications in 1959 that these expenses might soon begin to achieve the desired results. Several of the country's largest industrial firms were known to be experimenting privately with Elox equipment. In one of these, a special staff of some 15–20 research engineers was said to be working on production applications for the Elox process. While this company owned only 10–15 Elox units in 1958, it was understood that it was actively considering the purchase of approximately 1,000 electrical discharge machines in the period from 1959–64.[5] The exact timing of such orders, however, was unknown.

Obvious difficulties in foreseeing the timing of potential large orders such as those mentioned above had made it extremely difficult to predict the company's probable rate of future growth or to develop a detailed long-range plan for financing the increased volume of busi-

---

[5] This remark was interpreted to mean equipment of the general type produced by Elox, but would not necessarily be purchased entirely from Elox if other competitive models proved superior.

ness. As a result, specific needs were forecast only six months in advance. However, a general investigation of the possible sources of funds had been made in 1958. Although there was no existing need for short-term bank financing in 1958, the company had been granted an open line of credit of $250,000 from a local Detroit bank. It was understood that an additional sum of $500,000 might also be available if needed from large banks in Chicago and New York.

Management believed that it might also be possible to sell a block of debenture bonds in the event additional funds were needed. Such an issue might take the form of either a relatively high-yield [6] debt instrument which would be nonconvertible, or a lower-yielding [7] convertible debenture with the conversion price substantially in excess of the prevailing market price of the common at the time of the debenture issue. It was understood that it might be possible to raise as much as $1 million in this fashion and, further, that possibilities existed for private placement of the issue, which would preclude the expense of a public offering.

Another alternative method of raising funds would be the public issuance of common stock. Assuming favorable market conditions, this method would have the advantage of providing larger amounts of funds than other alternatives, but would entail the disadvantages of underwriting expenses and equity dilution. In early 1959, the company had 544,891 shares of common stock outstanding. Of this amount, approximately 65,000 shares, or 12 percent, were owned by management. The remainder was widely spread among some 2,500 stockholders. Other than the shares held by management, no large blocks were outstanding in the hands of any group or individual. As evidence of the extremely wide distribution of the issue, it was estimated by management that the 300 largest stockholders, including officers of the company, owned only approximately 50 percent of the shares outstanding.

Sales for the fiscal year ending April 30, 1959, were estimated at around $2.2 million, down slightly from the results recorded in 1958. Management believed that the existing physical facilities could handle a sales volume greatly in excess of these figures, and several estimates fell in the range of $4–$5 million. No additions to floor space would be necessary to handle this volume, and only a minor (from 10–15 percent) increase in machinery and equipment would be needed. At sales levels above these figures, however, additional physical facil-

---

[6] About 7 percent.
[7] From 5–6 percent.

Exhibit 29–1

ELOX CORPORATION OF MICHIGAN (A)

COMPARATIVE BALANCE SHEETS

	April 30, 1954	April 30, 1955	April 30, 1956	April 30, 1957	April 30, 1958
Cash	$112,275	$173,121	$106,666	$174,275	$160,524
Government securities	—	99,703	—	—	—
Notes and accounts receivable (net)	140,816	248,894	353,678	300,557	417,265
Inventories	163,178	208,556	327,262	385,337	329,411
Prepaid	6,699	14,082	13,409	6,706	16,443
Total Current Assets	$422,968	$744,356	$801,015	$866,875	$923,643
Investments	5,100	5,100	5,100	5,100	5,100
Machinery and equipment	$ 82,821	$122,924	$ 96,593	$153,967	$200,440
Buildings	71,458	99,754	204,764	213,670	215,283
(Allowance for depreciation)	(27,669)	(37,281)	(36,188)	(53,650)	(76,873)
	$126,610	$175,397	$265,169	$313,987	$338,850
Land	5,500	13,450	30,800	30,800	25,500
Net Fixed Assets	$132,110	$188,847	$295,969	$344,787	$364,350
Patents (net)	$ 24,181	$ 21,797	$ 31,263	$ 28,119	$ 24,955
Leasehold improvements (net)	—	3,277	—	—	—
Notes receivable	—	5,987	24,202	17,255	14,466
Deposits and other investments	—	4,720	12,290	12,184	7,083
Organization expense	889	889	889	889	—
	25,070	36,670	68,663	58,447	46,504
	$585,248	$974,973	$1,170,747	$1,275,209	$1,339,597

Exhibit 29–1—Continued

	April 30, 1954	April 30, 1955	April 30, 1956	April 30, 1957	April 30, 1958
Notes payable, bank	$ 30,000	—	$ 50,000	—	—
Notes payable, trade	—	—	12,524	—	—
Mortgage (current portion)	2,885	—	13,150	—	—
Land contract (current portion)	1,411	$ 1,869	—	$ 10,870	$ 11,457
Other	440				
	$ 34,736	$ 1,869	$ 75,673	$ 10,870	$ 11,457
Accounts payable, trade	$ 54,496	$ 94,093	$108,747	$126,049	$ 62,056
Withheld from employees	4,683	5,415	5,725	6,727	6,571
Customer's deposits	3,000	10,428	50,000	6,800	
	62,179	109,936	164,472	139,576	68,627
Accrued expenses	$ 46,114	$ 48,535	$ 51,010	$ 72,460	$ 73,217
Dividends payable	4,000	8,109	—	10,900	27,249
Accrued income taxes	90,065	149,464	91,369	139,337	136,849
	140,179	205,108	142,379	222,697	237,315
Total Current Liabilities	$237,094	$317,913	$382,524	$373,143	$317,399
Mortgage payable, bank	$ 18,726	—	$ 80,071	$ 57,964	$ 46,472
Land contract payable	15,705	$ 17,830	—	—	—
Debentures, 7%, due 5/60	6,475	—			
Deferred income (unfinished research project)	32,149	24,835			
	73,055	42,665	80,071	57,964	46,472
Class A stock: voting ($1.00 par)	$ 82,500	$360,000	$360,000	$360,000	$360,000*
Class B stock: nonvoting ($1.00 par)	17,500	184,981	184,981	184,981	184,981*
Capital surplus	17,500	69,414	69,414	69,414	69,414
Earned surplus	157,599	—	93,757	229,707	361,331
	275,099	614,395	708,152	844,102	975,726
	$585,248	$974,973	$1,170,747	$1,275,209	$1,339,597

* In mid-1958, all Class B stock was exchanged on a share-for-share basis into Class A stock. Thus, the company's capitalization consisted of 544,981 shares of voting common stock in early 1959.

SOURCE: Elox Corporation of Michigan, Annual Reports.

Exhibit 29-2

ELOX CORPORATION OF MICHIGAN (A)

COMPARATIVE INCOME STATEMENTS
(Fiscal Years Ending April 30)

	1951	1952	1953	1954	1955	1956	1957	1958	6 Mos. Ending Oct. 31, 1957	6 Mos. Ending Oct. 31, 1958
Net sales	$194,563	$633,996	$602,140	$936,910	$1,513,893	$1,638,388	$2,269,434	$2,324,334	$1,270,933	$1,131,626
Cost of sales	na	na	na	433,952	594,853	698,817	1,066,770	1,032,639	562,043	536,670
Gross profit	na	na	na	$502,958	$919,040	$939,571	$1,202,663	$1,291,696	$708,890	$594,956
Operating expenses	na	na	na	345,705	622,959	784,355	897,025	985,969	471,394	494,782
Operating profit				$157,253	$296,081	$155,216	$305,639	$305,726	$237,496	$100,174
Other income (expenses) net				3,606	1,633	31,989	(9,450)	10,966	7,205	(623)
Income before taxes	29,621	120,267	82,964	$160,859	$297,714	$187,205	$296,188	$316,722	$244,701	$99,550
Provision for taxes	9,890	63,627	44,500	90,000	149,609	93,447	149,338	157,849	124,505	49,016
Net income	19,731	56,640	38,464	$70,859	$148,104	$93,758	$146,850	$158,873	$120,196	$50,534
Cash dividends	—	3,750	4,125	7,983	22,559	—	10,900	27,249	—	—
Shares outstanding	75,000	82,500	352,716	400,000	544,981	544,981	544,981	544,981	544,981	544,981
Earnings per share	.26	.69	.11	.18	.27	.17	.27	.29	.22	.09
Dividends per share	—	.05	.05	.02	.045	none	.02	.05	—	—
Market price range* (over the counter; bid)					6-13	7-9¾	6½-10⅝	6-18⅛	—	—
Number of employees†	12	25	30	65	85	90	100	100		
Number of shareholders†	25	35	50	85	225	850	1,200	1,600		

Stock Splits and Stock Dividends
Fiscal 1951: 10% stock
Fiscal 1953: 4 for 1 split
Fiscal 1954: 25% stock

* Calendar years.
† Approximate.

Exhibit 29–3

ELOX CORPORATION OF MICHIGAN (A)

FINANCIAL POSITION OF SELECTED MACHINE TOOL COMPANIES, DECEMBER 31, 1957

(Millions of Dollars)

	Cincinnati Milling Machine Company	Brown & Sharpe Mfg. Company	Ex-Cell-O Corporation	Warner & Swasey Company	Kearney & Trecker Corporation
Current assets	$ 60.9	$18.7	$ 64.0	$27.4	$19.0
Fixed assets	24.9	11.0	44.9	16.8	8.7
Other	7.6	2.9	2.5	4.1	.9
Total Assets	$ 93.4	$32.6	$111.4	$48.3	$28.6
Current liabilities	$ 14.5	$ 1.7	$ 25.8	$ 4.3	$ 9.4
Long-term debt	—	—	10.5	9.4	2.4
Preferred stock	6.0	—	—	—	—
Common stock and surplus	72.9	30.9	75.1	34.6	16.8
Total Liabilities	$ 93.4	$32.6	$111.4	$48.3	$28.6
1957 sales	$148.3	$34.5	$168.9	$56.4	$32.4
1957 profits, after taxes	7.9	2.8	14.1	4.4	.9

SOURCE: Moody's Industrials, 1958.

Exhibit 29–4

ELOX CORPORATION OF MICHIGAN (A)

MACHINE TOOL SHIPMENTS* (1929–58)

Year	Shipments	Year	Shipments
1929	185	1944	497
1930	96	1945	424
1931	51	1946	335
1932	22	1947	306
1933	25	1948	289
1934	50	1949	249
1935	85	1950	306
1936	133	1951	632
1937	195	1952	1,125
1938	145	1953	1,192
1939	200	1954	892
1940	440	1955	670
1941	775	1956	886
1942	1,320	1957	844
1943	1,180	1958†	415

* Millions of dollars; metal-cutting types only.
† Preliminary estimate.
NOTE: These figures are for the machine tool industry as a whole.
SOURCE: National Machine Tool Builders Association, as reported in Standard & Poor's Industrial Surveys (Industrial Machinery), p. M 31.

ities would be required. Net income for the 1959 fiscal year was expected to approximate $100,000 after taxes, down somewhat from 1958 results. This drop in net was believed to be only temporary, however, and it was anticipated that a return to a higher profit margin would be achieved as sales resumed their upward trend.

While the precise timing of large orders such as those previously mentioned could not be predicted with any degree of certainty, management believed that a substantial increase in business, beyond extension of the past growth trend, might be expected from this source. Since such business would essentially be the result of past investment in research, development, and marketing, a high incremental profit, in the neighborhood of 30 percent before taxes, was expected on these orders.

With regard to the future of the company in the light of increasing competition, a feeling of cautious optimism prevailed. "We are coming to a point where we will have to begin to be concerned over competition," explained one Elox official. "We can't afford to sell our competitors short. We believe we have a good lead in the field today, but we know we'll be pressed harder to keep it in the future. Our competitors are bound to find ways of improving their equipment, and we just can't close our eyes to that."

Exhibit 29-5

ELOX CORPORATION OF MICHIGAN (A)

ADDITIONAL INFORMATION

(Fiscal Years Ending April 30)

	1953	1954	1955	1956	1957	1958
Sales	$602,140	$936,910	$1,513,893	$1,638,388	$2,269,434	$2,324,334
Expense breakdown:						
Cost of goods sold	39.0%	39.2%	37.7%	41.1%	45.4%	44.8%
Engineering and research	8.1	6.9	5.3	8.3	5.7	7.5
Selling and distribution*	26.8	25.3	28.2	31.9	26.9	28.4
General and administrative	12.1	11.5	9.2	9.2	8.0	6.3
Net operating profit	14.0	17.1	19.6	9.5	14.0	13.0
	100.0%	100.0%	100.0%	100.0%	100.0%	100.0%
Dollar backlog, April 30	$ 92,000	$165,000	$ 242,000	$ 507,000	$ 409,000	$ 260,000
Number of salesmen	8	10	12	12	14	18
Number of distributors	5	10	10	12	12	16
Number of servicemen	2	3	4	5	7	7
Number of people graduating from Elox operator's training school	0	45	87	91	109	114
* Includes:						
Salesman's expense (salary, commission, and travel)	10.7%	10.9%	5.6%	8.2%	8.5%	8.9%
Distributor's expense (discounts and commissions)	3.4%	0.3%	1.9%	1.6%	1.7%	1.7%

SOURCE: Company records and discussions with management.

In view of the prospects for increased competition, the management of the Elox Corporation of Michigan was engaged in a comprehensive review of the company's position in early 1959. The primary purpose of this analysis was to determine what policies the company should follow to retain its dominant industry position, considering the likelihood of increasing competition.

Exhibits 29–1 to 29–5 give financial and statistical information regarding the company and the machine tool industry.

30. UNITED–CARR FASTENER CORPORATION *

Experience with Elox Electrical Discharge Machining [1]

As of July, 1960, the United-Carr Fastener Corporation of Cambridge, Massachusetts, had owned and operated an Elox machine with quite satisfactory results for eight months and was planning to buy a second machine in the near future.

United-Carr manufactured over 20,000 different fastening devices, most of which were smaller than a half-dollar and fashioned out of thin sheet steel. The production of these devices was a high-speed operation generally performed by punch presses running up to 1,000 strokes per minute. Typically, the raw material, a strip of thin sheet steel (2 to 3 inches wide), was fed into one side of a set of progressive dies in the punch press. Driven by the force of a great flywheel on the press, these dies alternately opened and pressed together with each revolution of the flywheel. The raw material entering was drawn partly toward its desired shape by the first section of the dies, then progressed to the next section of the same dies, where it was drawn farther into shape, and so on until fully formed parts and trimmed off scrap emerged from the last section of the progressive dies. To stand up under this continual pounding process, the dies had to be made of very tough, hardened steel, and to form the desired shapes, many of which were quite complicated, the dies often had to be contoured into intricate shapes.

United-Carr made many of its dies in its own 40-man tool and die shop. It was for this shop that an Elox machine had been bought eight months earlier, and a second Elox machine would soon be bought. The first machine, capable of machining whole dies, had come into such demand in the shop that it had developed a backlog which was delaying work. The second machine would be smaller and was to supplement the first by adding capacity to machine only segments of dies, called inserts.

Prior to purchase of the first Elox machine, United-Carr had made

[1] Process developed by the Elox Corporation of Michigan. See also basic case, Elox Corporation of Michigan (A).

dies using its ultrasonic machine, and also using the traditional methods of cutting and grinding. Some diemaking work had also been performed on Elox machines in the tool and die shops of outside suppliers.

Management's reluctance to consider the possibility of using an Elox machine in the die shop of United-Carr had been overcome during 1958 by the development of improvements in the Elox process which enabled it to use electrodes that were more economical and practical because they were made of tougher metals such as steel and copper-tungsten instead of brass. Another influence in favor of Elox had been reports of favorable experience with a similar machine, the English Sparkatron, which was in operation in the plant of United-Carr Fastener Company of Australia, Limited. Finally, the conclusion of a brief economic study based on expected labor savings in the manufacture of one "typical" die made with an Elox machine was that the payback period might be as low as six months on a $27,000 Elox machine installation.

Foreign machines as well as the Elox were studied at tool shows by United-Carr representatives, and some of them, particularly the Japax, were considered to be the equal of Elox in performance. But Elox was favored because its domestic location seemed desirable in case of service or replacement problems. Only one Japax machine, a demonstrator on the West Coast, was then believed to be operating in the United States.

Although there was some contact through the local Elox salesman, United-Carr sent several of its shop and management people to the Elox factory in Michigan in forming the decision to buy the first machine. In these visits, which were believed to be quite justified in view of the large cost of the machine, United-Carr personnel studied the Elox machine in operation in Elox's own shop and discussed the machine with the president and other officers of Elox.

After eight months of operation, the Elox machine at United-Carr was performing satisfactorily. No repairs had been necessary, and the machinist who operated the machine, Mr. Moon, said that he could foresee no weak links where trouble would be likely to occur. The machine had proven its ability to do everything which Elox had claimed it would. It had been successfully used to cut very complicated shapes. It had cut corners with radii as small as .001 inches, holes with diameters as small as 0.020, and it had cut with ease through the hardest of metals, including carbide steel. Mr. Moon had performed some feats on the Elox machine which he claimed would have been impossible with conventional dicmaking methods.

According to Mr. Moon, operation of the machine was simple once it had been set up. Because the cutting took place very slowly, (roughly 45 minutes were required to cut through a one-inch steel plate) he often set the machine in motion on automatic feed, then left it to work at his bench on other parts. Devices contained in the machine automatically shut it off at the end of a cut or in case of any malfunction. Mr. Moon felt that there was little likelihood of danger, since the machine moved so slowly and the power level used (roughly 20 to 60 amperes at 60 volts) was so low. Learning to set dials controlling the power level and rate of feed was simple by referring to the reference handbook supplied by Elox.

The difficult art to learn in using an Elox machine, Mr. Moon said, was how to design electrode arrangements to perform the desired cutting. The electrodes had to be shaped and supported correctly, and they had to provide for a constant flow of oil under pressure in the immediate vicinity of the cutting arc to carry away chips so the chips would not interfere with the delicate feed process. In the case of cutting tiny round holes, Mr. Moon had made the electrodes of fine hollow wires. To keep these wires straight as they cut down into the workpiece, he had fashioned a precision plastic guide which would provide the wires with aim, support, and insulation. He connected a series of small neoprene hoses to the upper ends of the wires so oil could be pumped down through them to wash away chips.

Eloxing, Mr. Moon said, required a thorough knowledge of tool- and diemaking, but it also required a fresh approach and willingness on the part of the machinist to try things he hadn't tried before. Because the process was so new and its applications were so varied, its use constantly required innovation and novel approaches to diemaking problems. Mr. Moon had a drawer full of unique jigs and fixtures he had developed to accomplish new and different jobs. Occasionally, he was visited and consulted by Elox salesmen and by representatives from other shops, who learned new techniques from him and occasionally showed him ideas they had developed or seen for using the machine.

Some instructions for using the machine, together with data on materials, cutting rates, etc., were contained in a booklet that came with the machine. Three other volumes which also came with the machine were classified as catalogs by Mr. Moon, because they contained mainly descriptions of other Elox machines and fittings which were available. There was no manual on the servicing of the machine itself, and United-Carr did not want one because it did not wish to have its machinists burdened with learning the intricate mechanical and electrical composition of the machine. United-Carr preferred the assistance of the Elox serviceman, who they expected would attend within one or two days to any problems that arose.

The training course at the Elox factory had been very useful, according to the four United-Carr men who had attended it. Mr. Moon said it had been helpful to him in learning how to use and operate the machine. Mr. Wingard, who had been responsible for purchase of the machine, said that the course had performed a real service in convincing some of the United-Carr machinists that the machine could actually work effectively and was practical. Those men who had attended the course, he claimed, had come back very enthused about the machine.

Nevertheless, there were still some grounds, Mr. Wingard felt, for his original fear that the machine would not be fully accepted and used by the machinists in the shop. Only the youngest of the tool and die makers, Mr. Moon, had been willing to undertake the job of making the new machine work. Mr. Moon thought there was a natural reluctance on the part of the machinists to try the new machine—first, because none wanted to chance a failure in the eyes of his colleagues and, second, because there was a general feeling that specialization on one machine might associate a man with the position of machine operator, a lower status position than that of tool and die maker, which generally involved operation of many machines. Mr. Moon wished it to be quite clear that although he enjoyed working with the Elox machine and appreciated its effectiveness he did not want to be "tied down to it in any way."

United-Carr was considering the question of who should run the second Elox machine when it arrived. The effective performance of the first machine had led to its heavy usage, and before long it had developed a backlog. Consequently, a decision had been made to buy a second, smaller machine for $16,000 to augment the shop's Eloxing capacity. In selecting the second machine, United-Carr decided to buy an Elox again because the first machine had worked out so well. This decision had come close to reversal under the pressure of a Cincinnati salesman. At the time, Elox had released its Boston representative and had not yet found another. The Cincinnati man had represented his product so effectively that the men in the shop at United-Carr were swayed into favoring his machine. However, United-Carr management still felt that the features promoted by the Cincinnati salesman were not important enough to outweigh the security offered by the machine the company was used to.

31. TRIANGLE TOOL AND DIE COMPANY*

Experience with Elox Electrical Discharge Machining [1]

By 1960, the Triangle Tool and Die Company had operated one model Elox machine for six years, a second and later model machine for three years, and was planning to install soon a third and still later model Elox machine. In general, the company had gone through several years of problems with the Elox process and machining, but now was very pleased with both.

Triangle Tool and Die Company was a 50-man job shop located in Lynn, Massachusetts, and one of the largest independent tool and die shops in New England. Its jobs ranged from the design and manufacture of stamping dies for razor blade dispensers to the machining of high-speed turbine wheels. Mr. Feingold, the owner, estimated that about 5 percent of the output of his company was performed on his Elox machines.

The First Machine

Mr. Feingold first became acquainted with the Elox process from a description and pictures presented by an Elox salesman in 1954. Mr. Feingold saw what he thought were great diemaking possibilities in the process, and so he gave the salesman a $10,000 order for one machine, which could be canceled at the option of Mr. Feingold after he had had an opportunity to see the machine in operation at a forthcoming tool show in Philadelphia. The tool show performance satisfied Mr. Feingold, and he had the machine installed.

Immediately, problems began to occur. The manuals did not adequately explain how to run the machine, and some of the instructions had to be improved on. Elox subsequently revised these instructions. Mr. Feingold had visited the Elox factory, but decided not to participate in the factory training course. Technical difficulties were soon

[1] Process developed by the Elox Corporation of Michigan. See also basic case, Elox Corporation of Michigan (A).

encountered with the machine itself. Also it was found that in order to get the required accuracy it was necessary to make fixtures to position the electrodes. And the cutting efficiency of the machine was lower than had been anticipated. At that point, the management and machinists of Triangle became discouraged and questioned the wisdom of having purchased the machine.

Nevertheless, Triangle kept experimenting with the machine and gradually developed more effective ways of using it. Most of the problems were solved by trial and error and with help from the local representatives of Elox. Triangle was fortunate in having employees who were skilled in electronics so that they were able to perform minor repairs on the machine when it broke down. "But we liked to have the Elox repairman drop in when he was in the area. He did an excellent job," Mr. Feingold said, "and the machine always worked better when he left. In case of emergency, Elox was very cooperative in bringing a man in immediately. I think that servicing is one of the best-handled operations of the Elox company." Elox had recently hired a sales engineer for the New England area. This man, according to Mr. Feingold, had worked for several years in a large manufacturing company which operated over 40 Elox machines. His experience suited him very well to helping Elox users, and Triangle had benefited considerably from his calls. Mr. Feingold knew of two or three shops in his area which had given up trying to use their Elox machines during this period, as they were evidently unwilling to put in the time and effort to learn to use them to advantage.

The Second Machine

After about three years, Triangle had developed considerable skill in using the Elox machine. A number of jobs had been performed on it, such as drilling a 0.020-inch hole through a 0.125-inch diameter ball made of tungsten carbide, which would have been impossible with any other method. Triangle had also undertaken to make a turbine wheel for an aircraft engine manufacturer. Blades were put on this turbine wheel by cutting them right on the wheel with an Elox machine instead of using the conventional method of making blades separately and then fastening them to the wheel.

In this turbine wheel project, the single Elox machine of Triangle's would have become overloaded, and Mr. Feingold decided in the late summer of 1957 to augment his Eloxing capacity by installing a second new machine which was larger and cost about twice as much as the first one had cost. By this time, Mr. Feingold felt that the first machine had had a great deal of use, so he traded it in on the second and replaced the first with an identical, but nearly unused, second-hand machine purchased very cheaply from another shop.

With the second new machine, too, Triangle had many problems. Most of these were in the electronic power supply which once arced and nearly ruined an expensive part being machined, and another time completely burned out, requiring the replacement of $600 worth of tubes. Consequently, Elox consented to replace the power supply with another of the same type which had been in use in the Elox application shop.

With this new power supply, the second machine operated satisfactorily, and Mr. Feingold had no more trouble with it. Most of the servicing was performed by personnel of Triangle, using the pipe diagrams and circuit diagrams provided by Elox to find and correct difficulties as they occurred. By 1960, the two machines were the permanent charge of two machine operators in the Triangle shop. These operators had not been tool and diemakers. They were paid lower wages than tool and diemakers and did not make the electrodes. The electrodes and setups were made by experienced tool and diemakers, in accordance with designs developed in Triangle's engineering department. Gaining acceptance of the machines by shop personnel had "never been a problem," said Mr. Feingold, "because the machines did not threaten in any way to displace tool and diemakers."

The training program at Elox had never been used by Triangle Tool. The foremen were too busy in the shop to be able to go off to school, and with six years of Eloxing experience it was felt the personnel had sufficient understanding of the machine to be able to give new operators whatever training was needed. Triangle had, according to Mr. Feingold, both learned some from others about Eloxing and given help to others in using the process. Sometimes, Eloxing customers had been directed to his shop by Elox salesmen. In at least three cases, customers had later bought their own Elox machines as a result of the experience. Mr. Feingold thought that the ability of his shop to perform Eloxing had contributed significantly to its success and helped it to grow faster than competitive shops. On Mr. Feingold's desk was an artist's proposal for a 12-page advertising brochure on Triangle. The theme of this brochure was "pioneers and craftsmen in electronic machining." He expected that more of his competitors would adopt the process, but felt that Triangle's several years of experience were a great advantage.

"It's interesting the way this process has affected some other industries," said Mr. Feingold. "For instance, several companies have developed new electrode materials designed for use in electronic machining. A number of the punch-makers have started selling punches which are tipped with these materials. And the die set companies have started incorporating special insulation in their die sets [2] to make them suitable for use in electronic machining."

The Third Machine

In April of 1960, Mr. Feingold decided to buy another new machine of the latest model then available. The company would thus have three machines—one bought secondhand but of the same model as that bought new in July of 1954, a second model bought new in 1957, and the third latest model which was to be delivered in October of 1960.

The greatest problem in using the Eloxing machines, according to Mr. Feingold, was that of making the electrodes, which always wore out so fast. In some cases, he believed it had cost him more to make the electrodes than it would have cost to make the parts by conventional machining processes. No formal analyses of time required on the Elox machine as opposed to doing the same jobs by conventional methods had been made. This problem of electrode wear was, he said, his main reason for buying a new machine. The third machine was to have the capability to use steel electrodes for cutting steel, in contrast to his present machines which both required fast-wearing brass electrodes. The third machine was also to have hydraulic feed attachments which were supposed to permit greater cutting efficiency and also lengthen electrode life.

In choosing a machine, Mr. Feingold gave no consideration to competitors of Elox. He preferred to stay with machinery that his men were acquainted with rather than to chance the shift to an unknown machine. It would be a great mistake, he thought, to buy a foreign-made machine. "It is generally much easier to obtain parts and service from a domestic manufacturer," he said. "Also, many foreign machines are a problem to work on because of their use of metric threads and nut sizes."

---

[2] A die set consisted of two horizontal plates that were kept in alignment by accurately positioned vertical pins and bushings. The dies were then fastened to each of the horizontal plates so that the pins and bushings of the die set served to keep the dies properly aligned as the dies were brought together in use. By insulating the bushings, it became possible to mount the die set in the Elox machine so that dies could be Eloxed right in their die sets. Without the insulated bushings, it was necessary to Elox dies separately from the die set, then mount and carefully align them in the die set in order to use them.

32. ELOX CORPORATION OF MICHIGAN (B) *
Appraisal of the Company's Progress and Its Major Policies

Before visiting the Elox Corporation in September, 1964, the case writer had heard that Elox was considered to be a successful small company. He wondered what criteria should be used to measure the success of this particular company, and hoped that his visit would reveal clues as to why it had been successful. He was also interested in learning what basic plans the management of Elox might have for the future in order to assure its continued success.

As he drove into the company parking lot, he found that all available spaces were filled. He also noted a new addition to the main building. Inside the reception room he read the following sign:

This is Elox Corporation of Michigan.

We manufacture precision electrical discharge machine tools.

Dear Mr. Vendor or Guest ———

Welcome to ELOX. Please sign register and tell the receptionist the nature of your call. We know your time is valuable—if you do not reach your party in 10 minutes, check again with our receptionist. If the person you wish to see is still unavailable, the receptionist will explain the delay. If you have not reached your man in 20 minutes, your call will be referred to management for prompt attention.

Thank you for thinking of—

ELOX

Purchasing Agent Hours—Ron Klein, Tuesday and Thursday, 11 to 3 P.M. Friday, 10 to 2 P.M. Call limited to 10 minutes.

The company manufactured machine tools utilizing electrical discharge machining (EDM) instead of a cutting tool. The removal of metal was accomplished by electrical discharges between an accurately shaped electrode and the metal piece being worked on. Two

---

* Copyright © 1964 by the President and Fellows of Harvard College.

Exhibit 32–1

ELOX CORPORATION OF MICHIGAN (B)

COMPARATIVE BALANCE SHEETS
(Fiscal Years Ending April 30)

	1958	1959	1960	1961	1962	1963	1964
ASSETS							
Current Assets:							
Cash	$ 160,523	$ 99,306	$ 167,534	$ 221,167	$ 272,483	$ 475,795	$ 426,190
Notes and accounts receivable	417,265	396,257	402,619	808,723	962,891	1,048,120	1,221,909
Royalties receivable					19,002	15,534	26,339
Inventories, at lower standard cost or market	329,412	325,747	479,035	642,614	520,217	605,705	736,024
Prepaid expenses	16,442	14,638	6,490	7,246	11,052	13,422	14,529
U.S. Treasury bills, at cost		148,113					
Total Current Assets	$ 923,642	$ 984,061	$1,055,678	$1,679,750	$1,785,645	$2,158,576	$2,424,991
Property, Plant, and Equipment, at Cost:							
Land and land improvements	25,500	25,500	25,500	25,500	37,828	49,374	49,374
Buildings	215,282	234,402	235,246	235,246	345,386	347,865	357,172
Machinery and equipment	200,440	245,136	310,278	276,159	323,455	311,182	381,264
Less: accumulated depreciation	76,872	107,481	129,935	143,687	160,627	185,871	198,634
Net Property, Plant, and Equipment	$ 364,350	$ 397,557	$ 441,089	$ 393,218	$ 546,042	$ 522,550	$ 589,176
Other Assets:							
Patents (net)	$ 24,955	$ 21,791	$ 18,628	$ 15,464	$ 602,697	$ 547,634	$ 496,459
Notes receivable	14,465	10,822	7,813	68,943	41,625	22,062	86,559
Investment in foreign subsidiary* (at cost)	5,100	5,100	5,600	5,600	5,600	6,437	5,600
Cash value of life insurance on officer					1,300	2,300	3,362
Deposits and other	7,084	5,200	2,400	17,803	6,535	4,020	9,199
Total Other Assets	$ 51,604	$ 42,913	$ 34,441	$ 107,810	$ 657,757	$ 582,453	$ 601,179
Total Assets	$1,339,596	$1,424,531	$1,531,208	$2,180,778	$2,989,444	$3,263,579	$3,615,346

Exhibit 32-1—Continued

ELOX CORPORATION OF MICHIGAN (B)

	1958	1959	1960	1961	1962	1963	1964
LIABILITIES							
Current Liabilities:							
Notes payable to bank (unsecured)			$ 100,000	$ 100,000			
Mortgages payable to bank	$ 11,456	$ 12,047	12,647	13,278	$ 23,577	$ 13,859	$ 14,639
Accounts payable	68,626	140,658	81,530	225,484	196,408	207,980	207,466
Accrued expenses	100,468	60,439	65,519	162,227	179,695	209,768	240,900
Federal and state taxes on income	136,848	99,942	85,109	258,560	294,644	298,853	303,858
Total Current Liabilities	$ 317,398	$ 313,086	$ 344,805	$ 759,549	$ 694,324	$ 730,460	$ 766,863
Mortgage payable to banks, less portion due within one year..........	$ 46,472	$ 34,418	$ 21,766	$ 8,474	$ 155,903	$ 68,342	$ 53,704
Capital Stock:							
Common par value $1.00, authorized 750,000 shares; issued and outstanding shares	$ 544,981	$ 544,981	$ 544,981	$ 544,981	$ 634,387	$ 634,387	$ 634,387
Additional paid-in capital			69,413	69,413	975,108	975,108	975,108
Retained earnings	430,745	532,046	550,243	798,361	529,722	855,282	1,185,284
Total Stockholders' Equity	$ 975,726	$1,077,027	$1,164,637	$1,412,755	$2,139,217	$2,464,777	$2,794,779
Total Liabilities	$1,339,596	$1,424,531	$1,531,208	$2,180,778	$2,989,444	$3,263,579	$3,615,346

* Elox of Canada

pieces of equipment were required: an EDM machine in place of a conventional machine tool, and a power supply unit. (For further details about the equipment and its applications see Elox Corporation of Michigan (A). While in the reception room, the case writer met Earl Siegel, senior engineer, Advanced Development Manufacturing Engineering Services of the General Electric Company. Mr. Siegel, who was at Elox to check out a new EDM machine Elox had made for General Electric, had written several authoritative papers on EDM for the American Society of Tool and Manufacturing Engineers. He told the case writer that in 1959 EDM was used if the machining you wished to do could not be done by any other process. Today, based on General Electric's experience with 120 Elox machines, a decision whether to use EDM or conventional machines depends on the economics. For example, when either the materials, configuration, location, tolerance, or quality proves to be difficult with conventional machining, EDM may oftentimes be more economical. Whereas in 1959 EDM was generally used for tool and diemaking, it is now also being used in basic research engineering prototypes, and in production work. For example, EDM had opened up new engineering design concepts, especially with the new space-age metals such as tungsten, molybdenum, and titanium, which could not be machined any other way. Consequently, Mr. Siegel felt that EDM had the brightest future of all the newest machining processes available today.

Later on in discussions with members of the Elox management, the case writer learned that they agreed with Mr. Siegel's analysis of EDM, and were confident that most of the companies that could profitably use the process were not yet doing so. Although sales had more than doubled since 1959, the Elox management still felt an educational job remained to be done to show the many potential users what EDM could do to solve their problems and save them money. During the 1964 fiscal year that ended April 30th, sales had grown to $5,137,990, compared to the 1959 fiscal year sales of $2,236,879. Profits after taxes for these years were $393,441 and $101,300, respectively. Comparative balance sheets and operating figures as of April 30th are given in Exhibits 32–1 and 32–2 for the years 1958 through 1964.

Company Organization

Elox Corporation, in September, 1964, had approximately 4,000 stockholders and 175 employees. John S. Larkins, Jr., one of the original founders of the Elox Corporation, was the president and chief

Exhibit 32–2

ELOX CORPORATION OF MICHIGAN (B)

COMPARATIVE INCOME STATEMENTS

(Fiscal Years Ending April 30)

	1958	1959	1960	1961	1962	1963	1964
Net sales	$2,324,334	$2,236,880	$2,612,246	$3,607,017	$4,479,284	$4,677,163	$5,137,990
Cost of sales	1,032,639	1,027,823	1,246,703	1,785,789	2,222,615	2,216,149	2,466,070
Gross profit	$1,291,695	$1,209,057	$1,365,543	$1,821,228	$2,256,669	$2,461,014	$2,671,920
Operating expenses	985,959	1,012,220	1,198,716	1,318,811	1,558,967	1,752,403	1,982,702
Operating profit	$ 305,726	$ 196,837	$ 166,827	$ 502,417	$ 697,702	$ 708,611	$ 689,218
Other income (expenses) net	10,996	4,406	5,891	4,261	(3,995)	84,173	98,019
Income before taxes	$ 316,722	$ 201,243	$ 172,718	$ 506,678	$ 693,707	$ 792,784	$ 787,237
Provision for taxes	157,849	99,942	85,109	258,560	350,877	403,786	393,796
Net Income	$ 158,873	$ 101,301	$ 87,609	$ 248,118	$ 342,830	$ 388,998	$ 393,441

executive officer. Mr. Larkins, who was in his middle forties, was described by many of the Elox employees as brilliant, dominant, a fair but hard taskmaster, possessing drive and spirit, and as a man who preferred to do every job himself but had learned to be partly dependent on others. (One of Mr. Larkins' favorite extracurricular activities was coaching little league football. At a banquet held recently, he was introduced as the most demanding and successful coach in the area.)

Although there were no up-to-date formal organizational charts or job descriptions, Mr. Toggweiler, vice-president and treasurer, described the organization of Elox Corporation. Mr. Larkins, besides being president, served as the director of marketing and director of engineering. The company sales manager and R&D manager reported directly to Mr. Larkins. The company's mechanical engineering manager and electrical engineering manager also reported to Mr. Larkins on technical matters and reported to Mr. Toggweiler with regard to production and scheduling matters. Mr. Toggweiler, the company's only vice-president, reported directly to Mr. Larkins and was the only company representative besides Mr. Larkins to sit on the board of directors. The company's purchasing agent, controller, and sales service manager reported to Mr. Toggweiler and he was also responsible for production scheduling, personnel, and union negotiations.

Most of the Elox managers were in their early forties. Elox had recently hired a merchandising manager and a full-time patent attorney. Mr. Larkins explained that Elox couldn't really justify a merchandising manager this year, but would need one next year and wanted time to break him in. EDM, being a new and relatively unknown process, presented this problem to all new Elox sales and management personnel.

Mr. Larkins viewed his function as president as one of keeping all the business functional areas in balance. He felt keeping the proper balance between R&D, engineering, production, accounting, and sales would allow Elox to continue to achieve its budgeted profits. As president, he said he made many small decisions which, in total, were large ones; however, he doubted that he made three large decisions a year. In philosophizing on being president of a small company, he felt any small-company president must be willing to sacrifice and must also be a generalist. He also felt a small-company president has to be more competent than a manager of a larger firm, since in a small company there are no corners to hide in.

During a 90-day study of his time, Mr. Larkins found he spent about equal time among all the departments of the company. Mr. Toggweiler thought a breakdown of his own time would be as follows:

Purchasing, 2 percent.
Personnel, labor union, 20 percent.
Accounting, 10 percent.
Manufacturing, 20 percent.
Engineering scheduling, 5 percent.
Sales service department, 5 percent.
General business problems, 38 percent.

Mr. Larkins stated at lunch that Elox had a reputation of sorting out people and of letting people go. He felt in part that this reputation was true, since he considered that the company's past and future success depended on getting the right people to fit into the Elox organization. The company sales manager, who was also at lunch, jokingly said that when he had joined the company two and one-half years previously everyone gave him only thirty days to last.

In talking to various employees on what it was like to work for Elox, a representative description went about as follows: "Working for Elox is like working for a large family where everyone knows everyone. The work is challenging, demanding in time and ability, yet rewarding. Elox pays well if you do the job well. There is no room for the person who cannot do his job or the prima donna or department empire builder." One department manager summed up working for Elox as "a wonderful place to work if you want to produce and are capable of doing so."

Board of Directors

Information regarding directors of the company, including the amount of Elox common stock owned as of April, 1964, is given in Exhibit 32–3. Mr. Larkins was the largest Elox stockholder, owning approximately 8 percent of the outstanding common stock. Mr. Larkins said the role of the board of directors had changed over the years. "We now can get higher-quality men to sit on our board, and thus the board asserts more influence on company policies than they did in the past. Their job is to set overall external objectives and policies and approve major expenditures. Internal company policies are the responsibility of Elox management." The board also determines, under the company bonus plan, the amount given to the president and vice-president. Mr. Larkins said that the board was very inter-

Exhibit 32–3

ELOX CORPORATION OF MICHIGAN (B)

BOARD OF DIRECTORS

Name of Nominee	Principal Occupation	Has Served as Director Since	Securities of Company Owned Directly, Indirectly or Beneficially, or Which the Director Claims a Right to Vote
John S. Larkins, Jr.	President and chief executive officer, Elox Corporation of Michigan, Troy, Michigan	1950	53,589 shs. common stk.
Maynard R. Andreae	President, Syncro Corporation, Oxford, Michigan	1961	320 shs. common stk.
Gilbert H. Davis	Lawyer, Davis, Hayward, Rann & Slavens, Royal Oak, Michigan	1950	3,690 shs. common stk.
Charles L. Hall	Consulting engineer, Detroit, Michigan	1952	2,800 shs. common stk.
Kenneth D. Mann	Chairman, Firth Sterling Inc., Pittsburgh, Pennsylvania	1961	35,400 shs. common stk.*
Milton B. Pollock	Partner, Pollock & Richard, Business Management Consultants, Detroit, Michigan	1950	840 shs. common stk.†
Robert S. Toggweiler	Vice-president and treasurer, Elox Corporation of Michigan, Troy, Michigan	1957	540 shs. common stk.
L. Raymond Twyman	President of Interlox, Ltd., chairman of board of directors, Elox Corporation of Michigan	1957	110 shs. common stk.
Edmond F. Webb	President, Webb Engineering Associates, Franklin, Michigan	1956	7,260 shs. common stk.

* 200 shares owned by Kenneth D. Mann; 35,200 shares owned by Firth Sterling Inc., of which company Mr. Mann is chairman, and which shares he claims the right to vote.
† 400 shares owned by Milton B. Pollock; 440 shares owned by him as trustee, in which shares he claims no beneficial interest but has the right to vote.

ested in conveying to Elox stockholders and to the public that Elox was not a one-man corporation, but a company that had management in depth.

Plant Facilities—Production

The Elox plant was a modern one-story building on a four-acre lot, located in an attractive industrial area of Troy, Michigan, about 14 miles from downtown Detroit. Of Elox's 175 employees, 140 were at the Troy plant; of these, 25 were engaged in the assembly operation. Elox's policy was to concentrate its production effort in the final assembly of the EDM machines and power supply units, and to buy as many parts as possible from vendors. Mr. Larkins stated that this philosophy allowed them to free capital (that would have been used for production equipment) to be used for activities in the areas of R&D and marketing that no outside company could do for them.

Elox's power supply units were made by a wholly owned subsidiary, Caralox Company, in a modern one-story plant in Davidson, North Carolina. This subsidiary employed 35 people, of whom essentially all were involved in assembly work. The plant had 18,000 square feet and was located on 10 acres of land.

Elox employees at the Troy plant were represented by the International Union of Electrical Workers (IUE) and the United Automobile Workers (UAW). Both of these unions were members of the AFL–CIO. Elox's relations with the unions at the Troy plant were excellent, and there had never been a strike. The North Carolina plant had no union. There was about a 90-cent wage rate differential between the two plants. At both plants, the assembly department employees were paid on an hourly basis. Elox management was very pleased with the quality of the work done at both plants.

After completion of the Troy plant expansion, it was estimated that the two plants would be utilizing approximately 80 percent of their floor capacity, and could handle the assembly work for sales up to $9 million. Both plants worked only one shift a day.

Manufacturing costs were 48 percent of the sales dollar. Of this 48 percent, 5 percent represented overhead, 3 percent represented labor costs, and 40 percent represented purchases. Fifty percent of these purchases came from approximately three vendors. Negotiation with these vendors was the responsibility of Mr. Larkins and Mr. Toggweiler.

Engineering Department

Len Smith, a very agreeable person and one of the oldest company employees in years of service, had been the mechanical engineering manager for nine years. When asked what he thought were the company's major assets, he said that he felt that they were twofold—being the first company in the EDM field and taking advantage of it, and the spirit and attitude of the employees to stay first. When asked what he thought would happen to the company's spirit when sales began to level off, he answered, "We are not going to level off." Mr. Smith did feel that continued growth posed some possible problems. He felt without manufacturing facilities that Elox was quite dependent on vendors in regard to lead times and maintaining quality control. He felt that if competition increased there would be a need to cut down on delivery time which now ran about six to eight weeks on an EDM machine and power unit for a customer. However, at that time, he felt they could not economically justify the cost of equipment, plant space, and the training of new people that it would take to manufacture rather than just assemble their equipment. In his own department, he felt there was a need in the future for younger engineers to be trained to eventually take over, as it was becoming more difficult for older men to keep up with the new ideas and advances made in EDM equipment. In the past, Elox had preferred older and experienced engineers, since they had no formal training program and whatever learning was done had to be done by on-the-job experience. Mr. Smith felt that one of the joys of working for Elox was that the communication channels were always open, and an employee could see the whole picture. He hoped that this would continue in the future.

Accounting

Mr. Comings had been the controller of Elox Corporation for eight years. In reflecting on his work at Elox versus his previous job in the accounting department of a major auto firm, he felt that working for Elox was much more self-fulfilling. With Elox, he stated, "You have the opportunity to grasp all facets of accounting and see the whole picture."

He felt the company's main assets were a product more and more companies wanted, and "since we have the basic patents, they have to come to us and we are beginning to get more repeat business."

In considering future growth, he felt their only problem would be space. The way he planned to handle the future growth in the accounting department was by more complex equipment rather than more people. They presently had an IBM 632 for handling accounts payable, accounts receivable, and the payroll. They also had a Xerox Copier 9–14 for use by all the departments.

Marketing

Elox Corporation's sales and profits for the past seven years are shown in Exhibit 32–4. Of the 1964 sales of $5,137,990, 60 percent represented EDM machines and 40 percent represented the power

Exhibit 32–4

ELOX CORPORATION OF MICHIGAN (B)

SEVEN-YEAR COMPARISON

Excerpt from the April, 1964 Elox annual report:

The modest $4,443 increase in earnings does not truly reflect the activity of the past fiscal year. A profit position was maintained despite the expenditure of $200,000 for the purchase, and preparation for market of several new products. A new tungsten carbide hard facing device called the "Depositron" is an example of the use of a small portion of these funds. This device is already on the market and is contributing to our net profit for the current fiscal year. Other devices are being readied for the market as rapidly as possible.

NOTE: Elox common stock was selling at $8.75 a share as of 10/1/64. Its high per share for 1963 was $7.80. Prior to 1963, it had sold as high as $17.25 a share and as low as $2.25 a share.

supply units. The physical life of an EDM machine and power supply unit was estimated at 20 years or longer. A recent Elox development was a power supply unit that could be used for two EDM machines. The sales price of a standard EDM machine and power supply unit was approximately $20,000. The price of the power supply unit and EDM machine was about equal. An approximate percentage cost breakdown of the sales dollar would be:

Sales	100%
Manufacturing costs	48
Gross profit	52%
Research and development	11
General and administrative	6
Sales and service	22
Profit before taxes	13%

The power supply units which were well protected by Elox patents were more profitable than the EDM machines. Although some of the patents would run out in 1966, Elox had received recent patents on major improvements that maintained the strength of the company's position. According to Mr. Larkins, the strongest Elox patents were expected to be issued in the near future. According to Mr. Toggweiler, any company making EDM power supply units not licensed by Elox would be infringing on the patents of Elox.

Pricing, according to Mr. Larkins, was figured on a cost-plus-profit basis in conjunction with what the market would bear. Presently, Elox was on a seven- to eight-week back-order situation. However, he hoped to return to a four- to six-week back-order basis, which he considered to be more satisfactory.

The three largest customers of Elox were: General Motors (160 EDM machines), General Electric (120 EDM machines), Ford Motor (80 EDM machines). Chrysler, on the other hand, had purchased only one EDM machine. Ninety-three percent of Elox sales were in the United States, and 7 percent of their sales were overseas and in Canada. Elox's management felt they and their United States licensees accounted for 80 percent of the EDM sales in the United States. Elox itself accounted for about 56 percent of total United States EDM sales.

Elox's major competition in the United States was Cincinnati Milling Machine Company, Ingersoll Milling Machine Company, and Ex-Cell-O Corporation. Cincinnati Milling Machine Company had purchased over $250,000 worth of Elox power supply units during the previous year. Ingersoll and Ex-Cell-O were under a licensing arrangement from Elox to make their own power supply units. When asked why Cincinnati was not under a similar licensing arrangement, Mr. Toggweiler felt Cincinnati preferred to purchase the complete EDM power supply unit from Elox, due to Elox's experience, quality, facilities, and low production costs. Elox had also licensed several foreign producers of EDM machines, the largest being Charmilles, a Swiss company. Licensee royalties amounted to about $98,000 in the 1964 fiscal year ending in April. Elox had no plans for establishing assembly plants in Europe and preferred to continue to expand its selective foreign licensee arrangements.

Demonstration Room

Three thousand square feet of Elox's facilities made up the demonstration room. This room was used for EDM demonstrations for customers, teaching customer operators, and in teaching customer maintenance personnel. Mr. Larkins mentioned that this unique demonstration room, which also was used in teaching EDM to Elox employees, had taught EDM to over 3,000 people since it was started. The demonstration room was running two customer-operator training schools and one service-maintenance training school a month. These schools ran four and one-half days and had approximately twenty people in each school. Elox Corporation provided the instruction, lunches, and transportation from a motel, and the company that was sending the operator or serviceman paid his living and transportation costs. Pratt & Whitney, in Hartford, Connecticut, which had 40 Elox EDM machines, had sent as many as 17 men to this school at one time. This demonstration room contained the latest EDM machinery, which was valued at $150,000. Largely because of this demonstration room, there were always customers in the Elox building, producing a customer-oriented atmosphere throughout the Elox plant.

Sales Organization and Salesmen Compensation

In January, 1959, the basis of salesmen compensation was changed. Each of the 12 salesmen had previously received a salary, expenses, and a small commission. Under the new system, each salesman received only a 10 percent commission and was expected to pay his own expenses.

It had been hoped that this method of compensation would provide a greater incentive for the salesmen. However, by the fall of 1959, all but three of the salesmen had been switched to a new plan, which provided a salary and a small bonus if a quota was exceeded. It was a group quota established for all the salesmen in a district. If the quota was exceeded, all the district salesmen, as well as the district manager, shared equally in the bonus. The management said that the system of paying only a straight commission had been abandoned because: (1) it was feared that salesmen might neglect long-run customer relations in their efforts to make current sales; (2) it was difficult for new salesmen to earn enough under the straight commission plan; (3) the normal fluctuation in sales from month to month made it difficult for salesmen to plan their personal financial affairs. The three salesmen who stayed on commission did so on their own request. They were described as the company's best salesmen.

In March of 1959, the company had embarked on a program to expand its sales force. Since sales were made to the tool and die industry, it was reasoned that men who were experienced in this field would make good salesmen. The Elox Corporation advertised in local news-papers for men with tool and die backgrounds who were interested in training that would qualify them to sell Elox equipment to this industry.

About 200 men answered this advertisement; most of them had worked as machinists in the tool and die industry. Of these, 20 be-came students in a four-week night school conducted by Elox per-sonnel in the Elox plant. During these four weeks, the students stud-ied the theory of electrical discharge machining, learned to operate the Elox equipment, learned of the potential markets for EDM, and saw several movies on techniques of industrial selling. There was no charge to the students for this training, and they received no pay from Elox for this time.

At the end of the four weeks, eight of these men became Elox salesmen. Of the other 12, some were not offered jobs and some were not willing to move. These eight men moved to other sections of the country which had been only lightly covered by Elox salesmen. Their compensation was $500 to $600 per month plus a 1 percent com-mission.

"This program was unsuccessful," said vice-president Robert Togg-weiler, "but we learned one thing. A tool and die background does not necessarily qualify a man to be a salesman." By September, 1959, three of these eight men remained. Of the other five, two had resigned and three had been released. In the fall of 1959, management had decided that its nationwide sales force could be controlled better from district offices than from the home office. Four district sales managers were hired; these men were to supervise from three to five salesmen each in four different districts. The new sales managers all had engineering degrees and considerable experience in sales; they had been brought in from outside the company, because management did not believe that any of the Elox salesmen had the desired background.

The company continued to have manufacturers' representatives in areas where the sales volume did not justify having salesmen.

There was also a service organization with one serviceman located in each district. These men installed new machines and serviced exist-ing installations. The servicemen were scheduled by the district sales managers but were responsible to the service manager who was at the home office.

By September, 1964, the sales organization had grown to 14 direct salesmen, 9 servicemen, 5 regional managers, and 25 manufacturers' representatives. The compensation for the Elox salesmen was changed in September, 1963, from a salary to a commission arrangement of 5.5 percent on sales plus expenses. Since each salesman had an exclusive territory, a commission was split if a salesman sold an EDM machine in his territory that was shipped to another salesman's territory.

The salesmen spent most of their time selling the standard Elox EDM machines and power supply units rather than custom-made machines and component parts. The standard models accounted for the majority of Elox's sales, and they also contributed the highest percent profit per sales dollar. (In order to insure continued improvements and advances in their standard line, Elox spent the majority of its research and development dollars in this area.) Elox's management thought one possible way to continue their growth in the future would be to add related products that could be sold by their sales organization. An example of this was their recent announcement of a new device called the Depositron, which was used to impart a hard tungsten carbide facing to metal.

Manufacturers' representatives, who also had exclusive territories, received a 10 percent commission on the sale at the time the customer paid his Elox bill. Mr. Larkins recalled that five years ago the good manufacturers' representatives were not interested in taking on the Elox EDM line. However, now they were actively seeking Elox. The Elox servicemen were paid on a straight salary basis and serviced any Elox EDM user. They received their instructions from the home office in Troy, Michigan. The five regional managers were each responsible for approximately three direct Elox salesmen and also for the manufacturers' representatives in their region. These managers also were paid on a commission arrangement. Both the regional managers and the Elox salesmen could take a monthly draw against their future commissions.

Elox competition likewise sold EDM machines through a direct sales force and manufacturers' representatives. Mr. Larkins felt that in the future Elox would continue a middle-of-the-road sales policy between a direct sales force and manufacturers' representatives.

When Mr. Siegel, of General Electric Company, was asked whether he preferred to purchase major equipment such as EDM machines from the manufacturer's salesman or from a manufacturer's representative, he stated he preferred to buy from the manufacturer's salesman. His reasoning was that the manufacturer's salesman was generally better informed, since it was the only product he was selling.

Elox's Future

When discussing the future of the Elox Corporation, both Mr. Larkins and Mr. Toggweiler were most optimistic, as were all the employees of the company who expressed an opinion. Mr. Toggweiler said there was no concrete five-year plan of growth as such, but he felt they would continue to grow as they had in the past. To continue to grow, he said, "all we need are facilities, financing, and people. The first two we have and we can get the third."

Mr. Larkins felt that there was no reason for them not to continue their past growth. He saw no reason why the foundations of their profitable growth—(a) selling the best product at a reasonable price backed up by good service, (b) having all the functions of the business in balance and doing a passable job, and (c) freeing management's time and capital resources by having others do their manufacturing—could not be continued in the future.

Even though Mr. Larkins felt they had the facilities to more than double sales, he wanted Elox to continue growing at the rate they had in the past (see Exhibit 32–4). "We could probably double our sales, as many of our investors feel we should do, in a couple of years, but it probably would not be profitable and it would be a strain on our people. You can only grow so fast if you want to show the same profit margin we have had in the past."

33. CRAFTSBURG MANUFACTURING COMPANY *

The Strategy of Size, Expansion, and Competitive Position

Early in 1960, Alan Craig, president of the Craftsburg Manufacturing Company, and his associates on the management team were actively considering an expansion of the company's product line, facilities, and personnel. The company was engaged in the manufacture and sale of dining room furniture and operated one plant employing slightly over 100 people. Financial statements for the company are given in Exhibits 33–1 and 33–2, and data for the industry appear in Exhibits 33–3 and 33–4.

Craftsburg was a town with a population somewhat under 900 in the Adirondack region of northern New York. Most of the area was covered by forests, with relatively little farming; the forests were principally mixed northern hardwoods, including yellow birch and hard maple. Two towns with populations under 2,000 were 13 and 15 miles distant, and Stow, a town with 6,000 residents, which had been a textile center, was 21 miles away.

The Craftsburg management had been considering expansion for somewhat over two years. In August, 1959, inquiry developed the fact that a plant in Stow, built as a woolen mill and vacant for eight years, could be bought for $25,000. The main building was a well-built reinforced concrete structure with three floors and a basement, each 62 feet by 222 feet. An attached two-story building of wood construction had 2,500 square feet on each floor. They constituted, in effect, a single building equipped with sprinklers and adequate freight elevators. In addition, there was a powerhouse with two 125 h.p. boilers in good condition which would be suitable for heating the plant and providing steam for a wood lumber kiln. Each boiler was slightly larger than the single boiler of the Craftsburg plant.

Previous inquiries had not disclosed other facilities so well adapted to the purpose, and new construction on a one-story basis would cost approximately $8.00 per square foot. The building was basically in good condition and could be made ready for operation at moderate

---

Exhibit 33–1

CRAFTSBURG MANUFACTURING COMPANY (A)

INCOME STATEMENTS
(Years Ending December 31)

	1949	1950	1951	1952	1953	1954	1955	1956	1957	1958	1959
Net sales	$185,790	$264,649	$324,334	$348,582	$477,659	$527,817	$654,564	$772,143	$896,012	$952,631	$1,035,911
Direct labor	44,056	62,324	87,220	87,832	113,463	102,229	117,932	136,945	152,873	163,324	173,614
Cost of material	40,564	61,045	73,828	68,504	116,981	132,292	171,644	224,276	285,977	262,903	289,892
Overhead	50,772	67,779	86,349	76,621	96,472	99,455	142,218	151,041	146,600	200,094	219,168
Supplies (packing)	*	11,555	12,572	13,055	18,085	22,095	20,639	25,588	34,887	32,270	31,174
Other	17,643	5,330	(14,667)	1,169	(2,876)	5,662	4,763	(5,393)	(7,774)	3,852	(7,072)
Cost of manufacture	153,035	208,033	245,302	247,181	342,125	361,733	457,196	532,457	612,563	662,443	706,776
Sales expense	(27,602)	(28,537)	27,661	37,446	53,064	57,194	60,178	69,769	83,171	83,869	96,305
General and administrative expense		461	31,480	36,443	50,192	54,439	68,049	79,311	77,196	78,421	86,261
Other expenses	63		2,241	7,462	10,539	10,865	11,417	14,713	15,130	13,318	16,129
Total Cost	180,700	237,031	306,684	328,532	455,920	484,231	596,840	696,250	788,060	838,051	905,471
Net profit before taxes	5,090	27,618	17,650	20,050	21,739	43,586	57,724	75,893	107,952	114,580	130,440
Provision for federal income taxes	—	4,845	4,991	6,015	6,522	17,722	25,074	34,521	51,192	54,082	62,329
Net Profit after Taxes	$ 5,090	$ 22,773	$ 12,659	$ 14,035	$ 15,217	$ 25,864	$ 32,650	$ 41,372	$ 56,760	$ 60,498	$ 68,111

* Included in overhead.

Exhibit 33–2—CRAFTSBURG MANUFACTURING COMPANY (A)

COMPARATIVE BALANCE SHEETS (Years Ending December 31)

	1949	1950	1951	1952	1953	1954	1955	1956	1957	1958	1959
Current Assets:											
Cash	$ 11,535	$ 22,103	$ 4,658	$ 10,183	$ 6,426	$ 10,128	$ 17,969	$ 26,771	$ 46,991	$ 47,108	$ 90,789
Accounts receivable, trade	12,121	18,449	41,331	51,634	64,277	81,705	84,444	96,694	105,799	134,473	127,956
Advances for logs	116	3,904	337	3,459	5,852	64	—	—	521	45	80
Inventories	31,690	24,425	48,165	44,624	45,522	52,892	55,588	62,554	91,023	126,307	110,380
Prepaid insurance	2,405	4,294	9,440	7,053	1,917	2,950	4,071	5,698	6,513	9,497	10,859
Other	—	388	—	—	—			354	88		
Total Current	$ 57,867	$ 73,563	$103,931	$116,953	$123,994	$147,739	$162,072	$192,071	$250,935	$317,430	$ 340,064
Fixed assets (net)	$ 80,819	$ 77,320	$ 81,237	$ 82,345	$ 94,848	$103,630	$114,098	$102,603	$102,603	$107,960	$ 168,945
Due from affiliated company	—								6,178	2,154	3,051
Other assets (due from employees)	—	189	876	325	810	1,085	367	1,453	1,365	1,610	4,500
Cash surrender value of life insurance	—				1,258	1,865	2,472	3,078	3,707	4,287	4,929
Total Assets	$138,686	$151,073	$186,044	$199,624	$220,910	$254,319	$279,009	$299,205	$368,309	$433,441	$ 521,489
Current Liabilities:											
Accounts payable, trade	$ 739	$ 1,877	$ 1,509	$ 868	$ 315	$ 2,692	$ 1,272	$ 12,036	$ 8,600	$ 3,735	$ 16,901
Accruals	2,900	3,621	9,405	7,870	9,985	13,305	13,493	17,095	17,388	19,506	30,809
Notes payable, bank	22,469	6,278	13,481	6,741	13,068						
Equipment note, bank				5,677							
Taxes payable (federal)	—	4,845	5,074	6,015	6,522	17,722	25,074	34,522	51,192	54,632	59,654
Other	—		90	76	225	238	292	117	75	222	356
Total Current	$ 26,108	$ 16,621	$ 29,559	$ 27,247	$ 30,115	$ 33,957	$ 40,131	$ 63,770	$ 77,255	$78,095	$ 107,720
Mortgage payable	8,988	8,089	7,190	6,291	5,393	—					
Officers' accounts	—	—	11,779	16,039	19,698	29,277	35,393	7,336	2,987	13,148	11,742
Stockholders' Equity:											
Stock issued and outstanding	$110,143	$110,143	$110,143	$110,143	$110,143	$110,143	$ 88,078	$ 71,766	$ 71,766	$ 65,745	$ 258,840
Retained earnings	(6,553)	16,220	27,373	39,904	55,561	80,942	115,407	156,333	216,301	276,453	143,187
Total Equity	103,590	126,363	137,516	150,047	165,704	191,085	203,485	228,099	288,067	342,198	402,027
Total Liabilities	$138,686	$151,073	$186,044	$199,624	$220,910	$254,319	$279,009	$299,205	$368,309	$433,441	$ 521,489

Exhibit 33–3

CRAFTSBURG MANUFACTURING COMPANY (A)

FURNITURE MANUFACTURING RATIOS (%)*

	Industry		Case Goods Manufacturers†	
	Net Profit as % of Investment	Net Profit as % of Sales	Net Profit as % of Investment	Net Profit as % of Sales
1952	na	2.8	na	2.3
1953	6.7	2.5	5.9	2.9
1954	7.5	2.4	6.2	2.5
1955	10.4	3.6	7.1	2.4
1956	10.4	3.6	6.5	2.2
1957	7.2	7.6	5.1	1.9
1958	2.8	1.2	(2.2)	(.2)
1959	4.8	1.9	.7	.9

* All figures are after income taxes.
† Case goods were products such as dining room servers, cabinets, and hutches, as well as bedroom dressers and bureaus.

SOURCES: National Association of Furniture Manufacturers, Inc., "Furniture Manufacturers' Comparative Operating Ratios," 1955–57.

Exhibit 33–4

CRAFTSBURG MANUFACTURING COMPANY (A)

MANUFACTURERS OF CASE GOODS, 1959 DATA
NET SALES, $1 MILLION TO $2 MILLION
(Northern Mills)

	High	Average	Low
Net sales	100%	100%	100%
Cost of materials	55.4	36.8	23.9
Direct labor	27.8	19.4	11.3
Overhead	38.3	22.5	10.1
Sales expense	19.8	12.1	.1
General and administrative expense	11.2	6.5	3.2
Other	4.1	1.1	(.9)
Net (after taxes)*	7.2	.5	(6.6)
Net (after taxes)†	7.2	3.3	1.0

* Taxes exceed net because losses are averaged with gains.
† Includes only profitable manufacturers.

SOURCE: National Association of Furniture Manufacturers, Inc., "Furniture Manufacturers' Comparative Operating Ratios," 1955–59.

expense. It would provide good manufacturing space for the production of furniture. The availability of the building in Stow brought to a focus questions about expansion which had been considered by Mr. Craig and his associates for the preceding two years or more. Should they buy the building? Did the financial condition of the company warrant the expenditure?

Mr. Craig and his associates realized that other issues were likewise involved. What were the essential elements in the competitive strength the company had developed in its operation of the original plant? Might they be in part lost with expansion to a second plant? Could these elements of competitive strength be developed in a second plant 21 miles away?

History

The company had been under the present management since 1947, when it had been acquired by Alan Craig and his brother Edgar Craig. Alan Craig initially learned the sawmill and woodworking business from his father, who owned a sawmill and a sash and door plant in northern New York. The elder Mr. Craig was thoroughly versed in the art of selecting and sawing logs, and cutting lumber so as to maximize the amount of clear wood available for the products being manufactured.

For instance, in cutting out the material for a paneled door, any clear section long enough and wide enough to make the stiles (the vertical members at the hinge side and the knob side of the door) would not be cut up to make rails (the horizontal structural members). Wood long enough to make a rail would not be cut up for shorter vertical members between rails or for panels. If clear wood long enough for rails was not wide enough, it could be glued edge to edge to provide the requisite widths. Clear cuts not large enough for other uses might be used for the mullions in window sash. Full advantage was also taken of different sizes of doors and sash. During summer vacations from high school and college, Alan worked in the mill, gradually acquiring this art and skill of utilizing lumber economically.

After attending college and the Harvard Business School, Mr. Craig went to the West Coast, where he worked for two years in a small Oregon sawmill. In 1922, he left the West Coast and went to work for a well-known firm with interests in a series of lumber and woodworking plants, where he became manager of a succession of plants. Over the course of his employment there, he was successful in returning several unprofitable operations to profitable status, both by developing management and by introducing methods that resulted in more economical use of logs and lumber.

In the fall of 1947, the Craig brothers had first learned of the Craftsburg Manufacturing Company. The company was then in difficulty and was being run by a creditors' committee, which was anxious to obtain competent management for the plant and was willing to negotiate reasonable terms of sale. The committee said they felt the plant was then running at just about a break-even point.

A visit to Craftsburg and closer investigation of the facilities revealed that losses of close to $2,500 per year were being incurred. This discovery considerably chilled the Craigs' enthusiasm, and despite the presence of the representative of a large national department store chain who seemed anxious to purchase the entire output of the plant, they advised the committee that they were no longer interested. The committee was impressed with the Craigs, however, and requested that they seriously reconsider their decision. A second and more thorough investigation was subsequently arranged.

A consultant was hired to estimate costs of production for a dinette set consisting of a table and four chairs, using locally available wood and the existing plant and facilities. Estimates indicated a cost of $38 per dinette set on a volume of 70 units per week—a competitive figure. With this information, plus further encouragement from the department store chain and a favorable settlement on the existing $65,000 mortgage, the Craigs decided to invest in the company, although Alan Craig said later that he felt "the odds were about 5 or 10 to 1 against us."

The Craigs agreed to invest $43,000, an amount considered necessary to keep the company going. The company was to be operated by the Craigs. At such time as the Craigs and a committee of the townspeople were satisfied that the company was definitely regaining its health, stock was to be issued to them and to the Craigs. The townspeople were to receive a Class A stock, which was nonvoting and had a par value equal to the mortgage debt the townspeople held. The Craigs would receive a Class B stock, which held all voting rights and had a par value equal to the Craigs' investment. Both classes of stock were to share in whatever dividends were declared; but the Class B was to participate at $1\frac{1}{2}$ times any amounts paid as dividends on Class A stock, and its participation distributed in liquidation was three to one. The Class A stock was also to be callable at par. Within a year, the stock had been issued as agreed. Over the ensuing five years, all the Class A stock was redeemed by the company.

Operations commenced immediately and proved the validity of the cost estimates. Costs in the first week of operation were $38 per set, decreasing to $32 per set within the first month as volume increased to 110 units per week. At this point, however, inventory began to accumulate, because the chain was unable to purchase a significant amount of the plant's output due to a sudden slump in demand. Production was curtailed, and a hurried conference with Syracuse bankers proved to be of little help. Mr. Craig went to a personal friend, who was president of another chain, and explained his predicament. With this man's help he was able to get a suitable sales arrangement in Chicago for handling the line. At the suggestion of this Chicago company, Craftsburg began producing a more complete dining room group. Total designing costs amounted to approximately $6,000.

During this initial period, Alan Craig also introduced some organizational changes. Two foremen were released and replaced by four younger men. "It seemed to me that those old foremen just didn't know their jobs," said Alan Craig. "Under their direction, the mill failed twice and it was still losing money. Townspeople had poured $65,000 into this company, although I don't know where they got it. The 45 employees felt very insecure, and their morale was low. Still, these foremen took offense at my suggestions, and they wouldn't carry them out. Also, it seemed to me that they just plain hated hard work. So I let them go. To replace them, I looked for others who appeared to be young, hard-working, intelligent, and willing to take direction. Of course, I looked for them inside the plant. One of my fetishes is that, if possible, I will hire nobody from outside for a good job. Judging from my own observations, plus opinions of the townspeople and other employees, there seemed to be four young men who stood out from the crowd, the kind of men who were always eager to start work in the morning. In a small community like Craftsburg, it's pretty easy to learn all you want to know about people. You live with them and go to church with them and everyone knows everyone else. These young men were clean-cut, came from good families, and gave evidence of having the ability to carry responsibility."

After selecting the foremen as the nucleus of a supervisory group, Alan Craig realized the necessity of concentrating on production and on sales. While the two activities had to be carried on simultaneously, the nature of the sales arrangements described below made it possible for him to concentrate most of his time on production during the initial period. Alan Craig knew how to use wood efficiently in sawmill operation and in the production of many types of wood products, but he did not know how to build furniture.

After taking care of some obvious inefficiencies, such as bad housekeeping resulting in a cluttered floor and poor production flow which caused waste motion within the plant, he and the foremen went to a group of other furniture plants to get all possible information that would be useful in their own operation. They went especially to those companies manufacturing a very high quality of furniture. The executives of these companies were generous in giving the information about operations in their own companies.

Alan Craig and the foremen carefully observed the seasoning of wood prior to processing, the cutoff and ripsaw operations in which blanks for the parts were cut from incoming lumber, the preparation of parts, including accuracy in cutting for length and width, band saw operations for curves, and planing and sanding to give the best possible surface. Also, hand operations such as rounding off certain edges to improve the appearance and feel were noted.

They also observed wood bending and the fabrication of turned parts. Wood bending was done after steaming. With a steel band on the outside to take the tension, the wood part and the band were bent around a form having the curve desired, so the bending was accomplished by compression on the inside of the curve. The parts were dried in the fixture to set the curve. Round parts were made on a wood lathe, and subsequent sanding to get a good finish was somewhat difficult because of the shape.

Members of the group made a special study of finishing, including the materials used, the suppliers, the color, and resistance to damage in use, methods of application, the amount of hand rubbing, and inspection after finishing. The group observed the equipment used throughout the plants visited, the layout, the men assigned, the skills required, and scheduling, and inquired about wage rates and the balancing of production to keep equipment and men fully employed. Three factors to which they devoted special attention were the specifications established for parts, inspection against those specifications, and opportunities for more efficient use of wood throughout the process. They also observed the process of assembly and the structure employed to make the pieces fully useful over a long period of time. This included methods for making glue joints—such as those between pieces of wood assembled in panels—almost invisible, strong, and permanent.

In addition, members of the group went to technical meetings and read technical articles and bulletins such as those prepared by the Madison Laboratory of the United States Forest Service. One of the foremen was asked to make a continuing investigation of the seasoning of wood and of kiln operation. He attended conferences on kiln operation and made several trips to the Forest Products Laboratory at Madison, Wisconsin. The investigation of existing ways of making furniture was initiated almost immediately after acquisition of the company and continued at a somewhat decreased rate and on special production problems during the early years of the company, and to some extent up to the present.

At one of the plants visited, Alan Craig became acquainted with a man reputed to be one of the best furniture designers in the country, who was serving that company as a consultant. The lines of furniture were somewhat competitive but at different price levels. After discussing the matter with executives of the other furniture company, Mr. Craig hired the consultant to assist Craftsburg in design. The consultant was asked to assist in four main areas. The first was to design furniture that would meet the desires of customers and would sell. The second was to design units so strong and soundly constructed that they would retain their quality through years and generations of use. The third area was to design units that could be produced efficiently while attaining the objectives above. The fourth was to incorporate, as far as possible, raw material requirements whereby the lengths required for parts of the same thickness were balanced with differentials of two inches or less. That is, if clear wood in incoming lumber was not long enough for one part, it could be cut for a next shorter piece with a sacrifice of two inches or less.

The information obtained was not reduced to systematic written form, but was retained as a matter of feel and familiarity with the processes on the part of the group. It was discussed by Mr. Craig with the rest of the group and among the foremen themselves in terms of the Craftsburg operations.

When the books were closed on the first year, they showed a loss of about $23,000. The Craigs drew no salaries. The decision to produce the new line, however, turned out to be a profitable one. During the second year, the company made a profit sufficient to erase the previous losses and provide a small amount of retained earnings. Edgar Craig became less active during the next few years and eventually retired because of poor health.

Sales

Despite the financial success, the distribution arrangement was not altogether satisfactory to Craftsburg. Not only did the Chicago wholesaler exert an increasing degree of control over the company's prices and terms, but he also wished to own 50 percent of the company. An analysis of this proposal was made by Mr. Craig with the help of some financial advisers. As a result, Mr. Craig wrote the wholesaler to the effect that he considered the offer a bit low for the value. On receipt of this letter, the wholesaler called Mr. Craig to Chicago and proceeded to deliver him a sharply critical lecture on the entire matter. Mr. Craig wrote to the wholesaler, terminating their relationship. An arrangement was made whereby the wholesaler would continue to take the full output of the plant for six months, and 50 percent for the following six months, after which relations would cease, leaving Craftsburg with no sales outlet unless definite action were taken.

Alan Craig immediately devoted much of his time to attempting to locate a suitable replacement. It was his feeling that if he could locate just one man with outstanding sales ability and bring him into the management of Craftsburg, the bulk of his sales problems could be met. Mr. Craig finally located a man, then employed as a retail furniture buyer in a large department store, whom he considered to be extremely promising as a sales representative. "I screened some 15 applicants for the job," said Alan Craig. "Some I scratched right off, and others I was not sure of. I think I learned a lot through trial and error about picking sales representatives. The first three arrangements I had made for one reason or another had not worked out. It seemed to me that the buyer in this department store was the man we were looking for.

"I believe we needed a man who knew what would make furniture sell and wanted to sell it. It seemed to me that this buyer, Ralph Frantz, had these qualities. As a buyer, he had learned a lot about selling furniture by being the target of salesmen. In discussions, he appeared to have a good feel for what the customers wanted, and his reputation as a very successful buyer lent support to this conclusion. He had spent some time on the floor selling to customers of the store, so that he knew what factors of design, workmanship, and price would appeal to different segments of the market. He said that selling appealed to him as a profession. As a buyer himself, Mr. Frantz knew the problems and talked the language of other buyers to whom he might sell. He knew the problems of the store with regard to display, margins, and inventory turnover. It seemed to me that he had a lot of drive, and I thought his command of English, his appearance, and his good manners would speak well for the firm he represented.

"But I must admit that to a certain extent it was another shot in the dark. The man I had retained as a designer said I would be crazy to meet his demands. The designer said he didn't know of anyone who had ever been hired on a high salary as a furniture salesman for a manufacturer when he had no experience selling to buyers in furniture stores and furniture departments of department stores."

While this prospective representative whom Mr. Craig favored also professed a liking for the company, he said his present job paid him so well he could not afford to take the initial offer made him by Craftsburg. Although it required paying the candidate about double what he himself was receiving in salary, Mr. Craig decided that this man was the representative he was looking for. The man accepted the revised offer and thus began what Mr. Craig described as "the most pleasant association I have had in this business." After a somewhat slow start, the new sales head suddenly caught fire after six months and contributed greatly to the growth and success of the company thereafter.

"When we took over the plant, I didn't know much about sales," said Alan Craig. "The mill always ran for me, but I had quite a bit to learn about making and selling furniture. Ralph Frantz helped me a lot. We had many long talks about what people wanted in furniture and what they would buy at different prices. Together, we traveled to several cities, visiting stores and furniture shows and studying the furniture of other companies. Ralph pointed out to me the different styles and various ways of merchandising furniture. He also introduced me to other buyers he knew, and we kicked around different ideas with them, gradually developing our own sales policies.

"Now it works out pretty well. We are working a 45-hour week, our sales have grown consistently the past few years, and our order backlog has held fairly steady at about four to six weeks. Sales this year are about 5 percent higher than at this time a year ago.

"Our salesmen give exclusive distributorships in some communities. Most of the big companies aren't able to, but with our smaller volume we can, and as a result we think we get dealer loyalty and sales push that we otherwise would not have. Ralph and I picked the dealers carefully, choosing only those stores which sold good quality merchandise, had sound credit ratings, and showed promise of giving strong sales effort to our furniture. We don't advertise much, because we think it pays us better to concentrate our sales efforts on the buyers for the stores rather than the public, and let the stores sell it to consumers. Our intention is to design, construct, and price the furniture so that once it appears on the dealer's floor the customers will take it off quickly. We find that if the first piece moves off the floor quickly, it's not too hard to get the dealer to put a second piece in its place.

"Colonial is a continuing major style, so that although there are certain minor shifts in taste within it, the general pattern never goes out of date. This saves us the trouble of changing patterns, and it saves dealers from the danger of being caught with obsolete inventory. The construction is such that our furniture should be as serviceable after a generation as when it is bought new. We keep records on the volume of each item in the line. Ralph and I are continually weeding out items that move slowly, so that only the more popular items remain. However, our line keeps growing, because we always wind up adding more items than we drop. Ralph and the other salesmen are constantly proposing new items for which they have discovered a demand. To keep from hopelessly overburdening the plant, I have to see to it that we don't add too many new items. This often means I have to resist high pressure from the salesmen." A tabulation of items carried in the company's line during the past six years and the number of each sold during those years in shown in Exhibit 33–5.

"One segment of the market we try to emphasize," he continued, "is that composed of young married couples. We hope that the young wife who drops into the store during the week will find our furniture so appealing that she will bring her husband in on Saturday and convince him that they can fit it into their budget. We think almost every young couple wants one more piece of furniture, and our aim is to provide it. We can't possibly buy the kind of selling job that the young wife can do for us on her husband."

Production

Furniture-making operations were conducted in a single-story wooden plant located on a hill overlooking the nearby sawmill and commanding a broad view of the surrounding forest country. Lumber from the bolter saw was piled and stickered on kiln buggies and covered with tarpaulins until it went to the kiln. Full-length lumber from the sawmill was piled and stickered and carried by a forklift truck to the sawmill yard where the piles were placed on supports to keep the lumber off the ground. It was very important that the sticks (about one inch by two inches in cross section) placed between the layers of lumber to provide for air circulation be directly above those in lower layers and above the squared off logs used as supports for the pile, so that the weight would not cause bending. The ends of each board were coated to prevent too rapid drying at the ends and the production of end check. Partial air drying reduced the necessary time in the kiln. Sawmill and kiln operations are further described in Appendix 33–A.

When needed, lumber was moved from the sawmill yard to the kilns with a forklift truck and placed on kiln buggies. After kiln drying, which was performed in two steam-heated kilns on a cycle requiring 8 days for 1⅛-inch lumber and 18 days for all lumber thicker than 1⅛ inches, the lumber was kept in a section of the mill on kiln buggies for tempering. Tempering consisted of letting the lumber sit in the plant atmosphere for one to two weeks to permit the moisture content to become uniform throughout each piece of lumber. The wood then went to the cutoff and ripsaws and through the planer to become smooth, rectangular lumber cut to specific lengths. The cutoff and ripsaw operators were careful in trimming away defects to maximize the lengths of clear pieces of lumber. A long, although narrow, clear board was more valuable than a wider, but shorter piece, because several narrow pieces could always be glued to make a panel as wide as desired. The uniform lumber then went into a variety of different machines, where it was turned, sawed, bent, planed, shaped, grooved, and sanded into chair seats, tabletops, drawer fronts, legs, rungs, and other component furniture parts. These parts were assembled into furniture which was stained, sealed, lacquered, rubbed, waxed, and packed for shipment. A flow diagram of the Craftsburg production process appears in Exhibit 33–6.

Compared to the industry (Exhibits 33–1 and 33–4), Craftsburg was a relatively low-cost producer. Mr. Craig was not sure as to the exact quantitative importance of each source of savings. However, he had in the past computed the board footage of lumber going into each piece of furniture, and he had developed an approximate set of time standards. These standard times had been based upon those developed for the company during 1949 by an outside consultant. The consultant had estimated the production time required on the different pieces of furniture then made by Craftsburg, based upon his own experience and upon time studies he had performed at other plants. Mr. Craig had recently extended these estimates to form his own judgment of the time required to produce each item in the line as of 1959. As a check on these estimates, he had combined them with appropriate figures on usage of material and hourly labor costs and checked these against actual production costs. The results, he said, had been surprisingly close, differing only 1 percent to 5 percent depending on the year used.

Exhibit 33–5

CRAFTSBURG MANUFACTURING COMPANY (A)

Historic Sales per Unit in Line

Classification	Type	1954	1955	1956	1957	1958	1959
Chairs	CHA	1,615	1,308	982	197	22	—
	CHB	—	—	—	—	2,827	4,098
	CHD	1,612	1,317	3,057	3,346	2,963	4,139
	CHE	236	256	764	515	410	487
	CHH	640	289	144	—	—	—
	CHJ	—	—	—	4,183	4,463	4,605
	CHK	8,117	8,590	7,287	6,407	5,390	5,218
	CHL	1,593	5,653	8,369	9,211	10,223	11,816
	CHM	3,840	5,180	5,201	3,958	2,932	3,852
	CHN	248	10	—	—	—	—
	CHP	677	430	557	939	1,139	925
	CHR	348	257	219	35	8	—
	CHS	—	—	—	3,708	3,760	3,549
	CHT	1,410	1,375	1,253	1,326	1,243	1,514
	CHV	400	409	400	416	410	467
Total Pieces		20,736	25,074	28,233	34,241	35,790	40,380
Total Number of Types		12	12	11	12	13	11
Tables	TC	162	103				
	TD	1,723	1,833	1,551	1,250	1,298	1,070
	TF			422	403	317	104
	TG				286	554	605
	TH					779	987
	TI					305	560
	TJ					102	
	TJ2		292	866	667	727	600
	TJ3	44	94	6			
	TL	495	466	523	530	528	557
	TM	202	323	214	79	52	
	TN	290	601	758	615	491	567
	TR	1,185	1,990	2,130	1,558	1,539	1,346
	TV	196	217	208	373	256	410
Plastic laminates	TW				780	540	878
Plastic laminates	TW1				1,089	774	1,423
Plastic laminates	TW2						466
Plastic laminates	TW3				103	415	728
Total Pieces		4,297	5,919	6,678	7,733	8,677	10,301
Total Number of Types		8	9	9	12	15	14
Case goods	CAB						165
	CAC	443	573	713	764	755	1,024
	CAD	239	244	305	314	320	270
	CAL	190	213	324	330	421	454
	CAM	2					
	CAO	615	694	743	867	906	874
	CAP	624	486	644	726	686	806
	CAQ					130	
	CAS	268	336	370	478	396	607
	CAV	178	295	305	405	318	567
	CAW	103	101	136	150	163	252
Total Pieces		2,662	2,942	3,540	4,034	4,095	5,019
Total Number of Types		9	8	8	8	9	9

Exhibit 33–5—Continued

Classification	Type	1954	1955	1956	1957	1958	1959
Occasional tables	OTA	1,175	1,730	1,607	1,509	934	817
	OTB	3,350	4,569	4,935	5,151	4,265	3,235
	OTC	1,666	2,076	2,560	2,761	2,386	1,984
	OTC1	731	760	832	944	463	550
	OTD	267	235				
	OTF	198	116				
	OTH	873	795	959	1,085	868	619
	OTL	1,419	1,422	1,997	1,910	1,698	1,631
	OTM	960	931	1,314	1,115	1,108	953
	OTM2	841	640	816	1,117	1,086	879
	OTP	813	890	1,223	1,344	1,127	954
	OTU		264	789	1,089	1,001	746
	OTV			848	1,022	1,143	1,006
	OTW				571	416	246
Total Pieces		12,396	14,428	17,880	19,678	16,495	13,620
Total Types		11	12	11	12	12	12
Modern tables	MTA	626					
	MTB	770	10				
	MTC	956					
	MTD	116	42				
	MTE	157	37				
	MTF	87	28				
	MTN	132	53				
	MTO	35					
	MTP	93					
	MTQ	68					
		595					
Chain store furniture	CSA			778	622	538	
	CSB			1,296	895	486	
	CSC			415	414	92	
	CSD					2,883	1,746
	CSE					4,594	3,172
	CSF					2,365	989
Total Pieces		3,635	170	2,489	1,931	10,959	5,907
Total Types		11	5	3	3	6	3
Total Pieces of All Types		43,726	48,533	58,820	67,617	76,016	75,227
Total of All Types .		51	46	42	47	55	49

In going through other plants, he and the foremen believed they had been able to make close guesses on the total board feet and on total production times as contrasted with those at Craftsburg. They had concluded that most of Craftsburg's savings resulted from more economical use of lumber. In addition to effective use of lumber, the company also benefited from low lumber prices, realized in buying from the sawmill adjacent to the plant, which was also owned and operated at a profit by the Craigs.

Total production time per piece, they thought, was lower at Crafts-

Exhibit 33–6

CRAFTSBURG MANUFACTURING COMPANY (A)

FLOW OF PRODUCTION, AUGUST, 1959

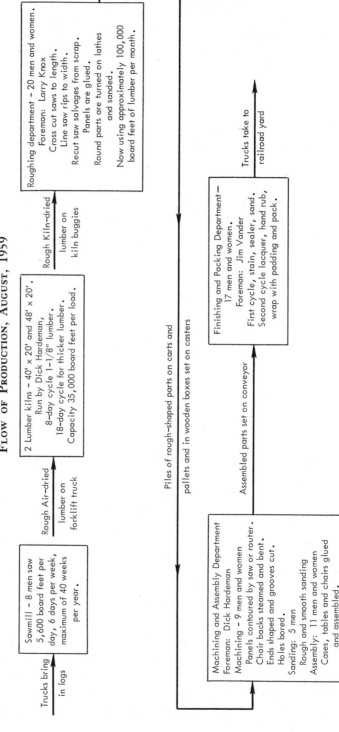

burg than at most other plants. Part of this saving was believed due to differences in the design of the furniture and the methods used for making it. Mr. Craig also thought the employees of Craftsburg tended to work somewhat harder and more efficiently than the average. "After you've been running a mill for a time, you get so you can tell by looking at a man whether he is working hard or not. When I saw a man loafing on the job, I used to point it out to the foremen and talk it over with them. With time and experience, the foremen got so they could spot and handle such things by themselves."

Finally, Mr. Craig believed his administrative and office expenses were significantly lower than those of the typical furniture company. Although there was no electrical or mechanical bookkeeping equipment other than a calculator, all clerical work was performed by one secretary, one clerk, and one bookkeeper. During the first year after taking charge, Mr. Craig had done all the bookkeeping himself at night after the plant had closed. Then, over a period of time, he had drawn in others from the plant and trained them in performing these functions. As of 1959, one man handled all incoming orders and accounts receivable; one woman typed orders, labels, and letters and did the filing; and a second woman made out the payroll, paid the bills, and kept the books. There had been no increase in the total number of supervisory and office personnel since 1953.

Management

Mr. Craig typically spent from three to four hours per day in the plant, mostly working out schedules and overseeing the activities of the shipping room. He liked to think that the plant ran by itself, which, in part, it did. The foremen handled customary problems themselves and did all the hiring and firing for their departments, but unusual problems, such as introduction of new techniques and new methods in the scheduling of parts were likely to be discussed with Alan Craig. He and the foremen worked constantly as a team, and all of them knew every man and woman in the plant. Mr. Craig frequently watched the furniture as it moved through the plant, often picking up parts to see that they were properly formed, planed, and sanded, and met other quality standards.

Until the past few months, Mr. Craig had held a meeting every two weeks with the foremen, to discuss problems, progress, and plans for the future, such as changes in methods, or purchases of new machinery. The meetings had been discontinued only because other demands had become so great on Alan Craig's time. He hoped he would be able to initiate them again in the near future.

Furniture parts [1] were manufactured in lots whose size depended on the composition of the order backlog. The parts passed through three departments in becoming completed furniture: first, the roughing department; second, the machining and assembly department; third, the finishing and packing department, as shown in Exhibit 33–6.

From the foremen of these departments, Mr. Craig received each week inventories of the number of pieces of each type of furniture in finished form, the number assembled but not yet finished, and the number in some stage of fabrication or assembly. With the number of pieces finished and ready for finishing in mind, he selected from the orders which had come in, starting with the oldest, those he could combine so as to ship the maximum number of full carloads. He then scheduled for finishing a sufficient number of units to complete such full carloads as were possible for the week. Freight rates were approximately 30 percent less for carload shipments. He estimated that 80 percent of the furniture was shipped in full cars. Next, he scheduled such partial carloads and truckloads as could be made up from the remaining pieces of furniture that were finished or could be finished during the week. This schedule of the minimum number of pieces to be finished during the week was posted in the finishing room.

From studying the remaining orders on hand, from his knowledge of the historic sales volume of each type in the line, and from the weekly in-process inventory, together with his frequent observations of the degrees of completion of different pieces in process, Mr. Craig then prepared a schedule of the number of each type of furniture to be assembled and the number of each type to be started from rough lumber during the coming week. Lot sizes were not standardized, but Mr. Craig never made them larger than 150 nor smaller than 75. He believed that if fewer than 75 were scheduled, the setup costs became excessive; while if more than 150 were started, the inventory thus created would become larger than the space available to contain it.

The schedule of pieces to be started was given to the foreman of the roughing department. Using standard parts lists, this foreman made another schedule which listed the number of each component part to be started into production in order to make up the number of furniture pieces called for on the schedule from Mr. Craig. For in-

---

[1] In this discussion, the word part is used to refer to a furniture component such as a top or a leg. The word piece refers to an assembled unit of furniture, such as a table or a chair.

stance, if Mr. Craig had scheduled 100 rocking chairs, the foreman would subdivide the requirement to 100 rocking chair seats, 100 backs, 200 rockers, 400 legs, and so on. Work would then begin on all the different types of parts needed in those chairs. A third list went to the foreman of the machining and assembly department, and told him how many pieces of each type were to be assembled during the week. To meet this schedule, he drew on parts produced by the roughing department, most of which had been produced the week before.

At the end of each week, Mr. Craig pulled together a number of small orders which had come in during the week and combined them so as to make one or two more truckloads in order to draw off as much additional work in process and finished inventory as possible. This usually required the rush production of a few pieces, which might be in various stages of completion. Consequently, the last few hours of the week were a very busy period.

Alan Craig alone had performed the basic scheduling function since taking over the company. However, in the near future he expected to teach this function to his son, Roy. After graduating from the local high school in 1951, Roy had attended Syracuse University, majoring in liberal arts, and had then spent two years in the navy as storekeeper on a large cruiser. During all his high school and summer vacations, Roy had worked in his father's plant, performing various machining and finishing operations.

On completion of his active military duty, Roy attended the Northwestern University Graduate School of Business Administration, where he received his M.B.A. Usually on Friday afternoon and often during the week, during graduate school, Roy visited the office of Craftsburg's Chicago representative, learning the selling points of furniture, how to merchandise it, and how to work with warehousemen and store buyers. Mr. Frantz took Roy with him on calls and spent a considerable amount of time explaining the selling end of the business, as he had with Roy's father. Roy had joined the company permanently after his graduation in the summer of 1959. At the start of 1960, he was working in the office, handling purchasing and minor customer complaints. He helped his father make up monthly financial statements, which Alan Craig prepared in longhand from the complete inventory taken monthly by the foremen and from the trial balance of the bookkeeper. Roy also spent several days per month on the road, visiting nearby Craftsburg customers.

As indicated previously, Alan Craig worked closely with the three foremen in running the plant. These were three of the same men he had picked on taking over and with whom he had studied the operations of other plants. Their job was that of seeing to it that people in the plant were kept busy and that Mr. Craig's schedules were met. In doing so, it was vital that each of them have a very clear picture of the requirements of the overall schedule, the needs of the other departments, and the number and location of all pieces in his own department throughout the day. Raw material started in the roughing department, proceeded to the machining and assembly department, and was completed and packed in the finishing and shipping department as indicated on the flow diagram, Exhibit 33–6. Ideally, each department was expected to be one week ahead of the next in production, but, in practice, the schedules were usually shorter.

Larry Knox ran the roughing department, which cut the lumber to length, fitted and glued the panels to be used in seats and case goods, and performed the turning operations. From the number of different pieces of each type ordered into production by Mr. Craig, Mr. Knox made his own weekly schedule of parts to be started and panels to be glued. Then his job became mainly one of seeing that sufficient rough lumber was brought in, telling the swing saw operator what lengths to cut, observing the flow of parts, and making sure that parts moved from one station to the next as needed. He was also training another man in the ways of running the department, so that if he was not able to be present his department would not be an additional burden on Mr. Craig and the other foremen. Until recently, he had been the only man in the plant familiar with running the kiln, a process which had a few months previously been taken over by the foreman of the machining and assembly department after he had learned the procedure from Mr. Knox.

From the roughing department, the lumber moved to the machining and assembly department, where it was further shaped, sanded, and assembled into furniture ready for finishing. This department was under the supervision of a second foreman, Dick Hardeman. Dick Hardeman ran his department so as to meet the schedule of parts to be assembled, which had been prepared for him by Alan Craig. His job consisted mainly of seeing that parts moved from one machine to another as they completed each stage of machining, and that the people of the department were never left without work to be performed.

The different types of furniture, with their correspondingly different shapes of component parts to be machined, required that setups frequently be changed on the various machines of the machining department. Dick Hardeman, who was also skilled in making jigs and fixtures, scheduled the changes of fixtures and, with the aid of one man who devoted himself exclusively to setups, made the changes. On his own initiative, Dick Hardeman had also undertaken to learn the kiln-drying process, and had asked Larry Knox to teach him how to run the kiln. Tending the kiln required careful periodic checks of moisture content in the wood being dried, and also periodic adjustments of the kiln controls. To make these adjustments, Dick Hardeman often had to visit the plant late at night and on weekends.

Jim Vander, the third foreman, ran the finishing department. Each day, he scheduled assembled furniture onto the finishing conveyor in such a way as to meet the required shipments. He also shifted the personnel of the department to accomplish the required packing. The finishing conveyor made two complete circuits with each piece of furniture to complete the finishing cycle. Furniture was covered with stain and set on pallets of the moving line from which fully finished furniture had just been removed. The stain dried as the conveyor moved toward a spray booth. In this booth, a coat of sealer was applied to form a base for lacquer. Over the remaining length of conveyor, the sealer dried and was sanded ready for lacquering. Then it began a second trip around the conveyor, during which lacquer was applied, allowed to dry, hand rubbed, and then unloaded as another load of furniture was put on.

Thus, the loading and unloading process was performed on every other circuit, each of which took from four to five hours. In between loads, the loading crew of three men and the staining crew of six were shifted by Mr. Vander to other jobs in the department, such as forming and stapling shipping containers, packing and loading furniture onto trucks, and finishing table legs, which were not finished on the conveyor. In the shipping room, Jim Vander spent a large proportion of his time working out schedules with Alan Craig. He also discussed the finishing and shipping schedules with the other foremen.

All the foremen were roughly the same age. Larry Knox was forty-two, Dick Hardeman was forty-one, and Jim Vander was forty-three. All had attended and graduated from the same local high school, and all had been discharged from the army within the same year.

Consideration of Expansion

As indicated previously, the company discovered in August, 1959, that an unoccupied building at Stow which appeared to be suitable for a second plant could be bought for $25,000. The company had been considering since 1958 the possibility of expansion to accommodate continued sales growth. The availability of this building at Stow had brought the question to a focus.

Craftsburg had been growing as a result of increasing demand for the company's products. Mr. Craig commented, "We have been growing at 5 to 10 percent per year, but it hasn't been our aim to become a big company. In fact, I was fairly happy with where we were two years ago. Of course, you have to consider the men of particular ability in your company. Unless you keep providing them with opportunities for growth, they may become dissatisfied."

The company growth which had been taking place steadily since 1948 had gradually increased the utilization of the company's facilities, until by 1960 Mr. Craig believed that the existing facilities were being used to capacity. During this period, sales had expanded from $185,790 to $1,035,911, the number of employees had grown from 40 to 100, and the manufacturing area in the existing plant had increased from 33,875 square feet to 45,125 square feet. As production had grown and new machinery had been added to increase capacity, the floor space had become more crowded, both as a result of space requirements of the new machinery and as a result of the larger volume of work-in-process inventory which had to be stacked and moved among the machines. The aisles through which parts were moved had become progressively narrower, and it appeared that any further crowding to permit increased output would only result in lower plant efficiency and, perhaps, lower productivity.

To meet the existing demand in 1959, the plant had been operating at full capacity, and even then it sometimes had difficulty in making deliveries. Mr. Craig commented: "About eight months ago, we began getting so many orders that we couldn't handle them all, and some of our customers were beginning to complain because we couldn't fill their orders on time. So we laid off all our salesmen south of the Mason-Dixon line. That cut off about $225,000 worth of sales per year, and we were able to fill orders on time again."

Mr. Craig's time also was in great demand. As discussed above, he spent three to four hours of each day in the plant, making out schedules and dealing with problems of production and shipping. The remainder of his day was generally spent in the company office, talking on the telephone with salesmen or customers, and handling correspondence, which he preferred to write out in longhand. The remainder of his time, often into the evening hours, was spent in analyzing figures on the company and the industry, planning budgets, and dealing with the longer-range problems of the company. He estimated that he also spent a total of approximately five weeks per year traveling to visit representatives and customers and to study displays at furniture stores and shows.

"We have been running this company by ear, and it has kept us awfully busy," he commented. "I don't have the time to work with the foremen as much as I used to. I used to spend an hour or so each day down at the sawmill, and now I almost never get down there. I simply can't spend as much time in the plant as I once did. I had thought that perhaps one thing that might help would be to ask Professor Hazelton, the labor relations expert whom my son Roy met at the Small Business Conference, to come up and spend a day or so here on a professional basis. Roy said Mr. Hazelton had a great deal of experience in industry and seemed to be the kind of man who would understand our operation. We don't want to lose the close contact we have always had with everybody in the plant.

"Perhaps Professor Hazelton could give us answers to a number of questions Roy has raised. What should we do if a union one day walked in with petitions signed by our employees? Should we start keeping some records other than those required for tax purposes on our employees? Should we initiate a suggestion system with rewards of money for good ideas submitted by the employees? Another thing I thought might free some of my time by making it easier for me to keep track of how well the plant is doing would be to set up some kind of a cost system. I think all we need is something that will show trends. We already have records on total payroll, total output, and recovery rates on lumber.

"We don't need standard costs for pricing, because we simply set our prices at the same level as those of our competitors. But we could use them to sense trends in our production operations. If we had standard costs for each type of furniture as it passed through each department of the plant, we could multiply these standard costs by the unit output of each department each month to detect trends of cost per piece for each department. My hope is that this would make it easier for me to determine how well we were doing."

Mr. Craig believed that his many activities in managing the company and personally overseeing operations were necessary in order to preserve his feel for what was going on. But he also recognized that these activities kept him so busy that it was questionable whether he could undertake the additional load of managing the installation, organization, and operation of additional facilities.

Alternatives

Mr. Craig could see some advantages in the possibility of extending the eixsting plant, rather than buying the Stow plant which was 21 miles away. On available land adjacent to the present plant an extension could be built. It would be possible, he thought, to extend the plant step by step, building only the area needed, rather than buying space all at once as in the Stow building. The estimated cost of such additional new construction was aproximately $8 per square foot. Also, he believed there would be advantage in retaining the entire facilities at one location so as to minimize the inconvenience and expence of transportation and communication between plants.

A major disadvantage of the Stow plant, in Mr. Craig's opinion, was its location. It was situated between a hill and a river, in a place where there would be very little room for expansion beyond the existing building, in case further expansion should appear desirable at a later date. Also, the proximity of the river led him to wonder whether the high humidity, which caused fogs and low mists along the river, would adversely affect the furniture produced or stored in the building and cause it to warp or crack. Experts that Mr. Craig had consulted on the subject were divided in their opinions. The top three floors of the plant were well above the high-water mark of the river, but the basement was only slightly above it and was usually quite damp. During a previous flood, the basement had become filled with water.

On the other hand, he saw a disadvantage in extending the existing plant in that he expected there would inevitably be some interruption of operations. He questioned whether the spirit of the plant could be maintained if the number of employees increased much over 100. In the event of a fire, he thought the company would be more vulnerable to business interruption and consequent loss of customers with only one plant.

Another problem of expanding at the present location would be that of obtaining men. There was currently no unemployment in the town of Craftsburg, and Mr. Craig estimated that men and women would have to be drawn from other towns which were from 12 to 20 miles away. Snow was deep in the wintertime. Should the Stow plant be used, there would be no problem of obtaining people in that town, but in either case there would be a need for training. He preferred to hire a person who had never done woodworking and teach him the way Craftsburg wanted it done, rather than hire a man who thought he knew how already.

There was also question as to which, if any, products should be added. The simplest expansion alternative would be simply to make a greater quantity of the existing dining room line. However, Mr. Frantz and the other five Craftsburg salesmen advocated that the company manufacture bedroom and living room furniture to complement the existing dining room line in colonial style. They informed Mr. Craig that several stores had customers who wanted matching sets for other rooms to go with their Craftsburg dining room pieces. The salesmen had concluded that the established Craftsburg name would have a carry-over value in selling other lines. Mr. Craig believed the company name was gaining in significance, but in view of the small amount of Craftsburg advertising, he wondered whether it would have a selling power great enough for new lines.

Should a new line be added, Mr. Craig believed it would be better to add bedroom furniture rather than living room furniture, because a living room group would pose additional production and styling problems in upholstering with which Craftsburg was not familiar. Bedroom furniture appeared to offer particular advantages insofar as it included a larger proportion of case goods than did dining room or living room furniture. Case goods included furniture characterized by a case, or boxlike structure, which might contain cupboards or drawers, as did bedroom dressers. Case goods required more internal framework which did not show and therefore could use more of the discolored but structurally sound wood in framework parts. This wood couldn't be used in panels and drawer fronts. The biggest cost in most case goods was lumber, which accounted for 35 to 40 percent of the cost. Mr. Craig estimated that 10 to 12 percent of the wood used in case goods could be discolored or contain small knots without affecting either strength or appearance.

The Stow plant did, he thought, offer great flexibility in that it would be equally suitable for any type of furniture. Also, whether bedroom, living room, or simply more dining room furniture were to be produced with the additional capacity, Mr. Craig estimated that the production equipment required would cost approximately the same. He expected it might take from six to eight months to ready the plant for production. His estimates of investments required for machinery and other facilities including the building were approximately as follows:

Investment Required	Annual Sales
$175,000	$240,000
200,000	400,000
250,000	700,000

He considered it very important that no new line should be produced which might hurt the quality reputation of Craftsburg. Therefore, he believed that any new production would have to be supervised with exceptional care, and that it would be desirable, insofar as possible, to plan against such production problems as would be likely to arise.

Should the decision to expand be made, Mr. Craig wondered who should be offered the opportunity of taking charge of the expanded portion. He also wondered when and how he should approach the man with this opportunity, considering the effect of the decision on the others in the company and on the man himself, who would have to move his home and family to Stow.

If the second plant were bought, should it be incorporated separately, or should it remain a department of the main company? If incorporated separately, how should the stock be owned? Should other members of the management team be permitted to participate in the ownership? Should other employees? These, Mr. Craig believed, were all decisions which depended on the basic decision of whether to expand, and if so, where?

He, himself, had no desire for Craftsburg to become one of the big companies in the industry. He definitely wanted it to be one of the very best. But he didn't think he would be able to stand still. As he summed it up: "There's nothing quite so hard for me as sitting back and not doing anything new in the world. In other words, if I don't do this, I'll have to think of something else."

APPENDIX 33–A
CRAFTSBURG MANUFACTURING COMPANY
Saw Mill Operations

The plant was on a hillside commanding a view of hills and valleys almost entirely covered with forests, including spruce, fir, and white pine, but principally mixed northern hardwoods, including yellow birch and maple. The area north to the St. Lawrence River and for 30 miles east, west, and south, from which the material for Craftsburg furniture would naturally come, was primarily forest land, with relatively little farming. This land will produce in perpetuity many times more in yellow birch and maple than the Craftsburg Company could ever use. It was a characteristic of the area that prior logging practices had taken many of the best trees. Very good logs remained, but when an area was being cut, loggers could bring out at relatively low incremental cost logs which would not yield full-length (12–18 foot) lumber of the higher grades under the grading system of the National Hardwood Lumber Association.

It is a characteristic of lumber that substantially perfect pieces can be cut from boards that will not grade high over a length of 10–18 feet. For instance, it would be impossible to tell by inspecting a 24- by 5-inch cutting whether it came from a board graded as No. 2 Common, No. 1 Common, Select, or F and S (first and seconds, treated as a single top grade). These grades are based on the extent of clear cuttings in a board.

Some 85 percent of the cuts used in furniture are 48 inches or less in length, with a large volume in the range 18–36 inches. The length of cuts needed for different types of furniture can be observed by measuring cuts in pieces of those types, making the measurement parallel to the grain. In utilizing lumber, Craftsburg took advantage of the skills which Alan and Edgar Craig had learned in their youth, together with extensions of those skills based on current experience. The furniture was designed so that clear wood too short for one cutting could be used for another cutting not over 1–4 inches shorter.

In the early years of the Craig management there was developed a method of cutting for length before sawing which is found very seldom elsewhere in the furniture industry. The company bought some bolts—logs under 5 feet in length—and developed others from crooked logs or those otherwise unfit for sawing on a long log mill. The bolts were sawed on a bolter mill, a saw especially adapted to this purpose. Most of the bolts were cut 50, 38, or 32 inches, although other lengths up to 5 feet could be cut if needed. Lumber from a 50-inch bolt was cut rough at the swing saw to 48 or 24 inches and finished at 46 or 23 inches. The 38-inch bolts were finished at 34 or 17 inches and the 32-inch at 29 inches. These lengths covered about 80 percent of the usage, with little end waste.

Logs with sound wood, but not suitable for full-length sawing, were bought at relatively low prices. A man with a light winch and a chain saw dragged a log out of the pile and cut out the clear sections between imperfections. For instance, a log from a forked tree with one fork cut off might show 87 inches clear below the fork with a diameter of 18 inches, and 44 inches clear at a diameter of 14 inches above the fork, but at an angle from the butt. It would be practically useless on a full-length sawmill. Or a log clear throughout its length, 18 inches in diameter under the bark at the small end, and 16 feet long, might have a regular bow or curve with the midway point from end to end on the inside face of the log 16 inches from a straight line drawn from end to end. This log likewise would be almost useless if sawed for long lumber. If cut into 4-foot bolts, the midway point in each bolt would be less than an inch from a straight line. Cutting a crooked log into the lengths used practically eliminated all crook.

After being squared off by slabbing to give one flat face, a bolt was turned with that face down on a light carriage, the next face was slabbed, and then lumber of the thickness desired was sawed by the operator, using guides and sets to move the bolt toward the saw and give the thickness desired. After the lumber on this face had been sawed, the bolt was rotated 90 or 180 degrees, and those faces were sawed to develop the best lumber from the outside of the bolt, leaving a core possibly 8 inches square, which was then sawed through and through without turning. Most of the lumber used was $1\frac{1}{8}$ inches thick, but if the bolt were adapted to that use, the operator could develop thicker lumber needed for chair seats, table legs, etc.

Immediately after sawing, the lumber was edged by sawing to give the widest square-edged board. However, a board from a 50-inch bolt with clear wood 4 inches wide at one end and 8 inches at the other was edged parallel to the bark, since this would give more recovery if finished as two 23-inch pieces. It was then piled on kiln buggies—light steel frames with double flange wheels, on which loads of lumber could be moved into temporary storage and then into the kilns on steel rails. The lumber was piled with stickers, 1 by 1½ inches or 1 by 2 inches, between the courses to provide for air circulation when in the kiln. If stored prior to going to the kiln, the loads were protected by tarpaulins to prevent warping and end checking. The kiln buggies were on rails on a platform which could be raised or lowered by a hydraulic cylinder similar to that used to raise cars in a garage, so the top of the load, as it was built up, could be kept at a convenient height. With one man in the yard, one bolter saw operator, an off-bearer taking lumber from the saw and edging it, and one man piling, the production was 3,000 board feet per day.

About 1955, paper companies began to buy hardwood pulpwood in the Craftsburg area. This led to a change in bolter operation. Loggers and pulpwood cutters tended to make logs not suitable for sawing into full length lumber into pulpwood. In 1959, the price per cord of hardwood pulpwood (83 cubic feet solid) at the roadside was $14. The fact that pulpwood had to be cut to 4-foot lengths made it impossible to recover all high-grade bolts for lumber; some high-grade sections were cut in two to get the 4 feet. A log not suited for full-length lumber might have a clear butt section of 6 feet, 2 feet of serious defect, and a clear section of 42 inches.

The company met this situation by offering to buy from loggers and pulpwood cutters yellow birch and hard maple bolts above a minimum diameter, in a range of lengths, and which met established specifications as to quality. The price in the fall of 1959 averaged $30 per M board feet, f.o.b. the Craftsburg Mill. One thousand board feet, log measure, equals approximately 1.7 cords. Technically, 1,000 board feet is nearly equal to 1 cord (1,000 sq. ft. 1 inch thick = 1,000/12 cu. ft. = 83.33 cu. ft.), but log measure is based on the volume of logs necessary to produce 1,000 board feet of lumber, and allows for the fact that hardwood is typically sawed 1⅛ inches, with a corresponding allowance for thicker stock, and allows also for the volume of solid wood in sawdust, slabs, and edgings. The price paid for high quality bolts made it advantageous for cutters to develop as many high-grade bolts as possible for sale to the company.

Beginning in 1955, the capacity of the bolter saw at approximately 3,000 board feet per 8-hour shift was no longer sufficient to supply the requirements of the mill. Some lumber was bought, but in 1956 the company established its own saw mill for 10- to 18-foot logs, in part because lumber could be obtained more cheaply by buying logs and doing its own sawing, and in part because it could saw lumber the way it wanted it, one factor being greater accuracy. Some lumber was sold at first, but in the fall of 1959 the entire production of the long log sawmill—approximately 7,600 board feet per day—as well as that of the bolter operation was used in the mill.

The lumber from the long log sawmill was piled, with stickers, at the sawmill, and was transported to the yard and placed on bunkers by a forklift truck, as described in the case. Care was taken to have the stickers in a vertical line, and directly above the bunkers, so that the lumber would not be bent by the weight of the pile. Also, ends were coated to prevent end checks from too rapid drying, and low-grade lumber was piled on top to prevent warping from too rapid drying in the sun. The piles of full-length lumber were carried to the kiln track and placed on kiln buggies for final drying in the kilns, since moisture content could be controlled and seasoning degrade could be minimized with final drying in the kiln.

It was the policy of the company to buy "woods run" logs, accepting many logs too crooked for use as full-length saw logs. In 1959, yellow birch veneer logs were selling for about $110 per M board feet at the roadside. Select maple logs were about $75 roadside. Loading and trucking costs to the point of use ran $15–$25. The company was buying yellow birch logs at $65 and maple at $65–$70 f.o.b. their mill.

Kiln Drying Lumber

The seasoning of lumber is a complex process. The moisture content of lumber from fresh logs, expressed as a percentage of the dry weight, may be over 100 percent. Reduction of the moisture content to approximately 26 percent—the fiber saturation point—involves little, if any, shrinkage. With reduction of the moisture content below this point, wood shrinks, the shrinkage in what would have been a circumferential direction in the log, parallel to the growth rings, being greater than radial shrinkage, perpendicular to the growth rings. The stress pattern during drying in pieces of lumber of the same dimensions thus will differ, depending on the direction of growth rings as shown in a cross section.

Loss from seasoning defects in lumber can be greatly reduced or eliminated if drying below the fiber saturation point is done in a kiln with complete instruments for control of the drying cycle, and if the operation of the kiln is in accordance with the methods best adapted to the lumber concerned. The Madison Laboratory of the U.S. Forest Service has devoted extensive research to the development of detailed schedules broadly recognized as standards in kiln operation. The objective in kiln operation is to reduce the moisture content to that desired in production, typically 5–8 percent; to do so while keeping the internal stresses within the elastic limits of the wood; to have the results as uniform as possible; and to keep the time for each load in the kiln at a minimum.

The Craftsburg Company had two kilns—one built in 1943 and another, somewhat larger, built in 1950. Both were fully instrumented, including instruments for automatic control of humidity and temperature in accordance with schedules set in advance for the entire drying cycle. Each kiln consisted of a masonry structure with doors at one end and rails on which loaded kiln buggies could be moved into the kiln and from the kiln to the tempering area, the axis of the lumber being lengthwise and the sticks separating the layers crosswise. With baffles on top of the loads and a clear space near each side wall, fans circulated air between the layers in the loads, and were reversed automatically at established intervals to reverse the air flow.

The time required in the kiln for each load, or the cycle, depended on the moisture content of the wood at the beginning, and was markedly affected by the thickness, being, in the practice of this company, 8 to 12 days for lumber 1 inch thick, 12 to 16 days for lumber 2 inches thick, and 16 to 20 days for bedpost stock 3 inches square. The cycle began with high humidity to prevent the outside of the boards from drying more rapidly than the inside to an extent which would cause too much tension from shrinkage on the outside and incipient or actual surface cracks. Heat was used to increase the rate of movement of moisture from the inside to the outside. As the moisture content of the lumber decreased, humidity was lowered until, at the end of the cycle, the humidity of the air was that required to balance a moisture content of 5–8 percent in the wood.

Seasoning defects may cause a lumber loss as high as 10 percent or even considerably more. These defects include end cracks, surface cracks, and warping, either in the board or after sawing. Case hardening is one cause of warping. It occurs when humidity is too low during the first part of the cycle so that the outside of a board is stretched and becomes set, but not stretched enough to cause surface checks. Then, when the entire board is at 5–8 percent, the outside is under compression. If such a board is ripped, or one surface is planed more than the opposite surface, it will warp or twist, either during manufacture or during later use.

Honeycombing is somewhat similar to case hardening. It is especially likely to appear in thick stock such as bedposts. With the outside under compression, the tension in the inside wood may become sufficient to cause internal cracks. When a bedpost, for example, is machined to its eventual shape, these open cracks may become part of the surface and be especially apparent when the finish is applied.

Lumber sawed at 1⅛ inches shrinks to about 1 inch after seasoning. This lumber typically is 25/32 inch thick when assembled, leaving only 7/32 inch for planing and sanding. If rough spots after planing are to be avoided, the limits on warping in a 4-foot cut are very small. In addition to lumber losses of 10 percent or considerably more, manufacturing losses can occur as a result of seasoning defects. For instance, after finishing, a tabletop may show surface cracks not apparent in the bare wood. With well-built kilns, instruments, and controls now available, and an operator competent in applying methods based on research and experience, these losses can be kept at a minimum.

Air drying in a yard works fairly well down to the fiber saturation point of 26 percent, but below that conditions cannot be controlled well enough to avoid excessive internal stresses. While good air drying is better than poor kiln operation, a competently operated kiln is, in substance, essential in producing furniture built to serve the grandchildren of the original purchasers.

The moisture content of furniture, with its coating of sealer and finish, in use in a house heated in the winter, tends to vary from 5–12 percent, but with the range somewhat dependent on climate. The makers of high-grade furniture manufacture at the lower end of this scale, about 5–8 percent, apparently because pressures involved in a piece going to 12 percent are less dangerous to sound construction than cracks which might open if furniture manufactured at 12 percent went to 5 percent in use.

The Craftsburg Company had excess kiln capacity and used kiln cycles somewhat longer than were required according to published schedules. Mr. Craig believed that longer cycles and a process of steaming and redrying to relieve stresses reduced losses from seasoning and added to the quality of the furniture when assembled. The lumber was kept in a tempering space, on kiln buggies, for several days after removal from the kilns to insure uniformity of moisture content throughout the loads.

Small Business Management
NOTES AND READINGS

1. THE RELATIVE POSITION OF SMALL ENTERPRISES IN THE AMERICAN ECONOMY*

This paper is intended to provide an understanding of the place of small enterprises in the American economy. It presents certain published data and the findings from various research studies which indicate the share of economic activity accounted for by these firms, as well as their profitability relative to larger companies.

Definitions

No effort is made here to utilize a single definition of a *small* enterprise. Various definitions have been used by government agencies and writers in the field, some based upon number of personnel, some based upon assets, and some based upon other qualifications. Naturally, the material presented in this paper must reflect the definitions used by those authors who conducted the research studies and compiled the data upon which the paper is based.

In this note, companies are arranged in categories according to number of personnel or total assets. When number of personnel is used, data are presented for all manufacturing companies, for companies with fewer than 500 employees, and for companies with fewer than 100 employees. When total assets are used as a criterion of size, data are presented for various asset size categories, such as for companies with assets of less than $1 million, with assets of $1 million to $5 million, and so on. The exact categories used depend on the data available and the author's judgment of the usefulness of various categories.

In the tables, when the term corporation is used the data relate to incorporated firms. When the terms business, firm, or company are used in the table, the data are not limited to corporations.

Limitations of the Data

In order to keep this note within manageable size, it is necessary to omit much material. For instance, very little is presented here about

---

489

the relative position of small firms in certain segments of the economy—such as retailing or construction. The data selected relate primarily to "small business as a whole" or to small manufacturing firms. In regard to research studies, only a few of the more significant or recent are summarized.[1]

Much of the data presented here is not so complete or so recent as might be desired. It is unfortunate that some of the most significant research studies in this area were conducted a number of years ago. In addition, certain of the statistics, gathered by government agencies, have been compiled for some years but not for others.

Relative Position of Industry Sectors

The tables below present data on the employment accounted for by industry sector and on the number of operating businesses by industry sector. Although there were changes reported during these periods, one can also note considerable stability in the relative position of these industry groups.

Position of Small Manufacturing Companies

In keeping with the area of concentration of this book, particular attention is devoted to the position of small manufacturing firms.

Three different measures of the relative position of small manufacturing companies are presented in this section. The position of these firms relative to all manufacturing firms is considered in regard to number of companies, employment provided, and total assets. The relative profitability of small manufacturing firms is considered later in the paper.

From the following tables it can be seen that a very high percentage of all manufacturing companies are small. Manufacturing firms with fewer than 50 employees or with fewer than 100 employees accounted for approximately 40 and 20 percent respectively of all manufacturing employment. Table 1–5 indicates that manufacturing firms with assets of less than $1 million accounted for approximately 9 percent of all assets held by manufacturing companies. Since the basis of

---

[1] Richard C. Osborn, *Effects of Corporate Size on Efficiency and Profitability* (University of Illinois Bulletin, Vol. 48, No. 7) (University of Illinois, Urbana, August, 1950), summarizes much of the research previously done in this area. A. D. H. Kaplan, *Small Business: Its Place and Problems* (New York: McGraw-Hill Book Co., Inc., 1948), also presents extensive data relating to these topics.

Table 1–1

Number of Full-time Equivalent Employees by Industry Sector

Year	All* Industries	Manufacturing Companies	Percentage of Total	Retail† Companies	Percentage of Total	Service Companies	Percentage of Total
1957 .	56,734	16,869	29.7%	7,570	13.3%	7,166	12.6%
1959 .	56,707	16,245	28.6%	7,795	13.7%	7,577	13.4%
1961 .	57,575	15,878	27.6%	8,013	13.9%	7,999	13.9%
1963 .	60,141	16,585	27.6%	8,454	14.1%	8,524	14.2%

Thousands of employees.

* Including government and government enterprises.
† Including automobile services.

Source: *Survey of Current Business*, July, 1960, for 1957; and July, 1964, for 1959–63.

Table 1–2

Number of Operating Businesses; Number of Manufacturing, Retail, and Service Companies

Year	Total Operating Businesses	Manu-facturing Companies	Percentage of Total	Retail Companies	Percentage of Total	Service Companies	Percentage of Total
1935 ..	3,065	206	6.7%	1404	45.8%	700	22.8%
1937 ..	3,215	215	6.7%	1490	46.3%	719	22.4%
1939 ..	3,306	223	6.7%	1559	47.2%	702	21.2%
1941 ..	3,364	235	7.0%	1590	47.3%	706	21.0%
1943 ..	3,045	239	7.8%	1400	46.0%	653	21.5%
1945 ..	3,258	263	8.1%	1456	44.7%	706	21.7%
1947 ..	3,879	331	8.5%	1673	43.1%	831	21.4%
1949 ..	3,965	312	7.9%	1693	42.7%	853	21.5%
1951 ..	4,067	323	7.9%	1672	41.1%	858	21.1%
1953 ..	4,188	331	7.9%	1859	44.4%	742	17.7%
1955 ..	4,287	326	7.6%	1875	43.7%	773	18.1%
1957 ..	4,471	332	7.4%	1926	43.1%	810	18.1%
1959 ..	4,583	323	7.0%	1977	43.1%	848	18.5%
1961 ..	4,713	322	6.8%	2011	42.7%	895	19.0%
1963p ..	4,797	313	6.5%	2032	43.4%	942	19.6%

Thousands of companies.
p Preliminary.

Source: Data for 1935–49 were obtained from A. Grimshaw, *Problems of the Independent Businessman* (New York: McGraw-Hill Book Co., Inc., 1955), p. 388. The source was reported to be *Survey of Current Business*.

Survey of Current Business, May, 1959, for 1951–57; and June, 1963, for 1959–63.

Table 1–3

NUMBER OF SMALL MANUFACTURING FIRMS COMPARED TO ALL MANUFACTURING FIRMS

Year	All Companies	Fewer than 500 Employees	Fewer than 100 Employees
1945	253.1—100%	249.2—98.5%	234.6—92.7%
1946	264.0—100%	260.5—98.7%	245.3—92.9%
1948	315.4—100%	311.6—98.8%	296.3—94.1%
1949	322.5—100%	319.1—99.0%	304.7—94.5%
1951	322.8—100%	318.9—98.8%	302.7—93.8%
1956	327.4—100%	323.7—98.9%	307.5—93.9%

Thousands of companies.

SOURCE: B. C. Churchill, "Size Characteristics of the Business Population," *Survey of Current Business,* May, 1954, for 1945–51; B. C. Churchill, "Size of Business Firms," *Survey of Current Business,* September, 1959, for 1956 data.

Table 1–4

PAID EMPLOYMENT FOR ALL MANUFACTURING FIRMS AND SMALL MANUFACTURING FIRMS

Year	All Companies	Fewer than 500 Employees	Fewer than 100 Employees
1945	16,922—100%	6,192—36.6%	3,112—18.4%
1946	14,663—100%	6,486—44.2%	3,339—22.8%
1948	15,864—100%	6,579—41.5%	3,432—21.6%
1949	14,950—100%	6,324—42.3%	3,394—22.7%
1951	16,820—100%	6,897—41.0%	3,592—21.4%
1956	17,661—100%	6,999—39.6%	3,696—20.9%

Thousands of employees.
Data are as of mid-March, each year.

SOURCE: *Ibid.*

Table 1–5

TOTAL ASSETS FOR ALL MANUFACTURING CORPORATIONS AND SMALL MANUFACTURING CORPORATIONS

Year	All Companies	Assets Less than $1 Million	Assets Less than $250,000
1940	60.5—100%	9.1—15.0%	3.7—6.1%
1945	91.0—100%	10.5—11.5%	3.7—4.1%
1951	160.9—100%	16.4—10.2%	5.9—3.7%
1953	176.8—100%	16.5—9.3%	6.1—3.5%
1955–56	201.4—100%	18.8—9.3%	6.5—3.2%
1957–58	224.9—100%	19.6—8.7%	7.0—3.1%
1959–60	252.1—100%	23.4—9.3%	8.0—3.2%
1960–61	262.3—100%	24.2—9.2%	8.6—3.3%

Billions of dollars.

SOURCE: *Statistics of Income, Corporation Income Tax Returns* (Washington, D.C.: U.S. Government Printing Office), as reported for the respective years.

classification in Table 1–5 is assets rather than number of employees, comparison between Table 1–5 and the other tables is impossible.

Examination of the data presented here for trends in the relative position of small manufacturing firms during the period covered suggests several conclusions:

1. The growth in the total number of manufacturing firms took place chiefly among the firms with fewer than 100 employees, with much of this growth concentrated in the years immediately after World War II.
2. Of total assets held by manufacturing firms, the percentage accounted for by smaller firms has declined, with the sharpest decline taking place during World War II.
3. The trends in regard to relative employment accounted for are not clear-cut. Firms with more than 500 employees lost a substantial number of employees from 1945 to 1946, probably associated with the readjustments to a peacetime economy. Thereafter, these large firms increased their share of total employment relative to the small firms.

From these data it appears that the relative position of small manufacturing firms has not changed dramatically during the period studied. This important conclusion is consistent with other studies which examined the relative position of small firms over longer periods.

One study of trends in the importance of small business (not limited to manufacturing firms) concluded: "All the economic indicators which measure the overall position of small business have shown remarkable stability throughout the past half century." [2] Another study which examined trends in the position of unincorporated business of all types commented: "It appears that for the most part small (unincorporated) business has managed, in overall measurements, to maintain its relative position in the economy." [3]

Contrasts among Industries

However, in individual industries the relative position of small companies has sometimes changed dramatically in fairly short periods. A number of studies of concentration in various industries have been conducted. The table below presents excerpts from one study in re-

---

[2] J. W. Markham, "Trends in the Relative Importance of Small Business," *Financing Small Business* (Federal Reserve System) (Washington, D.C.: U.S. Government Printing Office, 1958), p. 215.

[3] E. C. McKean, *The Persistence of Small Business* (Kalamazoo, Mich.: W. E. Upjohn Institute for Community Research, 1958), p. 45.

gard to changes in concentration for four particular industries in which the changes were most marked. Considerable variation among industries can be observed.

Table 1–6

CONCENTRATION IN FOUR SELECTED INDUSTRIES

Industry	Number of Firms		Percentage of Value of Shipments by Four Largest Firms	
	1947	1954	1947	1954
Fabricated metal products	430	1,017	31%	18%
Veneer mills	136	252	20	9
Mechanical stokers	46	25	55	78
Flour mixes	115	123	41	73

SOURCE: *Concentration in American Industry* (Report of the Subcommittee on Antitrust and Monopoly to the Committee on the Judiciary, U.S. Senate, 85th Congress, First Session) (Washington, D.C.: U.S. Government Printing Office, 1957), Table 42.

Discontinuances and Failures

The population of small manufacturing firms is dynamic, with each year seeing new firms being established, some firms being discontinued, and some small firms growing into the medium-size category. During 1953, as an example, 26,400 manufacturing firms were established and 31,500 manufacturing companies discontinued.

The "discontinuance statistics" receive prominent publicity and are often thought of as "failures." They are pointed to as an indication of the "plight of small firms." However, such conclusions may be misleading to those who might be considering starting a small firm or granting credit to one.

Since 331,000 such companies were in existence at the beginning of the year, this means that almost 9 percent of all manufacturing companies existing or established during the year were no longer in operation at the end of the year. Does this mean that creditors might expect to lose money in regard to 9 percent of the small firms that owe them money?

Only a small percentage of all discontinuances involve losses to creditors. Failed companies are defined as those involved in receivership, reorganization, or bankruptcy proceedings, or those which compromised with creditors out of court or ceased operations with loss to creditors. During 1953, 1,857 manufacturing firms were listed as failures, representing about 6 percent of all manufacturing firms discontinued in that year, and only about 0.5 percent of all manufacturing firms existing or established during the year.

Many of the 31,500 manufacturing companies discontinued in 1953 undoubtedly ceased operations for noneconomic reasons, such as retirement, sickness, or the founder's desire to take some other employment opportunity. Other discontinuances involved businesses that could have been continued profitably but were acquired by other companies or liquidated for various reasons. Of course, some businesses were continued when logical analysis would have indicated liquidation. Two observations might be made: First, the right to continue when things look dark is part of the new enterprise system. Second, many companies that are successful today survived early difficulties only because of the faith, hope, and obstinacy of their founders.

Relative Profitability of Small Companies

Conclusions about relative profitability must be drawn with care. Differences in accounting methods, compensation practices, and proportions of equity in the capital structure may affect reported profitability figures in ways that are difficult to evaluate.

Tables 1–7 and 1–8 present information on the profitability of manufacturing companies by asset size groups. The first table presents profits as a percentage of sales, and the second table presents profits as a percentage of stockholders' equity.

Examination of these two tables indicates that the average reported profitability of manufacturing companies during these years tended to be greater for large companies than for small ones. (Exceptions for rate of profit on stockholders' equity for 1956 and 1958 can be observed.) However, before drawing overall conclusions about the profit potential of small firms, one should examine other aspects of this matter.

For instance, the dividing line between salaries and profits is not well defined in many small companies. In a small company, pressures exist to adjust bonuses and salaries in order to minimize corporate profits and, therefore, corporate income taxes. The amount of officers' compensation can significantly affect reported corporation profits, particularly in small companies. For example, in 1941, for all corporations with assets below $50,000, officers' compensation totaled about 15 times reported net profits.

The data in Table 1–9, calculated by H. O. Stekler, show the effect of adjusting for officers' compensation. Rates of return after taxes on assets were calculated with and without officers' compensation included.

It is also enlightening to examine relative profitability when distinguishing between corporations showing a profit and corporations

Table 1-7

PROFITS PER DOLLAR OF SALES, BY ASSET SIZE
ALL MANUFACTURING CORPORATIONS EXCEPT NEWSPAPERS

(After Taxes)

Year	Under 250,000	250,000–1 Million	1–5 Million	Asset Size in Dollars 5–10 Million	10–25 Million	25–50 Million	50–100 Million	100–250 Million	250–1,000 Million	Over 1,000 Million
1954	0.0	1.4	1.9	3.1	3.9*	—	3.9	6.1†	—	—
1956	1.9	2.3	3.4	4.3	4.8*	—	5.4	4.9	6.4	8.9
1958	(0.6)	0.5	1.0	2.3	2.9*	—	3.6	3.6	4.1	7.0
1960	—	1.1‡	2.1	2.7	3.4	4.0	4.4	4.4	5.0	8.6
1962	—	1.0‡	1.8	2.4	2.9	3.5	3.6	3.6	4.3	8.5
1964	—	1.6‡	2.1	2.9	3.0	3.7	4.1	4.6	4.8	9.0

Data are for first quarter of each year.

* Asset size class is $10 to $50 million.
† Asset size class is $100 million and over.
‡ Asset size class is under $1 million.

SOURCE: Federal Trade Commission and Securities Exchange Commission, *Quarterly Financial Reports for Manufacturing Corporations*, (Washington, D.C.: U.S. Government Printing Office), as reported for the respective years.

Table 1-8

ANNUAL RATES OF PROFIT ON STOCKHOLDERS' EQUITY, BY ASSET SIZE ALL MANUFACTURING CORPORATIONS EXCEPT NEWSPAPERS

(After Taxes)

Year	Under 250,000	250,000–1 Million	1–5 Million	Asset Size in Dollars 5–10 Million	10–25 Million	25–50 Million	50–100 Million	100–250 Million	250–1,000 Million	Over 1,000 Million
1954	0.1	4.6	5.3	6.8	8.4*	—	8.4	11.7†	—	—
1956	15.6	11.5	10.4	10.9	12.2*	—	12.3	12.1	13.6	14.9
1958	(3.0)	2.1	2.9	4.9	5.8*	—	7.3	7.4	7.4	9.5
1960	—	5.0‡	6.3	6.4	7.4	8.4	9.2	10.2	10.2	13.0
1962	—	4.6‡	6.0	5.9	6.4	7.2	7.5	8.5	8.7	12.1
1964	—	7.4‡	7.0	7.7	6.9	7.8	8.8	9.7	9.7	13.8

Data are for first quarter of each year.

* Asset size class is $10 to $50 million.
† Asset size class is $100 million and over.
‡ Asset size class is under $1 million.

SOURCE: *Ibid.*

Table 1–9

COMPARISON OF RATE OF RETURN AFTER TAXES ON ASSETS
BY SIZE CLASS FOR ALL MANUFACTURING CORPORATIONS,
BEFORE AND AFTER INCLUDING OFFICERS'
COMPENSATION ADJUSTMENT
1955–57 Average

Asset Size Class ('000 Dollars)	Rate of Return* after Deducting Officers' Compensation	Rate of Return before Deducting Officers' Compensation
0–25	−13.9%	−9.4
25–50	−1.7	3.4
50–100	1.6	6.3
100–250	3.7	7.3
250–500	4.5	7.3
500–1,000	5.4	7.4
1,000–2,500	5.8	7.1
2,500–5,000	6.0	6.9
5,000–10,000	6.4	6.9
10,000–25,000	7.1	7.4
25,000–50,000	6.7	6.9
50,000–100,000	6.7	6.9
100,000–250,000	6.9	6.9
250,000 plus	7.0	7.1

* Rate of Return = Profit + Interest.

SOURCE: H. O. Stekler, *Profitability and Size of Firm* (Berkeley: Institute of Business and Economic Research, University of California, 1963), p. 39.

showing a deficit. Table 1–10, presenting data from 1955–56, shows that a higher percentage of small companies than of large ones are unprofitable. These figures are affected substantially by the business cycle; for instance, 86 percent of the smallest corporations incurred a loss in 1932, as compared to 60 percent of the largest firms.

Table 1–10

PERCENTAGE OF MANUFACTURING CORPORATIONS SHOWING
A LOSS IN 1955–56,* BY ASSET SIZE

Asset Size in Thousands of Dollars						
0–25	25–50	50–100	100–250	250–500	500–1,000	1,000–2,500
63.3%	42.7%	34.6%	24.0%	17.1%	14.6%	12.8%

Asset Size in Thousands of Dollars						
2,500–5,000	5,000–10,000	10,000–25,000	25,000–50,000	50,000–100,000	100,000–250,000	250,000 and up
9.1%	9.7%	7.0%	6.4%	3.0%	5.3%	1.0%

* Data are based upon business tax returns for accounting periods ending during the 12-month period from July 1, 1955, through June 30, 1956.

SOURCE: *Statistics of Income, Corporation Income Tax Returns, 1955–1956.*

Among unprofitable companies of all sizes, small ones seem to show larger relative losses (as percentages of equity) than do the large companies. Table 1–11 presents the results of a study of rates of return on equity for both income and deficit corporations in different size categories for the year 1946. Similar patterns can be observed for other years. Among corporations showing a profit, it can be seen that

Table 1–11

RATE OF RETURN ON EQUITY BEFORE TAXES IN 1946, FOR
INCOME AND DEFICIT MANUFACTURING CORPORATIONS
AND FOR BOTH COMBINED

Assets (thousands of dollars)	Income Corporations	Deficit Corporations	Both Combined
Under 50	33.5%	(75.8)	11.1
50–100	31.7	(39.1)	22.1
100–250	32.7	(35.4)	26.0
250–500	34.4	(31.5)	29.0
500–1,000	35.0	(31.7)	30.2
1,000–5,000	31.1	(22.4)	26.6
5,000–10,000	26.3	(18.3)	22.9
10,000–50,000	22.2	(13.9)	18.8
50,000–100,000	18.4	(12.5)	15.4
Over 100,000	10.4	(8.4)	9.9

SOURCE: *Statistics of Income, Corporation Income Tax Returns, 1946.*

smaller companies tended to show a higher return than larger companies.

Other factors, bearing on the relative profitability of large and small companies, should also be considered. For example, these profitability figures have been presented as returns on equity. Small corporations tend to have a lower percentage of equity and a higher percentage of debt in their capital structures than do larger companies. Thus, if rates of return were calculated as a percentage of total assets invested in the business, a portion (but not all) of the small company sector would compare less favorably with larger companies than in the studies presented here.

Another factor bearing on these studies of relative profitability relates to the age of the companies in the various size categories. Most of the new companies established each year would be classified as small companies during that year; in fact, most would be in the smallest size classes shown in Table 1–10. Some of these new companies should never have been started. Ill-conceived, ill-financed, and ill-managed, they pass from the scene as soon as their initial capital is exhausted. Other new companies, including some of the best managed, do not show a profit until several years after being founded. Money is plowed into product and market development. This increases expenses and reduces income in the early years, although it often results in large returns in future years. However, during the early years, lacking established product lines to contribute a profit, many of these companies show heavy losses. The substantial number of new companies in the population of small manufacturing companies undoubtedly exerts a depressing influence on the reported average of profitability of all small companies.

Some data are available to permit a comparison of the most profitable small companies with the most profitable large companies. Table 1–12 reports a study based upon a sample of 563 manufacturing and trading firms for the years 1927–29. With both manufacturing and trading firms, the small companies (defined as having assets less than $500,000) showed a greater dispersion in profitability.

These findings are not difficult to understand when one considers that large firms tend to represent the averaging of many factors contributing to profitability. Larger firms often have many products, with varying rates of profitability; larger firms have many people, some of whom may be very good, but some of whom are, inevitably, not outstanding; such firms often have many customers, compete in many markets, operate in different locations, etc. Considering the averaging effect of these many factors, one should not be surprised that large firms show less dispersion of profitability than small firms. It is probably also true that this averaging effect brings about greater stability in the profitability of large firms.

For a reader interested in a career in a smaller firm, the range of profitability among small firms is of real significance. He can see that the average profitability figures for small firms as a whole often compare poorly with those for larger firms. However, he knows that these averages are affected greatly by thousands of new or extremely ill-conceived small companies, many of which show substantial losses and give no promise of ever doing much better. He can also see that the most profitable firms in American industry appear to be small. In these companies, there is the happy blend of good management using adequate resources to exploit opportunities with high profit potential. The averaging effect mentioned in the above paragraph does not exert a depressing influence on the overall profitability of these small firms. The record of these companies demonstrates what can be done in small enterprises.

Table 1-12

Percentage Distribution of 563 Companies by Earning Rates on Capital for Different Asset Classes

(Ratio of Three-year Aggregates, 1927–29)

Asset Class	Number of Companies			Earning Rate				Average Rate of Earnings
		Loss	0–10%	10%–20%	20%–30%	Above 30%		

Asset Class	Number of Companies	Loss	0–10%	10%–20%	20%–30%	Above 30%	Average Rate of Earnings
A. Manufacturing							
0–$500,000	131	9.9	42.0	29.8	13.0	5.3	11.0
Above $500,000	210	7.1	61.9	23.3	6.7	1.0	8.0
Total, manufacturing	341	8.2	54.3	25.8	9.1	2.6	9.2
B. Trading							
0–$500,000	127	14.2	71.6	9.4	2.4	2.4	5.9
Above $500,000	95	5.3	75.8	17.9	1.0	0.0	7.0
Total, trading	222	10.4	73.4	13.1	1.8	1.3	6.3

SOURCE: W. A. Paton, *Corporate Profits as Shown by Audit Reports* (New York: National Bureau of Economic Research, Inc., 1935), p. 73, as reported in R. C. Osborn, *Effects of Corporate Size on Efficiency and Profitability* (University of Illinois Bulletin, Vol. 48, No. 7), p. 59.

2. CAREER OPPORTUNITIES IN SMALL BUSINESS

This note focuses primarily on problems and opportunities in securing a position with an established small company, and is addressed principally to the young man who is just completing his undergraduate or graduate training.

There is tremendous variety among small companies. The objectives and experience of the readers of this note are also undoubtedly quite diverse. Therefore, any generalizations must be considered with care to determine their applicability to a particular situation.

This can be illustrated by considering one of the arguments often advanced in favor of seeking a career with a smaller company. It is that a young man is more likely to achieve major responsibilities at an early stage in his career in a small firm because such a firm typically has a "greatly stretched" management. This probably describes accurately one of the major advantages of working for a smaller company, particularly a growing one. However, note the many exceptions which might be encountered. Some employees of larger firms have exercised great responsibilities in early stages of their careers, particularly when they are working in areas of activity new to the company. Likewise, many employees of smaller firms have been frustrated by one-man management, in which virtually no authority has been delegated to them. Nevertheless, generalizations about career opportunities in large and in small companies can be useful, if the reader does not assume them to be universally applicable but, rather, examines their specific applicability to each situation.

The first step is to follow the Socratic recommendation to "know yourself." This advice, so easy to give, is sometimes hard to follow. Nevertheless, it is essential to determine what one really wants (realizing that no job is perfect) and what features in a job are most and least important. A young man should also assess what he can contribute and the nature of his strengths and weaknesses. He might construct a profile of himself at present, and a profile of the position he would like to find.

If one's experience in the industrial world is limited, these judgments may be difficult to make. A man may not know what he wants, or he may feel that he will change so much over the next few years that today's judgments will not be applicable. Such feelings may direct him toward a career (at least initially) with a larger firm offering a training program that will allow him to "look around." They may lead him to dispose early of a military commitment, if he has not already done so, giving him time to mature his thinking.

With this process of self-examination underway and with the above-mentioned caveats about generalizations well in mind, we can consider some of the characteristics often associated with the large or small company environment.

The large company typically is organized so that its employees are more likely to become specialized. By contrast, I recall the executive of one small firm remarking, "As I drive to work each morning, I don't know what I'll be doing at ten o'clock, and don't even know which of the major functions of the business will be concerning me." The executives of many smaller firms carry such diverse responsibilities.

In general, large firms are more likely to feel they can afford an extensive period of training before new personnel are given major responsibilities. Many executives of smaller firms feel their new employees must be able and willing to pull their share of the load within a fairly short time of joining the company.

In regard to compensation, wide variations can be found, particularly among smaller firms. Many larger firms have policies such that the new member of the organization can, with some accuracy, forecast his salary increases for a considerable period into the future. By contrast, many smaller firms have never hired a man just out of college, and the thinking about what a new man is worth, particularly vis-à-vis older employees, may be very cloudy. Some smaller firms feel they cannot match the high starting salaries of the larger companies. However, some of these same firms are in a position over a longer period to handsomely reward, through salaries and, eventually, equity participation, executives who attain positions of key responsibility. As can be seen from cases such as Thermal Dynamics, the rewards to a stockholder-executive in a highly successful small company can be quite high. In some instances, these rewards have exceeded the best that large firms can offer.

Many people who start or buy businesses are motivated by the desire to be their own bosses. However, the man who hopes to join an established executive team of a small firm had better not have any illusions about dominating the situation. In fact, the graduates of many strong graduate business programs have unrealistic expectations about being "managers" their first day on the job. Unwilling to spend the time learning some part of the business from the ground up, they may create antagonisms which can permanently impair their effectiveness. In small as in large firms, it is necessary for people to work together; regardless of a man's qualifications, very few managers will wish to hire him if he can be happy only at the top.

Both large and small firms can be found which demand a heavy investment of time from ambitious young employees. In general, the small growing firm has a greatly stretched management; this often creates unique opportunities for the young man to exercise initiative. However, in taking advantage of these opportunities he may find that he is devoting more time to his job than he would in a larger firm.

Although an individual job in a large firm may be relatively narrowly defined, a larger organization encompasses great variety: it employs many people, often conducts operations in many locations, and sometimes operates in a number of industries. Thus, the employee of a large company, if he finds that he can't work well with his superior, can sometimes arrange a transfer or wait for the new assignment which often comes every few years. The member of a small company organization can often escape from his "frozen-in" position only by leaving the company. However, the opportunity for frequent moves in the large company is not an unmixed blessing, as the numerous large company executives who have had to move every few years can testify.

The young man considering a position with a small company also should recognize that the road to a successful relationship with his colleagues may not be so well paved as in most large companies. Many larger firms are used to "digesting" young college graduates each year. Their personnel policies, their training programs, their knowledge of the aspirations, the abilities, and the shortcomings often possessed by such men permit them to smooth the path. In smaller companies with little or no experience in training or supervising college graduates, too much may be expected, or not enough. Some of the persons in the small company may perceive "the college man" as a threat to their own opportunities, as a man who will be inserted above them in the organization. The perceptive new employee of a small company should recognize these potential difficulties.

He can indicate that he does not consider his college degree to have made him an expert on all the problems with which the others have been living. He can also indicate his willingness to teach what he knows to others and to "share the glory" with them. Thus, some of those who perceived him as a threat may actually decide that their opportunities are improved rather than diminished by his coming.

The above discussion describes some of the salient factors which tend to be helpful in distinguishing among career opportunities in companies of different size. The advice not to reason too much from generalizations, but to look at the specific situation, is repeated—because it is so important and so easily overlooked.

A young man may conclude, after consideration of these factors, that a small business career is probably not for him. This may be a very wise decision. Careers in smaller companies, like careers in accounting or law, are not for everyone.

Obstacles to Finding a Position in a Small Company

Assuming a man has decided that his career objectives can best be served by going with a smaller company, he finds many difficulties in realizing this ambition. In fact, the obstacles appear so great, particularly in contrast with the red-carpet treatment offered by some large corporations, that he may decide to take the easier path leading to a large company position, putting off until some indeterminate time the search for the right small company.

From the standpoint of a small company, there are a number of reasons why systematic programs to attract and hire college graduates are rarely undertaken. Small firms typically have only occasional needs for people to fill executive positions. Often, executives of such firms believe they cannot afford to carry a young man while he gains experience, so they search for an experienced man who can immediately carry responsibility. (In my opinion, this attitude is sometimes shortsighted and results in their getting a second-class experienced man rather than a first-class man who can be trained.) Executives of smaller firms sometimes feel they cannot compete with larger companies in attracting graduates of good schools; often they don't realize that there are young men graduating from college with a real interest in finding careers with smaller firms. In addition, in many small firms there is no single individual whose primary interest is hiring managerial people; rather it is a task assumed periodically by already busy executives. These needs and attitudes lead to an approach to hiring that is often not very systematic and usually not aimed at the young man just emerging from college. Typical approaches for the executives of small firms are to inquire among friends, public accountants, and lawyers, or to rely on chance encounters. The upshot is that applicants cannot be assured of finding good small business job leads through college placement offices, but rather should be willing to exercise imagination, ingenuity, and effort to find such leads.

From the standpoint of the young man seeking a career in a smaller firm, the lack of any systematic and easy way to learn "what small companies are seeking what kinds of people" at any given time is frustrating. If he seeks to go into the field, to contact particular companies, and to contact knowledgeable professional people who might know of openings, he is often overwhelmed by the immensity of the screening task. This occurs because the hundreds of thousands of smaller firms in our economy include many companies that would not have opportunities for or would not appeal to many young men. The following are just a few reasons why particular firms may not be of interest. There are companies that lack the profit or growth potential to appeal to an ambitious young man. There are firms in which the attitudes of the executives or owners lead to an environment not conducive to a satisfying career for a young man; a typical example is the owner-manager who is unwilling to surrender any authority. There are also family-owned firms, in which the real opportunities are reserved for sons or nephews. There are, as well, companies that do not seem suitable because of their location or the nature of their business. In addition, there are many businesses that might seem to be just what the young man is seeking but which, at the particular time he is searching for an opportunity, do not have an opening for him.

The purpose of the above comments is not to imply that there are no opportunities. Nevertheless, the proverbial needle in the haystack is analogous. It is no wonder that many young men choose the much easier path of allowing themselves to be wined and dined by large companies, and then choose career opportunities that may not really be what they want. (Some of these misplaced "small company executives" find satisfying careers in larger firms. However, some do not, and that is a tragedy for them, for their large company employers, and for the small businesses which might have benefited from their contributions.)

Approaches to Finding Opportunities in Small Firms

Unfortunately, there are no easy answers to the dilemmas described above. All that can be done is to suggest some approaches which have worked for some young men.

The advice given at the beginning of this note—to examine yourself, to decide what it is you really want—is the first step in any career planning. Having decided that a career in a smaller firm is appealing, the examination should not stop there, but should procced to a consideration of the kind of small company with which one would or would not wish to be associated. Does location matter? Remember that with many smaller firms you will not be transferred, but will probably make your home for many years in the same city. Does joining a family-held business in which the presidency might be reserved for members of the family bother you? Under what conditions might you be happy in such a situation? Other questions of this sort will occur to the discerning reader.

The likelihood of finding the right position may depend greatly on one's age and experience. For reasons already outlined, many smaller firms are extremely reluctant to hire men with no experience. To contrast two extremes, the young man with no working experience who is receiving his bachelor's degree is in a vastly different position from the young man who is receiving his master's degree and has worked for several years and knows what he wants. The first young man might well decide to go with a larger firm to get some experience and to give himself time to decide exactly what he wants. In such a case, he should be careful not to take just "any job" in "any large company." He should ask himself what kind of position he would like to be qualified to fill in a small company a few years hence and should examine the available opportunities accordingly.

Certain kinds of positions with larger firms offer considerable exposure to smaller firms, thereby providing the young man with an extended opportunity to judge whether he wishes to join such a company and also providing a detailed knowledge of particular companies' operations and personnel needs. Examples are positions with public accounting firms, management consulting firms, or firms that sell to small companies.

If he chooses to go with a larger firm initially with the expectation of later joining a smaller company, he should be very careful not to enter his initial job in a halfhearted way, thinking of it as merely a temporary position. This would be unfair to his employer, and would also greatly hamper his personal development.

The young man approaching the end of his academic work should make full use of his college placement office, even though most of the firms visiting these offices may be large ones. Some small companies send representatives to campuses to recruit; many of them write to such offices, describing opportunities that might be available. If the college offers an alumni placement service, examination of the opportunities listed through this service may be fruitful. For the graduate with considerable experience, contact with the executive placement services of some of the management consulting firms may be desirable.

One approach which offers promise for many young men can be summarized as going out to find the position, rather than waiting for it to come to you.

To narrow the field of search, the job hunter should make *some* of the above-mentioned judgments about what location, industries, and other factors are most appealing. In doing this he needs to strike a balance; if he is too particular, he may be unable to find an opportunity meeting his objectives. If he does not exercise some selectivity, then the screening task is too immense. It would be helpful in making these judgments and in his later search if he would gain as much background as possible through reading and conversations. Knowledge of the problems and opportunities of particular industries and localities and of the names and activities of particular companies could be gained through careful reading of trade publications, newspapers, and business directories.

Then he should make inquiries to learn the names of those men who might be most knowledgeable about the areas of interest, and he should seek to secure appointments with them. (It would be desirable if he could start with men he knows, even though slightly.) Commercial bankers or lawyers with a small company clientele are often good men to contact. The purpose of the appointment should not be to ask such men for jobs or for specific leads. This places them in an awkward position, unless they know something about the job hunter. Often the most useful approach for the young man is to ask for an appointment to secure advice about getting a job. Because these men are busy, interviews should be kept short unless there is a specific invitation to continue. At the end of the interview, the candidate might inquire as to who is knowledgeable about the field and able to give additional advice. This process then can be repeated.

It is probably advisable not to ask for an introduction to these persons, but to say you will call them yourself. This prevents imposing on the man who has provided help and also permits the young man to follow up quickly on the leads he has received.

Several benefits may accrue from this approach. The young man is likely to have gotten some frank appraisals of his opportunities and some good advice as to how to proceed. These comments may be particularly helpful, because they come from men who are peculiarly knowledgeable in regard to the very areas in which the young man's interest is greatest.

A second benefit is to learn the names of other persons whom this knowledgeable man regards as particularly qualified to give advice. This process can rapidly lead to those individuals who are most likely to be able to help the applicant.

A final benefit is that such interviews may lead to particular job openings which the adviser understandably might be reluctant to discuss before he has had an opportunity to learn something about the applicant. If the young man makes a good impression, he may learn about opportunities in particular companies and whom to contact in those companies. Some opportunities may not materialize until some time after the interview, when the adviser happens to encounter a small company searching for additions to its management team.

The approaches described above cannot ensure success. It may be that for a particular young man at a particular stage of his career the right opportunity may not be found in the time he feels he can devote to searching. In such a case, he may find it desirable to seek a position with a larger firm. This may be to his advantage if his lack of success implies unrealistic objectives or a lack of needed skills at that stage of his career. A period of seasoning with a larger firm may be just what is needed. He may discover, in fact, that he is very happy in a large company environment.

Study of the cases in this book can help to provide the reader with the background needed to decide whether a career in small business is for him. Personal conversations with those already in small firms can also add greatly to the understanding necessary to make an informed decision.

Finding career opportunities in smaller firms is not easy. However, neither is finding the right girl to marry. In both cases, the rewards of finding the right one can be great.

3. NOTE ON FINANCING SMALL BUSINESS ENTERPRISES *

Anyone who expects to participate in the ownership or management of a small business can look forward some day to the problem of raising money. The most common purposes would be to finance starting, buying, or expanding an enterprise or to provide funds for seasonal or other temporary needs of a going concern. The purpose of this note is to describe briefly some of the available sources and to review some of the considerations that might be useful to the seeker of funds. It is believed that he will be more successful in his search and more pleased with the results if the various alternative sources of funds are known and understood.

It is frequently stated that there is a shortage of capital for small business. Ordinarily, however, there seems to be adequate capital if the opportunities for lending or investing are sufficiently attractive. A seeker of funds needs first to develop an economically feasible and attractive project, then to find an appropriate source of funds, and finally to be well prepared with information and projections to make an effective and convincing presentation. In other words, if a man can demonstrate that without excessive risk he is able to make practical and profitable use of the funds desired and can generate the necessary cash flows, he can usually raise the money—whether he is a retailer laying in a stock of merchandise for the Christmas trade, a manufacturer buying a new piece of equipment, a contractor undertaking to build a school, or a potential entrepreneur attempting to buy a business concern.

In our free enterprise system, there is no central agency to which you can apply that has a simple standardized procedure for allocating funds among business applicants. The decisions and choices that determine which firms, ventures, or enterprises receive the funds they require are made by a vast array of independent financial institutions, business organizations, and individuals.

It might help to think of these arranged in a spectrum of sources, ranging from relatives and friends of the entrepreneur, through venturesome individuals able and willing to invest in speculative undertakings, venture capital firms, small-business investment companies, investment banking firms, finance companies, commercial banks, insurance companies, and savings institutions all the way to commercial paper firms that deal only with well-known, well-established companies with impeccable credit standings. Distributed along the spectrum at various points are numerous other sources of funds, such as community and state development corporations (e.g., Massachusetts Business Development Corporation), Small Business Administration, Area Redevelopment Administration, mutual funds and other investment companies, employee pension and profit sharing trusts, union funds, and a variety of ordinary corporations with funds for specialized expansion and acquisition programs.

Each of these entities has its own area of specialization, its own policies and objectives, and its standards and requirements as to such factors as credit worthiness, profit potential, and growth rate. Attitudes toward risk vary greatly; some leaders and investors are extremely conservative, while others can tolerate high risk if the speculative possibilities are sufficiently interesting. Voting control and management influence are important to some, while others prefer to be merely outside investors.

Many of the differences in investment interests, attitudes, and policies can be attributed to the personal preferences and experience of the individuals involved. Part of this is a matter of geographical location. Regional differences can often be traced to relatively greater familiarity with local industry. It would probably be easier to raise money for certain types of oil ventures in Houston or Dallas than in Chicago or Minneapolis, and the problems and opportunities of a tool-and-die-maker would probably be more realistically appreciated and appraised in Detroit and Cleveland than in Atlanta. In addition to these somewhat personal factors, financial institutions and government agencies are subject to a variety of statutory requirements and regulations that limit their freedom of action in numerous ways.

In view of these and other differences, it is not surprising that a proposal that would be given serious consideration by one man would be turned down cold by another, or that a venture scorned by three in succession would be eagerly snapped up by the fourth. It also is not surprising to find the differences reflected in the type of information requested and the type of analysis made. It will be noticed that some tend to concentrate their attention on risk factors and the soundness of balance sheet ratios, while others are more interested in future prospects, profit margins, and growth rate. Probably all lenders and investors will agree that the quality and character of management rank high in importance. It is interesting to note, however, that the characteristics they admire vary considerably. Some favor the thoughtful, prudent, cautious type; others prefer those who are aggressive, enterprising, and action-oriented. It is safe to say, however, that all lenders and investors give high priority to integrity, sound judgment, successful experience, resourcefulness, and determination to build a profitable business.

Somewhat as a counterpart to the spectrum of sources of funds, there can be visualized a spectrum of needs. This ranges from the man with nothing but a bright idea and a gleam in his eye, through embryonic firms in different stages of development, firms in business but struggling to survive, thriving companies that have passed the break-even point both as to profit and cash flow and now need funds for growth, to well-established enterprises able to internally generate all, or practically all, necessary long-term funds.

It is obvious that the problems, risks, and funds requirements for firms at these various stages would be quite different, and would present opportunities of widely varying attractiveness to the sources of funds mentioned earlier. The problem is to match up the source and the need with some degree of compatibility. This is not an abstract concept. An entrepreneur with a small company enters into a fairly close relationship with his financier, whether he sells common stock or borrows. For this relationship to be a happy and fruitful one, he should strive to get not merely the right amount of money at the right time, but the right kind of investor or lender. For example, if there are many uncertainties and a good chance of failure, it would seem most appropriate to have a knowledgeable and sophisticated investor in a high tax bracket. If it appears there may be a long period before cash returns are possible, he would do better to shun the funds of the impatient type who wants a quick return, or of the man who has other near-term plans for his money and would not want to be locked in. Even in an established, profitable small company, there are many opportunities for friction and conflict between company management and outside investors, particularly if there is no established market for the company's stock. Whenever it is difficult to withdraw funds or to readily dispose of an equity interest, it is important for the lender or investor to see eye to eye with the management on matters of financial policy, such as dividend payout, use of funds in expansion, raising additional capital, and similar matters.

It is generally necessary, when starting a company, for a person to use his own savings and those of people who believe in him and want to help him succeed. In many cases, these early funds come from relatives and friends. They are willing to act on their confidence in the entrepreneur and his hopes, and there may be little else to rely on. Typical arms-length investors act in their own interests, and before investing they like to see tangible demonstration that the hopes are realistic. The earlier they come into a venture (when important uncertainties are still unresolved), the greater the share of the venture they will require for the amount invested. Investors require an opportunity for profit proportionate to the risk. By way of contrast, after a company has established a profitable record of stability and growth, the terms on which funds can be obtained—whether short-term loans from a bank or long-term equity funds from investors— are much improved. The better terms, whether expressed as interest rate or as the percentage of the total equity given in exchange for a stated sum of money, reflect the increased confidence on the part of financial people in a management that has proved its ability to make a profit.

In other words, the founder of a firm is in a better bargaining position relative to the further progress he can make toward profitable operations before seeking venture capital. This is true whether he deals with individual investors, venture capital firms, or small-business investment companies—all of whom are available to provide financial support up to the point where the firm is able to go public.

Since the cost of outside money drops as an enterprise becomes better established, it is sensible and prudent to minimize the use of outside funds until they can be had on more favorable terms. This does not mean that a company should blindly forego opportunities for profitable investment, but it does suggest that management skill and effort in increasing inventory turnover, reducing the accounts receivable collection period, minimizing fixed assets, and eliminating extravagance and inefficiency will be well repaid in the form of a larger share of future ownership and profits.

Although a discussion of all factors determining the amount and type of outside funds to be raised is beyond the scope of this note, a word of caution may be in order. While there are strong arguments for making energetic efforts to reduce and postpone the use of outside funds, it is important and frequently critical to make realistic estimates of the future needs when dealing with banks, investors, and other sources. It is true that if you obtain too much your capital costs are unnecessarily high, but if you get too little you may run out of money at a time when it is impossible to raise more on favorable terms. It is usually easier and sounder to arrange for funds in advance rather than wait until a period of cash stringency arrives. If a realistic forecast, including an allowance for contingencies, indicates an amount considerably greater than would be needed immediately, it is frequently possible to arrange a commitment for the total amount with the privilege of drawing down funds as needed. A bank line of credit, against which the customer can borrow, is commonplace; and venture capital firms, SBIC's, insurance companies, and others can provide longer term or permanent capital under arrangements designed to meet the timing of a company's funds needs.

Although equity capital is much safer than debt for a small growing company, since it does not entail fixed charges or need to be repaid, there is usually a strong preference for the use of debt on the part of small business firms. There are certain obvious advantages. Assuming that earnings made possible by the borrowed funds exceed the net cost of the debt, there is a favorable leverage factor, and total earnings are increased. With the use of debt, it is not necessary to share the control, ownership, and future growth, as would be true if stock were issued. High taxes and the deductibility of interest, and long-term inflation which makes it possible to repay debt with depreciated dollars, increase the relative attractiveness of debt. It should be pointed out, however, that leverage works in reverse when earnings fall off, and if debt cannot be repaid, the owner may lose not only control but also his entire business through bankruptcy.

Commercial banks are the most common source of funds for small business, usually in the form of short-term loans, although term loans and accounts receivable loans are gaining in popularity. Generally, an enterprise is not eligible for bank credit until it is actually doing business and needs funds to finance accounts receivable and inventory. It is not possible to make sweeping generalizations applicable to all banks, except perhaps to say they vary widely in their attitude toward risk and in their interest in any particular type of loan. In large banks, there is variety within a bank; it is not unusual for one officer to feel justified in making a loan that another would turn down, perhaps on the basis of his familiarity with the particular field. In any event, a good relationship with a commercial bank is necessary for a small business. It is a logical first place to go for funds. If the banker cannot supply the funds, he will at least give advice as to the next move. If there has been a close, friendly relationship, the background of information and understanding the banker has developed enables him to extend, in good conscience, financial assistance that might not be possible for a new and unknown applicant. Much could be said on related topics: the various ways a commercial bank can serve a small business, factors to be considered in selecting an appropriate bank, how to get the most value out of a bank relationship, and so on. Since these matters are well covered in the literature, perhaps in this note it will be sufficient to point out that an effective relationship with an appropriate bank can serve as an important adjunct to a small firm's resources, supplying funds, information, and frequently guidance.

This does not mean that even the friendliest banker grants all loan requests. There are numerous reasons why a bank might decline to make a loan, or extend or increase one previously made. Basically, the interest rate charged has very little allowance for bad debt losses. When you compare the interest rate on a commercial loan with what the bank could earn on short-term government securities (with no risk and very little administrative expense), you will generally find a spread of from 0.5 to 2.5 percent to cover all the risk and most of the expense associated with commercial loans. Not many loans would have to get into trouble to wipe out the margin on all loans of this type in a bank's portfolio. If the banker's analysis indicates the customer might have trouble repaying the loan on time or, in fact, might not be able to repay it in full, he might suggest that the customer add equity to provide the needed permanent capital and also to serve as a protective loss-absorbing cushion. Or he might suggest applying to other lenders who make loans on longer terms and with greater risk than the bank does.

It is not unusual for a small business to need more funds than its bank wishes to lend. As mentioned earlier, there are numerous sources available. Finance companies, factoring firms, and leasing firms are well known. In different ways, these all permit a company, in effect, to turn assets (accounts receivable, inventory, plant, equipment) into cash. Savings banks and insurance companies make mortgage loans, although most insurance companies deal in fairly high minimum amounts. Venture capital firms, "finders" (individuals who, for a fee, bring together those seeking funds and those with funds seeking investment), and private investors provide funds in various forms, on various terms, to situations with varying degrees of risk and speculative appeal.

Several other sources are of particular interest to small business. Perhaps the most interesting development of this sort in recent years has been the organization of large numbers of small-business investment companies (SBIC's). These are authorized to invest in small business by means of equity, convertible debt, or debt. Full information regarding investment or loan limits, qualifications for obtaining funds, and the location of nearby SBIC's can be obtained from the Small Business Administration. The SBA itself provides funds to small business either by participating in a loan made by a commercial bank or by direct lending, if the small company can meet SBA qualifying standards but has been unable to borrow through normal channels. Again, full particulars are available from the SBA, at either Washington headquarters or a regional office.

In many states and local communities, business development corporations have been organized with private funds, frequently provided by banks and others with a stake in the economic well-being of a community. These corporations are usually prepared to make fairly long-term loans, for the benefit of the community, if there are reasonable safeguards against loss of principal.

At some point in time, if the company has an attractive record and interesting future prospects, an investment banking firm can be found to underwrite an issue of stock for sale to the public. This may be new stock, with the proceeds going to the company, or the stock of one or more of the founders, or some of both.

Going public is not necessary if a company is reasonably profitable and growth is not too rapid. However, with current high tax rates, a successful small company frequently has the potential to grow at a rate faster than can be financed with internal funds. Establishing a public market facilitates future financing and provides a market for both the founders' and investors' holdings. Raising equity funds through a public issue may be the only way to repay maturing debt obligations incurred in the course of early financing. For example, an SBIC may have bought convertible debentures. These may not be converted unless a public market is established, and it might be difficult to repay the debentures without raising new money.

Earlier it was suggested that there was no shortage of capital for a small business with attractive prospects. The problem is that any proposal must compete with other uses of funds. To elaborate on this idea, it might be helpful to visualize a vast flood of funds flowing through the spectrum of sources and being allocated as loans and investments by these institutions and individuals among the firms and individuals in the spectrum of needs referred to above. Although this flood varies with the ebb and flow of the economic tide, it is always substantial. Each person influencing any part of this flow of funds is faced with a wide choice of alternatives within the constraints of his investment or loan policy. Each person or company who would like to receive a portion of this flow should remember that his proposal or request should appear appropriate and relatively attractive to the person with whom he is dealing at a particular time. A small business seeking funds is in competition not only with others seeking funds for similar purposes but also with other forms of investment, including listed stocks, bonds, and even savings accounts.

The competitive strength or the ability of any particular type of proposal to attract either permanent or temporary funds depends on many factors, and changes from time to time and place to place. Railroads, canal companies, street railways, electric utilities, automobile companies, aircraft manufacturers, real estate syndicates, various types of mines, and, more recently, electronics, nucleonics, and space age companies have taken turns at being the glamour investments. At times, even new, unknown, and unproven ventures in favored fields have no difficulty raising funds on advantageous terms, at least until there is a shift in the investment interest or fashion. As mentioned earlier, important geographic differences in investment and lending tastes affect the relative attractiveness of particular types of opportunities.

The economic background has an important effect. In times of prosperity, the new, unproven, speculative firm has a much improved chance of attracting funds. The general atmosphere of confidence makes both investors and lenders less cautious; the emphasis is on opportunity rather than risk. There is more cash—both from ordinary income and sale of securities at a profit—available for reinvestment. Finally, there are fewer bargains among well-known stocks, both listed and unlisted. Price-earnings ratios are high, yields are low, and knowledgeable investors are consciously looking for new, unexploited opportunities. Conversely, in times of recession, investors are worried and cautious; risks are emphasized; reinvestment cash is less plentiful; blue-chip stocks are available at lower price-earnings ratios and higher yields. At a time like this, a request for funds for the new venture or the struggling small firm needs to be based on a really good opportunity, well prepared and well presented.

In the last analysis, probably the factor that, more than any other, determines which enterprises get the funds they apply for is the quality of the people associated with them. Economic conditions, market potential, financial resources, productive facilities could be identical; but two firms could still have vastly different prospects because of differences in such critically important management characteristics as

518 SMALL BUSINESS MANAGEMENT

intelligence, judgment, integrity, personality, drive, energy, education, experience, and others. Generally, the smaller or newer a company is, the higher the risk appears to a lender or investor. Similarly, the less experience record a company has, the more importance is attached to the records of the principals. In small, high-risk situations, the impression created by the individuals involved frequently is the determining factor in an appraisal of the credit worthiness or investment potential of the enterprise.

At any time or place or under any economic conditions, whether or not an entrepreneur gets the funds he seeks for either a new venture or an established company may largely depend on how well he has done his homework. His presentation, both written and oral, should show that he has made an objective appraisal of the financial prospects, that he has looked well into the future, and has realistic plans for meeting normal contingencies. He should show that he has learned what he could from the experience of others in similar fields. Sales estimates, rate of increase, return on investment, and his profit plan in general should indicate, without indulging in optimistically exaggerated forecasts, an attractive and feasible opportunity to use the funds profitably. He should have cash projections compatible with his other projections and plans, and there should be sufficient margin for error to accommodate the contingencies referred to above. His estimates of financial requirements should clearly show both amount and duration of need; and, if the proposal concerns a venture that is just getting started, the estimates should make adequate provision for acquisition of assets, working capital, start-up costs, losses to be expected during the breaking-in period, and all expenditures to be made before reaching the cash break-even point.

He should anticipate the questions a prudent lender or investor should ask, and should be ready with candid, factual answers. He should know his project and his business so well that he can answer unexpected questions. Intelligent and thorough preparation will result in a more effective presentation, will improve the chances for a successful negotiation, and should lead to better terms, greater confidence in the project on the part of the supplier of funds, and a more rewarding long-term relationship.

4. POTENTIALITIES AND PITFALLS OF FINANCING SMALL ENTERPRISES*

EDITOR'S NOTE.—This statement by C. Wrede Petersmeyer, then partner, J. H. Whitney and Company, New York (now president, Corinthian Broadcasting Corporation), was made during the Briefing Session on the Small Business Investment Act of 1958, sponsored by the American Management Association, New York, December 1–2, 1958. The statement was made approximately three months after the Small Business Investment Act became law, at a time when many people appeared to be somewhat overoptimistic about opportunities for profit in organizing and operating a small-business investment company. The situation called for someone to emphasize the dangers and problems associated with investments in many new and small business enterprises. This, Mr. Petersmeyer has done capably, against a backdrop of the investment policies and methods of a venture capital firm that had been, and since has been, an outstanding success in a difficult investment area.

As many of you know, the founder and senior partner of J. H. Whitney & Co. is fortunately a very wealthy man and also fortunately a very able businessman, Mr. John Hay Whitney, who is currently serving as Ambassador to Great Britain. Mr. Whitney is affectionately known and commonly referred to as "Jock" Whitney.

By way of illustrating the text of my remarks today, I am reminded of an event that happened a few years ago in our own firm that I think you might find interesting.

At that time, we were considering acquiring for a substantial amount of money a portion of a business of a very successful food company. Although the president of that company was a relatively young man, the patriarch, the prime mover and the founder of the company was his uncle, a rather elderly man, but still a very active man.

A great point was made during the course of our negotiations about the Horatio Alger rise of Uncle "Joe," who started as a fruit-cart peddler and, during the course of his career, had built up a very successful

---

* Reprinted from "Briefing on the Investment Act," a United States Government Printing Office publication dated December 31, 1958, printed for the Committee on Banking and Currency and the Select Committee on Small Business of the United States Senate.

enterprise. A time had been set by which we were to make our decision whether to go into this business or not, and we had not completed our investigation. We requested an additional two weeks in which to complete our investigation. While we were deliberating the progress of this particular project in our firm meeting, the telephone rang and it was the president of the company on the phone informing us that he was very sorry that his Uncle "Joe" had said that we could not have the extension of time. One of the partners commented in the firm meeting that, "You tell him that we must have the additional time. Otherwise, our answer will be 'No.' Tell him that our Uncle 'Jock' didn't start as a fruit-cart peddler and he has no intention of ending up as one."

I would like to cover today four areas: First, the background of J. H. Whitney & Co., and how it operates; second, the potentialities of financing new or small enterprises, based on our experience; third, the pitfalls of financing new or small enterprises, based on our experience; and, finally, some conclusions.

I am not going to be in the position of—I am sure the story a lot of you have heard—of the 5-year-old boy who was busy drawing on a blackboard, making pictures and his mother came in and said, "Johnny, what are you drawing?" He said, "I am drawing a picture of God." And she said, "But, Johnny, nobody knows what God looks like." And he said, "Well, they will when I get through."

I. The Background of J. H. Whitney & Co., and How It Operates

You might have chosen a better speaker today, possibly from a different organization than J. H. Whitney & Co., because J. H. Whitney & Co.'s prime purpose is not one of financing small business per se by any definitions or restrictions, but rather to provide equity capital for the development of growth companies in growth industries—the type of risk or venture capital that was provided in the early history of our country by private individuals, when the tax laws were somewhat different than they are now, and in the early days by banking houses. These are primarily situations that are not susceptible to bank financing, and also those that are not sufficiently large to be of interest to the general public.

J. H. Whitney & Co., along with American Research & Development Co.—incidentally, Bill Elfers here today and I were in the same class at Harvard Business School many years ago—and a handful of other companies, were pioneers in this field of providing new channels through which capital and enterprise could be brought together.

J. H. Whitney & Co., uses only its own funds, as far as equity investments are concerned. It makes use of bank financing wherever such is possible in financing the companies in which we take an interest. We do not deal in listed securities. We are not in the brokerage business. We hold no investments in listed securities except those of our companies that we started as embryo companies and that have grown to a point where they are now publicly held.

Mr. Whitney, for many years, probably from the time he was 20 years old, had been really a venture capitalist on his own, without a staff and without the kind of organization that he now has. Following the war, he came back to this country and decided he wanted to do something worthwhile with his funds. He felt he was in a position to take risks that others were not. He knew there would be new products, new processes, new companies that would grow as a result of the general stimulation of the economy in the postwar era.

As a consequence, he took his funds and divided them into three parts: First, into that needed for the security of himself and his family; second, a portion to establish a charitable foundation; and third, that needed to establish J. H. Whitney & Co.

The capital for J. H. Whitney & Co., which has previously appeared in the press was $10 million.

J. H. Whitney & Co., now has a staff, a total staff, of 33, all in New York. Of those 33, 13 are partners and the other 20 are secretaries, librarians, research people, accountants, and so forth. These partners, the 13 partners, have various backgrounds. Some are engineers, some have had production experience, some are lawyers, some are financial men, some are economists, some have marketing, merchandising, and general sales backgrounds.

Our cycle of operations encompasses the following four steps: First, screening out from the many propositions that come to us those with little or no merit and investigating those that are worth pursuing. That is done by informal teams of partners and staff whose fields of interest and experience and background are primarily in the areas that the proposition encompasses. We take on the services of consultants in fields in which we have little or no knowledge.

Second, making decisions on the investments that have been investigated sufficiently to be up for a decision. At some point, you must say we shall invest or we shall not invest. These decisions are pooled decisions; they are the result of the judgment of all of the partners in the firm who meet and combine their abilities in trying to decide whether this is something that our firm ought to go into.

Third, and probably the most time-consuming of all of the areas that we work in, is actively working with the companies in which we have investments, working with them to insure their growth and success. These 13 partners of J. H. Whitney & Co. hold a total of some 40 directorships in companies in which we are interested, and those are not once-a-month or quarterly or semiannual perfunctory directorship activities. These are working directorships. This type of director may be on the telephone every day, all day, or in meetings all day, or every day, or every week, or several times a month.

And, finally, in the cycle of operations of J. H. Whitney & Co. is the eventual turnover of investments through sale to the public or sale to some other organization, realizing a gain on those that are successful, and turning that money again over to reinvest in new situations.

During the past 12 years, we have been approached by over 7,000 entrepreneurs seeking capital, or an average of something over 500 a year. Of those 7,000, we have actually made investments in something over 50, in something less than 1 percent of the total that have come to us.

Just by way of illustration, you may be interested in the current work status reports in our firm and the kind of propositions that come to us. All of these that I will run down, just in a brief word, are propositions we have rejected within the last few weeks. I think you will see, when I get into the investment policy of J. H. Whitney & Co., some of the reasons why we rejected them. They still may be the types of propositions that will be interesting to some of you, because the investment policies you develop may be different from ours:

Participating in the commercializing of a new patented design of adjustable steps for use with house trailers; financing the expansion of test marketing of a pharmaceutical sold for the relief of pain; providing $200,000 to develop a direct-mail advertising list for a company which deals with the large automobile companies' advertising agencies; financing of television pilot films; providing capital for a company that is developing a skiing area with lifts in a town in Maine; providing capital to finance the construction of a gypsum mill in New Mexico; financing a children's fairyland where Mother Goose comes alive and Jack and the Beanstalk become real.

One from the Philippines, providing financing for two undisclosed inventions; providing undisclosed financial backing for a program of prospecting, drilling, and development work in northwestern Ontario; providing 3 to 5 million dollars of new capital to establish cattle- and meat-processing operations in Alaska; participating in financing for franchises for an operation of improving the quality of egg production; participating in the development of a new type of ruler with a sliding marker, which would mark small fractional distances once measured; providing 3 to 4 million dollars of additional capital for a metal-fabricating company; providing financing for an undisclosed new idea; financing development of a new type of helicopter, designed by a German and brought to the United States by the Armed Forces; providing a small amount of financing to complete the development of a new lightweight dense concrete panel; financing a continuation of developmental work on lead, silver, and zinc deposits in Idaho; financing the development of a 73,000-acre concession in Dutch Guiana; financing the exploitation of a special wing aircraft design; providing $500,000 for the conversion of 5,000 acres of land into irrigated farmland; providing unstated amount of capital to a small company that produces a roll-up ladder.

I could go on, but these give you some idea of the types of things that a firm such as ours, or a firm such as some of you may establish, will have to decide whether or not are of investment interest.

Those of you who may decide to enter this field may be interested in J. H. Whitney & Co.'s investment policy.

Let me say broadly that we are interested in those propositions that we think are worthwhile and that have a profit potential commensurate with their risk. Those are very broad criteria. There are a number of propositions that come to us on which we think we could make money, but in which we are not interested, because we do not think they meet our criterion of worthwhile. On the other hand, there are many ventures that are worthwhile that we do not think are economically sound. If the latter are sufficiently worthwhile, they will be referred to Mr. Whitney's foundation, which is where we think they belong.

So, broadly, they have to be financially attractive and they have to be something with which we would be glad to be associated.

Now, as to more specific policies: First, we are primarily interested in growth situations, in new or growth industries. Included in the fields in which we have substantial investments are frozen foods, electronics, certain phases of oil and gas operations, nuclear developments, uranium, new tool products and television broadcasting. Although we were originally interested only in new processes or new products, our policy has been broadened in recent years to include growth situations in growth industries, whether or not the given product or the process is a new addition to that field. To give you an example: We were not the first television broadcasters in the business.

However, television is certainly one of the most dynamic postwar industries; we felt that we could make a contribution in the field; we felt that the fact that we were not the very first broadcaster or were not broadcasters during the first few years or so of the birth of the industry is relatively inconsequential, providing we do something in this field that we think would justify our being in it.

Second, we are not interested in propositions that are still in the experimental or inventive stage. I will say "not primarily interested in them." This is the creative-inventive stage where we have found the risks extremely high, an area difficult to assess and one in which we are not very well able to assist. I am talking about the type of proposition in which somebody comes in with an idea of a product he would like to make and wants the capital to make the product to prove that it works. It is very difficult for a firm such as ours to assess the merit of such a proposition. We like to see and feel and touch the products intended to be marketed and on which the business is to be based.

Third, because our firm works very closely with the companies in which we make investments, we are primarily interested only in ventures in the continental limits of the United States. This, in recent years, has been extended to include Puerto Rico—I see one of the Puerto Rican representatives here today. We have made several investments in Puerto Rico.

Fourth, because small investments take as much time as large investments, we have generally found it not practical to make investments as small as, say, $50,000, unless such propositions involve unusual circumstances such as the need for first-round seed money, invested with the full knowledge that additional capital will be needed if the original capital proves the soundness of the product or process. What I am really saying is that generally propositions requiring total foreseeable capital of $50,000, with a potential of possibly tripling our money in 5 years, will not be of interest to our firm. I will discuss why in a little bit when I come to the economics of the venture capital business. Generally, the propositions that we go into are in the general area of $500,000 to $1 million.

Fifth, because we have found that new and relatively small companies need management assistance, probably at least as much as they need capital, it has, again, proved impractical for us to make investments in companies in which we do not have a sufficiently large equity interest to exercise an important role in the affairs of the company. This does not imply control. It implies a sizable stake in the company which we go into that enables us to lend some judgment and assistance, and, hopefully, to have such assistance be beneficial to the company.

Sixth, we have further eliminated companies whose sole assets are the services of individuals. By that, I mean financing advertising agencies, consulting firms, and so forth, because of the inherent difficulties of evaluating them, contributing to their operation, and, finally, because of the difficulties of realizing on such an investment.

(I think that same thing would apply to gasoline stations, drygoods establishments, and that kind of business.)

Seventh, obviously, the key of success in any business, and particularly in the businesses of the kind that some of you might be considering, is the quality of the management of the companies in which you make investments. We have to be satisfied, when we finance a business, that we are going to be happy with the management. If we have any reservations about management or if management is untried (which is often the case), we need to have enough of voice in the affairs of the company, for the company's sake as well as our own, to be able to make changes if such become necessary. If a situation, otherwise attractive, involved very weak management, we would probably not make the investment in the first place because our very last desire is to kick out the fellow that started the business we are financing. On the other hand, if there is a question about the ability of the fellow, and most people's abilities have to be proved, we would like a pretty strong voice in that business in order to effect changes if necessary.

Eighth, we are obviously interested in a return commensurate with the risks inherent in the venture capital field. This is a business that, by and large, is risky. We are not interested in making loans per se. We are interested in equity investments. We generally hope that if we are successful—if a company is successful, our investment will appreciate several times—3 to 5 times, let us say—in a period of 5 to 10 years.

Lastly, we are not interested in investments where there is obviously no way or no apparent way of realizing on them if they prove successful. We hope that we can ultimately bring our companies along to a point where they can be publicly financed or might be sufficiently attractive for acquisition by another buyer. So much for the background of J. H. Whitney & Co.

II. The Potentialities of Financing New or Small Businesses

You might be interested next in the potentialities of this business based on J. H. Whitney & Co.'s experience.

J. H. Whitney & Co., in the 12 years it has been in existence, we think, has been successful—not only financially, but also in terms of the satisfactions it has brought those associated with it. The satisfaction of seeing products brought to market that you would like to think would not be on the market were it not for you, the satisfaction of seeing small businesses grow and prosper, the satisfactions of seeing the managements of those companies grow and develop, the satisfaction of seeing the members of your own firm gain in breadth and experience over the years, and, lastly, the satisfaction, unattractive as it is sometimes, of learning from your mistakes and resolving that you won't make those same mistakes again.

As to financial results, J. H. Whitney & Co., has been successful. Obviously, the kinds of things we are in do not have, by and large, established market prices. But, based on our own evaluation of our investments, J. H. Whitney & Co.'s original capital, has almost quadrupled in 12 years. However, I am quick to point out that if in 1946, when J. H. Whitney & Co. was started, one had taken the same capital and put it into a diversified portfolio of listed securities, even those that do not have unusual growth possibilities, that capital would have tripled. We have not batted much better than we would have if we had put the capital in listed securities, with far less trouble and far less risk.

I would also like to point out that, of the 50 companies we have gone into, 250 percent of the 300 percent increase of J. H. Whitney's capital has been accounted for by 5 ventures, in each of which the amount of money at risk by J. H. Whitney & Co., was in excess of $2 million. Moreover, 1 of these 5 was an early success. Timing was on our side. If it had not been for one of these early successes, J. H. Whitney & Co. may not have been nearly so venturesome, nor able to make the later major investments that have accounted for a large part of its growth.

You might be particularly interested in those investments under $500,000 which we have made, which is more likely in the area a lot of you may be interested in. Of those, there are 38. A tabulation of those 38 shows this: In 15 of them, we lost all or substantially all of our money; in 6, we broke even—bailed out; in 4, we made some money, but an unfavorable rate of return on the investment; and, in

13, we were successful. And we would have done again those 13 out of the 38.

Some of these figures might be sobering to some of you after my previous remarks about the success of J. H. Whitney & Co.

Taking the 38 ventures as a whole of under $500,000 each, 38 both good and bad, the firm averaged slightly in excess of a 10-percent return or appreciation of capital over the full period of 12 years—assuming an average risk of 6 years, the return is something less than 2 percent a year. That is taking all 38 under $500,000. Even on the 13, that we would have done again, the percent gain over an average of 5 or 6 years has been some 54 percent, or a 9 to 10 percent return per year—just on the good ones. In neither case was the return on that money sufficient to cover the overhead of J. H. Whitney & Co.

Therefore, as you can readily see, our batting average has not been particularly outstanding in the so-called small investment field. This experience has partially dictated our trend toward investing more substantial amounts of money in a more limited number of enterprises, and more preferably in the fields in which we already have some experience.

I might point out that J. H. Whitney & Co.'s risks have been probably higher than those contemplated under SBIC, since we are primarily interested in new ventures with considerable growth possibilities rather than going small businesses that some of you might be interested in.

Finally, in the realm of potentials, one should not overlook the eventual development of knowledge in a field in which he has made a small investment that may lead to other investment opportunities in the same or a related field.

I will give you just three examples: One of our early ventures was the Minute Maid Corp., which was the pioneer of the frozen orange juice concentrate field. Our interest in Minute Maid led us into another investment in a company called Morton Packing Co., that makes frozen specialty products, meat pies and so forth. From our Minute Maid experience we also acquired some experience in the agricultural end of the orange juice business, which led to an investment in a grove operation in Florida. These things snowball—you start with one, and it may lead you down a path that you find most interesting. And you are better able to assess those opportunities because of your experience in the field.

Second, we made an investment many years ago in the community antenna field, which is a technical development in the television field involving the bringing of television to small communities that are cut off from signals from distant stations. That stimulated our interest in the television broadcasting field and led to an investment in a UHF station. It went broke, and we lost our money. But that interest in the broadcasting field led, a year later, to an investment in a television station in Tulsa, Okla., that has proved very profitable. Further, during the course of the last several years, we have built on that experience and now have 4 television stations and 2 radio stations. This is one of the major investments in J. H. Whitney & Co., today.

As a third example, we started in the oil and gas producing business, which led to investments in the oil refining field and in the tanker field. (We now have an interest in a company that has several tankers operating throughout the world.)

I would be reluctant to see any of the restrictions in the Small Business Investment Act so limit the activities of the SBIC's that they would not be able to make additional investments in fields in which they have an interest and have acquired experience.

III. The Pitfalls of Financing New or Small Enterprises

Now, as to pitfalls, for just a few minutes, and this is something all of you will be interested in. If you had a divining rod that would tell you as you touched on various propositions those that were good and those that were bad; if you could, at the same time, tell which managements are going to be outstanding and which are not; if this rod could tell you which companies would grow and prosper without additional capital, which ones would appreciate as rapidly as you hope at the time you make the investment, and which ones you would be able to sell out at the time you want to and realize on that investment, you would have it made in this business. Unfortunately, it doesn't work this way.

Obviously, one of the major requirements for a successful operation of a venture capital firm is an extremely able staff within the investment firm itself. There can be no greater pitfall than weakness in this area, because it leads to poor investigation, poor decisions, and poor assistance to the companies that you become associated with. It is the kind of business where every entrepreneur that comes to you is bubbling with enthusiasm about the good things about his proposition. A lot of that enthusiasm carries over to the people that they are approaching, and one almost has to become a devil's advocate, taking every single plus and finding out what is wrong with it. One can be carried away with the normal enthusiasm of projects. Every one sounds good to you when you are first in this game, based on my own experience. You soon find that most are not.

The requirements for a staff will vary. We think we need a well diversified group of people on our staff with various backgrounds, because propositions come in of every type covering a wide variety of fields of interest and types of industries.

I think that a good staff member in a company such as an SBIC needs, among other personal qualifications, three qualities: One, objectivity; two, a keen analytical ability; and, three, imagination. The lack of any one of these three attributes can jeopardize the success of a venture capital firm.

A second major pitfall, in our opinion, would be starting an investment firm of this type without adequate capital. A substantial amount of capital is needed for the four following things, which I will list and then elaborate on at a later time: One, sufficient capital to support a proper staff for investigation and assistance; two, sufficient capital to provide diversification of investments, without so small an investment in any one company that one cannot afford to watch and work with it; three, adequate capital to take care of the additional capital needs of ventures to which you are committed; and, four, adequate liquid capital to enable the firm to continue to look at new ventures.

Now, as to proper staffing for investigation and assistance: As I have indicated before, the cost of saying no in this business is extremely high. The something over 7,000 ventures we have looked at in 12 years would tax any staff. Facts must be checked, industries must be studied, and if the fields are new to the personnel, a liberal education must be gained in those fields. Sound decisions are only as good as the facts on which they are based, and factfinding is time consuming and costly.

Moreover, such staff talents are needed to assist the companies in which you have invested.

I think that it is safe to say—and I have some of my partners in this room—that better than 95 percent of the time of the partners of J. H. Whitney & Co., is consumed in working with companies in which we have investments. And, I think that, probably, has been the case even when we didn't have as many investments as we have now. We believe that the small businesses need guidance and need help, talents that are not available to them because of their size, at least as much as they need money.

Now it is, unfortunately, very difficult to generate income to offset the operating costs of a venture capital firm. By and large, the investments that are made are in companies that cannot afford, in our experience, to pay debt down at a given time, or to pay a particularly high interest rate. Moreover, the investments that are made, if they are in equities, are long-term investments. Generally, if the companies are going well, they need every dollar of capital to expand their operations. And if they are going poorly, they need every dollar to conserve their capital to stay afloat.

As a consequence, you are in a business where there is no substantial continuing income that you can rely on to support the operations of the firm.

Adequate capital, as I have just indicated, is needed to support a staff. You also need sufficient capital for proper diversification. Because of the risks inherent in financing new or small business, the capital obviously must be well diversified. And such diversification is feasible only with substantial initial capital. Diversity is a must in the operation of a sound venture capital enterprise.

Adequate funds, as I pointed out, are needed to take care of the additional capital needs of ventures that you are committed to. The amount of capital needed to provide additional capital if the company is successful is considerable, and if a company is unsuccessful, frequently it needs additional capital. So you have to keep a certain amount of your capital in reserve at all times to come to the rescue of the companies that you already have money in.

To give you three quick examples: a company that went well but needed additional capital, an example of one that did not go well although it needed additional injections of capital, and one of indeterminate success that needed additional capital.

In the early years of Minute Maid, between 1947 and 1949, the firm invested at various times something over half a million dollars in Orange Concentrates common stock. That was the early name of Minute Maid. Subsequently, another $450,000 was invested in Vacuum Foods, which was a subsequent name of the company—common stock. And, then, another $118,000 in Vacuum Foods preferred stock. So in 2 years the amount of money we had at risk in the Minute Maid situation had grown from half a million dollars to well over a million dollars. By then the company was going well, but it was growing faster than the capital available to support its growth. So, in 1950, we loaned Minute Maid an additional $550,000. At that time then we had better than a million and a half dollars in the company, after starting with what we thought was already a very sizable investment of half a million dollars. This is typical of companies in which we have had a part that have been successful—they need additional capital if they go well.

Second, we started a company a number of years ago in the printed circuit business. In August, 1952, we made an investment of $140,000 in the company. That was the initial capital that was required. Before the end of the first month, we increased our investment by some $30,000 to cover the first year's rent on a plant to house the operation. Then we had $169,000 in the venture. From December, 1952, which is only 3 months after the initial investment was made, to June, 1953, we had to put up another $220,000 in order to keep the company going. And, finally, we attempted to merge the company with another company, and even the merger costs were something like $15,000. So, we ultimately had an investment, or the investment had grown in something less than a year from $140,000 to over $400,000. It might be interesting to some of you to learn that we eventually lost virtually all of our money in this venture.

Third, we made an investment in a company to exploit a very interesting tool—a handheld power saw—maybe some of you own them now—called the Wright Power Saw. It combined the accuracy of a handsaw with a fixed blade with the mechanical advantages of a chain saw—a very attractive product. In April, 1950, we started with an investment of $80,000 to get the company started. Before the end of the year, we had advanced another $60,000 in the form of notes to the company. And, during the 5-year period thereafter, we made an additional $600,000 investment in the company. So we eventually had something slightly less than three-quarters of a million dollars in the company. The company was subsequently merged with another company that we thought could distribute the product more economically. We think we may ultimately recover our investment. But that company (a marginal one) like the ones that were successful and the one that was unsuccessful, needed ultimately far more capital than we ever expected it would need.

Lastly, you need adequate liquid capital to enable you to continue to look at new ventures. You can't be completely invested up in this business or you become an investment trust.

So much for the two major pitfalls that I have covered, which are the right kind of abilities in your staff and adequate capital to cover the requirements of the staff, for diversification, for standing back of the companies and continuing to look at new propositions.

The next pitfall is one of timing. You need early winners in this business. You can dissipate your capital extremely rapidly if your early ventures are unsuccessful, and the unsuccessful ones become unsuccessful much more rapidly than the successful ones become successful. We think we can tell pretty well by the end of the first year which ventures will be turkeys, but we cannot tell the ultimate success this early of those that look like they have a good chance of succeeding.

Next, the difficulty of assessing management abilities. I won't dwell on this. It is a major pitfall. A company is only as good as its management. I am sure all of you have had experience in hiring people—you are never sure unless you have worked with them over a period of time where their strengths and weaknesses are.

The next pitfall is the financing of projects too early in the game. We have had a lot of experience in this area. For example, we lost something like $460,000 in a company engaged in making an insulation board out of a volcanic ash, called perlite, many years ago. The product had basic characteristics that we thought were desirable, but we found after making the investment that the product could not be cut with a power saw without dulling its blades and that it could not be painted in as attractive a manner as competing products. In short we did not have a salable product at the time we made the investment and could not develop it to a point where it was salable. Until you know the product that you really propose to sell and on which you are staking your money, you are in a very risky business, and the kind of business in which the odds are stacked against you. Large going companies can expense such development and research costs with 50-cent dollars, whereas a new company is spending hard capital for such developmental costs.

As was pointed out earlier, another difficulty in this kind of business is becoming locked into investments with no apparent way out. Such investments may be successful in terms of developing a good, small profitable company, but trying to get it to a point where it is either large enough to be publicly marketed or sufficiently appealing to another group of investors is difficult. We have an investment in a company that makes stabilizing agents from seaweed, a very interesting operation. We have been in that company for 7 years now, I guess, and it has made a profit every year. However, it doesn't make enough of a profit to really be exciting to the public or another investor, and yet it will probably go on forever as a good, small profitable company.

So much for the major pitfalls. I would just like to wind up with some conclusions from what I have said.

We think that anyone starting a small-business investment company faces a dilemma regarding the size of its capital. Such a firm will either be investing in situations in which the risks are relatively small —and I personally doubt that low-risk capital is not available from established sources—or in relatively high-risk situations with attractive growth potentials. If the risks are small, the entrepreneurs are not going to be very excited about giving up equity through convertible debentures or a substantial amount of common stock. If the firm decides to go this route, it will need a very large amount of capital in order to cover its overhead out of the difference between the cost of its capital and its lending rate. For example, if it borrows money at 5 percent and lends it at 7 percent, let us say, a spread of something like 2 percent, it would have income of only $100,000 per year on total capital of $5 million—not adequate in our judgment to support a staff to make the investments or watch them.

On the other hand, the firm can invest in companies with considerable risks but with considerable growth potential. If it does this, it again must have sufficiently large amounts of capital to support the kind of staff and the kind of diversification that such risks entail. Anyone thinking of starting a small-business investment company must face realistically these economics.

The Small Business Investment Act alone does not open the golden gates of opportunities for investors to make money. Rather, it sets the stage for encouraging more to take the risks inherent in this field and for those seeking capital to have their day in court. We do not think that this type of business is suitable for the investor who may not be prepared to lose all of his money.

It would appear to us that the total initial capital requirements for such an investment firm would be in the area of several million dollars rather than in the area of hundreds of thousands of dollars. Too much can be lost too quickly, and the cost of an adequate organization comes too high.

5. THE LEGAL PATTERN OF BUSINESS FIRMS *

Any person visiting even the smallest business district of a town in the United States will observe, if he turns his attention to the matter, that the business which is carried on is owned in a variety of ways. There will surely be shops, dealerships, and services that are owned and operated by one person. Some of these may even have a sign showing the name of an individual and the abbreviation *Prop.*, indicating "Proprietor." Other activities will be found to be owned by a group of persons acting as partners. This will certainly be the case for any law office or medical center, and it will often be the case for other activities where a few persons have decided to join together to form a business. It is not always possible to judge that a firm is a partnership purely from its name, but the use of personal names (Smith & Jones) or the words *and Company* often furnish a clue.

Mixed in with these organizations, which are to be recognized as persons or groups of persons engaged in business, the observer will see, by the use of the abbreviation *Inc.* (Incorporated) or *Corp.* (Corporation) in the name, that certain firms are designated as having corporate form. Agencies, plants, and offices of larger businesses will be among those which bear the corporate designation. In most communities, for example, our observer is likely to find the business office of the local unit of the American Telephone and Telegraph Company, one of the largest private corporations in the United States. And, of course, on the shelves of all the stores the products of corporate business will greatly outnumber the goods that were made by other types of firms.

As he looks for the names which indicate that a business has corporate form, the observer will see the somewhat puzzling fact that many of the smaller firms are also incorporated. If he should conclude that there must be a variety of reasons why people choose to incorporate their businesses, he would be on the right track.

The differences between the types of ownership are of more than

* By Pearson Hunt, Professor of Business Administration, Harvard Business School, reprinted in slightly modified form by permission of the publisher and author from *Basic Business Finance* (rev. ed., Homewood, Ill.: Richard D. Irwin, Inc., 1961).

passing importance to all of us. Their significance begins to become apparent whenever one wishes to establish a relation with a firm that requires a commitment of some sort. Who is authorized to speak for the business? Will the business survive those who now speak for it? Where and how much is the ultimate liability of the firm, in case damage is done to me? How can I invest some of my funds in this firm? What participation in control would I have? Any one of these questions has different answers, depending on the type of business organization that is used. The reader should be able to answer them, among others, after study of this chapter.

Legal Patterns Fall into Two Groups

In order to indicate how some of the questions can be answered, it is necessary to identify the various bodies of rules within which a business must operate. We refer to these rules as *legal patterns*, of which several are available for choice by those who wish to set up a business organization. A complete treatise would describe even those, such as the *business trust* and the *joint stock company*, which are at present of small importance in the United States. The principal avenues of choice lead to the *corporation* on one side and to the *partnership* or to the *proprietorship* on the other, and our discussion will deal chiefly with them. The major concern of this material will therefore be to explain the characteristics of the corporation, on one hand, and the partnership-proprietorship, on the other, so that the reader can understand the factors that enter the decision-making process when the choice is being made for a firm. For the present the business trust can be regarded as very like a corporation, and the joint-stock company as a corporation except for the legal liability that attaches to its owners. A preliminary distinction can then be drawn between the partnership-proprietorship, which is simply a certain person or group of persons in business, and those businesses of corporate type, where there is a legal entity apart from the persons who own and operate the firm.

Present Importance of the Corporation in the United States

Since the corporation has become the predominant form of doing business in the United States, we can well begin our examination of the subject by a review of some important statistics about the varying importance of the corporation in various sectors of the economic activity of the nation. While we shall confine ourselves to the factual situation in the United States, it will be of interest to note that, in general, the same conditions will be found in any industrialized country where private enterprise plays an important part. Table 5–1 shows

Table 5–1

COMPARISON OF RELATIVE IMPORTANCE OF INCORPORATED
AND UNINCORPORATED ENTERPRISES AS MEASURED
BY PERCENTAGE OF TOTAL NET INCOME BEFORE TAXES,
BY INDUSTRY, FOR THE YEAR 1963

| Industry | Before-Tax Corporate Income | |
	Millions of Dollars	Percentage of Industry
All industries	$51,267	50.3%
Agriculture, forestry, and fisheries	86	0.6
Mining	929	85.9
Contract construction	521	9.8
Manufacturing	27,185	94.6
Wholesale and retail trade	5,406	30.2
Finance, insurance, and real estate	5,687	66.6
Transportation	1,084	54.1
Communication and public utilities	7,300	99.1
Services	554	3.7

SOURCE: U.S. Department of Commerce, *Survey of Current Business*, "National Income Number," July, 1964, Tables 44, p. 27, and 56, p. 31.

not only that one half of the business income is earned by corporations, but also that this form of business organization is dominant wherever large-scale units are needed for efficiency.

To explain more fully the reasons for the use of the corporate form, we now turn to an examination of its characteristics in some detail. They have been organized under the major headings: "Legal Entity," "State Sanction—Corporate Powers," "Financial Contracts," and "Tax Status." In each section, primary attention will be given to the corporation. The partnership-proprietorship and other patterns will be referred to only where there are major differences of concern to those selecting the legal pattern of a business.

Legal Entity

The reader should note that the American culture of today provides natural acceptance of the idea that one normally does business with an entity which is separate from the persons dealt with. One thinks of a business as separate from the personal interests of its owner. This division is a complex one, involving characteristics that are not always desirable, but it is important to recognize that it does exist. There is acceptance in our culture of the idea that a business unit is a separable entity, and the law has been specific in making the separation in the case of the corporation, so one can speak of the legal entity that exists in addition to the cultural entity that is generally accepted.

A useful definition of a *corporation* is: ". . . an association of persons which is in many respects treated as if it were itself a person. It has rights and duties of its own, which are not the rights and duties of the individual members thereof. . . . The rights and duties of the members descend to the successive members of the corporation." [1]

This statement is both the definition of a corporation and an explanation of the meaning of the term *legal entity*. The corporation has status before the law as a person. This means that courts will consider the corporation as a person which may enter into contracts, sue or be sued, and so on, quite independently of the individuals who own its securities. Thus, while the culture confers a sort of entity on any business unit, the law confines this privilege to the corporation. The other forms of organization are recognized only as groups of individuals.

It should be noted that the conferring of personality on the corporation does not mean that this kind of person has all the rights and privileges of a natural person. Obviously, there are many types of contract, such as marriage, that a corporation cannot enter into, and there are many types of conduct which corporations cannot undertake. There are, in fact, many laws limiting corporate privileges. The significant thing is that a corporation does have certain important elements of a separate personality in the eyes of the law.

Characteristics of the Corporation Associated with Legal Entity. Certain characteristics of a corporation may be associated with its legal entity. (1) There is the duty to have a corporate name, although as a privilege other types of firms may select names. (2) There is the privilege of a term of existence which is completely independent of the lives of any natural persons. (3) There is a provision for a board of directors to represent the owners, who may be a great many persons. (4) There is the privilege that the corporation may hold title to property and enter into contracts of all sorts without binding the individuals who own the corporation to the obligations it has under-

---

[1] Cecil T. Carr, "Corporation," *Encyclopædia Britannica* (11th ed.; New York: Encyclopædia Britannica Co., 1910–11), Vol. VII, p. 190.

taken. Finally, and often of great importance, (5) the separate entity is subject to different rules of taxation. This last matter will be the subject of a separate section.

The foregoing characteristics are available only in limited form, if at all, to the other forms of business organization, and none has all of them. A partnership operates under the rule—exactly contrary to that for the corporation—that any partner may act for the partnership in matters related to the business of the partnership, except where the limitation on the partner is indicated clearly and publicly.[2] The grant of such power to a partner is a necessary convenience if business is to be done efficiently, but it has served as the disruptive force that has caused the dissolution of many firms.

The Corporate Name.   The duty to select a corporate name includes as a requirement that the name indicate the fact of incorporation.[3] In the United States, this is usually done by using the word *Incorporated* as the last word of the corporate title. This is usually abbreviated and read as *Inc.* The word *Corporation* (Corp.) is sometimes used. One also finds *Limited* (Ltd.), which is the standard British and Canadian practice but appears in the United States only to lend a sort of prestige to the name. Some states have laws which permit the use of *The _____ Company* to distinguish a corporation. Other distinguishing words are used in other countries. The French *Société Anonyme* is worth noting because it points out the separate entity characteristic of the corporation.

Most states now permit any form of business unit to adopt a firm name. Often, there is some designation in the title that indicates the type of legal pattern that is used. Business trusts usually have the word *Trust* in their names.[4] Limited partnerships must indicate that some of the partners do not have unlimited liability, but do not do so in their names. In most states, the fact of limited partnership is disclosed in a Certificate of Limited Partnership, which is filed with the Secretary of State and is thus a matter of public record. The ordi-

---

[2] In such case the person is known as a *limited partner* and can take no part in the management of the partnership. He is simply a supplier of capital. A major difficulty faced by limited partners is that states other than that in which the partnership was formed may make the limited partner equally liable with the other partners for debts created in the outside state.

[3] Insurance *companies*, trust *companies*, and *banks* are usually corporations, though their names may not indicate the fact. These enterprises are incorporated under special laws regulating banking and insurance.

[4] The phrase *the trust problem* to designate the problem created by large-scale enterprise is a historical accident arising from the fact that the first "trusts" used the business trust form. Later, "trusts" used the corporate form much more frequently.

nary partnerships and other forms of business use the words *and Company* frequently.

Term of Life. Most corporations avail themselves fully of the privilege of indefinite existence by stating no termination date in their basic documents. Those that do usually find it easy to extend their life by amendment. One author has selected an apt simile by comparing the corporate society to a river. The water in the river, symbolizing the parties to the corporation, is ever changing. The general river, however, does not change; and one thinks of the river as the same entity, even though much water has flowed through it.

The characteristics of a corporation which have just been described can be summarized in the eloquent and frequently quoted words of John Marshall:

A corporation is an artificial being, invisible, intangible, and existing only in contemplation of law. Being the mere creature of law, it possesses only those properties which the charter of its creation confers upon it, either expressly or as incidental to its very existence. . . . Among the most important are immortality, and . . . individuality; properties by which a perpetual succession of many persons are considered the same and may act as a single individual.[5]

The historic rule is that a partnership must dissolve on the death, incapacity, or withdrawal of any partner, except a limited partner. The same is, of course, true of an individual proprietorship. A great many partnership agreements provide in detail the procedure to be followed on the withdrawal of a partner. A few states permit partnerships to survive without the signing of a new contract. Thus, in many cases a new partnership is formed to take over the affairs of the old one without any disturbance of the business. It must, however, be noted that no such arrangement can avoid the necessity of evaluating the interest of the withdrawing partner, or of paying this value to the partner, or his estate, or other representative. The payment may be made in notes of the new partnership, if this was provided for by the original partnership agreement, but any such notes must be payable in a reasonable time.[6]

---

[5] *Trustees of Dartmouth College* v. *Woodward*, 4 Wheat. (U.S.) 518, 636 (1819). In his first sentence, the learned justice was paraphrasing Sir Edward Coke. Case of Sutton's Hospital, 10 Coke's Reports 1, 32*b* (1613).

[6] The following quotations from a partnership agreement show the extent of complexity sometimes encountered in partnership agreements. Note that the partnership contract foresees problems of valuation as well as liquidation.

Profits and Losses. Salaries of partners shall be treated as expenses. Net profits or losses for each calendar year shall be entered as follows:

a) Net profits or losses up to and including 10% of the aggregate capital ac-

Despite the devices that can be created by advance agreement, the process of dissolution of a partnership and creation of a new partnership is usually a period of strain even with goodwill from all parties. It may impose severe financial burdens on the continuing business. Thus, the disadvantages of mortality lead many partnerships to shift to the corporate form. The same is true, of course, of the individual proprietor, if he desires to see his business continue after him.

The Board of Directors. In the proprietorship, the ultimate powers of decision are in the hands of the owner. In the partnership, as stated above, any general partner may act for the partnership. In the case of the corporation, most of the powers of ownership are placed in the hands of a board of directors. There are certain questions of such importance that they must be referred to a stockholders' meeting for a vote. These include decisions to merge with another firm, to change the privileges of a class of stockholders, and others of like importance. But in the normal course of affairs, the board of directors makes decisions as if the directors were owners, as long as its members act honestly and in good faith. From this situation of representative government comes the possibility—and often the fact—of a separation of ownership from control.[6a]

Adolph Berle and Gardiner Means, in their pioneering study,[7]

---

counts shall be credited or charged to partners in proportion to their capital accounts;

b) One-half of any remaining net profits or losses up through the next 6% of the aggregate capital accounts shall be credited or charged proportionally to the several capital accounts, and the other half shall be credited or charged against the partners in equal shares; and

c) All net profits or losses for each year over 16% of the aggregate capital accounts shall be credited or charged in proportion to the several capital accounts.

New Partners. New partners may be elected not less than 60 days after proposal for membership, by the vote of at least two-thirds of the members owning at least two-thirds of the firm's capital.

Withdrawal or Death of a Partner. A partner may withdraw at any time by agreement with the Executive Committee or by giving one year's notice. Withdrawal may be required by a two-thirds vote of members owning two-thirds of capital. Such withdrawal or death shall not work a dissolution of the firm. In case of the withdrawal or death of a partner, the interest of such former partner shall be determined and paid as follows:

a) The amount credited in his drawing account shall be paid on 30 days' notice.

b) His credit balance in the capital account, as shown by the last previous balance sheet plus or minus subsequent charges and corrections for the profit or loss of the year, with interest at 6% per annum until payment, shall be paid by the firm in 10 equal annual installments, with such anticipation in the payment of installments as the firm may decide. Such unpaid balances shall be treated as a debt of the firm.

[6a] Whether a director must be a shareholder is usually prescribed by a corporation's bylaws.

[7] Adolph A. Berle, Jr., and Gardiner C. Means, *The Modern Corporation and Private Property* (New York: Macmillan Co., 1933). Used by permission. The statistical section has become out of date, but the legal analysis is as cogent as ever.

defined location of the control of a corporation as follows: ". . . we may say for practical purposes that control lies in the hands of the individual or group who have the actual power to select the board of directors (or its majority). . . ." [8] In the active sense of day-to-day management, this definition is entirely true, and it is therefore appropriate to study first the location of the voting power which can be used at corporate meetings. Every corporation will have at least one class of shareholders whose members have voting power. In the majority of corporations, all the voting power is found in the common stock, on the basis of one vote per share.

Any shareholder may be elected a director at the annual meeting of the shareholders; but since his holding need be only one or a few shares, his own position as owner may be nominal. In the smaller firms, especially those *closely held* corporations where the ownership of shares is concentrated in a few hands, the membership of the board will be able to know the desires of the stockholder group, and to act accordingly.[9] In the larger, *publicly held* corporations, the directors may be unable to sense the desires of a group of shareholders of diversified characteristics. Although there has been a movement to persuade shareholders in the publicly held corporations to attend meetings, the proportion of such owners who do, in fact, attend has been and will continue to be small. Most persons entitled to vote at such meetings execute a *proxy*, which names someone who is authorized to cast the vote of the absent shareholder. There are, as our readers doubtless know, occasional proxy fights where opposing interests solicit the vote of the shareholder; but the majority of corporations have peaceful annual meetings at which the existing management, having solicited proxies, has a controlling majority of the votes at the meeting. The terms *management controlled* and *minority controlled* are used to describe corporations where the *proxy system* is relied on to provide the incumbent group with the votes needed to elect its nominees to the board of directors.

As far as the large, publicly held companies are concerned, the present situation has been aptly described by Mason:

The one-hundred-and-thirty-odd largest manufacturing corporations account for half of manufacturing output in the United States. The five hun-

[8] *Ibid.*, p. 69.
[9] In the past, three has usually been the minimum number of directors required by the statutes of most states, although a few states have permitted "a board of one or more directors." Recently, starting in 1961, several states, including Delaware, New York, and Illinois, have enacted laws providing that where all shares are owned by one or two stockholders the number of directors may be less than three but not less than the number of stockholders. (See E. George Rudolph, "Further Thoughts on the One or Two Director Statutes," *The Business Lawyer*, Vol. XX, No. 3 (April, 1965).

dred largest business corporations in this country embrace nearly two thirds of all nonagricultural economic activity. These or similar figures are reiterated with such frequency that they tend to bounce off our heads rather than to penetrate. But by now we are all aware that we live not only in a corporate society but a society of large corporations. The management—that is, the control—of these corporations is in the hands of, at most, a few thousand men. Who selected these men, if not to rule over us, at least to exercise vast authority, and to whom are they responsible? The answer to the first question is quite clearly: they selected themselves. The answer to the second is, at best, nebulous. . . .[10]

There are a great many factors to be appraised before one can form a judgment about the desirability of such a situation. Suffice it to say here that corporations are governed by elected boards of directors, which are supposed in legal theory to represent the interests of the owning investors. In many corporations, especially the closely held ones, they do. In other corporations, it is not easy for the members of the board to be identified as representatives of any ownership interest. Most directors in such circumstances act in what they believe to be "the best interests of the corporation"; but the exact meaning of that term is not clear—nor can it be, for the corporation is nothing more than an artificial being, with no interests of its own. One much-quoted attempt to provide guidance is the following:

. . . Business firms are man-made instruments of society. They can be made to achieve their greatest social usefulness—and thus their future can be best assured—when management succeeds in finding a harmonious balance among the claims of the various interested groups: the stockholders, employees, customers, and the public at large. But management's responsibility, in the broadest sense, extends beyond the search for a balance among respective claims. Management, as a good citizen, and because it cannot properly function in an acrimonious and contentious atmosphere, has the positive duty to work for peaceful relations and understanding among men —for a restoration of faith of men in each other in all walks of life.

. . . .

Those two words, "fair" and "reasonable," mark the asserted claims not only of a corporation's stockholders but of all other groups as well. Very few groups ever believe that they make unfair or unreasonable claims. But often what one group thinks fair is regarded as entirely unreasonable by another. It takes professional judgment, experience, and knowledge of the consequences of specific decisions to resolve all the claims and to keep all the groups in cooperative support of the joint enterprise.

This reconciliation of interest is not always as difficult as it may seem.

---

[10] Edward S. Mason (ed.), *The Corporation in Modern Society* (Cambridge, Mass.: Harvard University Press, 1959), p. 5.

It is in part a matter of recognizing true long-term interest, as distinguished from interests that may seem real because they are more immediate.[11]

In view of the widespread ineffectiveness of shareholder control, the reader may be disposed to conclude that the common shareholder should be considered as just another source of funds along with the bondholder and preferred stockholder. We disagree with this interpretation for two reasons: (1) The common shareholder alone possesses the legal right to control the management and the business, whether he exercises it or not; and (2) the common shareholder continues to bear the fundamental risks of the business, whether or not he dictates its policies. This leads us to the position that questions of financial policy *should* be determined from the point of view of the interests of the common shareholders *existing at the time the policy is being determined.* This interest, when determined, can then enter the balancing process implicit in the quotation from Abrams that we gave above.

Limited Liability.   As distinguished from other forms of business organization, the corporate form offers *limited liability* to its owners. The following comment has been made on the typical provision of corporation law on stockholders' liabilities:

Stockholders are liable to creditors of their corporation for unpaid stock subscriptions. In addition, the law in some states lists other conditions under which stockholders incur liability. Receiving unlawful distributions in the form of either dividends or payments on dissolution, or voting approval of other proposals which unlawfully reduce the corporation's capital are among [such] conditions.[12]

While the legal obligations of a proprietor or of any member of a partnership are described as *unlimited liability*, experience indicates that business creditors are reluctant to levy on personal assets, if only because of the cost involved. When they do, they often find that most of the assets in the partner's family are in the name of the wife or some other person not a partner. Such insulation from liability is common and expected. It reflects the cultural acceptance of the business as separate from the personal interests of the owners. Nevertheless, where one considers the incorporation of a small firm, the grant

---

[11] Frank W. Abrams, "Management's Responsibilities in a Complex World," *Harvard Business Review*, May, 1951, pp. 29–30.

[12] Commerce Clearing House, Inc., *Corporation Law Guide* (Chicago, 1959), par. 511 [par. 658].

of limited liability is often a factor of considerable weight in the decision.[13]

On the side of the publicly held corporation, where limited liability exists as a matter of law, it is now so universally a characteristic of securities that investors take it for granted. The need for this feature is therefore no longer an issue of the investment world. There is, however, one corollary of the grant of limited liability which corporate management needs to bear in mind. The capital contributed by the shareholders is to be kept separate from any earnings that may be received and held by the corporation. Dividends may not be paid out of such capital.

State Sanction—Corporate Powers

All the material above, which is centered on the legal entity enjoyed by the corporation, has implicit in it the fact that the corporation exists by the grace of legislative power. Artificial persons are created only by legislative action, and the sovereign has always been the agency on which depends the opportunity to create corporations.

General Incorporation Laws of the States. For some years past, beginning with New York in 1811, each of the states of the United States has had a "general corporation law," paralleled by a "general banking law" and the like, which permit persons to charter a corporation for any legal purpose, provided they meet certain requirements, which are the same for any applicant.[14] The terms of the laws vary greatly among the states, and some of the differences will be referred to where they are pertinent, but they have the common characteristic of the relative ease with which a corporation can be created. The necessary papers are drafted and filed, moderate fees are paid, et cetera, all within the terms of the statute and without real difficulty.

Incorporation is not difficult in any state, but few states match Delaware, where it is possible for a firm in Wilmington to advertise that out-of-state persons may employ it to handle all the necessary procedure of incorporation, with the result that:

Corporations are organized, by-laws adopted and records mailed to counsel on the same day. . . . The first meeting is held in Wilmington. Per-

---

[13] The limited liability feature of an incorporated business may be of little use if a banker or other creditor insists on having the debt contract personally endorsed by the principal stockholder(s).

[14] In the case of banks and other financial corporations, the minimum capital requirement may be substantial. Certain types of business, such as utilities, cannot be set up without a finding by a commission that they are "convenient and necessary."

sonal attendance of the incorporators is not required. . . . Thus the organization is brought up to the point of holding the first meeting of directors for electing officers and commencing business. This meeting may be held when and where convenient to the directors and forms are furnished as a guide for its procedure.

Many older corporations still do business under charters granted in the time when each charter was a separate legislative act. Some of them have unusually broad provisions. The charter of Dartmouth College deserves special mention, since it raised the constitutional question of whether a state could amend a grant of powers which it had made at one time. It was decided, in a famous opinion of John Marshall,[15] that the grant could not be amended. While this decision is still law, one should not be confused by its effect. The result has been that every existing general corporation statute contains a provision which reserves to the state the right to amend a charter granted thereunder.

Federal Corporations Result from Special Enactment.   No general corporation statute exists as a part of the federal law, though the Congress has the power to enact one, and bills have been submitted for the purpose. There is a general banking law, known as the National Banking Act, under which are chartered banks with the privilege, and duty, of carrying in their title the words *National Bank* (or N.B.A.). Similar laws provide for federal savings and loan associations, national farm loan associations, and other credit agencies; but for the formation of a general business corporation, one looks to the various states.

The federal Congress has chartered numerous corporations by special enactment. These fulfill some governmental purpose, often of a financial nature. The Federal Reserve banks, the Federal Land banks, the Reconstruction Finance Corporation, and the Inland Waterways Corporation are examples of the use of federal statute to create a corporation. On the other hand, the Congress has sometimes provided for the formation of a governmental corporation under state law. This is true, for instance, of the Commodity Credit Corporation of Delaware.

The Definition of Corporate Powers.   The saying "The corporation has limited powers" reflects the admitted fact that a corporation can have only the powers that the state permits it to assume. Nevertheless, the statement is misleading. In practice, those who form cor-

---

[15] *Trustees of Dartmouth College* v. *Woodward*, 4 Wheat. (U.S.) 518 (1819).

porations draft their own definition of powers and provide the powers they desire within the broad limitations of the general law.

At the time a corporation is formed, its powers will be defined by (1) the statutes of the state, which apply to all its corporations; (2) the *certificate of incorporation* (or *charter*, or *articles of association*), which is drafted by those desiring to form the corporation and applies only to the specific firm; and (3) the bylaws, further defining the corporation's powers, which are also drafted by the incorporators.

The Corporation Law. Corporations are subject to all law that affects business affairs, but the corporation statute of a state deals with the special characteristics of a corporation, and it is to the provisions of such a statute that one turns when the powers available to a corporation are to be described.

Anyone with imagination who studies carefully any piece of legislation will soon be able to think of situations where the application of the wording of the statute is uncertain. When lawyers speak of "untested" provisions of a statute, they refer to clauses whose meanings have not yet been the subject of a judicial decision. There is no other way to discover the meaning of a difficult clause than by waiting for a lawsuit to develop and observing the court's conclusion. Then it is said that the clause has been "interpreted."

For this reason, it must be realized that the corporation law of a state is far more than the text of the legislation. It includes this text and all the judicial decisions relative to it. From this fact flows a reluctance on the part of legislators to change long-standing and fully interpreted clauses of legislation. There is always uncertainty about the exact meaning of proposed provisions which may cause hesitancy in their use and costly litigation before their interpretation. Among the reasons for the popularity of Delaware in the past as a state of incorporation has been that its corporation law has been the subject of much litigation, so that at present the meaning of the statute is well settled.

Although from time to time judicial decisions tend to confuse rather than clarify the law, the longer the corporation continues to be the principal pattern used by business units, the more nearly perfected its law will be in every detail. Thus, as time has gone by, the greater has become the margin of preference for the corporation over the joint-stock company and the business trust.

Articles of Incorporation and Bylaws. Most general corporation laws make it clear that the state no longer values its privilege to limit the powers of corporations formed for general business purposes. In such circumstances, it is not surprising that a cautious draftsman may state the proposed powers broadly enough to avoid any necessity of later amendment. The case of the Public Works Emergency Leasing Corporation (Delaware, 1934) has been chosen to show how broad the powers may be, despite the more limited immediate purpose of the incorporators (in this instance, the Secretary of the Interior and two other government officials).

The articles of incorporation of this organization specify that it is to have perpetual existence. The powers include those:

> To undertake . . . any project eligible to be included in the comprehensive program of Public Works to be prepared pursuant to the provisions of the Recovery Act.
>
> To collect fees, tolls, and other charges in the construction of [public works].
>
> To cause maintenance and operation of edifices, structures, and buildings of every kind, nature, or description.
>
> To furnish, equip, operate, manage and maintain projects and structures of every kind, nature, or description, and to do any and all things necessary, suitable, or convenient in connection therewith, including without limitation the supplying of heat, steam, water, gas and electricity and transportation, telephone, and any other facilities or utilities necessary, suitable, or convenient.
>
> To carry on its functions in the State of Delaware or in any other State, Territory, or locality . . . without restriction or limitation as to amount.
>
> To acquire personal property of every kind, nature or description and in any manner to acquire, hold, use, or dispose of any franchises, licenses, grants, concessions, patents, trade marks, trade names, copyrights, or inventions granted by or existing under the laws of any government or subdivision thereof.
>
> To acquire, by purchase, exchange or otherwise, all or any part of or any interest in the properties, assets, business and goodwill of any one or more persons, firms, associations, or corporations engaged in any business for which a corporation may now or hereafter be organized under the laws of the State of Delaware; to pay for the same in any lawful manner; to hold, operate, reorganize, liquidate, sell, donate, or in any manner dispose of the whole or any part thereof; and, in connection therewith, to assume or guarantee performance of any liabilities, obligations, or contracts of such persons, firms, associations, or corporations, and to conduct in any lawful manner the whole or part of any business thus acquired.[16]

At this point, the reader is reminded that this description refers to incorporation under general laws, not under banking, insurance, or other special laws. The draftsman cannot entirely "encompass the

---

[16] Small wonder that a somewhat unsophisticated commentator found in this charter evidence of a conspiracy to socialize the nation!

world in the English language," as certain activities are in the purview of other laws. Thus, the extremely broad charter of the Chesapeake Corporation, a railroad holding company, conceded the following restrictions:

Nothing herein contained is to be construed as authorizing the Corporation to carry on the business of discounting bills, notes or other evidences of debt, or receiving deposits of money, or foreign coins, or buying and selling bills of exchange, or of issuing bills, notes or other evidences of debt for circulation as money. . . .

Nothing herein contained shall be . . . construed to give the Corporation any rights, powers, or privileges not permitted by the laws of the State of Maryland. . . .

Despite the possibility that narrow definitions of powers may prove embarrassing at a later time, a substantial number of cases exist where the powers that are taken are narrowly stated. This is particularly true of small firms, where the intent of the incorporators is to take advantage of certain of the attributes of the corporation without freeing the future management in every particular. Quite frequently in such firms one finds that the transfer of stock is limited to certain procedures that give the corporation's directors control over additions to the stockholder group.

Since the bylaws of the corporation are drafted to implement the articles of incorporation, it can be expected that they will not alter the conclusions suggested by the above paragraphs: that the general corporation law of most states does not, in fact, limit the freedom of incorporators to set up a corporation of their own design. While many corporations do operate with closely defined powers, many others do not, and the state is a passive agent. The legal pattern of the corporation need be no more restrictive than that of the noncorporate enterprise.

The state is also a passive agent in the taking of powers by firms that select patterns other than a corporation. A proprietorship is the most free of any special limitation on its business. Partnerships are, in most states, the subject of a special partnership law; but in making the partnership contract, a basic document similar to corporate articles and bylaws, draftsmen are as free when it comes to the particular matter of defining the nature of the business to be undertaken.

Important Distinctions Remain. The basic differences already referred to in this chapter are (1) that the corporation is a legal entity, and thus that its parties may separate its affairs from their own more completely than is possible under other legal forms; (2) that the corporation has the possibility of an unlimited term of existence; (3) that each member of a partnership, except a publicly announced limited partner, may act in the name of the partnership; (4) that a partnership must go through a dissolution on the death of a partner, and a new partnership must succeed it; and (5) that the liabilities of a corporation do not attach to its owners or its managers.

An important basic difference not so far mentioned, and one that cannot be avoided completely by clever draftsmanship, is the limitation put on a corporation's power to do business in any state. This limitation comes from the general recognition that a corporation is not a person in the sense used in the Constitution of the United States, which guarantees that each state shall confer on a citizen of any state all those rights which it confers on its own citizens. In contrast, an out-of-state corporation, "foreign" to a state in which it desires to do business, is always required to pay certain fees and to maintain a local office. In some states, it may be required to indicate which of its powers it proposes to use in the state; and in a few cases, it may be denied permission to do business at all. Such restrictions are possible under the general rule of a decision of the United States Supreme Court, quoted below, but the "comity" referred to in the quotation keeps the number of restrictions small.

. . . The corporation being the mere creation of local law can have no legal existence beyond the limits of the sovereignty where created. . . . The recognition of its existence even by other states . . . depend purely upon the comity of those states—a comity which is never extended where the existence of the corporation and the exercise of its powers are prejudicial to their interests or repugnant to their policy. Having no absolute right of recognition in other states, but depending . . . upon their assent, it follows . . . that such assent may be granted upon such terms and conditions as those states may think proper to impose. They may exclude the foreign corporation entirely; they may restrict its business. . . . The whole matter rests in their discretion.[17]

Although the comity of the states and reliance on laws of general application have kept the number of restrictions on foreign corporations small, the added expense alone results in the practice that most corporations incorporate in the state of their principal place of business. On the other hand, several large corporations have chosen as the state of their incorporation some state where the franchise taxes are low or some desired corporate practice is known to be legal.

Table 5–2 shows the state of incorporation and the state in which

---

[17] *Paul* v. *Virginia*, 8 Wall. (75 U.S.) 168 (1869).

Table 5–2

STATE OF INCORPORATION AND LOCATION OF GENERAL OFFICE OF TWENTY LARGEST UNITED STATES CORPORATIONS

Name of Company	Location of General Office	State of Incorporation
General Motors Corporation	Michigan	Delaware
Standard Oil Company (New Jersey) ...	New York	New Jersey
Ford Motor Company	Michigan	Delaware
General Electric Company	New York	New York
United States Steel Corporation	New York	New Jersey
Socony Mobil Oil Company, Inc.	New York	New York
Gulf Oil Corporation	Pennsylvania	Pennsylvania
Texaco, Inc.	New York	Delaware
Chrysler Corporation	Michigan	Delaware
Swift & Company	Illinois	Illinois
Western Electric Company, Inc.	New York	New York
Du Pont (E. I.) de Nemours & Company	Delaware	Delaware
Bethlehem Steel Corporation	New York	Delaware
Standard Oil Company (Indiana)	Illinois	Indiana
Westinghouse Electric Corporation	Pennsylvania	Pennsylvania
Armour and Company	Illinois	Illinois
General Dynamics Corporation	New York, Washington	Delaware
Shell Oil Company	New York	Delaware
Boeing Airplane Company	Washington	Delaware
National Dairy Products Corporation ..	New York	Delaware

SOURCE OF COMPANY NAMES: *The Fortune Directory of the 500 Largest U.S. Industrial Corporations,* Supplement to *Fortune,* July, 1960 (New York, 1960), p. 132. Copyright, 1960, by Time, Inc.
SOURCE OF OTHER DATA: *Moody's Industrial Manual, 1960,* except *Moody's Public Utility Manual, 1960,* for Western Electric Company, Inc.

the general office is located for the twenty largest United States industrial corporations (1960).

Financial Contracts

No single corporate characteristic does more to explain the corporation's overwhelming importance in the present-day American economy than its ability to create financial contracts of innumerable types. Any business may be referred to as a "bundle of contracts," for this phrase is used to point out that, as of any moment, the activities of any going concern, no matter what its form of organization, are defined in innumerable ways by the contracts into which it has entered. Such contracts, in fact, define the activities of a business from day to day far more than the basic documents referred to above. The bundle includes contracts of purchase and sale, contracts of employment, real estate lease contracts, and all the other types of business contracts that will be found to be in force in any going concern.

Contracts of the type just referred to do not distinguish a corporation. The distinction is found in the greater variety of financial contracts possible to a corporation because of its long span of existence and its ability to limit the liability of investors. When contrasted with the partnership or any business unit whose life is measured by that of some individual, the corporation offers much greater continuity, and thus the basis for long-term arrangements, such as bond or preferred stock issues. When contrasted with the joint-stock company, the corporation offers in its financial contracts less risk of loss, because of the feature of limited liability. Finally, the entity conferred on the corporation permits it to make contracts of the nature of mortgages on its property without the cumbersome detail that attends the use of instruments of this nature in connection with partnerships.

The term *corporate securities*, as used in finance, usually refers to stocks, bonds, and other evidences of contracts for funds.[18] Actually, existing security contracts, as used by corporations, vary in detail almost as widely as the range of the imagination, for there is as little restraint on the draftsman of corporate securities as on the draftsman of the articles of incorporation and bylaws that create the corporation. But examination of the innumerable corporate securities that have been issued shows three characteristics prevailing among them. Their terms are made *suitable* to the needs of particular buyers; they provide for the *division* of the contract among many investors; and they permit *transfer* of the benefits of the contract from one investor to another.

Suitability: Debt versus Ownership.   Much of the art of financial management is applied to the drafting of corporate financial contracts that are suitable to the circumstances of the corporation and the investor. But although the variety of individual cases is almost infinite, the contracts fall into two main classes: those which create debt and those which recognize ownership. The distinguishing characteristic of debt is that a contract of this nature contains a promise to pay money under stated conditions. The law conveys to the holder of a debt the right to enforce his claim by court action, if necessary. A contract of participation in ownership, on the other hand, does not contain a promise to pay but merely conveys an opportunity to participate in

---

[18] Originally, the term may have been restricted to contracts under the terms of which the promises were secured by the pledge of something of value—"the security"— but the use of the term is now far more general.

such distributions as shall be voted by the directors of the corporation. Thus, as a minimum, the holder of a debt of a corporation is
more certain of receiving payments according to the terms of his debt
contract than is the holder of a share in ownership.

Out of this distinction, with all the variety that can be applied in
individual cases, arises the possibility of drafting corporate financial
contracts that are suitable to a variety of investors. Those desirous of
relative certainty of payment will be offered debt contracts, broadly
referred to as *bonds,* or *notes.* Others, anxious to participate as owners when profits expand, will be buyers of shares of ownership, usually
referred to as *common stock* or *capital stock.*

A middle position, that of *preferred stock,* often appeals to investors desiring a larger return than that offered by debt contracts; but in
law this type of contract enjoys none of the certainty of a debt obligation. The dividend, though having priority over common stock, is
only paid when voted by the directors.

For example, the life insurance companies of the United States,
with investments in the securities of business and industry totaling
approximately $49.9 billion at the close of 1959,[19] are heavy buyers of
corporate bonds. Their investment policy, reflecting the nature of
their obligations, calls for an emphasis on safety of return rather than
on any prospect of great profit. Corporations obtain funds from this
enormous investing industry by creating bonds and preferred stocks
which confer a priority of claim on earnings (and perhaps also on assets). In return, the insurance companies agree to take a lower annual
return on their investment than would be required to satisfy a prospective buyer of stock under most market conditions.

Divisibility.   Any corporate financial contract may, and usually
does, provide that its terms shall apply ratably to each of many fractional parts evidenced by documents that shall be issued to a total representing the entire contract. Such parts may then be sold to as many
separate investors as desire to participate in the provisions of the financial contract.

For example, a corporate mortgage contract involving a loan of,
say, $20 million, may be evidenced by 20,000 bonds, each of $1,000
denomination. Each bond contains on its face a summary of the contract of debt. It is considered as evidence of a 1/20,000 interest in
the benefits of the contract.

The exact mechanism of accomplishing this result varies from case

---

19 Institute of Life Insurance, *1960 Life Insurance Fact Book* (New York, 1960),
p. 71.

to case, but the essence always is that many investors may participate by buying as much of the total issue as may suit their plans. The result is that a corporation may obtain enormous quantities of funds from the small purchases of many security buyers, including those who are not professional investors. In no other way could one obtain the great aggregations of wealth that have been accumulated by the major corporate businesses of the United States. In fact, the great corporations rely on "OPM"—Other People's Money—to use the designation made famous by Justice Brandeis.

The American Telephone and Telegraph Company can be used as an example. At the end of 1960, this corporation published a consolidated balance sheet showing assets totaling $22,558,283,000. It had obtained $2,090,611,000 of these assets by entering a variety of short-term contracts classed as "current liabilities."

The balance was made up in part of debt contracts totaling $7,232,-239,000. This sum represented a considerable number of issues and types of bonds issued by the parent company and its subsidiaries. The total number of bondholders is unknown, but it is undoubtedly very large.

Substantially all the remainder of the total assets of the company were represented by 223,518,483 shares of stock, owned by 1,911,484 shareholders. The average holding was about 117 shares.

Such an example serves to explain the essential feature of the financing of large corporations. The corporation, contrasting with the partnership-proprietorship, provides for the building of great sums out of small individual investments.

Transferability. The documents evidencing participation in corporate financial contracts can be made freely transferable, and in the typical case the contract so provides. Details vary from case to case, but the essence is that a holder of a security may transfer it at any time to some person who will take it. If the transaction is a sale, the price is negotiated between the investors. It must be recognized that the corporation is not a party to the transfer. It has received funds from the original investor, and subsequent transfers do not affect this sum. There is merely a transfer of parties on one side of the corporate contract. In fact, the corporation frequently receives no notification of the transfer. By contrast, a member of a partnership cannot sell his interest unless the transaction has the approval of a previously agreed number of the remaining partners.

No corporate characteristic is more responsible than this feature of transferability for the enormous growth of corporate enterprises.

Suitability provides a variety of investment media; *divisibility* provides the means for the accumulation of a great whole out of many small parts; *transferability* allows the investor to choose the time for his own purchase and sale.

Liquidity through sale is relied on by both small and large investors who would not be willing to commit funds to a single enterprise for as long as the business might need it. Thus is created a paradoxical condition in which businesses receive funds for long-term purposes such as the building of hydroelectric dams, while investors receive securities that may be converted into liquid funds by sale.

As a necessary result of the transfers that take place so frequently, there has developed the whole organization of security dealers and securities exchanges which are a vital part of the system of corporate finance.

Transferability, while it is a necessary condition for size, is not always a desired characteristic for small corporations. Frequently, the owners of a closely held corporation may reject the idea that any stockholder should be able to sell his interest to any one at any time. In such a case, the solution is provided by the inclusion in the articles of incorporation of provisions restricting transfer. Here, as elsewhere, the ingenuity of the draftsman is the limit to the terms of the limitation. The only general rules are that the limitation must be provided in advance, or imposed with the consent of the security holder, and that the limitation must apply equally to all the holders of any class of security to which it is applied.

An example frequently encountered among closely held corporations requires the security holder first to offer his security to the directors of the corporation. A procedure for setting the price for the sale is specified. If the directors do not act favorably within a specified time, the security holder is free to sell in the open market. It is of doubtful legality to forbid the stockholder to sell his holding in all circumstances.

Tax Status

A review of the major considerations that need attention before making the choice of the legal form of doing business must include the topic of income taxation. There is little difference in the treatment of the various types of business units as far as property and similar taxation is concerned. There is some disadvantage to the corporation because it must pay fees to maintain its corporate status in each

state wherein it does business, but such payments are minor considerations. On the other hand, there are significant differences between
the proprietorship, or the partnership, and the corporation in tax
treatment of income derived therefrom, and this can be of real importance in the choice of one or the other of these organizational
forms.

For those who have not studied the federal income tax law, a brief
introduction to some of its provisions is necessary. The reader will recognize that in our attempt to be brief, we shall necessarily describe a
complex situation only in approximate terms. First, the law recognizes
two types of income: *capital gains* and *ordinary income*. There are
also, of course, *capital losses* and *ordinary losses*. Capital gains or
losses result from transactions involving the sale of a capital asset, as
opposed to a product offered for sale, where the selling price is above
(or below) a value based on what was originally paid for the asset.
The most important type of capital transaction for the present discussion is the gain or loss resulting from the sale of a corporate security by an investor, who may seek his gain in this way rather than by
the receipt of dividends.

Ordinary income and losses result from the ordinary business activities of the taxpayer. This class includes, in the case of an investor,
interest and dividends on securities.

The distinction between capital gains and ordinary income is important because capital gains are taxed at rates equal to one half the
applicable rate for ordinary income, with a maximum of 25 percent.
When personal rates rise as high as 70 percent, this is a matter of considerable importance.

The tax law treats a corporation, which is a legal entity, as a separate taxpayer, and levies taxes on its ordinary income and capital gains
without reference to the way in which this income is distributed or retained in the business. Unlike the progressive personal income tax,
the corporate income tax since 1965 has been at a flat rate of 22 percent on all taxable income, plus a surtax of 26 percent of income in
excess of $25,000.

Any distribution to shareholders will then be considered part of
their personal income, and will be subject to a personal income tax at
a rate determined by the overall income situation of the individual
shareholder. There was modest relief from this double taxation of the
distributed income of corporations under the 1954 Code. Under that
code, the first $50 of dividends received was not included as taxable
personal income; and, in addition, a credit of 4 percent of dividends

received in excess of $50 was allowed as a deduction from the tax payable. Under the 1964 law, the 4 percent dividend credit was eliminated. Offsetting this, but only partially for many taxpayers, the dividend exclusion was increased from $50 to $100.

The idea of a separate tax on business income does not apply to the proprietorship or the partnership. As explained previously, business activity carried on under these forms is considered merely as an extension of the personal activities of the owner or owners; hence, business income is classed as personal income of the proprietor or partners. As personal income, it is subject to the personal income tax rates applying to the individual owners.

This basic difference in treatment has given rise to significant variations in the tax burden, depending not only on the legal form chosen for the business, but also on the ways in which the income of the business is handled. Whether these variations favor the corporate form or the partnership-proprietorship depends on the particular circumstances of the business and its owners and, at least in part, on circumstances which the owners may not be able to foresee at the time the legal form is chosen. Some of the more generally significant implications of these differences will be outlined in the remainder of this section.

At first glance, it might be concluded that a 48 percent levy on corporate income added to the personal tax on dividends to shareholders would make the corporate form distinctly unattractive from the tax point of view. This would be particularly true if all or a large part of the corporate earnings were regularly distributed in the form of dividends. On the other hand, if corporate earnings are retained in the business, they do not become personal income and therefore bear only the corporate tax, at least at that point of time. The opportunity of deferring, perhaps indefinitely, the receipt of the business earnings of a given period and the personal income tax associated therewith may be considered a major advantage by shareholders, particularly those whose personal income puts them in a tax bracket which is very high. There is a different opportunity, present only in a closely held company, to pay very high salaries to officers who are also shareholders. If such payments are allowed as "costs" by the income tax authorities, the corporate tax is avoided, although, of course, the personal income tax remains.

One important possible advantage of this aspect of the corporate form is the opportunity of using earnings for business expansion without being first subject to the personal income tax—an advantage which would have particular appeal for the owner whose tax bracket is above 48 percent. Further, the reinvestment of earnings makes possible their ultimate "withdrawal" as a capital gain rather than as dividend income, thus giving the advantage of the low capital gains tax. This results when there is an appreciation in the value of the stock as a result of reinvested earnings, with the shareholder receiving the benefit of the investment in a higher price for the stock when it is sold rather than in dividends during the time the stock is held.

There may also be some owners who have no desire to benefit from their investment during their lifetime. If the earnings can be reinvested without the depleting effect of the personal income tax and permanently retained in the business, the only tax that will bear on such earnings will be the tax on the value of the estate at time of death, a tax which would be paid in any case if the earnings were withdrawn and retained rather than spent.

It must be stressed, however, that the Internal Revenue Service has no intention of permitting the corporate form to be used simply as a device to avoid the personal income tax. The retention and reinvestment of earnings must have a valid justification in terms of normal and reasonable business practice. Although infrequently used, a special tax is provided by the Internal Revenue Code on the accumulated earnings of a corporation where it can be proved by the government that the purpose is to avoid the personal tax on dividends. The additional tax applies to unnecessarily accumulated earnings in excess of $100,000, and amounts to 27½ percent of the first $100,000, plus 38½ percent of accumulated earnings in excess of $100,000.

Even where it can be justified, the advantages of the corporate form arising out of the opportunity to defer the receipt of income may not be sufficient to outweigh the disadvantage of the added corporate income tax. There can be other disadvantages as well. The distribution received by the shareholder as dividends is personal income, regardless of its original source. The distribution received by the proprietor or partner retains the character as originally received by the business. Thus, a capital gain to the partnership is also a capital gain to the partners, whereas a capital gain to the corporation passed along as a dividend to its shareholders becomes personal income and is taxed as such. On the other hand, a potential advantage to the corporation lies in the handling of business losses. Because of the way the tax law stands, a net loss for a given year in a partnership could be used by the partners only as an offset against personal income in that year. A net loss to a corporation would have an advantage as a tax offset in certain past and future years.

From the foregoing, the reader can see that very few general statements can be made about the advantages of a corporate form of doing business from a tax point of view. The advantage will depend on the exact nature of the interests involved in the particular case, with emphasis probably being given to the degree of interest the owners may have in cash dividends in the near future, and to the uses the corporation may be expected to have for funds for expansion, debt retirement, and other purposes.

Probably in order to reduce the importance of the tax factor in the decisions of smaller businesses about the form of organization which they will use, the 1954 revision of the Internal Revenue Code provided that certain unincorporated businesses could be taxed as corporations and that certain small corporations could be taxed as partnerships. The reader is referred to Section 1361 for details. If a business once elects to be treated in one or another of these ways, it cannot change its choice at a later date without the consent of the Director of Internal Revenue.

The Effect of Size on Choice

The corporation has been said to dominate the business section of the American economy. This is true because large-scale enterprises almost exclusively use the corporate form in order to raise the great amount of funds they need. A few joint-stock companies exist, but they present no advantages to overcome the unlimited liability of their owners. There are some business trusts, but these have difficulty in gaining recognition because they have ill-defined terms of life and because they find that some states do not recognize them. They do provide a chance of greater centralization of control, but this is not often the determining factor. Thus, it is very seldom that a large-scale enterprise will adopt any form other than that of the corporation.

Much greater diversity exists among smaller firms. The advantage of security flotation loses much of its force. Instead, the factors of length of life, limitation of liability, centralization of management, fees, and income taxation assume greater importance. The result of such considerations on the selection of the form of organization varies with the details of a particular business and the predispositions of its managers.

6. A BRIEF ANALYSIS OF PATENT LAW FOR THE GENERAL PRACTITIONER *

The general practitioner should know a few basic facts about Patent Law. Preferably such facts should be elementary and should stem directly from an easily remembered statement of the basic reasons for having a patent system. This discussion will first outline the general object of the patent system, and then briefly cover certain aspects of the Patent Laws likely to be of interest to general practitioners, along with some specific answers to patent problems likely to arise in general practice.

General

The Constitution gives Congress power to "promote the Progress of Science and the Useful Arts by securing for limited times to Authors and Inventors the Exclusive Right to their respective Writings and Discoveries." (Article I, sec. 8)

The framers of the Constitution wanted to encourage contributions to scientific progress. This means that both inventions and public disclosure of inventions were to be encouraged. It does not follow automatically that once an invention is made, it then becomes a contribution to scientific progress. History amply demonstrates that in the absence of a suitable reward for disclosure, invention will be practiced in secrecy. When this happens, the inventor in a sense has a monopoly and science gains nothing. For instance coal, asbestos, gasoline (naphtha), alloys, and other important materials were once known in the ancient world, but because of secret use they disappeared when the persons who knew about them died. Penicillin or a substance very similar to it was evidently known to a group of Bohemian healers in the Middle Ages. Furthermore, a number of ancient arts still remain to be rediscovered. For instance, scientists are still trying to find out how the swords of Damascus were tempered. The framers of the Constitution evidently were aware of this and intended to encourage both inventions and disclosure of inventions.

---

* By Robert B. Russell. Reprinted with permission from *The Bar Bulletin*, April, 1950.

The reward to be given was specified in the Constitution and comprises exclusive use of the invention by the inventor for a limited period of time. It should be noted that Congress was not given power to determine what type of reward should be given. All Congress could do in this respect was fix the time period (seventeen years) and the details of administration.

The phenomenal production of patents since 1836 and the concurrent tremendous strides of scientific progress in the United States are strongly indicative that the patent system has been highly successful in attaining its object. In operation, the system turns scientific research into an extremely competitive field. Big and little corporations alike stand on comparatively equal ground in research because of it. In fact, if the little corporations couldn't get the reward of exclusive use, they would have no defense against the sales organizations of the big corporations and on the other hand, the large corporations couldn't be expected to conduct costly researches if their competitors could immediately reap the benefits of the developments made. Perhaps large corporations derive benefits from our patent system, but it does not mean that the system fails, because without the system the big corporations would lay less emphasis upon research and the lone inventors would be absolutely without defense or incentive. Furthermore, there can be no doubt that the researches conducted by the big corporations tremendously promote scientific progress. And finally, although it cannot be empirically proved, many people consider that the most significant result of the competitive field of scientific research created by our patent system is that the United States has many more competent technicians than any other country in the world. This fact no doubt contributed heavily to our discovery of the atomic bomb before the Germans did.

Another thing to remember about our patent system is that it provides an opportunity for the introduction of many inventions to the market which would never reach the market if patents were not available to protect the risk capital involved in launching them. Frequently inventions are so radical that the market has to become "re-educated" to the new concept before the new invention will be accepted. Without patent protection capital cannot be found to carry the project through the lean, re-education period. An ancient but yet apt illustration of this is the history of the development of the water closet. It was invented in England during the reign of Queen Elizabeth I. The inventor applied for a patent in order to secure the capital outlays of his financial backers. The patent was refused, and the invention was abandoned. It lay dormant for over 100 years, after which time it gradually came into use.

The basic things to remember, however, about the patent system are that it was designed to promote scientific progress (and the Useful Arts), that it strives to accomplish this by rewarding those who contribute to progress, and that a contribution to progress is not merely a scientific advance but is a scientific advance accompanied by a disclosure to the public.

How Much Scientific Advance Is Necessary to Constitute Invention?

A good definition of what amounts to invention has never been developed. The cases contain numerous attempts to define it, but none as yet has succeeded. Learned Hand's formula is to estimate what a man skilled in the art would have known before the invention was made and then try to decide whether the invention would have been obvious to such a man. Another formula involves probing into the inventor's mind to see if he had a "flash of creative genius." This standard has been rejected by Congress, 35 USC #103. ("Patentability shall not be negatived by the manner in which the invention was made.") None of these formulae is certain, and consequently you can't tell in advance how the court will decide. Incidentally, this element of uncertainty makes patent cases which turn on the question of invention highly dependent upon excellence of counsel in argument.

The general practitioner need not concern himself with the niceties of defining invention. In general, if a valuable contribution has been made to the progress of science, it should be rewarded, and the general practitioner can at least tentatively assume that it may be patented. Commercial success is an indication of invention if it is not attributable primarily to salesmanship, rather than the intrinsic value of the invention itself.

Not All Scientific Advances Are Patentable

One difficulty in administering the patent system is that of determining what types of contributions should qualify for the reward. It isn't practical to reward every conceivable type of contribution to progress. Suppose, for instance, a person gets an idea for making gasoline out of kerosene. Should he be granted a patent on the idea? The practical answer is simple. It is impossible to determine whether or not the idea is a true contribution to progress unless it is worked out in detail and actually appears to be operative. Furthermore, if ideas as such were patentable, millions of people would try to take out patents on the mere hope that the idea might prove practical in the future. Congress has resolved this problem by permitting the reward to be given only for specific, thoroughly worked out and described, operative embodiments of ideas. The statutory classes for patentable subject matter are as follows (35 USC #101, 161):

1. Process
2. Manufacture (article, product)
3. Machine
4. Composition of Matter (drugs, alloys, etc.)
5. Certain types of Plants

While it might seem that the statutory classes narrow the field of patentable contributions to progress, in actual practice almost every contribution of value may be embodied in some form to bring it within one of the classes. For instance, a contribution may be nothing more than a mathematical formula for which there is no statutory class, but usually a machine can be constructed in accordance with the formula, thereby bringing it within the statute and rendering it patentable probably to cover all machines so constructed.

An example of something not within the statutory classes is "a way of doing business" (which cannot be called a process). The "Drive-in Theatre" patent has been held invalid for this reason. Also arrangements or organizations of printed matter are not patentable even though amounting to definite contributions. It is sometimes said that the discovery of a function of nature cannot be patented. For instance, you cannot patent the process of exposing wheat to sunlight to raise its vitamin D content, even though your discovery of the fact may have been a valuable contribution.

Conversely the Patent Office will not enter applications for perpetual motion machines although in a sense they fall within one of the statutory classes.

How Do You Know When You Have a Patentable Invention?

When a person wants to know if he has made an invention, the standard procedure after determining it is within a statutory class is to make a preliminary search in the Patent Office Library to see how close the prior patents come to the proposed invention. Obviously if the subject matter of an alleged invention was known before, the invention cannot be called a contribution to science and therefore, a patent cannot be obtained upon it. The patent law way of stating that a proposed invention does not make a contribution is to say that it is "anticipated in the prior art." Ways in which an alleged invention may be anticipated include: prior public use, prior sale, prior publication, and prior offer for sale; in fact, anything that qualifies as prior public knowledge suffices. The effect of anticipation is operative even though the inventor himself is the one who published the article or sold the device, but in order to prevent hardship, the inventor is permitted to file a patent application any time up to one year after the invention became part of the public knowledge, without losing his rights to the invention.

Preliminary searches, of course, are not infallible, but often they demonstrate that it is useless to file a patent application and thereby they save the inventor the considerably greater expense of preparing the application. When the preliminary search appears favorable, a patent application is usually filed, and then the Patent Office conducts a much more thorough search of the prior art. Because of this extensive search made by the Patent Office, the cases hold that there is a presumption of validity of issued patents, but, of course, this presumption can be overcome by showing that the Patent Office erred or did not have available evidence of prior public knowledge.

In general, the Patent Office does not attempt to discover evidence of public use, sale or offer for sale. While this might appear to be a serious weakness, it is in part justified by the fact that each applicant for a patent must execute an oath to the effect that he knows of no such prior public use, etc. Furthermore, it would be very difficult administratively to conduct searches on a scale broad enough to include public use and sale, etc.

What Does the Patent Cover Once You Get It?

The patent laws require that the patentee "distinctively claim" that which he alleges to be his invention. The reason for this requirement is to prevent the patentee from vaguely stating what he considers to be his invention and then attempting to assert his patent to cover more than he actually contributed to the progress of science. Therefore, each patent application is accompanied by a set of claims each of which amounts to a separate and concise definition of the invention or inventive subdivisions thereof. Claim drafting and interpretation is a highly developed art the details of which need not concern the general practitioner. The important feature is that you cannot infringe a patent unless your device, process, etc., has every element of one of the claims of the patent, or an obvious equivalent of every element of one such claim.

It has often been said that you never know how much your patent covers, or much less, you are not even sure your patent is valid at all, until it has been tested in court. This statement is perhaps theoretically correct, but it gives the misleading impression that the operation of our patent system is highly uncertain. Such is not the case. As compared to certain foreign patent systems, ours is highly reliable. In France, for instance, inventors are not required to distinctly claim their inventions but may merely describe the invention and then claim vaguely "all of the inventive features embodied in the foregoing description." In France it is easy to get patents and once you get them, their scope and validity are not at all clear. As a result there is far less faith in their system than ours and in turn their system is less effective in promotion of progress.

Problems Relating to Inventorship

Often several people independently make the same invention and the question then arises as to who should get the patent. Here again the general practitioner should relate the problem to the basic aims of the patent system. One aim is to create a race for invention, and therefore the first inventor should normally receive the reward. On the other hand disclosure is also to be encouraged, so it may turn out that if the first inventor is negligent in disclosing or filing for a patent a second inventor who is diligent may be given the reward.

Inventorship conflicts in the Patent Office are called Interference Proceedings. Such proceedings are generally complicated and, unless handled with great care, may give rise to damaging estoppels against the parties. While the general practitioner need not concern himself with the details of Interference Proceedings there are two practical points he should bear in mind. First, the inventor's own word is not acceptable to prove the date of conception. For this reason, inventors should make a full written disclosure of an invention as soon after conception as possible and then have several witnesses, preferably people who understand the invention, sign and date the disclosure. The natural inclination is for inventors to keep their ideas absolutely secret so others will not steal them, but to follow the natural inclination greatly weakens the inventor's chances of winning an interference. It should be noted that putting a written disclosure in a sealed envelope and mailing it to yourself for purposes of obtaining a postmark on it, will probably not suffice for purposes of establishing conception dates. The second important fact to remember relates to reduction to practice; i.e., building a working model. If it can be shown in Interference Proceedings that the first inventor in point of time was not diligent in reducing his invention to practice, then he may lose out to a later inventor. For this purpose, filing an application for patent has the status of constructive reduction to practice. In addition to this, if the inventor delays too long in filing for a patent after an actual reduction to practice, even though the invention has not been used publicly, he may lose his rights. The reason for this is that a person should not be allowed to hold his invention back for a number of years and then reap the benefits of a patent thereafter. There is no fixed time, however, for this penalty; the only guide is that the delay should not be unreasonable. In general it is good advice to recommend filing a patent application as soon as possible.

Design Patents

Design patents are in a separate category from mechanical patents, and are granted for inventive ornamental designs. However, since it is difficult to define or prove inventiveness of ornamental designs, design patents are looked upon with some disfavor. It may be said that they afford protection against closely similar articles.

Trademarks

Trademark protection is essentially based upon the common law right of protection against unfair competition. For this reason registration of a trademark in the Patent Office is not necessary. To prove the common law case, however, you have to show among other things that (1) your mark is known in the market, (2) is recognized in connection with your goods, (3) is valuable, and (4) that the mark of the infringer is confusingly similar to your own, and since registration of the mark helps establish the first three of these points, it is generally advisable to register.

There is no need to hurry for registration of trademarks. In fact, registration of trademark in the Patent Office cannot be obtained until the trademark has been used in interstate commerce. Furthermore, most states provide for registration of trademarks after use on an intrastate scale.

Trademark registrations may be renewed every twenty years indefinitely.

Copyrights

Copyrights apply to all types of works of art. Even some types of labels may be copyrighted. However, copyright protection must not be confused with trademark protection. To recover for copyright infringement the infringer must have copied your work of art regardless of the existence of confusing similarity.

Copyright protection is part common law and part statutory. The common law protects authors, etc., against piracy or plagiarism of unpublished works, but once the work of art is published the only protection is statutory. Therefore, general practitioners should be aware of the one fatal error likely to be committed by the uninitiate. In order to obtain a valid copyright registration, the first publication of the work of art must bear the notice of copyright. This generally includes the word "Copyright" followed by the year of publication and the name of the proprietor, that is, owner of the copyright. The proper procedure is to have the book published with proper notice of copyright and then to apply for copyright registration.

Copyrights last for 28 years and may be renewed for only one additional 28-year period.

Some Practical Considerations

Patent Pending.   Patent pending in itself has no legal significance. All it amounts to is a warning that in the future there may be a patent covering the item in question. Patent Pending often remains affixed to articles on the market long after the patent application on them has been abandoned. In a sense, this is a fraud on the public and might be stopped by the FTC, but I am not aware of any direct action that can be taken by competitors against the perpetrator. However, there is an action available against a person who falsely marks an item patented; called a *qui tam* action.

Kept Inventors.   It is standard practice in business to require research personnel to agree to assign to the company all inventions developed by them during their term of employment and for two years afterward. Such agreements, particularly the two year clauses, are thought by some to be oppressive. However, they are valid, and are justified by the necessity for protecting the investment of the company in research.

Disclosure of Ideas and Unjust Enrichment.   If a would-be inventor has an idea and takes it to a company for the purpose of selling it to them, an unjust enrichment situation may arise before the company is aware of it. If nothing is said about remuneration, the implication is that the company will not use the idea without remunerating the would-be inventor. Thus a company may turn an idea down when it is offered, then use it several years later and become liable to pay the original offeror. This proposition holds true for all ideas, not merely patentable ideas. For instance, a large recovery was made against a cigarette company in the following situation. X suggested to the company that they run an advertisement showing two men in riding clothes, one offering the other a cigarette, and the other saying, "No thanks, I have my 'advertized brand.'" The company turned X down, but several days later their sales department independently arrived at very much the same idea and ran an ad showing two men on a golf course doing exactly the same thing. X recovered a substantial sum of money.

The only safe way to prevent such an unjust enrichment situation from arising is to entertain ideas only on the understanding that there will be no obligation to pay for them even if they are used. If such is made clear, of course, there is then no harm in telling the offeror that he may receive something if the company elects to reward him.

Licensing.   It is well known that licenses tying the sale of unpatented articles to the licensed patent are in violation of the Antitrust laws. Likewise other licenses linking a number of patents together or fixing prices in connection with patents may be illegal. The general practitioner should beware of these.

Forming Corporations around Patents.   The general practitioner should know that it may not be wise to form a closely held corporation exclusively to own patents. The earnings of such a corporation are strictly classifiable as personal holding company type income,* 80 percent of which must be distributed. Furthermore, expenditures for obtaining patents must be capitalized in a corporation, whereas they probably are deductible expenses for a partnership. Of course, these drawbacks may be outweighed by other considerations.

Patent Suppression

The question of patent suppression has only a small relationship to the problems of the general practitioner. The principal reason the

---

* EDITOR'S NOTE.—The 1964 tax law establishes a flat 70 percent tax on undistributed personal holding company income if 60 percent of the corporation's income is personal holding company income.

general practitioner should know something about it, is that an appealing argument can be made against the patent system based upon fears of patent suppression, and unless the general practitioner, as he sits as a judge or legislator, has an understanding of the problem, he may be led to a hasty and false conclusion.

Patent suppression rarely occurs. There are numerous rumors about it, but I know of none that can be proved. The rumors usually come from a confusion with the problem of secret use or else they are fostered by disgruntled inventors who overestimate the value of their own inventions. Sometimes companies develop and patent machines which are superior to existing equipment, but they obviously cannot convert immediately to the new machinery. Gradual conversion takes place, however, in such instances and, therefore, they can hardly be called cases of patent suppression. On the other hand the problem of secret use of inventions is serious. The patent system, however, cannot be blamed for secret use of inventions because the entire emphasis and incentive of the patent system is directed toward public disclosure of inventions.

Without going further into the pros and cons of the alleged problem it is evident that proposed changes in the patent system to prevent patent suppression must necessarily be directed toward a reduction in the scope of the patent grant, and it then becomes a problem of balancing what is to be gained thereby against what is lost. We in the patent field know how quickly inventors turn towards a reliance upon secrecy the minute the scope of the patent grant is reduced because such was the immediate effect of certain Supreme Court decisions of the past decade holding apparently strong patents invalid for lack of invention. This tendency toward secrecy was particularly noted in the chemical field. Balanced against losses of this type would be the supposed benefits to be gained from the elimination of at best a doubtful problem.

Of course, much more can be said about this and other related problems. In general the question of patent suppression arises concurrently with Antitrust problems, and is often confused with them. The principal thing to bear in mind is that violations of the Antitrust laws should be punished as such, by compulsory licensing of patents, etc., if need be, but that a general reduction in the scope of the patent grant, to apply to all patentees, would be accompanied by substantial losses in research incentive.

7. NOTE ON MAJOR APPROACHES TO SECURITY VALUATION *

The purpose of this note is to provide some background for the study of cases on valuation of securities, a subject that will be developed in the cases and class discussion. The note is intended not as a discussion of the broad subject of valuation, but rather as an introduction to some of the methods employed in *security* valuation treated in later cases,[1] although the valuation of business concerns as units is not basically dissimilar to the valuation of specific ownership or debt securities. Further, attention will be focused on common stocks, avoiding questions related to the valuation of fixed income securities.

The need for arriving at an evaluation of securities in terms of dollars arises most frequently in one of the following situations:

1. In pricing an issue of new securities.
2. In appraising for purposes of sale, purchase, or taxation existing securities for which current market values have not been established or are not considered appropriate to the specific purpose.
3. In mergers, reorganizations, exchange, or refunding operations in which one security must be measured against other securities that may be exchanged.
4. The investment appraisal of securities to determine whether in the investment analyst's judgment those securities should be bought or sold at current market prices.

Kinds of Value

The term value is used in economic, business, and legal phraseology with a wide variety of meanings.[2] Some of the many kinds of value confronting the student of finance are: *assessed value* for purposes of property taxation; *condemnation value* awarded as payment in takings by right of eminent domain; *book value* as derived from accounting statements; *reproduction value* of existing fixed tangible

---

[1] For extended discussion of the general subject of valuation, see J. C. Bonbright, *The Valuation of Property* (2 vols.; New York: McGraw-Hill Book Co., Inc., 1937).

[2] Bonbright opens his treatise on value, cf. p. 3, with the following quotation from a decision by Justice Holmes: "A word is not a crystal, transparent, and unchanged, it is the skin of a living thought, and may vary greatly in color and content according to the circumstances and the time in which it is used."

business assets; *going-concern value* of assets of at least potentially profitable business enterprises; *liquidating value* of assets on dissolution of a business; *collateral value*, representing the amount that may be borrowed on the pledge of an asset; *fair value*, used as a base for public regulation of utility rates; *sale values*, representing the anticipated realizations on sale under various conditions; *market value*, usually determined from actual prices, or bids and offerings in some sort of "market" (which implies the existence of potential buyers and sellers), though it may be imputed by estimate; *fair market value* that adds to the concept of market value the assumption of the existence of a large number of buyers and sellers, and sometimes the assumption that those buyers and sellers are well informed and entirely rational in their evaluations. The value derived under this last assumption is also called *intrinsic value* or *investment value*, distinguishing it from market price.

Despite the variety of the concepts of value indicated above, most of the methods of security valuation fall into three main categories: those based on the capitalization of earnings concept, those that emphasize physical assets, and those that stress actual or imputed market prices. The outlines of each major approach will be drawn in succeeding pages.

It will soon be apparent that there is no single, always reliable method of determining *the* value of a business or its securities that can be applied to all situations. Often, several methods of getting at an answer, or various combinations of methods, will be useful in a particular situation. In supporting his decision in an evaluation case, *Northern Pacific Railway* v. *Adams County*, Judge Webster effectively expressed the views of those who favor an eclectic or composite approach to valuation when he wrote: [3]

I feel that in both reason and authority it is infinitely safer, where a number of relevant evidential factors are available, to give a composite view based upon all relevant elements and give to each in the exercise of sound judgment that weight and consideration which the peculiar facts of the case in hand justify and require. By using in combination a number of factors, each evidential element serves as a check and balance upon others. . . .

Further, it must be emphasized that the purpose of the particular valuation and the point of view of the evaluator will strongly influence the selection of approach. Typically, valuations are undertaken for a definite purpose and from a definite point of view, and the

---

[3] I.F. Supp. 163 (E.D. Wash., 1932), rev'd., 72F (2d), 816 (C.C.A. 9th, 1934).

choice of approach and the final appraisal will inevitably reflect that purpose and point of view. For example, a businessman who is considering the purchase of the majority stock of a street railway company with intentions of liquidating the company for the scrap value of its property would obviously approach the problem of placing a value on the stock in a way different from that of an investor who plans to acquire the stock for the income it may produce from continued operation.

The Capitalized Earnings Approach

The capitalized earnings approach to the evaluation of common stocks rests on the philosophy that the current value of property depends on the income it can be made to produce over the years. Hence, it is argued, ownership shares in the assets of a business concern are properly valued on the basis of the earning power of the business. It is the earning power that will provide income to the shareholder, and it is income that he values rather than the physical assets themselves.

The basic validity of the concept that value rests on earning power, or potential earning power, is seldom challenged. It is in the application of the concept to actual situations that major questions arise.

There are two main steps in the process of valuation by the capitalized earnings method. First, the analyst must arrive at an estimate of the future income that the investment will produce. Then, he must decide how much he is willing to pay for the claim to those future earnings. In the more tangible terms of one share of common stock, what will be the earnings per share of common stock of a given company? Then, assuming the analyst has arrived at an estimate of $5.00 a share per annum, how much should he pay for the anticipated earnings stream of $5.00 a year?

Estimate of Earnings. The task of arriving at a reasonable estimate of future earnings is not an easy one. The analyst knows that the profits of a particular concern will be influenced by movements of the economy as a whole, by conditions within a particular industry, and by the effectiveness of the individual company within its industry. Taking General Motors as an example, the future of GM will clearly be affected by conditions of world economy, of national economy, of the industry, and of the competitive effectiveness of GM within the industry.

In practice, an analyst seldom has the time and resources to undertake a complete weighing and cataloging of all the factors that will bear on the future profits of a particular company. Usually, the analyst works from the basis of earnings reported by the company for recent years, adjusting the figures upward or downward in accordance with his appraisal of the total effect of factors he thinks will affect the fortunes of the company. Although future earnings may be expected to vary from year to year, it is usually considered impractical to attempt a precise forecast of annual variations for many years into the future. What is commonly done is to forecast smooth trends—upward, level, or downward. Not infrequently the forecast is simply of average earnings over the years.

Let us assume that the analyst, either as a result of a painstaking and reasonably complete consideration of the various factors that may affect General Motors' profitability, or as a result of a "horseback estimate" by way of a quick mental adjustment of recent earnings figures, forecasts earnings of $3.50 a share. What value then should be placed on a share of stock? How much is the probable earnings stream of $3.50 worth?

Rate of Capitalization.   The process of putting a valuation on an estimated earnings stream is known as the "capitalization of earnings." It should be clear that the amount of the valuation will depend *both* on the estimate of earnings and on the rate of capitalization selected. And although the process of estimating future earnings, dealing as it must with an uncertain future, is an inexact one, the selection of an "appropriate" rate of capitalization is even less exact and objective.

In general, the selection of a rate of capitalization is determined by the relative certainty of the estimated earnings actually being realized. The more certain the prospective buyer is that the earnings will materialize, the more he will pay for the claim to the earnings. On the other hand, where uncertainty is great or, in other words, where the risk is believed high, the buyer will insist on a high rate of return. For example, in the case of a small concern producing a highly competitive item of uncertain demand, the buyer of stock may insist on a price that will yield a return of 25 percent on his investment. That is, he would capitalize estimated earnings of $5.00 a share at 25 percent and reach a valuation of $20 for one share of the stock. ($5.00 ÷ 25% = $20.00). This relationship is also widely expressed another way— that the risk justifies a value of "four times earnings."

If, however, the business in question were a very stable one with every prospect of steady earnings at the $5.00 level, the buyer might well be willing to accept a capitalization rate as low as 5 percent, in which case he would value one share of stock at $100. ($5.00 ÷ 5% = $100) or "twenty times earnings."

In the example of the high-risk situation above, the analyst might prefer to adjust for the risk by writing down the estimate of earnings to, say, $2.50. To the extent that he has thus made allowance for the risk factor through a conservative estimate of earnings, a duplicate allowance for the uncertainty would not be made through the capitalization rate. In other words, if the earnings estimate were written down from $5.00 to $2.50 to allow for the risk, then a capitalization rate of 12.5 percent rather than 25 percent would be in order.

Since the factors that go to determine the risk in a particular situation are complex, and weighing them is a matter of judgment, it is apparent that the selection of a capitalization rate appropriate to the risk is subjective.[4] It is also clear that a small change in the rate of capitalization applied will make a substantial change in the final valuation figure.

In practice, many analysts tend to classify industries by groups and to develop rules of thumb governing appropriate rates, however questionable on theoretical grounds. Thus, for many years, it was widely felt that the more stable industrials with good prospects were "worth" about 10 times conservatively estimated earnings.

At this point, the student may ask, "What about dividends?" He might well point out that the preceding approach makes no distinction between the two alternative uses of earnings—reinvestment within the corporation or payment to shareholders. As a result, the approach contains the implicit assumption that a dollar of retained income is as valuable to the investor as a dollar received in the form of a dividend. If the analyst is not prepared to accept this assumption, and increasing numbers are not, then presumably a company's dividend policy must be taken into account as an additional factor affecting the value of its common stock. On this point, Graham and Dodd write:

> Our conclusions (in a preceding chapter) were that dividends were basically the most important single factor in valuation from the standpoint of the ordinary public stockholder; that earnings were chiefly important because of their bearing on present and future dividends; and that average market prices were influenced (and properly so) to a preponderant degree by the company's pay-out policy.[5]

---

[4] On this subject of selection of a capitalization rate, Bonbright, cf. p. 264, comments: ". . . a scrutiny of the available literature will yield surprisingly few answers to some of the most fundamental and elementary problems involved in the choice of a capitalization rate."

[5] B. Graham and D. L. Dodd, *Security Analysis* (3d ed.; New York: McGraw-Hill Book Co., Inc., 1951), p. 586. The authors' suggested formula for estimating the value of railroad and industrial common stocks is as follows: Value = earnings multiplier x (expected dividend + one-third expected earnings), p. 454. The "earnings multiplier" in this formula is not necessarily the conventional price-earnings ratio.

In countering this argument, supporters of the capitalization of earnings approach might point out that few American concerns have an established dividend policy under which a definite percentage of earnings are paid out as dividends over the years. Numerous factors influence the policy of boards of directors with respect to dividends, and consequently it is extremely difficult to estimate the percentage of earnings that will actually be disbursed as dividends in the future.

The analyst might also argue that the directors would not vote to retain the earnings in the business unless they believed the funds could be profitably employed and that the reinvestment would ultimately lead to higher dividend payments. If the stockholder is forced to sell, it is argued that his investment will have gained in value by reason of the reinvested earnings, and he will be able to realize on the gain in the form of high prices when he sells. Radio Corporation of America might be cited as an example. The company never paid a common dividend from the time of its organization in 1919 until 1937, yet the market price of the stock was markedly influenced by the substantial reinvestment of earnings from 1919 to 1928. A more recent example is Texas Instruments, Incorporated, which has not paid any common dividends, yet enjoyed a considerable rise in the market price per share (1953 price range, $5.75–$5.38; 1959 range, $193.50–$61.25). Other analysts have observed, however, that a comparison of two companies with the same earning power and general position will invariably show a higher selling price for the stock of the company which pays larger dividends.

Analysts will undoubtedly continue to disagree about the logic of the capitalization of earnings approach, for the problem has no simple answer. If there is a trend of opinion at the present time, however, it appears to be in the direction of giving greater weight to the dividend factor.

Asset Approaches to Valuation

Several methods of valuation can be termed asset approaches, since they center attention more on the assets to which the shares of stock have claim than on income data. Among the more significant of these concepts of value are book value, reproduction value, and liquidation value.

As the terminology suggests, *book value* is derived from the asset values shown on the company's own books and presented in its most recent balance sheet. The excess of assets over debts represents the accounting net worth of the business and, hence, the book value of the stockholders' investment. Where preferred stock is outstanding, a value for the preferred shares must, of course, be deducted to determine the net worth applicable to common. The net worth available to common stock divided by the number of common shares outstanding yields book value per share.

Many refinements on this direct method of computing book value are in use. Some analysts prefer to exclude from net worth some or all of such intangible assets as goodwill, patents, bond discount, organization expense, and deferred charges. Others analyze reserve accounts and add to net worth those reserves which are felt to be essentially segregations of surplus. A few inject a measure of the capitalized earnings approach by allowing goodwill (or even adding it when none is shown on the books) if the earnings have been large enough to support a contention that the concern has a going-concern value in excess of the stated value of the tangible assets.

Despite the variance in method of computation, book values are relatively easily and simply determined. To the unsophisticated, they are exact and clear cut, and until relatively recent times were widely accepted as standards of security value.

The student of accounting, however, will immediately recognize that the figures for book value for a particular company will be influenced by the accounting policies of that company. The variations between companies in accounting for current assets are relatively small. The lack of standardization of accounting practice is particularly significant in the valuation of fixed assets and in the treatment of intangibles such as patents and goodwill. Hence, a concern with a rigorous depreciation policy would show lower net fixed assets and, thus, lower book values than would a similar concern that had charged less depreciation.

When book values are used in valuing the security of one company against that of another, the analyst must attempt the often difficult task of reconstructing reported figures so as to get them on a comparable basis.

Even if a concern follows "conventional accounting practice" in all respects, it will arrive at its balance sheet values by reference to conventions rather than sheer logics of value. Hence, inventories are carried at cost or market, whatever is *lower*. More important, fixed assets are typically carried at historical cost less depreciation rather than at current values.

An even more important weakness than the influence of vagaries of accounting convention and practice is the failure of the book value approach to give consideration to the earning power of the assets as the real test of their worth. For example, the Coca-Cola Company of Delaware has reported earnings averaging $6.79 per share of common stock over the last 10 years (1950–59). Yet, the book value per share on December 31, 1959, including $9.40 per share of goodwill carried on the books of the company, amounted to only $51.55. Clearly, the book figures, even with the inclusion of the goodwill on the books of the company, is no reasonable indication of the worth of the Coca-Cola stock (1959 price range of common stock, $169.00–$119.25).

Book values are most useful in appraising companies whose assets are largely liquid and subject to fairly accurate accounting valuation (i.e., banks, investment trusts, and insurance companies), but even in these instances book values used alone are seldom reliable standards of value.

Reproduction value, or the cost of reproducing the assets of a concern at current prices, is of significance mainly in the case of public utilities where it sometimes becomes a factor in the determination of rate schedules by governmental regulatory bodies. As a single standard of value it is seldom used. A major objection lies in the inescapable fact that the typical business is much more than the sum of its physical assets. While costs of replacing physical properties can be calculated with some exactness by painstaking appraisal, the cost of duplicating the business organization—its experience, know-how, and reputation—apart from the physical assets is most difficult of determination.

When physical assets are the principal things of value to a concern, however, and when they can be readily reproduced, the cost of reproducing the assets will tend to serve as a ceiling on valuations reached by other methods. For example, in the case of a concern the principal asset of which is a residential apartment house, few buyers would pay more for the shares of the apartment house concern than the cost of erecting and getting into operation a similar apartment house, regardless of the earnings of the present concern.

On the other hand, *liquidation values* tend to put a floor under valuations reached from other approaches, since many firms will purchase concerns when valuations placed on the business become so low as to create an opportunity for worthwhile profits through their liquidation. During depression periods when earnings are low or nonexistent for a number of firms, liquidation values may become widely significant.

It might be noted at this point that even in the liquidation approach the valuation of the assets is based indirectly on their potential earning capacity. Unless they are to be sold for scrap value, the assets will ultimately find a market in someone who feels that he can use the assets effectively—that is, make them earn him a profit.

In certain cases, in which the majority stock of a concern is being valued, a combined capitalized earnings and asset approach may be appropriate. The appraiser may find, after valuing the shares on the basis of the earning power of the business, that the concern owns certain assets which may be sold or distributed to security holders without impairing the earning capacity of the company. Redundant cash, government securities, or unused plant may fall in this category. These "extra" assets may properly be valued without reference to the earning power of the business, and their net realization value added to the capitalized earnings value in the final determination of the worth of the stock. This is known as the redundant asset method.

Conversely, when additional investment by the purchasers is needed in order to realize the estimated earning power, the additional investment required may appropriately be subtracted from the value arrived at by capitalized future earnings based on the assumption that the additional investment will be made.

Market Value Approach

Another major approach to value looks to the prices set for the security in actual transactions between buyer and seller—to "the bloodless verdict of the marketplace." Proponents of this approach argue that actual market prices are set by buyers and sellers acting in basic self-interest. Thus, they are appraisals of supposed experts who are willing to support their opinions with cash. Therefore, they maintain that the prices at which sales take place are practical expressions of value which are definitely to be preferred to theoretical or "ex cathedra" views of value.

Supporters of market price as a standard argue that the market price at any particular time reflects the value of the security sold in relation to all other securities or opportunities for investment, and that all values are basically relative. Hence, the price of a security in a free market serves as an effective common denominator of all the current ideas of the worth of a security as compared to other investment opportunities. Also, market price is a definite measure that can readily be applied to a particular situation. The subjectivity of other approaches is avoided in favor of a known yardstick of value.

Whatever truth is embodied in these arguments, there are many problems in applying market price as a standard of value.

In the first place, recent market prices are available for the common stocks of only the larger American companies. There were some 400,-000 corporations in existence in this country on December 31, 1958. Of these companies, only 2,933 had securities listed on national exchanges. Further, "listing" does not in itself create an active group of buyers and sellers, and many listed stocks are traded on a very desultory and infrequent basis.

Where there are few prospective buyers and sellers for a security, a thin market is said to exist. Markets are particularly thin for many securities traded in the over-the-counter market, where one will often find such wide spreads between bid and asked prices as "16 bid 19 asked." The dumping of a relatively small number of shares on such a thin market may suffice to depress market prices substantially.

Further, the market price for a particular stock on a given date may be sharply influenced by intentional manipulation of the price through such devices as "dumping" or the development of a "corner" on the market for the shares. Also, stabilization, or price support activity, is legal in a number of instances and is typical during the period in which a new issue is being marketed by the underwriters.

Another question often arises in the valuation of large blocks of securities. Recorded sales prices for the date in question may be based on the sale of a hundred or two shares. Is it fair and appropriate to apply the price set on a small scale to a large block of shares?

A more basic objection frequently raised is the contention that the market itself tends to exaggerate major upward and downward movements in stock prices. For example, it is argued that in 1929 speculative influences pushed common stock prices for certain widely traded stocks far beyond "reasonable" levels. Conversely, it is claimed that prices in 1932 were so depressed by purely psychological factors and by technical pressures for liquidity as to be manifestly poor standards of long-run value.

Partially in answer to some of the objections above noted, the theory of fair market value, or intrinsic value, has been developed. Under this approach, fair market value is the value at which a sale would take place if there were willing buyers and willing sellers actually in the market, and each equipped with full information on the security and prepared to act in an entirely rational manner. This concept does meet most of the objections stated, yet *per se* it raises a need for other standards of valuation than market quotations and suggests recourse to something like capitalized earnings as a more valid appraisal of "intrinsic worth."

At any rate, largely because of their ease of application, market prices are widely used by the courts and by tax authorities, although not to the exclusion of other standards where they are deemed appropriate.

Regardless of theoretical weaknesses of market price as a measure of intrinsic value, where a market price exists for even one share of stock it will inevitably affect the appraisal of a prospective buyer or seller—however large the potential transaction. The seller will in ordinary human nature hesitate to take a price much less than the price label established in the market, and the buyer will resist evaluations substantially higher than the market quotations.

The foregoing discussion of valuation processes should not be interpreted as minimizing the influence of bargaining, or horse trading, in fixing exchange prices in other than auction markets. It should be apparent that valuation is truly an inexact process by which evaluators in their own minds reach an *approximate area of value*. Often, like Judge Webster, the evaluators may use various approaches in arriving at an approximation of value. Within the area established in the minds of the prospective buyer and the prospective seller, the final price will be developed by the bargaining process. Hence, our concepts of area of value should be regarded as establishing the boundary lines within which the pulling and hauling of bargaining will establish a price at which an exchange will take place.

Selected References

BONBRIGHT, J .C. *The Valuation of Property.* 2 vols. New York: Mc-Graw-Hill Book Co., Inc., 1937.

CLENDENIN, JOHN C. *Introduction to Investments,* chap. 4. New York: McGraw-Hill Book Co., Inc., 1960.

GRAHAM, B., DODD, D. L., and COTTLE, S. *Security Analysis,* Part IV (esp. chap. 32). 4th ed. New York: McGraw-Hill Book Co., Inc., 1962.

JOHNSON, R. W. *Financial Management,* chaps. 22 and 23. 2d ed. Boston: Allyn and Bacon, Inc. 1962.

8. SMALL MANUFACTURING ENTERPRISES *

The objectives of those interested in small manufacturing enterprises are that these enterprises shall be strong, vigorous, and profitable, and that their strength and their numbers shall increase year by year. This means that firms now having rough going will be enabled to overcome their most serious current difficulties and go on to lay the foundations for a strong competitive position. It means further that firms already successful will have opportunities to compound their success. It looks forward to all these firms, together with new firms, being a hard-hitting, strong, and profitable part of our total manufacturing process.

The attainment of these objectives means a reversal of the trend toward bigness of the last 90 years. Are such objectives realistic?

The most important single fact in this whole problem is that a substantial segment of small manufacturers have shown that these objectives can be met. At every stage of our history part of the small manufacturers have been strong and profitable. Approaches based on "doing something for small business" in a spirit of weakness and of failure are unrealistic unless they also recognize the achievements of firms that are successful. The objectives are in part attained already; among some 300,000 existing industrial enterprises with personnel of 100 or less, an important segment is made up of firms now strong in competition and substantially more profitable than large corporations.

In the light of these objectives two problems can be stated:

1. Is strengthening of small manufacturers as a sector of our business structure in the public interest—in the interest of the nation as a whole?

   What courses of action will make the industrial climate more conducive to the strength and growth of these enterprises? By what agencies of government and/or by what other groups should these courses of action be undertaken?

2. What courses of action within the group of small manufacturers themselves will be most effective and most feasible in accomplishing these objectives more fully than at present?

   What action should be collective among the firms? What is the re-

* By W. Arnold Hosmer. Reprinted from *Harvard Business Review*, Nov.–Dec., 1957.

sponsibility of each firm individually? What are the foundations on which an effective overall program of action can be based?

These problems need to be examined with as much of the power of imaginative management thinking as can be brought to bear. Imaginative thinking is as necessary in management as in technical fields.

Among the 300,000 small firms are executives as able as any in large corporations. The very ablest are limited in both cases, but men as able as the operating executives of large corporations exist in hundreds, in fact in thousands, among these small enterprises—men whose experience is rounded because they have to deal with all of the problems of an enterprise, not with one function. These hundreds, these thousands, of men have used imaginative thinking in management of their own companies, but their skills have not been applied equally to the small enterprise problem as a whole.

Means for bringing this proved management experience and ability to bear represent the most fruitful single approach toward the general problem. A basic strength is big men in small enterprises.

The emphasis in this article is on searching out and developing policies and methods which will advance the problem of small industrial enterprises measurably toward a solution. The emphasis is not on statistical description but on courses of action—on doing something about it. After an examination of the factors that make these small manufacturers what they are—so dramatically different and so important to the economy—we shall focus on two areas for action: taxation considered from the operating point of view and the strategy of size.

A Dominant Force

Small manufacturers are defined in this study as those with total personnel of 100 or less. We could spend much time on definitions, but men—and women—are the essential element, and we shall use 100 as the dividing point.

The basic distinction is direct management. Of course direct management does not exist in all smaller firms, but at the point of about 100 in personnel subtle changes typically occur which distinguish those with personnel below 100 from those above.

These small firms have been the dominant form of industrial organization for centuries, in fact since the beginning of industry. In Europe in the sixteenth century, visitors went to see the Plantin Press because it was a "large" enterprise—with 56 in the factory itself and another 20 or so working in their homes.[1] In this country for over 200 years, from 1620 to 1820, we had substantially no manufacturers with personnel over 100. For the next 50 years, small firms were still dominant.

From 1870 to the present, almost 90 years, the emphasis has shifted to large-scale operation, large companies. In public discussion, in the press, and in the attention of our public financial markets, the emphasis is on large units, though in actual production manufacturing has not gone as fully toward large-scale operation.

Even defining "small" with a limit of 100, these small manufacturers bulk large in the total economy:

They give employment to more than twice as many persons as the nine largest corporations in the country, including General Motors, U.S. Steel, General Electric, Ford, Bethlehem Steel, Standard Oil (N.J.), Westinghouse, Western Electric, and Chrysler. If foreign employees of these large companies were excluded, we could add Goodyear to make an even 10 and still have twice as many persons in the small firms.[2]

Total personnel in these small manufacturing firms is greater than that in our 44 largest corporations. If the proprietors of enterprises carried on as single proprietorships or partnerships were added to the figures in Table 8–1 to give total personnel in these small firms, we could add another six

Table 8–1

TOTAL MANUFACTURING FIRMS BY NUMBER
OF PAID EMPLOYEES

Employee Size Classes	Number of Firms	Number of Employees
0–3	137,300	144,000
4–7	51,900	287,000
8–19	57,300	731,000
20–49	38,900	1,218,000
50–99	17,400	1,211,000
Total 0–99	302,800	3,591,000
100–499	16,160	3,305,000
500–999	2,060	1,420,000
Total 100–999	18,220	4,725,000
Total 0–999	321,020	8,316,000
1,000 and over	1,850	8,503,000
Total of all classes	322,870	16,819,000

SOURCE: *Survey of Current Business*, May, 1954, p. 23; figures on total employment in large companies, *The Conference Board Business Record*, December, 1952, p. 144.

---

[1] Dr. Raymond De Roover, "The Business Organization of the Plantin Press in the Setting of Sixteenth Century Antwerp," *Gulden Passer*, 34e Jaargang, 1956, p. 116.

[2] Figures on employees of corporations from *The Conference Board Business Record*, December, 1952, p. 144.

large corporations and have total personnel greater than that in our 50 largest corporations.

Frontier of Industry.   The center of this whole subject is in the men and women carrying on these enterprises. Many thousands would probably be equally content in large corporations, but they are not the ones who give the group its special character, a character peculiarly difficult to describe. I shall use the frontier as an analogy:

The frontier built men. The pioneers who pushed our frontier westward from the seaboard were resourceful men and women—willing to depend on themselves and impatient with old restrictions. Self-reliance of this order is possibly the most distinguishing feature of small manufacturing enterprises.

The frontier was rough. Many of the pioneers failed in their objectives— to have a farm of their own, a store, a sawmill. Men—and women—faced dangers they knew about and went on, in spite of sickness, Indians, cold, and privations. Many did not have the ability and fortitude to stand the rigors of frontier life. But the failure of those who did fail did not prevent the westward movement of the frontier. Nor did the proportion of failures present the creation of new farms, new enterprises, and new communities.

Here again, small manufacturing enterprises are peculiarly like our frontier. Some do fail, but the proportion of failures has not kept new people from starting out, nor has it prevented success and achievement as a whole.

The frontier was a changing and a boiling scene. The constant problems were not a matter of a little better or a little worse, a change in some percentage up or down. They were a matter of life and death, where wrong decisions could end a venture. The men of the frontier knew this, and the men operating small enterprises are painfully aware of it.

The frontier was complex, and also selective. New communities were established with all of the relationships required in church, town meeting, and grist mill. There probably were drifters and ne'er-do-wells in every group, but the self-reliant men predominated and natural leaders led, just as they do today in small enterprises.

As on the frontier, there is a drama, a breadth of human relations, in a small management team forging a strong competitive position, an excitement these men at least find lacking in large corporations. Doubtless, men who are running some of these enterprises do not measure up. Tragedy, sometimes stark tragedy, is mingled with success, often outstanding success. Thus, in spirit, in difficulties, and in opportunities, these small enterprises are the frontier of today. The central fact is the relative pattern of success and failure. The driving force is the expectation of success. And it is a driving force against which large corporations can never wholly prevail.

The same theme keeps recurring: "The big companies can be

taken. We are doing it now. If we could only get an even break in taxes and financing, we could really take them." Or, from a man recently retired as president of a fairly large company, "That company is just as vulnerable to competition from a small firm giving customers reliable service and precision as our competitors were 40 years ago."

Here, then, is the problem: Does the relative frequency of success warrant a growing stream of our ablest young men seeking their careers in these small enterprises? Does the frequency pattern of success warrant equity investment? And if not within the present industrial climate, what changes can be made to bring the requisite conditions about?

The Leaders

Within the group of some 300,000 industrial firms is a smaller group, possibly 30,000, which is an especially significant element in our business structure. This group consists of firms with the highest quality of management. The quality of management cannot be measured statistically, and it requires the best of judgment to appraise it; but in determining whether a firm should be considered a member of this select group we can be guided by what it has achieved or, for new firms, by our appraisal of the men.

It is obvious that the quality of management differs throughout the entire group of over 300,000. In many of these firms the management is tragically poor, whereas at the other end of the spectrum one finds management teams which can match anything to be found in the departments and divisions of large corporations and in the top management teams of most of them. High quality shows up in two areas:

1. The man or men carrying responsibility—particularly the existence of a cohesive management team.
2. Management techniques such as well-devised records, careful engineering in product development, scheduling of purchasing and production against sales, and systematic financial planning.

If we think of small manufacturers as an array, a spectrum, based on the quality of management, the 10 percent with the highest quality of management, no matter how defined or selected, are a significantly different group.

Table 8–2 sets forth the author's estimate of the personnel involved in such firms, to show the order of magnitude. The percentages used for estimating here are based on observations of a large number of firms, and follow those observations in reflecting a higher percentage of firms with a notably high quality of management in the larger classes.

On this basis, even the selected group of 30,000 firms out of 300,000 employ more persons than General Motors, and more than Chrysler, Ford, and Standard Oil (N.J.) combined, with Eastman Kodak included for good measure.

Table 8–2

ESTIMATED COMPOSITION OF SELECTED GROUP OF 30,000
BEST MANAGED FIRMS AMONG TOTAL MANUFACTURING FIRMS
EMPLOYING LESS THAN 100

Employee Size Classes	Percentage of Class in Selected Group*	Selected Group Number of Firms	Selected Group Number of Employees
0–3	5%	6,900	7,000
4–7	10	5,200	23,000
8–19	15	8,600	73,000
20–49	15	5,800	183,000
50–99	20	3,500	182,000
0–99	10	30,000	468,000

* Estimated percentages applied by author to total number of firms in corresponding size class (Table 8–1).

Blazing the Trail. What about the position of these 30,000 best managed firms as leaders of the whole 300,000 small manufacturing enterprises, as leaders not only of those already in existence but of those yet unborn—a point of focus for the aspirations of men seeking to establish enterprises equally successful?

The 30,000 have sweated out the difficulties, have developed products that customers will pay for, at attractive prices, and in view of the whole range of other suppliers. In every phase of operations one can find among these leaders firms which have pounded out highly successful solutions. In each of these areas the instances show the diversity and flexibility in adaptation needed in successful competition. The very fact of diversity is an important feature in showing what can be done. For instance:

Among the 30,000 firms one could find at least 1,000 highly successful instances of the handling of cost-price relationships, of selling against existing facilities and acquiring facilities in terms of available markets, of pricing in terms of learning curves, of policies to meet seasonal variations in demand—of the whole complex of factors in this area. To see the achievements of firms like these makes the top managements of our largest corporations think in terms of mergers.

But, while the 30,000 are effective leaders in one sense, in another sense they are not. They have blazed the paths of effective operation. They have not so far been equally effective in leading others along these paths.

The medical profession has developed effective means of accomplishing this second part of leadership—the extension of the best methods and the best skills broadly through the profession. In the field of business administration in the last 40 years, we have developed a whole series of methods for the careful examination and dispersion of new ideas and new methods. But this process has not operated by any means as well among small enterprises as it has among larger competitors. Why? There are two related reasons:

(1. The tradition of "full disclosure" of financial statements and other facts has become well established among large corporations, especially among those with listed securities. The custom of disclosure is not established in anywhere near the same degree among these small enterprises.

(2. Firms such as our 30,000 are highly competitive. Our large corporations also compete, but I am convinced that the rigors of the competitive game are greater among these small enterprises. The whole reaction against big business in the last 75 years has assumed the fact of competition among small firms.[3] The assumption is correct. If one of these small firms has worked out a strong competitive position, there are limits to the extent of disclosure and assistance to other firms one can reasonably expect.

How Profitable? Unfortunately, we do not know just how profitable the small manufacturers are. Opinions formed by citing instances out of 300,000 firms are subject to obvious error—understatement as well as overstatement. Table 8–3 gives earnings and related figures, both in dollar amounts and in percentages. It is limited to 114,000 firms organized as corporations out of 322,000 in total. Size classes are based on assets, not men, but taking $10,000 of assets per man (probably too high), firms with under $1 million correspond roughly to those with 100 and under in personnel.

In interpreting the figures for income measured as a return on equity—for instance, 16.2 percent for the $500,000 to $999,990 class as compared with 18.7 percent for the $100 million and over class—one needs to allow for these facts among others:

In general, the averages for these 100,000 firms are lower than they should be to be comparable with the averages for large firms, because

---

[3] See J. D. Glover, "The Attack on Big Business" (Boston, Division of Research, Harvard Business School, 1954).

Table 8-3

INCOME OF MANUFACTURING CORPORATIONS BY ASSET SIZE CLASSES, 1952

Asset Size Class (thousands of dollars)	Number of Firms		Income before Taxes (millions of dollars)		Equity (millions of dollars)		Dividends (millions of dollars)		Income before Taxes—% of Equity	Income after Taxes—% of Equity	Dividends—% of Equity	Dividends—% of Income after Taxes
	In Class	Cumulative	In Class	Cumulative	In Class	Cumulative	In Class	Cumulative				
$0–50	38,146		–$21,733		$326,639		$4,432		–6.7%	–1.9%	1.35%	–20.4%
50–100	13,282	56,428	67,936	$46,203	725,129	$1,051,768	10,635	$15,067	9.4	4.5	1.46	24.0
100–250	23,683	80,111	265,864	312,067	2,180,158	3,231,926	36,701	51,768	12.2	6.4	1.68	13.8
250–500	12,786	92,897	379,279	691,346	2,658,886	5,890,812	58,160	109,928	14.3	6.4	2.20	15.4
500–1,000	8,571	101,468	612,386	1,303,732	3,780,539	9,671,351	92,474	202,402	16.2	6.9	2.42	15.1
1,000–5,000	9,019	110,487	2,275,093	3,578,825	12,530,777	22,202,128	366,742	569,144	18.2	7.6	2.90	16.1
5,000–10,000	1,471	111,958	1,333,978	4,912,803	6,935,821	29,137,949	251,473	820,617	19.2	8.0	3.62	18.9
10,000–50,000	1,359	113,317	3,730,194	8,642,997	18,477,580	47,615,529	879,041	1,699,658	20.2	8.6	4.25	23.5
50,000–100,000	179	113,496	1,527,837	10,170,834	8,096,594	55,712,123	418,165	2,117,823	18.9	7.9	5.18	27.4
100,000 and over	215	113,711	10,056,876	20,227,710	53,784,136	109,496,259	3,546,963	5,664,786	18.7	8.5	6.10	35.4

SOURCE: Based on *Statistics of Income for 1952* (Washington, D.C.: U.S. Government Printing Office, 1955), Part II, p. 55, Table 4, and p. 80, Table 6.

(a) among the small firms are most of the thousands of new firms formed each year that obviously need several years to get themselves on a going basis, (b) many of the more successful small firms disappear each year by merger with large firms or by growing beyond the $1 million limit, (c) a share of current earnings of the small firms takes the form of salaries.[4]

In particular, many of the most shrewdly managed small firms, including many of the 30,000 leaders, plow back all amounts otherwise available for earnings into research and into development of their product lines and marketing structures, along with other expenditures to strengthen their competitive position.

Small firms show a greater diversity in earnings. It is possible—indeed probable—that the upper two to three deciles of the several size groups below $1 million show the highest rate of return in industry.

The 30,000—the upper decile in management—may not at present show high earnings, for the reasons stated above, but if the rate of building earning power is added, the facts are there to get equity capital flowing, to get investors probing among the whole 300,000.

The basic data exist—in tax and other reports made out so laboriously—to test, and I believe to support by a solid foundation of evidence, the statements made above. At present the formulations, for instance in the Treasury Department's *Statistics of Income*, are not set up to answer operating questions. However, reformulation is possible in operating terms, using the abilities of operating men to ask the right questions and all the capacities of data processing. In my opinion this would be the most important single thing the government could do in the interest of all small enterprises, with the single exception of taxes.

In summary, the objectives stated in the beginning of this article are in part attained; the problems there stated have in part been solved. We have an inventory of proved experience and proved achievement. In the interest of the entire 300,000 enterprises now in existence and of perhaps another 200,000 not yet established a remaining problem is to make this proved experience more articulate, more directly available for the entire group.

Democracy in Taxation

Our emphasis is on management. But it is impossible to release the full dynamic force of management under the present tax laws. The proposals below are made from the point of view of men operating small enterprises. Instead of minor technical tax concessions, let us be-

---

[4] See Joseph L. McConnell, "Corporate Earnings by Size of Firm," *Survey of Current Business*, May, 1945, p. 6.

gin with proposals that would really solve the problem. The purpose is to release enough of the dynamic forces among small enterprises so that by the end of a very few years the public revenue will be increased, not decreased.

I am definitely among the company of those who think our tax laws create a preferred position for large corporations.

This preferred position is the crux of the problem. As J. Keith Butters and John Lintner summarize their conclusions:

7. In almost every respect high taxes are less repressive on large, established corporations than on small, growing firms.

(a). High taxes reduce the profit expectancy of new expansions by large companies much less severely than they restrict similar expansions undertaken by small . . . companies.

(b). Large, established companies have substantial amounts of funds becoming available from their noncash expenses in addition to whatever earnings they may be able to retain after taxes. These funds may be used to finance the introduction of new products and technical innovations.

(c). Finally, large, established companies generally can acquire new capital on much more favorable terms than can small companies. In addition to their ability to float common stock with relative ease, they can usually issue preferred stocks or bonds—alternatives available to small companies only on a limited scale, on more expensive terms, and usually at great risk to the common stockholders.

8. Thus, unless special adjustments are made to relieve the burden of a flat-rate corporate tax on small companies, such a tax would tend to promote an increased degree of industrial concentration in addition to restricting the growth of small, independent companies.

9. It would be possible substantially to relieve the tax burden on most small, growing companies without greatly diminishing Federal revenues. This study clearly emphasizes the need for such relief. But it makes no attempt to examine the many problems which would arise in formulating the precise character of this relief.[5]

The strength of the small business position is that *it does not ask for treatment as a privileged class, but for elimination of the present preferment for large corporations.*[6] Advocates of small business who depart from this weaken the whole position of small business. The rea-

---

[5] *Effect of Federal Taxes on Growing Enterprises* (Boston, Division of Research, Harvard Business School, 1945), pp. 3 and 4. It is my understanding that Professors Butters and Lintner believe the carry-back and carry-forward have ameliorated the situation somewhat but that in substance it is as stated in the quotation above. I do not wish to imply that they have approved or disapproved the proposals in this article.

[6] See Maurice H. Stans, "What Small Business Needs," *Accounting Review*, October 1946, pp. 369, 371.

sonable tax objectives of small enterprises can be attained within the bounds of balancing out the present preferences for large corporations.

The proposals of the Cabinet Committee on Small Business, in my opinion, do not have sufficient bite in terms of actual business operation to accomplish the purpose.[7] The first, reducing the tax on the first $25,000 from 30 percent to 20 percent with a maximum effect of $2,500, would be expensive in terms of the public revenue. Would it be effective in any basic sense? Would this $0 to $2,500 help in working-capital problems, or getting equity capital flowing, or leading to a change in the competitive position of many small firms?

Much the same questions can be raised about the rest—do they go beyond concessions of a technical nature, do they redress the tax balance, do they release the dynamic forces that can create business and create public revenue?

The proposals below may or may not be the best available, they may or may not reduce the initial public revenue more than the Cabinet Committee proposals, but they do have the capacity to release dynamic forces.

1. A provision that dividends declared from earnings made while a company has personnel of 100 or less be not taxable in the hands of the recipients, regardless of the date of declaration. A flexible upper limit would be advisable, for instance, by decreasing the percentage of earnings subject to the right by 1 percent for each 4 additional personnel with the right disappearing at 500. Possibly a provision would be necessary that not over 20 percent of the earnings of a year could be declared in dividends until the third succeeding year.
2. Optional depreciation, whereby a manufacturer could take the depreciation on assets in any year he chose, likewise with a flexible upper limit. In adjusting depreciation a company could also adjust taxable income as between years. This has broader effects than at first appear. Provisions would be needed to prevent abuses, and to limit the right to bona fide operating companies.
3. In order to give incentive to original "seed" money, a provision that gains arising out of the first $50,000 of investment in an independent enterprise be not subject to either the capital gains tax or inheritance tax. Like the provisions above, it would not apply prior to the date of enactment. This would almost certainly increase the public revenue both in the short run and in the long run.
4. Either elimination of stock option provisions or action making them equally available to small companies. It is usually impossible to get valuation on small company stock as a basis for options.

---

[7] Cabinet Committee on Small Business, *Progress Report* (Washington, D.C.: U.S. Government Printing Office, 1956).

5. A right to issue stock to employees in limited amounts per year—possibly $3,000 or $5,000—without the stock's being taxable income of the employee. With careful provisions to prevent abuse, it is almost certain the public revenue would be increased, through leading more able young men into this field.
6. Before a judgment is made that any group of provisions favorable to small business is too costly budgetwise, careful examination of three subjects: a tightening up of regulations and more rigorous administration on deductible expenses, a question whether very high salaries should be deductible in full, and a similar question on professional fees and fees in the snowballing use of consulting firms on "48-cent dollars." The effect would fall principally on large corporations.

These may or may not be the most effective and feasible means of balancing out the present preferred tax position of large corporations. If better means exist, let us get them out in the light—stated, analyzed, and criticized, along with those above, so that judgments can be made on the basis of as complete facts and as careful analysis as can be brought to bear.

I am thoroughly convinced that the above proposals, if enacted, would not go beyond the point of balance; they would not create a preferred position for small business. I am just as thoroughly convinced that action less forceful would leave the preferred tax position of large corporations possibly reduced but still in existence.

On the dividend proposal, a man of broad experience in the financial field made the following comments:

(a) This is strong enough to get equity capital actually moving.
(b) It would lead the investment industry to do the imaginative thinking and research necessary to learn how to make this kind of investment.
(c) It would facilitate proprietorships and partnerships incorporating when the business facts warrant it and close corporations giving up their close position to issue stock broadly in shares, subdivided to meet investment demands.

Effect on the Public Revenue. What would be the effect on the public revenue? The dividend proposal in substance seems to be in operation already on something like 75 percent of taxable income involved; the transfer of earnings from the generating enterprise to the owners without double taxation already exists in proprietorships, partnerships, and in those close corporations where such transfers are made through salaries. The second proposal would be a matter primarily of deferral of some part of depreciation, but some companies could adjust income to $25,000, getting more use of the lower rate.

The third and fifth would almost certainly increase public revenue, and the fourth might well have the same effect *if* option provisions for large corporations were tightened up.

The major question is whether the provisions above hit at the actual roadblocks in attaining the stated objectives. If those roadblocks are, in fact, removed, the dynamic force in small business, the plans of men with solid records of achievement, will create jobs and expanding volumes of business, not only within the firms themselves but in purchases of materials, of capital equipment, and of houses by men holding new jobs, together with all their increased purchases of goods and services within their communities.

In short, if present taxes are as repressive as they appear to be, provisions removing their repressive effects may increase rather than decrease the public revenue.

The Strategy of Size

The objectives stated at the beginning are rugged—yet have been met by the 30,000 leaders among the small manufacturing enterprises. Are they attainable by the rest of the 300,000 and the 200,000 yet unborn?

Throughout many segments of business, large companies have a position no small enterprise can meet in competition. Not only do they have funds for the great investment required, but the investment banking structure is keyed primarily to meet their needs. They can expand to the point where they enjoy the benefits of lowered cost in large-scale production. Funds for research enable them to do basic exploration and development work in the main line of their industries and in the variants and byways which may prove important in the future; and their patent counsel are busy in weaving a fabric of protection for them. The national marketing structure is heavily directed toward mass distribution for large firms.

There is no gainsaying that, within the particular segments of business where the advantages of large-scale operation apply, the large companies generate a competitive strength which a small business can counter with difficulty, if at all. But does this mean, as is so often assumed, that the competitive advantage of size operates evenly throughout the entire economy? Are there not other areas accounting for a substantial part of national production where the competitive forces are reversed and where the advantage actually lies with the small enterprises?

Such areas do, in fact, exist. And men operating in the field believe they are large, encompassing a potential volume of business substantially greater than that which has been captured by small companies up to now. But the picture is complex. Some of the unsuccessful small enterprises are bucking the tides of size in a field they never should have entered. In contrast, the great majority of successful small companies operate where the competitive tides are running with them rather than against them.

What are the segments of business in which the competitive forces favor small enterprises? Where can the imagination and initiative of management teams develop profitable operations in a climate conducive to their success?

Limited National Volume. Products whose total national demand is of the order of $1 million to $5 million are a natural area for small enterprises. No one company is going to control all the volume. General Electric, for instance, has no reason to be in such a market, and even much smaller companies will be scattering their shots unduly if they try to compete for this type of business. Yet a company with personnel of 100 or less, conducted with aggressiveness and initiative, can meet one or more markets of that size and do very well. Competitive advantages may be even greater in markets of $100,000 to $500,000.

All industries have struck a rough balance of size, with a distribution among large, medium, and small companies. This balance, which depends on the workings of a whole series of factors, is not static. It is dynamic, moving in slow adjustment to the elements which influence overall profitability. The fact that our largest companies have shown increasing sales over the last 10 years of an expanding economy does not necessarily mean that the balance is moving toward greater size; limited and inadequate evidence indicates there is a time lag before small enterprises pick up volume in segments where competitive forces favor them.

The advantage arises only if the product is, in fact, separate. If it is a pressure gauge of a special type used on high-pressure boilers, but is only one item in a large line of gauges using similar know-how and manufacturing methods, it is manifestly not a separate product.

But if it requires special knowledge and background, special methods and skills in manufacture, and contact with customers by men with particular backgrounds, then the product can be considered a separate item. One instance—somewhat extreme, to be sure—is engraving engines. These devices are designed to engrave grids for use in spectroscopes with 12,000 to 15,000 uniform lines per inch, uniformly spaced. Shrewd men have found hundreds of such products and are finding them in every new major product—although it is the major products alone which hit the headlines.

Charles H. Kline, in "The Strategy of Product Policy," gives a breakeven analysis in which the cost of a product of limited volume was compared for a small and a large company:

As a general rule, the smallest economic unit that has the facilities to undertake a given operation performs it most efficiently. That is why, when large companies enter low-investment businesses, they very often run into difficulties. . . .

The product in question was a semifabricated material with a small but assured market potential of about $200,000 annually. The investment in plant equipment necessary for this volume of sales was about $25,000.

. . . The large corporation needed a sales volume of $216,000 per year to break even on this product. The small company, however, could make money anywhere above the breakeven point of $55,000 in annual sales. . . . At the breakeven volume of $216,000 for the large company, the small company would net $72,000 before taxes. . . .

Actually this analysis was made by the large corporation after several years of poor operating results. When this cost study became available, the product was dropped.[8]

Regional Products. Some products are manufactured and sold more advantageously within a specific region than they are in a national market. Though in some instances excessive freight rates account for this advantage, service is more often the determining factor. The local manufacturer may be able to deliver within 24 hours, by his own truck or otherwise; and the customers are close enough so they can go over blueprints with his engineers, if it is an industrial product. He or his engineers can get to the customer's plant for immediate conferences to iron out difficulties. On other occasions the local manufacturer can handle his inventory and emergency production facilities so the customer can rely on fast action when he needs it, without the disconcerting uncertainties of delivery from a plant 1,000 miles away.

The regional businessman may be able to do more of his selling direct, and arrange long-term agreements with one or more customers or distributors that give him a steady basic volume. In addition, there is an intangible advantage in keeping one's finger on the pulse of a concentrated market.

When added up, the conditions are very similar to those characteristic of limited national demand which I have discussed. If the regional volume is large, it may be worthwhile for a major company to

---

[8] *Harvard Business Review*, July–August, 1955, p. 94.

compete for the business, possibly through a series of local plants, located in each of the promising regions. But the regional volume often will not warrant the overhead, nor the special effort required to compete through delegated responsibility and a decentralized organization.

Short Runs, Special Lots.   The very nature of mass production limits the number of sizes, types, or models which can be turned out profitably. It is true, of course, that the requirements of most customers are met by the mass-produced types, but in all industries some customers have special needs based on unique uses or individual tastes. As our economy becomes more mature, while still remaining dynamic, apparently the demand for nonconforming models is increasing.

Short runs of special styles create management difficulties and increase costs for large companies in both production and marketing. The more completely mechanized mass production becomes, the greater the problems in these unusual orders. Delivery is delayed, cost is high, and the administrative process of the mass producer is clogged.

With sharper cost controls, many large organizations are finally coming to recognize that they are losing money on these short runs and special models. The small manufacturer, on the other hand, is often so organized in both sales and production that he can handle small lots and special types much more inexpensively and efficiently than can his bigger colleague.

Consequently, many large corporations have worked out cooperative arrangements with small firms to take over this business. The president of one small company I know of, for instance, negotiated arrangements with two large corporations under which the big firms referred customer inquiries and orders for short runs to his concern. These agreements have been in existence for a number of years, to the mutual satisfaction both of the large companies and of the small one. Needless to say, the plan has been highly profitable to the small firm.

High Precision.   Throughout industry the trend toward higher precision and closer tolerances is notable. In mass production, where high precision depends primarily on machines, it can be achieved on a high volume basis without undue problems in administration. But when high precision depends on craftsmanship or on fine manual skill, it is difficult for a large company to manage production because of its series of echelons and departments. The direct management characteristic of a small enterprise makes it easier to meet very close tolerances and keep spoilage down. As the president of one small company said,

"It is remarkable how competition drops out on the short side of two ten-thousandths of an inch."

Small-Scale Mass Production. We commonly assume that mass production insures continuously decreasing cost in proportion to rising sales volume and a growing work force, reaching its ultimate with such companies as General Motors, U.S. Steel, and General Electric. But, while this may be true of some industries, it certainly is not true of every one. Substantially all the economies of mass production are often realized at a remarkably low scale of operation.

Thus, many small enterprises with personnel of 100 or less are competing successfully on a mass-production basis. For instance:

One company with special machinery and methods for manufacturing a component used in the products of some eight large corporations turned out a volume greater than that of a whole department in any one of those companies. Consequently, it was able to set up mass-production methods which simply were not feasible for any of its customers.

As the proprietor pointed out, "Every once in a while one of the big outfits tries to make the item itself, but it runs into quality difficulties and comes back to us. I keep five or six of the big users supplied, and my prices are very satisfactory. My 15 men know the operation far better than my customers do."

In the component business, success for the small company depends on the nature of the item, the production process, and the sales volume. But the possibilities are not limited to parts: even on completed products, a company with personnel of 100 or less may achieve most of the economies of mass production. Many instances exist in the plastics and metalworking industries. To illustrate:

A 12-man firm with which I am acquainted makes special types of pumps for a segment of the chemical industry. The motors, bearings, and several other parts are standard items, the castings are purchased from a foundry on a steady-run basis, and requisite machining is done on special machine tools that are as automatic as any company could use.

As more and more standard components become available, the required volume for economical production of finished products will be even further reduced. Also, the standard components themselves are a highly appropriate product for mass production in a small plant, as we have seen. Finally, machine tools which give a small plant substantially all the advantages of mass production have been developed in many lines. The obstacle for the small manufacturer, then, is not equipment or cost; it is capital and marketing. If these can be overcome, the potentials of mass production in small firms are large—and intriguing.

Uneven Growth. We are accustomed to a rapidly expanding gross national product. This growth is not even, but rather is the sum of a complex multitude of changes, with some industries declining or even virtually disappearing, others increasing their volumes at varying rates, and still others appearing for the first time. Furthermore, within each industry some lines move up in volume and others down, and within each line some items lose their markets and others require sudden increases in volume. Possibly this might be called the internal dynamics of industry.

It is quite impossible for any large company manufacturing several complex lines of products to keep all of them in the correct adjustment to current demand. Similarly, for industry as a whole the adjustment of available supply to current demand takes place irregularly and is marked by both overproduction and delivery delays.

Such a dynamic, changing pattern leaves many gaps which can be filled by small manufacturing enterprises with their greater speed of decision and closer contact among production, engineering, and sales. It is dangerous, to be sure, for individual products may become obsolete, but a demand so great that it causes delivery delays may well be evidence of a fertile future market. The period of short supply can give the small manufacturer a chance to become established.

The familiarity or "feel" for an industry acquired by the management team of an aggressive small enterprise enables the executives to spot and appraise these competitive opportunities. Probably they will eliminate four out of five of the situations for various reasons, but the fifth alternative is likely to be highly profitable. One test question, to be put to prospective buyers, has proved helpful in classifying the possibilities: "Would you be willing to negotiate a reasonably long-term arrangement for a basic volume if we went into this field?"

The real achievement, then, is to spot a field where present delay portends a growing long-term demand, do realistic market research, concentrate limited engineering and other know-how on needed improvements, design alternative innovations, and secure solid patent protection. Big companies cannot protect their flanks on thousands of existing products; they have to concentrate their engineering and research in a few new fields. The entrepreneur can take advantage of this weakness.

Time of Executives. The allocation of top-management time and the amount of delegation key executives are forced into are crucial factors in business operation. Roughly speaking, senior executives may spend up to 2,500 hours per year on the affairs of their company;

meetings of the board or its committees may total 150 hours, exclusive of other services rendered to the organization by its directors.

In General Electric, with sales in 1956 of over $4 billion, the time per $1 million of sales, on this bassis, comes to about 37 minutes a year for executives and 2.2 minutes for directors. Even in a company with $100 million in sales, the breakdown is 25 hours for executives and 1.5 hours for directors.

Any such operation is so unlike one in which all 2,500 hours of senior executive time are concentrated on $1 million in sales as to be an altogether different type of business. And in a really small business, with sales of less than $1 million, the concentration on problems that are small in dollar volume but important in policy formation becomes even more intense.

The question of delegation is also significant here. In the case of products with market potential of $1 million—$10 million which demand separate know-how—and not all do, of course—can delegation meet the competition of direct management? At the end of the delegation process a large company can bring to bear the full time of the men in charge. But delegation may have to operate through four or five echelons or levels of authority. Is the process of delegation that good?

Can delegation produce a cohesive management group; or are production men, engineers, cost men, and salesmen separated by organizational walls and forced to communicate through channels? They have the prestige of a big company, its special services, and its financial strength. But are they authorized to make decisions, or must they get recommendations approved? Will this take three weeks? And most important, have they been trained in a field where initiative and drive paid off, or have they had 20 years of training in playing it safe?

Here we have another point of balance—a flexible balance moving with the type of product, the total volume, and the quality of management which the small enterprise or its large competitor can bring to bear. A company with $100 million of total sales may find that on $60 million in large volume lines mass production with well-devised delegation and control gives it a tremendous competitive advantage. On another $20 million it may have little, if any, advantage. But if the last $20 million is in separate lines averaging $1 million, can it stand the competition of small firms with the same quality of management?

In short, *can* delegation work that well? And are 25 hours per year of top-management time enough?

Selling Service.   Service is one of the main products sold by small manufacturers. It is as complex as the situations it is called on to meet.

It means personal contact, knowing the men in the industry, knowing all the details of one's own segment of the industry—including sources of material and parts, production, designing, flexible scheduling, and control of inventories to meet the special needs of particular customers. It means being a man people like to do business with. Intangible as these advantages may be, they add up to a significant part of competition in action.

Beating large competitors in the service area is by no means easy. Being able to forecast delivery and come through better on promises, keeping quality a bit higher and more dependable, staying a little ahead in design, holding costs low enough to give sea room—all these take a management team able to get things done and to use to the full all the advantages of direct management. The basic fact is that this service can be concentrated on a segment of the market, with 1,000 to 2,500 hours per $1 million in sales instead of 5 to 50 hours at the top.

No firm can expect to reap the benefits of service on every order, of course, but it can be decisive in some cases. Thus:

One buyer used the flexibility of a small firm in giving a telephone order on Wednesday for material he *had* to have the next Monday morning. He got the material. A little later this buyer reverted to a penny-counting approach on a large order, and was on the verge of turning over some good business to a large competitor of the small firm. But the competitor had not been able to meet the Monday delivery, so the president of the small firm got the order and was able to negotiate a "retainer volume" arrangement for future business. The retainer arrangement has operated to the mutual satisfaction of both parties.

With some customers, a good supplier can establish a position leading to a long-term profitable relationship; with others, no small supplier can do business and live. One of the necessary skills in operating a small business is to know which is which.

A further type of service is used very effectively by some large companies and not at all by the majority—research and development contracts. It is still true that most of the important technical breakthroughs have been made by small firms or by one or more persons working alone. Many additional small firms have the engineering competence and the concentrated know-how of a management team to tackle problems on a major product, or to develop new products on order.

Why buy up small firms to get the benefit of their creative thinking? Why not negotiate contracts to use the creative capacity of teams concentrating on limited areas? Such team operations can make come alive engineers who in a large engineering department would sit at a drafting board, period.

Conclusion

The objective of small manufacturing as a strong and profitable part of our economy is attainable. Many thousands of firms have attained such a position already.

Nevertheless, the problem of small business still remains, both as a national problem and as acute problems for many thousands of firms. For the nation, industrial democracy in action, the breeding ground of industry, is cramped and repressed. For individual firms, competition is made harder by artificial restrictions on the flow of equity capital and unnecessary impediments in sales.

The most effective solutions are to be found, first, in the removal of restrictions and, second, in a more widespread use of management methods proved in competition.

The dynamic forces in small manufacturing can only be realized if we have tax provisions developed from an operating point of view and sufficient in their effects to balance out the existing preferred position of large corporations. With these dynamic forces released, the imaginative power of direct management will find an even fuller scope within the strategy of size.

The leaders in management—described here as the 30,000—have blazed the trail. They represent an inventory of proved experience. The interests of the remainder of the 300,000 firms now having rough going, and the 200,000 yet unborn can best be served by using that inventory of proved experience—the results of big men in small enterprises.

BIBLIOGRAPHY

The literature on small business is extensive, and any brief bibliography can provide but a starting point for the selective reader. This literature includes material written for a number of different audiences. Some books and articles within this field have been written primarily for those interested in the characteristics of "small business as a whole"; some have been written for the present or prospective manager who is presumed to have relatively little background in administration; and some have been prepared for the experienced and knowledgeable manager or the prospective manager who has considerable training in administration. This bibliography lists some material prepared for each of these audiences, but the emphasis is upon the last mentioned above.

Books

CHRISTENSEN, C. ROLAND, *Management Succession in Small and Growing Enterprises*. Boston: Division of Research, Graduate School of Business Administration, Harvard University, 1953.

DAY, JOHN S. and DONHAM, PAUL, *New Enterprises and Small Business Management*. Homewood, Illinois: Richard D. Irwin, Inc., 1959.

FEDERAL RESERVE SYSTEM, *Financing Small Business*, Report to the Committee on Banking and Currency and the Select Committees on Small Business, United States Congress. Washington, D.C.: U.S. Government Printing Office, 1958.

FLINK, SALOMON, *Equity Financing for Small Business*. New York: Simmons-Boardman, 1962.

HOAD, WILLIAM N., *Third Small Business Case Book*. Ann Arbor: Bureau of Business Research, School of Business Administration, University of Michigan, 1955.

KAPLAN, A. D. H., *Small Business: Its Place and Problems*. New York: McGraw-Hill Book Co., Inc., 1948.

KRENTZMAN, HARVEY C., *Administrative Management for Small Business*. Washington, D.C.: U.S. Government Printing Office, 1965.

MACE, MYLES L., *The Board of Directors in Small Corporations*. Boston: Division of Research, Graduate School of Business Administration, Harvard University, 1948.

MAYER, KURT B. and GOLDSTEIN, SIDNEY, *The First Two Years: Problems of Small Firm Growth and Survival*. Washington, D.C.: U.S. Government Printing Office (Small Business Research Series No. 2), Small Business Enterprise, 1961.

MILLER, HARRY, *The Way of Enterprise*. London: Andre Deutsch, 1963.

OSBORN, RICHARD C., *Effects of Corporate Size on Efficiency and Profitability*. Urbana: University of Illinois Bulletin, Volume 48, Number 7, August 1950.

PRESTON, LEE E., (ed.), *Managing the Independent Business*. Englewood Cliffs, N.J.: Prentice-Hall, Inc., 1962.

PROXMIRE, WILLIAM, *Can Small Business Survive?* Chicago: H. Regner, 1964.

ZWICK, JACK, *A Handbook of Small Business Finance*. Washington, D.C.: U.S. Government Printing Office, 1965.

Articles

BOYCOTT, A. E., "On the Sizes of Things, or the Importance of Being Rather Small," *Contributions to Medical and Biological Research, Volume One*, New York: Paul B. Hoeber, 1919.

CALDER, GRANT H., "The Peculiar Problems of a Family Business," *Business Horizons*, Fall, 1961.

COATES, CHARLES B., "The Case of the Lonesome Loan," *Harvard Business Review*, November–December, 1964.

COOPER, ARNOLD C., "R & D Is More Efficient in Small Companies," *Harvard Business Review*, May–June, 1964.

COPELAND, F. W., "When Companies Reach the Awkward Age," *Duns Review & Modern Industry*, July 7, 1962.

DAKE, LELAND E., "Why Some Growth Companies Are Faltering," *Business Horizons*, Autumn, 1963.

DEARDEN, JOHN, "Profit-Planning Accounting for Small Firms," *Harvard Business Review*, March–April, 1963.

DOODY, ALTON F. and DAVIDSON, WILLIAM R., "Growing Strength in Small Retailing," *Harvard Business Review*, July–August, 1964.

FREEDMAN, HARRY S., "Scientific Management in Small Business," *Harvard Business Review*, May, 1950.

HOSMER, W. ARNOLD, "Small Manufacturing Enterprises," *Harvard Business Review*, November–December, 1957. (This article is included in this book.)

KRENTZMAN, HARVEY C. and SAMARAS, JOHN N., "Can Small Business Use Consultants?" *Harvard Business Review*, May–June, 1960.

MILROY, ROBERT R., "The Small Business Corporation—Proceed With Caution," *Business Horizons*, Summer, 1960.

NEWMAN, LOUIS E., "Advice for Small Company Presidents," *Harvard Business Review*, November–December, 1959.

Problems and Opportunities in Small Business (entire issue), *Iowa Business Digest*, February, 1959.

PUGH, OLIN S., "Small Business Investment Companies," *Business Topics*, Autumn, 1963.

SCHLAIFER, ROBERT, "Big Business and Small Business: A Case Study," *Harvard Business Review*, July, 1950.

Small Business (entire issue), *Law and Contemporary Problems*, Winter, 1959.

"Where Sick Companies Can Turn For Advice," *Business Week*, August 15, 1964.

WHITE, ROGER B., "How to Get Team Unity in a Small Enterprise," *Business Horizons*, Fall, 1958.

There is also a journal devoted exclusively to management problems of smaller companies. It is the *Journal of Small Business Management*, published quarterly by the National Council for Small Business Management Development.

Management Research Grant Program

Over two-hundred research projects have been conducted at various universities and research institutes with funds provided by the Small Business Management Research Grant Program.[1] A wide range of subjects has been investigated, including inquiries of very broad interest and inquiries of interest primarily to particular industries or geographical area.

The full reports can usually be purchased by writing to the universities where the research was conducted. Summaries, describing in two to four pages these reports, are issued by the Small Business Administration and are entitled "Management Research Summaries." Complete lists of the Summaries which are available can also be obtained from the Small Business Administration.

It is unfortunate that limitations of space prevent our listing all of these research studies. The following list includes some of those of most general interest.

CHAMBERS, EDWARD J. and GOLD, RAYMOND L., *Pilot Study of Successful and Unsuccessful Small Business Enterprises Within Montana*. Missoula: Bureau of Business and Economic Research, Montana State University, 1963.

COLLINS, ORVIS E. and MOORE, DAVID G., *The Enterprising Man*. East Lansing: Bureau of Business and Economic Research, Michigan State University, 1964.

DAVIDS, L. E., *Characteristics of Small Business Founders in Texas and Georgia*. Athens: Bureau of Business Research, University of Georgia, 1963.

---

[1] Unfortunately funds for the continuation of this program have not been appropriated for several years. The authors believe that the continuation of this program would be extremely valuable to the smaller business segment of our economy. Professor Hosmer has indicated reasons for the support of this program in testimony before the Select Committee on Small Business, United States Senate, March 22, 1960.

Davidson, T. L., *Some Effects of the Growth of Planned and Controlled Shopping Centers on Small Retailers.* Storrs: School of Business Administration, University of Connecticut, 1960.

Deran, Elizabeth Y., *The Successful Shopkeeper: A Study of Retailer Survival in Nine Communities.* Champaign: Bureau of Economic and Business Research, University of Illinois, 1963.

Eckey, David C. and Robbins, W. David, *The Use of Consultants by Manufacturers.* Richmond: School of Business Administration, University of Richmond, 1964.

Friedland, S., Dymaza, W. A., and Moranian T., *The Financing of Manufacturing Activities in New Jersey.* New Brunswick: Rutgers, The State University, 1963.

Gort, Michael, *The Pattern of Changes in the Size Structure of Business Firms.* Chicago: Graduate School of Business, University of Chicago, 1964.

Havighurst, Clark C., *Deferred Compensation for Key Employers: A Planning Guide for Small Businessmen and Lawyers.* Durham: Small Business Studies, Duke University School of Law, 1964.

Hoad, William N. and Rosko, Peter, *Management Factors Contributing to the Success or Failure of New Small Manufacturers.* Ann Arbor: Bureau of Business Research, Graduate School of Business Administration, The University of Michigan, 1964.

Hooker, Raymond W., *Attitudes of Wisconsin Bankers Towards Small Business Financing.* Madison: Department of Economics, University of Wisconsin, 1961.

Karger, Delmar W. and Jack, Andrew B., *Problems of Small Business in Developing and Exploiting New Products.* Troy: School of Management, Rensselaer Polytechnic Institute, 1963.

Lewis, E. H. and Hancock, R. S., *The Franchise System of Distribution.* Minneapolis: Research Division, School of Business Administration, University of Minnesota, 1963.

Malinowski, Zenon S. and Kinnard, William N., Jr., *The Place of Small Business in Planned Industrial Districts.* Storrs: Institute of Urban Research, University of Connecticut, 1963.

O'Neal, F. Hodge and Derwin, Jordan, *Expulsion or Oppression of Business Associates: "Squeeze-Outs" in Small Enterprises.* Durham, N.C.: Duke University Press, 1961.

Rotch, William, *Management of Small Enterprises: Cases and Readings.* Charlottesville: Bureau of Population and Economic Research, University of Virginia, 1964.

Stekler, H. O., *Profitability and Size of Firm.* Berkeley: The Institute of Business and Economic Research, University of California, 1963.

Small Business Administration Publications

The Small Business Administration publishes a number of booklets and pamphlets. For instance, there is the "Starting and Managing Series," in which each publication of the series deals with problems of a particular kind of business. There is also the "Management Aids Series," in which each booklet includes a number of articles on particular management problems, such as determining salesman's compensation or deciding on plant location. Full information about these and a wide range of other SBA publications can be obtained from SBA offices.

Other Bibliographies

ELLIS, JESSIE (CROFT), *Small Business Bibliography*. Boston: F. W. Faxon Company, 1959.

Federal Handbook for Small Business, A Survey of Small Business Programs in the Federal Government Agencies. Washington, D.C.: U.S. Government Printing Office, 1962.

PITTSBURGH UNIVERSITY, Bureau of Business Research, *Small Business Bibliography*, 2nd Edition. Pittsburgh: 1958.